EXPERT SYSTEMS IN
ECONOMICS, BANKING AND MANAGEMENT

EXPERT SYSTEMS IN ECONOMICS, BANKING AND MANAGEMENT

edited by

L.F. PAU
Technical University of Denmark

J. MOTIWALLA
Institute of Systems Science, Singapore

Y.H. PAO
Case Western Reserve University, U.S.A.

H.H. TEH
Institute of Systems Science, Singapore

1989

NORTH-HOLLAND
AMSTERDAM • NEW YORK • OXFORD • TOKYO

330·028
E 96

ELSEVIER SCIENCE PUBLISHERS B.V.
Sara Burgerhartstraat 25
P.O. Box 211, 1000 AE Amsterdam, The Netherlands

Distributors for the United States and Canada:
ELSEVIER SCIENCE PUBLISHING COMPANY, INC.
655 Avenue of the Americas
New York, N.Y. 10010, U.S.A.

Library of Congress Cataloging-in-Publication Data

Expert systems in economics, banking, and management / edited by L.F.
  Pau ... [et al].
        p.   cm.
    A collection of some of the papers presented at the 2nd
International IFIP/IFAC/IFORS Workshop on Artificial Intelligence in
Economics and Management, held in Singapore, Jan. 9-13, 1989.
    Includes bibliographical references.
    ISBN 0-444-88060-7
    1. Business--Data processing--Congresses. 2. Management--Data
processing--Congresses. 3. Banks and banking--Data processing-
-Congresses. 4. Economics--Data processing--Congresses.
5. Artificial intelligence--Congresses. 6. Expert systems (Computer
science)--Congresses.   I. Pau, L.-F. (Louis-François), 1948-
II. International Federation for Information Processing.
III. International Federation of Automatic Control.
IV. International Federation of Operational Research Societies.
V. International IFIP/IFAC/IFORS Workshop on Artificial Intelligence
 in Economics and Management (2nd : 1989 : Singapore)
HF5548.2.E965   1989
330'.028'5633--dc20   89-22938
                                                             CIP

ISBN: 0 444 88060 7

PRINTED IN THE NETHERLANDS

PREFACE

Artificial Intelligence in Economics and Management:
What For and How?

1. INTRODUCTION

This volume is an edited collection of some of the papers presented at the 2nd International IFIP/IFAC/IFORS Workshop on artificial intelligence in economics and management, held in Singapore, January 9-13, 1989, with the International Federation for Information Processing (IFIP) as the main sponsor, and the Institute of Systems Science, National University of Singapore, as organizer. It was attended by more than 230 persons, with a geographical coverage extending to all of Asia, North America, Europe, Australia, Middle-East and South America. Over 130 papers were submitted, and 57 accepted by the International program committee.

It was a follow-on to the 1st workshop on Artificial intelligence in economics and management, held in Zürich in 1985, which had resulted in the book (1) which is still the earliest reference volume as to developments in that area. At that time, the major issue were still:

- what is artificial intelligence (AI)?
- why artificial intelligence in economics and management?

The first question found its justification by the fact that only few economists, banks, financial services, management departments had then yet been exposed to A.I. through knowledge based systems (KBS), natural language analysis (NL), intelligent front-ends (IFE), or symbolic programming environments.

The second question originated in a need for arguments or justifications for pay-offs, if A.I. development work was to be initiated (2).

Underlying both was an issue of interdisciplinary research and training, as few AI researchers had ventured into meaningful economic, financial and management problems, and even fewer economists or business administration specialists had received any AI education.

As evidenced by the papers, panels, posters tutorial lectures, and conversations at the 2nd Workshop the situation had changed in 1989.

2. AI IN ECONOMICS AND MANAGEMENT: WHAT FOR?

A wide variety of applications have been developed as prototypes, and even as operational systems in finance, banking, services, accounting, consulting, organizational strategy, marketing, economics, scheduling, and production planning, as evidenced in Part I of this volume. Furthermore, the survey chapter provides an extensive and structured collection of known projects, organizations involved, and tools/methods used, as to substantiate further the claim to the shear size of the wave of efforts over the past 3 years.

More fundamentally, the users are largely in charge themselves of not only the
initiative, but also the development of AI applications in the above areas.
The first consequence is that the implementations and solutions almost invariably are merging conventional programming or methods, with some originating in
AI research, thus leading to integration. The second consequence of this natural push for solutions to real or new problems, often unsolvable previously, is
that application/generic or completely specific tools emerge, distributed on a
wide commercial basis.

There are still of course areas where the applications pose significant yet
unresolved challenges to AI and to other techniques, such as macroeconomics in
a broad sense, policy analysis, public services, portofolio and risk management,
legal knowledge, forecasting, intelligent information analysis.

3. AI IN ECONOMICS AND MANAGEMENT: HOW?

As it appears from Part I, most applications developped so far have relied on
rather standard AI tools or methods, blending them appropriately with similarly
rather established concepts or methods from other disciplines (such as economics
and decision support systems), to provide novel solutions. Consequently, specifications can be drawn of the features of a few general purpose tools specifically aiming at applications in economics, finance, banking, services, and management.

The chapters in Part II point at new AI methodologies, software engineering aspects, neural processing, and user interface designs for further improvements.
Furthermore, a number of trends emerged from the discussions and panels.

Reasoning work emphasizes higher level planning with lower level actions, constraint propagation, and the concurrency of algorithms. This will impact the
internal architecture of the AI solution software, but also the reasoning models,
with a much heavier emphasis towards behavioral or rational expectation models
first pioneered in economics research.

In terms of cognitive models, there is evidence of an integration of connection-
nist/neural approaches and symbolic representations. This is essential for
meaningful explanation and case analysis capabilities.

Contrary to the mainstream of AI research, but possibly for valid reasons,
qualitative reasoning is barely present in practical implementations, although
some basis for it exists in macroeconomics, securities trading, and risk analysis.

Knowledge representation concepts are more and more influenced by logics,
although default reasoning and scale perception are still unresolved. But inter-
estingly enough, the knowledge representation paradigms encountered e.g. in
financial and other services, tend to accomodate the data structure requirements from data base and user interfaces, with object oriented approaches
having a clear lead.

In general, much work still needs to be done in terms of report generation,
explanation facilities and dialogue, integration with hypertext or multi-media
facilities, and of course on natural language analysis.

And beyond, the validation of knowledge, controlling access to it, and its
legal or social implications are still largely open issues which may further
limit the use of AI in economics and management.

4. CONCLUSION

Today, the proper controlled infusion of AI as an ingredient to novel or more
efficient solutions to practical problems, does offer a significant pay-off.
However, the tools must be largely improved in terms of their integration with
other user-driven facilities (data bases, report generators, explanations),
and must be made more robust. At the same time, research should not be ignored,
out of self-satisfaction, as very major progress needs to be done especially in
reasoning, case analysis, and learning, while reincorporating the often forgotten
contributions from economics, social theories, decision systems , and finance.

L.F. Pau
J. Motiwalla
Y.H. Pao,

April 1989

References

(1) Artificial intelligence in economics and management, L.F. Pau (Ed),
     North Holland, Amsterdam, 1985

(2) L.F. Pau, Artificial intelligence in economics and management: why?,
     in (1), pp. v-ix

ACKNOWLEDGEMENTS

The 2nd International IFIP/IFAC/IFORS Workshop on artificial intelligence in economics and management, was hold in Singapore 9-13, 1989, with:

SPONSORS

*   IFIP   (International Federation for Information Processsing)
                (main sponsor)

*   IFAC   (International Federation of Automatic Control)

*   IFORS   (International Federation of Operational Research Societies)

in cooperation with:

*   AAAI   (American Association for Artificial Intelligence)

*   ACM-SIGART (Association for Computing Machinery - Special Interest Group
                for Artificial Intelligence)

*   IEEE-CS   (Computer Society of the Institute of Electrical and Electronics
                Engineers)

*   IPSJ   (Information Processing Society of Japan)

*   SEARCC   (South East Asia Regional Computer Confederation)

with support from:

*   IBM Singapore Ltd

*   Digital Equipment Singapore Ltd

*   Texas Instruments Singapore Ltd

ORGANIZER

Institute of Systems Science (ISS), National University of Singapore

CO-ORGANIZER

SCS (Singapore Computer Society)

CHAIRMAN

J. Motiwalla, ISS, National University of Singapore

PROGRAM COMMITTEE CHAIR

L.F. Pau, Technical University of Denmark

Y.H. Pao, Case Western Reserve University

H.H. Teh, ISS, National University of Singapore

ORGANIZING COMMITTEE CHAIR

D. Narasimhalu, ISS, National University of Singapore

CONTENTS

Contents

Expert Systems in Economics, Banking and Management
L.F. Pau et al. (Editors)
© Elsevier Science Publishers B.V. (North-Holland), 1989

1

APPLICATIONS OF ARTIFICIAL INTELLIGENCE IN BANKING, FINANCIAL SERVICES AND ECONOMICS

L.F. Pau, Technical University of Denmark
Bldg. 348/EMI, DK 2800 Lyngby, Denmark

Abstract: This paper surveys approximately 200 actual applications development projects carried out by companies and institutions, with specification of the nature of the AI project goals, of most development environments, and of project partners. The goal of this survey is to identify methodological as well as software tool needs resulting from these development projects. The application areas covered are: banking, finance, insurance, economics, auditing, commodities trading, tax planning, general management.

1. THE MOTIVATIONS FOR THE USE OF AI

In the areas of banking, financial services, insurance, economics, and related industries, the main operational motivation for initiating, and eventually fielding, systems solutions using some significant portion of artificial intelligence (AI) techniques, are the following:

G1:   development of computer based solutions allowing for the handling of tasks of a high relative complexity, as measured vs. operator skills, thus leveraging skills/staff, and reducing risks; the complexity involves achieving a compromise between: providing a consistent level of information, wide range of capabilities promoting specific goals, and providing training capabilities;

G2:   setting up computer based information services, with user specific information screens, and dialogue functions, offering a time - and/or competitive edge over other actors operating in the same domain, thus pooling knowledge for actions initiated by the user;

G3:   replacing paperwork, information consolidation and cumbersome control procedures, in rather routine based operations involving usually distributed agents/sources, and where a high consistency is needed reflecting a common policy;

G4:   outright labour, quality, time and money savings in centralized routine tasks, with reduced errors;

G5:   ability to upgrade a solution software incrementally with a higher software writing productivity.

As examples of the above motivations, we can mention those presiding in a few case examples:

G1:   lending advisors (e.g. Wells Fargo Bank/Syntelligence)

G2:   bond portfolio planning and trading systems with market interpretation (e.g. Salomon Brothers)

G3:   real estate appraisal for credit granting (e.g. Security Pacific Bank)

G4:   money transfer telex conversion into standard formats (e.g. Citybank Information re-
        sources/Cognitive Systems Int.; Sumitomo Bank/Digital Equipment

G5:   cash point machines network management and fault diagnosis (e.g. BRED, Bankcontak
        Belgium)

The classes of motivations may be further related to the location of the need in terms of the organizational element where the solution is needed; a framework for the location of the solution need is the following (see also [B-17]:

L1:   front-office services facing the end customer (e.g. pension planning advisory system)

L2:   general support functions (e.g. document filing and routing)

L3:   product or service specific support functions (e.g. credit card charge authorizer, back of-
        fice functions)

L4:   internal policy making and related information analysis (e.g. matching products to cus-
        tomer needs)

L5:   auditing compliance and security functions (e.g. accounts auditing)

2. SURVEY OF DEVELOPMENT PROJECTS

Whereas a number of studies have tried to survey applications, markets [F-9] or generic solutions (e.g. risk management, underwriting), it is the aim here to go back to more technical aspects.

The attached tables survey approximately 200 actual applications development projects.

First, we consider each development project as aimed at providing a solution to an actual problem defined by a specific capability to be implemented. This implies that the solution approach and architecture will typically always involve the integration of whatever resources are needed (conventional programming, artificial intelligence tools, databases, user interfaces, computer architectures).

Next, this survey does not deal at a high priority with the AI experience level of the developers and users, nor with the state of actual fielding or testing of the solution.

Next, the projects are grouped by application categories, thus revealing immediately which are the classes of problems resulting in the largest estimated effort level. There may of course be wide differences between the specific aspects highlighted in different projects within the same category. For example, an investment advisory system running on a mainframe is quite different from a simple one running on a PC.

Last, some entries are incomplete, and a few unchecked, owing to project secrecy, unjustified publicity, unclear data about their status, etc.; and of course the survey is in no way making any claim for exhaustivity.

3. DEVELOPMENT AND DELIVERY ENVIRONMENTS

The survey clearly shows a clear trend towards three types of development and delivery principles:

- multi user applications, which are software packages embodying complex, widely accepted, and open knowledge (e.g. product advisors, self-service sales assistants, personal financial planning systems)
- hybrid environments, which offer integration facilities whereby heterogeneous inference, knowledge representation, languages and database query languages can be blended together, but where no application specific knowledge resides initially
- application generic shells, also called inclination shells, with built-in functions and standard knowledge, but allowing for end user customization of the knowledge (e.g. Lending Advisor from Syntelligence)

In all instances, there is a growing emphasis towards:
- back office/workstation/mainframe integration with the corresponding portability requirements on the development environment
- distributed use over a network with data and knowledge servers (eventually distinct)
- incorporation of validation and software maintenance procedures
- multilingual knowledge acquisition tools or languages
- report generation for results and explanations
- imbedded training modes or facilities
- incorporation of diverse user interface drivers (e.g. terminal drivers, videotext drivers)
- incorporation of menu layout and customization facilities, including the ability to freeze or free some dialogue sequences, and soft key programming features
- parsers for standard economic/financial on-line information services (e.g. various Reuters, Dow Jones, Telerate or Datastream services)
- interfaces to, or true rule-based spreadsheet capabilities

4. GENERIC DOMAIN UTILITIES

Regardless of the development and delivery environments, a number of common calculations, regulatory databases or generic knowledge bases can be identified which must be included in most solutions. They make up upgrades or specific user-developed additions to multi-user application environments, hybrids as well as application generic shells; seen from a different perspective they constitute one major set of capabilities which distinguish environments in economics /banking/ finance from other AI applications:

Calculations:
- rates of return
- accounting balance calculations
- tax calculations
- actualisation indexes
- times series analysis
- trade commissions/fees

Procedures:
- risk ranking
- account profitability
- protocol verification e.g. for fraud control
- client profiles
- multi attribute scoring
- econometric model re-estimation around a nominal path
- linear programming algorithms
- set-up of search screens, e.g. based on ratios

Knowledge bases:
- trading instrument descriptors (frames) dictionaries of variables applicable in selected industries
- cross-impact tables
- in the future: legal/regulatory knowledge bases
- simple truth maintenance systems
- balanced trade generators, e.g. for swaps or securities/futures trades

Client relation knowledge base (for each client):
- expectations and commitments agreed between the parties
- preferences of each party
- procedures which are agreed between the parties in normal cases
- history of the relationship
- client attributes, incl. risk profile

Furthermore, generic applications at an advanced level may require specific search/inference algorithms, as well as user interfaces with some adaptive features, none of which are found elsewhere (see [E-3]).

5. INFERENCE CONTROL AND CONFLICT RESOLUTION STRATEGIES

Existing AI environments usually provide forward and/or backward chaining to control the search for knowledge elements in the knowledge base. Forward chaining matches these elements with rule antecedents in order to fire consequent actions. Backward chaining matches elements of the knowledge base to rule consequents in an attempt to verify rule antecedents.

Forward chaining from observed facts and backward chaining from goals or likely hypotheses minimize the search space, and are often used in problem types G3, G4, G5. In the other instances, typically for problem types G1, G2, both are used simultaneously, and associated with backtracking, because inference then aims at exploiting the knowledge structure to explore alternatives under control of conflict resolution strategies.

A control resolution strategy produces a subset of knowledge elements with validated antecedents that may be fired. This strategy attempts to select the most applicable inference control strategy in order to reach a solution at the earliest possible time. Some of the conflict resolution strategies are as follows, and are increasingly important in banking/finance/economic applications:

R1: First found: the first applicable knowledge element that is found is used first, which means that it should often be dismissed when knowledge is added incrementally

R2: Least recently used: the applicable knowledge element the least recently used is chosen; this is relevant in e.g. trading systems.

R3: Most recently used: counterpart to R2.

R4: Antecedent ordered: priorities attached to the antecedents of e.g. rules are used to resolve conflicts. This is helpful when there is a natural or "administrative" ordering of importance amongst the antecedents.

R4: Consequent ordered: the same as R4, except that priorities are attached to the consequents of the rules; this is typical of risk assessment.

R5: Most complex first: the rule that has the most antecedents or consequent clauses (depending on whether the inference engine is chaining backward or forward, respectively), will be fired first.

R6: Simplest first: same as R5, except that the rule with the least number of clauses is chosen; this is typical of applications of type G3, where the solution should process most cases except unique exceptions

R7: Global priority: as well as assigning priorities to the antecedents and consequents of rules, a rule may be assigned a priority as a whole: this happens in most finance and auditing systems.

The solution requirements should always specify which of the above or customized conflict resolution strategies should be implemented, otherwise poor user satisfaction and confidence will be the outcome.

REFERENCES

This bibliography is aimed at giving as complete as possible an overview of the technical build-up and requirements for applications of artificial intelligence in banking, financial services and economics. Descriptions of work in end-user organizations are emphasized, as opposed to basic research disconnected of user driven solution requirements. The references are organized into the following application categories:

A: Auditing
B: Banking
C: Commodities trading
E: Economics
F: Finance and financial services
G: General references and surveys
I: Insurance
M: Management
T: Taxation

A-1   **Parker-Jervis, George,** Accountants called to Account, The Observer, 6 September 1987.

B-1   **Donaldson, H.,** A critic of knowledge based systems or AI, Creativity & innovation network, Oct.-Dec. 1983, 172.

B-2   Financial Technology Bulletin, Bath House, 56 Holborn Viaduct, London EC1A 2EX.

B-3   Journal of financial and quantitative analysis.

B-4   Journal of money, credit and banking.

B-5   Tipi: taking the grief out of home loans, Expert System user, May 1987, 20-23.

B-6   Les systèmes experts et la banque, Banque et informatique, 1st part. No 32, jan/feb 1987, 71-82, 2nd part : No 33, March 1987, 34-39.

B-7   **Slahor, L.,** AI in banking: intelligent workstations or mainframes, Proc-IEEE COMPEURO´87, May 1987, Hamburg, Cat. IEEE-CH-2417-4/87,851.-

B-8   Proceedings Bank AI´88, SWIFT, La Hulpe, Belgium, 1988.

B-9   **Pinson, S.,** A multi attribute approach to knowledge representation for loan granting Proc.IJCAI´87, p.588-

B-10   **Ben-David, Arie; Sterling, Leon,** A prototype expert system for credit evaluaion, in: Artificial intelligence in economics and management, L.F. Pau (Ed), North-Holland, 1986.

B-11   **Bond, Alan H.,** AI simplifies banker/customer relationships, Applied Artificial Intelligence Reporter, Vol4, No 4, University of Miami, April 1987

B-12   **Carter, Chris and Catlett, Jason,** Credit assesment using machine learning, Proceedings of the third Australian conference on applications of expert systems, Sydney, May 1987

B-13   **Dodwell, Bernard,** Credit evaluation for commercial loans, Expert systems in the city, Banking Technology conference, London. January 1987.

B-14   **Duda, Richard; Hart, Peter; Reboh; Rene, et al,** Syntel: using a functional language for financial risk assesment, IEEE Expert, Fall 1987.

B-15   **Hovenaars, M.N.,** Experiences at NMB bank, Presentation at banking applications and artificial intelligence - SWIFT international conference, Brussels, May 1987.

B-16   **Klahr, Philip,** The Authorizer´s Assistant: a large financial expert system application, Proceedings of the third Australian conference on applications of expert systems, Sydney, May 1987.

B-17   **Marmier, Edouard,** An overview of artificial intelligence activities at Credit Suisse and the Swiss brokerage convention prototype, Presentation at Banking applications and artificial intelligence - SWIFT international conference, Brussels, May 1987

B-18   **Van Reesema, S,** Expert systems on a PC in mortgages, business loans and leasing, Expert systems in the city, Banking Technology conference, London, January 1987.

B-19   **Serre, J.M.; Voyer, R.,** Tipi, an expert system written in Le Lisp for a French bank, The second international expert systems conference, Learned Information, 1986.

B-20   Journal of banking and finance + Studies in banking and finance, North Holland

B-21   **Makowski, Paul,** Credit scoring branches out, Credit Management J., March 1987, 26-31

E-1   **L.F. Pau (Ed),** Artificial intelligence in economics and management, North Holland, Amsterdam, 1986

E-2   **Williams, Thomas,** A graphical interface to an economist´s workstation, IEEE Computer Graphics and Applications J., August 1984

E-3   **L.F. Pau,** Inference of functional economic model relations from natural language analysis, in [E-1]

F-1   Special issue on financial applications, IEEE Expert, Vol 2, no 3, Fall 1987.

F-2   **Alexander, T.,** Why computers cannot outthink the experts, Fortune, Aug. 20 1984, 99-108.

F-3   Expert Systems J., Vol 1, no 2, oct, 1984, p.102.

F-4   **Stansfield, J.** , COMEX: a commodities support system , IJCAI-77, 1977, Vol 1 p. 109.

F-5   Expert System Journal, Vol 1,no 1, July 1984, p. 9.

F-6   **Roycroft, A.E.**, ACCI, in: Bramer M.A (ed), Research and development in expert systems Cambridge Univ. Press, 1985, 127-39.

F-7   **Bonarini, A.**, Man machine interaction and inferential architecture for financial planning, in: G.P. Katz (Ed), ESPRIT´85, North Holland, 1986.

F-8   **Frenkel, K.A.**, Toward automating the software development cycle Comm. ACM, Vol 28, no 6, june 1985, 578-89.

F-9   Expert systems in banking and securities, OVUM Ltd, London,1988.

F-10   **A.R. Blair, R. Nachtmann, J.E. Olson**, Forecasting foreign exchange rates: an expert judgment approach Socio. Econom. Planning Sciences, Vol 21, no 6, 363-369, 1987

F-11   **Behan, Joseph**, Case Study: the Security Pacific Automation Company, Expert systems in financial institutions, Institute for International Research, New York, September 1987

F-12   **Behan, Joe and Lecot, Koenraad**, Overview of financial applications of expert systems, Security Pacific. 1987

F-13   **Berber, Philip R.**, AI in action in the dealing room: the current state-of-play in the USA, Systems Designers, April 1987

F-14   **Dulieu, Mike; Fish, Alan**, Artificial Intelligence in the dealer/computer interface, BankAI´87, Swift international conference, Brussels, May 1987.

F-15   **Firlej, Maureen**, Tactical dealer information system: dilemmas of using valuable knowledge, KBS 87, Online Publications, 1987

F-16   **Iwasieczko, B; Korczak, J; et al**, Expert systems in financial analysis, in:Artificial intelligence in economics and management, L.F. Pau Ed), North-Holland, 1986.

F-17   **Krutchen, Dale**, An expert financial portfolio management advisory system, The second international expert systems conference, Learned Information, 1986.

F-18   **Lubich, Nancy Irene**, The application of artificial intelligence in the financial services industries, Proceedings of the third Australian Conference on applications of expert systems, Sydney, May 1987

F-19   **Norris, Graeme** A knowledge based system for investment appraisal, Knowledge based systems´86 , Online, July 1986

F-20   **Reiter, R.** FX: A foreign exchange expert advisory system, The second international expert systems conference, Learned Information, 1986; Shap, Keith (Ed), Artificial Intelligence in financial trading, Intermarket, February 1987.

F-21   **L.F. Pau**, An expert system kernel for the analysis of strategies over time, in [E-1]

G-1   **Andren, John**, Future issues in implementing expert systems, Expert systems in financial institutions, Institute for International Research, New York, September 1987.

G-2   **Cook, Sandra**, Knowledge representation for financial expert systems, Presentation at banking application and artificial intelligence SWIFT international conference, Brussels, May 1987

G-3   Les systèmes experts en France, La lettre de l´Intelligence artificielle, No 38, May 1988, p.8-12.

I-1   **Jenny, C.J.**, Requirements on expert systems as seen by an insurance company, Zurich Insurance Co., April 1984.

I-2   Texas Instruments AI letter, Vol 3, no 12, dec 1987.

M-1   **Reitman, W.**, The financial advisor and the operations advisor, 1st. Int. Symp on AI and ES Berlin, AMK,12-22 , May 1987.

M-2   **Halloway, C.**, Strategic management and AI, Long range planning, Vol 16, no 5, 1983,89-93.

T-1   **Shpilberg, D.Lynford et al**, Exper Tax: an expert system for corporate tax planning, Expert Systems, Vol 3, no 3, july 1986,136-

T-2   Expert System user, October 1987, 6-

T-3   **Parker, R.**, An expert for every office, Computer design, Fall 1983, 37-46.

Field	Problem	Company/ development	Implementation architecture	Product/Prototype name
ECONOMICS	NL front-ends to economic forecasting	FEDERAL RESERVE	Forecasting quarterly model + Judgement scripts	
	Judgemental forecasting	BATELLE	NL inference of model relations by semantic analysis	[E-3]
		FEDERAL RESERVE	Dempster-Shafer uncertain rules	
		FSI-ECO	Rule based	ECO
	Economic tutorial aids and explanations	ECRC	CAI + explanation facilities	
		DIGITALK	SMALLTALK	ECONOMICS DISCOVERY
	Choice of intermediate economic targets	T.U. DENMARK/ NATIONAL BANK	Reallocation amongst endogeneous and exogeneous variables and monetary targets	[E-3]
	Political risk analysis	Frost and Sullivan		Political risk service on 85 countries
		COMPUTER TEACHING CORP/ Univ. Illinois	Policy goal percentaging analyses in PLATO/TENCORE	P/G analysis [E-3]
	Market forecasting	ESI (UK)	Model building from expectations, and factors; PROLOG-2, statistics, FORTRAN	EMEX

Field	Problem	Company/ development	Implementation architecture	Product/Prototype name
INSURANCE	Property and casualty underwriting	- SYNTELLIGENCE/AIG/ ST PAUL & CO/ FIREMANS FUND/ IBM	SYNTEL data flow model	Underwriting Advisor [F-11]
		- METROPOLITAN LIFE INSURANCE - NIPPON LIFE INSURANCE - EQUITABLE LIFE	Prolog	
		- CIGNA - TRANSAMERICA INSURANCE/AI Corp. - LIBERTY MUTUAL INSURANCE/AI Corp. - AETNA/DIGITAL EQ. - STATSKONTORET (S)/ EPITEC	ART	KBMS KBMS
	Claims processing	CIGNA		
	Reinsurance underwriting	SCANDIA AMERICA GROUP	International reinsurance	
		HM 6 V Research Oy (SF) KANSA Insurance		
	Insurance vending machines	BANK OF AMERICA	Contract life cycle models, and regularity knowledge base	
	Fire insurance underwriting	PROTECTION MUTUAL INSURANCE (Illinois)		
	Life underwriting	MONY Financial services (US)	IBM ESE	CLUES

Field	Problem	Company/ development	Implementation architecture	Product/Prototype name
	Insurance brokerage	PROFESSIONAL NETWORKS/UK)/ MOORGATE	Product selection for small brokers; CRYSTAL	ADVISA

Field	Problem	Company/ development	Implementation architecture	Product/Prototype name
BANKING	Credit scoring, evaluation, and granting	KREDIETBANK (B)/ Systems Designers (UK) CULLINET	SAGE shell to analyse numeric credit taker data	Loan approcal adviser
			Car loan credit scoring	APPLICATION EXPERT [B-6]
		Univ. Sydney	Credit card applications; ID3 algorithm	[F-4]
		CREDIT AGRICOLE (F) BRED (F); Univ. Paris	SNARK shell	PATRILOG CREDEX [B-10]
		Intelligent Environments Ltd, (demo)	Production rules, and inclusion of financial calculation functions	CRYSTAL
		DKO Bank (SGF)/Nokia	PC Based	Loan analysis
		CAISSE D'ESPAGNE/ACT Information/Arthur Andersen (F)	Evaluation of "prêts conventionnés", rulae based in Le-Lisp shell Antinea	TIPI [B-5]
		BARCLAYS BANK (Israel)	C-PROLOG	[E-3]
		SYNTELLIGENCE/IBM	SYNTEL dataflow functional language; on MVX-XA(PL/1), IBM-PC/C	SYNTEL [F-4] LENDING-ADVISOR
		HELIX TECHNOLOGY/ AIS	Basic + Prolog + d Base III	
		CHASE MANHATTAN IDM/CARISMA SRL	Prolog and frames + discriminant analysis	CRES

Field	Problem	Company/ development	Implementation architecture	Product/Prototype name
BANKING		BANCA DI SAN PAOLO di TORINO/DIGITAL	Family credit repayment	SPACE
		AMERICAN EXPRESS	ART shell and data base interfaces; authorizes credit card charges	Authorizer Advisor
		INFERENCE CORP./ SYSECA (F)	Credit card authorizer	
		BANCA DI PARMA/ DIGITAL		
		BANQUE HERVET/ EVALOG (F)	Loan risk	EVENT
	Selecting public funding	ARTHUR YOUNG	NEXUS shell	[F-6]
	Commercial lending	FIRST NTL-BANK OF ATLANTA	Leasing contract analyzer	
		AGRILEASING (I)	Leasing evaluation	ALVIN
		BAIL GESTION (F)/CIC	Leasing advisor	
		OKOBANK (SF)/NOKIA	Agricultural loans; XIPLUS and/C	MATIAS
		Nederlandsche Middenstandbank (NL)	Lending advisor	
		BARCLAYS BANK (UK)/ DIGITAL		
		TECH.UNIV. DENMARK (DK)/ NYKREDIT	Loans for mixed property; rule based CLEOPATRA.	

Field	Problem	Company/development	Implementation architecture	Product/Prototype name
BANKING	Job control and back office operations	LCEXAM (US)/STANDARD CHARTRED BANK N.Y.	Examining letters of credit for compliance to UCP400 CCode	META-PSS
		UNION BANK OF SWITZERLAND	Consolidate and prepare all 15000 operational daily batch programs in COBOL. Knowledge based task scheduling. VM/PROLOG and DEDALE shell	
		BANCA NAZIONALE DEL LAVORO (I)/MESARTEAM	Blackboard architecture	
	Computer facilities audit and tuning	COGNITECH (F)	Administrative documents	SADR
		BAYERISCHE VEREINS-BANK	Shell Insight 2	
	Pricing package	FIRST NTL CHICAGO	EDP Audit	
		MIDLAND MONTAGU (UK)		
	Bank operations and money management	SPICER & PEGLER BANCO CAT. DEL VENETO (I)		E/G/I
	Reduce settlement costs	FINANCIAL CLEARING AND SERVICES		

Field	Problem	Company/ development	Implementation architecture	Product/Prototype name
BANKING	Generate and check money transfer wires	- CHASE - SWIFT - COGNITIVE SYSTEMS7 CITY BANKL/GECOSYS - SECURITY PACIFIC - SUMITOMO BANK (J)/ Nihon DEC	Semantic nets	TELEX READER TEXPERT
	Inkasso recovery	CYBERCREDIT FINAN-CIAL SYSTEMS		CYBERCREDIT
		SEGIN (F)/Editions juridiques Lamy	Object based layered model	Distributed by videotex
	Discretionary account surveillance	COOPERS & LYBRAND	Mixed chaining, in Goldworks	
	Bank telemarketing and client advisory services	PROPHECY DEV.CORP.	Frame based semantic nets	PROFIT TOOL
		IBM		FAME
		ZENTRAL SPARKASSE (A)		
		CCF (F)		
		CIF (F)	Bank acc. budgetting and loan	
		Stadtsparkasse München (FRG)		
		COOPERS LYBRAND (UK)	Advice on pension schemes	CLASP

Field	Problem	Company/development	Implementation architecture	Product/Prototype name
FINANCE	Securities trading	MORGAN STANLEY (US)		Automated securities trading
		INTELLIGENT TECHNOLOGY GROUP (US)/ STARWOOD CORP.	Pattern recognition of stock groups relative to market	
		IBM	Options trading; constrained logic programming [F-4]	
		INFORM (UK)	Chart analysis	TRADERS ASSISTANT
		CRITERION SOFTWARE (US)	Technical analysis	BREAKOUT
		GSI (CH)/Vanilla (UK)	Offline trading on PC	TRADEMASTER
		SECURITY PACIFIC NTL BANK (US)	Predict FOREX	Security [F-5]
	Foreign exchange; currency trading instrument choice	GECOSYS (B)/G.B.	FOREX message analysis	DEAL-READER
		ATHENA GROUP PROPERTY DEV.CORP.	Rule based " "	FX CONTESSA
		CHEMICAL BANK (US)	FOREX auditing	
	Bond portofolio management	SALOMON BROTHS.	Reassignment to increase convexity quants	
		CIGNA (US)	Bond underwriting, with client financial review	SURETY AIDE
	Financial planning and stock portofolio management	ACASTE (F)	Financial analyses, spread-sheet and text processor	CHARIS

Field	Problem	Company/development	Implementation architecture	Product/Prototype name
FINANCE		SKANDINAVISKA (EN-SKILDA BANKEN (S)/EPITEC SPARDA-BANK (FRG)/GMD	BABYLON shell	EVA
		INTELLIGENT TECHNO-LOGY (UK)		Intelligent portofolio management INC services
		APPLIED EXPERT SYSTEMS/J HANCOCK MUTUAL LIGE INS./N.Y. LIFE INSURANCE/TRAVELERS/FUJI XEROX/GOLD HILL	Rule based, with KB decomposition; runs on Xerox workstations; LOOPS	PLAN POWER, [F 4] CLIENT PROFILING
		GENERALE DE BANQUE/COGNITIVE SYSTEMS/DEC	Rule based with KB decomposition	LE COURTIER
		TEKNEKRON SYSTEMS SANWA BANK		
		CRITERION SOFTWARE (US)	Rating system	Intelligent Market/Equities system
		A.D. LITTLE		PFPS
		KNOWLEDGE BASED NETWORK SYSTEMS		
		STERLING WENTWORTH		PLANMAN, BUSINESS PLAN

Field	Problem	Company/development	Implementation architecture	Product/Prototype name
FINANCE		OBJECTIVE FINANCIAL SYSTEMS		OBJECTIVE F.S.
		CAP SOGETI/CSELT/ Philips MBLE		ESTEAM ESPRIT P316 [F-10]
		NOVACAST (S)		STOCKMASTER
		CITYMAX (UK)	Portofolio management	EQUUS (ESPRIT project)
		QUINARY (I)	Frames + propagation network	PECUNIA
	Securities trading regulations + auditr	MOORGATE PNL	Logic based data base queries	ADVISA
		BEAR, STEARNS SECURITY PACIFIC		
		NEW YORK STOCK EXCHANGE	Detect illegal trades and insider dealings	ALERT
	Mortgage and pensions underwriting	SOFTSERV/COMCAP	Rule based (SAVOIR)	Mortgage selector
		POLYTECNIC WALES (UK)	Mortgage valuation; SAVOIR	
		ARTHUR ANDERSEN/ TEXAS INSSTRUMENTS	Rule based regulatory assessment of loan features	Mortgage loan analyzer [1-2]
	Dealing rooms/desks	IBM PHILLIPS & DREW (UK)	what - if analysis prior to trade	ORBIT project FS-GILTS

Field	Problem	Company/ development	Implementation architecture	Product/Prototype name
FINANCE		HELIX FINANCIAL SYSTEMS (UK)	Interest rate arbitrage and what-if displays	OPPORTUNITY
		ICL/ FUTURE SYSTEMS (UK)	Gilts and money market trading	FS-DEALER
		Alvey ARIES Club/LOGICA	Fundamentals analyst + Technical analyst	TAURUS
		A.D. LITTLE	Brokers scratchpad + Traders workstation in Goldworks	TRADERS ASSISTANT, EQUITY TRADER, CASH TRADER
		CANADIAN IMPERIAL BANK COMMERCE	DIGILINK to Reuters, and CRYSTAL for swaps	
		KNOWLEDGE ASSOCIATES (US)	PROLOG controlled dissemination of financial data	FINANCIAL QUOTE SYSTEM
	Stock-selection	DOW JONES	NL to financial databases	
		SALOMON BROTHERS		
	Securities trading regulations + audit	INTELLIGENT TECHNOLOGY GROUP	Rule based + simulation	
		WAGNER & STOTT	Object based	
		BANKERS TRUST		
		UNION BANK OF SWITZERLAND		

Field	Problem	Company/ development	Implementation architecture	Product/Prototype name
FINANCE		Intelligent environments (UK)	CRYSTAL	

Field	Problem	Company/ development	Implementation architecture	Product/Prototype name
TAX PLANNING AND ANALYSIS	Business tax planning	SYSTEM SOFTWARE (UK)	PAYE, National insurance, company organisation; used CRYSTAL shell	Business advisor taxation [T-2]
		COGNITIVE SYSTEMS (US)	Automated tax assistant	[T-3]
	International tax	COOPERS & LYBRAND	Ruled based, in GCLISP on PC, with forward chaining	Expert-TAX [T-1]
		COOPERS & LYBRAND (USA)		CLINTE
	Legal tax evluation	UNIV. MANCHESTER/ INLAND REVENUE (UK)	Advisor shell for apportionement of close company income	ACCI [F-9]
	Personal tax planning	US Dept. Housing/ Dept. of Treasury	Prolog	Tax consulting system [E-3]
		Legal knowledge Systems Inc.		Tax payer (DAN)
	Tax code analysis	US TREASURY		
	Forms scanning	US TREASURY/BBN	Rule based	
		Deutsche Kreditgenossn- schaft BIM (FRG)		
	VAT	ERNST & WHINNEY (UK)	VAT validation	VATIA
		CUSTOMS (DK)/ CRI	VAT validation	ESKORT

Field	Problem	Company/ development	Implementation architecture	Product/Prototype name
PERSONNEL MANAGEMENT	Salary increase equalization	UNIV. SAARLANDES	Backward chaining	LST-1
	Corporate personnel management	AI CORP/SECURITY PACIFIC	Intellect NL. front-end	
AUDITING	Verify balances, and match ratios against sector data and trends	Deutsche Kreditgenossenshact BIM (FRG)	Semantic nets + Prolog + Basic	Portable Adviser
		T.U. DENMARK	Backward chaining	ESE DEMO
		COOPERS LYBRAND		
		FIRST NTL. BANK OF CHICAGO (US)	Rule based	
	Asset and liability balance sheet analysis	BANQUE DE FRANCE (F)		COSIE
		IBM		
		EXPERTeam (F)	Production of financial reports, with spreadsheadet and knowledge based financial analyzer; on TI Exp	FINEXPRO+ CREDIT EXPERT
		SEC/Arthur Andersen (US)	Financial analysis of EDGAR filings, using ratios and notes; uses KEE shell on Symbolics	Financial statement analyzer (FSA) [F-4]

Field	Problem	Company/ development	Implementation architecture	Product/Prototype name
AUDITING	Screening financial disclosure filings	SEC/A.D. LITTLE/ ARTHUR ANDERSEN/	NL parser ELOISE coupled to EDGAR document management system	
	Real estate appraisal	SECURITY PACIFIC		
	International transfer pricing for sales	DATA GENERAL (US)	Pricing of parts shipped abroad; GOLDWORKS + MVLISP	

Field	Problem	Company/development	Implementation architecture	Product/Prototype name
COMMODITIES	Movements in crude oil and product prices	SHELL	Conflict resolution + policy + trade models	
		SKYLINE CORP. (CH) BP Oil	Integrated spread-sheets	
	Bauxite prices	UNCTAD/Brazil	Disequilibrium model	
	Commodities trading	MIT	Frames	COMEX [F-7]
PROJECT MANAGEMENT	PERT management integrated with business and financial modelling	PANSOPHIC	Coordinating models	INGOT
		AMACONSULT (CH)	PERT models	
MANAGEMENT DECISIONS	Formulate, think through and justify decisions	DECISION SUPPORT SOFTWARE	Group decision making and hierarchy	EXPERT CHOICE
	Corporate financing and budgetting in relation to strategic decisions (new plant, product)	PALLADIAN SOFTWARE	Mixed chaining + specialist models	MANAGEMENT ADVISOR
	Entreprise wide information management	IBM	Asset management	EWIN, CASES
	Financial decision making instruction	Arthur Andersen	LOOPS7KB hierarchy	FSA

Field	Problem	Company/ development	Implementation architecture	Product/Prototype name
MANAGEMENT DECISIONS	Payment of company car tax	Intelligent Environments LTD (demo) & HM & V Research OY (SF) / VALMET Oy	Production rules and inclusion of financial calculation functions	CRYSTAL
	Pricing system	TRANSAMERICA INSURANCE/AI CORP.	Process control pricing system by salesman	
	Analysis of general ledger files	HUMAN EDGE SOFTWARE	Identity troublesome business areas by NL queries	Intellect
		DATEV (FRG)		HEXE
	Building surveying	ROYAL INSTITUTION CHARTERED SURVEYORS (UK)	Building selection and surveying	

Expert Systems in Economics, Banking and Management
L.F. Pau et al. (Editors)
© *Elsevier Science Publishers B.V. (North-Holland), 1989*

Qualitative Reasoning in the Commercial Lending Decision:
The Role of Naive Mathematics

Lisa Braden-Harder, R. Bhaskar and Seshashayee S. Murthy

IBM T.J. Watson Research Center

P.O. Box 704

Yorktown Heights, NY 10598, USA

1 Introduction

Commercial lending decisions, an important class of economic decisions, have generally proven harder to model and less amenable to AI than personal credit decisions.[1] This is not surprising, because commercial lending is riskier as it involves larger loan amounts. Also evaluating a business enterprise from the point of view of a lender is more complex than simply predicting an individual borrower's ability to pay back a loan. The essence of this complexity stems from the fact that the bank lending officer makes *qualitative judgements* about a the business making the loan application. In this paper, we use recent work on qualitative reasoning in physical domains[10] to model the qualitative judgements of a loan officer.

Our approach is to examine verbal protocol data for evidence that the loan officer uses qualitative judgments. The verbal protocol data we use is about a lending decision that has already been studied in the accounting literature on commercial lending[12,13]. We examine the data for evidence that the qualitative judgements made can be captured by a set of Q-spaces proposed in work on design[10]. The method of analyzing the data is novel, but not completely original; we use a full-blown natural language parser along with a variety of dictionary driven tools on the protocols and examine the output of the parser for evidence of Q-spaces using fairly mechanical rules. Using such a natural language parser is the logical extension of a fairly long line of research[2,3,7,8,14,15]. The natural language parser we use is the PEG (PLNLP English Grammar) system, which is the result of a fairly long-standing research program in our laboratory. Information about PEG is summarized in [11].

The rest of this paper is divided as follows: first, in Section 2 we describe Q-spaces and the general problem of qualitative reasoning. Next we describe, in Section 3 the method we use for protocol analysis, and the commercial lending problem in Section 4. Finally in Section 5 we describe the subset of the data that we analyze in detail, and what we found.

---

[1]This paper is exclusively about these decisions as made by lending institutions in the United States for domestic customers; no international aspects are considered.

2   Qualitative Reasoning and Naive Mathematics

Qualitative reasoning provides a broad picture of the functioning of the world by taking a step back from the details provided by a quantitative approach. In reasoning with numbers the aim is to break the real number line into broad, qualitatively distinct classes, and describe the working of a system in terms of these classes. Such reasoning has mathematical aspects to it, but these aspects are often concealed by the surface nature of the task being performed; hence the term *naive mathematics*[1]. DeKleer [6] defines the qualitative values a variable can have $A_0 \ldots A_z$ as representing disjoint abutting intervals that cover the entire number line. We term the set of these values a *Q-space*[10]. Within a particular domain, a Q-space will have implicitly defined operations and endpoints, and we shall call such domain-dependent Q-spaces *naive algebras*. In this context, it is possible to describe the aim of qualitative reasoning as the reduction of the cardinality of the Q-space while still retaining the information available from doing the analysis using quantitative values. This has two benefits.

1. Complete quantitative information is not always available about the variables being analyzed. This is true in managerial decision-making, but it is also true even in more precise domains such as engineering design. Yet, one has to make decisions using this partial information. In some cases, the partial information can be used by representing the variables in qualitative form. By using the smallest possible Q-space in which to perform the analysis, we are able to deal better with incomplete information.

2. Using qualitative descriptions and reasoning it is sometimes possible to form a clear picture of a decision problem, even if it is impossible or difficult to cast it into a form such as an optimization problem. Thus one can get a better understanding of the workings of the system at some convenient level of detail. In essence using a small Q-space gives a broader picture of the workings of a system.

Commercial lending requires qualitative reasoning of the kind that can take place in a Q-space. For example, it is possible to examine the average age of the accounts payable of a company, and by examining whether the average age is increasing, determine if the company has been alleviating a cash flow problem by delaying payment of current liabilities. Even though the calculations are made in the space of ordinary numbers, the inferences are of form, *increasing age*, *decreasing age*, and so on.

We use a set of 3 Q-spaces to model the assessments of the loan officer. These spaces are essentially as follows:

Q-space 1 *-, 0 and +*, ie the value of any variable is assigned one of these three values.

Q-space 2 *0, small, medium, large*

Q-space 3 This is a refinement of Q-space 3. Each of the three non-zero categories of Q-space 2 is further divided into three categories, corresponding approximately to small, medium and large.

Although it is possible to elaborate this set of Q-spaces, we simply choose those that seem, *a posteriori*, to actually fit the data. In earlier definitions, for example in [10], four Q-spaces are proposed.

Our use of these Q-spaces will be as follows: examine the verbal protocol data for evidence that some variable is actually being assigned a value in one of these spaces. Identify the evidence, and attempt to mechanize the search for the evidence through the parser.

3   Method for Protocol Analysis

Automatic analysis eliminates the time-consuming task of hand-encoding protocols and provides increased reliability and validity. Other research has been done in this area [2,3,7,8,14,15], but only one of these systems, PAS(Protocol Analysis System), attempts to encode protocol segments using some linguistic analysis[14,15]. In PAS-I, a linguistic processor containing a keyword grammar is used to map each segment into its propositional form from which it can be mapped into a problem space. Waterman and Newell[14] argued against more complete linguistic analysis of the protocols because of the complexity of such a task. In addition, they held that syntactic analysis would not be useful for segments that were not complete, grammatical sentences. Our work differs from theirs in two important respects: (1) we have incorporated some natural language tools that enable us to do more detailed linguistic analysis and (2) we have selected the less complicated task of mapping segments into Q-spaces.

Our approach is to use general natural language tools with no specific domain dependencies. One of these tools, the PLNLP English Grammar, PEG, is a broad-coverage syntactic parser. This bottom-up parallel parser provides an approximate parse for a majority of English segments. It is robust; as part of the CRITIQUE text analysis system[11], the parser has been used to analyze over two million words of text. The PEG parser handles ungrammatical sentences and sentence fragments acceptably in a majority of cases because most of the sentence fragments that we have encountered contain some structure which the parser is able to identify and combine into clauses. Likewise, ungrammatical segments have not presented a problem thus far. Perhaps because the PEG parser can identify many common English errors. (Its first application was text-critiquing.)

3.1   Procedure

Our method for mapping segments into appropriate Q-spaces involves parsing each segment, comparing the results with a list of target words that might indicate some qualitative or quantitative reasoning, and then identifying modifiers that might indicate a more detailed Q-space. The parser generates a parse tree for each segment (See Figure 1) and an underlying record structure with additional information. For this tree the sentence is *Once again saw that healthy jump in 75 to 76 and again for 76 to 77.*

The subsequent processing currently uses only four types of information generated during parsing: syntactic structure, part-of-speech assignments, base forms, and quantity markers. The structure describes possible clause boundaries and modifier attachments. For example, the syntactic structure of the sentence in Figure 1 shows that the adjective *healthy* is modifying the noun *jump*. A syntactic parser cannot always disambiguate modifier attachments, but it can reduce the number of possible attachments. This task is easier for shorter segments, which are predominant in the protocol, because there are very few possible attachments. Part-of-speech assignments (e.g. noun, verb) for each word are also provided by the parser. If multiple parses are generated, more than one part-of-speech

Once again saw that healthy jump in '75 to '76 and again for '76 to '77.

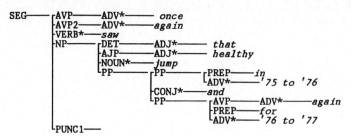

Figure 1: A Sample Parse Tree

assignment may be made. Also available is the base or uninflected form for each word. (In the example, *see* is identified as the base form of *saw*.)

After the segment has been parsed, the next step is to traverse the parse tree and the underlying record structure in search of target words and modifiers. Each segment is processed independently. No attempt is made to use contextual information, for instance, to resolve pronoun references. As mentioned before, part-of-speech and base form assignments are made for each word. This information is compared with a list of target words. If a match is found, the syntactic structure can then identify any modifiers (adjectives or adverbs) that might be of interest. Modification of a target word usually indicates a subdividing of the Q-space (i.e. a move to a more detailed Q-space). If the phrase includes a target word, it is a candidate for the Q1 space. If the target word is modified by an adjective or adverb, then the segment is a candidate for the Q2 problem space. Additional modification indicates a Q3 space. To identify segments for the other Q-spaces, quantity markers are used. Dollar amounts, for example, are noted while years are excluded.

An extensive list of target words is essential for this processing to be successful. To generate such a list, we identified several sets of words that might indicate some qualitative reasoning (acceptable/unacceptable, short/long) using a concordance of frequent words in the protocol. Of course,.a manually generated list would be very limiting. According to Ericsson and Simon[7] on average, half of the words in a protocol are used only once. The list of target words was automatically extended using the synonymy relations that appear in the Collins Thesaurus. This was done by means of indexes into the synonym dictionary that have been generated by Chodorow, et al[5]. With this information, it is possible to "sprout" synonyms over several levels (i.e. find synonyms of synonyms) to create an extensive list of related words grouped by part of speech[4].

3.2 Conclusions about Protocol Analysis Method

This combination of a natural language parser and on-line synonyms has been used to successfully map segments into Q-spaces for several episodes of the protocol. The syntactic parser provides syntactic structure, part-of-speech assignments, and base forms that improve the accuracy of word matching over standard string or pattern matching. Synonyms are useful for automatically extending a list of target words and determining the "closeness" of two words. This approach takes advantage of the wealth of domain information that has been encoded by humans in dictionaries over hundreds of years. By incorporating dictionary information automatically, we have avoided hand-coding domain-specific information and thus, the system could be easily transferred to other domains.

Although this method was developed to identify Q-spaces, it could be extended to do more extensive content analysis. Consider the task of identifying statements about trends. Many such segments could be identified using the procedure mentioned above. If the word *increase* were sprouted (because it might suggest a trend), the sentence in figure could be classified as a trend statement because synonyms of *increase* include *jump,* (as well as *build up, upturn, rise* and a hundred more). Segments that mention time (e.g. year, 75) would also be of interest as in the sentence *It's getting more significant every year.* Constructions that include *have been, is getting* etc. followed by an adjective might also indicate a trend. Another clue might be the presence of domain-specific words (e.g. accounts receivable). These and other linguistic clues could be used to extract appropriate segments. Such clues include generated synonyms that are phrases, and techniques for assigning confidence factors to control incorrect matches[4].

4 The Commercial Lending Task

The commercial lending task in its simplest form consists of evaluating a set of financial statements of the borrower. There are some general restrictions on the kind of financial statements that are considered acceptable; in general they must be prepared according to generally accepted accounting principles, or GAAP; they must be certified by auditors. Other than these, most lenders do not usually impose many restrictions on the kind of information that must be supplied by a potential borrower. If the loan is to be a secured loan, then some additional information may be required about the security itself, or in some cases, information needed for implementing such arrangements as a lock box, assignment of receivables, etcetera.

Even in its bare essentials, a commercial lending decision involves analysis along one or more dimensions. We list some of these dimensions below, though this selection of dimensions is simply idiosyncratic. Several selections are possible, and here we use one that is similar to a conventional characterization of the lending decision.

Payback and Cash Flow A borrower must have the cash flow to sustain a payback as agreed; chiefly, this view requires an analysis of the cash flow situation of the borrower, an analysis of its existing commitments; the flow of funds statement is the chief source of data here.

The Business Relationship A loan may be either to an existing customer, or to a new customer; in either case there is an opportunity to evaluate the potential or history of a continuing relationship with a borrower. Information such as account history, Dun and Bradstreet ratings, etc. may be useful here.

The Industrial View A loan may provide an opportunity to evaluate an industry; in particular, it may be possible or necessary to carry out the conventional 2 ×2 analysis of market share of an individual borrower versus market growth; for example in a "tight money" situation, a lender may choose not to lend for market expansion in an industry with low market growth.

The Design View Sometimes, it may be *necessary* for a bank to lend to a particular borrower; in such a case the decision problem is one of *designing* a loan that fits certain conditions, such as varying the payback period, the interest rate, the kind of security, and so on.

4.1   The Specific Problem

The specific task posed to the subjects was a loan decision about a hypothetical company called the "Dawson Stores Case."[2] Five conditions were imposed on the nature of the task in order to make it both tractable and realistic. These conditions were as follows.

1. Four years of full financial statements were presented to the subject in order to insure that a realistic and adequate information set was available to the bank lending officer. Three years of statements are often a requirement at many banks.

2. Sufficient supplemental information was available if requested by the subjects. This was done in order to insure that the subjects did not terminate the task due to a perceived lack of information.

3. The loan was of sufficient size to require formal financial analysis.

4. No evaluation of collateral is required.

5. The loan does not violate any legal or policy restrictions of the bank.

The subjects were all lending officers employed at banks in either Boston or Columbus [12,13].

5   The Data

In this paper, for reasons of brevity, we shall discuss part of the behavior of exactly one subject, Loan Officer P. We have broken down the verbal protocol into 35 episodes, which collectively lasted about 42 minutes. The subject reached a positive decision (ie "make the loan") at that time. Of these 35 episodes, we discuss just one episode, which in sequence was Episode 7. The verbalization of the subject for this episode is shown in full in Figure 2. The subject is talking about the number of days needed to collect receivables. The figure 56 days is essentially a measure of receivables turnover and is given by dividing the average balance of accounts receivable by the average daily net sales[9, pp. 11-32]. The assessments being made here are about various current assets, such as receivables, inventory, etc. in relation to sales. There is an attempt by the subject to convert the problem to a qualitative

---

[2]The data that we use was collected as part of an earlier study that one of us participated in[13]. The materials for this case were constructed by Ray Stephens as part of his doctoral work at the Harvard Business School[12]. We are grateful to Professor Stephens for developing these materials.

1. (Reads 25 seconds)

2. Cash has been building up *nicely*.

3. Receivables appear to be turning over *respectably well* based on revenues

4. of a million eight.

5. Need to figure out what the days turn will be.

6. (Uses calculator).

7. 114 days.

8. I guess the thing that disturbs me is maybe what is being taken for

9. granted - what doesn't accord with their operations seems to be a *little*

10. *bit long* for a retail store.

11. 114 days?

12. (Uses a calculator again).

13. Alright, it's 56 days.

14. (Uses calculator.)

15. Inventory turn is about the same, 67 days.

16. (Uses calculator.)

17. Accounts payable is 49 days,

18. cash cycle – it *looks like* about a 74 day.

19. For a 1/31 year end this is possibly a *good* master charge candidate -

20. speed it up somewhat -

21. around 56.

Figure 2: Loan Officer P, Episode 7.

one, with all assessments being of the same dimension, viz. days. As a result, qualitative judgements made here can be simple total or partial ordering judgements. Such qualitative assessments are what we seek to discover through automatic protocol analysis using the PEG parser.

For the episode we have described, we found that the subject used Q-space 2 and Q-space 3. This can be understood by looking at the somewhat *lispified* output of the protocol analysis provided in Figure 3. In this episode, we see that of the 11 sentences spoken by the subject in this episode, six of them involve qualitative modifications to a judgement, such as *well* (Segments 1 and 2), *a little bit long* (Segments 9 and 10), etc. In each of these cases, the qualitative assessment (i.e., assignment to a Q-space) takes place after a number is either read or calculated. The full analysis, shown in the figure, gives a complete picture of this.

6   Conclusion

We conjecture that these qualitative assessments which are both the result of numerical calculations and their cause, have to be thought of conceptually as though they were *goals*. However, a collection of qualitative assessments is satisfactory not when they reach some particular value, as is the case with goals, but when they are somehow not in conflict with one another. If one part of a set of qualitative assessments does not reach conclusions *similar* to other parts, then the assessment continues and is refined till the conflict is reduced.

```
Episode P7: Current Assets
(Remark (Reads 25 seconds))
((Text (Cash has been building up nicely.)
  (MLI cash 0)
  (Trend (Trend 4 3 1 3) (PHRASE has been 0))
  (Trend (Increase 1 1 1 3) (PHRASE build up 0))
  (QA-2 (Well 1 1 1 12) (ADV nicely) (modifies build up)
  (Syntopic Cash))
((Text (Receivables appear to be turning over respectably well
                  based on revenues of a million eight.)
  (MLI turn over 0 )
  (MLI revenues 0 )
  (Assessment (Look 1 2 2 9) (VERB appear))
  (QA-1 (Well 1 1 1 12) (ADV well))
  (QA-2 (Adv respectably) (modifies well))
  (Value 1000000 8)
  (Syntopic Receivables))
((Text (Need to figure out what the days turn will be.)
  (MLI days turn 0 )
  (Assessment (Explain 2 1 1 2) (Calculate 2 1 1 2) (PHRASE figure out 0))
  (Assessment (Request 2 2 1 2) (NOUN need)))
(Remark (Uses calculator))
((Text (114 days.)
  (Value 114))
((Text (I guess the thing that disturbs me is maybe what is
       being taken for granted)
  (Assume (Assume 1 1 1 4) (PHRASE take of granted 0))
  (Assume (Assume 1 1 1 4) (VERB guess))
  (QA-1 (Surprise 2 1 1 4) (VERB disturb))
```

Figure 3: Analyzed text of Episode 7
Page 1

```
 (Approx (Possibly 1 1 1 2) (ADV maybe))
 (Syntopic what))
((Text (what doesn't accord with their operations seems to be a little
       bit long for a retail store.)
 (Assessment (Look 1 2 2 9) (PHRASE seem to be 0))
 (QA-1 (Fit 1 1 3 9) (VERB accord))
 (QA-2 (Little 1 3 3 10) (ADJ little) (modifies long))
 (Adj bit retail their))
((Text (114 days?)
 (Value 114)
(Remark (Uses a calculator again))
((Text (Alright, it's 56 days.)
 (Adv alright)
 (Value 56)
 (Syntopic 56 days))
 (Remark (Uses calculator.))
 ((Text (Inventory turn is about the same, 67 days.)
   (MLI inventory turn 0 )
   (QA-1 (Equal 1 1 1 6) (PHRASE the same 0))
   (Value 67)
   (Syntopic Inventory turn))
 (Remark (Uses calculator.))
((Text (Accounts payable is 49 days.)
  (MLI accounts payable 0 )
  (Value 49)
  (Syntopic payable))
((Text (cash cycle, it looks like about a 74 day.)
  (MLI cash 0 )
  (Assessment (Look 1 2 2 9) (PHRASE look like 0))
  (Approx (Adj about))
  (Value 74))
((Text (For a 1/31 year end this is possibly a good master charge candidate.)
  (Value 31)
  (Approx (Possibly 1 1 1 2) (ADV possibly))
  (QA-1 (Healthy 2 1 1 2) (Acceptably 2 2 2 2) (ADJ good))
  (Adj master)
  (Syntopic this))
((Text (speed it up somewhat, around 56.)
  (Approx (About) (PREP around))
  (Value 56))
```

Figure 3: Analyzed text of Episode 7

Page 2

References

[1] Bhaskar, R. (1986). Crypto-Mathematical Tasks in Problem Solving: The Domain of Naive Mathematics. IBM Research Report, RC 11916. Yorktown Heights, NY: IBM T. J. Watson Research Center.

[2] Bhaskar, R. and H. Simon, H. A. (1977) "Problem Solving in Semantically Rich Domains: An Example From Engineering Thermodynamics. *Cognitive Science* 193-251.

[3] Brown, Charles (1986) The Verbal Protocol Analysis Tool (VPA): Some Formal Methods for Describing Expert Behavior. *2nd Symposium on Human Interface* pp. 561-567.

[4] Chodorow, M. S., Byrd, R. J. and Heidorn, G. E. (1985) "Extracting Semantic Hierarchies from a Large On-line Dictionary," *Proceedings of the Association of Computational Linguistics*. 299-304.

[5] Chodorow, M., Ravin,Y. and Sachar, H. (1988) "A Tool For Investigating the Synonymy Relation in a Sense Disambiguated Thesaurus," *Proceedings of the Association of Computational Linguistics, Conference on Applied Natural Language Processing.*

[6] de Kleer, J. and Brown, J.S. (1984) A Qualitative Physics Based on Confluences. *Artificial Intelligence* 24 (1984) 7-83.

[7] Ericsson, K. A. and Simon, H. A. (1984), Protocol Analysis: Verbal Reports as Data. Cambridge, Mass: The MIT Press.

[8] Konst, L., Wielinga, B. J. and Elshout J. J.(1983), Semi-Automated Analysis of Protocols from Novices and Experts Solving Physics Problems. Proceedings of the IJCAI, pp. 97-99.

[9] Lev, Baruch. (1974). Finacial Statement Analysis: A New Approach. Englewood CLiffs, NJ: Prentice-Hall.

[10] Murthy, S. S. (1988). Qualitative Reasoning at Multiple Resolutions. Proceedings of AAAI, 1988. pp. 296-300.

[11] Richardson, S. and Braden-Harder, L. (1988). The Experience of Developing a Large-Scale Natural Language Text Processing System: CRITIQUE. Proceedings of the Association of Computational Linguistics, Conference on Applied Natural Language Processing. 195-202.

[12] Stephens, R. G. (1978) Use of Financial Information in Structuring and Improving Decison Processes for Bank Lending Officers. DBA thesis. Boston, Mass.: Harvard University Graduate School of Business Administration.

[13] Stephens, R. G., Schank, J. K. and Bhaskar R. (1980) Accounting Information and the Lending Decision: A Process Tracing Perspective. WPS 80-46. Columbus, OH: College of Administrative Science, The Ohio State University.

[14] Waterman, D. and Newell, A. (1971) Protocol Analysis as a Task for Artificial Intelligence, **Artificial Intelligence.** Vol. 2, Nos. 2 and 3 pp. 285-318.

[15] Waterman, D. and Newell, A. (1973). Pas-II. IJCAI, 1973, pp. 431-445.

[16] Winterfeldt, D. and Edwards W. (1986) Decision Analysis and Behavioral Research. New York: Cambridge University Press.

Expert Systems in Economics, Banking and Management
L.F. Pau et al. (Editors)
© Elsevier Science Publishers B.V. (North-Holland), 1989   35

A CLEVER SCREENING SYSTEM FOR
COMMERCIAL LOAN APPLICATIONS*

Jean ROY and Jean-Marc SURET

Department of Finance and Insurance
Faculty of Business Administration
Laval University, Québec G1K 7P4 (Canada)

The system supports commercial credit analysis via two modules. The first one proposes a diagnosis of past financial statements. The second one provides tools to
evaluate both requests for long term debt and for lines of credit. It is able to identify
major weaknesses which should lead to rejection.

1. INTRODUCTION

The system was developed for the "Fédération des Caisses populaires Desjardins de
Québec". This organization oversees the operation of some 320 local credit unions which
manage some 6 billion dollars worth of assets. The credit department is staffed with some
twenty credit analysts who handle some 10 000 loan applications per year, 6 500 of them being
of the commercial type. Thus the task though complex is repetitive and requires about 3,5 hours
on average to be performed. Also because commercial credit is a relatively new activity for this
organization, it has grown at a rate of more than 25% per year over the last three years. This
strong growth has put pressure on hiring and integrating new human ressources. Finally, one
must note that before our intervention, the credit department did not make use of computers
beyond word processing. So the context was ideal to consider the development of a decision
support system that would integrate as much knowledge as possible and thus improve productivity and relieve the overloaded employees.

The research project was jointly funded by a state agency and the financial institution. The
development team consisted of four persons: a credit analyst acting as expert, two finance professors, one of whom was an ex-credit analyst himself, and a programmer. The system that was
developed part-time over a period of eight months has two major modules: one aimed at the
analysis of historical financial statements, the other used to evaluate the project to be financed.
Overall, the system displays twenty-six different screens and prints these on a thirteen page
report. The modules will be described in the next two sections. Finally, we will conclude with
an evaluation of the strengths and weaknesses of the system.

---
* The authors gratefully acknowledge financial support from the "Centre francophone pour la
recherche en informatisation des organisations" and the "Fédération des Caisses populaires
Desjardins de Québec".

2.   ANALYSIS OF HISTORICAL FINANCIAL STATEMENTS

Traditionally, financial statements analysis is performed by computing financial ratios and interpreting these by comparing them with those of the industrial sector and with those of previous years to detect trends. The approach taken in the system is to implement and improve this process. To achieve this goal, the system behaves as follows.

First, it displays a title screen and then asks some general information: identification of the borrower and of its industrial sector, identification of the local credit union where the application originated, and the name of the analyst using the system. The system then links to two data bases. First, it extracts from Statistics Canada's *Corporation Financial Statistics* file the aggregate balance sheet and income statement of the industrial sector of the borrower. Ninety-four accounting items are retrieved from one of the 182 industrial sectors available. Secondly, it gets the total deposits and capital of the credit union and computes the maximum amounts that can be lent to a single borrower according to the type of loan, i.e. unsecured, secured by a mortgage or a mixture of both. Screens number 3 to 7 are used to input the information contained in past financial statements: income statement, statement of retained earnings, balance sheet, flow of funds and supplementary information taken from the notes. The system allows the input of the financial statements taken at any three dates: a typical case would be two yearly and the last interim statements.

Then the systems computes some thirty ratios for each date available and for the industrial sector used for comparison. These are eventually displayed as such in four screens and allow the analyst to generate his own interpretation. However, the system will further propose an interpretation and an evaluation of the financial results of the borrower. To perform this task two approaches are used. First, the system performs a systematic decomposition of financial ratios, called structured financial analysis. Secondly, it computes financial health indicators that are obtained either as discriminant scores or via an iterative dichotomization procedure. As these two procedures represent the knowledge in this part of the system, they will now be described in some detail.

2.1   Structured Financial Analysis

Clearly the most important concept in credit analysis is the evaluation of the capacity of a borrower to reimburse his debt. Different ratios can be computed to evaluate this capacity, some typical ones would be: debt/assets, the "times interest earned" and the cash-flow over the due within one year. However, academic research, such as that conducted by Gombola *et al.* [3] and Frydman *et al.* [2], has shown that the ratio with the best predictive power is that of cash-flow (net profit + depreciation) over total debt. This ratio has the advantage of being insensitive to the maturity structure of debt and, thus, measures long term solvency rather than liquidity. The system will generate a judgment as to whether the solvency of the firm is much worse, worse, similar, better or much better than the industry average.

Then it will proceed to explain the relative position of the firm with regard to its industrial sector. To obtain an explanation, the solvency measure is decomposed as shown below:

$$CR = \frac{CF}{TD}$$

$$CR = \frac{CF}{S} \cdot \frac{S}{TA} \cdot \frac{TA}{TD}$$

CR : capacity to reimburse

CF : cash-flow (net income plus depreciation)

S : sales

TA : total assets

TD : total debt

Thus, solvency is explained as the product of three major factors: profitability of sales, productivity of assets and capitalization. The system uses this factorization to generate the following type of diagnosis:

"The capacity to reimburse of the firm is the x% lower than the industry average because its profitability is y% lower, its productivity z% lower or its capitalization is w% lower than the industry average."

Further decomposition of the profitability and productivity measures are obtained as follows:

$$\frac{CF}{S} = (S - E_1 - E_2 ... - E_n - D + D)/S$$

$$= 1 - E_1/S - E_2/S ... - E_n/S$$

E_i : expense i

D : depreciation

Thus to explain profitability, one needs only to examine several ratios of expenses to sales. The system breaks down expenses in four conventional categories, which cover the various types of input to the production process, namely: material, men, machines and money. The system can then explain the profitability measure as below:

"The profitability of the firm is x% higher than the industry average because its expenses for material are y% higher or its expenses for wages and salaries are z% higher or its expenses for equipment are u% higher or its interest expenses are v% higher than the industry average."

Similarly, the productivity measure is decomposed as :

$$\frac{S}{TA} = \frac{S}{(A_1 + A_2 + ... + A_n)} = \frac{1}{(A_1/S + A_2/S + ... + A_n/S)}$$

So, to explain the overall productivity of assets, we break down the assets in various categories; specifically the system focuses on accounts receivable, inventory and fixed assets relative to sales. These three ratios are traditional turnover measures. Again the system will be able to generate a diagnosis of the following form:

"The productivity of the firm is x% lower than the industry average because its account receivable are y% higher or its inventory is z% higher or its fixed assets are w% higher than the industry average."

The two-level decomposition process involves all major components of the balance sheet and income statement. So even if it is very summary, it is in a sense complete. It proceeds from the general to the particular and quickly points out the strengths and weaknesses of the firm. From this diagnosis, the analyst can scrutinize further if need be.

2.2   Financial health indicators

Another approach to integrate knowledge in the system is to exploit the results of researches aimed at predicting corporate bankruptcy. Discriminant analysis has been the major statistical technique used for this purpose. Altman and Lavallée [1] have conducted such a study on 54 Canadian firms and have obtained the discriminant function shown below:

$$Z_c = -1,626 + 0,234X_1 - 0,531X_2 + 1,002X_3 + 0,972X_4 + 0.612X_5$$

Z_c : discriminant score

X_1 : sales/total assets

X_2 : total debt/total assets

X_3 : current assets/current liabilities

X_4 : net profit after tax/total debt

X_5 : rate of growth of net worth - rate of growth of assets

A score above zero predicts survival and below zero bankruptcy. An uncertainty zone exists between $-0,71$ and $1,05$. This method should predict correctly 81,5% of the times. Our system computes this score for the firm under consideration and interprets the result.

Similarly, Legault and Véronneau [4] have obtained a discriminant function based on 173 manufacturing firms based in the Province of Québec, which is the area of operation of our financial institution. The study done for the Institute of Chartered Accountants of Canada got the following function:

$$Z_{ca} = -2,7616 + 4,5913X_1 - 4,5080X_2 + 0,3936X_3$$

Z_{ca} : discriminant score

X_1 : (net worth + debt due to shareholders)/total assets

X_2 : (profit before tax and extraordinary items + interest expense)/total assets

X_3 : sales of previous year/total assets of previous year

A score above -0,30 predicts survival. The average score of surviving firms is 0,7 and the average score of bankrupt firms is -1,2. This method should give a correct prediction 83% of the time. Again our system computs this score and interprets it. Thus we are able to strengthen or weaken the prediction generated by the previous discriminant function.

Finally, the system generates another prediction of survival or bankruptcy based on a classification three procedure developed by Frydman *et al.* [2]. The procedure is implemented via the five following rules:

1. If $X_1 \leq 0,1309$ and $X_2 \leq 0,1453$, then bankruptcy is predicted.

2. If $X_1 \leq 0,1309$ and $X_2 > 0,1453$ and $X_3 \leq 0,025$, then failure is predicted.

3. If $X_1 \leq 0,1309$ and $X_2 > 0,1453$ and $X_3 > 0,025$, then survival is predicted.

4. If $X_1 > 0,1309$ and $X_4 \leq 0,6975$, then survival is predicted

5. If $X_1 > 0,1309$ and $X_4 > 0,6975$, then bankruptcy is predicted.

X_1 :   cash-flow/total debt

X_2 :   retained earnings/total assets

X_3 :   cash/total sales

X_4 :   total debt/total assets

This classification scheme was obtained with the CART (Classification and Regression Trees) software, which implement a variation of the basic ID3 algorithm (Iterative Dichotomization). Based on a sample of 200 US firms, this classification predicts correctly 81% of the times.

Thus the analyst is given three global measures of financial health; he can see to what extent they agree and eventually form his own judgment accordingly. The last screen of this section is in fact given to the analyst who can integrate his comments to the final report printed by the system. We believe that this approach of leaving the final word to the user has crystalized the idea that man and machine are working in collaboration rather than in competition. This has been significant, we believe, in inducing acceptance of the system by the users.

3.   EVALUATION OF THE PROJECT

The following module allows the user to analyze the project to be financed. Two screens are used to describe the sources and eventual uses of funds. From this information, the system generates a pro-forma balance sheet and computes several pro-forma ratios relative to the anticipated financial structure of the borrower. Then the system helps the user at forecasting the next income statement, which eventually gives an estimate of the expected cash-flow for the coming year. The capital and interest due within a year is recalculated taking into account the new debt and this amount is compared to the expected cash-flow. Finally, the critical ratio of cash-flow to total debt is evaluated and a judgment of its adequacy is generated. To complete the analysis, the system computes the critical level of sales that would generate a cash-flow equal to the capital to be repaid in the coming year. This "break even" level is compared to the actual and forecasted level of sales to estimate the risk of default. These constitute the basic elements of the analysis of the new long term debt. The system also supports the analysis of an application for a line of credit.

The basic approach to evaluate the line of credit that can be offered to a borrower is to calculate it as x% of accounts receivable plus y% of inventory. The two percentages are adjusted with regard to the quality of the assets used to secure the line of credit. However, three other rules are used that may pull down the potential line of credit. First, the line of credit must not exceed the owner's net worth. Second, it should not be more than 15% of sales for a manufacturing firm or more than 10% of sales for a service business. Finally, the line of credit should be approximately equal to the net working capital. This last rule is based on the rationale that short term assets should be financed about equally by the line of credit, the suppliers and long term capital. Accordingly, our system applies these rules and displays whether the proposed line of credit would comply.

A broader analysis of short term financing is also conducted. Once the maximum line of credit is known, the required contribution of the owners of the firm to short financing is computed: this is called the required working capital. Then the system forecasts the expected working capital, based on the description of the project and the expected income statement. This allows to anticipate any liquidity problem.

Once the long term and short term analyses are completed, the system helps the user via nine questions to estimate the risk premium to be charged to the borrower over the prime rate of interest.

Finally, the system displays a summary screen showing three long term solvency measures, the three financial health indicators recomputed on a pro-forma basis and four criteria to compare the requested line of credit to. These ten critical values are used as a screen to filter the loan application. The system identifies whether the borrower is weak relative to any of the ten benchmarks, in which case it suggests that a serious motive for rejection exists.

Again the user is given the last screen to input his comments. He or she may point out any element that may affect the relevancy of the analysis or the reasons why the suggestion of the system should be overridden.

4. CONCLUSION

Although the initial trust for this project was to explore the potential of knowledge-based systems for credit analysis, great care was taken to avoid the "solution in search of a problem syndrome". Rather a careful analysis of the user's needs led to building a multi-faceted tool that involves data-base, spreadsheet, word-processing and expert-system functions. It then seemed natural to use the GURU software which offers all these functions; however, it eventually proved cumbersome. Also it was realized that the same content could be offered to the user using LOTUS 1-2-3, provided one accepts to lose the separation of rules and data. Considering the relatively small size of the knowledge base, which is made of some one hundred "if statements", the lost was considered small with respect to several important advantages such as the ease to distribute to final users already familiar with spredsheets, the speed of execution and the ease to maintain and modify. Another important advantage is the fact that the user is offered an open system where it is possible to extend the analysis within the system as may be required in a particular instance.

Our experience is interesting, we believe, because it shows how expert-system concepts can be integrated in applications that may look traditional. The screening system described in this paper does not pretend to be a truly expert-system. However, one should be convinced by now that it contains a very significant amount of knowledge with regard to credit analysis. We deliberately proceeded to a detailed description in order to illustrate the various flavors of knowledge present in the system.

Obviously, some of the finance and accounting knowledge is embedded in the formulas used to compute various variables and in the order in which these are displayed. Some knowledge has been acquired through a theoretical decomposition of the problem. Another type of knowledge comes from formal empirical research. Finally, some rules are basically heuristics used by practionners. This eclectic approach to gathering knowledge gives strength, we believe, to the system.

In closing, several limitations of the system need to be mentioned however. The system is strongly dependent on the availability of past financial statements and a clearly identified industrial sector that can be used for comparison purposes. This implies that is is not appropriate for projects that are start-ups or firms that do not neatly fall into the industrial classification of Statistics Canada. Also the system is basically designed to study one firm at a time. It is not able to deal with situations where several affiliated companies are involved in the same loan request. Despite these limitations, the users have found the system very helpful and the development effort is still in progress.

REFERENCES

[1]   Altman, E.I. and Lavallée, M.Y., Business failure classification in Canada, Journal of Business Administration, Summer 1981, pp.147-164.

[2]   Frydman, H., Altman, E.I. and Kao, D., Introducing recursive partitioning for financial classification: The case of financial distress, The Journal of Finance, March 1985, pp. 269-291.

[3]   Gombola, M.J., Haskins, M.E., Ketz, J.E. and Williams, D.D., Cashflow in bankruptcy prediction, Financial Management, Winter 1987, pp.55-65.

[4]   Legault, J. and Véronneau, P., CA-Score, A warning system for small business failures, Bilans, June 1987, pp.29-31.

Expert Systems in Economics, Banking and Management
L.F. Pau et al. (Editors)
© Elsevier Science Publishers B.V. (North-Holland), 1989

USING INDUCTIVE LEARNING FOR ASSESSING FIRMS' FINANCIAL HEALTH

Michael J. SHAW and James A. GENTRY

Department of Business Administration and Department of Finance,
respectively, University of Illinois at Urbana-Champaign, Champaign,
Illinois, 61820, U.S.A.

The research described in this paper stems from the vision that,
just as AI is useful in the medical domain for analyzing symptoms
and diagnosing diseases, it can also provide powerful tools for
assessing the health of corporations by looking at their financial
performance. In this paper, the financial performance is evaluated
by a cash flow model. Inductive learning is then used for deriving
rules for assessing the financial health. The application in business loan evaluation is described.

1. INTRODUCTION

This paper describes an ongoing research effort to develop a knowledge-
based decision-support system (DSS) that specializes in assessing firms'
financial health for commercial banks. The system, referred to as MARBLE (a
decision-support system for managing and recommending business loan
evaluation), is a knowledge-based DSS that uses decision rules for evaluating
commercial loans. The MARBLE system was designed to use the lending judgment
of experienced loan officers [21]. It was constructed in collaboration with a
commercial bank in Chicago.

Although there are many types of bank loans, commercial banks are a primary
source of credit for companies that do not have easy access to capital markets.
In general, the risk characteristics of companies seeking bank credit are
greater than companies needing credit in the capital markets. Thus, determining which business loan applicant should be extended credit and how much
credit are major decisions for commercial bank lending officers and credit
analysts. Assessing the financial health of a company requires careful analysis of both quantitative financial statement information as well as qualitative information concerning the outlook for the company. Having the necessary
information, the correct credit analysis model, and the ability to interpret
the information correctly is a task of bank lending staff. A knowledge-based
expert system with features such as explanation ability, heuristic inference,
reasoning with uncertainty and structured representation of knowledge is an
invaluable tool in the loan decision-making process.

In addition to the common expert-system design, MARBLE is also equipped
with the learning capability. Learning is an important feature of any intel-

ligent system. There are two aspects in decision-support tasks where learning
comes into play: (1) learning decision rules for the knowledge base, i.e.,
the knowledge-acquisition process and (2) refining existing rules by observing
prior problem-solving experience, i.e., the knowledge refinement process. To
achieve these learning functions, MARBLE must be equipped with an inductive
inference engine that is complementary to the deductive problem solver. Thus,
an important design issue concerns the inductive learning technique for rule
learning and knowledge acquisition.

There are practical incentives to introduce inductive learning into MARBLE.
First, an important part of the DSS contains decision rules used by experienced
loan officers, but we observed that it is not easy to acquire knowledge from
loan officers in the form of rules. Second, there may not be an expert in
evaluating business loans because the evaluation is highly judgmental. We
observed that it is often difficult to achieve a consensus among loan officers
on the best set of rules to use. Third, even when the decision rules have
been determined and employed, MARBLE needs a means to refine the rules continuously. These problems can be resolved by incorporating an inductive-
learning component in the knowledge-based DSS.

The objectives of the paper are to develop MARBLE and show how it employs
production rules that represent the basic knowledge of a bank lending system;
to present an overview of the business loan application process; to develop
MARBLE as an integrated problem-solving model structured around the business
loan decision making process; to explain the inductive learning method; to
present a cash flow model for assessing financial health; and finally to
present an empirical study of a MARBLE application.

2. ASSESSING FINANCIAL HEALTH AND LOAN EVALUATION

Assessing the firm's financial health is the major task in loan evaluation.
Typically, the evaluation of a business-loan application is a subjective decision process made independently by loan officers and credit analysts. The
loan-granting decision is based on the analysis of a firm's historical and
pro forma financial information and on the interpretation of qualitative information concerning its product markets and industry characteristics, and the
overall performance of management. The loan-evaluation decision is traditionally analyzed by statistical linear models, such as regression analysis
[17], or polytomous probit analysis [10], or recursive partitioning [11]. As
pointed out by Haslem and Longbrake [9] and Dietrich and Kaplan [10], statistical analysis with linear models cannot capture the subjective judgments and
the qualitative evaluation so important in the lending decision. In essence,
the approach used by MARBLE is akin to the heuristic simulation method employed by Cohen, Gilmore, and Singer [5], which simulates the decision process

of loan officers. MARBLE, however, employs production rules as the basic
knowledge representation, which has been pointed out as an effective model of
the human decision-making process [1]. In addition, the knowledge-based expert technology enables MARBLE to be equipped with uncertainty reasoning,
explanation, and incremental refinement capabilities. As will be shown, inductive learning can be applied to enhance MARBLE's performance further by
automatically acquiring decision rules for loan classification. There are
two schools in the development of mental models for describing learning processes: (1) the connectionist model, which describes mental processes in
terms of activation patterns defined over nodes in a highly interconnected
network; and (2) the production-system model, which describes mental processes
as symbol manipulation in a production system [1] [15] [16]. The method we
use for incorporating learning in MARBLE is the second approach in which
learning is achieved by rule-augmenting.

The evaluating of a business loan application is based on information presented in the financial statements plus qualitative information related to
company and industry characteristics, the quality of management, the ability
to repay the loan, and the availability of collateral. Frequently the qualitative information is of greater value to the lending decision than the financial statement analysis. The evaluation of a firm's credit worthiness is
based on a credit score for each of the characteristics. When the credit risk
score is calculated, the risk classification of the applicant is established
by comparing it to an objectively determined standard.

If the loan is approved, the bank establishes the terms of the loan with
the customer in order to assure repayment. The final phase of the process involves organizing all the data and information used in the decision process
and storing it in the loan documentation file. This file is the basis for
future performance reviews.

3. DECISION SUPPORT TASKS

A DSS is usually linked to an external database and a model base that is
characterized by a large amount of data and program modules. The problem
solver of MARBLE can be viewed as a production system [3] [15] where production rules are used to represent (1) procedural knowledge, (2) decision heuristics, and (3) model abstraction. Procedural knowledge is the knowledge
about the essential steps of making a given decision, which is mostly related
to information collection. For example, in evaluating a company's credit-
worthiness, the supporting information includes the performance measurement
of the management, the outside credit rating of the firm, if available, and
credit analysis of the firm's financial data. Because the decision heuristics
are rules of thumb used by loan officers that are inherently judgmental, this

class of rules requires considerably more effort to obtain and refine. The
rules generated by inductive learning belong to this category. The third type
of rule is used to represent the model knowledge available for decision support; these rules indicate the application requirements of each model and the
precedence relations between models.

With these different types of decision-support knowledge, the problem
solver serves as a bridge that links the decision maker's problem environment
with the appropriate models, data, and decision rules residing in the DSS.

The basic inference mechanism for accomplishing decision support tasks in
a knowledge-based DSS, such as MARBLE, is based on the problem-solving theory
established by Newell and Simon [16], which treats problem solving as a process of search through state space. A problem is defined by an initial state,
a desirable goal state, a set of operators that transforms one state into
another, and a set of constraints that an acceptable solution must meet.
Problem-solving under this theory involves the selection of an appropriate
sequence of operators that will succeed in transforming an initial state into
a goal state through a series of steps. For decision-support tasks, the steps
selected in the process are primarily information processing activities that
result in a plan of action. Problem solving utilizes information from the
knowledge-base, external database, dynamic database (sometimes referred to as
blackboard), and a model base. In the case of MARBLE, the model-base can contain program modules for financial analysis, mathematical programming routines,
forecasting, simulation, or regression algorithms. The external database
typically contains the historical loan data and financial information of companies applying for loans. Therefore, special care must be taken to handle
the interface between the system's knowledge-base, model base, and database.

4. INDUCTIVE LEARNING

The ability to learn has long been recognized as an essential feature of
any intelligent system. Dietterich et al. [6] categorizes learning methods
into four areas based on their behavioral characteristics: rote learning,
learning by being told, learning from examples, and learning by analogy. Most
existing knowledge-based systems use "learning by being told" for acquiring
problem-solving knowledge. That is, the system acquires its domain knowledge
from experienced decision makers in the field, e.g., experienced loan officers
in the case of MARBLE, and transform the knowledge into the representation
form in the knowledge-base.

Inductive learning can be defined as the process of inferring the description of a class from the description of individual objects of the class.
Training examples are given in the form of instances and described by a vector
of attribute values. Each class can be viewed as a concept which is described

by a concept recognition rule as a result of inductive learning. If an input data instance satisfies this rule, then it represents the given concept. A concept is a symbolic description expressed in some description language that is TRUE when applied to a positive instance and FALSE when applied to a negative instance of the concept.

The process of inductive inference is itself a problem-solving process where solutions, the inductive concept descriptions, can be obtained through searching [14] [19] [20] [22]. Concept descriptions are derived through a sequence of transformations to generate the goal descriptions. The states are defined by the possible symbolic concept description, structured in a search space called the hypothesis space. Based on this paradigm, the inductive inference system consists of these components: (1) the hypothesis space which organizes all the concept descriptions by a partial ordering; (2) the class of transformation rules being considered, such as the generalization rules; (3) the set of training examples; and (4) the criteria for a successful inference, such as the simplicity of hypothesis generated, goodness of fit, completeness, and consistency [2].

Generalization is essential for making inductive inference. If a concept description Q is more general than the concept description P, then the transformation of P to Q is called generalization. P is said to be more general than Q if and only if there are more instances covered by P than by Q. Based on the concept of generalization, inductive inference can be viewed as a process of generalizing the initial descriptions as observed from examples and intermediate concept-descriptions until the inductive concept-descriptions consistent with all the examples are found. Thus, the generalizations relations between concept-descriptions provide the basic structure to guide the search in inductive inference. This generalization relation can be accounted for in inductive inference by ordering concept-descriptions according to their degree of generality/specificity and by using transforming rules to achieve generalization.

The input to the MARBLE's inductive learning component consists of three parts: (1) a set of positive and negative examples, (2) generalization rules and other transformation rules, and (3) the criteria for a successful inference. The resulting output is a set of decision rules consisting of inductive concept description for each of the classes. The inference process used in MARBLE for inductive learning is based on the star methodology developed by Michalski [12] [13], in which negative examples are used in the learning process to constrain the search space for the inductive concept descriptions. In other words, the inductive learning algorithm uses negative examples to ensure that the learning process would only search through those descriptions consistent with positive examples and not covered by negative examples.

5. THE CASH FLOW MODEL

Cash flow information is a basic ingredient for analyzing the financial
health of a company. Cash flow components have been found useful in the prediction of bankruptcy, bond ratings, and loan risk classification [7] [8]. We
have developed a cash flow model consisting of 12 major components. The 12
cash flow components are operating, receivables, inventories, other current
assets, payables, other current liabilities, financial, fixed coverage expenditures, investment, dividends, other asset and liability flows, and change in
cash and marketable securities. A net flow is determined for four of the
components, namely operating, other assets and liabilities, financing, and
investment. A cash inflow has a positive sign and a payment has a negative
sign. The algebraic sum of the components are equal to the change in cash and
marketable securities. The revised format for the cash flow analysis and the
acronyms for each variable are presented below.

Operating Flows

	Inflows	(OI)
minus:	Outflows	(OO)
equals:	Net Operating Flow	(NOF)

Working Capital Components   (NWCF)

Determine if each NWCF is either an inflow or outflow:

	Inflow (I)	Outflow (O)
ARF	ARFI	ARFO
INVF	INVFI	INVFO
OCAF	OCAFI	OCAFO
APF	APFI	APFO
OCLF	OCLFI	OCLFO

Other A&L Flows

	Inflows	(OA&LI)
minus:	Outflows	(OA&LO)
equals:	Net Other A&L Funds Flow	(NOA&LF)

Financial Flows

	Inflows	(FI)
minus:	Outflows	(FO)
equals:	Net Financial Flow	(NFF)

Investment Flows

	Inflows	(II)
minus:	Outflows	(IO)
equals:	Net Investment Flow	(NIF)

Dividend Outflows   (DIV)

Fixed Coverage Expenditure Outflows   (FCE)

Net Inflow (-) or Net Outflow (+)
    Sum of the above cash flow components

minus: Change in Cash (CC)
         (Ending Cash-Beginning Cash,
            where a - = Outflow and a + = Inflow)

equals: zero

The cash flow components contained in the revised cash based model are presented in equation (1).

$$NOF_t + ARF_t + INVF_t + OCAF_t + APF_t + OCLF_t + NFF_t$$
$$+ FCE_t + NIF_t + DIV_t + NOA\&LF_t - CC_t = 0 \qquad (1)$$

Because the interrelationship among the components is complex, equation (2) is presented in a sources and uses format of a most likely case. Excepting changes in cash and marketable securities, a source (S) would be a positive number and a use (U) would be negative. As a first cut, the following equation presents a formulation of the cash flow model and the most likely source/use classification of each component for a financially healthy firm.

$$\underset{(S)}{\overset{+}{NOF_t}} + \underset{(U)}{\overset{-}{ARF}} + \underset{(U)}{\overset{-}{INVF}} + \underset{(U)}{\overset{-}{OCAF}} + \underset{(S)}{\overset{+}{APF}} + \underset{(S)}{\overset{+}{OCLF}} + \underset{(S)}{\overset{+}{NFF_t}} + \underset{(U)}{\overset{-}{FCE_t}}$$

$$+ \underset{(U)}{\overset{-}{NIF_t}} + \underset{(U)}{\overset{-}{DIV_t}} + \underset{(U)}{\overset{-}{NOA\&LF_t}} - \underset{(S)}{\overset{+}{CC_t}} = 0 \qquad (2)$$

The percentage contribution is calculated by dividing each component by the total cash flow (TCF), which is equal to either the total inflow (TI) or total outflow (TO). In evaluating management performance with the Cash Flow Components, a hierarchy of relationships emerge [4] [18]. Analyzing the chronological trend of each component and evaluating their interrelationships provides a solid framework for interpreting the financial health of a firm. In turn it reflects the success of management strategies and policies during the period of analysis. For example:

NOF_t/TCF_t - What proportion of the total inflows are generated from operations? The closer the ratio is to 1.0 the stronger the financial health of the firm. That is, the firm is not dependent on external sources of capital and does not have to sell assets.

NIF_t/TCF_t - What proportion of the total expenditures are flowing to capital investments? The higher the proportion, the stronger the financial health. That is, the firm has opportunities in which it is willing to make a long-run investment commitment.

NFF_t/TCF_t - What proportion of the total inflow of funds are from external sources? An increasing trend, especially of debt, may indicate an increase in financial risk.

FCE_t/TCF_t - What proportion of total outflows are used to cover fixed expenditures? The lower the ratio, the stronger the financial health of a firm, because the level of financial risk is lower.

DIV_t/TCF_t - What proportion of total outflow is devoted to dividends? An outflow to dividends has a positive meaning for investors, while a zero outflow carries a mixed signal. In a growing firm, a ratio of zero means the firm is retaining all of its dividends for reinvestment. In a declining firm or a firm approaching failure, a zero flow to dividends indicates cash resources are being used to finance assets or repay trade credit or short-term debt and/or interest.

6. AN EMPIRICAL STUDY

To test the performance of the inductive inference method for rule learning in the domain of loan evaluation and risk analysis, we have conducted an empirical study using real-world data. Loan risk classification and the classification of a bankrupt firm are based on accounting information. Because loan information is held by banks and considered private, we have used public financial information to classify the risk of bankruptcy. This study uses financial data for predicting bankruptcy. The task for the inductive inference engine is to perform concept learning about the characteristics of bankrupt firms. The learned rules based on such data are used as part of the risk analysis in MARBLE.

In the empirical study, we apply the inductive inference algorithm to the problem of bankruptcy prediction. To identify the relevant attributes for learning the characteristics (concepts) of bankrupt firms, we adopted the cash-based funds flow components which include funds from operations (NOF), working capital (NWCF), financial (NFF), fixed coverage expenses (FCE), capital expenditures (NIF), dividends (DIV), and other asset and liability flows (NOA&LF).

The ratio of these components to the total net flow (TNF) form the first seven attributes of each example. The eighth attribute is a scale measure, calculated by total net flows/total assets (TCF/TA). Thus, each training example consists of the following eight attributes (1) NOF/TCF, (2) NWCF/TCF, (3) NOA&LF/TCF, (4) NFF/TCF, (5) FCE/TCF, (6) NIF/TCF, (7) DIV/TCF, and (8) TCF/TA.

The data are obtained from the bankruptcy study conducted by Gentry et al.
[7]. The Standard and Poor's Compustat 1981 Industrial Annual Research File
of companies, and the Compustat Industrial Files were used to determine companies that failed during the period 1970-81. Balance sheet and income
statement information for the failed companies was used to determine the funds
flow components. There were a total of 29 companies of which the complete
financial statement information for the year before the failure date was
available. These companies are used as positive examples. Furthermore, each
of the 29 failed companies was matched with a nonfailed company in the same
industry, based on asset size and sales for the fiscal year before bankruptcy.
The same set of financial data are provided for each of these nonfailed companies, which serve as negative examples of the concept. The objective of the
analysis is to determine whether the inductive inference engine can effectively discriminate between failed and nonfailed companies by the financial
data available. The rule learning program is written in PASCAL on PDP 11/780.

The set of training examples are the funds flow components of the failed
and nonfailed firms. To test the predictive accuracy of the rules generated
by the inductive inference algorithm, we use the holdout sample technique and
use half of the sample for rule learning; the rules are then tested on the
remainder of the sample. The selection of training examples out of the set of
data is based on a degree of representativeness of each data case. The training examples are selected so that they are most distant from each other and,
therefore, are the most representative examples. The beam search version of
the inductive inference algorithm is used with beam-width = 10.

The result of using the learned rules to test against the holdout sample is
shown in Table 1, which shows that the learned rules are quite effective in
predicting and classifying. Since the inductive learning algorithm is both
consistent and complete, the original positive and negative examples can be
classified with perfect accuracy. Accordingly, Table 2 shows the learned
rules classify the whole set of data cases, 29 failed firms and 29 nonfailed
firms, with 86.2% accuracy, compared with 83.3% accuracy resulting from the
logit model used in Gentry et al. [7], the rules generated by inductive learning appear to provide a valid decision aid for determining whether a firm has
the characteristics of bankrupt firms.

Shaw [23] showed a comparative study on different types of inductive learning methods. In practice, it is important that the inductive learning algorithm used can accommodate noise in the training data. Besides classification
correctness, computation efficiency, conciseness of concept descriptions, and
the dimensionality of the learned rules should also be considered.

TABLE 1
The Prediction Accuracy of the Inductive Learning
Procedure Using Holdout Example

	Total Number of Testing Cases	Number of Correct Prediction	Percentage Correct
Failed Firms (Positive Examples)	15	11	73.3%
Nonfailed Firms (Negative Examples)	15	11	73.3%

TABLE 2
The Classification Accuracy of the Inductive Learning
Procedure Using the Whole Example

	Total Number of Testing Cases	Number of Correct Prediction	Percentage Correct
Failed Firms (Positive Examples)	29	25	86.2%
Nonfailed Firms (Negative Examples)	29	25	86.2%

7. SUMMARY

Assessing the financial condition of a firm is a highly judgmental task in which qualitative as well as quantitative financial information should be used. Whereas the traditional statistical methods have trouble dealing with qualitative information, AI methods can provide powerful tools for the task. Using the business loan evaluation exercised in commercial banks as an example, this paper describes the inductive learning method for characterizing a firm's financial performance through cash flow components.

REFERENCES

[1] Anderson, J. R., The Architecture of Cognition (Harvard University Press, Cambridge, MA, 1983).
[2] Angluin, D. and Smith, C., Inductive Inference: Theory and Methods, Computing Surveys, Vol. 15, No. 3 (1983), pp. 237-269.
[3] Buchanan, B. and Shortliffe, E., Rule-Based Expert Systems (Addison-Wesley, Reading, MA, 1984).
[4] Chen, K. H. and Shimerda, T. A., An Empirical Analysis of Useful Ratios, Financial Management, Vol. 10, No. 1 (1981), pp. 51-60.
[5] Cohen, J. J., Gilmore, T. C., and Singer, F. A., "Bank Procedures for Analyzing Business Loan Applications," in: Cohen, K. J. and Hammer, F. S. (eds.), Analytical Methods in Banking (1966), pp. 219-49.
[6] Dietterich, T. G., Lonclon, R., Clarkson K., and Dromey, R., Learning and Inductive Inference, in: Cohen, D. and Feigenbaum, Ed. (eds.), Handbook of Artificial Intelligence (Kaufman, Los Altos, 1981), pp. 323-525.

[7] Gentry, J., Newbold, P., and Whitford, D., Classifying Bankrupt Firms with Funds Flow Components, Journal of Accounting Research, Vol. 23, No. 1 (1985), pp. 146–160.

[8] Gentry, J., Newbold, P., and Whitford, D., Predicting Industrial Bond Ratings with a Probit Model and Funds Flow Components, Financial Review, 1988.

[9] Haslem, J. A. and Longbrake, W. A., A Credit Scoring Model for Commercial Loans, A Comment, Journal of Money, Credit and Banking, Vol. (1972), pp. 733–34.

[10] Kaplan, R. S. and Dietrich, J. R., Empirical Analysis of the Commercial Loan Classification Decision, Accounting Review, Vol. 58, No. 1 (1982), pp. 18–38.

[11] Marais, M. L., Pattell, J. M., and Wolfson, M. A., The Experimental Design of Classification Models: An Application of Recursive Partitioning and Bootstrapping to Commercial Loan Classifications," Journal of Accounting Research, Vol. 22, Supplement 1984, pp. 87–113.

[12] Michalski, R. S., A Theory and Methodology of Inductive Learning, in: Michalski, R., Carbonell, J., and Mitchell, T. (eds.), Machine Learning (Tioga, Palo Alto, 1983).

[13] Michalski, R. S. and Larson, J., Selection of Most Representative Training Examples and Incremental Generation of VL1 Hypotheses: The Underlying Methodology and the Description of Programs ESEL and AQ11, UIUCDCS-R78-867 (Department of Computer Science, University of Illinois, Champaign, IL, 1980).

[14] Mitchell, T., Generalization as Search, Artificial Intelligence, Vol. 18 (1982), pp. 203–26.

[15] Newell, A., Production Systems: Model of Control Structures, in: Chase, W. G. (ed.), Visual Information Processing (Academic Press, New York, 1973).

[16] Newell, A. and Simon, H. A., Human Problem Solving (Prentice-Hall, Englewood Cliffs, 1972).

[17] Orgler, Y. E., A Credit Scoring Model for Commercial Loans, Journal of Money, Credit and Banking (1970), pp. 435–45.

[18] Pinches, G. E., Eubank, A. A., Mingo, K. A., Caruthers, J. K., The Hierarchical Classification of Financial Ratios, Journal of Business Research, Vol. 3, No. 3 (1975), pp. 295–310.

[19] Quinland, J. R., Discovering Rules from Large Collection of Examples: A Case Study, in: Michie, D. (ed.), Expert Systems in the Micro Electronic Age (University Press, Edenburgh, 1979).

[20] Rendell, L., A New Basis for State-Space Learning Systems and a Successful Implementation, Artificial Intelligence, Vol. 20 (1983), pp. 369–92.

[21] Shaw, M. and Gentry, J., Using an Expert System Incorporating Inductive Learning for Evaluating Business Loans, Financial Management (1988).

[22] Shaw, M., Applying Inductive Learning to Enhance Knowledge-based Expert Systems, Decision Support Systems, Vol. 3, No. 4 (1987), pp. 319–332.

[23] Shaw, M. J., An Integrated Framework for Applying Machine Learning in Decision Support Systems, BEBR Working Paper No. 1484, Department of Business Administration, University of Illinois, Champaign, IL, 1988.

Expert Systems in Economics, Banking and Management
L.F. Pau et al. (Editors)
© *Elsevier Science Publishers B.V. (North-Holland), 1989*

Toward a Domain-Specific Tool for Underwriting Commercial Insurance

Nancy A. Broderick and Peter Politakis
Intelligent Systems Technology Group
Digital Equipment Corporation
Marlboro, MA 01752

Abstract

CLUE is a prototype that provides assistance to an underwriter in making decisions about writing or declining a given commercial lines property risk. A major goal of this application is to implement a domain-specific tool that could be easily tailored with a client's underwriting criteria. The foundation of such a tool are embodied in an architecture that supports: the distinction between general underwriting knowledge and class of business dependent underwriting knowledge; information originating from potentially many sources including user input, database retrieval, and external routines; and a customizable set of rules for combining underwriting criteria in order to reach an underwriting decision. Currently, the classes of business handled by the prototype include bakeries and convenience stores; we plan to experiment with other classes that could replace or extend these. CLUE has been developed in a rule-based VAX Lisp environment and also in Neuron Data's Nexpert Object.

1   Introduction

CLUE, the Commercial Lines Underwriting Expert, is a prototype to provide assistance to an underwriter in making a decision regarding whether to write or decline a given commercial lines property risk. This document describes the application with a goal to implement a domain-specific tool that could be easily tailored with a client's underwriting criteria. A small set of classes of business is handled by the prototype; we plan to experiment with other classes that will extend the scope of the system. Currently, the application has been developed in a rule-based VAX Lisp environment and also in Neuron Data's Nexpert Object.

The task of the underwriter, and thus the system, is to evaluate a given risk and determine whether that risk is worth writing. Based on the sources of information available, the system guides the underwriter through evaluation of the producer, insured, and property components of the risk. The producer is the agent submitting the business and the insured is the applicant requesting property insurance. If an unacceptable situation is detected during the analysis of the risk, the session will end with the recommendation to decline the risk. Otherwise, evaluation of the producer, insured, and property components continues. The session concludes with a decision regarding whether to write or decline the risk, an overall rating of the risk, information supporting the analysis, and notes of interest to the underwriter.

From our experience, we believe we have the foundations required to design and implement a domain-specific underwriting tool. The foundations for such a tool are embodied in an architecture we have developed that supports:

- general underwriting principles
- the distinction between general underwriting knowledge and class of business dependent underwriting knowledge
- underwriting analysis based on information available at different levels of detail
- information originating from potentially many sources including user input, database retrieval, and external routines
- a customizable set of rules for combining underwriting criteria in order to reach an underwriting decision.

2 The Problem

2.1 Characteristics of the Problem

The underwriting process may be viewed as a classification/interpretive type problem. On a high level, the task of the underwriter is to examine the details of a particular risk and to classify the risk as either a write or a no-write case. This gives the process a classification flavor. On another level, the evaluation of a risk with regard to the class of business has an interpretive side. Many questions are asked during the process of deciding whether or not to write the risk. These questions are asked as needed and used for continual evaluation of the risk. As the evaluation proceeds, intermediate conclusions are drawn to help capture and explain the final write/no-write decision.

In the case of commercial lines property underwriting, the type or class of business plays a key role in determining the set of criteria necessary for evaluation of the risk. Each class of business requires attention to information that is important for that particular type of business operation. Therefore, underwriting a property risk is largely a class of business driven analysis of the risk information. Determination of which criteria are important as well as how to evaluate those criteria is crucial to the underwriting task.

The underwriter draws on a variety of sources for information in order to reach a decision. The underwriter may have only general descriptive information for use in analyzing the risk, or may have a more complete and detailed description of the risk via supporting reports and documentation. In either scenario, the underwriter may be called upon to reach a decision regarding the risk. As such, the underwriting task becomes a decision making process based on the sources of information that are available to the underwriter while the risk is being analyzed. The underwriter must make a decision based on the amount and quality of information available. In keeping with this, one of the goals of the system is to form an evaluation based on, and consistent with, the information available.

For example, if the underwriter has only the application to work from, a decision must be made from the limited information available on the application. The application may include general information such as name and address of the insured, description of business operations, and property information such as building construction type, building age, number of years the insured has been at the current location, general exposure information, fire rating, and some comments. Details of common hazards (e.g., heat type, fuel type, wiring) as well as special hazards information is generally not available on a commercial lines application. The underwriter must make an assessment based on a higher level of information. If more detailed reports are available, the underwriter can make a more well informed decision. For example, risk control reports aid in property risk evaluation as they contain details of construction, occupancy, protection, and exposure. Financial reports aid in the evaluation of the insured.

Another characteristic of the underwriting process is the ability to handle missing information. Often information useful in making a decision may be unknown or uncertain. The underwriter must make best use of whatever limited information is available in order to evaluate the risk.

All of the above characteristics of the underwriting process support a knowledge-based solution approach. That is, the type of problem - classification/ interpretive - is a fairly well understood paradigm in knowledge-base systems. Also, current knowledge-base shells generally support a feature to group rules. This feature allows the contextually relevant rules (class of business specific) to be active at any point and, in general, supports reasoning at different levels of detail. Furthermore, the use of default values to questions helps with the possible large set of unknown values the underwriter must work with.

In addition, the very nature of the underwriting domain provides justification for a knowledge-based solution. The ability to combine, in a consistent fashion, the detailed expertise of underwriters that specialize in certain types of risks, makes the availability of such a system very desirable from both a production and training perspective.

2.2 Basic Flow

Two versions of the prototype were developed. Each version guides the underwriter through the analysis of the property risk. The evaluation of the risk is based on the combined evaluations of the producer, insured, and property components of the risk. If an unacceptable situation is detected during the analysis of the risk, the session will end with the recommendation to decline the risk. Otherwise, evaluation of the producer, insured, and property components continues. Each of the producer, insured and property components produce a qualitative rating. These ratings are combined, in a final component module, to form a qualitative rating for the overall risk, as well as a decision whether to write the risk.

The first version of the prototype was implemented with a Lisp-based, rule-based tool. Rules were separated into rule blocks associated with the different component evaluations. This first version was tutorial in nature with features providing help for each question, explanations for why a question was asked and why a conclusion was reached, as well as a facility for retracting an answer and continuing the inferencing based on a new value. Furthermore, all questions, except those pertaining to the producer (available on-line), were asked of the user. The resulting detailed interactive dialogue supported the tutorial aspect of the first version.

The second version of the prototype was developed in Nexpert Object. The object representation strengthened the model, allowing a richer, more natural definition of the knowledge base. Rules were separated into knowledge islands with context links used to conditionally cross from one knowledge island to another. Each of the producer, insured, property, and combining evaluations modules were implemented as separate knowledge islands. This version of the prototype was developed with less emphasis on the tutorial aspects of the first version and with more emphasis on creating a production environment for the underwriter. The information available for the producer and the information from the incoming application are stored in a relational database. Only information not found in the database is asked of the user during evaluation of the risk. This feature limits unnecessary data entry on the part of the user and helps achieve a more productive environment for underwriting analysis.

The basic flow of both implementations of the prototype, proceeding through the modules for evaluation of the producer, insured, and property, is guided in a forward chaining manner. Within each module, the evaluation is determined with a backward chaining strategy.

2.3 Size

The dimensions of the prototype model for the classes of bakeries and convenience stores are noted here. The size was similar for both implementations of the prototype. The number of findings are 89, variables 26, conclusions 33, and rules 255. We are currently experimenting with other classes to assess model complexity.

Expert Systems in Economics, Banking and Management
L.F. Pau et al. (Editors)
© Elsevier Science Publishers B.V. (North-Holland), 1989

An Artificial Intelligence Approach to Predicting Bond Ratings

Soumitra Dutta   Shashi Shekhar

Computer Science Department
University of California
Berkeley, CA 94720, U.S.A.

Abstract

The *default risks* of most bonds are rated by various independent organizations, e.g., Moody's and S&P. These ratings are often used by investors to define allowable bond purchases and to measure the risk characteristics of investments in bonds. It is not known what model, if any, do these rating agencies use for rating the various bond issues. Past researchers have used multi-variate regression models to relate the corporate bond ratings with the financial ratios of the corporations, but have had limited successes. In this paper we present results from an initial attempt at predicting bond ratings by using the **neural network** model from the domain of artificial intelligence and comparing the results with those obtained by using regression models.

1. Introduction

The *default risk* of a bond is the possibility that promised coupon and par values of a bond will not be paid. The default risks of the most actively traded bonds are rated by various independent organizations. Standard and Poor's and Moody's are the largest of these rating agencies concentrating upon corporate and municipal issues (in the USA). Table I shows the top three ratings given by S&P and Moody's.

TABLE I : Definitions of Ratings Given by S&P and Moody's

Moody's	Standard & Poor's	Definition*
Aaa	AAA	The highest rating assigned. Capacity to pay interest and principal very strong.
Aa	AA	Very strong capacity to pay interest and principal. Differ from highest rated issues only in small degree.
A	A	Strong capacity to repay interest and principal but may be susceptible to adverse changes in economic conditions.

*Adapted from S&P's *Bond Guide* and Moody's *Bond Record*

Though these ratings reflect each agency's opinion about an issue's potential default and not its relative investment merits, they are often used to define allowable bond purchases by certain investors. For example, the Comptroller of Currency has stated that bank investments must be of *investment grade* (i.e., in the top four rankings). These ratings have a significant effect on the offering yield on bond issue. These ratings are also used by institutional portfolio managers as a metric to reflect the risk of their investments in bonds.

To evaluate a bond's potential for default, rating agencies rely upon a committee analysis of the issuer's *ability* to repay, *willingness* to repay, and *protective* provisions for an issue. It is not known what model, if any, do these rating agencies use for rating the various bond issues. The situation is complicated by the fact that all the various aspects analyzed by the ratings committee are not known completely and some features such as *willingness* to repay are affected by a number of variables which are difficult to characterize precisely. Thus it is not possible to accurately define a regression model which performs the required ratings of bonds. This is the main reason for the poor results yielded by conventional statistical analysis techniques.

Our aim in this project is to use the **neural network** model from the domain of artificial intelligence to predict bond ratings and compare our results with those obtained by using multivariate regression models for bond rating.

The paper is organized into six sections. Section 2 gives a precise definition of the problem of bond rating and describes the work in bond rating done by other researchers and discusses the limitations of the statistical techniques used by them. Section 3 provides a brief introduction to the neural network model and shows how it can be used for learning to predict bond ratings. It also compares the regression model with the neural network model. Section 4 describes the objectives of our experiment and the procedure of data collection and experimentation. Finally, sections 5 and 6 discuss the results and conclusions respectively.

2. Rating the Bonds

2.1 The Problem Statement

The task of assigning ratings to the different industrial bond issues can be posed as a *classification* problem: given a set of classes and a set of input data instances, each described by a suitable set of features, assign each input data instance to one of the classes. For our study, the different bond issues form the set of input data instances and the various bond ratings (AA, B, etc.) form the set of possible classes to which the input bonds can belong. Each bond instance can be described by a set of features which represent important financial information about the company issuing the bond. Formally, we state the problem now:

Let B represent the space of n bonds, $B_1, B_2, ..., B_n$, and R be the set of possible (mutually exclusive) m bond ratings, $R_1, R_2, ..., R_m$. Let F represent the k dimensional feature space, $F_1, ..., F_k$, describing each of the bonds. Each bond B_i can be considered as a k-tuple $(F1_{Bi}, F2_{Bi}, \cdots , Fk_{Bi})$ in the Cartesian space $F_1 \times F_2 \times \cdots \times F_k$. And rating the bonds involves finding the one to one mapping function f

$$f : F_1 \times F_2 \times \cdots \times F_k \rightarrow R$$

The mapping produced by this function f, i.e., the ratings assigned to the various bonds is determined by the rating agencies, but a precise functional form or a mathematical model of this function f is not known. There is some consensus on what financial information about the company can affect the ratings of its bonds and thus the feature space is defined. Past researchers have tried to approximate the function f by using various multi-variate regression models, with limited success. In this paper, we attempt to use a neural network for modeling the function f, with the input vector space being given by $F_1 \times F_2 \times \cdots \times F_k$ and the output vector space being given by R.

2.2 Review of Past Research

For determining the rating of bonds, rating agencies use both the financial data of the company and other qualitative factors, such as their subjective judgement concerning the future prospects of the firm. However, researchers in finance have concentrated upon quantifiable historical data for the firm and provisions of the bond issue. The typical financial variables used include proxies for liquidity, debt capacity, debt coverage, size of issue etc. They usually take coded bond ratings as an independent variable and use statistical techniques like regression to get a model of bond ratings.

[HORR 66] regressed coded ratings with fifteen financial ratios. Subject to the magnitudes of cross-correlations, he chose six ratios out of the fifteen, which had highest correlation with ratings. These were total assets, working capital over sales, net worth over total debt, sales over net worth, profit over sales, and subordination. Another regression between the ratings and the new set of variables, gave a model. This model was correct for 58% of Moody's ratings during the period 1961-64.

[WEST 70] has a similar approach, using logarithmic forms of nine variables including earning variability, solvency period, debt equity ratio and outstanding bonds. His model correctly predicted 62% of Moody's rating during 1953.

[POGU 69] used a regression model with dichotomous (0-1) dependent variable, which represents the probability of group membership in one group of pair. They ran separate regressions for each pair of successive ratings (e.g. Aaa and Aa, Aa and A, A and Baa etc.) with the following independent variables: debt over total capital, income over assets, income over interest charge. Dummy variables were used for broad industry effects. This approach involved at least (n - 1) regressions for n-rating groups. A bond is assigned to the group in which its probability of occurrence is the highest. This method predicted 8 bonds out of 10 in hold out sample from the period 1961-66.

[PINC 73] screened the initial 35 variables via factor analysis, and used multiple discriminant analysis to develop the final model. They used the following variables- subordination (0-1), years of consecutive dividend, issue size, income over assets, income over interest charge, and debt over assets. Bonds were classified on the probability of group membership. This model predicted roughly 65% and 56% of the Moody's ratings for hold out samples in the periods 1967-68 and 1969.

2.3 Limitations of Statistical Models

These approaches (based on multiple regression) have had limited success (60 % correctness) in predicting bond ratings, even after considering as many as 35 financial variables and performing a large number of iterative regressions (n-1 iterations for n ratings). This suggests that the assumption of a regression model for bond rating may not be correct. Statistical techniques always require the assumption of a certain functional form for relating dependent variables to independent variables. When the assumed functional form is not correct, the statistical techniques merely confirm that, but do not predict the right functional form. Neural networks do provide a more general framework for determining relationships in the data and do not require the specification of any functional form. Our results show that neural networks perform consistently better than regression.

3. The Neural Network Model

3.1 Introduction

A Neural network is a multiple layered network consisting of simple processing elements called "units" that interact with each other using weighted connections. A simple three layered neural network is shown in figure 1.

Every connection has a scalar weight, and each unit computes a weighted sum of the incoming values and passes this sum through a nonlinear function, with the resulting value becoming the units output. Each directly observable feature is represented by an input unit, whose value represents the magnitude of a continuous quantity, or probability that a discrete feature is present. Each of the possible hypotheses that we wish to evaluate is represented as an output unit.

Each unit has a "state" or "activity level" that is determined by the input received from units in the layer below. The total input, x_j, received by unit j is defined as

$$x_j = \sum_i y_i w_{ji} - \theta_j$$

where y_j is the state of the i'th unit (which is in a lower layer), w_{ij} is the weight on the

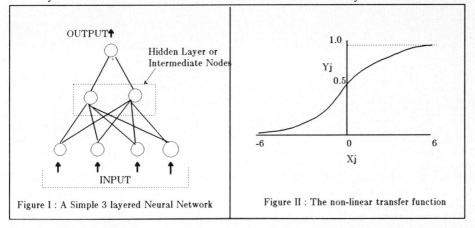

Figure I : A Simple 3 layered Neural Network

Figure II : The non-linear transfer function

connection from the i'th to the j'th unit and θ_j is the threshold of the j'th unit. The lowest layer contains the input nodes and an external input vector is supplied to the network by clamping the states of these units. The state of any other unit in the network is a monotonic non-linear function of its total input (see figure 2).

$$y_j = \frac{1}{1 + e^{-x_j}}$$

All the network's long term knowledge about the function it has learned to compute is encoded by the magnitudes of the weights on the connections.

In the simplest of these networks (2 layered), the input units are directly connected to output units, by a set of connections with modifiable weights. Given a set of input vectors and the desired output for each input vector, we can iteratively find a set of weights that will perform the mapping, if such a set exists. The two layered neural network is similar to regression, but more powerful. First, there is no need to specify any functional form for performing the mapping and second, the non-linear summation at each unit leads to a better fit. This is validated by our results (see section 5). Unfortunately for many interesting recognition tasks there is no set of weights in a simple two layered network that will do the job. In most cases, one can not treat the lowest-level features as independent sources of evidence and simply add them up. It is necessary to introduce one or more intermediate layers of hidden nodes (historically named as the *hidden layer*), which combine the raw observations into higher order features more useful in determining the output. Consider for example the problem of deciding whether to grant a bank loan to a particular customer. Various important features of that customer's financial history (e.g., past loans taken) are fed as input to the neural network. The fact that this customer failed to repay one small loan in the past cannot be directly used as evidence against or for granting the loan, instead we have to look at entire credit history of the customer and trends in his repayment of loans. It is necessary to extract out higher order features about the customers financial record (e.g., good prospects for future solvency) to decide whether to grant the loan or not. The tasks needing hidden nodes, can be categorized in terms of how many input units must connect to each hidden unit in a three(or more) layered network. This determines the order of statistics that can be extracted. Standard algorithms for determining the optimal number of layers and the optimal number of nodes in each layer have yet to be developed. In particular, such a choice is very dependent on the application domain of the neural network. If the input vector space consists of extremely low level features, then we need a larger number of hidden layers to successively extract out the higher order features from the input data. A smaller number of hidden layers suffices if the input data is itself representative of some higher order features. In our particular study, for reasons of efficiency, many higher order features were chosen in the input vector space and thus it was seen that the performance of the neural network did not improve significantly with an increase in the number of hidden layers (see section 5).

3.2 Learning in Neural Networks

Rather than programming them, we train neural networks by example. We show a neural network examples from the input vector space along with the correct response in the output vector space. The network adjusts the weights on the connections between the units in accordance with the shown examples and can reproduce the correct result when shown another input vector subsequently.

The network has parameters of weights on the connections, and learning which of the exponentially many possible combinations are relevant for predicting the output, is a hard problem. *Back Propagation* is one of the techniques used to learn these weights. It involves two passes each time an input-output vector is presented. In the forward pass, activity starts at the input nodes and passes through the layers to compute the activity levels of all units in the network. In the backward pass, we start at the output unit and back propagate the derivative of the error (the difference between actual output vector and desired output vector) through the same network in the reverse direction. The error with a given set of weights is defined as

$$E = \frac{1}{2}\sum_{j,c}(y_{j,c} - d_{j,c})^2$$

where $y_{j,c}$ is the actual state (weight) of unit j in input-output training example c (in the forward direction) and $d_{j,c}$ is its desired state (weight). This allows the network to compute, for each weight, the gradient of output error with respect to that weight. For a hidden unit, j, in layer J the only way it can affect the error is via its effects on the units, k, in the next layer K. So the derivative of the error $\partial E/\partial y_j$ is given by

$$\frac{\partial E}{\partial y_j} = \sum_k \frac{\partial E}{\partial y_k} \frac{dy_k}{dx_k} \frac{\partial x_k}{\partial y_j}$$

where the index c has been suppressed for clarity. The weight is then changed in the direction to reduce the output error. Our neural network simulator uses global optimization for changing the weights simultaneously, and avoids the problems of conflicting local weight adjustments. Thus learning works by gradient descent on an error surface in weight space. The learning procedure is computationally expensive and very slow. Further it can get stuck in local minimas due to the gradient descent method, though in practice this is a minor problem.

To summarize, learning in a neural network essentially refers to learning the appropriate weights on the various connections in the network. For this, we use a set of training input and output vectors and allow the neural network to obtain (by using back propagation and global optimization as described above) the weights on connections which best produce the output vectors corresponding to the input vectors. To verify how well the neural network has learned to predict the output vector, we can use the same set of weights (on the connections) learned during the *learning phase* and check the accuracy of the output for a new set of input vectors. We shall refer to the input vectors used for learning the weights as the *learning* sample and the input vectors used for testing as the *testing* sample. It is important to note that neural networks do not ask for the mapping from the input to the output space to be specified; instead they determine this mapping by suitably adjusting the weights on the inter-unit connections. Another important advantages of neural networks is that they are very robust to noisy inputs and have the ability to *abstract* out the "ideal" from a non-ideal training set (the hidden layers abstract out the higher order features from the input vectors).

3.3 Regression Analysis vs Neural Network Models

Regression can give us the parameters of a functional form but not the correct functional form. The neural-network model helps us for determining the functional form as well the parameters. It does not require us to guess any functional form, but determines the functional form by itself. It tunes the functional form and parameters to fit the learning examples, as closely as desired. We can specify both, the desired size (number of parameters) of the model (neural network) and the error tolerance for the model. This gives us a more general framework for discovering relationships existing in data . As expected we found that it consistently outperformed regression methods for predicting bond ratings (see section 5).

However we note that the statistical models are useful in determining the right set of independent variables, which determine the dependent variable to the largest extent. This is difficult to do with neural networks, as the hidden layers (intermediate layers) of a neural network extract the higher order features from the input variables to decide the output, the output is not influenced directly by the inputs. The weights on the connections for a two layered network can give the relative importance of the input variables, but for any three or higher layered network, such a discrimination from the weights on the connections becomes very difficult.

4. Data Collection and Experimentation

4.1 Selection of Variables

Based on the results of [HORR 66] and [PINC 73], we selected ten financial variables for predicting bond-ratings. The influence of a variable on the bond-rating and ease of availability of data, were the primary factors in the selection of the variables. These are listed in table 4.1.

The definitions of most of the variables are self explanatory, but some of the variables need further explanation. Variable #2 gives the ratio of the total funded debt to net property. It is a key factor in analyzing the underlying outstanding debt of utilities, railroads, steel companies, etc., where investment in property is a major consideration in providing the structure for earn-

Table 4.1 : Financial Variables used to Predict Bond Ratings

Var	Definition	Var	Definition
1	Liability / (Cash + Assets)	2	Debt Proportion
3	Sales / Net Worth	4	Profit / Sales
5	Financial Strength	6	Times
7	past 5 year Revenue growth rate	8	next 5 year Revenue growth rate
9	Working Capital / Sales	10	subjective Prospect of Company

ings. This ratio is a less important indicator for service companies. Variable #5 is the financial strength of the company as mentioned in the *Valueline Index*. Variable #6 gives the number of times available earnings cover fixed charges. Charges include interest on funded debt, other interest charges, amortization of debt discount and expenses and similar charges. Variable #10 is a subjective measure of the future prospects of the company as decided by comments from Valueline and the S&P Bond Guide.

Our first experiment uses all the ten variables in predicting the bond rating. Then we used only the first six variables to predict the bond ratings. The correlation matrix of the the input data is shown in *table 4.2*. Most of the entries in the matrix are small and hence the chosen variables are independent (as desired).

Table 4.2 : Correlation Matrix

Var#	1	2	3	4	5	6	7	8	9	10
1	1.0									
2	-0.3	1.0								
3	-0.31	0.17	1.0							
4	-0.25	-0.08	-0.67	1.0						
5	0.0	-0.27	0.3	0.01	1.0					
6	0.19	-0.32	0.23	0.09	0.59	1.0				
7	0.06	0.13	0.22	0.11	0.26	0.27	1.0			
8	-0.32	0.34	0.21	0.27	0.31	0.28	0.53	1.0		
9	0.28	-0.16	-0.5	0.26	-0.18	-0.17	-0.10	-0.24	1.0	
10	-.02	-0.04	0.19	0.06	0.5	0.2	0.3	0.39	-0.19	1.0

4.2 Data Collection

Bond ratings and values of the financial variables for a set of industrial bonds, are taken from the April 86 issues of the Valueline Index and the S&P Bond Guide. Bond issues of forty seven companies were selected at random and we used thirty of them to perform the *learning*, i.e., to train the neural network (obtain the weights on the different connections) and obtain the regression coefficients. The rest seventeen of the bonds were used to test the neural network and regression performance. All the selected bonds had approximately the same maturity date (1998 - 2003).

4.3 Linear Regression Model

We used the Berkeley I.S.P. (Interactive Statistical Package) for multiple regression analysis to get a set of regression coefficients and their respective t-statistics. The t-statistics was significant for every regression coefficient. The regression coefficients obtained were then used to predict the ratings of both the learning sample(to see how well the regression model fitted the learning sample) and the testing sample of new bond issues (to see how well the regression coefficients predicted the ratings of the test bonds). The results are summarized in next section.

4.4 Neural Network Model

To build a neural network model for predicting bond ratings, we first *train* the neural network. For each bond issue, we apply the relevant financial variables at the input units and the corresponding bond-rating at the output unit. The learning algorithm of the neural network simulator adjusts the weights on the inter-unit links suitably to produce the right mapping of the input (the financial data describing each bond issue) onto the output (the corresponding bond rating). To save computation time we can specify a tolerance on the total error of fit. The error in the mapping of the learning sample is calculated by running the neural network with the learned set of weights on the input (learning) data and comparing the output ratings with the actual ratings of the learning sample. The weight adjustment in neural network model can be stopped after the actual output is within the specified tolerance of the desired output.

After the learning phase, i.e. model building phase, we freeze the parameters of the neural network. The financial ratios of test case bonds are now used as the inputs of the model and we compare the output of the model with the ideal rating of the bond.

We experimented with different neural network configurations (2 layered , 3 layered, different number of hidden nodes in 3 layered neural networks, etc.). The total permissible tolerance was kept constant for different neural network configurations. We compare the performance of the various neural networks against regression analysis and the performances of the various neural network configurations against themselves in next section.

Finally we repeated all the above experiments with a smaller number of variables (variables #1-#6 of the ten variables initially chosen).

5. Results

Table 5.1 to 5.4 summarize the results of our experiments. The models were expected to recognize if a given bond belongs to class of all the bonds with AA rating. This problem naturally classifies the responses of prediction models into four different categories, described by the pairs of (actual, predicted) columns in the table 5.1.

Table 5.1 : Possible Classifications of Responses

Actual	Prediction	Description
Accept	Accept	S&P rating is AA and rating of model is also AA
Accept	Reject	S&P rating is AA and rating of model is not AA
Reject	Accept	S&P rating is not AA but rating of model is AA
Reject	Reject	S&P rating is not AA and rating of model is also not AA

The column *actual* is *Accept* if and only if the given bond is actually rated AA by S&P. For an ideal model, our test results should only belong to the first and fourth rows of table 5.1 where the ratings given by S&P and the model coincide. Rows 2 and 3 of table 5.1 are the undesirable cases and represent false negatives and false positives respectively. We report the statistics for the learning case and testing cases, separately to bring out the important features of our study. In table 5.2 we list in detail the results of our study of the regression and neural network models for the four possible response classifications described in table 5.1. High values in the columns under *Predicted/Actual in %* for the response pairs (Accept, Accept) and (Reject, Reject) point to a good model while high values for the response pairs (Accept, Reject) and (Reject, Accept) point to an inferior model. The values are listed separately for the learning and testing phases for both neural networks and the regression analysis. This shall help us to better compare neural networks and regression analysis. For example (from table 5.2) during the learning phase,the regression model correctly classified 61.5 % of AA bonds as AA bonds , and 64.8% of non-AA bonds as non-AA. Similarly (also from table 5.2), during the testing phase the neural network model (both the two layered neural network and the three layered neural network) correctly classified 83.% of the AA bonds as AA and 81.9% of the non-AA bonds as non-AA.

5.1 Interpretation of Results

The data of table 5.2 is summarized in tables 5.3 and 5.4 for comparison. The % entries in tables 5.3 and 5.4 essentially represent the % of correctness of prediction of the two models (regression and nerual network) and are obtained by computing a weighted average of the corresponding entries in table 5.2 for the response pairs (Accept, Accept) and (Reject, Reject). The weights are given by the actual number of bonds in the respective categories. We also list the absolute error as` tot_sq_err for each model to give an idea of goodness of fit by various models. The *tot_sq_err* gives the sum of the squares of the errors in prediction (i.e., the differences between the numerical values of the actual and predicted bond ratings) in all the cases.

Table 5.2 : Performance of Regression and Neural network using 10 variables.

Phase	Classification		% correct using 10 var			% correct using 6 var		
	actual	predicted	Regress.	2 L N-net	3 L N-net	Regress.	2 L N-net	3 L N-net
Learning	Accept	Accept	61.5	76.9	92.3	61.5	76.9	76.9
	Accept	Reject	38.5	23.1	7.7	38.5	23.1	23.1
	Reject	Accept	29.4	17.6	0.0	35.2	17.6	17.6
	Reject	Reject	64.8	82.3	100.0	64.8	82.3	82.3
Testing	Accept	Accept	50	83.3	83.3	50	83.3	83.3
	Accept	Reject	50.0	16.7	16.7	50.0	16.7	16.7
	Reject	Accept	27.2	18.1	18.1	27.2	18.1	18.1
	Reject	Reject	72.8	81.9	81.9	72.8	81.9	81.9

Table 5.3 : Results (Learning)

# Variables	Neural Net		Regression
	2-layers	3-layers	
6	80% tot_sq_err =0.2365	80% tot_sq_err =0.1753	63.33% tot_sq_err = 1.107
10	80% tot_sq_err =0.2241	92.4% tot_sq_err =0.0538	66.7% tot_sq_err = 0.924

Table 5.4 : Results (Testing)

# Variables	Neural Net		Regression
	2-layers	3-layers	
6	82.4% tot_sq_err =0.198	76.5% tot_sq_err =0.1939	64.7% tot_sq_err = 1.528
10	88.3% tot_sq_err =0.1638	82.4% tot_sq_err =0.2278	64.7% tot_sq_err = 1.643

From tables 5.2 to 5.4 we can draw the following observations.

Neural networks consistently out_perform regression in predicting bond ratings from the given set of financial ratios. Both in the training and learning samples the total squared error for regression analysis is about an order of magnitude higher than that for neural networks (see tables 5.3 and 5.4). Also, the success rate of prediction for neural networks is considerably higher than that for regression analysis, e.g., the success rate during the testing phase for the two layered neural network (10 variables) is 88.3% as compared to 64.7% for the regression model.

Table 5.5 : Results (Testing)

# Variables	Neural Net		Regression
	2-layers	3-layers	
6	82.4% tot_sq_err =0.198	76.5% tot_sq_err =0.1939	64.7% tot_sq_err = 1.528
10	88.3% tot_sq_err =0.1638	82.4% tot_sq_err =0.2278	64.7% tot_sq_err = 1.643

From tables 5.2 to 5.5 we can draw the following observations.

Neural networks consistently out_perform regression in predicting bond ratings from the given set of financial ratios. Both in the training and learning samples the total squared error for regression analysis is about an order of magnitude higher than that for neural networks (see tables 5.4 and 5.5). Also, the success rate of prediction for neural networks is considerably higher than that for regression analysis, e.g., the success rate during the testing phase for the two layered neural network (10 variables) is 88.3% as compared to 64.7% for the regression model.

There is no appreciable difference in results when we consider only a subset of the chosen variables. During the testing and learning phases, the success rate does improve with an increase in the number of variables , but this improvement is not significantly large. During the learning phase, the total squared error decreases substantially for a three layered neural network when we use 10 variables instead of 6 (from 0.1753 to 0.05380), but the total squared error increases for the 3 layered network with 10 variables during the testing phase. There also seemed to be no appreciable difference for the regression results for the two sets of variables.

For the different configurations of neural networks, we observe that during the learning phase the total squared error decreases for a neural network with a larger number of layers, but there are no significant differences in results during the testing phase. We see that given the training sample, we can obtain a better fit (with respect to the training sample) using a larger number of layers in the neural network but the additional layers do not seem to add to its predictive power as evidenced during the testing phase. This result can be understood in light of our earlier comments (see section 3) regarding the required number of hidden layers in a neural network. Our input financial features of a bond are relatively high level abstractions and thus there is no significant improvement in prediction with an increase in the number of hidden layers.

The results obtained during the testing phase by our regression analysis are comparable to those obtained by previous researchers (see section 2). The poor performance of the regression models indicates that the linear multivariate model is inadequate for explaining the rating of bonds. This is particularly significant considering the fact that past researchers have built some very sophisticated models for regression analysis using as many as 35 variables and n-1 iterations for n ratings. This lends support to our premise that there are substantial gains to be achieved by applying non-traditional techniques such as neural networks to domains such as bond rating which lack a well defined mathematical model.

It was observed by us that whenever the neural network model is in error it is off by at most one rating . In contrast, regression analysis was often off by several ratings. We have not presented details to here due to space limitations.

6. Conclusions

In this paper we have demonstrated the usefulness of applying concepts from the domain of artificial intelligence to that of of management. For many problem domains lacking in a precise mathematical model, neural networks present a much more powerful computational tool than standard statistical techniques like regression. This is validated by our results which show that neural networks consistently outperformed regression while predicting bond ratings. Our regression model was simple, but the prediction rates of our neural networks are significantly higher than the best obtained by past researchers using multi-variate regression models.

This work demonstrates the the power of neural networks for bond prediction, though the performance can be improved in several ways. Our choice of input variables can perhaps be improved upon and this can be done by repeating the experiment with many different sets of variables and seeing which set of variables gives the best results. Another obvious improvement that can be achieved is by considering different industry sectors separately. A larger number of learning examples and test cases should help in increasing the quality of and confidence in the results. We are confident that with further experimentation, significantly higher accuracy can be obtained by our neural network model.

7. Acknowledgements

We would like to thank Prof. Andrew Rudd, Business School, U.C.Berkeley for introducing us to the problem of bond-rating and providing valuable insights from time to time. We also thank Rajesh Mehra of the quantitative finance research group, BARRA, for providing data related to several bond issues. We are grateful to Dr. Shabbir Rangwala, Mechanical Engineering., U.C.Berkeley, for his help with the neural network simulator.

References

For Bond Rating

[ANG 75]   J.S.Ang, K.A.Patel, "Bond Rating Methods: Comparison and Validation", *Journal of Finance*, Vol. 30, No.2, May 1975

[HORR 66]   J.O.Horrigan, "The Determinantion of Long Term Credit Standing with Financial Ratios", Empirical Research in Accounting: Selected Studies, 1966, *Journal of Accounting Research.*

[PINC 73]   G.E.Pinches, K.A.Mingo, "A Multivariate Analysis of Industrial Bond Ratings", Journal of Finance, March 1977.

[POGU 73]   T.E.Pogue, R.M.Soklofsky, "What is in a Bond Rating?", Journal of Financial and Quantative Analysis, June 1969.

[REIL 76]   F.K.Reilly, M.D.Joehnk, "The Association between Market-Determined Risk Measures for Bonds and Bond Ratings", Vol.31, No.5, December 1976.

[WEST 70]   R.R.West, n Alternative Approach Predicting Corporate Bond Ratings", *Journal of Accounting Research*, Spring 1970.

For Neural Network Models

[AART 87]   E.H.L.Aarts, and J.H.M.Korst, "Boltzmann Machines and Their Applications", in *Lecture Notes in Computer Science#258* on Parallel Architectures and Languages Europe, Springer-Verlag 1987.

[CARP 87]   Carpenter & Grossberg, "A massively parallel architecture for a self organizing neural pattern recognition machine", Computer Graphics, Vision, and Image Processing, January 1987

[FAHL 87]   Fahlman,S.E. and G.E.Hinton, "Connectionist Architectures for Artificial Intelligence", *IEEE Computer Magazine*, January 1987, special issue on AI.

[GROS 86]   Grossberg, "Competitive Learning: From Interactive Activation to Adaptive Resonance", *Cognitive Science*, June 1986

[HOPF 85]   J.J.Hopfield, and D.W.Tank, "Neural Computation of Decision in Optimization Problems", *Biological Cybernetics*, Vol. 52; No. 2, Springer Verlag, New York, 1985.

[RUME 86]   M.Rumelhart, et.al., "Parallel Distributed Processing: Explorations in the Microstructure of Cognition", Bradford Books, Cambridge, MA, 1986 (Chapters 1,2,4,5,7,8,9,13,14,17,18,20).

Expert Systems in Economics, Banking and Management
L.F. Pau et al. (Editors)
© *Elsevier Science Publishers B. V. (North-Holland), 1989*

RASF--Automating Routine Analysis of Financial Data

Lin, Zhangxi

Economic Information Centre of Fujian
45 Guping Road, Fuzhou 350003
P. R. of China

ABSTRACT: RASF is a pilot expert system based on a financial database for analysing financial conditions in routine way. It trys to ultilize the techniques of knowledge engineering currently available integratedly. By emulating the activities of an analyst, RASF will hand out a piece of analysis report according to the results of reasoning.

1. INTRODUCTION

Routine analysis of statistical data is a regular work in economic management. In the case, an analyst reads all the latest arrived data thoroughly, checks them by various comparison, tests them with some models. With the help of some related material and his/her domain knowledge, the analyst would give out an analysis report to his/her superior or departments concerned. This is always done in the managements of finance, material, transportation, banking,etc. To decision makers this work is especially important, for the reports which have been elaborately configured contain adequate amount of refined information and will benifit them in saving much time to gain validated information from large amount of data. It is a pity that although the application of computer has occupied an absolutely superior position in economic management and the techniques of database have been widely used in this field [1], the routine analysis of well managed data have to be done in manual way.

It is positive that the report submitted by a senior analyst may be satisfactory. But not everyone can do the job in same level within certain time. As the amount of data referred is getting larger, and the factors concerned become complicated, the drawback of conventional approach would be evident [2].

RASF (Routine Analysis System for Finance), which is aimed to develop the techniques of knowledge-based system in management, is a pilot expert system based on a financial database for analysing financial conditions in routine way [3]. To emulate a financial analyst, RASF will try to scan newly updated data in databases, reveal out the abnormal conditions reflected by them, reason about them, reache some opinions and finally draft out an analysis report.

RASF is intended to integrate up the latest techniques available for its target. For example, the techniques of Model Base[4] is to be introduced into RASF so that the system will provide better quantitative analysis results. RASF could be considered as an extension of financial database[5], or an approach to improving management productivity. What it will behave must be more friendly, more accessible and of a level of intelligence.

2. LIGHTS FROM SAMPLE REPORTS

After twenty-three pieces of monthly industrial enterprises finance reports of Fujian province have been studied, following results are obtained:

a). The configuration style of reports is tied to certain format. Generally, the explaination of main indexes, analysis of causes and prediction of next cycle are included, In analyzing main indexes, a straightforward method is used and opinions are put forward after some inferences. To illustrate the condition more clearly, sometimes more detailed information which may be considered being of lower level is processed in same way. Causality analysing starts from abnormal value of some indexes, including fine ones and unpleasant ones. Related indexes are listed out and other information is involved. Obviously, picking out the causality of the facts is in the light of domain knowledge. The prediction of future is rather rough. Occasionally, a number of suggestions to certain issues may be raised.

b). It could be seen that there are some facts and information in reports which might not be put into the financial database adequately, such as those of power supply, prices changing, marcket conditions, policy changing, the management level of enterprises, etc. The knowledge cover a large range of area and most part of it is not well structured, that means it is difficult to organize it in a regular way. The problem is, that the more the knowledge is involved in a report, the higher the level of the report would be.

c). The causality analysing is the key problem in reports. Sometimes it is necessary to analyse a cause deeply and progressively. Thus, the discussion have to be extended further and very detailed examples would be mentioned.

d). Indexes in reports are mostly presented with their values, also uncertain expressions are used, such as "rather better", "nearly the same as", "not very satisfactory", "greatly increaced", etc. Therefore, writers of reports sometimes have to qualify the values of some indexes with some statement for the literal sack.

There are following key problems which have to be solved in RASF:

. How to represent various sources of knowledge integratedly and make full use of them simultaneously;

. How to emulate the inference mechanism of manual problem solving process;

. How to configure out a coherent writing of report.

Consequently, a integrated method of knowledge representation must be introduced and an elaborate global data base must be used as the basis of problem solving.

3. THE STRUCTURE OF RASF

The structure of RASF is shown in Figure 1. We can see that there are several components around the Main Control System--MCS.

Financial Database--FDB is a basic member in the system. Typically, it stores and manages such indexes as:

. gross product of industry,

. total profit of industrial enterprises,

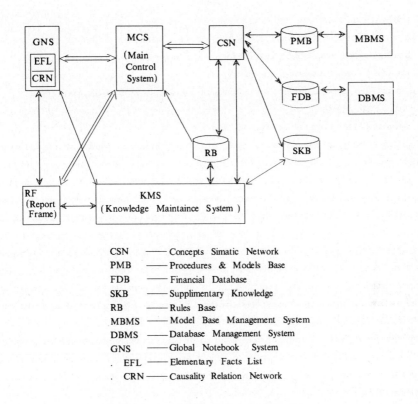

CSN ——— Concepts Simatic Network
PMB ——— Procedures & Models Base
FDB ——— Financial Database
SKB ——— Supplimentary Knowledge
RB ——— Rules Base
MBMS ——— Model Base Management System
DBMS ——— Database Management System
GNS ——— Global Notebook System
. EFL ——— Elementary Facts List
. CRN ——— Causality Relation Network

Figure 1 . The Structure of RASF

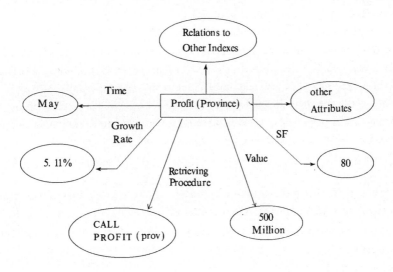

Figure 2 . The Attributes of "Provincial Profit"

. fiscal levy,

. financial income of industry,

. general debility of enterprises, etc.[6]

The data of FDB are updated monthly.

Besides FDB, there are three main kinds of knowledge sources in RASF:

. Rules Base--RB [7],

. Supplementary Knowledge Base--SKB,

. Concepts Semantic Network--CSN with Procedures and Models Base--PMB which is subject to CSN.

All the concepts in FDB, RB and SKB, which will play their roles in reasoning, are placed in CSN. So that, from the point of view of MCS, there is a unified expression of knowledge to the system. MCS can address knowledge sources through CSN and mustn't care where a concrete value comes from. Every concept has its attributes (see the example in Figure 2). To gain its value, a procedure link to it in PMB must be used, which could retrieve the data from FDB or SKB through a given path. In another situation, procedures are applied to calculate the data subject to facts previously known. Of course, various kinds of models including both deterministic and stochastic ones [8] should be stored in PMB in addition to retrieving procedures.

SKB is used for management of relevant facts which may not be involved in FDB,such as power supply condition of certain period, selling situations of some products, the effects of policy changing, etc. Every fact is expressed in SKB as a first class predicate.   For example, we have this fact:

"It is a drought season so that the power supply is not good in May, this would affect the production of following two month."

The fact will have this format in SKB:

> MONTH (power-supply) = May and
>
> NOT (CONDITION (power-supply) = good).

In addition, we may obtain two rules:

(1) If current season is drought then it is mostly happened that power supply is bad.

(2) If power supply is bad then the production of two coming month will be affected.

Global Notebook System--GNS [9] is a working data structure changing all the time when RASF is analysing the data. It employs blackboard structure technique to approach a rather complex goal and is composed of two parts as following:

. Elementary Facts List--EFL, which records facts or assertions gained during problem solving;

. Causality Relation Network--CRN, which is a stretching system for placing the consequences of causality inferred. CRN has the similar characters as CSN, and is different in that it is for placing the facts and assertions which are currently obtained and it emphasizes their causality relations which will be applied to compose the essay. Moreover, a value reflecting effective degree is attached to every relation in CRN.

GNS has an initial state just before the system starts running. This state may consist of a few index nodes with some primary relations between them which could be immigrated from CSN. While running, RASF keeps refreshing and extending CRN with facts and rules and adding new information into EFL in the meantime just like writing something onto a notebook. To indicate the termination of this phase, a flag is used and also state testing must be performed. When the state of GNS is contented RASF will stop analysing data and turn to configure the report according to what the notebook registered.

4. KEY POINTS OF RASF

There are a number of key points which embody main idea of dealing the issues RASF has addressed [10].

a). The expression of uncertain concepts.

There are two occasions RASF has to tackle uncertainty problem. One of these is reasoning with facts like "Some raw material is short-supplied in most of factories". In this case, we could not get exact information about how many factories are lack of raw material, the uncertainty factors have to be introduced when reasoning with this fact. Another occasion is for the literal requirement when drafting the report. In this occasion RASF must give each index, which will be explicitly mentioned in the report, a qualitative conclusion, such as "not ideal", "greatly increaced", "slightly affeted by", etc. Therefore, a strength factor--SF is set in RASF for each index to indicate the assessment of it. The value of an SF can be calculated according to that of corresponding index by certain algorithm. In the other hand, the description patterns in several levels are set to express the degrees of indexes qualitatively and each level is linked to a different value range of SF. So that, RASF can work alternatively between categories of quantitative and qualitative.

b). Reasoning.

Nonaccurate reasoning is necessary to RASF. As we have discussed above, each index in use is to be set an SF which will play a important role in reasoning. The principle will follow those being employed in the systems like MYCIN [11].

Default reasoning [12] is also used in RASF, for there are so much knowledge a management-oriented expert system has to touch upon that it is impossible to manage all the knowledge in a moderate size of system. By using default reasoning technique, RASF could reach a satisfied result with incomplete knowledge.

Suppose there is a default:

"Normally, the yearly growth rate of gross product is between 4.8% and 5.2%."

It is meant that we could consider a value 5.1%, which indicates the growth rate of gross product for a factory in this year, normal, as it is in a normal range. But if there is a fact in SKB which points out that the normal growth rate of this factory must be greater than 6% this year for some reasons,then RASF would reach a contrary result.

c). Report drafting.

An analysis report consists of hundreds of sentences in a organic way. There are certain links between sentences which have their complex structures. If information collected in

GNS is enough for report composition, then the problem remained is how to organize it
into a smooth and reasonable configuration.RASF takes frame-based representation [13] for
the job of writing. The Report Frame--RF, which is extracted from the reports written by
manual, has a tree structure. It possesses global configuration of the report as well as most
of patterns of analysing sentences. Some of branchs or leaves can be pruned if no more
information could be matched to RF during composing. Although the patterns of sentences
vary in a large arrangement, they are reduced much in economic analysis reports.Here are
samples of sentence patterns used in RASF:

    . Declarative pattern, which states a fact;

    . Asserting pattern, which gives out a judge about something;

    . Causality pattern, which describes relations of facts;

    . Enumerating pattern, which enumerates all facts concerning a given index;

    . Suggesting pattern, which raises a suggestion.

      The report editing rules are used for report configuring. With the rules, RASF
automatically ascertains the situation of current work and could determine, according to
the context,when and where an adequate conjunction to be used or which adjective could
fit the sentence better.

    d). Knowledge acquisition.

      Knowledge acquisition is always a key issue in knowledge based systems. RASF's
knowledge comes mainly from the reports previously accumulated month after month.
Although it is a shortcut to go, there are still many things to do. Therefore, RASF must
provide a well-designed man-machine interface for knowledge updating. We have a DBMS
for FDB's maintainance and a Model Base Management System--MBMS for PMB's
maintainance. The updating of other knowledge sources, such as SKB, RB, GNS, CSN and
RF, is performed by Knowledge Maintainance System--KMS. KMS must be friendly and
can help user to keep all sources of knowledge coordinated.There must be an interactive
facility for users to add knowledge while RASF is running. When the system turn out that
the knowledge currently used is not sufficient to solve problem, it should ask user to input
information according to its query. Of course, the new concepts involved in these
knowledge must already exist in CSN, otherwise the system would ask user to define them
in advance.

5. DEVELOPING RASF

    Now, a primary logic design of the system is formed and a media-term scheme for the
project of RASF is put forward. In the first phase, the main idea of RASF is to be tested
in IBM PCXT using an expert system building tool--GURU [14][15], industrial enterprises
financial data of province being used. Some key techniques of the system is being studied.
GURU is a meticulously developed tool for expert system in solving management-oriented
problem with its integrated power of data management, electronic spreadsheet, natural
language processing, reasoning capability, data communication, graphing and so on. But we
have met some difficulties when designing a ingenious blackboard system with the

facilities GURU provided and English version of GURU cannot meet the requirements of Chinese information processing. Nevertheless, GURU is still a convinient environment for a series of research work. A more suitable tool of artificial intelligence, which should be capable of operating under the environment of Chinese, would be choosen for RASF in next phase.

6. ACKNOWLEDGMENTS

It is a pleasure to acknowledge that a number of conversations with Professor Lin Yaorui and Professor Shi Chunyi have helped to shape this paper. Professor Wu Zhongmin has kindly taken time to give detailed advices about the procedure of submitting the paper. Mr Chen Shengsheng and Mr Liu Qun have helped a lot in paper typesetting and data collecting seperately. Mr Zhang Yaonian has contributed in checking literal issues.

REFERENCES:
[1]   Yao, Qinda,   Database Design   (Higher Educational Publishing House, 1987), in Chinese.
[2]   Lin, Zhangxi and Lin, Yaorui,   The Application of Techniques of Artificial Intelligence to Timetable Scheduling,   Journal of Tsinghua University,Vol.24,No.2, 1984,pp.1-9, in Chinese.
[3]   Dayal, U. & Smith, J. M., PROBE: A Knowledge-oriented   Database Management System, in: Brodie, M. L., et al (eds.),   On Knowledge Base   Management Systems-- Integrating   Artificial Intelligence and Database Technologies   (Springer-Verlag New York Inc., 1986), pp.227-257.
[4]   Tu, Xuyan et al, Large System Cybernetics and Multilevel Intelligent Management System, International Meeting of Data for Development International Association (1988), in print.
[5]   Stonebraker, M., Triggers and Inference in Database Systems, in: Brodie, M. L.,et al (eds.), On Knowledge Base Management Systems--Integrating Artificial Intelligence and Database Technologies (Springer-Verlag New York Inc., 1986), pp.297-314.
[6]   Zhang, Zhengyuan et al, Financial Management of Industrial Enterprices (Shandong People's Publishing House, 1982), in Chinese.
[7]   Hayes-Roth, F., Rule-based Systems, Comm. of ACM, Vol. 28, No. 9, Sept. 1985, pp.922-932.
[8]   Li, Zhuoli,   Practical Econometric Models and Economic Forecasting   (Tsinghua University Publishing House, 1981), in   Chinese.
[9]   Nii, H. P., Blackboard Systems: The Blackboard Model of Problem Solving and the Evolution of Blackboard Architecture, The AI MAGZINE Summer, 1986, pp.38-53.
[10] Lin, Yaorui et al, The Principles and Practices of Expert System (Tsinghua University Publishing House, 1988), in Chinese.
[11] Waterman, D. A., A Guide to Expert Systems (Addison-Wesley Publishing Company, 1986).
[12] Etherington, D. N.,   Formalzing Nonmonotonic Reasoning Systems, Artificial Intelligence, Vol. 31, No. 1, Jan. 1987, pp.41-85.
[13] Fikes, R. and Kehler, T., The Role of Frame-based Representation in Reasoning, Comm. of ACM, Vol. 28, No. 9, Sept.1985, pp.904-921.
[14] Simons, G. L., Expert Systems and Micros (NCC Publications, 1985).
[15] Holsapple, C. W. and   Whinston, A. B.,   Manager's   Guide to Expert Systems Using GURU (DOWJONES-IRWIN, 1986).

Expert Systems in Economics, Banking and Management
L.F. Pau et al. (Editors)
© *Elsevier Science Publishers B.V. (North-Holland), 1989*

Qualitative Modelling in Financial Analysis

Irene M.Y. Woon and Peter Coxhead

Department of Computer Science and Applied Mathematics
Aston University, Birmingham B4 7EG
United Kingdom

Qualitative modelling has traditionally been applied in the domain of physical systems, where there are well established and understood laws governing the behaviour of each component in the system. This paper investigates the validity of applying the theory in the domain of financial analysis where such laws may not exist or if they do, may not be universally applicable. Because of the inherent differences in the nature of these two domains, we argue that a different qualitative value system ought to be used. We show the features of such a system and discuss the main issues resulting from its use.

Introduction

Analysing the financial 'health' of a company, based on its annual financial statements, has always been of great importance, but is even more vital today with fast-moving international markets. Such an analysis has both quantitative and qualitative aspects. The quantitative aspects are clear: the raw figures in the financial statements must be re-cast and transformed to generate extra information for various purposes (e.g. reporting by product line or reporting by cost centre), and to produce indices of performance. Computer assistance with this task is readily available, ranging from the ubiquitous spread-sheet to major specialised packages, e.g. FCS, ESI. However, the figures alone are not enough: the human expert needs to interpret them. For example, if the sales/profit ratio is below the industry norm, management needs to know why this has happened. Does it suggest any long term problems? How could it be corrected?

One way of aiding human judgement in this qualitative area seems to be by the use of expert systems. It is clear that when such judgement can be regarded as being carried out by the application of rules, rule-based expert systems can attain the level of human performance, e.g Prospector, Xcon. Such systems have been proposed in the area of financial analysis. However, rule-based systems offer only shallow knowledge (Ganoe 84, Iwasieczko *et al.* 86). At present, the most hopeful model for reasoning based on deep knowledge seems to be that broadly known as 'qualitative physics' (Forbus 84, de Kleer & Brown 84, Kuipers 84).

'Fluid' model of a company

Since qualitative physics has been successfully applied to fluid flow systems, it is interesting to find that, quite independently, financial analysts have been offered models of company finances which use fluid flow analogies (Helfert 82, Van Horne 83). The company is viewed as a system of reservoirs and pipes through which funds are 'pumped' (see Fig. 1). The reservoirs represent the accumulation of assets or liabilities that build up during the course of business activity, such as the accounts receivable reservoir or the cash reservoir. Pipes connect the reservoirs, channelling funds to and from them, thereby affecting their levels.

A pump is used as a surrogate for the complex set of interactions that typically occurs between the firm and its environment, resulting in its current sales. These funds, together with other sources of input into the system, e.g. shareholder's contributions, are employed to carry out the normal activity of the business, which in turn generates sales and maintains the entire cycle of flow. The regulating activity of management is represented by a series of valves, each valve being placed on the inlet/ outlet pipe to a reservoir, e.g. the valve setting at the selling expenses outlet might represent management's inclinations to invest in advertising.

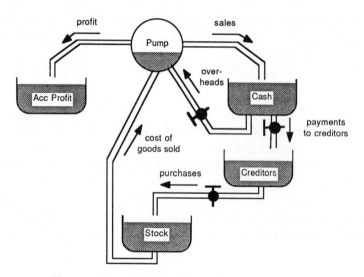

Figure 1 - Example of a 'fluid' model of a company

Qualitative description of the model of a company

The funds flow model of a company must be described by a formal qualitative model. The choice of such a model is still the subject of active research; we have chosen to follow the general approach of de Kleer and Brown (de Kleer & Brown 84). However, their research has generally attempted to analyse real physical systems; here, the attempt is to analyse a *model* of a real-world situation, so that an over-precise description would not be sensible, since the model itself is already an abstraction. Following de Kleer and Brown, we have attempted to proceed as follows. The funds flow model is described in terms of a set of variables and the relationships among them. All variables, whether flow rates, levels, or valve or pump settings, are reduced from their full quantitative value to one member of a qualitative set. The relationships among the variables lead to equations (confluences) connecting their qualitative values. Only certain sets of values satisfy these equations and thus define a potentially large but finite set of states which describe the model. This state space can be used to attempt to answer such questions as: given that the present fixed asset/net worth ratio is too high, how could this have arisen? The strategy is to find the paths from the states in which this is true to states in which the ratio is normal, and argue that following these paths offers a way of correcting the situation, if this is the requirement; alternatively, following them in reverse offers an explanation of how the situation could have occurred.

The first issue that arises is what qualitative value set should be used. In physical systems, value sets such as {negative, zero, positive} are useful. In the financial area, analysts' main concerns are to chart and explain departures from 'normality'. Thus a more useful qualitative set appears to be {low, normal, high}. Relationships among variables result, in the first instance, in equations connecting *quantitative* values. Thus for example, the model in Fig. 1 implies that:

$$\text{cost of goods sold} + \text{overheads} = \text{profit} + \text{sales} \qquad (1)$$

Expressing this in qualitative terms requires not only the replacement of quantitative values by qualitative ones, but also that the necessary operations on such values are defined. The principle used was a simple one: any expression involving only 'normal' values should always evaluate to 'normal'. Tables 1a to 1c define the basic operations needed. In certain cases, e.g. adding 'high' and 'low', the result can be any one of 'high', 'normal' or 'low', i.e. is ambiguous. The value 'ambig' is used solely as an abbreviation for the expression 'high | normal | low'. The tables for multiplication and division are identical to those for addition and subtraction respectively and so have been omitted. Note that as with quantitative arithmetic, subtraction corresponds to the addition of a negated value. However, a significant difference from quantitative arithmetic is the identity of qualitative addition and multiplication and qualitative subtraction and division. Equality poses some problems which are discussed further below; for the present, disregard Table 2, and assume only that identical qualitative values are equal. The operation of taking the qualitative value of a variable is expressed by the use of square brackets: thus [credit sales] means the qualitative value of the credit sales. Using this notation and the operator tables, we can re-write (1) as the *qualitative* equation (confluence):

$$[\text{cost of goods sold}] + [\text{overheads}] = [\text{profit}] + [\text{sales}] \qquad (2)$$

(It might be better to use e.g. Q+ or Q= instead of + or = to stress that qualitative addition or equality is involved, but this notation becomes clumsy in more complex formulae; it should be assumed that when qualitative values are involved, the operators are also qualitative.)

Constants can be used in qualitative equations. For example, the relationship between credit sales, accounts receivable, cash collections and bad debts might be expressed by the equation:

$$[\text{credit sales}] - [\text{cash collections}] - [\text{bad debts}] - [\text{accounts receivable}] = \text{normal} \qquad (3)$$

Suppose that cash collections and bad debts are 'normal'. Equation (3) then becomes:

$$[\text{credit sales}] - \text{normal} - \text{normal} - [\text{accounts receivable}] = \text{normal} \qquad (3a)$$

Since Table 1b shows that subtracting 'normal' leaves values unchanged (i.e. 'normal' is a right identity for subtraction), (3a) can be re-written as:

$$[\text{credit sales}] - [\text{accounts receivable}] = \text{normal} \qquad (3b)$$

This implies that, for example, if the value of credit sales is 'normal', then accounts receivable must be 'normal' (since only 'normal' - 'normal' yields 'normal' according to Table 1b). Thus Equation (3) produces constraints on the qualitative values of the variables involved; only certain sets of values will satisfy the equation.

Table 1a - Addition Operation: [x] + [y]   Table 1b - Subtraction Operation: [x] - [y]

[y]\[x]	low	normal	high
low	low	low	ambig
normal	low	normal	high
high	ambig	high	high

[y]\[x]	low	normal	high
low	ambig	high	high
normal	low	normal	high
high	low	low	ambig

Table 1c - Negation Operation: -[x]   Table 2 - Equality Operator: [x] = [y]

[x]	-[x]
low	high
normal	normal
high	low

[y]\[x]	low	normal	high	ambig
low	true	false	false	true
normal	false	true	false	true
high	false	false	true	true
ambig	true	true	true	true

The precise properties of the value system need further investigation, since they determine how equations involving them ought to be written so as to express the exact semantics of any situation. Since qualitative addition and multiplication are identical as are qualitative subtraction and division, it is usually only necessary to discuss addition and subtraction, with any conclusions transferred automatically to multiplication and division respectively. The qualitative value system put forward here has the following properties, which can be verified by use of Tables 1a to 1c.

(i)   As in quantitative algebra, addition is a commutative operation, whereas subtraction is not, i.e. for all qualitative values [x] and [y]:

$$[x] + [y] = [y] + [x]$$
$$[x] - [y] \neq [y] - [x]$$

(ii)   As in quantitative algebra, addition is an associative operation, whereas subtraction is not, i.e. for all qualitative values [x], [y] and [z]:

$$[x] + ([y] + [z]) = ([x] + [y]) + [z]$$
$$[x] - ([y] - [z]) \neq ([x] - [y]) - [z]$$

(iii) As in quantitative algebra, multiplication and division are distributive over addition and subtraction, e.g.:

$$[x] * ([y] + [z]) = ([x] * [y]) + ([x] * [z])$$

However, the identity of multiplication with addition and division with subtraction means that qualitative addition and subtraction are also distributive over qualitative addition and subtraction, e.g.:

$$[x] + ([y] + [z]) = ([x] + [y]) + ([x] + [z])$$

(iv) The set of qualitative values, Q = {low, normal, high}, has an identity for addition and subtraction, viz. 'normal', since for all qualitative values [x]:

[x] + normal = [x]

[x] - normal = [x]

(v) Each element of Q does not have a strict additive or subtractive inverse element. Since as noted in (iv), 'normal' is the identity for both operations, a strict additive inverse would require that for every [x], $[x]^{inv}$ existed such that:

$$[x] + [x]^{inv} = normal \qquad (4)$$

Table 1a makes clear that this is not so. This is highly inconvenient as it appears to prevent the re-arrangement of equations, which generally involves the implicit addition of inverses in order to transfer terms from one side to another. One solution is to define the additive inverse as the negation (Table 1c), as in ordinary arithmetic, and also extend the equality operator via Table 2 so that a value of 'ambig' appearing on one side of an equation is equal to any value on the other side. (A similar approach can be used for subtraction.) Equations can now be solved in the usual way. For example, consider the equation:

$$[x] + high = normal \qquad (5)$$

There are two ways of solving this equation to find [x]. Firstly, we can substitute each of the three possible values of [x] into (5) in turn, checking which satisfy it. Only [x] = low does so, since the left-hand side of (5) is then 'ambig', which is qualitatively equal to the right-hand side 'normal', according to Table 2. Secondly, we can re-arrange (5):

[x] + high = normal

⇒   [x] = normal - high = low

Whichever method is used, the definitions of inverse and equality ensure that the same answer is obtained. However, since 'ambig' has been taken to equal 'normal', equations which would yield the same quantitative solutions can yield different qualitative solutions: in particular, ambiguity is possible.

To summarize: properties (i), (ii) and (iii) taken together mean that qualitative expressions involving +, -, * and / can be written as if they were normal quantitative expressions evaluating from left to right. To ensure the correct evaluation of nested expressions, parentheses may be needed when the operators - and / are used. Common variables in equations can be factored, since all the qualitative operators are distributive; this means that expressions may be simplified without any loss in accuracy. Property (v) however means that equations which are quantitatively equivalent are not necessarily qualitatively so.

Problems with defining confluences

The consequence of these considerations is that, although the use of qualitative reasoning seems at first sight quite straightforward, in reality the situation is rather more complex. The use of qualitative arithmetic involves a paradox. Its advantage is that it allows a system containing many variables with wide ranges of values to be described using a value system that involves only a few values. Yet it is precisely this reduction and consequent imprecision which produces the greatest difficulty in the use of qualitative reasoning, namely ambiguity. Ambiguity results from the occurrence of a large set of possible solutions to an equation or set of equations. For example, consider Equation (3). If the value of any one of the four variables is 'ambig', then the left-hand side will evaluate to 'ambig', regardless of the values of the other variables, so that the equation will be satisfied. Since each set of values of the variables defines a state, when this happens there may be a computationally intractable number of possible states to investigate. It appears that such unconstrained solutions tend to be less commonplace in the description of physical systems, where most of the work in qualitative reasoning has been carried out, largely due to the nature of the domain area and the description which is appropriate. Domain areas involving business matters tend to be more complex and less well structured and consequently are less well constrained. There are various ways of reducing ambiguity, such as the use of knowledge and heuristics and the use of quantitative data, and ultimately these will have to be used. However, it appears that the degree of ambiguity may also be affected by the way the qualitative model is expressed i.e. the way in which the equations are written. As there does not appear to be any published research into this issue, this paper seeks to present some of the conclusions we have reached, based both on theoretical considerations and on practical investigation using a Prolog program to solve sets of qualitative equations. In the following equations, the unknown variables will be represented by [x] and [y]; other variables are to be regarded as known.

1. It does not matter how a single equation is written. For example, given the values of [a], [b] and [c], precisely the same set of values of [x] satisfy all the alternative forms of the same 'semantic' equation given below:

$$[x] = [a] + [b] + [c]$$
$$[x] - [a] = [b] + [c]$$
$$[x] - [a] - [b] = [c]$$
$$[x] - [a] - [b] - [c] = normal \qquad (6)$$

   (The evaluation of the equations proceeds as it does with normal mathematical equations. Thus, the ordering of items on one side of the equation is also irrelevant, e.g. Equation (6) may also be written as: $[x] - [b] - [a] = [c]$.)

2. The factored form of an equation should be used if one exists. For example, Equation (8) will lead to less ambiguous results than Equation (7):

$$[x] = ([a] * [b]) - ([c] * [b]) \qquad (7)$$
$$[x] = [a - c] * [b] \qquad (8)$$

   This is due to the fact that information is lost whenever quantitative values are converted to qualitative values. In particular, [a] - [c] is only weakly qualitatively equal to [a - c]: for example, if a = high and c = high, [a] - [c] yields 'ambig', whereas if the quantitative values of a and c were used, the qualitative value of (a - c) could be determined precisely. To minimise loss of information, all calculations should be carried out as far as possible using quantitative values before converting to corresponding qualitative values.

3. Simplification of a set of equations leads to less ambiguity if there are common items to be cancelled out.

Consider the two equations:

$$[a] + [c] = [x] + [c] \tag{9}$$
$$[a] = [x] \tag{10}$$

They are not fully equivalent, and in particular (10) is less ambiguous than (9) because the common element [c] has been cancelled out. The underlying reason is that cancelling involves adding the inverse which in qualitative arithmetic may yield 'ambig':

$$[a] + [c] = [x] + [c]$$
$$\Rightarrow [a] + [c] + [c]^{inv} = [x] + [c] + [c]^{inv}$$
$$\Rightarrow [a] + \{normal, ambig\} = [x] + \{normal, ambig\} \tag{9a}$$

Unless [c] = normal, $[c] + [c]^{inv}$ = ambig, which means that (9a) is true regardless of the values of [a] and [x], i.e. the solution is [x] = ambig for any value of [a].

4. Simplification of a set of equations leads to less ambiguity if unknown variables can be replaced by known variables so that there are no unknowns in the equation.

Consider the two sets of equations:

(i) $[x] = [a] + [b]$
  $[y] - [x] = normal$

(ii) $[x] = [a] + [b]$
  $[y] - [a] - [b] = normal$

The set of qualitative values of the four variables which satisfy both these sets of equations is the same. The reason appears to be that in substituting [a] + [b] for [x], there is still one unknown left.

However, consider the sets of equations:

(iii) $[d] = [x] - [a]$
   $[b] + [x] - [a] = 0$

(iv) $[d] = [x] - [a]$
   $[b] + [d] = 0$

In this case, set (iv) gives less ambiguous results than set (iii), as substitution leaves the second equation of the set with no unknowns. Thus, it seems advantageous to write equations so that where there is dependency it is expressed in terms of a known quantity, rather than an unknown quantity.

5. Simplification of a set of equations leads to less ambiguity if unknown variables can be replaced by known variables, followed by cancellation of common variables.

Consider the next two sets of equations:

(i) $[x] = [b] - [a]$
  $[a] + [x] = normal$

(ii) $[x] = [b] - [a]$
  $[b] = normal$

In set (ii), [x] has been substituted and the common items have been cancelled out and this leads to less ambiguity. Substitution without any cancellation has no effect as in:

(iii) $[x] = [b] + [c]$
   $[y] = [x] + [b]$

(iv) $[x] = [b] + [c]$

         $[y] = [b] + [c] + [b]$

Sets (iii) and (iv) produce an equal number of solutions i.e. valid values of the variables.

These conclusions provide guidelines in the formulation of confluences to describe the flow of funds within a company. Referring to Figure 1, it can be seen that flows in and out of the pump need some form of synchronisation. The difference between the sales flow and the cost of goods flow can be attributed to the markup the company sets on the volume of goods. Suppose the confluence equations describing this are written as:

[selling price] * [volume] =[sales]   (11)

[cost price] * [volume] = [cost of goods sold]   (12)

[sales] - [cost of goods sold] - [overheads] = [profit]   (13)

and further suppose that cost price and profit are normal while selling price and volume are high. Substituting these values into Equations (11) - (13) and solving, we obtain:

high * high = [sales] $\Rightarrow$ [sales] = high

normal * high = [cost of goods sold] $\Rightarrow$ [cost of goods sold] = high

high - high - [overheads] = normal $\Rightarrow$ [overheads] = ambig

But in fact, overheads in this instance is known and is not ambiguous, since if the markup on the volume of goods is high and the volume transacted is high but the profit is only normal, this can only be because the overheads are high. This implies that the relationships expressed by Equations (11) - (13) are not quite appropriate. The examples in Equations (7) and (8) give an idea on how such a relationship can better be expressed. If we rewrite (13) by substituting in the values of [sales] and [cost of goods sold] to give:

([selling price] * [volume]) - ([cost price] * [volume]) - [overheads] = profit

we see that this corresponds to (7). The equation that will correspond to (8) and consequently produce more accurate results is:

([selling price] - [cost price]) * [volume] - [overheads] = [profit]   (13a)

Reworking (13a) with the values given previously, we get :

(high - normal) * high - [overheads] = normal

$\Rightarrow$ high - [overheads] = normal

$\Rightarrow$ [overheads] = high

If we extend the model shown in Figure 1 to include a debtors reservoir with credit sales flowing into it and cash collections flowing out, a set of equations relating to current assets may be:

[current assets] = [debtors] + [cash] + [stock]   (14)

[cash collection] + [cash sales] - [payments to creditors] - [overheads] = [cash]   (15)

[credit sales] - [cash collection] = [debtors]   (16)

[cash sales] + [credit sales] = [sales]   (17)

Suppose that current assets, debtors and stock are normal and sales is low. What can be inferred about the state of the other variables? We can proceed by substituting (15) and (16) into (14):

[current assets] = [credit sales] - [cash collection] + [cash collection] + [cash sales]

                          - [payments to creditors] - [overheads] + [stock]   (14a)

We could reduce (14a) even furthur by substituting (17) into it to arrive at:

[current assets] = [sales] - [cash collection] + [cash collection]

$$- \text{[payments to creditors]} - \text{[overheads]} + \text{[stock]} \qquad (14b)$$

We can then cancel out the common element [cash collection] and proceed to solve the equation as:

normal = low - [payments to creditors] - [overheads] + normal

Substituting the result of Equation (13a) into this will give us:

normal = low - [payments to creditors] - high + normal

$\Rightarrow$ normal = low - [payments to creditors]

$\Rightarrow$ [payments to creditors] = low

Equation (14a) as it is written is unsolvable if [cash collection] is unknown, and if it were known to be high or low, then [payments to creditors] would be ambiguous. It is essential to rearrange equations so that the unknowns cancel each other out.

Future Work

The previous section has assumed the qualitative values of the flows, pumps and valves. There are several ways these may be derived and used to drive the qualitative model. We have chosen to use published ratios to derive these qualitative values. It is common for analysts to compare company ratios to the pertinent average industry ratios. They commonly use terms like 'higher than industry average', 'lower than normal', 'normal' or 'all right' to describe how the company ratios are perceived (which of course fits well with the qualitative value set we have been using). This adds another dimension of difficulty into designing the overall system. The division operation is identical to the subtraction operation, so that when both elements of the ratio are either high or low, the result of the ratio is ambiguous i.e. it satisfies all values. There may be suffcient constraints generated from other ratios or confluences to pinpoint the values of the individual elements, but experience shows that frequently this is not possible. Our current approach to controlling this situation has been to divide the solutions into two sets; one containing values that are common to all candidate solutions and the other those which are different. The latter set requires further disambiguation by additional information - the simplest of which is to query the user, or by the use of heuristics, which is the subject of continuing research. Once this has been done, qualitative values for the pump, flows and valves can be derived and questions on how the company is doing, what options are open to it, or how it can improve itself can be answered.

References

de Kleer, J and Brown, J.S. (1984). "A Qualitative Physics based on Confluences", *Artificial Intelligence*, **16**(1-3), 7-83.

de Kleer, J. (1986). "Reasoning about Multiple Faults", *Proceedings - AAAI-86 Fifth National Conference on Artificial Intelligence.*, 132-139.

Forbus K. (1985). "The Role of Qualitative Dynamics in Naive Physics", *Formal theories of the Commonsense World*, Hobbs, J.R and Moore, R.C (eds), Ablex Publishing Corporation, pp.185-226.

Ganoe, F. (1984). "Knowledge Based Decision Support for Financial Analysis", *Proceedings of the 1984 IEEE Conference on Systems, Man and Cybernetics*, 229-232.

Helfert, Erich A. (1978). *Techniques of Financial Analysis*, Prentice-Hall.
Iwasieckzo, B., Korczak, J., Kwiecień, Muszyńska, J. (1986). "Expert System in Financial Analysis", *AI in Economics and Management,* Pau, L. F (ed), Elsevier Science Publishers B.V., North-Holland, pp. 113-120.
Kuipers, B. (1984). "Commonsense Reasoning about Causality: Deriving Behaviour from Structure, *Artificial Intelligence,* **16**(1-3), 169-203.
Van Horne, James C. (1983). *Financial Management and Policy,* Prentice-Hall.

Expert Systems in Economics, Banking and Management
L.F. Pau et al. (Editors)
© *Elsevier Science Publishers B.V. (North-Holland), 1989*

Port-Man – An Expert System of Portfolio Management in Banks

Y. Y. Chan,   T. S. Dillon,   E. G. Saw

Department of Computer Science,
La Trobe University, Bundoora,
Victoria 3083, Australia.

Abstract

Port-Man is a banking advisory system that uses a combination of frames and rules as its knowledge representations. The system selects of a list of investment products which would most closely match the investor's investment criteria. The selected products are ranked according to the rates of return and risk levels. Frames are used in the system to specify the explicit context and function of the rules. Functions and rules are also grouped and attached to frames. They will be executed if the attached frames are active. Hence the process of Port-Man can be viewed as a sequence of frames activations. The system may restart the consultation for a different set of inputs if some changes to the input data have been made without going back to the beginning. Port-Man is written in a new expert system language called XL and the syntax and features of XL are also discussed in the paper.

Keywords : Expert System, Frames, Investment Banking, Expert System Language.

1   Introduction

One of the major areas of service provided by the banking industry is to help people to plan the financial aspect of their lives. To be able to function effectively, banks must be able to advise their customers on the best possible arrangement that would suit their individual investment needs. This implies that the investment advisor must have a knowledge of the products offered by the bank and the ability to recognize the customer's needs and match these needs with the appropriate products. Currently this service is performed by the bank officers. One of the problems is the non-consistency of the advice given from these officers. Certain products could be well known to some officers but are ignored by others. Hence, the same investment situation could lead to different advice from different bank officers. The problem would be more marked when the branches are more decentralized.

Furthermore the consultation process is usually complicated and may take some time. This delay could lead to investors impatience with the process, with the likely loss of the client to the bank. Hence the development of an expert system would greatly increase the provision of banks service to its customer as it could make this service more readily available and greatly speed up the process.

Port-Man is a banking advisory system designed to assist bank officers to give advice on personal investment in a bank. It helps to speed up the consultation process and standardize the experience of the the the bank's financial consultants. The task of the system is to select a range of bank products that will satisfy the criteria for investment. The selected products are ranked according to the rates of return and risk levels. A cash projection for each selected product can be displayed. Moreover, various side effects for the investor, such as tax variation or pension adjustment, will be taken into consideration. Upon request, the system will give an explanation of how a product is selected. In addition, the user may query the system during the consultation process. Finally, Port-Man allows the user to change any previous input or investment criteria, and the system will then restart the process at the appropriate stage.

2   Consultation Stages

In general, the consultation process of Port-Man can be divided into 4 stages:

1. Information Acquisition;

2. Product Selection;

3. Choice Refinement;

4. Explanation.

2.1   Information Acqusition

Initially Port-Man acquires personal information about the investor. In case the investor has made a previous consultation with the system, Port-Man searches for the personal record of the investor from the data base. The subsequent consultation will then update the record accordingly. Otherwise, a new record will be created for the consultation. A minimum set of questions about the investment objectives and criteria will be asked via a form orientated screen. More specific questions will be asked only if needed in later stages.

2.2 Product Selection

In this stage, Port-Man searches for the feasible products for the investment. Products are divided into different groups according to the product features, such as interest type, capital growth and etc. The product groups form an up-side-down tree, with the most general group as the root node and the more specific sub-product groups as the successor nodes in the tree.

The search algorithm may then be considered as a tree search algorithm. Starting from the root node, the algorithm traverses to the successor nodes in a depth first search manner. Upon entry to a successor node, the algorithm attempts to match the investment criteria with the features of the product group. If the matching succeeds, the algorithm continues its search to this node and to any successor nodes. If the matching fails, the algorithm prunes the branch from that node and backtracks to another unvisited branch of the most recent predecessor node. If the matching is undecided, the algorithm will request more information from the system, which will then collect the desired information by rules, if-needed functions or direct queries to the user. Consequently, most interactive query-answer dialogs will take place at this stage.

No matter the matching is successful, failed or undecided, the system records the decision made and the corresponding justifications. Moreover, each piece of information will have a record of its own justification as well.

2.3 Choice Refinement

Once the feasible products are found, the system considers the various side effects that the products may have for the investors. Warning messages will be given if the investor's tax situation is affected or if his/her pensioner card entitlement is jeopardized by any of the selected products. Also, if the investor is a pensioner, the effective net return after the reduction of the pension will be calculated and displayed. Furthermore, if the user has any subjective opinion on the future change in interest rates, the system will highlight all the products that may be chosen in the case of any change in interest rates. It may even recommend the period of investment for some of the selected products. Finally, the system ranks the selected products according to the rates of return and the risk levels.

2.4 Explanation

It is an optional stage where the user may question the system on how or why a product is selected. Recall that the system has recorded every decision and justification as it traverses along the product tree. A reverse list of the decision record may answer the "how" question and the appropriate justification records could answer the "why" question. In addition, the justification of the adjustment actions made in the choice refinement stage are also recorded so that more specific questions may be answered at this stage.

The explanations are mainly menu-driven. Currently, details of products, description of rules and arithmetic formulae may also be displayed by means of menus. In addition, the menu facility is also incorporated in most of the query-answer dialogs to assist the user to answer the system queries in the product selection and choice refinement stages. Moreover, some of the investment criteria/parameters can also be changed via the menu facility. If there are some changes in the investment parameters, the system will restart the consultation process from the appropriate stage, depending on the changed parameters. Thus, it allows the user to make several investment plans at a minimum of input and process time.

3   Knowledge Representation

In Port-Man, frames are the major components of knowledge representation, while production rules are used to represent the control knowledge of product selection. System parameters, personal details of investors, investment criteria, features of products are all represented in frames. Even the rules are grouped together and are attached to the appropriate frames. In general, Port-Man has six classes of frames:

1. Customer Frames;

2. Target Frames;

3. Product Frames;

4. Variable Frames;

5. Control Frames;

6. Objective Frames.

3.1   Customer and Target Frames

The personal record of each investor is internally represented by a customer frame. The slots consist of personal facts about the investor and a history of previous consultation with

Port-Man. New information collected from the present consultation will also be inserted into the frame. For each consultation, a separate target frame will be created for the investor.

A target frame records a particular investment objective and investment criteria. The required product features and their justifications are all recorded in the target frame. In addition, a target frame has a set of attached rules to guide its search along the product tree.

3.2   Product Frames

As mentioned in the previous section, the products in Port-Man are classified into different groups, which form a hierarchical tree. Internally, Port-Man represents each product/product-group (we will call it product group in general) by a product frame. A product frame is therefore a node in the hierarchical tree. It describes the common features of the product group. It also has a set of attached rules to guide the search for the sub-product groups. The general structure of a product frame is as follows:

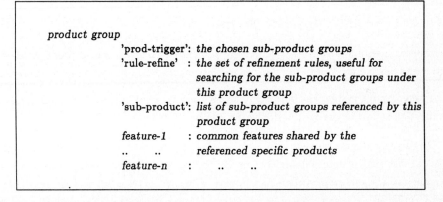

Figure 3.1: The Structure of a Product Frame.

3.3   Variables Frames

In Port-Man, each system parameter has a corresponding variable frame. A variable frame is used to control and record how its value is derived. The rules required, the if-needed functions, the value derived and the context of the parameter are all held in the variable frame. For instance, the parameter **Invest-Amt** has the following structure :

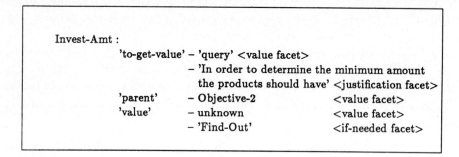

Figure 3.2: The frame structure of the variable **Invest-Amt**

The 'value' slot is to store the value of the the parameter. The 'Find-Out' is the name of an user-defined function used to derive the value of the parameter. The 'parent' slot indicates the dynamic relationship of the variable frame with another frame and is particularly useful for explaining a chain of "why" queries from users. The 'to-get-value' slot is used to specify how the unknown value is deduced. The justification facet of the slot gives an explanation on why the variable is required by the system.

3.4   Control and Objective Frame

The control frame is used to represent higher level tasks, e.g., the review task and the consultation task. The frame contains a list of tasks to be performed. A task is an action to be taken by the system and consists of a function that is to be executed. The name of the function is held in the control slot of the frame.

The objective frame is created dynamically by the system whenever Port-Man performs a goal or task. It has slots defining the purpose or reason for the goal along with the name of either the variable frame or previous objective frame from which the goal originated. Hence in this way all the active objective frames are linked together. The objective frame will be deleted once its goal or task is completed.

The frame representation provides the system with a very modular control methodology. Most frames have some attached rules or functions. These rules or functions define the complete control within the attached frames. They also control the next frames to be activated. Hence the process can be considered as a sequence of frames activation. For instance, the search algorithm in the product selection stage is implicitly defined by the attached rules and functions in the product frames. Such methodology is found to be particular suitable in Port-Man because of the frequent changes in bank products. Maintenance can be achieved by removing unwanted product frames, inserting new product frames or updating existing product frames in the knowledge base. The search algorithm can also be specially tuned for some particular product groups. A major problem encountered in large expert systems is in the maintenance of the attached rules and the rules which activate the frames. For example, if a product is to be replaced by a new product, we have to remove the rules attached to the old product frame and allocate a new set of rules to the new product frame. Besides, we may need to update the context of the rules that activate the removed frame. A lot of searching will be involved, especially if the rule base is large. We will address this problem in the next section.

4 Implementation

Port-Man is implemented in XL and X-Tract, an expert system environmrnt developed by ISR, an Australian company. XL provides both syntactic and functional level manipulations of frames and rules. The following subsections discuss how the variable frames and rules in Port-Man are constructed in XL.

4.1 Implementation of Variable Frames

As was mentioned in the previous section, system parameters in Port-Man are represented by variables frames. In general, frames in XL have the following structure :

```
Frame-name :
          Slot-1 – <value facet>
                   <certification facet>
                   <justification facet>
                   <if-needed facet>
              ...      ...
              ...      ...
          Slot-n –    ..      ..
                      ..      ..
```

Figure 4.1: The general frame structure in XL

where Frame-name must be a symbol while Slot-i and facets may be symbols or strings. Strings are written as 'strings'. Facets may also be constants except the if-needed facet which must be a string. The value facets of a slot can be retrieved by a binary function **of**.

For example, refer to figure 3.2, the statement

'parent' of Invest-Amt

returns the symbol **Objective-2**. However, if the value facet contains the logical value
unknown[1], the function specified by the if-needed facet, if it exists, will be called automatically. Therefore, the statement

'value' of Invest-Amt

results in calling the function **Find-Out**, whose value will be returned. Moreover, if the
if-needed facet is missed, a system event relevant event function (**RELEVENT**) will be
called instead. The **RELEVENT** function may be redefined by users. Therefore, it is
useful to define a general **Find-Out** algorithm as **RELEVENT** function.

XL allows all facets of a slot to be assigned by a XL statement called **remember**.
remember has the following syntax :

remember frame-name, slot, value[,certification ,justification ,if-needed]

Hence, the various facets of the 'value' slot in the figure 3.2 could easily be assigned by the
statement :

remember Invest-Amt, 'value', unknown,,,'Find-Out'

4.2   Implementation of Rules

Port-Man associates rules with the frame which defines the context in which the rules
are applied. For example, if the rules are used to deduce the interest type, they will be
grouped and attached with the **Interest** variable frame.

The grouping of rules is enhanced by XL facilities. XL internally indexes rules by means
of two master control frames (MCF's) called the **lhs-frame** and **rhs-frame**. Elements of
the expression comprising the antecedent of a rule are stored as a slot name of the **lhs-
frame** while the rule name is placed in the value facet of the slot. Similarly, elements of the
expression comprising the consequent of a rule are stored as the slot name of the **rhs-frame**
with the rule name in the value facet. An element of an expression may be a constant, a
string, a frame or a function name. The frame properties of MCF's, allows the rules to be
grouped together by means of one **expand** statement. The syntax of **expand** in frames is :

expand [all] [lhs/rhs] relation [control-frame], pattern, object-frame [,funct-name]

---

[1]XL has 3 logical values : yes, no, unknown

The keyword **relation** specifies that the expansion is in respect to frames. In brief, the **expand** passes the **object-frame** and all the information of the slot that matches, in depth first search manner, the **pattern** of the **control-frame** or **object-frame** (if **control-frame** is missed) to the user-defined function called **funct-name**. The keyword **all** ensures the expansion continues until all the slots are examined or that the **function** returns a logical value **no** at the top level. Hence, we may associate the rules whose consequents are relevant to an element, say 'fixed', to a frame called **Fix-Set** by the following statement :

expand all relation rhs-frame, 'fixed', Fix-Set, rule-filter

Thus, if a rule is given certain *keys* in the context, the grouping of rules can be made directly from the MCF's using the *keys* as the **pattern**. The maintenance can also be made automated using the *keys*.

5 Conclusion

In summary, Port-Man uses a combination of rules and frames as the knowledge representations. To facilitate the system solution and to reduce the search space, the products with similar features are grouped together. Rules are used to guide the system selection of the investment products and are attached to various slots in the frames. Hence, the control becomes modular and local to the frames.

The explanation stage allow the user to examine the current chain of reasoning during the consultation and how the system arrived at the solution. This stage is designed not only to justify the chosen products, but also to help the bank consultants to feedback their experience and to make recommendations to the system. In addition, Port-Man allows the user to change the values of system parameters. In this way, it provides an efficient means to run the consultation using a different set of inputs.

Port-Man is implemented in XL. The tools provided by XL simplifies the building and manipulation of frames and rules. Consequently, the knowledge engineers can devote more time and concentration on the implementation of expertise knowledge.

Acknowledgement

We gratefully acknowledge the help of Mr Colin Watts of ISR, Mr John E. Coulston and Mr Bruce A. Esler of the ANZ bank. We also wish to thank ISR for providing the XL software, Olivetti for providing the hardware, the Victorian Department of Industry and

Technology and Resources for financial support that enabled us to acquire the XL system and the ANZ bank for their assistance in the development of the project.

References

[1] Aikins J.S., "Prototypical Knowledge for Expert System", Artificial Intelligence 20 (1983) pp. 163 - 210.

[2] Buchanan B.G. and Shortliffe E.H., Rule Based Expert System, (Addison Wesley 1984).

[3] Chan, Y.Y., Saw E.G. and Dillon, T.S., "An Expert System for a Portfolio Management Using Both Frames and Production Rules", Proceedings of Avignon'88 General Conference (France, 1988).

[4] Davis, R. and King, J., "An Overview of Production Systems," Machine Intelligence 8 (New York, 1977).

[5] Kunz, J., Fallat, R., McClung, D., Osborn, J., Votteri, B., Nii, H., Aikins, J., Fagan, L. and Feigenbaum, E "A Physiological rule based system for interpreting pulmonary function test results", Working Paper HPP-78-19, Heuristic Programming Project, *Dept. of Computer Science, Stanford University, (1978).*

[6] Ogawa, H., Nanba, H. and Tanaka, K., "An Active Frame for Knowledge Representation", 6th International Joint Conference of Artificial Intelligenca (Tokyo, 1979).

[7] Podbury, C.A. and Dillon, T.S., "An Intelligent Knowledge Based System for Maintenance Scheduling in a Power System" Proceedings of the 9th PSCC (Lisbon, Portugal, 1987).

[8] Shortliffe, E.H., Computer Based Medical Consultation : MYCIN (American Elsevier, New York, 1976).

[9] Tan, P.L., Loo, S.L., and Dillon, T.S., "An Intelligent Assistant to MAnage Incomplete Queries Based on Extended Data Frames", Proceedings of the ACSC-ll Conference (Brisbane 1988).

[10] Winston, P.H., "The Commercial Debut of Artificial Intelligence", Proceedings of the 2nd International Confrence on the Application of Expert Systems (1986).

[11] X-Tract Development Guide (Intelligent Systems Research, Australia 1987).

[12] X-Tract System Reference Manual (Intelligent Systems Research, Australia 1987).

Expert Systems in Economics, Banking and Management
L.F. Pau et al. (Editors)
© *Elsevier Science Publishers B.V. (North-Holland), 1989*

KNOWLEDGE ACQUISITION AND REASONING WITH A CANONICAL GRAPH MODEL IN PERSONAL FINANCIAL PLANNING

B.J. GARNER and E. TSUI

Division of Computing and Mathematics
Deakin University
Geelong, Victoria 3217
Australia*

A *canonical graph model* [1] for personal financial planning is described. Domain rules are encoded within the knowledge base via a man-machine dialog in (near) natural language. Reasoning with the rule base is facilitated by a *general purpose inference engine* (GPIE) [2]. Key requirements for good natural language interfaces to rule-based systems are identified and an annotated rule encoding and execution session is included. Perhaps the most notable achievement of this research is that a novice can create, modify and communicate with a rule base in near natural language, irrespective of the internal and intermediate representations in the computer and how the knowledge was originally acquired.

1. CURRENT PROBLEMS

A recent comprehensive survey [3] of expert system (knowledge based systems) tools indicates the availability of many tools/shells for custom development. While these tools provide structured design phases for the encoding of expert knowledge and basic mechanisms (eg. forward chaining, backward chaining, mixed strategy) for reasoning with knowledge, they are seen to be unsuitable for use by non-specialists for the following two reasons:

1. Domain (Expert) knowledge is encoded through a highly structured interface, often in the form of screen windows, template application, menu driven systems and/or programming in a specific language.

2. Though not mandatory, the user is often assumed to possess knowledge about the implementation language (eg. C, Pascal, Prolog, Lisp) of the tool/shell. Two such examples are ART [4] and KEE [5].

As a result of the above problems, knowledge engineers are often required to encode the requisite expert knowledge for a knowledge base in a format that is specific to the individual tool/shell. Apart from the above problems and the

---

* This research is funded by the Australian Research Grants Scheme under contract number A48615479

consequent knowledge acquisition bottlenecks, current expert systems tools/shells also lack functionality [6]. Typical deficiencies would be:

1. Inexact matching [2] between rule assertions and given data is either inadequate or not provided in most tools/shells (eg. EMYCIN, ROSIE and OPS5). In [6], this issue is referred to as *resolution inference* in expert systems. The applicability of a rule base is severely limited if inexact/partial matching between (given) data and rule assertions is not supported.

2. An inadequate framework for representing *structural knowledge* [7] in the knowledge base impairs the reasoning (inference) engine's ability to perform any "*deep*" reasoning (ie. uncompiled, non-heuristic) with its knowledge structures. Therefore, most expert systems are only capable of performing an *heuristic classification* task [8]: abstracting a given problem to a class of problems, followed by mapping the class of problem directly to a class of solution, and finally specialising the deduced class of solution to a specific solution. Without a framework for the representation of structural knowledge, the applicability of the rule knowledge to generic and specific instances is limited.

3. Every one of the tools/shells surveyed uses its own knowledge representation scheme, and therefore, domain (expert) knowledge cannot be shared among these systems. Systems that are developed from these shells normally function as advisors, decision support systems and diagnostic systems. The feasibility of using these tools/shells to develop system(s) to solve problems in other areas of artificial intelligence (eg. natural language understanding, planning and machine learning) has not been demonstrated. The fact that these tools/shells rely on specific knowledge representation scheme(s) casts doubt on the *semantic richness* and *extensibility* of the formalism.

4. While these tools/shells provide a basic reasoning mechanism, there is typically no guideline (or methodology) for the formulation of *control knowledge* (or *strategic knowledge*) [8] for a particular application. For example, out of the eight expert systems shells surveyed in [3], only two systems (Expert-Ease and TIMM) provide an induction technique as a basic reasoning function, only one system (ES/P Advisor) provides the resolution of horn clauses as a basic reasoning function and none of the systems provides meta level control in the selection of rules to trigger.

5. Efficiency issues in the processing of assertions in a rule base have largely been ignored.

In this paper, we report recent progress on the development of a *rule encoder* that, together with the *general purpose inference engine* developed by the research group and reported elsewhere [2], aims to solve the above problems in knowledge acquisition and reasoning (refer Figure 1). The *Rule Encoder* (RE) provides an user-driven environment for the encoding of expert knowledge, in the form of rules, within the knowledge base. The *General Purpose Inference Engine* (GPIE) provides matching (both *inexact* and *exact*) between data and assertions and, in addition to conventional inference techniques, it supports meta level control and strategies for reasoning under uncertainty. A rule base in the domain of personal financial planning [9] [10] has been developed to exemplify these points.

2. NATURAL LANGUAGE INTERFACES TO RULE-BASED SYSTEMS

There is a great deal of merit associated with knowledge acquisition through a natural language dialog for the knowledge engineer. As stated in [11] *"The most natural and practical manner for a person to communicate to a computer is through natural language."* However, for the designer of a natural language acquisition system, capturing (semantic) knowledge from natural sentences is an extremely difficult task.

Prior to a discussion of the merits of the *Rule Encoder*, it is important to review the key requirements for good interfaces to rule-based systems. Key characteristics are defined for an *"ideal"* natural language interface to a rule based system on the basis of domain-independence (ie. portability), rule management considerations and extensibility (ie. flexibility).

1. *The lexical analyser of the parser and rules in the rule base should be clearly separated.* This is analogous to the segregation of the declarative and control knowledge in typical expert systems. The more general a lexical analyser is, the easier it is to adapt it to other rule bases in the same domain. If the knowledge captured in the parse trees corresponds to (part of) the knowledge in the rule base (eg. rule assertions/facts), then the interface for the rule base becomes very tedious to maintain, since whenever the rules are modified, the associated

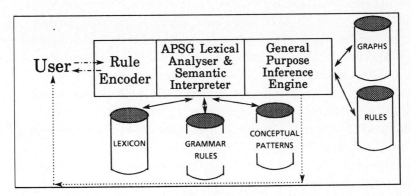

FIGURE 1
Communication with a rule base in natural language

semantic/syntactic analysis techniques embedded in the parser have to be recreated. In addition, the parser for such systems would become highly domain specific, and therefore, not easily adapted to similar applications. In [12] and [13], an intelligent tax advisory system based on a natural language interface to a rule based system has been reported, but the leaves of the parse trees are required to correspond exactly to the (rule) facts in the rule base. As pointed out in [13] *"The leaf nodes of the (verb category) hierarchies point directly to the facts of the expert system."* In [12], the authors admitted that *"Since each rule is selected according to the selection procedure contained within the interpreter, this procedure influences the structure of the rules and the control information that must be explicitly encoded into the system.".* To quote from [14], *"The lack of automatic construction of the hierarchies and automatic classification of propositions in them is currently a limitation in our system. If, for a given domain, a certain tree has to be extended, such extension will have to be done by hand. Also, propositions have to be hand encoded in the hierarchies. This makes transportability to other domains more difficult".*

The *Rule Encoder* developed in this research does not impose any commonality between the parse trees and the rules. The only shared knowledge between the parser and the rule base is the lexical knowledge of all the tokens in the entire system. In the RE, knowledge in the parse trees is translated into conceptual graphs [15], and graph matching techniques [1] are then applied to correlate input data (represented as graphs generated by the parser) and rule assertions.

2. *There should be an intermediate formalism (eg. conceptual graphs) underpinning the entire system.* Communication between the interface and the rule base should be via the intermediate formalism. For the RE, this intermediate formalism is conceptual graphs. The system described in [12] and [13] maps captured knowledge in the parse trees directly to the LISP atoms in the program. The DETEKTR (Development Environment for TEKTronix TRoubleshooter) system [16] maps user input directly to PROLOG facts with consequential inflexibility.

3. *The same natural language interface should be capable of being used to construct a rule base from scratch, as well as interacting with an existing rule base.* It is important to have a natural language interface to an existing system, but it is equally important that the same interface can be used to build a new rule base. The design methodologies described in [12] and [16] give no indication as to how their approach can be applied to couple/interact with existing rule based systems. The RE described below is capable of the dual roles of building and interacting with rule bases.

One common characteristic of all the above approaches is that these are all knowledge-based approaches. When a rule is encoded into an intermediate form, implicit knowledge that is often embedded in the meaning of a rule, but is lacking from the utterance, can be made explicit.

3. THE RULE ENCODER (RE)

Prior to the development of the *Rule Encoder*, rules in a CGM (Canonical Graph Model, [1]) were encoded using the *Rule Acquisition System for Conceptual Structures* (RASCS) [17] and the *Knowledge Base Editor* (KBE) [1]. However, this (manual) process of encoding rules soon becomes a tedious task for the user (knowledge engineer), because with this method, in order to create a rule, all the graphs involved in the rule have to be prior encoded by the *Knowledge Base Editor* (KBE) in the form of user-prepared template assertions. For example, the rule "*if experience level is high and financial service is currently used then skill required can be high*" would require three graphs, and altogether, nine (user-prepared) assertions for creation. Further interaction with the RASCS is required to codify the rule (using the graphs) in the CGM. Another drawback in the use of the KBE and RASCS to encode rules is the fact that both modules require the user to conceptualise, in this case to represent, knowledge in the CG formalism. This is seen as an unreasonable assumption of the user. The *Rule Encoder* is aimed to eliminate this pre-requisite.

The primary aim of the *Rule Encoder* (RE) is to enable the user to encode rules in (near) natural language statements. This does not mean that user-input is totally unrestricted nor do the authors claim that the RE can process all forms of sentences. In fact, the RE employs a combination of pattern/template matching, grammar parsing and semantic analysis techniques to encode the requisite rule base knowledge. In addition to rule encoding facilities, the RE also provides an environment for rule base management, all editing facilities for the maintenance of a rule base, and functions for governing the integrity of data graphs in the directory. It provides access to GPIE for rule consistency, redundancy and subsumption checks [10] [2] and for reasoning with the rule base.

For example, a user-input proposition can be matched by, but not limited to, the following templates

> *IF ... , THEN ...*
> *PROVIDED THAT ... , ...*
> *BECAUSE ... , THEREFORE ...*
> *THE RESULT OF ... IS THAT ...*
> *NOT UNTIL ... , ...*
> *NOT AFTER ... , ...*

where "..." can be taken as a list of assertions separated by AND/OR operators. Assertions are strings of characters that if interpreted successfully, lead to sets of graphs corresponding to the semantics of the assertions being automatically created. These graphs are then recorded in a *rule predicate* (in PROLOG) [1] [17] which is later accessed by GPIE when reasoning with the rule base. For example, the proposition *"if financial risk is low and tax advantage is moderate then buy options"* has three assertions.

To interpret assertions, the RE uses the *Semantic Interpreter* (SI) developed in [18]. The SI adopts the *Augmented Phrase Structured Grammar* (APSG) developed in [19]. For each syntactically correct assertion, the SI applies semantic analysis strategies to construct/compose a set of *canonical graphs* [15] [1] for the assertion. For example, the result of interpreting the assertion *"skill required can be high"* is the graph

$$[SKILL]->(DEGREE)->[HIGH].$$

(Details of the parsing strategies and the semantic analysis techniques used in the *Semantic Interpreter* can be found in [18] and [1].)

There are two advantages in dividing the interpretation of an input proposition into a template matching phase and a semantic analysis phase:

1. Contemporary progress (publications) in AI supports a rule assertion in the form of either a simple short sentence, a string of symbols or a phrase. At this stage, there is little point in designing a *"grand"* and versatile parser that attempts to encompass all possible forms of sentences since the complex knowledge structures hence generated would probably be difficult, if not impossible, to be represented in rule form.

2. By using templates to extract assertion(s) from a proposition, the machine processing time for the average rule is acceptable, since a template matching method is purely syntax-based.

3. It may reasonably be expected that most experts can formulate their domain knowledge as simple sentences (assertions) suitable for the SI to encode. There is (almost) universal agreement on a common lexicon for each area of expertise eg. telegraphic transfer, banking, accounting, auditing etc. Besides, common words and idioms in a particular domain can easily be added to the system's lexicon.

Finally, if all the assertions in a proposition can be interpreted successfully, and corresponding canonical graphs generated, then a rule predicate is stored in the PROLOG memory. This rule predicate captures all the necessary knowledge about a rule in terms of the graphs in the rule, the logical relationship between the graphs on both sides of the rule and groups of all the concepts in the rule that share identical value. These groups are called *binding groups* in [17] (and [1]) and they are automatically detected by the RE. For example, the subjects of each of the assertions in a rule normally form a binding group.

The use of the rule encoder to capture domain knowledge in a rule form is viewed as a significant achievement in knowledge acquisition for CGMs. This research builds on the work that has been done on reasoning with (conceptual) graphs and on semantic parsing strategies for language understanding. Paradigms developed for the RE, SI and GPIE have now been merged to produce an integrated tools environment. Rules are processed by GPIE and the results can be conveyed to the user either in the form of displayed graphs or sentences (via a *language encoder* for graphs). The integrated module becomes a powerful rule acquisition module of high practicality (see Figure 1).

Perhaps the most notable achievement of this research is that a novice can now create, modify and communicate with a rule base in near natural language, irrespective of the internal and intermediate representations in the computer.

4. THE GENERAL PURPOSE INFERENCE ENGINE

As stated earlier, reasoning with the rule base in the CGM is facilitated by a *graph-based inference engine* [2]. This inference engine is capable of flexible control structures and inexact matching and can complement an expressive intermediate notation, such as conceptual graphs. The *generality* of the rule set (in a CGM) is transparent to the inference engine, thereby permitting reasoning at various levels, through specialisation and instantiation of rule assertion graphs. By general purpose, the authors mean that such a shell is both *flexible* and *efficient*. To provide flexibility in an Inference Engine (IE) shell, the following issues were considered:

- The ease of tuning the shell to model conventional inference techniques (eg. forward chaining, backward chaining and mixed strategies);
- The provision of inexact matching between data and assertions/rules;
- The switching of inference modes (strategies) during an execution session;
- Ease of extension of the basic shell for reasoning under uncertainty, meta-level control and other user-specified variations to the default modes; and
- integration of the shell into an existing Knowledge Engineering toolkit

By efficient, the authors mean that scanning/searching of the rules in the rule base during execution is restricted to a minimum. In GPIE, the efficiency of executing a rule is achieved at the expense of *compiling* (transforming) the rule set prior to execution and having enough memory storage for the compiled (transformed) rules. Similarly, the system described in [12] relies on the generation of *rule maps* to enhance the efficiency of processing rules.

5. THE PERSONAL FINANCIAL PLANNING RULE BASE

We have developed a rule base for personal financial planning. An initial set of *"IF-THEN"* rules in English has been extracted from [9]. In [9], a LISP based program that processes rules has been reported but consideration of the knowledge representation issues involved in the *conceptualisation* of expert knowledge is patently inadequate nor does it address the problem of efficient rule processing. As a result, the system presented in [9] is incapable of demonstrating the form of inexact matching between data and assertions such as the *General Purpose Inference Engine* (GPIE). In the conceptual graph formalism, each rule assertion is represented as a *canonical graph*, which consists of a set of connected concept and relation nodes. More specifically, by representing knowledge in conceptual graph formalism, domain knowledge is represented by its *primitives* (ie. a set of labels for concepts and relations), and appropriate semantic relations between these primitives are explicitly stated.

Technical issues associated with the conceptualisation of the personal financial planning rule base are reported in [10]. There are 97 rules and 160 assertions in the rule set. There exist 3 clusters of connected rules - identification of investment objective(s), diversification of investment and estimation of life insurance cover. Depth of the inferences may range from one to three levels. The *index file* ([2], [1]) generated by the *Rule Compiler* consists of 97 compiled rule indices, 422 graph indices and amounts to 29.3Kbyte of storage.

6. A SAMPLE EXECUTION SESSION

In this section, an annotated execution session with the RE (hence the SI and GPIE) is presented. In this case study, the user encodes the rule *"if experience level is high and financial service is currently used then skill required can be high"* for the knowledge base, loads the rest of the rule base, checks and compiles the entire set of rules, and finally, invokes the GPIE to perform forward and backward reasoning on the rule set. (User input is in **bold** and annotations are in *italics*. The session has been slightly edited to enhance readability.)

RuleEncoder> **if experience_level is high and financial_service is currently used then skill required can be high.**

(The user types in the above proposition and the Rule Encoder starts to identify the assertions in the proposition and builds a canonical graph for each of the assertions.)

(1567) Identified "experience_level is high " as an assertion

SI: SYNTACTIC ANALYSIS FOR "experience_level is high " STARTS AT 15:06:58

SI: SYNTACTIC ANALYSIS FOR "experience_level is high " FINISHES AT 15:07:08

(1567) Identified "financial_service is currently used " as an assertion

SI: SYNTACTIC ANALYSIS FOR "financial_service is currently used " STARTS AT 15:07:45

SI: SYNTACTIC ANALYSIS FOR "financial_service is currently used " FINISHES AT 15:08:05

(1517) There exists 2 graphs for the last assertion

(1568) The generated graphs are:

Name: temp800
[FINANCIAL_SERVICE] -
>   ->(DEGREE)->[STATE]
>   <-(OBJ)<-[USE].

Name: temp798
[USE] -
>   ->(OBJ)->[ENTITY]
>   ->(OBJ)->[FINANCIAL_SERVICE].

Enter only temp798 temp800 : **temp800.**
(The user is asked to choose a canonical graph to represent the last assertion.)
Processing resumes ...
(1567) Identified "skill required can be high " as an assertion
SI: SYNTACTIC ANALYSIS FOR "skill required can be high " STARTS AT
15:10:37
SI: SYNTACTIC ANALYSIS FOR "skill required can be high " FINISHES AT
15:11:13
(1519) Internal representation for the proposition
    " if experience_level is high and financial_service is currently used , then skill
required can be high " is encoded (Rule 12)
RuleEncoder> **display rule 12.**
(Display the encoded rule and the associated canonical graphs.)
LHS:
[[EXPERIENCE_LEVEL] -
>   ->(DEGREE)->[HIGH].
> ->(AND)->
[FINANCIAL_SERVICE] -
>   ->(DEGREE)->[STATE]
>   <-(OBJ)<-[USE].]
->(THEN)->   /* Causal Relation */
RHS:
[SKILL] -
>   ->(DEGREE)->[HIGH].

     ...   .

RuleEncoder> **compile.**
(Proceeds to the Rule Consistency Checker and Rule Compiler.)
(1571) Proceed to Rule Consistency Checks (RCC) and Rule Compiler (RC) in GPIE
...
(1036) Rule Consistency Checker (RCC) invoked ...
(1018) RCC: Checking for (local) rule integrity ...
(1021) RCC: Checking for (local) rule conflict and (local) rule redundancy ...

(1023) RCC: Checking for (global) rule conflict, (global) rule redundancy and rule subsumption ...
(1029) RCC: Checking for (global) rule completeness ...

   ...   .

(1120) GPIE: RC: Proceed to generate indices for compiled rules ...
(1015) RC: Generating indices for rule predicates ...

   ...   .

RuleEncoder> **list rules.**   *(List of rules in the rule base.)*
(1534) The following rule(s) is (are) recorded
2 3 4 5 6 7 8 9 10 11 12 13 14 15 16 17 18 19 20 21 22 23 24 25 26 27 28 29 30 31 32 33
34 35 36 37 39 40 41 42 43 44 45 46 49 50 51 52 53 54 55 56 57 58 59 60 61 62 63 64 65
66 67 68 69 70 71 72 73 74 75 76 77 78 79 80 81 82 83 84 85 86 87 88 89 90 91 92 93 94
95 96 97 98 100
RuleEncoder> **what if income is moderately secure, emergency reserves are inadequate and you are an aggressive risk-taker ?**
(The user poses a set of assertions to the system and forward chaining is carried out by the GPIE on the set of given assertions.)
(1578) GPIE deduction(s) terminated with the following assertions:
Assertion with graph name 'r4r1' and linear form:
[LIQUIDITY] -
                    ->(DEGREE)->[HIGH].
(Canonical graph for "Liquidity is high".)
Assertion with graph name 'r16r1' and linear form:
[FINANCIAL_RISK] -
                        ->(DEGREE)->[HIGH].
(Canonical graph for "Financial risk is high".)
RuleEncoder> **what leads to skill required is high ?**
(The user poses a goal for the system to verify. Backward chaining is invoked to deduce all the assertions that can lead to the above goal.)
(1578) GPIE deduction(s) terminated with the following assertions:
Assertion with graph name 'r12l1' and linear form:
[EXPERIENCE_LEVEL] -
                        ->(DEGREE)->[HIGH].
(Canonical graph for "Experience level is high".)
Assertion with graph name 'r12l2' and linear form:
[FINANCIAL_SERVICE] -
                        ->(DEGREE)->[STATE]
                        <-(OBJ)<-[USE].
(Canonical graph for "Financial service is currently used".)
RuleEncoder> **quit.**

7. CURRENT RESEARCH

The authors are furthering the RE/GPIE approach to provide a *true* interactive knowledge base (IKBS) environment eg. one that can identify and keep track of user-goals in a dialog. We aim to complete an intelligent advisory system in the near future. Key extensions to the GPIE reasoning modes are:

(i)   intelligent backward chaining;

(ii)   a mechanism for the detection and variation of user goal(s); and

(iii)   mixed reasoning strategies.

ACKNOWLEDGEMENTS

The authors would like to thank Dickson Lukose for his contribution to the implementation of the financial planning rule base, and for suggestions on extensions to the SI. His technical support was most appreciated.

REFERENCES

[1]   TSUI, E. (1988); *Canonical Graph Models*, Ph.D. thesis, Division of Computing and Mathematics, Deakin University, October, 1988.

[2]   GARNER, B.J. and TSUI, E. (1988); *General Purpose Inference Engine for Canonical Graph Models*, to appear in Knowledge Based Systems, December, 1988.

[3]   GILMORE, J.F., PULASKI, K. and HOWARD, C. (1986); *A Comprehensive Evaluation of Expert System Tools*, Applications of Artificial Intelligence III, J.F. Gilmore, Editor, Proc. SPIE 635, p2-15.

[4]   INFERENCE CORPORATION (1987); *ART reference Manual*, Version 3.0, Inference Corporations.

[5]   FIKES, R. and KEHLER, T. (1985); *The role of Frame-based representation in reasoning*, Communications of the ACM, Vol. 28, No. 9, p904-920.

[6]   CROMARTY, A.S. (1985); *What are current expert systems tools missing ?*, COMPCON '85, February 25-28, San Francisco, p411-418.

[7]   CLANCEY, W.J. (1983); *The Epistemology of a Rule-Based Expert System - a Framework for Explanation*, Artificial Intelligence 20, p215-251.

[8]   CLANCEY, W.J. (1985); *Heuristic Classification*, Artificial Intelligence 27, p289-350.

[9]   PINC, J.D. (1984); *FINPLAN: A Prototype Expert System for Personal Financial Planning*, M.S. Thesis, University of Florida, 1984.

[10]   GARNER, B.J. and TSUI, E. (1988); *A Canonical Graph Model for Personal Financial Planning*, Technical Report 88/3, Xerox AI Laboratory, Deakin University, June, 1988.

[11]   SILVESTRO, K. (1987); *A Knowledge-base acquisition tool*, Proceedings of the 7th International Workshop on Expert Systems and Their Applications, 13-15 May, 1988, Avignon, France, p419-434.

[12]   DATSKOVSKY-MOERDLER, G., McKEOWN, K.R. and ENSOR, J.R. (1987); *Building Natural Language Interfaces for Rule-based Systems*, IJCAI-87, p682-687.

[13]   DATSKOVSKY, G. (1988); *Structure from Anarchy: Meta Level Representation of Expert Systems Predicates for Natural Language Interfaces,* Applied ACL, *1988.*

[14]   DATSKOVSKY-MOERDLER, G. (1988); *Structure from Anarchy: Meta Level Representation of Expert System Predicate for Natural Language Interfaces,* Proceedings of the Second Conference on Applied Natural Language Processing, 1988.

[15]   SOWA, J.F. (1984): *Conceptual Structures,* Addison-Wesley, Reading, 1984.

[16]   FREILING, M., ALEXANDER, J., MESSICK, S., REHFUSS, S. and SHULMAN, S. (1985); *Starting a Knowledge Engineering Project: A Step-by-Step Approach,* The AI Magazine, Fall, 1985, p150-164.

[17]   GARNER, B.J., LUI, D. and TSUI, E. (1986); *On better goal type interpretation,* Proceedings of the First Australian AI Congress, November 18-21st, 1986,Melbourne.

[18]   GARNER, B.J., LUKOSE, D. and TSUI, E. (1987); *Parsing Natural Language through Pattern Correlation and Modification,* Proceedings of the 7th International Workshop on Expert Systems and Their Applications, May 13-15, 1987, Avignon, France, p1285-1299.

[19]   HEIDORN, G.E. (1975); *Augmented Phrase Structure Grammars,* in Theoretical Issues in Natural Language Processing, 10-13 June, 1975, Cambridge, Massachusetts, p1-5.

Expert Systems in Economics, Banking and Management
L.F. Pau et al. (Editors)
© Elsevier Science Publishers B.V. (North-Holland), 1989

KNOWLEDGE BASES FOR ECONOMIC FORECASTING

Odile PALIES

LAFORIA – Institut de Programmation – University P. et M. Curie
4 place Jussieu – 75252 Paris Cedex 5 – France

Jean-Marc Philip

HENDYPLAN S.A.
59 rue du Prince Royal – 1050 Bruxelles – Belgique

Economic forecasting is actually provided through econometric models
which have obvious limitations. Especially, they are invalid to the
analysis of the economy in the very short term and they cannot compute
some variables, as exchange rate, by the projection of long term
tendencies. Knowledge-based systems hold out several new
possibilities : mixing quantitative and qualitative reasoning, explicit
representation of economic processes and economists'expertise. This
paper presents two prototypes build with Artificial Intelligence
technics ; one to analyse the current economy situation and the other to
compute exogenous variables of an econometric model.

1 – INTRODUCTION

Most firms need economic forecasting as data for decision making in
economic or financial domains. But if they wish to well-integrate these data in
their strategy building, they must understand how and why this result has been
achieved [1]. Economic forecasting is actually provided through econometric
models. Most of the time, even the economists who develop the model do not
control how interdependencies between each variable work, because their own
analysis is qualitative, based on heuristic rules.

On the other hand, several others limitations from econometric models may be
pointed out [2].
  - As they give an averaged view of the economy, they are of limited use in the
    very short term forecasting, which however is an important factor for
    industrial or financial decision makers.
  - Running econometric models requires the values of all the variables when
    economists diagnose many situations only via the analysis of some
    informations that are easily accessible in current data bases.
  - Many factors are out of the scope of the model (exogenous variables,

unestablished links, non-quantifiable phenomena). Classifying the variables into endogenous, exogenous and out of model variables depends on the possibility to compute them rather than on an economic theory.

A knowledge-based approach provides a framework which allows to **describe explicitly the economic agents process and the economists' behaviour** and to deal with quantitative and qualitative scaled variables. These technics may actually be improved into two directions in order to overpass some limits of econometric models. The first one is aimed at replacing econometric or technico-economic models by cognitive and qualitative reasoning. The second one links an econometric models with an expert system to explain and compute exogenous variables.

In this paper, we present two prototypes of expert systems : ECO to analyze the economy in the very short term, and KARL to compute the exogenous variables used by the simultation software KEOPS.

2 – ECO : ECONOMIC ANALYSIS IN THE VERY SHORT TERM

In the very short term, economic forecasting can be influenced by occasional or temporary events. Economists must find the factors that **explain the disturbance of economic tendencies**. But these events are of various kinds and must be dealt with in various manner ; decisions about interest rates are objective data, the degree of popular confidence enjoyed by a government is subjective. They are available in different data bases or news, and collecting them is expensive and difficult. On the other hand, only a small part of them are relevant to a specific situation. The economists use heuristic expertise to select them.

```
IF    industrialists on capital goods = "optimist"
AND   NO increase in public-sector investment
AND   balance of industrialists' treasury = UNDETERMINED
THEN  opinion of industrialists on capital goods =
      "discredited"
```
FIGURE 1 : A rule to question the user in ECO

We realize an expert system ECO [3] which simulates the economists' behaviour. ECO interprets well-plotted data, such as those obtained from INSEE's (the French statistical agency) periodic polls of industrialists. When it diagnoses a discrepancy between industrialists' forecasting and economic tendencies, it must find the **occasional** events which are assumed to explain this phenomenon.

The forecast and the economic tendencies are computed with informations from data bases connected to ECO. But, some occasional events are not directly accessible in these data bases (for example : public investments, politic decisions). ECO must ask the user about these lacking data and must argue why these events are of some interest (the ECO's rule of the figure 1 ask the user about the public investment decisions and the balance treasury state). In any case, even with **incomplete information**, ECO provides a forecast.

ECO is build on the expert system generator Intelligence Service (from TECSI Software). Its knowledge base can forecast the production in four branches (automobile, intermediate goods, capital goods, and consumer goods) and changes in prices. The knowledge base of each domain is structured according to the same architecture (fig. 2) :

1 rules to **compare qualitative variations** of the economic tendencies with industrialists'forecasting,
2 rules to **research selective information** if the rules of the first step cannot explain the industrialists' forecast,
3 rules to **give the ECO forecast** on a specific domain and to combine the results of all the branches.

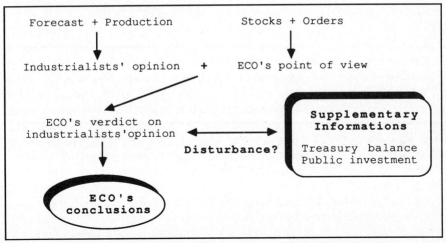

FIGURE 1 : Structure of a forecast system for Capital Goods

The expert system approach allows us to provide a production forecast, which is based, in most cases, only on well-plotted data and, in others cases, to question only on very specific information.

3 – KARL : EVALUATION OF EXOGENOUS VARIABLES

Such fundamental variables as the rate of exchange are often treated as **exogenous** variables of econometric models because they cannot give satisfactory forecasts when they are estimated over the past, even with the most sophisticated methods. Such variables are determined by the **anticipation of the future** of economic agents. Endogenous variables of econometric models, such as trade current or balance of the United States, now are essential variables for explaining variations of the dollar even if they were not significant over the last decade.

A knowledge-based approach to the representation of the anticipation behaviour of economic agents is better adapted to explain variations of such variables than classical quantitative methods used to build econometric models.

Our aim is to help in evaluating exogenous variables, all the while taking into account the endogenous variables that influence them. In this way, the range of modelled variables can be increased without increasing correspondingly the number of equations used in the econometric model.

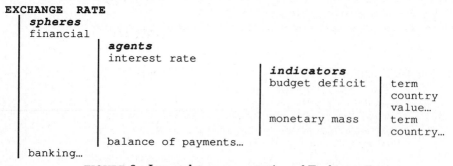

FIGURE 3 : *Incomplete representation of Exchange Rate*

In KARL, our prototype written in Prolog, distinct economic spheres are described (economic, banking, political, international). Each exogenous variable is semantically represented in each sphere by a list of indicators and may have different behaviours, formalized by a set of production rules (fig. 3). Each indicator is calculated for each country and for each term, and the result provides us with the old and the new values.

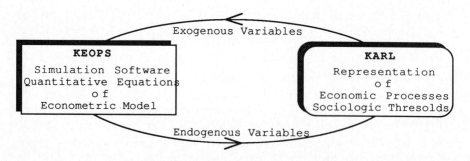

FIGURE 4 : *Linking KARL and KEOPS*

KARL may then be linked to a classical econometric model by the following process (fig 4). Beginning with the exchange rate, for example, we start from the last value known in the data base. This value is included in an econometric model which is supported by the simulation software KEOPS [4]. After the first period, the model gives the results of all endogenous variables used as data of the expert system KARL (current trade, budget deficit, economic growth rate, inflation rate ...). These new values of the variables enable to build indicators of KARL's knowledge base. The mixing of the variations of these variables with heuristic rules gives a new value for the level of the dollar.

The KARL's rules integrate both reasoning about economic processes and expert **interpretation of sociologic thresholds** (fig. 5). By mean of the link existing between the expert system and the econometric model, the result of the first one is included as input of the second one. So, the simulation software computes an estimated variation of the dollar for the following period, and so on. Regarding the results of the model, the rules released in the expert system will be different at each period.

```
effect_Exchange_Rate (middle_term,usa,budget_deficit,2,V) :-
    calcul_var (usa, budget_deficit, R) ,
    R > deficit_thresold ,
    decision (usa, politic, "military_expansion") ,
    value (usa, exchange_rate, budget_deficit, A) ,
    V = A * R.
```

FIGURE 5 : Examples of KARL's rules

This approach, which uses both rules and equations, by linkage or by mixing, can be justified from a theorical viewpoint, because a part of the economy does not necessary work close to an equilibrium. A weakpoint of classical econometric models is that they always provide an equilibrium. On the other part, a strong argument in favour of knowledge based systems is their ability to **represent evolutive mechanisms** which govern economy.

Then, explaining the value of the dollar not by simple observation of the past, but by heuristics, which represent anticipation behaviour of economic agents reacting to figures given in prevision by an economic model, is better adapted to forecast the evolution of such variable.

The aim of the present research is to improve KARL's approach to modelize interactions between exogenous and endogenous variables of an econometric model. We built a skeleton of essential economic processes which is able to explain the forecast provided by qualitative and quantitative cooperation. The first validation of KARL has been made in the determination of the variation of the dollar. This knowledge base can be completed, improved and personnalised by financial experts.

4 - CONCLUSION

These two prototypes, ECO and KARL, prove the interest of explicit representation of economic processes and of expert reasoning to explain and control their interdependencies.

This idea can be extended to many other explaining variables of econometric models (short term and long term interest rates, scrapping rate, investments ...). As a matter of fact, this approach could be extended even to all endogenous variables which depend of qualitative or anticipation effects ; variables left in the econometric model are the only one responding to mechanical effects.

Actually, we wish to implement a knowledge-based software which is well-adapted to economic forecast. We will develop on a multi-agent language, called MERING IV [5], including a description of each economic agent, a representation of its own ability and behaviour and a knowledge base to communicate with others economic agents. The inference process will be supported by a formal qualitative reasoning [6].

REFERENCES

[1] Fontella E., "Macro Economic Forcasting and Expert Systems", *l'Economique et l'Intelligence Artificielle*, (Congrès AFCET, Aix-en-Provence 1986), pp. 169-173.
[2] Paliès O., Mayer J., "Economics Reasoning by Econometrics or Artificial Intelligence", *Theory and Decision,* vol. 26, (Reidel ed. 1989), in print.
[3] Paliès O., Corcos E., Mayer J., "ECO : un système expert pour l'analyse de conjoncture", *l'Economique et l'Intelligence Artificielle*, (Congrès AFCET, Aix-en-Provence 1986), pp. 175-178.
[4] Hendyplan S.A., "KEOPS : User's Manuel", (copyright DON/E 1985-86), Mai 1988.
[5] Ferber J., "Des objets aux agents ; une architecture stratifiée", *Actes du 6ème congrès RFIA,* (AFCET, Antibes, Novembre 1987).
[6] Bourgine P., Raiman O., "Economics as reasoning on a qualitative model", *l'Economique et l'Intelligence Artificielle*, (Congrès AFCET, Aix-en-Provence 1986), pp. 185-189.

Expert Systems in Economics, Banking and Management
L.F. Pau et al. (Editors)
© *Elsevier Science Publishers B.V. (North-Holland), 1989*

ESTIMATING UNOBSERVABLE DECISIONS THROUGH BUSINESS SURVEYS: PRELIMINARY RESULTS

Claudio G. Gianotti

Dipartimento di Elettronica,
Politecnico di Milano,
P.zza Leonardo da Vinci 32,
20133 Milano,
Italy.

ABSTRACT

Business surveys are qualitative and quantitative data reporting the opinion of economic entities (firms, families, etc.) about the current status, the past trends and the expected short-term variations of some key indicators. This paper argues that methods from the Artificial Intelligence research in qualitative reasoning can be applied to the economic analysis of the surveys; formal methods of qualitative reasoning over qualitative data have never been reported in the economic literature. A simple example is discussed.

1. INTRODUCTION

The purposes of this paper are:
- to introduce business surveys (or tests) as a source of qualitative information with relevant applications in economics;
- to explain the techniques used in the economic literature for dealing with this kind of information, and evaluate them from the perspective of Artificial Intelligence;
- to show how such data may be used for estimating unobservable decisions in firms;
- to propose Forbus' theory of qualitative interpretation of measurements as the basis for integrating quantitative and qualitative data within the qualitative framework.

2. BUSINESS TESTS

Business tests are short-term economic surveys conducted in more than 40 countries; as an example, [1] and [2] report the results of the French and Italian inquiries, upon which this paper is based. Surveys are generally repeated three to four times a year, although some variables are inquired monthly. In the following, only surveys in the industry are considered.

Business tests consist mostly of questions whose answers are stated in qualitative terms. The forms are supposed to be filled in directly by the manager(s) of the firm. The answers are aggregated on a sectorial basis; the aggregated results are then published.

Each test contains two groups of questions: the first one includes questions about the (current or past) state of a variable, the second one includes questions about the

variable's (current or past) trend. Answers to questions concerning the state of a variable must be chosen among alternatives like:
- high, normal, low; good, satisfactory, poor;
and similar. Correspondingly, answers about trend are chosen among:
- increasing, stable, decreasing; improving, stable, worsening;
and similar. Under this respect, surveys are close to the standard, single landmark qualitative reasoning approach ([3]): the answers can be interpreted as the partial state of an underlying qualitative sectorial model (which is not explicitly represented). The state is partial because the inquiries do not cover the whole range of interesting economic parameters; moreover, some of them are available in reliable numeric form (e.g. exchange rates).

Results are expressed as the percentages of firms choosing each of the three possible alternatives. Percentages are noted as P_+, P_- and $P_=$, with the following definitions:
- P_+ is the percentage of firms answering "increasing" or "higher-than-normal";
- P_- is the percentage of firms answering "decreasing" or "lower-than-normal";
- $P_=$ is the percentage of firms answering "stable" or "normal".
P_+, $P_=$, P_- must sum up to 100.
The *balance* $(P_+ - P_-)$ is often used for plotting graphs; it gives a rough estimate of the sectorial trend, if it is assumed that the firms responding "stable" have experienced (on the average) no change.

As an example, here is a list of questions from the french inquiries (a more complete list can be found in [4]):
- stock level;
- liquidity;
- factors limiting investments;
- trends of delivery time;
- order-book level;
- investment trends;
- foreign demand trends;
- selling price expectations;
- expected profits;
- expected evolution of inflation.
Future and past trends in general refer to a period of three to four months from the date of the inquiry.

There are some good reasons for preferring qualitative inquiries to the more traditional quantitative surveys:
- timeliness: business tests can be answered and processed rapidly (within a few days), while quantitative data need more time (several months) before being

published in a reliable form. Hence qualitative inquiries are important because they provide the most up-to-date source of information available to the analysts;
- breadth: questions often address parameters which are either not measurable (e.g. feelings about the economic environment) or difficult to measure reliably (e.g. stock);
- reliability: correct trends are easier to perceive than correct magnitudes. For this reason, qualitative data are believed to be less error prone;
- subjectivity: qualitative questions are the only way to get information about expectations;
- ease-of-use: good results (e.g. short-term forecasting) can be achieved with limited processing.

Qualitative inquiries however also raise subtle problems: beside the indecision formulas (well-known in the AI literature) resulting from the addition of qualitative variables of different sign, qualitative data from business tests have other limitations on their own (see [5] for a deeper discussion):
- ambiguities in the questions: the requested assessment of the stock level refers to the current demand or to the forecasted demand?
- ambiguities in the answers: should "normal level" be interpreted as the "desired level" or the "programmed level"?
- context-dependent interpretation: e.g. the long-term trend establishes the "normal level", while short-term oscillations are reported as variations from that level. The "normal level" after a recession is likely to be quantitatively different from the "normal level" after an expansion. This remark is valid for both the qualitative into quantitative transformation and vice versa (e.g. suppression of the trend);
- firm's bias: e.g. amount of statistical data used for answering the questions;
- personal bias: optimistic vs. pessimistic, interested vs. not interested and so on;
- ambiguities in the epistemological status: answers about the future trend of variables controllable by the management (endogenous variables such as production) are to be interpreted as intentions; answers about the trend of variables not controllable by the management (exogenous variables such as foreign demand) are to be interpreted as judgements. Hence forecasting errors are imputable in the first case to plans revisions, in the second case to lack of knowledge.

3. WHY ARE BUSINESS TESTS IMPORTANT FOR ECONOMICS AND AI?

Business tests raise the problem of integrating qualitative and quantitative information in a consistent line of reasoning, which is crucial to both economics and Artificial Intelligence (AI).

Economic analysis is traditionally based on quantitative information (either in the form of time series or cross-sectional data): statistical techniques are used to estimate the value of unknown parameters in models of the interactions among variables. However, the trend toward the formalization of less structured problems and the increased emphasis on individual attitudes (expectations) is focusing the interest on methods of representation and manipulation of symbolic knowledge.

From the AI side, qualitative reasoning (see [3], [6], [7], [8]) has been conceived as a way of representing causality starting from a complete mathematical model of the system under analysis; however, in many cases, and most notably in the practice of economics, the model is partly unknown, and must be identified (or elicited) from large amounts of information, both quantitative and qualitative: hence the need for an integration.

Moreover, the transformation between qualitative and quantitative information is relevant for many tasks in which qualitative reasoning applications have been proposed: e.g. think of a robot, receiving numeric data from its sensors, basing its reasoning on a qualitative model, and performing some action through its actuators. The AI literature has to some extent taken into account only the diagnostic part of the problem (Forbus [9] developed a theory for translating measurements into qualitative data, see section 6); however, the general problem of quantifying qualitative information and vice versa is far from being solved.

4. ESTIMATION THROUGH QUANTIFICATION

Business tests include examples of judgmental forecasts. A large part of the literature about business tests deals with the problem of quantifying the answers, so that they can be included into quantitative models (with the purpose of increasing the accuracy in the short run) and used with the conventional statistical methods.

Pioneering work on this topic was done by Anderson and Theil (see [10], [11], [12], [13], [14]); subsequent work has been presented for instance in [15], [16], [17], [18], [19]. Some of the above references also report applications and comparisons with forecasts using only quantitative information.

The most simple method of quantification (already mentioned in section 3) is based on the following assumption:

$$\frac{\Delta Y_t}{Y_t} = k * (P_+ - P_-) + c + e$$

where Y_t is the corresponding numerical index, k is a positive constant, c is a constant and e is the error term.

The method is debated because it ignores $P_=$; this implies that different percentage weights may well result in the same balance. Nevertheless, balances are widely used since they are easy to compute.

As a more complex example, consider the approach proposed in [15] and applied in [19].

Basing on the short-term model for stock demand, the production plan is estimated (sectorial series for the monthly production exist), and hence the sensitivity of production to variations in the demand can be tested for different sectors; from this information, it is possible to deduce which strategy for stock management is more adequate for reproducing the behavior of each sector (note that the strategy is unobservable). The role of qualitative enquiries can be appreciated by looking at the equations for the inventory smoothing strategy:

$$\Delta S_t^p = \partial * (S_t^* - S_{t-1})$$

$$S_t^* = a + b * D_t^e$$

$$P_t^p = D_t^e + \Delta S_t^p$$

$$\Delta S_t = \Delta S_t^p + \mu * (D_t^e - D_t)$$

$$P_t = D_t + \Delta S_t$$

where:
D_t^e is the expected demand;

S_t^* is the optimum level corresponding to the expected demand;

ΔS_t^p is the programmed adjustment of the stock level;

P_t^p is the programmed production;

∂ is a smoothing factor due to uncertainties in the forecast and other difficulties;

μ accounts for the fraction of the forecast error charged to the stock;

P_t, D_t, ΔS_t are the real levels and variation.

Both D_t^e and ΔS_t^p are not observable; hence the hypothesis of an inventory smoothing policy is impossible to test from the time series available. Qualitative questions about ΔS_t^p are on the contrary included in the business tests:

- an answer "normal" is assumed to mean that the stock level is close to the programmed level for the next period ($|\Delta S_t^p| \leq c * S_{t-1}$, with c = constant);

- an answer "lower than normal" is interpreted as $\Delta S_t^p < -(c * S_{t-1})$;

- an answer "higher than normal" is interpreted as $\Delta S_t^p > c * S_{t-1}$.

The constant c (defining a kind of indifference interval) is assumed be equal for all respondents; its value is either set a priori equal to a few percentage points, or is estimated.

The interpretation of the qualitative data as numeric values is based on the following considerations/assumptions:

- each manager answers on the basis of a subjective probability distribution for ΔS_t^p

(due to the uncertainties in D_t^e);

- the answer depends on the position of the median of the distribution with respect to the interval $[-c * S_{t-1}, c * S_{t-1}]$;
- the distributions for all managers have the same form;
- the aggregation (sum) over all distributions results in a standard normal distribution for the median, denoted $f(m)$.

The mean and variance of the normal distribution are then computed from the following constraints:

$$P_+ = \int_{c*S_{t-1}}^{\infty} f(m)\,dm \qquad P_- = \int_{-\infty}^{-c*S_{t-1}} f(m)\,dm$$

A similar procedure can be applied to the expected demand.
The process is repeated for different inventory models, and the results compared with the available data (for actual demand, production, inventory levels); the best fitting model is then chosen as a guess for the sectorial policy in stock management.

As a general commentary to quantification, consider the following remarks:
- in principle, it does make sense (although it may be difficult) to try to recover the quantitative information from qualitative answers based on quantitative data (i.e. from a qualitative observation of a quantitative event), provided that the underlying parameter has been measured in the past, and time series are therefore available;
- even if a quantification is possible, this process always involves assumptions which could turn out to be arbitrary; moreover, see section 2 for a discussion of the limitations of qualitative information. Hence, complicated quantification methods are not justified;
- it is not possible to recover quantitative information from judgmental answers (no underlying quantitative event), or from answers based on measurements not available outside the firm (no quantitative series).

One consideration which has been largely neglected in the literature about business tests is that the converse problem of translating quantitative data into qualitative series is more tractable, due to the reduced precision of the target representation; therefore it might be more convenient (and sound) to keep the business tests in qualitative form and to transform instead the quantitative information needed (see [20] for a a short discussion).

5. AN ALTERNATIVE APPROACH

An approach overcoming the above criticisms should:
- define a model in which target variables are expressed as a function of the parameters inquired in business tests, and of other available data;
- compute *trends* for the target variables.

These trends can then be compared to the measured values (if some exist); from statistical regularities and eventually inconsistencies, it should be possible to estimate unobservable decisions at the micro-level.

Such a model should be designed as follows:
- inputs to the model are the answers to the surveys and qualified quantitative data;
- the model itself consists of a set of constraints, derived from accounting identities, economic causalities (company's or sectorial models), consistency checks;
- the output of the model is either a consistency assessment, or an estimation of unobservable strategies.

As a simple example consider the problem of an outside analyst trying to establish a company's investment. The investment figures as they result from the financial sheets may be not accurate, because of, for instance, write-offs or fiscal convenience; on the other side, due to the stability of the investment policy in most firms, the short-term trends of investments as reported in business tests are likely to be accurate. A comparative analysis could therefore suggest if (and which) corrections are needed.

6. QUALITATIVE INTERPRETATION OF MEASUREMENTS

Forbus [9] proposed a theory for qualitative interpretation of measurements.

The interpretation is based on the idea of segmentation; using domain dependent knowledge, quantitative time series are partitioned into sequences of measurements (segments) corresponding to the same qualitative value of the underlying parameter. In business tests, this amounts to the determination of the indifference interval defining the "stable" resp. "normal" state. If a quantitative value exceeds the upper bound of the interval of indifference, then the qualitative interpretation of the measurement is "increasing" resp. "above normal"; this interpretation holds until the value is greater than the upper bound of the indifference interval. In the opposite case (numeric value smaller than the lower bound), the qualitative interpretation is "decreasing" resp. "below normal".

The series of the parameters affecting the same model can be segmented independently; segments are then merged together in the sense that the crossing of any segment boundary is seen as a transition in the qualitative model.

Parameters in models using business tests may be:
- qualitative (e.g stock);
- quantitative (e.g. accounting data, macroeconomic data);
- both qualitative and quantitative (e.g. production);
- unobservable (e.g. production costs, strategies).

From the existence of unobservable parameters, it follows that qualitative or quantitative measurements do not determine completely the state of the system; the model, however, by imposing consistency constraints among the parameters, reduces the number of acceptable interpretations.

Changes in the unobservable parameters are detected indirectly; namely, whenever no qualitative change in the measured values occurs, then:
- either the model is effectively in the same (qualitative) state;
- or there is a qualitative change in an unobservable parameter (hidden transition).
Hidden transitions are detected from the fact that the qualitative interpretation of the successive measurements forces the system into a state which is not causally related to the previous one; the constraint of preservation of causality then supports the assumption that some hidden transitions between the two observed states must have happened.
The main assumptions of the qualitative interpretation theory:
- there must exist a model;
- there must exist domain-dependent criteria for qualitative interpretation;
- numeric data are in the form of time series;
- events shorter than the time interval between two measurements are not relevant,
are all easily met in business tests, but the second one, in the sense that it is difficult to elicit the required criteria, and that these criteria are not stable over the time: by comparing the qualitative and quantitative series for the same parameter, it has been shown in [21] that the same numeric data may cause different qualitative judgements over time (depending on attitudes and trend evolution). However, the arbitrariness of such a step should be acceptable when compared with the stronger assumptions behind quantification; moreover, pre-processing of the quantitative series could be used as a mean to account for the continuous shift in the subjective reference point (e.g. trend and seasonality).

7. AN EXAMPLE
Consider the following simple models for production and inventory smoothing:

PRODUCT. SMOOTHING   INVENTORY SMOOTHING

$$P_t^p = D_t^e + \Delta S_t^p$$

$$\Delta S_t^p = \partial * (S_t^* - S_{t-1})$$

$$S_t^* \sim k * P_t^p \qquad\qquad\qquad S_t^* \sim k * D_t^e$$

$$\Delta P_t^p \sim \frac{1}{1-k\partial} \Delta D_t^e \qquad\qquad \Delta P_t^p \sim (1+k\partial) * \Delta D_t^e$$

Production smoothing strategies aim at keeping changes in production small, using inventories as a buffer; hence the production changes *less* than the demand. Inventory smoothing strategies on the contrary focus on the achievement of an optimal stock level; hence the production changes *more* than the demand.

The following table shows how the inventory strategy (unobservable decision) in a firm during a given quarter can be estimated using the qualitative answers to the questions concerning the expected demand, the programmed production, the programmed variation in the stock, the capacity exploitation. The table was developed under the following simplifying assumptions:
- answers to the business surveys are available at the micro-level;
- state at time t-1 is as planned by the firm;
- production is only limited by the capacity and not, for instance, by the supply-side;
- stock must be produced by the firm.

D_t^e	P_t^p	ΔS_t^p	CE	STRATEGY
↗	↘	X	X	Production Smoothing
↘	↗	X	X	Production Smoothing
↗	→	→↘	m	Saturation
↗	→	↘	<m	Production Smoothing
↘	→	↗	<m	Production Smoothing
→	↗	↗	X	Stock build-up
→	→	→	X	Stable
→	↘	↘	X	Stock build-down
↗	↗	↗	X	Indecision
↗	↗	→	X	Inventory Smoothing
↘	↘	↘	X	Indecision
↘	↘	→	X	Inventory Smoothing

with: ↗ → ↘ :resp. increasing, stable, decreasing
X   :don't care
m   :maximum exploitation
<m   :exploitation lower than maximum

Sectorial knowledge is helpful in establishing explanations for the guessed strategy: e.g. the commercial sector normally uses inventory smoothing; production smoothing could hence be motivated by speculation.

8. CONCLUSIONS

The research is preliminary in the sense that:
- more examples are needed at the micro level, in order to understand to which level of insight the tests can be used;
- a better coupling with quantitative data (financial statements) must be searched for; the numeric information should be checked for consistency against the tests, and guidelines for diagnostic reasoning should be defined.

ACKNOWLEDGEMENTS
The author wishes to thank: Prof. L.F.Pau, for the initial idea of applying AI to qualitative inquiries, and for his support; M. Halim, for her generous support; and J.P.Cling, G. Ferrari, V. Maniezzo, J.L.Roos, A. Rossena, for useful suggestions.

REFERENCES
[1] INSEE: Enquête mensuelle auprès des chefs d'entreprise, since 1962.
[2] ISCO/MONDO ECONOMICO: Indagine mensile sull'industria.
[3] De Kleer, J. and Brown, J.S.: "A qualitative physics based on confluences", Artificial Intelligence 24 (special issue on qualitative physics), 1984.
[4] Devillers, M.: "The use of Business Surveys in Short-term Forecasts. The French Experience", 16th CIRET Conf. Proc., Washington, D.C., 1983.
[5] Vogler, K.: "Content and determinants of judgmental and expectation variables in the IFO Business survey", 13th CIRET Conf., Munich, 1977.
[6] Forbus, K.D.: "Qualitative process theory", ibid.
[7] Iwasaki, Y. and Simon, H.A.: "Causality in device behavior", Artificial Intelligence, 29.
[8] Kuipers, B.: "Common sense reasoning about causality: deriving behavior from structure", Artificial Intelligence 24, 1984.
[9] Forbus, K. D.: "Interpreting measurements of physical systems", Proc. 5th AAAI Conf., Philadelphia, 1986.
[10] Anderson, O. Jr.: "The business test of the IFO-institute for economic research, Munich, and its theoretical model", Revue de l'Inst. Int. de Statistique, vol. 20, 1952.
[11] Theil, H. and Cramer, J.S.: "On the utilization of a new source of economic information", 16th Europ. Conf. of the Econometric society, Uppsala, August 1954.
[12] Theil, H.: "Recent experiences with the Munich Business Test", Econometrica, April 1955.
[13] Anderson, O. Jr., Bauer, R. K., Fuhrer, H., Petersen, J. P., Wolfsteiner, M.: "Short-term entrepreneurial reaction patterns", 17th Europ. Conf. of the Econometric society, Kiel, Sept. 1955.
[14] Theil, H.: "Measuring the accuracy of entrepreneurial anticipations", 17th Europ. Conf. of the Econometric society, Kiel, Sept. 1955.
[15] Carlson, J.A. and Parkin, M.: "Inflation expectations", Economica 42, 1975.
[16] Artus, P. and Bournay, J.: "Productions et importations industrielles", Annales de l'INSEE, n. 26-27, 1977.
[17] Menendian, Claude: "Les tests conjuncturels comme moyen de prevision de l'indice de la production industrielle", 14th CIRET Conf., Lisbon, September 1979.
[18] Batchelor, R. A.: "Aggregate expectations under the stable laws", Journ. of Econometrics, 16, pp. 199-210, 1981.
[19] Conti, V. and Visco, I.: "The determinants of "normal inventories" of finished goods in the Italian manufacturing sector", 2nd. Int. Symp. on inventories, Budapest, 1982.
[20] Piatier, A.: "Business cycles surveys - Their utilization for forecasting", 14th CIRET Conf., Lisbon, 1979.
[21] Anderson, O. Jr. and Striegel, W.: "Business surveys and Economic research. A review of significant developments", 15th CIRET Conf., Athens, 1981.

Expert Systems in Economics, Banking and Management
L.F. Pau et al. (Editors)
Elsevier Science Publishers B.V. (North-Holland), 1989

SEQUENTIAL CAUSALITY AND QUALITATIVE REASONING IN ECONOMICS

Ron Berndsen and Hennie Daniels

Institute for Language Technology and Artificial Intelligence (ITK)
University of Tilburg
Hogeschoollaan 225, P.O. box 90153
5000 LE Tilburg, The Netherlands. phone 13-669111 ext 2026 or 2914
Telex 52426 KUB NL

In this paper we apply formal qualitative reasoning to a simple economic model. First, we bring together the lines of thought in
comparative statics and the approaches from the field of qualitative
reasoning. It is shown that the theories of causal ordering and
mythical causality applied to the static model do not clarify the notion of economic causality. Then we propose a concept of explicit
causality embedded in qualitative models which closely follows the
way of economic thought.

1. INTRODUCTION

Qualitative reasoning and constraint propagation have been studied mainly
in the context of physics and electronic circuit analysis [Bob 84]. However,
the exploration of these ideas in economic theory is being considered.
Differences between quantitative and qualitative models are discussed and illustrated by the Classical macro-economic theory of output and employment in
[Far 86]. Constraint propagation techniques are applied to a model concerning
the equilibrium of the commodity and labour market [Bou 86]. In [Pau 86] qualitative arguments occuring in government texts addressing economic subjects
are mapped into a formal grammar. Qualitative dynamics (Kuipers' formalism) is
applied to a Keynesian model [Ber 88].
 Application of QR-techniques undoubtedly contributed towards the formal understanding of economic reasoning.
However, part of the new methods in QR closely corresponds with earlier results published in economic literature. The similarity between the theory of
confluences [Kle 84] and comparative statics [Sam 83] has been pointed out in
[Iwa 86a]. In fact, a profound treatment of qualitative statics in economics
was already described in [Gre 81]. This was not recognized as far as we know
by the QR-society at the time of writing this paper.

In economic theory prediction is merely a form of extrapolation if there is no understanding of the causes of the observed events [Sim 57]. The understanding of a sequence of events is usually done by forming a causal chain. Although QR has contributed to the formal description of causality, some difficulties and open questions still remain, especially in economics [Iwa 86a, Kle 86, Iwa 86b]. We believe that we can overcome these problems by implementing the theory of causality as described in [Hic 79].

These ideas are illustrated in a Keynesian model which consists of three parts: the multiplier function, the investment function and the liquidity-preference theory. In the static model, we compare the method of confluences [Kle 84] with the approach of sign solvability [May 81]. It is shown that the theories of causal ordering [Sim 57] and mythical causality [Kle 84] do not clarify the notion of economic causality. One way to get around this problem is to consider a dynamic model in which a standard notion of causality can be defined. This dynamic model can be described in terms of qualitative simulation [Kui 87] or the theory of confluences [Kle 84]. In the first case the theory of causal ordering in mixed models applies [Iwa 88]. In the second case the same explanation can be derived from mythical causality and inter-state behaviour. In both cases the causal ordering corresponds to the intuitive notions of causality. However, we believe that it is unsatisfactory to derive the causal structure from a somewhat arbitrary dynamic model. We feel that the *explicit* representation of causality should be considered as part of the *economic modeling proces*. In [Hic 79] Hicks considers two different kinds of causality: contemporaneous causality and sequential causality. In contemporaneous causality a variable A having a causal link to a variable B directly influences B and hence cause and effect occur in the same time period. In economics, sequential causality, takes place in two steps: a change in A leads to decisions based on it which have their effects on B. The decision-making is an intermediate stage in the causation taking place. There is always a time-lag between cause and effect in the case of sequential causality.

The qualitative model consists of standard symbolic constraints originating from balance sheet equations and constraints representing contemporaneous causality. Relations between economic entities that correspond to sequential causality complete the model with so-called causal constraints. The above considerations lead to a natural extension of qualitative models.

2. CAUSALITY IN THE STATIC MODEL

2.1. The Keynesian model

The economic model that is described below is the monetary sector of the well-known Keynesian model (see e.g. [Den 81,Ch. 4],[Sam 83,Ch. 9]). This part of the model explains the transmission mechanism of money i.e. the effects on the economy of a sudden change in the money supply. The static model consists of the following equations :

$$y = f(I) \qquad \text{multiplier function} \qquad (2.1)$$

$$I = g(r) \qquad \text{investment function} \qquad (2.2)$$

$$M_1 = M_1(y) \qquad \text{transactions money demand} \qquad (2.3)$$

$$M_2 = M_2(r) \qquad \text{speculative money demand} \qquad (2.4)$$

$$M_d = M_1 + M_2 \qquad \text{total money demand} \qquad (2.5)$$

$$M_d = M_s \qquad \text{money market equilibrium} \qquad (2.6)$$

M_1 and f are increasing functions of y and I respectively. M_2 and g are decreasing functions of r.

The main feature of the Keynesian monetary model is the liquidity-preference theory. This theory states that the demand for money (M_d) can be divided into three distinct motives: the transactions motive, precautionary motive and the speculative motive. Both the transactions motive and the precautionary motive depend on the level of income (y) and therefore they are treated here as one (M_1). According to the speculative motive money is preferred to interest-yielding assets (e.g. long-term government bonds) if the return from money is higher than the return from those assets. This is the case when interest rates are relatively low, so the speculative motive (M_2) depends inversely on the interest rate. The total demand for money (M_d) is defined as the sum of the money demanded by the combined motives, namely the transactions motive, the precautionary motive, and the speculative motive. The money supply (M_s) is determined by the actions of the monetary authorities and is therefore treated as exogenous.

Equations (2.1) and (2.2) represent the multiplier function and the investment function respectively. The multiplier function links income (y) and investment (I). The level of investment is determined by the interest rate. When the interest rate is large there are few projects which are profitable. Hence the interest rate and level of investment are related inversely.

The above mentioned equations only hold when the system is in equilibrium.

2.2. Causal ordering

The theory of causal ordering can be found in [Sim 57]. This technique derives a causal ordering among variables in a system of n equations and n unknowns. We rewrite the equations (2.1) to (2.6) in canonical form:

$$
\begin{array}{llll}
f_1(Y,I) & = 0 & f_1 = Y - f(I) & ; \quad f' > 0 \quad (2.7) \\
f_2(I,r) & = 0 & f_2 = I - g(r) & ; \quad g' < 0 \quad (2.8) \\
f_3(Y,M_1) & = 0 & f_3 = M_1 - h(Y) & ; \quad h' > 0 \quad (2.9) \\
f_4(r,M_2) & = 0 & f_4 = M_2 - i(r) & ; \quad i' < 0 \quad (2.10) \\
M_d - M_1 - M_2 & = 0 & & \qquad\qquad\quad (2.11) \\
M_d - M_s & = 0 & & \qquad\qquad\quad (2.12) \\
M_s & = c_1 & & \qquad\qquad\quad (2.13)
\end{array}
$$

I = investment   ; M_d = total money demand
Y = nat. income ; M_1 = transactions money demand
r = interest   ; M_2 = speculative money demand
c_1 = constant > 0 ; M_s = money supply

The total causal ordering is as follows:

$$M_s \longrightarrow M_d \longrightarrow \{Y,I,r,M_1,M_2\}$$

The only minimal complete subset of zero order is M_s and M_d is the derived structure of first order. The derived structure of second order consists of $\{Y,I,r,M_1,M_2\}$. The resulting ordering is correct if we keep in mind that the model describes equilibrium positions for a given value of the money supply. After a disturbance in the money supply, equilibrium is only restored when money supply equals money demand (money market equilibrium). Hence the other variables change only after the total money demand has changed caused by a change in the money supply. This explanation is quite unsatisfactory. A similar example in physics has been given in [Iwa 88].

2.3. Qualitative comparative statics

Comparative statics is a technique to compare equilibrium states. In qualitative comparative statics one is only interested in the qualitative change of the endogenous variables. Samuelson stated the sign solvability problem that occurs in qualitative comparative statics in 1947. Since then quite a number of people have contributed towards the solution of this problem ([Lan 62,65],[Gor 64],[Bas 68]). In general the equilibrium equations read:

$$f(x,\alpha) = 0 \qquad\qquad\qquad (2.14)$$

The vector of endogenous variables is x and α is an exogenous parameter. In order to investigate the new equilibrium position after a small variation in the parameter α we differentiate (2.14) with respect to the parameter α:

$$\sum_{j=1}^{n} \frac{\partial f_i}{\partial x_j} \frac{dx_j}{d\alpha} + \frac{\partial f_i}{\partial \alpha} = 0 \qquad\qquad (i = 1,\ldots,n) \qquad (2.15)$$

The formalism can be applied to the model presented in section 2.1. In this case Y, I and r are the endogenous variables and M_s corresponds to α (M_1 and M_2 can be eliminated by simple substitutions). If we rewrite (2.15) in matrix notation we get:

$$\begin{bmatrix} \dfrac{\partial f_1}{\partial Y} & \dfrac{\partial f_1}{\partial I} & \dfrac{\partial f_1}{\partial r} \\[2ex] \dfrac{\partial f_2}{\partial Y} & \dfrac{\partial f_2}{\partial I} & \dfrac{\partial f_2}{\partial r} \\[2ex] \dfrac{\partial M_d}{\partial Y} & \dfrac{\partial M_d}{\partial I} & \dfrac{\partial M_d}{\partial r} \end{bmatrix} \begin{bmatrix} \dfrac{dY}{dM_s} \\[2ex] \dfrac{dI}{dM_s} \\[2ex] \dfrac{dr}{dM_s} \end{bmatrix} = \begin{bmatrix} -\dfrac{\partial f_1}{\partial M_s} \\[2ex] -\dfrac{\partial f_2}{\partial M_s} \\[2ex] -\dfrac{\partial M_d}{\partial M_s} \end{bmatrix} \qquad (2.16)$$

where

$$\begin{aligned} f_1 &= y - f(I) &&; f' > 0 \\ f_2 &= I - g(r) &&; g' < 0 \\ M_d &= h(Y) + i(r) &&; h' > 0 \text{ and } i' < 0 \end{aligned}$$

(2.16) is equivalent to

$$\begin{bmatrix} + & - & 0 \\[1ex] 0 & + & + \\[1ex] + & 0 & - \end{bmatrix} \begin{bmatrix} \dfrac{dY}{dM_s} \\[2ex] \dfrac{dI}{dM_s} \\[2ex] \dfrac{dr}{dM_s} \end{bmatrix} = \begin{bmatrix} 0 \\[2ex] 0 \\[2ex] + \end{bmatrix} \qquad (2.17)$$

It can easily be seen [May 81] that (2.17) is sign-solvable. The solution is given by

$$\begin{bmatrix} \dfrac{dY}{dM_s} & \dfrac{dI}{dM_s} & \dfrac{dr}{dM_s} \end{bmatrix}^T = [+ \ + \ -]^T.$$

The same results are obtained by the confluence approach of de Kleer and Brown in the next section.

2.4. Mythical causality

The static Keynesian model can be formulated in terms of confluences starting from the equations given in section 2.1:

$$\partial_1 Y = \partial_1 I \qquad (2.18)$$
$$\partial_1 I = -\partial_1 r \qquad (2.19)$$
$$\partial_1 Y = \partial_1 M_1 \qquad (2.20)$$
$$-\partial_1 r = \partial_1 M_2 \qquad (2.21)$$
$$\partial_1 M_d = \partial_1 M_1 + \partial_1 M_2 \qquad (2.22)$$
$$\partial_1 M_d = \partial_1 M_s \qquad (2.23)$$

A confluence is a constraint with qualitative derivatives and variables which can take on a value from the set $\{+,0,-\}$. An assignment of a value to each variable in a set of confluences in such a way that all confluences are satisfied is called an 'interpretation'. Due to ambiguities, it is possible that a state has more than one interpretation.

The set of confluences describes the difference between two equilibrium states. The solution of this set of confluences can be found by constraint propagation. The order in which the variables are determined is called mythical causality. It is called mythical because all the changes take place at the same instant. It is important to note that the differential ∂_1 is the differential with respect to M_s and not with respect to time (compare [Kle 86]). The unique interpretation of the set of confluences after a money supply shock is given by

$$[\partial Y, \partial I, \partial r, \partial M_1, \partial M_2, \partial M_d, \partial M_s] = [+,+,-,+,+,+,+]$$

There are two ways to propagate the disturbance through the confluences which lead to two different so-called causal explanations:

$$\partial M_s = + \rightarrow \partial M_d = + \rightarrow \partial M_1 = + \rightarrow \partial Y = + \rightarrow \partial I = + \rightarrow \partial r = - \rightarrow \partial M_2 = +$$

$$\partial M_s = + \rightarrow \partial M_d = + \rightarrow \partial M_2 = + \rightarrow \partial r = - \rightarrow \partial I = + \rightarrow \partial Y = + \rightarrow \partial M_1 = +$$

Both explanations do not represent the intuitive notion of causality. Thus neither mythical causality nor causal ordering (section 2.2) are capable of capturing the right explanation. A clear difference between the two methods is that mythical causality provides the signs of the changes of the variables after a disturbance. But the signs are not always unique. When a feedback loop is involved it is necessary to use one of the heuristics to solve the confluences. The kind of causality which appears in static models is not very helpful in understanding the behaviour of a system. The reason of course is, that in a static model no time elapses between cause and effect i.e. all the effects are instantaneous. This only makes sense in case one variable is simply a definition in terms of the other variables (e.g. a balance-sheet equation). In any other case it is more natural to assume that the cause preceeds the effect. In fact, that is the way a causal account is normally given: as a sequence of events over time describing the phenomenon. The theory of causal ordering is extended to dynamical systems by Iwasaki [Iwa 88]. This is discussed in the next section.

3. CAUSALITY IN A DYNAMIC MODEL

3.1 Causal ordering in a mixed model

A mixed structure consists of static and dynamic equations. A mixed structure can be obtained from a static model by replacing one or more static equations with their dynamic counterparts. Or from a dynamic model by replacing dynamic equations with corresponding static equations. It is important to know which equations should be altered. In the Keynesian model or more general in economics, knowledge about which equations should be dynamical can be derived from economic theory. In the static model (equations 2.7-2.13) we alter the equation describing the money market and the equation representing the investment function. In the first case, the idea is that when the money-market is in disequilibrium the interest rate is changing. In case of an excess supply (demand), the interest rate decreases (increases). Equation (2.8) is replaced by the dynamic equation (3.2) because entrepreneurs have a desired level of investment that depends upon the interest rate and can differ from the actual level of investment. If the actual investment is lower (higher) than the desired investment, entrepreneurs increase (decrease) their investments. The mixed model is given by

$$f_1(Y,I) \quad = 0 \tag{3.1}$$

$$f_2(I,r) \quad = \dot{I} \tag{3.2}$$

$$I \quad = c_2 \tag{3.3}$$

$$f_3(Y,M_1) \quad = 0 \tag{3.4}$$

$$f_4(r,M_2) \quad = 0 \tag{3.5}$$

$$M_d - M_1 - M_2 = 0 \tag{3.6}$$

$$M_d - M_s \quad = \dot{r} \tag{3.7}$$

$$r \quad = c_3 \tag{3.8}$$

$$M_s \quad = c_1 \tag{3.9}$$

The causal ordering of this dynamical model is depicted in figure 1.

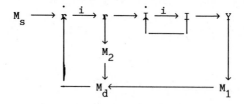

FIGURE 1.

Causal ordering in the dynamical model

This causal diagram closely follows the intuitive notion of causality in the Keynesian model. A change in the money supply causes the interest rate to change because the money-market is in disequilibrium. This has two effects. Firstly, investment will change because the desired level of investment is changed. Secondly, the speculation money demand changes. The change in investment influences transaction money demand via a change in national income. As a result, M_d changes which asserts a feedback causing the interest rate to change. The dynamic equations produce the correct causal ordering. In the next section, we propose a way of implementing causality in a model explicitly by using so-called causal constraints.

3.2 Causal constraints in Kuipers' formalism

In this section we consider a dynamic version of the Keynesian model using a modification of Kuipers' formalism. In this approach, the qualitative behaviour of a system is determined by propagating transitions of variables through a set of constraints. A constraint restricts combinations of transitions of variables which take place at the same time-point or interval. The causal constraint which we define below, restricts transitions of variables in adjacent time intervals. This makes it possible to represent causality in an explicit way. This intuitive notion of causality (cause preceeds effect) is termed sequential causality by Hicks [Hic 79]. The model in Kuipers' notation is given by

ADD(C,I,Y)	National Income	(3.10)
ADD(M_1,M_2,M_d)	Total money demand	(3.11)
M^+(M_1,Y)	Transaction money demand	(3.12)
SC^+(Y,C)	Consumption function	(3.13)
SC^-(r,I)	Investment function	(3.14)
SC^-(r,M_2)	Speculation money demand	(3.15)
DERIV(r,M_d- M_s)	Money market	(3.16)

M^+, ADD and DERIV are defined in [Kui 86]. SC^+ and SC^- are defined below. SC^+(X,Y) holds at $\langle t_i, t_{i+1} \rangle$ for :

QDIR X at $\langle t_{i-1}, t_i \rangle$ = inc and QDIR Y at $\langle t_i, t_{i+1} \rangle$ = inc
QDIR X at $\langle t_{i-1}, t_i \rangle$ = dec and QDIR Y at $\langle t_i, t_{i+1} \rangle$ = dec
QDIR X at $\langle t_{i-1}, t_i \rangle$ = std and QDIR Y at $\langle t_i, t_{i+1} \rangle$ = any

SC^- is defined analogously.

In the computation of the qualitative behaviour we ignore uninteresting landmarks by taking the projection of the state on QDIR. Therefore, we can combine one I-transition and one P-transition to a single transtion from interval to interval. In doing so, we get a modification of the constraint propagation as given in [Kui 86]. Figure 2 illustrates the qualitative behaviour of the system after a money supply shock. The system moves from one equilibrium state to the next in as few transitions as possible. Figure 3 shows oscillating behaviour. In figure 2 and 3 +, 0, - denote respectively inc, std and dec.

	I0	I1	I2	I3	I4	I5	I6	I7
Y	0	0	+	+	+	+	0	0
I	0	0	+	+	-	-	-	0
C	0	0	0	+	+	+	+	0
r	0	-	-	+	+	0	0	0
M_1	0	0	+	+	+	+	0	0
M_2	0	0	+	+	-	-	0	0

FIGURE 2.

	I0	I1	I2	I3	I4	I5	I6	I7
Y	0	0	+	+	-	-	+	+
I	0	0	+	+	-	-	+	+
C	0	0	0	+	+	-	-	+
r	0	-	-	+	+	-	-	+
M_1	0	0	+	+	-	-	+	+
M_2	0	0	+	+	-	-	+	+

FIGURE 3.

4. CONCLUSIONS

Formal methods of qualitative reasoning can be used to support intuitive e-
conomic reasoning. In economic reasoning causal models play an important role.
They are almost always used in an implicit way. Mythical causality and causal
ordering applied to static models often do not give a satisfactory explanation
of causality. In dynamical models, the result of both methods may coincide
with the intuitive notion of causality. But it seems somewhat unnatural to
make static models dynamic just to obtain a causal explanation of the effects
resulting from a perturbation of the equilibrium state. Therefore we feel that
the explicit representation of causality should be considered as part of the
economic modeling process. A first attempt in the form of causal constraints
is given in this paper.

References

[Bas 68] Bassett J.,Maybee J. and Quirk J. (1968) Qualitative economics and
the scope of the correspondence principle, *Econometrica* **26**.
[Ber 88] Berndsen R.J. and Daniels H.A.M. (1988),Application of constraint
propagation in monetary economics in: *Proceedings of expert systems &
their application* Avignon,France.
[Bob 84] Bobrow et. al. (1984) Special issue on qualitative reasonin-
g, *Artificial Intelligence* **24**.
[Bou 86] Bourgine P. and Raiman O. (1986),Economics as reasoning on a qualita-
tive model in: *IFAC Economics and artificial intelligence* Aix-en-
Provence,France.
[Den 81] Dennis G. (1981),Monetary economics,Longman,London.
[Far 86] Farley A.M. (1986),Qualitative modeling of economic systems in: *IFAC
Economics and artificial intelligence* Aix-en-Provence,France.
[Gor 64] Gorman T. (1964),More scope of qualitative economics, *Rev. of econo-
mic studies* **31**.
[Gre 81] Greenberg H.J. and Maybee J.S. (eds.) (1981),Computer-assisted analy-
sis and model simplification, Academic Press,New York.
[Hic 79] Hicks J. (1979),Causality in economics,Basil Blackwell,Oxford.
[Iwa 86] Iwasaki Y. and Simon H.A. (1986),Causality in device behaviour-
, *Artificial Intelligence* **29**.

[Iwa 86] Iwasaki Y. and Simon H.A. (1986),Theories of causal ordering: reply to de Kleer and Brown, *Artificial Intelligence* 29.

[Kle 84] De Kleer J. and Brown J.S. (1984),A qualitative physics based on confluences, *Artificial Intelligence* 24.

[Kle 86] De Kleer J. and Brown J.S. (1986),Theories of causal ordering, *Artificial Intelligence* 29.

[Kui 86] Kuipers B. (1986),Qualitative simulation, *Artificial Intelligence* 29.

[Kui 87] Kuipers B. (1987),Qualitative simulation as causal explanation, *IEEE Transaction on systems, man and cybernetics* 17.

[Lan 62] Lancaster K. (1962),The scope of qualitative economics, *Rev. of economic studies* 29.

[Lan 65] Lancaster K. (1965),The theory of qualitative linear systems, *Econometrica* 33.

[May 81] Maybee J.S. (1981) Sign solvability in: Greenberg H.J. and Maybee J.S. (eds.) (1981),Computer-assisted analysis and model simplification, Academic Press,New York.

[Pau 86] Pau L. (1986),Inference of functional economic model relations from natural language analysis in: Pau (Ed.) *Artificial intelligence in economics and management* Elseviers Science Publishers,North-Holland.

[Sam 83] Samuelson P.A. (1983),Foundations of economic analysis,Harvard University Press.

[Sim 57] Simon H.A. (1957),Models of man,Wiley & Sons,Inc.,New York.

Expert Systems in Economics, Banking and Management
L.F. Pau et al. (Editors)
© Elsevier Science Publishers B.V. (North-Holland), 1989

ANALYSIS OF DATA FOR ECONOMIC RATIONALITY
An Expert Systems Approach

Kuan-Pin Lin and Stan Perry

Department of Economics and Systems Science Ph.D Program,
Portland State University, P. O. Box 751,
Portland, Oregon 97207, U. S. A.

Abstract

Non-parametric data analysis and explanation fit in well with the rule-based expert systems approach. With added human-computer interface, this rule-based inference engine implemented in PROLOG is a complete expert system capable of analyzing and explaining economic rationality in observed data.

1. INTRODUCTION

This paper introduces ADER, a rule based expert system constructed to analyze data for economic rationality. The techniques and principles of logic programming are applied to build and explain a knowledge base containing behavior information about economic data. It provides an integrated framework for non-parametric data analysis based on the similar decision criteria of consumers and producers.

A non parametric frame for analyzing rational choice was originally proposed by Samuleson [16]. His concept for testing utility maximization is now recognized as **revealed preference theory** (see Houthakker [8] and Richter [14]), and has been developed in the context of both consumers and producers. The non-parametric approach is useful in economics for data analysis independent of functional form and parameter estimation. Notable contributions to the field have been made by Afriat [1], [2], Diewert and Parkan [5], [6], Hanoch and Rothschild [7], Varian [16], [17], [18], [19] and many others. Recent works of Lin [11], Lin and Perry [12], show how to logically test data for consistency with consumer and producer behavior.

In the following, we first summarize the behavioral conditions necessary for optimization and related axioms of consumer and producer choice. Then we describe the computer implementation of ADER using a simple example for illustration. Case studies showing the application of ADER to well known sets of consumer and producer data conclude the paper. Future extensions will emphasize improved program efficiency and include provisions for handling very large databases in a microcomputer environment.

2. ECONOMIC RATIONALITY

A primal assumption in economics is that humans are optimizers; consumers maximize utility while producers maximize profit or minimize cost. We define economic rationality as behavior that is consistent with optimization.

Samuleson's insight was that economic data should reflect economic rationality, but perfect rationality is a strong assumption for empirical implementation. If a data set contains observations that violate perfect rationality, an approximate rationality index should be measured indicating the maximum factor ranging from 0 to 1 that when applied to the data removes all violations of rationality. Economists are assumed to deal with data observations with approximate rationality only, although economic theories often assert that the perfectly rational individual would always behave in a way consistent with optimization.

In the following we briefly summarize the rational choice behavior of consumers and producers as a set of logical IF/THEN rules. These basic rules consist of several definitions about preference relations and the derived axioms about maximizing or minimizing rationality. Given a set of data observations satisfying these rules, the existence of a classical utility or production function is warranted. Properties on these functions such as differentiabilty, homotheticity, and separability can be further analyzed. Interested readers can refer to Varian [16], [17], [18], Lin [11], Lin and Perry [12] for background information about the subject.

2.1 Utility Maximizing Rationality

Utility analysis is founded on the observation that consumption at a given price reveals a point on the utility function. Given a rationality index, the optimization principle implies that if the consumer could increase utility by choosing a different commodity bundle they would do so. Failure to choose the prescribed bundle from a finite set of bundles is considered a violation of rationality.

For consumers with rationality index r, choosing between commodity bundles i and j, with price vectors P^i, P^j and quantity vectors Q^i, Q^j the necessary rules are as follow:

(U.1) Given a rationality index r, i is **directly preferred to** j if $rP^iQ^i \geq P^iQ^j$.

(U.2) Given a rationality index r, i is **strictly directly preferred to** j if $rP^iQ^i > P^iQ^j$.

(U.3) Given a rationality index r, i is **preferred to** j if there is a path from i to j via k, l, ... , and m such that i is directly preferred to k, k is directly preferred to l, ..., and m is directly preferred to j.

(U.4) **Weak Axiom of Revealed Preference**: Given a rationality index r, if i is directly preferred to j and $Q^i \neq Q^j$ then j can not be directly preferred to i for all i and j.

(U.5) **Strong Axiom of Revealed Preference**: Given a rationality index r, if i is preferred to j and $Q^i \neq Q^j$ then j can not be directly preferred to i for all i and j.

(U.6) **Generalized Axiom of Revealed Preference**: Given a rationality index r, if i is preferred to j then j can not be strictly directly preferred to i for all i and j.

2.2 Cost Minimizing Rationality

The cost minimizing producer prefers the least expensive combination of inputs that will produce the desired level of output. Failure to choose the cheapest feasible input-output combination is considered a violation of cost minimizing rationality. Two types of rationality failures are possible in cost minimization: input-based and output-based violations. This results in two versions of the weak axiom of cost minimization, the first places the approximate rationality index on the input decision while the second places the index on the output decision. Of course both versions are identical if there is perfect rationality. See Lin and Perry [13] for possible interpretation of rationality index in production context.

Let W^i and X^i be vectors of input prices and quantities respectively, and Y^i is output quantity for each data observation i. A cost minimizing producer choosing between input-output combinations i and j should follow the rules:

(C.1) **Input-based Weak Axiom of Cost Minimization**: Given a rationality index r,

$\quad$ if $Y^j \geq Y^i$ then $rW^iX^i \leq W^iX^j$ for all i and j.

(C.2) **Output-based Weak Axiom of Cost Minimization**: Given a rationality index r,

$\quad$ if $rY^j \geq Y^i$ then $W^iX^i \leq W^iX^j$ for all i and j.

2.3. Profit Maximizing Rationality

The rationality criterion for profit maximization is relatively simple. The producer must choose the largest possible profit; failure to do so is considered a violation of perfect rationality. Again, in the case of violations of perfect profit maximizing rationality, an approximate index can be applied to either the input or the output decision. While analysis of multiple outputs is possible, we have restricted our analysis to a single output.

Given an observation i, let P^i and Y^i be the price and quantity of output; W^i and X^i be the price and quantity vector of inputs. For profit maximizing producers with rationality index r, choosing between production decisions i and j, basic rules of profit maximization are:

(P.1) **Input-based Weak Axiom of Profit Maximization**: Given a rationality index r,

$\quad P^iY^i - rW^iX^i \geq P^iY^j - W^iX^j$ for all i and j.

(P.2) **Output-based Weak Axiom of Profit Maximization**: Given a rationality index r,

$\quad P^iY^i - W^iX^i \geq rP^iY^j - W^iX^j$ for all i and j.

3. IMPLEMENTATION

ADER, Analysis of Data for Economic Rationality, is implemented in Turbo Prolog [4] for IBM-PCs. The ADER program uses pull-down menus and windows extensively to handle model selection, data input, data analysis, knowledge explanation, and system control. There are three models - utility maximization, cost minimization, and profit maximization. Our strategy for implementation is similar for each model: read the data and construct the preference relations; perform data analysis for various rationality axioms, and provide explanations about the knowledge on preference relations and axiom violations.

The most basic facts in the inference engine of ADER are data observations of prices and quantities. Data input must be expressed in the form

$\quad$ N P_1 P_2 ... P_n Q_1 Q_2 ... Q_n

where N is a label or identifier. N may be alpha-numeric but numerals should not precede other characters. P_1 through P_n and Q_1 through Q_n represent numeric lists of prices and quantities respectively. Note that for production analysis P_1 and Q_1 represent the output price and quantity, while other Ps and Qs are input prices and quantities.

As an example, the following three observations of consumer data taken from Koo [9] can be read directly from a text file:

```
1  1  1  2  3 10  5
2  1  1  1  7  6  6
3  1  2  1 11  7  2
```

These data are stored internally using the functor format $data(N,P,Q)$. Knowledge about preference relations among data observations are generated when data analysis for an appropriate model is requested. For each of three models considered here, the relation **directly preferred to** or $drp(N1,N2,C)$ is extracted first from data observations using a forward chaining procedure. Where N1 and N2 are the observation identifiers and C is the model specific "cost" of direct traversal from N1 to N2. Figure 1 below summaries the inequality relations of drp for utility maximization, cost minimization, and profit maximization models, using the notations introduced in section 2. Once drp is known, its transitive closure **preferred to** or $rp(N1,N2,Path,C)$ can be computed and added to the knowledge where Path is the traversal path between the observations N1 and N2 with C the corresponding cumulative "cost". A version of Warshall algorithm [20] is used for this computation. Moreover, directed acyclic graph techniques are called on to prevent cycling around paths already tested. Depending on the application in mind, this cumulative traversal cost between any two observations can be minimized.

	Utility Maximization	Cost Minimization	Profit Maximization
$drp(i,j,C)$ for $0<r\leq1$	$rP^iQ^i \geq P^iQ^j$	$rW^iX^i \leq W^iX^j$	$P^iY^i - rW^iX^i \geq P^iY^j - W^iX^j$ or $P^iY^i - W^iX^i \geq rP^iY^j - W^iX^j$

Figure 1. Definitions of drp Relations.

Given a model, an axiom and an index, the relational knowledge about economic data is computed and stored as outlined above. After the embedded knowledge of drp and rp have been extracted from the data, the knowledge is searched for violations of the desired axiom. This is usually just a search of the knowledge base for evidence of rule inconsistencies, but may require additional computations or generation of new knowledge. Any axiom violations, when found, are asserted into the knowledge base in the form of $violation(A,N1,N2)$ where A is the name of the axiom under investigation. Figure 2 presents the major components of the inference engine and the associated knowledge contents expressed as Prolog terms.

	Analysis	Explanation
Facts Rules	Data Definitions Axioms	data(N,P,Q) drp(N1,N2,C) rp(N1,N2,Path,C) violations(A,N1,N2) .....

Figure 2. Analysis and Explaination Components of ADER.

Rationality testing works as follows. Each axiom is first instantiated with a rationality index of 1.0, resulting in the maximum number of violations if they exist in the data. ADER offers an option to continue with a lower rationality index if desired. A binary search is implemented in ADER to compute the largest index that removes all violations for the data. The following listing shows the partial contents of the knowledge base after testing the Koo data above for consistency with the generalized axiom of revealed preference with rationality index 1:

model("utility","generalized_axiom",1)
data("1",[1,1,2],[3,10,5])
data("2",[1,1,1],[7,6,6])
data("3",[1,2,1],[11,7,2])
drp("1","3",0.95652173913)
drp("2","1",0.94736842105)
drp("3","2",0.92592592593)
rp("1","3",[ ],0.95652173913)
rp("2","1",[ ],0.94736842105)
rp("3","2",[ ],0.92592592593)
rp("1","2",["3"],0.88566827697)
rp("2","3",["1"],0.9061784897)
rp("3","1",["2"],0.87719298246)
violation("generalized_axiom","1","2")
violation("generalized_axiom","2","3")
violation("generalized_axiom","3","1")

At this point, an explanation of information in the knowledge base is possible. ADER explains the logic of knowledge deduction about preference relations and rationality violations. It provides a menu-driven explanation of available knowledge that is based on a limited trace of the knowledge generation processes discussed above. For instance, continuing on Koo's example, if we request an explanation of the relation *rp(1,2)*. ADER produces this message:

With rationality index 1.0000 rp(1,2) BECAUSE drp(1,3) AND drp(3,2)

drp(1,3) BECAUSE the expenditure in obs 1 is greater than or equal to the expenditure in obs 3 given the prices in obs 1

drp(3,2) BECAUSE the expenditure in obs 3 is greater than or equal to the expenditure in obs 2 given the prices in obs 3

In addition, depending on the model selected and the axiom tested, explanations of other information such as preference structure and orderings are also available. In particular, the *best* and the *worst* of the preference order can be identified as well as identification of any data points that are not connected. The *disconnected* points give some indication of the degree of branching in the preference order. If all data points are connected the preference is a simple order. Other structures such as *isolated* points and *cycles* can also be identified from the knowledge base.

The following list shows the knowledge base of Koo's example after searching for an approximate rationality index that permits validation of the generalized axiom of revealed preference. It shows that with rationality index 0.955, there are no more violations of generalized axiom. In terms of preference ordering, data observation "3" is the best while "1" is the worst.

```
model("utility","generalized_axiom",0.955078125)
data("1",[1,1,2],[3,10,5])
data("2",[1,1,1],[7,6,6])
data("3",[1,2,1],[11,7,2])
drp("2","1",0.99091446696)
drp("3","2",0.96848636174)
rp("2","1",[ ],0.99091446696)
rp("3","2",[ ],0.96848636174)
rp("3","1",["2"],0.95968714691)
best("3")
worst("1")
```

4. CASE STUDIES

Two sets of data taken from consumption and production studies are applied to demonstrate non-parametric data analysis for economic rationality using ADER. First, the British consumption expenditure data used in Landsburg [10] provides a suitable data set for testing consistency with utility maximization. For testing producer rational choice, the U.S. manufacturing production data utilized in Berndt and Wood [3] is used.

4.1 Consumer Rational Choice

The British data set consists of prices and quantities of nine consumption categories of goods and services for the years 1900-1955. In his study of taste change in Britain, Landsburg [10] tested this data for consistency with the strong axiom of revealed preference and found no violations.

Running ADER to test utility maximizing rationality, the first step in the analysis is to select the **Utility Maximization** model, this limits the rule domain to utility analysis. After loading the data set, an axiom is chosen for analysis from the **Analysis** menu.

The British data set is free from violations of the weak, strong, and generalized axioms of revealed preference with rationality index 1.0. Consulting **Others** from **Explanation** menu after proving the generalized axiom shows that 1955 was the most preferred year in the knowledge base while the bundle available to consumers in 1918 was ranked the worst. In addition, a number of bundles are not connected, indicating a branched preference ordering. There are neither cycles nor isolated points in the data.

4.2 Producer Rational Choice

The U. S. manufacturing data utilized by Berndt and Wood [3], has been widely used by researchers to test new econometric methods for production analysis. A fundamental question that seems not to have been answered about this data is whether it is consistent with the behaviors of cost minimization or profit maximization. The data summarizes input prices and quantities for capital, labor, energy, and materials from 1947 to 1973 for the U. S. manufacturing. The output price and quantities are composites produced from the associated inputs.

After loading the data into ADER we are able to answer several questions about the Berndt and Wood data. We find that the data does violate both profit maximizing and cost minimizing rationality. ADER produces the following results in response to the *weak_axiom_1* or input-based weak axiom of cost minimization:

weak_axiom_1 fails at 1959 to 1961 with rationality index 1
weak_axiom_1 fails at 1960 to 1961 with rationality index 1
weak_axiom_1 fails at 1971 to 1969 with rationality index 1

At this point an explanation of the failures as well as knowledge concerning data relations can be requested. Instead, we search for the maximal approximate rationality index:

weak_axiom_1 succeeds for this data with rationality index 0.9912109375

For the output-based weak axiom of cost minimization or *weak_axiom_2*, ADER finds identical violations with rationality index 1.0. However, the binary search finds a somewhat lower approximate rationality index:

weak_axiom_2 succeeds for this data with rationality index 0.98095703125

Moving on to test profit maximization, ADER rejects perfect rationality for both input and output based profit maximization. As a matter of fact, two versions of profit maximizing rationality are rather poor based on the calculated index: 0.504395 and 0.817383 respectively.

The above examples demonstrate some applications of ADER to analyze data for rational choice behavior of consumers and producers. Common assumptions made by economists may overestimate the rationality of humans. Of course, many interpretations of less than perfect rationality can be offered, and this is the subject of ongoing research (see also Lin and Perry [13]).

REFERENCES

[1] Afriat, S., The Construction of a Utility Function from Expenditure Data, *International Economic Review* 8 (1967), 67-77.
[2] Afriat, S., Efficiency Estimation of Production Functions, *International Economic Review* 13 (1972), 568-598.
[3] Berndt, E. R. and Wood, D. O., Technology, Prices, and the Derived Demand for Energy, *Review of Economics and Statistics* 57 (1975) 376-384.

[4] Borland International, Turbo Prolog 2.0, 1988.
[5] Diewert, W. E. and Parkan, C., Test for Consistency of Consumer Data and Nonparametric Index Numbers, University of British Columbia, Discussion Paper 78-27, 1978.
[6] Diewert, W. E. and Parkan, C., Linear Programming Tests of Regularity Conditions for Production Functions, University of British Columbia, Discussion Paper 79-01, 1979.
[7] Hanoch, G. and Rothschild, M., Testing the Assumptions of Production Theory: A Non-parametric Approach, *Journal of Political Economy* 80 (1972), 256-275.
[8] Houthakker, H. S., Revealed Preference and Utility Function, *Economica* 17 (1950), 159-174.
[9] Koo, A., Revealed Preference - A Structural Analysis, *Econometrica* 39 (1971), 89-97.
[10] Landsburg, S., Taste Change in the United Kingdom 1900-1955, *Journal of Political Economy* 89 (1981), 92-104.
[11] Lin, K.-P., Modeling Economic Rationality: Revealed Preference Theory and PROLOG, *Proceedings of the First International Conference on Economics and Artificial Intelligence*, 271-272, Aix-en-Province, France, 1986.
[12] Lin, K.-P. and Perry, S., A Logic Programming Approach to Revealed Preference Theory, *Computer Science in Economics and Management* 1 (1988), forthcoming.
[13] Lin, K.-P. and Perry, S., Non-parametric Tests of Producer Behavior, Portland State University, Working Paper, 1988.
[14] Richter, M. K., Revealed Preference Theory, *Econometrica* 34 (1966), 635-645.
[15] Samuelson, P. A., *Foundations of Economic Analysis*, Harvard University Press, 1947.
[16] Varian, H. R., The Nonparametric Approach to Demand Analysis, *Econometrica* 50 (1982), 945-973.
[17] Varian, H. R., Nonparametric Tests of Consumer Behavior, *Review of Economic Studies* 50 (1983), 99-110.
[18] Varian, H. R., The Nonparametric Approach to Production Analysis, *Econometrica* 52 (1984), 579-597.
[19] Varian, H. R., Testing for Optimal Choice Behavior, University of Michigan, Working Paper, 1987.
[20] Warshall, S., A Theorem on Boolean Matrices, *Journal of the American Association of Computing Machinery* 9 (1962), 11-12.

Expert Systems in Economics, Banking and Management
L.F. Pau et al. (Editors)
© *Elsevier Science Publishers B.V. (North-Holland), 1989*

ASSESSMENT OF EXPERT SYSTEMS IN TAX CONSULTANCY

H.A.M. Daniels
Faculty of Economics
Institute of Language Technology
and Artificial Intelligence
P.O Box 90153, Tilburg
The Netherlands

P. van der Horst
Information Systems
Postbank N.V.
Bontekoekade 4
2516 LA The Hague
The Netherlands

In this paper we propose a method for cost/benefit analysis
of so-called "hand-me-down" expert systems. This method is
based on the substitution principle of capital and labor.
These issues are illustrated in the case Expattax, an
expert system developed at Coopers and Lybrand, Rotterdam.

1. INTRODUCTION

Expert systems are among the most promising applications of
Artificial Intelligence until now. This is due to their ability
to engage in judgemental reasoning, like domain experts, and to
reach a comparable level of performance. The decline of initial
investment costs accelerates the widespread utilization of these
systems. It has been recognized that expert systems in financial
industry is a fast growing area [Wat86][Hum87]. The early developments originate from financial institutions and consultancy firms
in the United States [Shp86]. European banks and consultancy
agencies are preparing for new regulations of a European
commonmarket after 1992. Faced with an increased competition
these institutions want to incorporate new technologies in their
basic activities in which expert systems play a key-role [Ben88].

To exploit the full potential of expert systems it is important
that management identifies the opportunities in the organization.
A checklist of questions that should be considered to obtain a
sound judgement about a possible application can be found in
[Wat86]. For fiscal legislation the answers to these questions
are affirmative. Apart from that, tax consultancy also has the
characteristics as described in [Leo88] such as a frequent use of
questionaires and a slowly changing knowledge domain, which are
also positive factors.

Once the opportunities have been determined the next step will
be the selection and evaluation of beneficial projects. In the

assessment of expert systems one should take into account both qualitative and quantitative aspects. However, we believe that management is more interested in quantitative operational benefits of expert systems instead of vague promises, although the qualitative benefits may dominate in the long run [Str85] [Sha88]. There is no doubt that insufficient understanding of the benefits and the inability to quantify them will cast any development effort in a negative light [Far88].

In the next session we provide a method for cost/benefit analysis that applies for a large class of expert systems, so called hand-me-down expert systems [Leo88]. In section 3 we will address some important issues on development aspects and project management of this type of expert systems. In section 4 these general issues are illustrated in a case study.

2. COST/BENEFIT ANALYSIS

A cost/benefit analysis should serve as a guiding principle for management to evaluate the different opportunities that have been identified. Therefore this analysis ex ante is even more important than a similar ex post evaluation. The cost of development and maintenance are relatively easy to quantify. However, the benefits are more difficult to determine. The costs of an expert system consist of hardware, software, the wages of the expert and the knowledge engineer, and the costs of maintenance throughout the economical duration of life of the expert system. The benefits of expert systems can be devided in two categories: benefits on the operational level and benefits that have a strategic impact. The benefits on the operational level can be calculated using the substitution principle of capital and labor. In this section we give a generic method applicable to so called hand-me-down expert systems. The strategic benefits are of a qualitative nature. We quote the most important that are often mentioned in literature (see e.g. [Far88], [Mic86], [Rau86]).

- structured knowledge conservation
- knowledge distribution
- learning system
- consistent decisions
- marketing instrument

These qualitative factors are well known but are, in general, difficult to quantify. Some remarks on the impact of the strategic benefits for the case at hand are given in section 5.

In the analysis two different kinds of experts are identified. The first is the expert who has the knowledge to solve a particular problem. This expert participates in the development of the expert system (let us call him E1). E1's knowledge is handed down by means of the system to a second expert (E2) who is going to perform the same task with the expert system. This is why such systems are often called hand-me-down expert systems. The resulting benefits are twofold: E1 is freed to solve more demanding problems and the costs of performing routine tasks are reduced. In most cases a small fraction F of time of E1, compared to the old situation, is still needed in the new situation. Let T1 denote the time spent by E1 to give one advice without expert system; let T2 denote the time spent by E2 to perform the same task with expert system. To calculate the cost savings we compare the costs in the old situation to costs in the new situation. Let W1 and W2 denote the fees of E1 respectively E2. The cost of the expert system is C and the total number of consultations during the economical duration of life is denoted by N. In C the costs of hardware and software, development and maintenance are included. The cost of performing the task in the old situation is given by:

T1*W1

The cost of performing the task in the new situation is given by:

F*T1*W1 + T2*W2 + C/N

The amount of cost savings per task equals:

(T1*W1)*(1-F)-(T2*W2 + C/N)

Important factors in this analysis are N, W1 and F. Pairs of F and N that result in zero profit form the curve of break-even-points. This curve divides the area of F and N combinations in two parts: the area consisting of profitable combinations and its complement. Figure 5 in section 3 shows this curve for Expattax. In figure 4 the dependence of the total profits as a function of F are given in the case of Expattax.

3. CASE STUDY

3.1. The domain of Expattax

Fiscal legislation consists of a large quantity of rules, which can be divided in two parts: jurisprudence and heuristics. The fiscal expert tries to describe the problem of a client in juristic language. Problem solving consists of two phases: one being the problem description and the other problem solving. These phases can be executed by different experts [Sph86]. The rules of fiscal legislation are complex and sometimes seem contradicting to novices. Only skilled experts can tackle seemingly contradictory situations. The output of a fiscal expert is an advice and the impact of implementing this advice.

Expattax is an expert system that deals with problems concerning expatriate tax payers in The Netherlands. These problems are scattered about a wide range of fiscal fields. The cases that occur frequently can be handled by Expattax. Expattax is a rule based system implemented in the shell Xi Plus. The core system consists of four knowledge bases:

1) Resident,
2) Incomtax,
3) Estattax,
4) Securtax.

These separate modules contain isolated chuncks of knowledge which will be described shortly.

3.2. Knowledge bases.

Resident, the diagnostic systems that determines the fiscal status of the client. A tax status depends on whether the client is coming to The Netherlands or leaving The Netherlands, the profession of the client, the marital status of the client and so on. Different treaties describe different solutions to (different) situations. The most common regulations are the OECD Guidelines. These guidelines provide answers to most of the questions concerning residence determination. Many other tax regulations refer to these guidelines. Dutch Tax Law also has specific regulations, e.g. the so called 35% regulation. It can change the tax status of the client from resident into nonresident tax payer under certain conditions. Sometimes the client has a dual residence. Only in exceptional cases the client has to pay tax in both countries.

Incomtax, the incomtax module. Incomtax determines the taxable income of a client in The Netherlands. Once the tax status of a client is defined (resident or non-resident) one proceeds solving a specific problem for the non resident tax payer. Therefore two

questions have to be asked:
1) is the client taxable in The Netherlands and for what sources?
2) what is his taxable income and his tax liability ?
To calculate taxable income of the client one has to identify the clients sources of income. These sources are described in article 49 of the Dutch Income Tax Act. Together these sources form the gross income. To calculate the net income one has to deduct several costs. The taxable income equals net income minus deductable losses. The deductable items are contained in the Dutch Income Tax Act in article 48.

Estattax, the real estate module. Estattax is the knowledge module to calculate the income from real estate. This module is automatically started when in the module Incomtax a value for income from real estate is needed. In Estattax three groups of real estate purchasers/owners are identified. Group one consists of real estate owners who leave The Netherlands, group two consists of people coming to The Netherlands and buying a house, group three consists of real estate investors. All possible real estate deductions for expatriate tax payers are taken into account.

Securtax, the social security module. This module will investigate whether an expatriate tax payer must pay social security taxes in The Netherlands. To check this a lot of tax treaties have to be evaluated. For different professions different tax treaties are relevant. Also the importance of the treaties are different in each single case.

3.3. System Development
The development of expert systems is similar to the development of standard information systems. However there are two main differences: most expert systems are developed using a prototyping approach, and secondly in the development team of expert systems the domain expert plays an important role. In expert system development four project phases identification, conceptualization, formalization and implementation, testing and validation can be distinguished [Jac86]. A prototyping approach is practically feasible because high level development tools like expert system-shells are available. In a standarized approach these phases follow each other sequentially and reports at the end of each period mark the starting point of the next. In a linear development process one tries to minimize feedback to preceeding phases. In rapid prototyping the development process consists of a large number of cycles in which all of the phases

previously mentioned are present. These cycles reflect the incremental approach of the development of the expert system. Different versions of the system are validated by the user and the expert. As the project evolves, the cycles tend to stretch because the experience of the project team is growing and less feedback is required.

When a new version or part of the system becomes available the expert evaluates the reasoning capabilities of the system and gives feedback information to the knowledge engineer. It is important to provide high level tools for communication between the expert and the knowledge engineer. In this way the knowledge engineer and the expert can communicate at the conceptual level and the expert is not burdened with unneccessary details of implementation. For tax experts directed reasoning graphs and AND/OR trees turned out to be convenient tools.

3.4. Knowledge representation

Expert legal knowledge is considered at three hierarchical levels. At the ontological level we consider the unrefined expert knowledge, the formal decision process as well as informal principles and strategies used by experts. This will be called the material system. The epistemological level consists of the formalized and structured knowledge. The formalization and structuring of unrefined knowledge is a time consuming activity and it constitutes about 70% of the knowledge engineer's work. Graphical schemes are appropriate to record the expert knowledge at this level. Examples are given below. The complex of formalized and structured knowledge is called the conceptual system. At the lowest level the knowledge is represented in the syntax of Xi Plus, rules, facts and demons. This is called the operational system. The operational system is the final mutation of the expert knowledge.

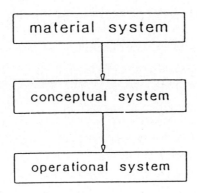

FIGURE 1. Mutation of expert system-knowledge.

To describe knowledge at the conceptual level two different graphical techniques have been used: (1) AND/OR graphs and (2) directed reasoning graphs (DRG). An AND/OR graph is a useful device to represent 'static' knowledge. It does not indicate the 'dynamical' reasoning process of the expert but it describes hierarchical relations of concepts. The mapping of knowledge from AND/OR graphs into Xi Plus is illustrated with an example from the Incomtax module. The taxable income for a non resident tax payer is equal to the gross income minus the deductions and minus the offsetable losses according to article 48 of the Dutch Income Tax Law. The gross income is equal to income from business, income from substantial interest, income from real estate and income from labor. The deductions are equal to self employment deduction and social security contributions.
The AND/OR graph of this example is given in figure 2.

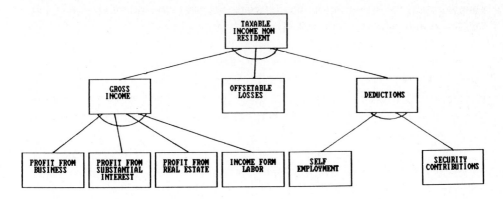

FIGURE 2. AND/OR graph Taxable Income.

The implementation in Xi Plus reads:

fact 1.   taxable income = net income - offsetable losses

fact 2.   deductions = self employment + security contributions

fact 3.   gross income = business profit + real estate + substan-
             tial interest + employment

Directed reasoning graphs is a graphical technique for recording "dynamical knowledge". We have developed this representation scheme to obtain a faithful and adequate representation of the reasoning process of the expert. The charts indicate in which order the various steps in the problem should be followed to reach a solution. DRG's serve as a communication tool between the knowledge engineer, the expert and the expert system shell.

When an expert solves a problem he can use two sources of knowledge: literature and experience. Because experience is instantaneously available, it is the first tool the expert uses to solve the problem. He will try to identify similarities with other problems solved in the past. Similar cases are solved in more or less the same way. Experts only use handbooks to check solutions or to fill in gaps. Experts are able to make large short cuts in reasoning and spend their time mainly on the issues that have rarely occurred in the past. Clearly an expert system cannot operate this way. A large number of simple problems have to be solved sequentially to solve the complete problem. On the other hand the system shouldn't ask for information not needed. The DRG's are of great help, because they demand a clear representation of time ordered steps in the reasoning process. In DRG's four symbols are used: rectangles, diamonds, arrows and rectangles with vertical lines. Rectangles represent a starting point or a choice option (this choice requires a certain expertise). Rectangles with vertical lines represent a conclusion. Diamonds represent yes/no - questions (this choice requires only common sense knowledge). Arrows show the direction to the next step in the reasoning process.
Figure 3. is an example of a DRG representing the procedure to determine whether or not a client has a dual residence. From this DRG the next rule can be derived:

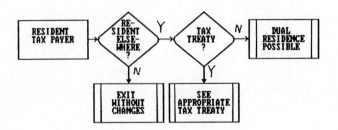

FIGURE 3. DRG of dual residence.

rule 1.   if the client's tax status is resident
            and the client has a residence somewhere else
            and the Netherlands have no tax treaty which regulates
            dual residence
            then the client has a dual residence

From the examples it is clear that AND/OR graphs and DRG's can serve as a powerful tool in the conceptualization and implementation phase.

Expattax consists of 400 rules, 60 demons, 50 facts, 6 queries and 170 questions. Most of the questions have help files available. Expattax has 140 help files and 60 report files.

3.5 Cost/Benefit analysis applied to Expattax

The application of the cost benefit/analysis as given in section 2 to Expattax is straightforward.

$W1$ = \$125.00/hour; $T1$ = 8 hours. So the cost of an advice without using Expattax is \$1000.
$W2$ = \$65; $T2$ = 2 hours; F = time E1 with Expattax/ time E1 without Expattax. In our case F is estimated to be 1/8. The economical duration of life of Expattax is assumed to be 3 years. The number of total advices per year = 40, so N = 120.

The cost C of Expattax consist of:
hardware   \$ 7,500
software   \$ 5,000
consultance of E1   100*\$125 = \$12,500
knowledge engineer   \$ 6,750
maintenance 3*\$1,000   = \$ 3,000

Total costs C   = \$34,750

The total development cost of Expattax are relatively low. The
system is of moderate size and the knowledge engineer was a
graduate student who could do the job at relatively low salary.
It should be noted that an empirical formula exists to estimate
expenditure of a expert system once the size of the system is
known. This formula relates the development costs of the system
to the total number of rules. We now apply the results of section
2 to this particular case.

Cost of an advice with expert system:
0.125*1000 + 2*65 + 34,750/120 = $ 544.60

So the savings are: 1000 - 544.60 = $ 455.40 and the total savings
are N*455.40 = $ 54,648 in three years.

Important parameters are F an TA. Usually TA is known to the
company but F has to be estimated. Figure 4 shows the relation
between the fraction F and the profits per advice where TA is
kept fixed, TA = N/3 = 40. In figure 5 the curve of break-even-
points divides the area of TA and F pairs in two parts: the area
consisting of profitable combinations and its complement.

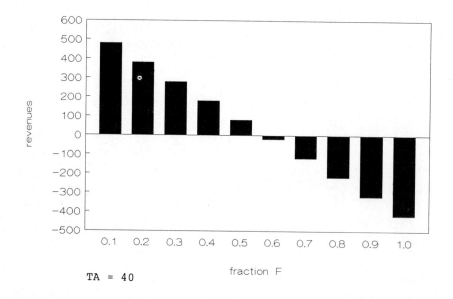

TA = 40   fraction F

FIGURE 4. Relation between fraction of time (F) and
          the profits per advice

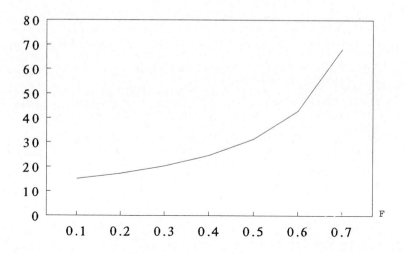

FIGURE 5. break even points, profits = 0

4. CONCLUSIONS

The domain of fiscal legislation is particulary suitable for the application of expert systems. In each individual case the cost/benefit analysis can be carried out to estimate the potential operational benefits. This method can be used to select the most promising projects. Critical success factors are project management, knowledge acquisition, and knowledge representation.

In assessing expert systems one should take into account both operational and strategic aspects. Qualitative (strategic) benefits as described in section 2 were all present in the case at hand. The knowledge was distributed to several sites and the system is used as learing tool for unexperienced fiscal "experts". It is expected that the number of advices will augment in a common European market and the company will use the expert system to increase her market share.

The existence of a competative environment introduces significant issues of security. Since the highly structured knowledge accumulated in an expert system is of strategic importance the protection of this software demands high priority.

REFERENCES

[Ben88]: M. Bensimon, M. Ducamp, L. Nguyen, Les systemes experts en milieu financier, Proceedings of the eighth international workshop on expert systems and their applications, Vol. 2, Avignon 1988.

[Cou87]: D. Couger, S.C. McIntyre, Motivation Norms of Knowledge Engineers Compared to those of Software Engineers, Journal of Management Information Systems Winter 1987-1988, Vol. 4, Nr. 3.

[Dha87]: V. Dhar, On the Plausibility and Scope of Expert Systems Management, Journal of Management Information Systems Summer 1987, Vol. 4, Nr. 1.

[Far88]: P.M. Farrel, J. Pingry, Expert Systems in Manufacturing, Proceedings of the eighth international workshop on expert systems and their applications, Vol. 2, Avignon 1988.

[For87]: R. Forsyth, Software Review: Expertech Xi Plus, Expert Systems, February 1987, Vol. 4, Nr. 1.

[Hum87]: B. Humpert and P. Holley, Expert systems in finance planning, Expert Systems, 1987, Vol. 5, No. 2.

[Jac86]: P. Jackson, An introduction to expert systems, Addison-Wesley, 1986.

[Kur88]: K. Kurbel, W. Pietsch, Projekt management bei einer Expertensystem-Entwicklung, Infortmation Management 1988, No. 1.

[Leo88]: D. Leonard-Barton, J.J. Sviokla, Putting Expert Systems into Work, Harvard Business Review, March - April 1988.

[Mic86]: R. Michaelsen, D. Michie, Prudent expert systems applications can provide a competitive weapon, Data management, July 1986.

[Mic83]: R. Michaelsen, D. Michie, Expert systems in business (Recent developments in expert systems point toward success for this technology in business environments), Datamation, November 1983.

[Pau86]: D.A. Waterman, J. Paul, M. Peterson, Expert systems for legal decision making, Expert Systems, October 1986, Vol. 3, Nr. 4.

[Rau86]: W. Rauch-Hindin, Artificial Intelligence in business, science and industry, Prentice-Hall 1986

[Sha88]: L. Shafe, R. Willocks, The strategic implications and applications in finance, Implementing applications: some practical examples, Proceedings of the eighth international workshop on expert systems and their applications, Vol. 2, Avignon 1988.

[Shp86]: D. Shpilberg, L.E. Graham, H. Schatz, ExperTAX: an expert system for corporate taxplanning, Expert Systems, July 1986, Vol. 3, Nr. 3.

[Str85]: P. Strassman, Information payoff, The transformation of work in the electronic age, Free Press, p. 100, 1985.

[Tor87]: Torsun,PAYE, a tax expert system, Research and development in expert systems III: Proceedings of expert systems 1986, the sixth annual conference of the British computer society specialist group on expert systems, Cambridge university press, 1987.

[Wat86]: D.A. Waterman, A guide to expert systems, Addison-Wesley 1986.

[Wei88]: J.R. Weitzel, K.R. Andrews, A Company / University Joint Venture to Build a Knowledge Based System, MIS Quarterly, March 1988.

Expert Systems in Economics, Banking and Management
L.F. Pau et al. (Editors)
© *Elsevier Science Publishers B.V. (North-Holland), 1989*

A DECISION PROCESS APPROACH TO EXPERT SYSTEMS IN AUDITING

Varghese S. JACOB, Assistant Professor
Andrew D. BAILEY, Jr., Arthur Young Professor of Accounting

Faculty of Accounting and Management Information Systems
The Ohio State University, Columbus, Ohio 43210-1399

The process of audit opinion formulation is complex. We analyze this
complex audit decision process as a special case of a more general
decision process model. The results of the analysis are used to
classify and analyze existing expert systems in auditing. In order
to adequately address the complete audit, we propose a network of
specialized, communicating expert processors each of which deals
with a specific decision problem within the context of an audit.

1. INTRODUCTION

We view auditing as a complex pattern of judgments and decisions. It is a
sequential activity with feedback and feedforward loops. Within many of the
sequential stages we find imbedded a complete and complex set of judgment and
decision activities. In order to provide a more general view of the audit
judgment and choice process we combine a general model of judgment and choice
from the psychological literature with a more traditional description of the
audit process. The integration of these two views makes it possible for us to
classify recent developments in expert systems (ESs) as they apply to auditing.
Based on this review, we propose an interacting network of expert processors to
overcome some of the limitations of the systems.

2. DECISION PROCESSES

In describing a general decision process we integrate the views of Simon [18]
and Einhorn and Hogarth [6]. The resulting six stages of any judgment and
decision activity are (see Figure 1): a) Intelligence Activity; b) Information
Acquisition; c) Design Activity; d) Choice; e) Action; f) Review Activity/
Learning.

3. THE AUDIT DECISION PROCESS

We view the audit process to be composed of thirteen stages, an extension
and variation on the stages described in Felix and Kinney [7] (see Figure 2).

  a) Orientation - The auditor gains knowledge about the client's operations
     and its environment and makes a preliminary assessment of risk and
     materiality;
  b) Preliminary Evaluation of Internal Controls (ICs);

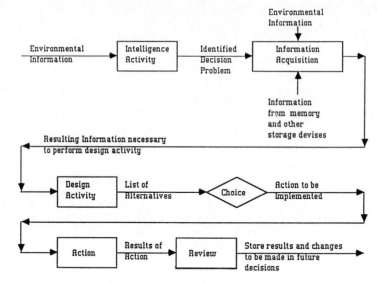

Figure 1:   The Decision Process

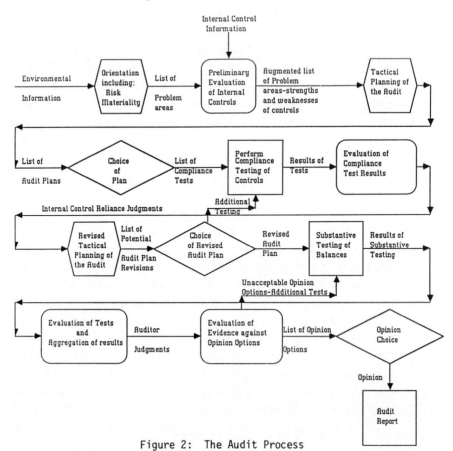

Figure 2:   The Audit Process

c) Tactical Planning of the Audit;

d) Choosing a Plan for the Audit;

e) Compliance Test of Controls;

f) Evaluate Internal Controls Based on Compliance Test (CT) Results;

g) Revision to the Preliminary Audit Plan;

h) Choosing a Revised Plan for the Audit;

i) Implementation of Substantive Tests (STs);

j) Evaluation and Aggregation of Results;

k) Evidence Evaluation - This could lead to further tests or form the basis of the auditor's choice of opinion;

l) Choosing an Opinion which classifies the client's financial statements;

m) Audit Report.

The audit process revolves around the information acquisition decision (IAD) and the opinion decision. The orientation phase of the audit process is the intelligence activity for both IAD and the opinion decision. The auditor is searching the environment for conditions which can be construed as problem areas requiring special attention during the audit. Special attention translates into additional information gathered about the specific area.

The next nine stages of the audit relate to information acquisition. Information acquisition is of paramount importance in auditing. Obtaining complete information about the client's operation is not practical, therefore decisions as to the information acquired have to be made. The preliminary evaluation of ICs forms the information acquisition phase for the generation of various possible audit plans. The auditor analyzes various methods of acquiring information from the client and chooses a plan to sample the available information.

The compliance test of controls is the first stage of the action activity for the IAD. This is followed by a review activity - the evaluation of the controls based on the compliance tests. The review activity may lead to a modification of the audit plan. The modification may result in additional compliance tests being performed and changes in the originally planned substantive tests. The second stage of the action phase for the IAD is the implementation of the substantive tests. The next phase of the process is the review phase of the IAD, where the results from all tests are evaluated and aggregated. This is followed by the design phase of the audit opinion decision. During this phase the evidence obtained is analyzed with respect to the opinion options. The auditor may choose one of the opinions as the decision, or perform further tests if the opinion options are deemed unsatisfactory. The auditor's choice of the opinion is then reflected in the audit report - the action activity for the audit opinion decision. The review/learning phase exists and becomes apparent when the auditor performs the next audit on the same or similar firm.

Table 1 compares the audit process with the general decision process. The

imbedded nature of the decision process within the audit process is easily demonstrated in several ways. Table 2 demonstrates this relationship by providing example decisions that need to be made within the context of each stage of
the audit process.

TABLE 1
THE AUDIT DECISION PROCESS

Audit Process	Decision Process
1. Orientation	Intelligence - IAD/OD
2. Preliminary Evaluation of Controls	IA-IAD
3. Tactical Planning of the Audit	Design - IAD
4. Choosing Plan of Audit	Choice - IAD
5. Compliance Test	IA-OD/Action - IAD
6. Evaluation of Internal Controls	Review - IAD
7. Revision of Audit Plan	Design - IAD
8. Choosing a Revised Audit Plan	Choice - IAD
9. Implementation of Substantive Tests	IA-OD/Action IAD
10. Evaluation and Aggregation of Results	Review - IAD
11. Evidence Evaluation	Design - OD
12. Choosing an Opinion	Choice - OD
13. Audit Report	Action - OD

IA - Information Acquisition
IAD - Information Acquisition Decision
OD - Opinion Decision

TABLE 2
DECISIONS MADE WITHIN THE AUDIT

Audit Process	Decision Made
	Decide on:
1. Orientation	Materiality & Risk
2. Preliminary Evaluation of Controls	Controls which need extensive testing
3. Tactical Planning of the Audit	Staffing decision; feasible plans
4. Choice of Plan	Plans to be implemented
5. Compliance Tests	
6. Evaluation of Internal Controls	Status of controls tested
7. Revision of Audit Plan	Feasible revisions to audit plan
8. Choosing a Revised Audit Plan	Plans to be implemented
9. Substantive Testing	
10. Evaluate Tests & Aggregate results	Evidence to be used
11. Evidence Evaluation	Opinion options
12. Opinion	Opinion to be rendered
13. Audit Report	Form of report

4. EXPERT SYSTEMS IN AUDITING

Expert systems are generally built in narrow problem domains. All of the
systems developed to date can be categorized within one or two of the phases of
the audit process. The systems typically deal with only one of the accounting
control cycles (see Table 3). Table 4 summarizes the dimensions of the decision process captured by each of the fourteen systems. As shown in Table 3,
the fourteen ESs can be classified by the major audit process activity they
perform. Readers are also referred to Messier and Hansen [15] and O'Leary [16]
where some of these systems are reviewed. Tables 3, 4 and 5 provide information concerning the: audit stage addressed, general decision process stage
addressed, and implementation characteristics of the audit ESs respectively.

TABLE 3
EXPERT SYSTEMS IN AUDITING

ES \ Audit Process	Orientation	Pre Evaluation of ICs	Tactical Planning	Evaluation of ICs	Evidence Eval.	Choosing an Option
AUDIT-PLANNER	X					
TICOM		X				
ARISC		X	X	X		
ICES		X	X			
INTERNAL-CONTROL ANALYZER		X				
INTERPRETER		X	X			
EDP-XPERT		X		X		
DS			X			
AUDITOR					X	X
CFILE					X	X
LOAN PROBE					X	X
EXPERTAX					X	X
AOD					X	X
GC-X					X	X

Orientation - None of the fourteen systems explicitly performs the orientation phase of the audit. However, AUDITPLANNER developed by Steinbart [19] for studying auditors planning stage materiality judgments can make recommendations on planning level materiality for the overall audit.

Internal Control Analysis and Compliance Test Planning - A number of ESs have been developed to perform internal control analysis. TICOM [1] is designed to aid the auditor in modeling a system following which the auditor can query TICOM to evaluate the internal controls of the modelled system. ARISC [14], Internal Control Expert System (ICES) [9], INTERNAL-CONTROL-ANALYZER [8] and INTERPRETER [13] focus on internal control evaluation. The primary difference between these systems is the specific accounting cycle considered for analysis. EDP-XPERT [10,11] is designed to assist an auditor in making judgments about the reliability of controls in a computing environment.

TABLE 4
PHASES OF THE DECISION PROCESS CAPTURED BY AUDITING EXPERT SYSTEMS

	Intelligence	IA	Design	Choice	Action	Review
AUDITPLANNER		X	X[d]	X		
TICOM		X				
ARISC	X	X	X[a]	X		
ICES		X	X[a]	X		
INTERNAL-CONTROL-ANALYZER		X	X[a]	X		
INTERPRETER	X	X	X[a]	X		
EDP-XPERT	X	X	X[a]	X		
DS		X	X[b]			
AUDITOR		X	X[a]	X		
CFILE		X	X[a]	X		
LOAN PROBE		X	X[a]	X		
EXPERTAX	X	X	X[a]	X		
AOD		X	X	X		

a - Only Evaluation; b - Suggests Alternatives   IA-Information Acquisition

Tactical Planning of the Audit - Arthur Young's Decision Support Software [3]

focusses on audit planning to the extent that it suggests possible audit procedures to be performed. The system focusses the auditor's planning stage efforts on the areas of greatest risk.

Opinion - The expert systems which perform this function can be classified into two sub-groups, one's that deal with a specific account and those that deal with the overall audit.

Specific Account Systems - The specific account opinion judgments are made by: AUDITOR [5] which deals with the adequacy of allowance for doubtful accounts, CFILE [12] which assists auditors in assessing bank loan loss reserves, LOAN PROBE [20] which appears to be an extension of CFILE and also performs loan loss evaluations, and ExperTAX [17] is designed to aid in the corporate tax accrual and planning process.

Going Concern Decisions - The systems which deal with the overall audit opinion are Audit Opinion Decision (AOD) [4] and GC-X [2]. AOD aids an auditor in making decisions pertaining to the going concern opinion. The system is primarily designed to guide the user through the decision process specified by detailed professional standards. GC-X, on the other hand, evaluates the information input by the user to make a going concern judgment.

TABLE 5
FEATURES OF EXPERT SYSTEMS IN AUDITING

Expert System	Language/Shell	Representation	Problem Domain
AUDITPLANNER	EMYCIN	Rules	Planning Stage Materiality
TICOM	PASCAL	Procedures	External Control Modelling
ARISC	Galen	Rules	Internal Control Evaluation in Purchasing Cycle
ICES	EMYCIN	Rules	Internal Control Evaluation Sales and AR
INTERNAL-CONTROL ANALYZER	EMYCIN	Rules	Internal Control Evaluation Revenue Cycle
INTERPRETER	INTERLISP	Frames/Rules	Audit Planning-Internal Control Evaluation & Compliance Tests
EDP-XPERT	AL/X	Rules	Internal Control Evaluation in Computer Environments
DS	PASCAL	Decision Tree	Tactical Planning
AUDITOR	AL/X	Rules	Bad Debt Allowance
CFILE	INSIGHT 2	Rules	Assessing Bank Loss Reserves
LOAN PROBE	INSIGHT 2	Rules	Loan Less Reserve for Banks
EXPERTAX	Common LISP	Frames/Rules	Corporate Tax Accrual and Planning
AOD	XINFO	Frames	Going Concern
GC-X	LISP	Rules	Going Concern Decision

5. A NETWORKED EXPERT SYSTEM FRAMEWORK FOR AUDITING

An ultimate objective in this area might be to develop an ES that supports all aspects of the audit in an integrated manner. However, even if practicable in other respects, limitations on computing capacity and time required to search the enormous knowledge base would likely render such a global model unusable. Rather than a single, massive, global model, we propose a network architecture. Each node in the network will either represent a processor running an ES addressing a small component of the total audit or an ES designed to integrate and evaluate the results produced by other ES nodes.

The network orientation offers a number of advantages: first, it is a practical recognition of our inability to build a global audit ES due to our lack of understanding about both auditing and expert behavior when complex and interrelated decisions have to be made; second, as demonstrated by those systems already reviewed, practical and effective ESs can only be constructed within narrow domains, an aspect which can be exploited in the networked framework; third, a networked system can operationalize both the parallel and sequential features of an audit; and finally, the architecture is more efficient from a computing point of view and will potentially yield to the new developing parallel processing environments.

The network structure will be based on the audit process model. The network will involve a sequence of decisions beginning with the ORIENTATION phase and the specification of planning materiality and risk and concluding with the list of opinion options and choice. In addition, the network will be partitioned according to the more detailed levels of an audit. The depth of specificity will depend upon the results of future research efforts and our increasing ability to capture audit expertise.

A key factor to consider in developing a networked system for auditing is the interrelationships between the various cycles and accounts. For example, the Purchasing (PcR) and Treasury Cycles (TC) are clearly related. The two cycles and their related accounts provide correlative evidence about each other, e.g., the current ratio and inventory turnover. The needed information exchanges are achieved by having each node possess the knowledge pertaining to decisions in its limited problem domain and enough knowledge about the information interrelationships, such that it can query the other nodes for information whenever necessary.

Figure 3 represents an aggregate view of the network for the development of auditing ESs. The initial evidence source has been labelled environmental. Information from this source includes several components: the audit firm's database which may contain historical information about the client, public databases such as LEXIS, NAARS and finally the client's database. The processors marked MT and R in Figure 3 support the determination of the audit materiality and risk. AUDITPLANNER is an example of an ES supporting the materiality criteria judgment. The Statistical Expert System (SE) provides advice on planning data accumulation and analyzing data collected.

In the ORIENTATION phase, the processors will pay particular attention to the transaction processing cycles: Treasury Cycle (TC), Production Cycle (PC),

Purchasing Cycle (PrC); Revenue Cycle (RC), and Closing Cycle (CC). The information generated by the processors in the orientation phase are fed to the processors performing the preliminary evaluation of controls, e.g., TC-ICE in Figure 3. An example of a system which fits this category in the PrC is ARISC. The results from these processors are than analyzed by the processors responsible for the TACTICAL PLANNING (TPA) of the audit where an integration of the information collected so far takes place.

The role of compliance test processors (e.g., TC-CT in Figure 3) is to exe-

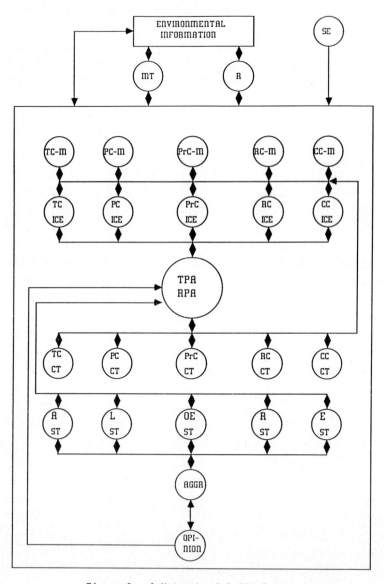

Figure 3: A Network of Audit Expert Systems

cute the tests designed in the Tactical Planning Stage and to analyze the results. The results are fed back to the internal control evaluator which then
reports back to the audit plan review processor (RPA).

The TPA initially integrated other ES results and decided upon the preliminary plan for compliance and substantive tests which were then designed by the
appropriate processors. After completion of the compliance tests, the RPA integrates these results and decides on the revised substantive test plan. Like
the compliance test processor, the substantive test processor's primary function is to implement the tests and to analyze and evaluate the test results.

The results from all the evaluations and tests for each of the cycles and
accounts are than transmitted to the processor which aggregates the results
from the various cycles and accounts (AGGR). The aggregated information is fed
to the processor which analyzes the results and renders an opinion (OPINION).
If the opinion is unacceptable further tests may be required. This is achieved
by linking the processor which makes the opinion decision to the processor
performing the planning of the audit.

One could specialize the processors further, for example, disaggregation
of the Revenue Cycle (RC) node in Figure 3.

6. CONCLUSION

The audit process is complex, with many interrelated decisions being made on
the way to the final opinion decision. Research in developing ESs in the area
has taken a piecemeal approach. This initial step is understandable and possibly appropriate, however, if the goal is to develop an ES which considers the
audit as a whole, the approach is clearly inadequate. In order to consider the
audit as a whole one needs to take into account the interrelationships between
the accounts and cycles. Decisions made in one cycle or account could affect
the decisions in other cycles or accounts. A networked ES framework with
communication between the processors is one way to conceptualize the needed ES
efforts to operationalize the audit.

REFERENCES

[1] Bailey, A.D., et.al., "TICOM and the Analysis of Internal Controls," The
    Accounting Review, (April, 1985), pp. 186-201.
[2] Biggs, S.F., and M. Selfridge, "GC-X: A Prototype Expert System for the
    Auditor's Going Concern Judgement," Working Paper, University of Connecti-
    cut, (January, 1986).
[3] Broderick, J.C., "A Practical Decision Support System," A. Bailey, Ed.,
    Auditor Productivity in the Year 2000: 1987 Proceedings of the Arthur
    Young Professors Roundtable, The Council of Arthur Young Professor, Reston,
    Virginia, (1988), pp. 131-168.
[4] Dillard, J.F., and J.F. Mutchler, "Knowledge-Based Expert Systems for Audit
    Opinion Decisions," Technical Report submitted to the Peat, Marwick,
    Mitchell Foundation, (1986).

[5] Dungan, C.W., and J.S. Chandler, "AUDITOR: A Microcomputer-Based Expert System to Support Auditors in the Field," Expert Systems, (October, 1985) pp. 21-221.
[6] Einhorn, E.H., and P.M. Hogarth, "Behavioral Decision Theory: Processes of Judgement and Choice," Annual Review of Psychology, (1981), pp. 53-88.
[7] Felix, W.L., and W.R., Kinney, "Research in the Auditor's Opinion Formulation Process: State of the Art," The Accounting Review, (April, 1982), pp. 245-271.
[8] Gal, G.F., "Using Auditor Knowledge to Formulate Data Model Constraints: An Expert System for Internal Control Evaluation," Ph.D. Thesis, Michigan State University, (1985).
[9] Grudnitski, G., "A Prototype of an Internal Control Expert System for the Sales/Accounts Receivable Application," Audit Judgement Symposium, University of Southern California, (1986).
[10] Hansen, J.V., and W.F. Messier, "A Knowledge-Based, Expert System for Auditing Advanced Computer Systems," European Journal of Operational Research, (September, 1986a), pp. 371-379.
[11] Hansen, J.V., and W.F., Messier, "A Preliminary Investigation of EDP-XPERT," Auditing: A Journal of Practice & Theory, (Fall, 1986b), pp. 109-123.
[12] Kelly, K.P., G.S. Ribar, and J.J. Willingham, "Interim Report on the Development of an Expert System for the Auditor's Loan Loss Evaluation," Auditing Symposium, VIII, University of Kansas, (1986).
[13] Kelly, K.P., "A Knowledge-Based Theory of the Audit Planning Process," Working Paper, (1987).
[14] Meservy, R.D., A.D. Bailey, and P.E. Johnson, "Internal Control Evaluation: A Computational Model of the Review Process," Auditing: A Journal of Practice and Theory, (Fall, 1986), pp. 44-74.
[15] Messier, W.F., and J.V. Hansen, "Expert Systems in Auditing: The State of the Art," Auditing: A Journal of Practice and Theory, (Fall, 1987), pp. 94-105.
[16] O'Leary, D.E., "The Use of Artificial Intelligence in Accounting, B.G. Silverman Ed., Expert Systems for Business, Addison Wesley, Reading, Massachusetts, (1987), pp. 83-98.
[17] Shpilberg, D. and L.E. Graham, "Developing ExperTAX: An Expert System for Corporate Tax Accrual and Planning," Auditing: A Journal of Practice and Theory, (Fall, 1986), pp. 75-94.
[18] Simon, H., The Science of Management Decision, Prentice-Hall, Englewood Cliffs, New Jersey, (1977).
[19] Steinbart, P., "Materiality: A Case Study Using Expert Systems," The Accounting Review, (January, 1987), pp. 97-116.
[20] Willingham, J.J. and G. S. Ribar, "Development of an Expert Audit System for Loan Loss Evaluation," A.D. Bailey, Ed. Auditor Productivity in the Year 2000: 1987 Proceedings of the Arthur Young Professors Roundtable, The Council of Arthur Young Professors, Reston, Virginia (1988), pp. 171-184.

Expert Systems in Economics, Banking and Management
L.F. Pau et al. (Editors)
© *Elsevier Science Publishers B.V. (North-Holland), 1989*

**CONNECTIONIST EXPERT SYSTEMS
FOR INTELLIGENT ADVISORY APPLICATIONS**

CHEE LAI KIN
Institute of Systems Science,
National University of Singapore

TAN AH HWEE
Department of Information Systems and Computer Science,
National University of Singapore

Abstract

Two prototype systems were built for an advisory application in the area of career guidance. The first prototype is built using a structured rule-based knowledge representation and backward inference paradigms. This prototype demonstrated the feasibility of using a current expert systems approach. However, for the full-scale implementation and eventual maintenance of the live system, a number of key issues have to be resolved. These include further extensive knowledge acquisition from multiple human experts; choice of implementation vehicle for mass deployment and the approach for maintaining the system as current as possible, given the high volatility of the knowledge domain. The second system which used the connectionist model as knowledge base was then developed to explore to what extent this paradigm can help overcome or provide alternatives to these issues. Both systems make use of 'shells' for prototype development.

1. INTRODUCTION

Connectionist Expert Systems are expert systems that use connectionist models as their knowledge bases. Connectionist models are basically highly interconnected networks of simple computing elements. Such networks can be constructed from training examples by currently available machine learning techniques. As such, there is the potential of employing this approach to automate the development of expert systems for advisory/classification problems.

The objectives for the second prototype using the connectionist approach are to investigate the following:-

* using examples (generated from the earlier prototype) to automatically build the connectionist expert system

* how easily can the knowledge from the earlier prototype be transferred to the connectionist expert system

* by way of feeding new set of training examples, can the maintenance problem be reduced drastically

* to what extent can connectionist expert systems handle noisy and incomplete information for this class of applications

The authors' opinion is that connectionist expert systems are not meant to replace current expert systems as this approach is still new. This paper describes the above issues, the feasibility and potential of how both the connectionist and the current Expert Systems paradigms can be synergistically applied to create an even more advanced, interdependent and adaptive computing technology, resulting in real economic value to this class of advisory expert systems in general.

1.1. Current Expert Systems Approach -
Overview of the Career Guidance Advisory System

This system provides career guidance to users who are seeking the vocations that best suit their interests, abilities and work value profiles. The system will assess these end-user's profiles before recommending a list of suitable vocations as shown in Fig.1.

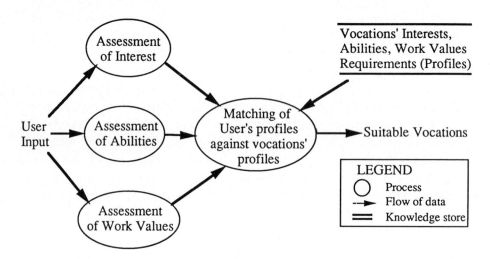

FIGURE 1
Knowledge Flow Diagram of
Career Guidance Advisory System

The knowledge base essentially contains the instruments for assessments of the three different profiles and the corresponding profiles requirements for each of the vocation for recommendation by the model. Fig.2 illustrates that the matching of the end-user's profile to that of any particular vocation is a multi-dimensional set of rules. The knowledge base for this prototype is structured as in Fig.3. The current scope of functionality of the prototype has yet to include the complexities of educational guidance and provision of occupational information. The knowledge domain on vocations and its profiles can be volatile to reflect the current economic directions and industry trends of a particular nation.

Assessment On:	INTERESTS	ABILITIES	WORK VALUES
Process Steps:	Step 1: Answers from user are translated into scores Step 2: Highest two are taken and translated into Interest codes	Step 1: User gives self ratings against a list of abilities Step 2: All those with ratings above a certain threshold value are selected	Step 1: Answers from user are translated into scores Step 2: All those with scores above a certain threshold value are selected
Matching Rules:	Codes must match exactly with those of "suitable vocations"	User's ability profile must match >= 60% with those ability profile of "suitable vocations"	User's work values profile must match 60% with those work values profile of "suitable vocations"

FIGURE 2
Simplified Functional Requirements for Career Guidance

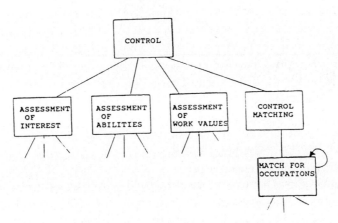

Note:

i) The various rules required are defined for each module of the knowledge base. The modules are linked together in a hierarchical manner. Each module has its own control strategies and scope of inferencing.

ii) the "match for occupations" can have a number instantiations depending on the total number of vocations in the knowledge base.

iii) the "control" module is to control the overall inferencing mechanism for the system.

FIGURE 3
Approach using Structured Rule-based Expert System

The prototype is implemented on a multi-user mainframe expert system shell called ESE, of structured rule-based paradigms. Currently, it supports approximately 30 vocations and consists of around 200 rules.

1.2. Current Expert Systems Approach - Implementation Issues

In the current approach, the process of eliciting knowledge from the human experts is key to the quality and development of the system. The current process is unstructured, time-consuming and a recognised bottleneck. In the career guidance system, the problem is compounded by the need for several interdisciplinary human experts. The overlapping knowledge presents additional difficulty to resolve. On the part of the human experts, they have to be articulated in provision of their knowledge, which frequently is not the case especially the more experienced ones. Past cases or examples have to be painstakingly analysed for a thorough understanding before the knowledge can be adequately represented for the building of the knowledge base.

The system needs to have the potential to be deployed on a large-scale basis. The implementation vehicle is desired to be an economically viable one. Using the current Expert systems paradigm, the fully developed system is envisaged to be quite massive and complex in nature. Reasoning is done by searching through the knowledge base, and if this is large, performance can be affected.

Once deployed, the system and especially the knowledge base has to be maintained. Knowledge bases are a lot more active and knowledge is continually improved upon and new things are being learned to necessitate the changes within the system. Not only new knowledge has to be entered into the knowledge base but outdated or incorrect knowledge must be removed. For example, over time, new occupations may be included and existing ones may have to be revised accordingly. Changes have to be done carefully so as not to skew the preordained reasoning mechanisms. Current expert systems are not able to learn i.e. acquire more knowledge from existing knowledge and consultations performed.

2. CONNECTIONIST EXPERT SYSTEMS

2.1. Connectionist Models (an overview)

Connectionist models are basically highly interconnected networks of simple identical computing elements. A computation is performed collectively by the whole network with the activity distributed over all the computing elements. The operation of the basic component is shown in Fig.4. At each point in time, each unit U_i has an activation value, denoted $a_i(t)$. The activation value is passed through a function f to produce an output value $O_i(t)$ which propagates through a set of unidirectional connections to other units in the system.

Associated with each connection is a weight W_{ij} which determines the amount of effect that unit i has on unit j. All input to a unit U_j must be combined by some propagation rule (usually addition) and then the combined inputs to a unit, net_j together with its current activation value $a_j(t)$, determine a new activation value $a_j(t+1)$ via a function **F**. These systems are plastic in the sense that the pattern of interconnections undergoes modification as a function of experience.

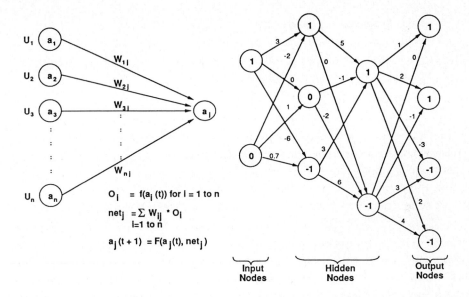

$$O_i = f(a_i(t)) \text{ for } i = 1 \text{ to } n$$

$$net_j = \sum_{i=1 \text{ to } n} W_{ij} \cdot O_i$$

$$a_j(t+1) = F(a_j(t), net_j)$$

Input Nodes   Hidden Nodes   Output Nodes

Fig. 4   Operation of the Basic Components   Fig. 5 A 3-layer Perceptron

There are already quite a number of well established connectionist models such as Multi-layer Perceptrons[3,6], Interactive Activation and Competition Networks[4], Inference Networks, Enhanced Perceptrons[5], Hopfield Networks, Kohonen Networks and Fukushima Networks etc.

As our problem domain, Career Guidance, is of an diagnostic nature, Multi-layer Perceptrons and Enhanced Perceptrons would be the most appropriate network structure.

2.2. Multi-layer Perceptrons

Multi-layer perceptrons[3] are feed-forward networks having layers of nodes with links connecting each other. A three-layer perceptron with two layers of hidden units is shown in Fig.5.

In our application, the activation of processing unit U_i at time t is $a_i(t)$ and can take value among *-1*, *0* and *1*. The output function is chosen to be an identity function ie. the output level of a unit is equal to its activation value. The pattern of connectivity is represented by a weighted matrix **W** in which each entry, W_{ij}, represents the strength and sense of the connection from unit i to unit j. The rule of propagation, **p** is a weighted summation of inputs to a unit, such that

$$net_j = sum (W_{ij} * O_i) \quad \text{for all } U_i \text{ connecting to } U_j$$

The activation rule **F** is a threshold function, such that

$$a_j(t+1) = \begin{array}{l} 1 \text{ for } net_j > 0 \\ -1 \text{ for } net_j < 0 \\ 0 \text{ for } net_j = 0 \end{array}$$

2.3. Logical Reasoning and Inferencing

After defining the basic structure, the propositional meaning is then incorporated. Each node in this context, represents a certain assertion and its activation value gives the truth value of the assertion. Under this assignment,

$$\begin{array}{lll} \text{assertion is} & \text{true} & \text{if } a_i = 1 \\ & \text{false} & \text{if } a_i = -1 \\ & \text{unknown} & \text{if } a_i = 0 \end{array}$$

The process of logical reasoning and inferencing can be demonstrated using a sample problem that determines the personality type of a person.

Personal profiles
U_1 : like chess puzzles
U_2 : like science courses
U_3 : like music
U_4 : participate in scientific fair
U_5 : write or draw well
U_6 : take part in concert

Conclusions
U_7 : Artistic
U_8 : Investigative
U_9 : Artistic and Investigative
U_{10} : not able to conclude

The real numbers in the output nodes are biases that should be added to each net_j. Now if we assign *true*(+1), *false*(-1) or *Unknown*(0) to each input node and calculate the value of other nodes, we are able to obtain the personality type from output node's activation. For example, if the person likes science courses (a_2=1) and chess puzzles(a_1=1), has participated in scientific fair(a_4=1) and concert(a_6=1) before but doesn't like music(a_3=-1) and cannot write or draw well(a_5=-1), we can conclude that the person has an Investigative personality(a_8=1) by verifying

$$net_8 = -2.5+(1.5)(1)+(2)(1)+(-1)(-1)+(2)(1)+(-1)(-1)+(-1)(1) > 0$$

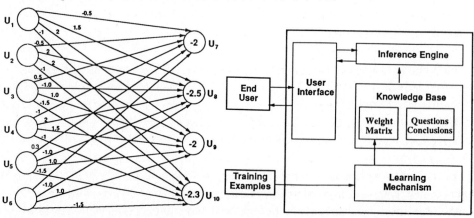

Fig. 6   **Connectionist Structure for Determining Personality Types**

Fig. 7 **A Connectionist Expert System**

In addition to the 6 by 4 weight matrix, We must also provide questions for obtaining personal profiles and conclusion texts which report the finding to the user. The network, questions, conclusions and and the weight matrix constitute the knowledge base for a connectionist expert system shown in Fig.7.

2.4. Learning Algorithm

A connectionist model learns through the modification of weight matrix as a function of experience to effect the change in the heuristic knowledge. There are a few algorithms suitable for our purposes, namely the Pocket Algorithm[1,2] and the back propagation algorithm[3] etc.

2.5. Inferencing Mechanism

During the consultation, questions are asked in a heuristic order to obtain the attributes of the user and the appropriate values are assigned to the corresponding input nodes. The input nodes, once obtain their value will propagate the values to the next layer (*forward chaining*). S.I. Gallant[1,2] pointed out that it is usually possible to deduce the activation for a cell without knowing the values of all of its input. In fig.3., for example, if we know that the person likes chess puzzles but not music, have participated in scientific fair and cannot write or draw well, then we can conclude that he/she is investigative without knowing the rest of his/her personal profiles.

After the forward chaining, If some output nodes are activated, the corresponding conclusions are reported to the user. Otherwise, *backward chaining* occurs. S.I. Gallant[1,2] uses Conf(U_i) (*an estimate of the likelihood that an unknown variable U_i will eventually be reduced*), to choose the next question to be asked. The system then tries to infer forward again until some conclusions are reached.

The arrival of the conclusions is explained by listing those decisive inputs that contribute to the outcomes. All the inputs that have positive contribution are first listed. Then those inputs with largest absolute value of weight are picked from the list one by one until the inputs picked are sufficient to make the inference.

2.6. Interactive Activation & Competition Properties

In the above discussion, we assume that the input nodes are independent and do not take the advantage that the activation value of a input node can contribute to the determination of that of the other input nodes. Not only this stops us from checking the consistency of the input attributes, when the number of input nodes becomes large, it is going to bore the user with unreasonably huge number of questions.

The Interactive Activation and Competition Networks[4] seems to offer us the solution. For those input attributes that support each other, we link them by a excitatory connection and for those contradict to each other, by inhibitory connection. The activation value of a input node is changed based on a function that takes into account both the current activation and the net input from the other input nodes.

After the incorporation of this properties, the system will still try to make conclusions using the original inferencing mechanism. But when the number of questions asked exceeds a certain tolerance limit, the activation values of those input nodes known so far will be used to infer the unknown activation values of the other input nodes. After the activations stabilize, the full set of input values is used to infer forward to derive the values of the output nodes. This allows us to derive conclusions by only asking a controlled number of questions and to resolve contradictary input attributes.

3. IMPLEMENTATION

3.1. Connectionist Expert System Developer (CESD) Toolkit

A graphical package CESD Toolkit which serves almost the same purposes as the current expert system shells, is first developed. It is implemented on APOLLO DOMAIN DN580 and uses Graphical Primitive Routines (GPR) for graphical display and DOMAIN/DIALOGE for interactive manipulation. The coding started in June 1988 and the overall skeleton was not finalized until mid August.

I   Knowledge Base

The knowledge base when saved is in a text file format. When it is loaded into the system, a work buffer will be used to hold its content. Any modification on the expert system will be effected on the work buffer content.

II   System Components

There are four main components working in a collaborative manner. Fig.8. shows an overview of their inter-relationships.

(1) Graphics Editor

    CREATE   for building a new expert system

    EDIT   for editing an existing expert system

The operations supported are *Insert node, Delete node, Alter weight, Change question text, explanation text and conclusion text.*

(2) Filing System

    LOAD   reads in a selected (text file format) knowledge base and assigns the content to the work buffer.

    SAVE   saves the work buffer content to a selected text file.

(3) Learning Mechanism

The function **LEARN** reads in training examples from a chosen example file generated earlier on and modifies the weight matrix of the expert system in the work buffer according to some learning algorithm

(4) Consultation

Activating **CONSULT** starts a dialogue kind of consultation. Explanation facilities like WHY and HOW are also implemented. **TUTORIAL** guides naive users on how to make use of this package. Some basic concept on the operations of a connectionist expert system is also provided.

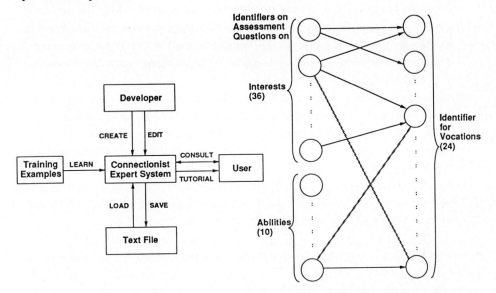

Fig. 8 System Components of   Fig. 9 Career Guidance Expert System
        CESD Toolkit   Using Connectionist Architecture

3.2. Career Guidance Advisory System

There are 36 factors on interests, 10 factors on abilities and the other 45 factors on work values. Due to the limited size of the job pool(24 at present, will be expanded to over 300), the 45 factors on work values are taken out. So in our implementation, this corresponds to 46 input nodes and 24 output nodes as shown in Fig.9.

The present model employed is single-layer perceptron. The result is very satisfactory. Given a set of personal profiles, the system is always able to find the correct match. With the incorporation of the interactive activation and competition properties, we are even able to cut down the number of questions asked by 50%.

4. CONCLUSION

We have presented both the current approach and the connectionist approach for constructing expert systems (and in particular, the connectionist approach in detail). The current approach has been well studied and widely accepted whereas the latter is still new and immature. However, through our findings, we can conclude the following :

(1) The automated generation of knowledge bases is attractive as it does not involve deriving heuristics and writing rules etc. The only factor that may reduce its credibility is the considerable effort in collecting training examples and validating the quality of the examples collected.

(2) The training part in the connectionist approach can take up extensive computing resources but once the system is trained, very minimal hardware and software support is needed.

(3) Connectionist expert systems have minimal maintenance problem as the refinement of knowledge can be achieved by feeding in new set of training examples. Modification of rules or control information as in current rule-based expert systems is not required.

(4) Connectionist expert systems are generally more robust. As the knowledge is represented by the connectivity of the network, malfunction in a portion of the network will cause degrading of the system performance but not total failure. Error tolerance is also promised by this new technology, ie noisy and incomplete input can still be accepted.

This paper does not mark the end of the project. CESD Toolkit still needs several enhancements to make it more presentable and user friendly. The Career Guidance Advisory System has yet to be expanded to a full size job pool of 300 jobs. Another line of research is to try building the system on other types of connectionist model like Enhanced Perceptron to further explore the potential and limitations of the connectionist expert systems.

ACKNOWLEDGEMENTS :

The authors would like to acknowledge the valuable contributions from the team of experts from the Institute of Education who provided the expert knowledge on career guidance and counselling, and especially Dr. Sim Wong Kooi and Mrs. Lun Chor Yee, who are the driving forces behind this joint project with the Institute of Systems Science. We also thank Professor Teh Hoon Heng and Dr. Tan Chew Lim for many of their ideas and comments on the implementation approaches. And of course, Dr. Juzar Motiwalla and the management of the Institute of Systems Science for the ongoing encouragement, resources and support towards this ongoing project.

REFERENCES

[1]   Gallant S.I., Connectionist Expert Systems, Comm. of the ACM Feb 88
[2]   Gallant S.I., Automatic generation of expert systems from examples.
       In proc 2nd Intl Conf AI Applicatn IEEE Press, New York,1985, pp.313-319.
[3]   McClelland, J.L., and Rumelhart, D.E., Eds. Parallel Distributed Processing:
       Explorations in the Microstructures of Cognition. Volume 1 & 2.
       MIT Press, Cambridge, Mass. (1986).
[4]   McClelland, J.L., and Rumelhart, D.E., Eds. Explorations in PDP:
       A handbook of Models, Programs, and Exercises.
       MIT Press, Cambridge, Mass. (1988).
[5]   Hoon Heng Teh & Wellington C. P. Yu,
       A Controlled Learning Environment of Enhanced Perceptron.
[6]   Richard P. Lippman, An Introduction to Computing with Neural Nets.
       IEEE ASSP Magazine, Apr. 1987, pp. 4-22.

Expert Systems in Economics, Banking and Management
L.F. Pau et al. (Editors)
© *Elsevier Science Publishers B.V. (North-Holland), 1989*

CATA: AN EXPERT DATABASE FOR INTELLIGENT TRAVEL ASSISTANCE

Anna BODI

Graduate School of Management, Monash University,
Clayton, Victoria, 3168, Australia.

John ZELEZNIKOW

Department of Computer Science, La Trobe University,
Bundoora, Victoria, 3083, Australia.

CATA is an intelligent flight planning assistant. It is an expert database, which asks the user to input his destination, constraints, rules and goals. The output is a list of flights meeting the traveller's specifications; together with an alternative list, which may not quite meet the user's rules or constraints, but optimizes his goals. CATA is written as a deductive database, and uses heuristic rules to prune its search of the database. Unlike other air-travel related expert systems, CATA does not attempt to model the traveller. Instead, CATA complements existing Computer Reservation Systems by providing comprehensive individually tailored advice and information to the traveller.

KEY WORDS   Expert Databases, Decision Support, Travel, Knowledge Representation.

COMPUTING REVIEW CATEGORIES I.2.4, H.4.2, H.1.2.

1. INTRODUCTION

Computers have been significant in the airline industry for more than thirty years. Many of the earliest programs were designed for airline reservation systems. They were often written in machine code, or else some now obsolete programming language.

Currently most airline companies' Computer Reservation Systems (CRSs) would be unrecognizable as an extension of the CRSs of the early 1950s. They perform not only reservations, but also make difficult calculations, such as load factors and fuel required.

None of these systems, however, explicitly help the consumer plan a complex individual itinerary. Whilst they will tell a traveller how to get from point A to point B, with any intermediate stops specified, they will not quote him the cheapest seasonal fare, or suggest that flying Melbourne-New York-Melbourne is a much cheaper alternative for a voyager wishing to travel Melbourne-Philadelphia-Melbourne. (Philadelphia is only 150 km from New York, and there are excellent coach connections from all three major New York airports.)

A travel agent may be able to provide this information. But this of course depends on the availability of an excellent travel agent. Good agents are not always easy to find, at least in the Australian context [1].

CATA is a computer aided travel assistant to help the customer plan his itinerary. A prospective voyager indicates which cities he wishes to visit and then indicates his own rules, for example:

(1) he wants the cheapest fare;

(2) he is willing to pay up to $200 extra if he can visit Chicago;

and constraints, for example:

(1) he will not fly Continental;

(2) he is not prepared to have more than three connecting flights each way;

(3) each section of the trip must take no more than thirty hours.

CATA will then produce a list of those flights meeting the traveller's rules and constraints, in descending order of the customer's chosen priority. Whilst it provides expert advice to the voyager, it does not try to become an expert system, in that it does not try to model a travel agent (the expert). Instead, it provides intelligent access to an extremely large and dynamic database.

We begin with a survey of the current state of automation in the airline industry, and show how CATA fulfills an important function. A summary of the capabilities of CATA follows. A more detailed discussion of the implementation of CATA will follow in a later paper. We conclude by showing that the use of artificial intelligence techniques/knowledge based systems, like CATA, can bring competitive advantages to the tourism industry, as well as to other areas including banking.

2. AUTOMATION IN THE AIRLINE INDUSTRY

The airline with the best developed information technology will get the tightest grip on its markets, especially in a deregulated or liberalised environment. (Deregulation of the airline industry in United States occurred in 1978, it will occur in Europe by 1992, and may occur in Australia after 1991). The computer is increasingly seen as an essential management and commercial weapon in the struggle to survive [2].

For example, yield management has become critical for protecting profits in a deregulated or liberalised industry, and ad hoc methods of monitoring and forecasting yield are no longer suitable in complex and volatile trading conditions. However, whilst there are cases of automation helping airlines' decision making (e.g., flight planning, routing, baggage management, weather service), the major use of computers has been the routine transaction processing of CRSs.

2.1. Computer Reservation Systems

The major requirement of a CRS is to handle a heavy transaction processing load. It must quickly identify if seats in a given category are available on a given flight, and if the seats are then booked, ensure that no-one else is allocated the booked seats.

At the moment, there is tremendous competition between the airline companies to have travel agents use their CRS. In the United States, most major airlines have their own CRS, although Northwest and TWA share the PARS system [3]. The dominant CRSs are those of American Airlines (Sabre) and United Airlines (Apollo). Both airlines are now competing to sell management systems, as well as reservation systems, to the travel trade. So important are the CRSs, that many airline companies now see them as a major source of income. As Robert Crandall, chairman and president of AMR Inc. (American Airlines' parent company) points out, the operation of a major reservations system is an excellent form of diversification [2]. It does more than boost revenue for the airline. It cushions earnings against instability in the industry. Revenue is based on the number of reservation transactions, not on the value of the fares. While a fare war may damage airline operating revenue, it increases reservations revenue by increasing traffic. Indeed, the Sabre system produced nearly one-third of the 1986 operating profit of AMR. Flying aircraft has turned out to be much less profitable than running CRSs.

Until recently, most CRSs were unfairly biased against competing airlines' flights [4]. If the owner of the system has flights between the required cities, then its flights always appear first. So if a CRS were queried about flights between Los Angeles and Boston, it would list its own company's flights (which may stop in Chicago) first, even though a competitor may fly from Los Angeles to Boston non-stop. Thus the CRS will boost the owner's profitability at the expense of the customer. Whilst the controversy about the bias of CRSs has been settled in the United States, it is still a major international problem [4].

The control of CRSs has become so important to the airline industry that European and Asian consortia have been developed to thwart the dominance of American companies. Amadeus (Lufthansa, Air France, SAS, Iberia) and Galileo (British Airways, KLM, Swissair, Austrian Airlines, Alitalia, Aer Lingus) are the European newcomers, whilst Abacus (Cathay Pacific, Singapore Airlines, Thai International) and Fantasia (Qantas, JAL) are underway in Asia.

Whilst commercial PARS offers a lowest farefinder option, [3], CRSs are primarily reservation systems. Any passenger information they supply is secondary to their goals.

Thus, despite the competitiveness, and the high richness and complexity of CRSs, these systems do not provide comprehensive individual information and advice to the traveller. CATA complements CRSs by providing such information.

2.2. Artificial Intelligence Techniques in the Airline Industry

Most of the major uses of artificial intelligence in the airline industry have helped provide information to the airline. They have generally been involved in automated navigation and planning load factors.

Recently however, there has been some work performed on providing intelligent assistance for the prospective traveller.

2.2.1. Expert Systems

An expert system is a computer program using expert knowledge to attain high levels of performance in a narrow problem area.

Bose and Padala [5] have developed Globetrotter, a personal flight plan scheduler. It bases its decisions on the user's constraints which may include cost, class, flight times etc. Unfortunately the system also makes assumptions based on the user-provided information. The assumptions and other constraints are used to limit the search for an appropriate flight. Whilst this technique shortens the search space (an important step), it also, in our opinion, makes unwarranted assumptions about the traveller. Instead of querying the customer for his specific requests, it makes a naive model of the user (such as business or pleasure traveller), and provides an itinerary consistent with this model. For example, one of the rules is

R8: if (type-of-traveller (business traveller)) - >
then   (assumable (important (date-of-travel))),
         (assumable (important (time-of-travel))),
         (assumable (not (important (cost-of-travel)))),
         (assumable (important (town-of-origin))),
         (assumable (important (town-of-destination))).

CATA does not make a model of the traveller, and will therefore have a larger search space, but it will avoid making vague generalizations about the traveller. Globetrotter reasons with incomplete knowledge by constructing a model of the traveller. CATA does it by asking him for more rules and/or constraints.

2.2.2. Expert Databases

Deductive databases are a generalization of relational databases. They allow for rules (of the form 'if A then B') as well as facts, and by using the Domain Closure Axioms and the Closed World Assumption (see [6]), they allow inferences to be made about negative information.

The current version of CATA is written in PROLOG. Recently, there have been research teams developing languages specifically designed for implementing deductive databases. Two such languages are RDL1 [7], developed at INRIA in Rocquencourt, France and LDL [8], developed by M.C.C. in Austin, Texas. These languages are superior to PROLOG in their implementation of databases, because of their ability to handle sets (while Prolog only deals with a tuple at a time), and their ability to efficiently handle updates and objects. When these languages become commercially available, they may be used in the final version of CATA.

The heuristics of CATA draw on the airtravel expert database developed by Freitag and Biernath [9]. Its aim is to find optimal time flight connections between airports depending upon user-supplied constraints. It uses a number of important heuristics to reduce the search space:

(1) it searches for shortest paths, i.e. minimum number of nodes (connections);
(2) it restricts search to international airports;
(3) it does not leave the smallest geographic region common to the start and destination airport; and,
(4) it considers only the best connecting flights with respect to an overall flight time estimate.

These heuristics will be used in CATA, subject to the user-defined rules and constraints.

The air travel expert database is written as a deductive database, extended with LISP function calls and aggregate functions, and uses a relational database system MERKUR.

We shall extend Freitag and Biernath [9] by:

(1) providing for user rules and integrity constraints; and,
(2) providing intelligent advice to the user, by seeking his major goal, and then providing him with an optimal solution by possibly modifying some of his rules, and/or constraints.

3. CATA

CATA is an intelligent assistant to aid flight planning. It does not check whether seats are available on a given flight nor make reservations. It is written as a deductive database, and uses many of the heuristics of Freitag and Biernath [9].

3.1. CATA Facts

A copy of the International Official Airlines Guide is stored in a relational database in CATA. Also stored is a complete list of current prices, including each different class of flights.

CATA also requires a map of the world for three reasons:

(1) to compute the shortest distance between the town of origin and the town of destination;
(2) to determine all possible routes within the given constraints, between the town of origin and the town of destination; and,
(3) to allow the inference engine in CATA to deduce when two towns are 'sufficiently close together' so that if a traveller wishes to journey between points A and B, but his goal

is the lowest possible fare, then the engine may suggest he travel to point C to minimize his outlay.

3.2. The CATA Knowledge Base

The CATA knowledge base will include goals, rules and constraints. Each of these will be defined by the user.

Each traveller is asked to specify his major goal(s), for example, minimum cost, least number of connections, shortest flight time. A traveller may give his goals a priority ranking. He may, of course, have no goals.

Often a traveller is prepared to put up with extra inconvenience (e.g. paying more, having more connections or stopovers) if he can visit extra cities. For instance, he may wish to find the cheapest fare Melbourne-Paris-Melbourne. He may be prepared to pay an extra $400 if he can also visit Boston on his way back, and an extra $200 if his outward leg takes less than 26 hours and his return leg takes less than 22 hours.

CATA allows the user to input up to a fixed maximum number of rules. He may rank the rules, so that if a conflict occurs (in which case the system would report that no itinerary meets the traveller's requirements), then CATA would use the maximum number of rules that did not produce a conflict.

The traveller can also specify constraints, which will often involve negative information, for example:

(1) he will not fly Aeroflot or Air India or Pan American;

(2) he will not make a connection in an Arab country; and,

(3) no flight can be more than ten hours, and his total flying time must be no more than sixty hours.

Positive constraints can also be specified. For instance, a traveller may specify that he must stop in Honolulu.

3.3. The System

Given an input of start and destination airport, goals, rules and constraints, CATA will search the database, retrieving relevant information, and outputting it in decreasing value of the goals; for example in terms of increasing price.

CATA has a further reasoning capability. After the first search has been concluded, CATA will conduct a second search to see if the value(s) of the goal(s) can be increased by modifying or omitting some of the rules or constraints. For example, the value of the goal (decreasing the price) may be increased by flying into London rather than Paris.

How do we decide where to search for alternatives (B1, B2, ..., Bn) rather than flying into a city A, which the user specified? One way would be to consider all of those cities B with an international airport, lying within a predefined distance of A. However, there are often other more important criteria than the distance from Bi to A. Such criteria may include:

(1) the price of travelling from A to B;

(2) the time involved in travelling from A to B;

(3) the difficulty in travelling from A to B.

For instance, the traveller may wish to travel from Melbourne to Lugano (Switzerland) and return.   Whilst Milan is the closest airport, it has many disadvantages:

(1) it is in a different country, so would involve crossing international borders an extra two times;

(2) Milan airport has no station, so the traveller would have to catch a bus/taxi to the station;

(3) Zurich airport has a station with excellent connections to Lugano and most major European cities.

As well as having a database of distances between cities, CATA will also store a set of values $c(Ai,Aj)$, listing the convenience of travelling from Ai to Aj.   Initially these values will be inputted by the CATA systems programmers. Eventually it is hoped that CATA will have the ability to intelligently calculate the choice function c. To prune the database, we shall only consider those cities Bi lying within a predefined distance of A.

For the specific query specified above (Melbourne-Paris-Melbourne), the proposed itinerary may be:

Continental: Mel-NY-Paris-Bos-Hnl-Mel

Cost: $1803

- - - - - - - - - - - - - - - - - -)   further

- - - - - - - - - - - - - - - - - -)   solutions

- - - - - - - - - - - - - - - - - -)

BUT WHY NOT TRY

Continental: Mel-NY-Lon-Bos-Hnl-Mel

Cost: $1590

It is intended that CATA have a good user interface, by using natural language and having menu features. A detailed description of the CATA software will appear in a later paper.

4. DISCUSSION

To quote Woolley [2]:

Curiously, for such a technology-oriented industry, the airlines are not so far down the automation road as some other industries such as banking. In the 1980's, the airlines have failed to take advantage of many of the opportunities which technological development could provide.

Barry Tate, manager of industry automation for IATA (International Air Transport Association) has said:

> By failing to recognize the effect that automation is having, airlines will risk losing control of the marketing of their products. Arrival of third parties on the scene, with good computer and communications facilities, could radically alter the traditional methods of selling airline seats.

Because of the high competitiveness of banking (see Bodi and Zeleznikow, [10]), the customer is being given increasing control, especially with regard to electronic banking. Thus in banking the customer frequently interacts with computer systems (generally using Automated Teller Machines). Automated banking has the advantage that the major customer transaction is cash withdrawal, which can be done through an ATM. Home banking has not been successful, probably because it does not provide the facility to withdraw cash.

The trend to automation has taken a different complexion in the airline industry. To perform even the simplest transaction in most CRSs requires the availability of a trained operator. Most systems are very difficult to use. There are some minor exceptions. For instance, it is possible to buy a Boston-New York shuttle ticket through an automated vending machine by using a credit card, but the machine will not sell the cheaper tickets.

Thus, despite the competitiveness and huge richness of CRSs, in general they do not provide individual information and advice to the traveller. Whilst CATA does not provide reservations, it provides important advice. Good travel agents offer useful advice, but even the best could not match the accuracy and comprehensiveness of CATA. In particular, agents could not efficiently search a large dynamic database, and provide the unusual routes that most adequately fit the traveller's requests. They certainly could not give the alternative itineraries CATA provides.

CATA is an important tool in giving airlines a competitive edge. It might even have unexpected spinoffs, for example, in distributing passengers from the overloaded Oriental route to Europe, to a routing through the United States. Once one airline provided CATA to its clients, the others would be under pressure to follow.

CATA would be an invaluable aid to travel agents. It would allow them to quickly and efficiently plan a travel itinerary to meet their client's specifications.

REFERENCES

[1] Travel Agents on Trial, Choice (March 1988) 33-37.
[2] Woolley, D., Automation in the Airlines: An Essential Marketing Tool, Interavia 11 (1986) 1269-1271.
[3] Preble, C., Northwest, Trans World Discuss Joint Ownership of PARS System, Aviation Week and Space Technology (November 3, 1986) 93-95.
[4] Rek, B., Computer Reservations Controversy Spreads, Interavia 8 (1987) 819-820.

[5] Bose, P.K. and Padala, A.M.R., Reasoning with Incomplete Knowledge in an Interactive Personal Flight Planning Assistant, in: Proceedings Seventh Avignon Conference on Expert Systems (Avignon, France, 1987) pp. 1077-1092.

[6] Ullman, J.D., Principles of Database and Knowledge-Base Systems, Volume 1 (Computer Science Press, Rockville, Maryland, 1988).

[7] Simon, E. and De Maindreville, C., Deciding Whether a Production Rule is Relational Computable, in: Gyssens, M., Paredaens, J. and Van Gucht, D., (eds), Proceedings 2nd International Conference on Database Theory, Springer Lecture Notes in Computer Science, Volume 326 (Springer Verlag, Berlin, 1988) pp. 205-222.

[8] Zanioli, C., Design and Implementation of a Logic Based Language for Data Intensive Applications, in: Kowalski, R.A. and Bowen, K.A., (eds), Proceedings 5th International Conference on Logic Programming (M.I.T. Press, Boston, 1988) pp. 1666-1688.

[9] Freitag, B. and Biernath, O., An Airtravel Expert Database, in: Proceedings 3rd International Conference on Data and Knowledge Bases, Jerusalem, June, 1988, in print. Also available as Technical Report TUM-18804, Technische Universitat Munchen, Munich, West Germany (February 1988).

[10] Bodi, A. and Zeleznikow, J., Software Design for Electronic Banking: Managing the User-Computer Interface in: Proceedings 16th Annual ACM Computer Science Conference (ACM Press, New York, 1988) pp. 140-146.

Expert Systems in Economics, Banking and Management
L.F. Pau et al. (Editors)
© Elsevier Science Publishers B. V. (North-Holland), 1989

EXPERT SYSTEMS AND SOCIAL WELFARE BENEFITS REGULATIONS: THE BRAZILIAN CASE *

Celso Escobar Pinheiro and Daniel Schwabe

Departamento de Informática
Pontifícia Universidade Católica do Rio de Janeiro
R. M. de S. Vicente 225, Rio de Janeiro, RJ 22453
BRASIL

An expert system designed to determine entitlement and values of Social Welfare Benefits is presented. This system is also able to explain its reasoning and to give advice on how to proceed in order to become entitled when an applicant fails to conform to some rule.

1 INTRODUCTION

This paper describes an expert system designed to determine entitlement and values of Social Welfare Benefits, explain its reasoning and give advice on how to proceed in order to become entitled when an applicant fails to conform to some rule.

The Brazilian Social Welfare legislation is made of laws, rules and normative acts, compiled in three large books known as CLPS, RBPS and CANSB.

This legislation is applied by clerks at the Instituto Nacional de Previdência Social (INPS) which supplies them with a collection of handbooks containing step-by-step procedures on how to apply the law on most common cases and how to fill and dispatch the required forms. We will refer to those handbooks from now on as Benefit Regulations.

The project was contracted by the INPS in order to obtain a system to teach clerks about Benefit Regulations and help them give information about Benefit values to the general public. The main need for such a computer system was the fact that one could not, for example, simply ask an INPS clerk how much one's Benefit would be if one retires on a particular date. One would have to formally require it and go through the whole process of entitlement, having to resign oneself to the final results (if calculations were correctly done). Another problem was the fact that clerks often have different interpretations on the legislation when applied to cases not described in the Benefit Regulations.

There are three main types of Benefits: retirement, sickness leave and pension. Retirement has three modes: old age (65 year for men and 60 years for women), contribution time (30 years for men and 25 years for women) and special hazardous activities (15, 20 and 25 years of service).

Benefit values are calculated over a period of time known as PBC (Calculation Base Period) comprised of the most recent contributions to the INPS (last 12 or 36, depending on the case).

One can have many activities over which contribution is made to the Social Welfare system, at the same time, within the PBC. For this reason, it is necessary to establish a composition of non-concurrent activity periods known as the Main Activity. The remaining periods are called Secondary Activities and their contributions have a lower weight on the Benefit value calculations. Thus, the system must establish all permitted compositions in order to indicate their corresponding Benefit values.

Most of the problems found during the formalisation of the Benefits Regulations were due to misunderstandings between our generalizing and logical approach and the case-by-case regulations format. Another source of problems was the fact that several legal rules were ambiguous and incomplete, which required consensus from experts to be added to the system rules.

*This research was partially supported by a contract with DATAPREV.

The SIB (Benefits Information System) development was started on August 1986 and the final product was considered validated by the INPS on June 1987. It was developed in Prolog, using an extended *and/or* graph to represent the rules of the Benefit Regulations.

Other authors [2,4,6,11,12] have worked on the representation of legal rules as a logic program, although they were not intending to produce usable systems. Most recent works are from W.P.Sharpe (1984) that presented a Prolog representation for the Statutory Sick Pay provisions contained in the British Social Security and Housing Benefits Act ; M.J.Sergot (1985) that presented a formalization of the British Nationality Act ; and T.J.M.Bench-Capon, G.O.Robinson, T.W.Routen and M.J.Sergot (1987) that presented a formalization of the British Supplementary Benefit legislation.

2   FORMALIZING LEGISLATIONS

The "general" problem found when formalizing legislations is due to the open textured nature of the legal domain [7,9]. This means that in spite of the vast number of common cases handled by any legislation, there will always be a possibility of a case where that legislation does not apply smoothly, requiring some further interpretation or choice. This is directly related to the fact that any law is expressed in natural language, involving heavy commonsense understanding.

For this reason, the law is usually applied on the basis of past cases. To decide whether a specific rule does or does not apply to a case, the court discusses similarities and differences between current and past cases.

Obviously, this is not a proper domain for traditional rule- based systems application. However, there are many legal areas where the law is applied by clerks and in most of those cases there are written regulations on how to interpret the relevant law and how to execute its legal procedures.

This particular subset of the legal domain is what we found of interest for the development of expert systems since its "openings" can be carefully isolated from the deduction system by asking the user about those items which require any level of judgement.

Our experience showed that it is possible to start the knowledge acquisition process directly from the legal regulations of the target domain to a conceptual structure responsible for the organization of all the knowledge of the future system.

This process can be understood as an elaboration cycle that starts with the translation of conceptual rules to executable rules, followed by the execution of test cases. In the event of mismatch on the expected results, the first thing to be done is to review the coding of rules. If this does not solve the problem, there could have been misunderstandings between experts and designers that were reflected as ill-formed conceptual rules. In this case, rules should be reviewed with experts in order to detect errors and correct them. Sometimes the problem is due to Regulation omissions so, in this case, there must be a consensus between experts as to the modifications to be done on the conceptual rules in order to include their solutions in the system knowledge.

3   KNOWLEDGE REPRESENTATION

3.1   Conceptual Structure

The conceptual structure used for the development of the SIB was an extended *and/or* graph [14] where each node represents a conceptual rule and its direct descendants represent the necessary conditions to satisfy the rule. A node without descendants represents either a "raw" fact or a calculation procedure which is too obvious to be explained to the user by the final system. In other words, this graph contains all the necessary information to generate stylized explanations of the regulations.

A rule of the form

```
R if ( A and B ) or C
```

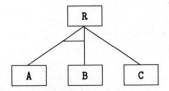

Figure 1: . *And/Or* graph for R if (A and B) or C

can be represented graphically as a graph node R and its descendants A, B and C as in Figure 1, where the union between arcs R–A and R–B indicate the conjunction of conditions A and B.

We have used explicit negation on nodes representing negative concepts. This led the system to handle only affirmative rules, which we think is a more "human" way of reasoning. In other words, if we have a rule, say,

A if (B and (not C)) or D

we would describe C instead of not C , stating that node C was a negative node on the conceptual graph. For example, we had a conceptual rule

Claimant has 60 contributions without loss of the insured status
IF:
  Claimant has 60 contributions between a certain date and the end of the PBC
AND
  Claimant did not loose the insured status between this date and the end of the PBC.

whose negative condition was trasformed to

(NOT) Claimant loose the insured status between this date and the end of the PBC.

The first condition above corresponds to an operation of counting backwards 60 months of contribution from a limit date (the end of the PBC), over a composition of periods of activity, determining the date that corresponds to the last contribution counted. This condition was considered as a "terminal" node as the system is not supposed to explain how to do counting operations.

The second condition generated a new rule that explains how a claimant looses his insured status instead of explaining how he does not loose it.

3.2 Rule Generation

The coding of conceptual rules was done in Prolog, requiring the introduction of parameters to represent factual values such as dates, periods of time, values of contributions, etc.

On the example given above, descriptions like a certain date and this date were substituted by formal parameters to eliminate ambiguity. This led to the following Prolog code:

```
has_60_contrib_without_status_loss (Activity) if
    has_60_contrib_between (Date,End_PBC,Activity) and
    not (status_loss_between (Date,End_PBC,Activity)).
```

The parameter Activity was included to allow the same predicate to handle all permitted compositions of activity periods for one claimant. At this level of abstraction, Activity represents a concept which is data independent. At lower levels, where it was necessary to manipulate its periods of time, we had to have in mind, when coding, the data structure used to represent such compositions.

Periods of time were described by functional symbols (functors) as:

```
date (Day,Month,Year)
month (Month,Year)
interval (date(D1,M1,Y1),date(D2,M2,Y2))
begin (date(Day,Month,Year))
end (date(Day,Month,Year)) .
```

Time was considered linearly and the mapping between calendar dates and integer numbers was made by a predicate

```
time (date(D,M,Y),N) .
```

We have also developed some basic predicates to handle basic temporal relations between periods of time, having been inspired by the event calculus and temporal logic of various authors [1,5,8,10,13]. For example, some functions defined are

before (Period1,Period2) is true if the last day from Period1 comes before the first day from Period2.

between (Period1,Period2) is true if the first day from Period1 comes after or is equal to the first day of Period2, and the last day from Period1 comes before or is equal to the last day from Period2.

before* (Period1,Period2) is true if the last day from Period1 comes before or is equal to the last day from Period2, and the first day from Period1 comes before the first day from Period2.

To clearly state the temporal aspect of relations involving time, we have described all of them by database facts of the form

```
holds (Relation,Period) .
```

To determine if a relation holds during a specific period of time, we have used the predicate

```
holds_on (Relation,Period) .
```

For example, let us suppose that a claimant had two jobs, one from May 10, 1973 to August 3, 1978 and the other from February 15, 1979 to December 20, 1987. Those facts can be represented by

```
holds (active (job_code(1)), interval (date(10,5,1973),date(3,8,1978)))
```

and

```
holds (active (job_code(2)), interval (date(15,2,1979),date(20,12,1987))) .
```

We could, by applying the predicate holds_on , deduct that

```
holds_on (active (job_code(1)), month(10,1978))
```

is false and

```
holds_on (active (job_code(2)), date(10,4,1983))
```

is true.

Let us now illustrate the methodology employed by taking a closer look at some Benefit Regulations. Item 2.1.c from BS/INPS/DG of 12-10-81 establishes that the INPS clerk must verify "if the claimant ceased to contribute for more than 12 months counted from the end of his job (...) to the date of requirement."

Item 2.1.d says:

"if the answer to item 2.2.c is affirmative, extend the term (...) up to 24 months for the claimant who has paid 120 or more contributions, without occurrence of an interval without contributions that brings on the loss of the insured status."

Item 2.11 says:

"the loss of the insured status will occur after the 2nd. month following the expiration of terms indicated in items 2.2.c and 2.2.d (...)."

Those concepts were represented in the conceptual graph as:

[Rule 131]
The loss of the insured status between a date D and the end of the PBC occurs
IF:
[Rule 140]There exists an interval which is the largest of all existing intervals
          without contributions between these dates
AND
[Rule 141] The interval brings on the loss of the insured status.

It should be noted that rule 140 was not explicit on the regulations text, having been included after discussions with legal experts, as the text refers only to intervals occuring after the end of the last activity.

Rule 141 was expressed as:

[Rule 141]
The interval brings on the loss of the insured status
IF:
[Rule 150] The interval is greater than 14 months
AND
[Rule 151] The interval is equal or less than 26 months
AND
[Rule 152](NOT) There are 120 or more contributions up to the beginning of the interval,
          without intervals that bring on the loss of the insured status
OR
[Rule 153] The interval is greater than 26 months.

Curiously, there is a recursive concept on the above Regulation, which was represented inside rule 152 by the string the loss of the insured status , characterizing a graph structure.

The translation to Prolog predicates was done quite straightforwardly:

```
status_loss_between (D1,D2,Activity) if
    largest_interval_between (D1,D2,Activity,Interval) and
    brings_on_status_loss (Interval,Activity).
brings_on_status_loss (interv(Begin,Months),Activity) if
    Months > 14 and
    Months <= 26 and
    not (have_120_contrib_by (Begin,Activity)) and !.
brings_on_status_loss (interv(_,Months),_) if
    Months > 26 and !.
```

Rules like `largest_interval_between` are what we called "procedural rules" that is, their bodies do not represent any concepts derived from the conceptual structure as their corresponding nodes have no descendants. For this kind of rule, Prolog was used as a procedural programming language, making heavy use of lists, backtracking and recursion, loosing its "naturelness" and data structure independence.

3.3   Explanation Structure

The SIB, as built, included an internal representation of the *and/or* graph which was used as a basis for explanations about the Benefit Regulations.

Each node of the graph was represented by a database predicate of the form

```
node (Code,Type,Descendants,Text)
```

where `Code` is an arbitrary integer number ; `Type` is a symbol that states if it is an affirmative or negative node ; `Descendants` is a list where each element is a sub-list containing the codes of the nodes that compose a conjunction of conditions to satisfy the node corresponding rule ; `Text` is a string of characters that contains the text for the node condition.

On the previous example, the corresponding node for rule 141 was represented by

```
node (141,aff,[[150,151,152],[153]],''The interval brings on
     the loss of insured status'')
```

An interface with the user was provided to allow him to "navigate" through the graph, inspecting each rule at a time. This was accomplished by means of an "interpreter" responsible for the adequate concatenation of texts contained in each node, restoring the original conceptual rule.

Another type of explanation required by the INPS was a detailed report about the deduction steps that justify the system results. As this report would be given to Benefit claimants we have standardized its format and supressed many intermediary deduction steps that would be of no practical interest to the public.

To achieve this result we have introduced, in the relevant rules, special database predicates designed to record "history" facts during the execution of the system rules, allowing its later recovery at report time. For example, on the predicate

```
satisfies_retirement_conditions (Mode,MST,Class,N) if
    (...)
    option (N,36,[Main|_]) and
    satisfies_minimum_contrib (60,Main) and
    assertz (hist_contrib (N,36)) and
    satisfies_specific_conditions (N,Main,Mode,MST,Class).
```

the command `assertz` creates a fact whose presence on the database represents that the claimant has paid the minimum of 60 contributions on the `option` (composition of activities) with code N and a PBC of 36 months.

At report time, for each database option , the system verifies if there is a corresponding `hist_contrib` fact. If this does not happen, it indicates the failure of `satisfies_minimum_contrib` predicate and a message ''The minimum required number of contributions was not satisfied on this option.'' is printed, justifying the refusal to the claimant.

We have developed a prototype version of the SIB allowing interative explanation about each deduction step. To obtain this result, we introduced a mechanism to record an internal representation of the rules execution graph, including key- parameter values and descriptions. It should be noted that this solution was adopted because we had no access to the internals of the interpreter itself, and no "meta-predicates".

Each node of this graph was represented by a database fact

```
ex (Code,Result,Param_List,Descendants)
```

where `Code` is the integer number associated to each executed rule ; `Result` is a symbol that indicates success or failure of the rule's corresponding predicate ; `Param_List` is a list where each member is a functor

```
par (Text,Value)
```

where `Text` is a string that describes the meaning of a parameter of the referred predicate and `Value` is its content ; and `Descendants` is a list where each member represents the result of the execution of each condition of the referred predicate by means of a functor

```
res (Code,Result,Param_List)
```

where each of its parameters has the same meaning described above, but applied to each rule condition.

As it was not possible to modify our Prolog inference mechanism, it was necessary to modify predicates that represent conceptual rules in order to implement the control mechanism for the "trace" facts generation. For example, rule 131 predicate previously shown was changed to

```
status_loss_between (Cod,D1,D2,Activity) if
    RC = 131 and
    begin (RC) and
    largest_interval_between (RC,D1,D2,Activity,Interval) and
    brings_on_status_loss (RC,Interval,Activity) and
    !  and
    push (res (RC,true,[par (''date D'',D1),
                        par (''end of PBC'',D2)],Cod).
status_loss_between (Cod,D1,D2,_) if
    RC = 131 and
    !  and
    push (res (RC,false,[par (''date D'',D1),
                         par (''end of PBC'',D2)],Cod) and
    fail.
```

The initialization procedure is made by the predicate

```
begin (Rule_Code) if
    asserta (ex (Rule_Code,start,[],[])).
```

and the push (Result,Cod) predicate acts in two levels of the rules execution graph: it appends the res functor to the list of results from the ex fact with code Cod (the superior level) , and it records the result (true or false) and the key- parameter descriptions and values (the par functors) on the ex fact with code RC (the current level) .

The additional failing clause had to be included to allow the recording of predicate failure results with their corresponding parameters values.

The original explanation "interpreter" was slightly modified to show, after each rule test, its corresponding execution result and, after each of its conditions, a message stating if it failed, succeeded or was not tested. In the case of having been tested, the condition's parameters texts and values are also shown.

For example, an explanation about the execution of rule 131 had the following text, when considering an hypotetical case where the claimant has lost his insured status:

WHY the condition [Rule 131]
"The loss of the insured status between a date D and the end of the PBC occurs"
was satisfied ?
To satisfy this condition it is necessary that
[Rule 140]There exists an interval which is the largest of all existing intervals
            without contributions between those dates
≫ the condition above was satisfied.
            ≫ date D = 05/07/81
            ≫ end of PBC = 30/11/87
            ≫ interval beginning = 15/03/84
            ≫ months in interval = 28
AND
[Rule 141] The interval brings on the loss of the insured status
≫ the condition above was satisfied.
            ≫ interval beginning = 15/03/84
            ≫ months in interval = 28

The structure behind this system output is the database fact

```
ex(131,true,[par(''date D'',date(5,7,1981)),
            par(''end of PBC'',date(30,11,1987))],
   [res(140,true,[par(''date D'',date(5,7,1981)),
                  par(''end of PBC'',date(30,11,1987)),
                  par(''interval beginning'',date(15,3,1984)),
                  par(''months in interval'',28)]),
    res(141,true,[par(''interval beginning'',date(15,3,1984)),
                  par(''months in interval'',28)])])
```

This explanation structure allows the user to investigate either why a certain condition was
satisfied or why it has failed. On both cases, the system will show all the corresponding rule conditions
and their execution results, so the user can go on looking for further explanations until he is satisfied
or he comes to rules where no explanations are given because they reflect commonsense knowledge
(as judged by the experts) or "raw" facts.

3.4   Advice Giving

There are certain types of information that cannot be derived from the results obtained from the
deduction process [4], for example, questions about how to proceed in order to conform to the
conditions of a rule that was not satisfied.

We have solved this problem by creating additional "advice rules" directly associated with rules
that express concepts that were potentially questionable in that sense.

For example, the conceptual "advice rule" for the case where the claimant does not have the
minimum number of contributions required for entitlement was:

[Rule 200]
To calculate the number of additional contributions required for entitlement
IT IS NECESSARY:
[Rule 210]To determine the last interval without contributions that has brought
            on the loss of the insured status
AND
[Rule 220] To count the number of contribution months occurred after the end of
            this interval

AND

[Rule 230] To subtract the number of contribution months just counted, from the minimum number of contributions required for entitlement.

The conclusion to the execution of the above example rule is the message

Conclusion of [Rule 200]:

IT IS NECESSARY TO CONTRIBUTE FOR ADDITIONAL 43 MONTHS !

The user can ask the system, at any moment during explanations, how to proceed to satisfy a rule by typing a command followed by the rule's code. If there is a corresponding "advice rule", it is executed and its code and conclusions are shown on the screen. If not, the message No advice for this rule is printed.

As those rules have the same pattern as regular rules, the user can also investigate their deduction steps in the same way already described.

4 CONCLUSION

The SIB has 3 modules: one for the acquisition of claimant data, one for the execution of rules and presentation of results and justifications, and one for explanations about Benefit Regulations. The Prolog code has around 8200 lines and the executable code requires aproximately 500 Kbytes of memory on an IBM PC compatible machine.

The conceptual structure is an extended *and/or* graph developed on the basis of the explanations to be given by the system to the user. The final system graph has 294 nodes and its conceptual rules correspond to 175 Prolog predicates.

The SIB was a success in terms of its performance on real cases and also in terms of the adequacy of its rule coding based on the explanation conceptual structure. It showed that it is worthwhile using logic programming for the representation of legal regulations.

5 REFERENCES

1. Allen, J.F., Towards a general theory of action and time, *Artificial Intelligence* No.23 (1984), pp. 123-154.

2. Bench-Capon, T.J.M., Robinson, G.O., Routon, T.W. and Sergot, M.J., Logic Programming for large scale applications in Law: a formalisation of Supplementary Benefit Legislation, Imperial College of Science and Technology, London, 1987.

3. Hart, H.L.A., *The Concept of Law*, Oxford, Clarendon Press, 1961, pp. 124-125.

4. Hustler, A., Programming Law in Logic, Research Report CS-82-13, 1982, Department of Computer Science, University of Waterloo.

5. Lee,R.M., Coelho,H. and Cotta,J.C., Temporal Inferencing on Administrative Databases, *Information Systems*, Vol.10, No.2, Pergamon Press Ltd., 1985, pp. 197-206.

6. McCarthy, L.T., Reflections on TAXMAN: An experiment in Artificial Intelligence and Legal Reasoning, *Harvard Law Review* 90, 1977, pp. 837-893.

7. Popp, W.G. and Schlink, B., JUDITH, a computer program to advise lawyers in reasoning a case,*Jurimetrics Journal* 15, 1975, pp. 303-314.

8. Rich, E., *Artificial Intelligence*, McGraw-Hill Book Co., 1983.

9. Rissland, E., AI and Legal reasoning - report of a panel, *Proceedings of the Ninth International Joint Conference on AI* , Los Angeles, California, 1985, pp. 1254-1260.

10. Sadri, F., Three recent approaches to Temporal Reasoning, DOC 86/23, Department of Computing, Imperial College, London.

11. Sergot, M.J., Representing Legislation as Logic Programs, 1985, Technical Report, Department of Computing, Imperial College of Science and Technology, London.

12. Sharpe, W.P., Logic Programming for the Law, Research and development in Expert Systems, *Proceedings of the Fourth Technical Conference of the British Computer Society Specialist Group on Expert Systems* , University of Warwick, 18-20 December 1984, pp. 217-228.

13. Shoham, Y., Temporal logics in AI: semantical and ontological considerations ,*Artificial Intelligence* No.33 (1987), pp. 89-104.

14. Winston,P.H.,*Artificial Intelligence*, Addison-Wesley Publishing Co., 1984, pp. 182-187.

Expert Systems in Economics, Banking and Management
L.F. Pau et al. (Editors)
© *Elsevier Science Publishers B. V. (North-Holland), 1989*

THE DYNAMIC RESCHEDULER:
CONQUERING THE CHANGING PRODUCTION ENVIRONMENT*

MATHILDE C. BROWN**

Andersen Consulting, Arthur Andersen & Co.
33 West Monroe Ave.
Chicago, IL 60603

ABSTRACT

The Dynamic Rescheduler (DR) is an automated assistant for managing change and adjusting an active schedule to accommodate new events in the production environment. The application provides a shop floor supervisor with an intelligent rescheduling assistant that is capable of considering more alternatives in a limited amount of time than is manually possible. This intelligent aid uses techniques of hypothetical reasoning and constraint-based rescheduling to generate alternative adjusted schedules. Using heuristics and rescheduling knowledge, DR generates alternatives, tests them for feasibility, and evaluates them against the current set of goals. The application allows a supervisor to react intelligently and on a timely basis to changes on the shop floor. This chapter describes the reactive scheduling problem, investigates alternative solutions to the problem, and discusses the architecture, knowledge, and processing details of the Dynamic Rescheduler solution.

1. INTRODUCTION

Reacting to changes and new requirements on the shop floor is a serious problem in today's factories. In fact, many companies have to reschedule up to 80 percent of their planned production. The Dynamic Rescheduler (DR) uses techniques of hypothetical reasoning and constraint-based rescheduling to solve reactive scheduling problems. The first part of this chapter will introduce shop floor scheduling and the reactive scheduling problem. A discussion of potential solutions, including various AI techniques, will follow. The next section will examine the technical aspects of DR and explain how the application would solve a typical reactive scheduling problem. Finally, the last section will describe future development directions.

2. SHOP FLOOR SCHEDULING

Scheduling the production of orders is a vital step in planning and controlling the production environment. The scheduling problem involves allocating resources over time to perform a set of tasks [2]. In the manufacturing environment, scheduling is the assignment

---

* Much of the material presented in this paper was previously presented at the 3rd IEEE Conference on Applications of Artificial Intelligence, San Diego, 1988.
** Currently at Stanford University, Palo Alto, CA.
  Electronic Mail Address: MBrown@sumex-aim.stanford.edu

of jobs or work orders to work centers on the shop floor for a given period. Based on scheduling decisions, work orders can be completed, and planned production is possible.

Once production is scheduled for a period, a monitoring and control function is necessary. This function ensures that the schedule is being met by comparing the work order status and machine status to the schedule. The monitoring and control of production is potentially affected by several objectives. One objective may be to meet scheduled due dates whenever possible. Another may be to maximize resource utilization. If problems occur, they must be handled and their effects minimized to ensure prompt customer service and high product quality. The shop floor must be able to respond quickly to demands and changes.

3.   THE REALITY - THE NEED FOR RESCHEDULING

In addition to meeting these production objectives, shop floor personnel responsibilities often include the following:

- Controlling the flow of orders through the work centers
- Keeping others aware of changes in due dates and order requirements
- Acting as a liaison between automated manufacturing systems and the shop floor
- Evaluating the feasibility of order completion in view of current conditions
- Ensuring all work is completed on time [8].

Because of this large load of responsibilities, personnel on the shop floor would be better able to respond to problems if manufacturing activities occurred as planned. However, no matter how well planned the original short-term schedule is, the shop floor is too dynamic for a plan to be valid for an entire day or even a single shift. Machine reliability, operator and tooling availability, and changes in the demand and order requirements all contribute to scheduling and shop floor problems. Because the schedule is generated as a plan to utilize given resources, conflicts result when resource changes occur. For example, it was recently reported that typically 16 percent of scheduled production cannot be met because tooling is not available [7].

Adjusting the schedule to accommodate unexpected situations, changes in order requirements, and other environmental conditions is known as rescheduling or reactive scheduling. Various research [6,9] has shown that the need for rescheduling is commonly due to the following situations:

- Changes in customer request dates
- Late deliveries
- Engineering changes
- Erratic yield from production
- Resource unavailability (i.e., tooling, operators, down equipment)

Although rescheduling on the production floor is a problem for many companies and may be required for as much as 80 percent of the work orders [6], most companies do not have a formal approach to rescheduling. Typically, rescheduling decisions are made quickly and with a limited amount of information and analysis. If a machine goes down in a traditional environment, the processing time for the current operation is often increased to handle the problem. This usually results in missed due dates. If a rush order is received, it is merely placed on a machine without regard for the best placement or the resulting bumped orders. Although the rescheduling problem becomes temporarily subdued, the quick manual solution chosen may have detrimental side effects and long-term consequences, such as missed due dates and an increase in work-in-process.

4.   PRESENT SOLUTIONS

Many potential automated solutions for shop floor reactive scheduling have been investigated. One approach is to treat rescheduling as a scheduling problem and to use existing scheduling technology to address it. But many of the approaches to automated scheduling have not provided complete solutions. For example, research has provided optimal solutions that minimize mean flow time for certain shop floor scenarios, such as the open shop, one-machine problem [9]. But these shop floor configurations rarely exist in actual production environments. A number of other scheduling approaches, such as MRP-II and dispatching rules, have been shown to be useful for specific parts of the problem, but have not yielded complete scheduling solutions on their own. Some of these approaches are described below.

4.1.   MRP-II

A Material Requirements Planning (MRP-II) system can develop a long- term master production schedule. However, the underlying techniques cannot be used to generate a feasible short-term schedule (a schedule for a week or other short length of time). This is because a system scheduling for the short-term (or rescheduling) must generate a feasible plan, i.e., one that uses only available resources. Availability restrictions, however, imply utilizing finite capacity scheduling techniques instead of the infinite resource capacity assumptions made by most MRP-II systems.

4.2.   Dispatching Rules

Various dispatching rules (also referred to as priority rules, or rules for selecting the next order for a work center) have been used as part of some scheduling systems. For example, many companies select the next order for production based on the due dates of the orders. However, exclusive use of priority rules may result in an inflexible and incomplete solution. It has been shown that priority rules are best for specific circumstances and should be chosen to suit definite goals [4]. Also, many automated priority rules do not handle nonquantitative factors. Factors such as the importance of the customer, the nature of the order, and whether the order is for a customer or for safety stock inventory are difficult to represent and incorporate with priority rule techniques [9].

4.3.   Heuristics

Both of the previous techniques suffer from the combinatorics of the scheduling problem. When selecting the next job for a machine, optimal solutions theoretically can be found in a finite number of computational iterations. However, it has been shown that as the size of the problem grows and becomes more realistic in terms of machines and orders, the amount of time it takes to arrive at an optimal solution is too long to be feasible. The combinatorics involved when a system tries to find an optimal short-term schedule make the problem too large to solve using only the above techniques.

To counteract these problems, considerable work has been conducted with heuristics. Most schedulers or dispatchers use simple heuristics on a daily basis to solve their scheduling and rescheduling needs. Incorporating some of these simple rules into automated scheduling systems has yielded solution methods better equipped to handle large problems. As Melnyk notes, "Since little progress has been made in finding optimal solution procedures for models of realistic size, the search for and investigation of simple, effective, but nonoptimizing decision rules remains an important research thrust" [9].

4.4.   AI Solutions

More recently, artificial intelligence (AI) techniques have been used successfully to solve shop floor scheduling problems. For example, the PEPS prototype uses a data base of priority dispatching rules and selects the appropriate one for an existing scheduling context [12]. This offers multiple priority rule alternatives for varying circumstances. ISA was the first operational AI-based scheduling system. ISA allocates plant capacity and inventory to orders to provide firm delivery dates to customers of DEC [10].

Some of the AI techniques used to solve scheduling problems include rule-based reasoning, constraint-directed search, and frame-based representation. One of the more recent research areas is constraint-based scheduling. The shop floor domain has many potentially conflicting constraints. To schedule production in this situation, constraints must be selectively relaxed. Thus, the problem solving strategy must be one of finding the best solution that meets a subset of the constraints. Constraints can serve to restrict the number of alternatives considered and to assist in selecting the best solution [5,13].

Opportunistic reasoning allows the most promising activities to be performed depending on the existing problem state. This additional AI technique has proven successful when intelligent focusing of problem solving is desirable, as is the case with scheduling problems [11].

However, modeling the scheduling system after the human scheduler does not provide the best automated solution. Human scheduling decisions are usually made as a reaction to a crisis. Also, the decisions are often locally greedy, or solve only the immediate situation without consideration of other areas or the resulting effects [14]. An AI system in this area should not seek to replicate the human scheduler or supervisor, but to extend his capabilities by doing more problem solving than was manually possible.

To summarize, many AI techniques have been used successfully to help solve the scheduling problem. Other traditional techniques, such as priority rules, have proven successful for portions of the scheduling problem. These techniques must be combined and used together to develop an integrated scheduling solution. Arthur Andersen & Co. has developed the foundation for an integrated AI-based application that combines many of these techniques to address the unique requirements of reactive scheduling. A brief summary of the problem area and a description of this application follow.

5. CONQUERING THE RESCHEDULING PROBLEM

Most rescheduling decisions are made manually. Often, in the short time frame a shop floor supervisor has available to react to a change in the production environment, the supervisor does not consider long- term consequences of manual schedule adjustments. An automated rescheduling system could be used to aid the supervisor in responding to changes and new situations by considering a number of alternative schedules that accommodate the change and by recommending the 'best' alternative.

The Dynamic Rescheduler (DR), an automated rescheduling application, has short-term schedule information from an area controller or other scheduling function. It receives messages regarding problems such as a down cell or a new or rush order; these messages are received from the controller or manually entered into the system. The system then adjusts the active schedule to respond to the problem, and displays the best adjusted schedule to the supervisor for confirmation.

The application was developed by two people over a six-month period on Symbolics and DEC hardware. It is built on the Automated Reasoning Tool (ART™) software from Inference Corp. The following sections will describe the architecture, knowledge, and processing details of the Dynamic Rescheduler application.

6. ARCHITECTURE

Figure 1 shows a model of DR. A flexible window-oriented interface allows the user to interact with the system. Emergency messages can be input to the system manually through the user interface, or downloaded from the controller. The user interface consists of a hierarchy of windows and conversations for various production problems. It uses a familiar Gantt chart display of the schedule information, which graphically shows how jobs have been scheduled over work centers in an area. In addition to the schedule display, other windows also display information to the user. Responses are input via the keyboard or mouse.

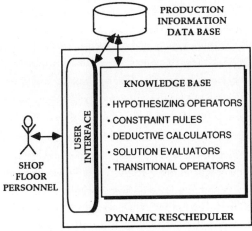

Figure 1

The knowledge base consists of domain-specific rescheduling knowledge in rule format. (The detailed rule hierarchy and structure will be discussed later.) The knowledge base also contains the control strategy of the rescheduling process. The declarative knowledge in the data base consists of schemata representing the schedule information, work order requirements, cell information, and product details that have been downloaded or input by the user.

7.   RESCHEDULING KNOWLEDGE

The rescheduling knowledge of DR is based in part on the approaches to scheduling described in the previous section. It consists of portions of MRP-II and dispatching rule techniques as well as heuristics and AI approaches to scheduling. The structure of the rescheduling knowledge in DR is similar to the following two levels of decision-making in scheduling as defined by Ow and Smith:

- Strategic level: Within a particular scheduling scenario, strategies and goals may differ
- Tactical level: Alternative ways of achieving the strategies [11].

DR's knowledge can be categorized into goals, which are similar to the strategic level of goals and preferences of the system, and heuristics, which are the tactical level rules and operators for achieving the goals.

7.1.   Goals

Within the strategic level of decision-making, various goals may exist and may be pursued at different times. These goals can be similar to the criteria by which traditional dispatching rules have been judged, such as the following factors:

- Job lateness with respect to due dates
- Percentage of jobs late
- Work-in-process inventory
- Machine utilization
- Schedule stability

DR has many production goals, similar to those mentioned above, to guide its rescheduling. The most important goal is to meet due dates, or minimize tardiness. This is achieved with an iterative process of constraint relaxation. The application's secondary goal is to maximize the schedule stability. The stability goal can be met by fixing the active schedule as much as possible. Yamamoto and Nof found that their scheduling/rescheduling approach, which was fixing the existing schedule prior to rescheduling around a down machine, was more successful than other scheduling approaches for the same problem [15]. DR also fixes as much of the existing schedule as possible when rescheduling. The amount the schedule is fixed can be adjusted by relaxing this constraint as needed.

As illustrated in Figure 2, the system enters the most constrained goal state first. For example, the first goal state, which corresponds to an active rule set, may be to meet all due dates by fixing the schedule. If no alternative schedules can be found, the next less-constrained goal state is entered by using a transition network approach to control and constraint relaxation. This process continues until the system selects a feasible rescheduling solution. However, if the system is unable to reschedule because the amount of rescheduling necessary is excessive, it is best simply to schedule again starting from a blank slate.

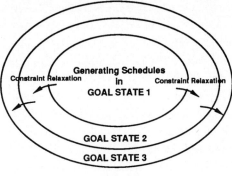

Figure 2

7.2.   Heuristics

The rescheduling knowledge of DR consists of a rule base of knowledge and incorporates many of the previously mentioned techniques. Using techniques of hypothetical reasoning and constraint-based rescheduling, the system identifies the best schedule with the least detrimental long-term consequences. The application also utilizes opportunistic reasoning in its rule base. All of the rules, which are described below, can be active at the same time. Thus, if a rule is applicable in the current context of rescheduling, it will be placed on the agenda.

The rescheduling knowledge of the system is divided into the following types of rules:

a. **Hypothesizing operators**. The hypothesizing operators are rules that generate alternative hypothetical schedules. Given an active schedule and a new situation in the production environment, they generate all of the possible schedules that accommodate the change. These rules perform schedule manipulation depending on the current goal state. Thus, the hypothesizing operators are part of the tactical level of decision-making in the system. These rules are responsible for generating the alternatives that potentially meet the current goals or strategies.

b. **Deductive calculators**. The deductive calculators calculate and determine facts, such as an estimated end time of an order based on its start time and production duration over a cell.

c. **Constraint rules**. The constraint rules evaluate each alternative generated by the operators. Those not meeting particular constraints for the current goal state will be eliminated. These rules have the greatest potential influence in the application. If a constraint is ever violated, the appropriate rule will fire to ensure that the infeasible alternative is eliminated from further consideration.

Various constraints may be active depending on the goal state of the system. Again, these constraints are implemented in rules that opportunistically fire when a conflict develops while rescheduling in a certain goal state. Some of the schedule restrictions used by DR follow. The first three are discussed by Smith, et al. [13].

- Causal Restrictions: Precedent constraints on the order of   operations
- Physical Constraints: Functional restrictions; for example, certain machines can produce certain part types, or they can produce only one part at a time
- Resource Unavailability: A down or previously scheduled cell or machine
- Temporal Restrictions: The order due date in some situations, for example

d. **Solution evaluators**. Alternatives that satisfy all of the constraints are feasible and potential rescheduling solutions. The solution evaluators judge the alternative solutions and select the 'best' one for the current goal state based on various heuristics. This is an additional set of rules at the tactical level of scheduling decision-making in the application.

e. **Transitional operators**.   The transitional operators relax constraints when necessary and perform the transitions between processing and goal states.

When the application enters a goal state, the hypothesizing operators generate alternative schedules using any calculations necessary from the deductive calculators. The constraint rules constantly evaluate the alternatives for feasibility. Once all feasible schedules are generated, the solution evaluators select the best solution. If no alternatives are feasible, the transitional operators relax constraints and enable the application to enter a different goal state to attempt to generate more alternative solutions.

The above rules contain some additional heuristics for rescheduling. Both backward and forward scheduling techniques are used when placing rescheduled orders. Also, if multiple orders must be rescheduled, the system ranks the orders by priority, if priorities have been specified. If not, then the orders are ranked for rescheduling by relative urgency. This is consistent with an MRP-II planning system. Additional heuristics are used to shift orders on the schedule and to evaluate alternative solutions during rescheduling.

The time representation utilized allows the system to manipulate order sequences such as 'before' another order, 'after' another order, and 'in conflict' with another order (containing, during, and overlap) [1].

8. TYPICAL SCENARIO

This section describes an example of how the system would be used. An MRP-II master production schedule is produced assuming infinite capacity for a long time period by another function. A short-term schedule is developed either manually or automatically for a period. If a change occurs while the short-term schedule is being followed, the information is sent to DR automatically or input by the user. For example, if a cell goes down in the area, that information is input, along with an estimated down time. The system displays the active schedule in Gantt chart format to the user, and then determines the impact of the new information. The affected schedule is displayed and the user can request DR to reschedule.

The rescheduling knowledge is then activated. If the down cell causes multiple orders to be bumped, they all must be rescheduled. DR ranks them by priority or relative urgency. The highest priority or most urgent order is rescheduled first. DR initially tries to reschedule by affecting as little of the schedule as possible. The active schedule is fixed and various heuristic hypothesizing operators determine and construct all possible ways of placing the first bumped order. If rescheduling is not possible by leaving the existing schedule as is, the constraints are relaxed. The system enters the next goal state and tries to reschedule by moving other orders within their due date time frames. The alternatives generated are evaluated by potential performance based on current goals. If no feasible alternatives are generated, then the meeting-due-dates constraint is further relaxed. If rescheduling was possible and all bumped orders have been rescheduled, the best alternative schedule is displayed to the user for confirmation.

In summary, the architecture and the knowledge of DR incorporate many heuristic and AI techniques. The application provides the shop floor supervisor with an intelligent scheduling assistant that is capable of considering many more alternatives than manually possible. The supervisor is able to react intelligently and on a timely basis to changes on the shop floor.

9. FUTURE PLANS

The system in its current implementation provides a solid framework for a customized reactive scheduling system. Depending on the specific needs of users and their shop floors, the system will be customized with specific preferences and constraints. The integration requirements will also be unique to a plant location. Additionally, many possible enhancements for future development have been identified.

The system is currently equipped to respond to inconsistencies. When an emergency has rendered the original schedule invalid, rescheduling is invoked. However, it does not identify areas for schedule improvement automatically. Changes in the production environment do not always require rescheduling. They may indicate a possible schedule change that would improve the performance of the schedule in a key area. Thus, incorporating this type of ability into DR would provide additional benefit to a user.

A major development and research thrust is to investigate the applicability and feasibility of incorporating machine learning capabilities into DR. A rescheduling system that could learn additional constraints and rules from the user would obviously be a more flexible assistant to a supervisor or other shop floor personnel. Various techniques of machine learning, such as explanation-based learning and apprentice techniques, are currently being researched. One approach or a combination of approaches will be developed for DR.

10. CONCLUSIONS

DR demonstrates the power of heuristic techniques as well as the applicability of AI techniques to the scheduling problem. The foundation for a customized rescheduling application has been laid. The application will be customized in the future for specific users with the rescheduling knowledge and heuristics of a particular shop floor. Some of the above enhancements will also be incorporated into the system. With a combination of priority rules, heuristics, constraint-based scheduling, and other AI techniques, the Dynamic Rescheduler illustrates a feasible solution to the rescheduling problem.

ACKNOWLEDGEMENTS

Lisa Canapari Curtis was a major contributor to the development of the Dynamic Rescheduler. Thanks also to the rest of the project team, Beth Quevillon, Bruce Johnson, and Sue Kellom for their contributions to this application. Special thanks to Brad Allen for his expertise and guidance. Thanks also to Chun Ka Mui, Bill McCarthy, Beth Quevillon, and Larry Downes for their constructive criticism of this paper and to John Lawler for the graphics work in this paper.

REFERENCES

[1] Allen, James F., "Maintaining Knowledge About Temporal Intervals", Communications of the ACM, Vol. 26, No. 11, Nov. 1983, pp. 832-843.
[2] Baker, Kenneth R., Introduction to Sequencing and Scheduling. John Wiley & Sons, Inc., 1974.
[3] Blackstone, J. H., Jr., D. T. Phillips, and G. L. Hogg, "A State-of-the-Art Survey of Dispatching Rules for Manufacturing Job Shop Operations" International Journal of Production Research, Vol. 20, No. 1, 1982, pp. 27-45.
[4] Conway, Richard W., "Priority Dispatching and Job Lateness in a Job Shop", Journal of Industrial Engineering, Vol. 16, No. 4, July-August 1965, pp. 228-237.
[5] Fox, Mark S. and Stephen F. Smith, "ISIS - A Knowledge Based System for Factory Scheduling", Expert Systems, Vol. 1, No. 1, 1984, pp. 25-49.
[6] Hall, R. W., "The Rescheduling Problems: Nemesis or Opportunity?", Midwest AIDS 1975 Conference Proceedings, Cincinati, 1975.
[7] Mason, F., "Computerized Cutting-Tool Management", American Machinists & Automated Manufacturing, Vol. 130, No. 5, May 1986, pp. 105-132.
[8] Melnyk, Steven A. and Phillip L. Carter, Production Activity Control: A Practical Guide. Dow Jones-Irwin, Homewood, IL, 1987, pp. 51-100.
[9] Melnyk, S. A., P. L. Carter, D. M. Dilts, and D. M. Lyth, Shop Floor Control. Dow Jones-Irwin, Homewood, IL, 1985, pp. 157-216.
[10] Orciuch, E. and J. Frost, "ISA: Intelligent Scheduling Assistant", First Conference on Artificial Intelligence Applications, IEEE Computer Society, December 1984, pp. 314-320.
[11] Ow, Peng Si and Stephen F. Smith, "Towards an Opportunistic Scheduling System" Nineteenth Annual Hawaii International Conference on System Sciences, Honolulu, HI, January 1986.
[12] Robbins, James H., "PEPS: The Prototype Expert Priority Scheduler.", AUTOFACT 1985 Conference Proceedings, November 1985, pp. 13-10 - 13-34.
[13] Smith, Stephen F., Mark S. Fox, and Peng Si Ow, "Constructing and Maintaining Detailed Production Plans: Investigations into the Development of Knowledge-Based Factory Scheduling Systems" AI Magazine, Fall 1986, pp. 45- 61.
[14] Steffen, Mitchell S., "A Survey of AI-Based Scheduling Systems", Fall Industrial Engineering Conference, Boston, December 1986.
[15] Yamamoto, M. and S. Y. Nof, "Scheduling/Rescheduling in the Manufacturing Operating System Environment" International Journal of Production Research, Vol. 23, No. 4, 1985, pp. 705-722.

Expert Systems in Economics, Banking and Management
L.F. Pau et al. (Editors)
© *Elsevier Science Publishers B. V. (North-Holland), 1989*

AN INTELLIGENT CLASSIFICATION AND FORMULATION OF NETWORK PROBLEMS

CHAE Y. LEE

Korea Institute of Technology
Taejon, Korea

The purpose of this paper is to develop a knowledge based system that classifies and formulates many network problems usually appears in production and distribution management. Three knowledge beses for the detailed classification, general formulation and specific modeling are constructed. An approach via query and answer graph is employed for the systematic rule generation. Several different factors are considered even in the same category of the network to identify the detailed classification. Problem definition, general formulation and proposed algorithms are provided for the novice users to easily generate data dependent models of their own problems. Pascal programs that easily communicate with databases are installed for the specific formulation phase. Side constraints that necessarily follows the network problems are also examined to enhance the system flexibility.

1. INTRODUCTION

Many problems that arise in the management of production, distribution and vehicle routing are closely related to the network flow problems. These problems are thus need to be identified and solved as a specific subclass of network problems. The research on the network problems, however, has been concentrated much more on the efficient algorithms and their complexities than on the classification and formulation of the related problems. A few recent research [4, 5] on the automatic modeling of mathematical programs are thus very promising to the nonexperts who can not verify and formulate the problems even with many available computer codes.

We in this research consider various network flow problems [2] and some other linear program (LP) based networks. The knowledge bases to classify and formulate the network problems are constructed in such a way that the expert system first identify the category and detailed subclass of a given network and then formulate the problem. For the classification rules the structures and the characteristics of related networks are catefully compared and examined. The goal of the formulation is to provide the values of the coefficients of each network model which is presented at the stage of general formulation. Side constraints that usually occur in the network models are also taken into account in the specific formulation phase.

2. CLASSIFICATION OF NETWORK PROBLEMS

We first classify the network flow problems into seven categories by identifying the problem specific characteristics of each network. Detailed classification and generation of the knowledge bases will then be followed.

2.1. Seven Categories of the Related Problems

The network flow problem as a subset of mathematical programming is defined as a network problem that carries flow. One specific example of the problem is the well known transportation problem. We in this study consider linear program based network flow problems in which the cost related to each flow is linear.

The network flow problem [2] in linear program includes maximum flow problem, shortest path problem, assignment problem, transportation and transshipment problem. The transshipment problem as the most general model is called the minimum cost network flow problem. The schematic relationships of these problems are shown in FIGURE 1. The central point in the figure is the minimum cost network flow problem. Other problems listed to the left are less general in the sense that they are specializations of the minimum cost network flow problem.

We here consider another class of network problems which is seeking optimal trees and traversals. These problems are especially abundant in cable networks, pipelines and vehicle routing problems. The minimum spanning three problem and the traveling salesman problem [3] are the typical examples.

By including the above two problems into the network flow problems we have the following seven categories of network problems to be examined for the automatic classification :

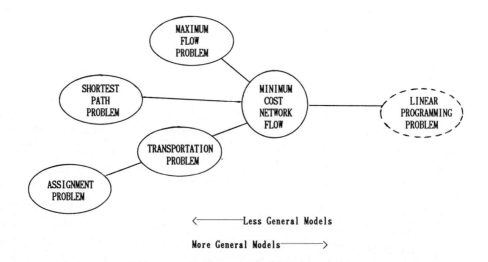

FIGURE 1   Relationships of Network Flow Problems

1. maximum flow problem
2. transportation problem
3. minimum cost network flow problem
4. matching problem
5. shortest path problem
6. minimum spanning three problem
7. traveling salesman problem

2.2. Detailed Classification

In the previous section we classified the linear program based network problems into seven categories. This classification is the first stage of the expert system to be developed. To connect each class of network problem with the existing algorithms in the mathematical programming more detailed classifications need to be followed. This detailed classification is thus the prestage of the formulation of each problem and construction of databases.

The following two factors are considered for the network flow problems :

- single or multi-commodity flow
- balanced or unbalanced supply and demand.

The transportation problem as an example is classified as either single commodity or mulit-commodity transportation problem. The single commodity transportation problem is then classified into balanced or unbalanced transportation problem. Two types of problems are considered for the multi-commodity transportation problems. When the supply and demand and the movement of each commodity are independent, the problems is handled as a number of single commodity transportation problems. However, when one or more commodities are dependent in the process of supply, demand or movement, the problem becomes a special case of transportation problem which requires side constraints to formulate. Thus the classification of the transportation problem (the second goal in the knowledge base) is described as

2. Transportation Problem
    2.1 Single Commodity Transportation
        2.1.1 Balanced Transportation
        2.1.2 Unbalanced Transportation
    2.2 multi Commodity Transportation
        2.2.1 N Single Commodity Transportation
        2.2.2 Special Case of Transportation

Different factors are applied to each class of network problems and the results are shown in TABLE 1 which is the list of goals of our expert system.

2.3. Generation of the Knowledge Base

The knowledge base for the classification of the network problems consists of two stages. Rules in the first stage classify a specific problem into one of the seven categories. The seven categories in our knowledge base are first divided into the following three groups according to the problem characteristics :

1. Flow problems
2. Tree/Path/Traversal
3. Matching

The flow problems include maximum flow, transportation and minimum cost network flow problems. The minimum spanning three, shortest path and traveling salesman problems are varified in the second group. Finally the third group includs matching which is the general case of assignment problem.

TABLE 1   Goals in the Classification of Network Problems

1. Max Flow Problem
    1.1 Single Commodity Max Flow
    1.2 Multi Commodity Max Flow
2. Transportation Problem
    2.1 Single Commodity Transportation
        2.1.1 Balanced Transportation
        2.1.2 Unbalanced Transportation
    2.2 Multi Commodity Transportation
        2.2.1 N Single Commodity Transportation
        2.2.2 Special Case of Transportation
3. Min Cost Network Flow Problem
    3.1 Single Commodity Network Flow
        3.1.1 Balanced Network Flow
        3.1.2 Unbalanced Network Flow
    3.2 Multi Commodity Network Flow
4. Matching Problem
    4.1 Bipartite Matching
        4.1.1 Cardinality Matching
        4.1.2 MaxMin Matching
        4.1.3 Weighted Matching
            4.1.3.1 Balanced Assignment Problem
            4.1.3.2 Unbalanced Assignment Problem
    4.2 Nonbipartite Matching
5. Minimum Spanning Tree Problem
6. Shortest Path Problem   .
    6.1 Shortest Path With No negative Arcs
        6.1.1 Shortest Path Between A Specified Pair Of Nodes
        6.1.2 Shortest Path Between Each Pair Of Nodes
    6.2 Shortest Path With Negative Arcs
        6.2.1 No Negative Cycles
        6.2.2 Negative Cycles
7. Traveling Salesman Problem

To generate the classification rules we partly use a tree structured queries and answer graph which represents the order of queries and the related answers. An example of the query and answer graph is shown in FIGURE 2. Questions related to the classification of the three flow problems are shown in the graph. Any type of queries can be employed to lead to goals. Related answers are yes or no, one-of, or any simple response to the query.

Based on the query and answer graph production rules are generated both for the general and detailed classifications. Sample rules are illustrated in FIGURE 3.

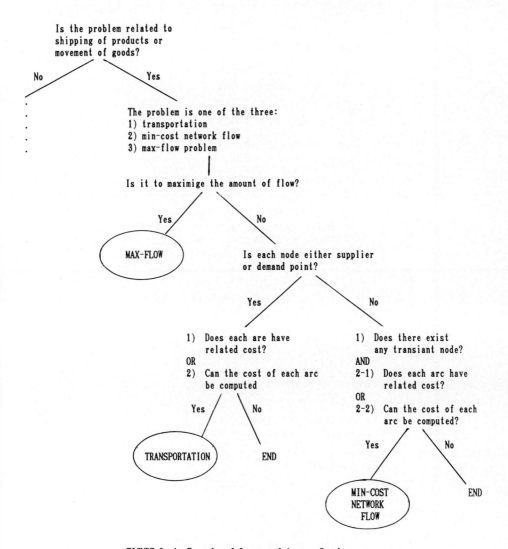

FIGURE 2   An Example of Query and Answer Graph

3. FORMULATION OF THE NETWORK PROBLEMS

Once a problem is classified as a specific subclass of network problems, it needs to be formulated as a model. General and specific formulations are discussed together with the side constraints encountered in the network problems.

3.1. General Formulation

One of the advantages of network problems in linear programming is that each subclass has its own general formulation. The term general is used in the sense that the formulation is data independent. Data dependent specific formulation will be discussed in the next section.

Since each problem type has a distinct linear programming model, the general formulation is presented as the result of the detailed classification. In other words, the search of a

```
!
! Min Cost Network Flow Problem
!
RULE 3
IF  The problem is in category network flow.
AND NOT It is to maximize the amount of flow.
AND NOT Each node is either supplier or demand point.
AND It has one or more transient nodes.
AND Each arc has related cost.
OR  The cost of each arc can be computed.
THEN Min Cost Network Flow Problem
!
RULE 3.1
IF  Min Cost Network Flow Problem
AND It has only one commodity.
THEN Single Commodity Network Flow
AND DISPLAY single commodity network flow
!
RULE 3.1.1
IF  Single Commodity Network Flow
AND total supply is equal to total demand
THEN Balanced Network Flow
!
RULE 3.1.2
IF  Single Commodity Network Flow
AND total supply is greater than total demand
THEN Unbalanced Network Flow
AND DISPLAY dummy demand node
!
RULE 3.1.2
IF  Single Commodity Network Flow
AND total supply is less than total demand
THEN Unbalanced Network· Flow
AND DISPLAY dummy supply node
!
RULE 3.2
IF  Min Cost Network Flow Problem
AND Not It has only one commodity.
THEN Multi Commodity Network Flow
AND DISPLAY multi commodity network flow
!
```

FIGURE 3   Sample Rules

goal in the knowledge base leads to the determination of the problem type and the general formulation. In our system the following information is presented with regard to the general formulation :

1. Problem definition
2. Formulation
3. Proposed Algorithms

This general formulation is a prestage of the specific formulation in which real data need to be obtained as explained in the model. The general formulation thus provides an important information to the novice users. The general formulation of the single commodity minimum cost network flow problem as an example is shown in FIGURE 4.

```
DISPLAY single commodity network flow

          Single Commodity Network Flow Problem


 1. Problem Definition

     The minimal cost network flow problem has the added feature
   of allowing a (partial or complete) shipment to pass transiently
   through other sources and destinations before it ultimately
   reaches its designated destination. In essence, the minimal
   cost network flow model automatically seeks the minimum cost
   route between a source and a destination without having to
   determine such a route a priori.


 2. Fomulation

        Minimize   SUM(i) SUM(j) c(i,j)*x(i,j)

        subject to
          SUM(j) x(i,j) - SUM(k) x(k,i) = b(i)    i = 1, 2, ... , m
          0 <= x(i,j) <= u(i,j)                    for all i and j

          SUM(i) is the summation of all i
          SUM(j) is the summation of all j
          c(i,j) = unit shipping cost along the arc (i,j)
          x(i,j) = amount of flow on the arc (i,j)
          u(i,j) = upper bound of x(i,j)
          b(i) > 0 : amount of supply at node i
          b(i) < 0 : amount of demand at node i
          Assumption : SUM(i) b(i) = 0


 3. Algorithms

        Network simplex method
        Out - of - Kilter algorithm
        Any LP code based on simplex method
```

FIGURE 4   Example of General Formulation

3.2. Specific Formulation

One important goal of the expert system in this research is to provide a specific formulation for the given network problem. It is the result of this stage that enables the users to apply computer codes or softwares to obtain the solution of the model.

Since network problems range in size from small paradigm problems to complex one with hundreds of thousands nodes and arcs, acquisition and storage of the coefficient data becomes an issue of the specific formulation. Pascal based data generation programs are employed in our system. The program is designed such that the coefficient data are fed either directly from the terminal or through the interface with the database. In any case the following three types of coefficients are stored in the program :

1. Cost coefficients
2. Right-Hand-Side coefficients
3. Constraints coefficients

By the nature of the network models many coefficients of the constraints are zeros which need not be stored in the program. Thus, to reduce the memory size in our program only nonzero elements are stored for the coefficients of the constrains.

3.3. Consideration of the Side Constraints

One of the most important issues in the network problem is the side constraints. The existence of any side constraint in a specific network problem obstructs the use of related solution algorithms. It means that if a network problem has side constaints, the problem is no more in the frame of the general formulation which is presented in Section 3.1. To overcome such a problem we first examine the types of side constraints in network problems and then consider the classification and formulation of the constrains.

3.3.1. Side Constraints in Flow Problems

The main constraints in the flow problems are so-called flow conservation constraints. In the flow network each node has the flow conservation constraint which equates the amount of inflows to the amount of outflows. Each arc in the network also has a constraint which is called arc capacity constraint. It represents the upper bound of the flow that passes the arc. Since any constraint in the network is related either to the arc or to the node, the possible side constraints in the flow problems are the one related to the nodes.

The following four types of side constraints are considered in our system :

1. Inflow-Limit constraint
2. Inflow-Comparison constraint
3. Outflow-Limit constraint
4. Outflow-Comparison constraint

The Inflow-Limit constraint restricts the total amount of inflows at a node while the Inflow-Comparison constraint is the restriction among the amounts of inflows. The Outflow-Limit and Outflow-Comparison constraints are defined in the same way.

For the formulation phase of each of the above side constraints different information is required. The information required for the Inflow-Limit constraint as an example is shown below.

- Index of the related node k
- Indices of node i from which node k receives inputs
- Quantity limit of inflows at node k
- Form of inequality ($\leq, \geq, =$)
- Each coefficient of the variable x_{ik}

The acquisition of the above knowledge will successfully accomplish the modeling of minimum cost network flow problems with the Inflow-Limit constraint.

3.3.2. Side Constraints in Tree/Path/Traversal Problems

For the minimum spanning three problem, we define the following two types of side constraints :

1. In-Arc constraint
2. Out-Arc constraint

The In-Arc constraint includes a certain arc in the minimum spanning tree while the Out-Arc constraint prohibits the arc as a solution. These two types of side constraints are also applied to the shortest path problem.

In the shortest path problem, however, side constraints related to a node need to be considered in addition to the arc constraints. In a network one would like to have the shortest path pass through a specific node. Thus the following four types of constraints are considered in the shortest path problem :

1. In-Node constraint
2. Out-Node constraint
3. In-Arc constraint
4. Out-Arc constraint

For the traveling salesman problem it is quite clear that the same side constraints are applied as in the minimum spanning tree problem.

3.3.3. Side Constraints in Matching Problems

The matching problems that usually arise in the production management are bipartite matching in which each arc in the graph has one end in a set S and the other end in another set T. Therefore the side constraint in the bipartite matching is to restrict a noed in the set S or T. By defining the side constraints as

1. S constraint
2. T constraint

we can easily formulate them with the indices of nodes in the two sets. As an example if node 1 in the set S has to be assigned to either node 2 or node 4 in the set T, then the side constraint is given as

$$x_{12} + x_{14} = 1$$

In the following section we discuss the functional components of our system together with the features included in it.

4. SYSTEM DESCRIPTION

A prototype expert system is developed by compiling the knowledge base and Pascal programs in an expert system shell [7]. The system's control structure makes use of a goal driven inference engine. The pascal engine which is accessible from the inference engine receives inputs either directly from the users or from the database.

The knowledge in the system is partitioned into three knowledge bases. The knowledge base for the classification is designed first to categorize the network problems and then to perform the detailed classification at each class. Explanation of the special terminologies and supplementary information are provided in the knowledge base.

General formulation of each subproblem is contained in the second knowledge base which aids users for the detailed model description.

To formulate the problem specific model and treat the side constraints a Pascal program is installed for each network of the seven categories. Specially reserved words in the knowledge base are used to access the Pascal programs. The interaction of the knowledge base and the Pascal programs are controled by the two engines.

5. CONCLUSIONS

A prototype knowledge based expert system is developed that classifies and formulates various network problems in linear programs. An approach via query and answer graph is employed to construct the knowledge bases that are the most important and difficult part in the expert system development.

Three knowledge hases are built for the classifications, general formulations and specific formulations of the network problems in seven categories. Several different factors are taken into account for the detailed classification phase. Types of side constraints in each problem are defined and added to the specific formulation. Pascal programs are also made use of to represent the coefficient data in the model.

To improve the performance of our expert system the knowledge base refinement phase [1] is expected. the addition, deletion, and alteration of rule-components in the existing knowledge bases will clearly enhance the system's empirical adequacy.

1. Ginsberg, A., S.M. Weiss and P. Politakis, Automatic Knowledge Base Refinement for classification Systems, Artificial Intelligence, Vol.35, No.2.
2. Jensen, P.A. and J.W. Barnes, Network Flow Programming, John Wiley and Sons, 1980
3. Lawler, E., Combinatorial Optimization, Networks and Matroid, Holt·Rinehart·Winston, 1976
4. Mills, R.E., R.B. Fetter and R.F. Averill, A Computer Language for Mathematical Program Formulation, Decision Sciences, Vol.8.
5. Murphy, F.H. and E.A. Stohr, An intelligent System for Formulating Linear Programs, Decision Support Systems, Vol.2, 1982.
6. Nilsson, N.J., Principles of Artificial Intelligence, Springer-Verlag, 1982.
7. INSIGHT2, Level Five Research Inc., 1985.

Expert Systems in Economics, Banking and Management
L.F. Pau et al. (Editors)
© *Elsevier Science Publishers B.V. (North-Holland), 1989*

EXPERT SYSTEMS FOR SOFTWARE PROJECT MANAGEMENT

Dr. Roberto Meli, Dr. Elisabetta Tesi
ELEA SpA - Olivetti Formazione / Consulenze
Centro Strategie e Metodologie Sistemi
Firenze (ITALIA)

The subject of this study is the use of Expert Systems in the field of Information Systems Project Management. This is a complex field in which various tasks converge, and we believe that many of these lend themselves to the use of Expert Systems (E.S.) to render them more efficient and manageable. For this reason we singled out project planning, with particular emphasis on forecasting of project variables for the formation of our prototype, which was developed using a rule-based shell. Following the preface which gives a general outline, the first part of the text introduces the theme of Project Management and defines our frame of reference. The second part describes the prototype of our Expert System (Sistema Esperto per la Pianificazione [SEP]).

1. PREFACE

The SEP project was the brain child of the initiative "Systems Research and Analysis" (Analisi e Ricerche sui Sistemi [ARS]), promoted by ELEA in an effort to supply a concrete response to the growing neccessity for a link between advanced technological research (at both international and university levels) and the practical needs of the business world. Our prototype is part of a "package" of consultancy, training and products, offered by ELEA, related to Project Management as well as Expert Systems.

We believe that a study of this kind can serve on the one hand to diffuse and strengthen the use of Expert Systems, and on the other to propose a means of support for the managerial activities that until now could be automated only in part with traditional technologies. Another of our goals was to gather experience of the use of methods, tools and techniques in order to continue a more ambitious and widespread plan of research on Expert Systems development methodologies.

The philosophy of Project Management, already established in many work environments due to the type of jobs done (engineering, for example), is also becoming important in the field of information systems development. The characteristic expertise of a Project Manager evolves from a purely technical one to a managerial one: from expert in programming languages and structured techniques, the Project Manager is becoming a specialist in public relations, communication and the integration of the varying parts of an organization. The much-needed training of an ever increasing number of Project Managers is hindered by the slowness of the acquisition and practice of managerial capacities. An E.S. can therefore play an important role in the formation of these new Project Managers.

2. PROJECT MANAGEMENT OF BUSINESS SYSTEMS

In this section we will roughly outline what we mean by Project Management and the domain which we chose for the formation of our prototype.

A business system project can be defined as a complex effort, generally more than six months long, which requires interrelated tasks followed out by various organizations with well-defined goals and budgets. The project also represents a means of growth for modern companies. The way in which such projects are managed, as well as the role and relevance of the Project Manager, depend on variables such as size, typology, philosophy, existing organizational structure, financial resources (etc.etc.) of the company in question.

Within a project, two distinct though strongly related processes coexist: Production and Direction.

Production can be described as the group of activities that allows to pass from identification and definition of a user problem to the creation of a solution in the form of an organizational/informational system. Such tasks are, for the most part, of a "technical" nature, such as the planning and analysis of interviews, analysis of data and man/machine interfaces, software engineering, systems testing. *Direction*, on the other hand, can be seen as the group of activities carried out with the intent to evaluate economically the Production process and its expected results, begin it, guarantee its adhesion to forecasts in terms of time, means and costs, and finally end it. In other words, the directional activities are those which allow the transformation of a gathering of individuals and resource materials into a stable organization, capable of reaching collective goals within determined limits of quality, time and costs. Such functions are for the most part of a "managerial" nature such as: motivation of the work group and interested outsiders, acquisition of an efficient internal and external leadership, solution of possible conflicts, preservation of social relations. Moreover, the two processes share a group of activities which have both managerial as well as technical connotations. Some of these "mixed" functions are: interviewing, planning of project commitments, cost/benefit analysis, quality control, project presentations. For example, cost benefit analysis, based on "technical" reasoning, has relevant "managerial" implications. Diagram 1 outlines the above concept, emphasizing the directional process, on which we will concentrate our attention.

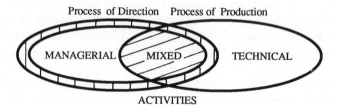

diagram 1

An efficient directional process consists of four fundamental phases: Planning, Organization, Action, Feedback. These four stages, for which the Project Manager is responsible, are continually recycled from the beginning to the end of the project (as shown in diagram 2).

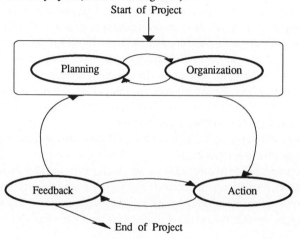

diagram 2

Planning is divided in two distinct parts: "Forecasting" and "Prescription." The former attempts to foresee the resources(persons, time, equipment, money, etc.) necessary for the completion of a project. At this point estimating skills as well as forecasting methods and models become quite important. The latter consists of a "prescription," a detailed outline of the tasks necessary for the development of the project to be carried out by the group. Network planning techniques are generally used for this scope. A computer based information system is also a quite useful support. These two aspects of the Planning phase are conceptually distinct though closely related and often chronologically inseparable.

Organization essentially consists of the identification of the best criteria for the choice of personnel, the definition of the internal structure most appropriate for the nature of the project, the assignation of tasks, responsibility and goals, and so on.

Action is based on the ability to motivate employees, win a position of leadership, detect and resolve conflicts, communicate efficiently, cure public relations, interpret non-verbal messages, resolve technical and personal problems, use creative techniques, and so on.

Project *Feedback* can be either internal or external. Internal feedback consists of the measurement of the project's progress and the assurance of its coherence to the original plan. Clearly an effective interpretation is based both on the ability to assess the reality without influencing it and the correct usage of such tools as structured walk-through, meetings, progress reports, etc. Product/process quality control and the development of external contracts become very important elements. External feedback, on the contrary, is that which the project gives to the surrounding environment (top-management, users, clients, etc.) and takes place for the most part during presentations of the project.

A project is never an isolated effort within a company, and the study of the relationship between projects is of the utmost importance. The analysis, planning and control of the so-called Project Portfolio are significant tasks which are the competence of the Planning Committee or of the information systems Manager. It is essential that both levels of management (project and multi-project) are synchronized and consistent.

All of the above mentioned activities (and others) make up the methodology of Project Management, developed by ELEA, which provides techniques and criteria for their effective application. In order to develop the prototype of our Expert System, we singled out the Planning phase, with particular emphasis on the euristic field of Forecasting.

2.1. The problem of forecasting

To begin with, our use of the term *Forecasting* refers to the evaluation of a quantity that will reveal itself in the future, obtained through the application of a rational and conscious method such as a *Forecasting Model*. That is to say, a formula or a group of formulas that allow the project variables of interest to link between themselves. A compound forecasting model can be made up of different relationships or partial models, each one suitable for a particular circumstance. Henceforth, for simplicity's sake, we will indicate forecasting models without distinguishing between compound or partial models. *Estimating*, on the other hand, can be thought of as the primitive or intuitive elementary aspect at the basis of a forecast. For example: a forecast may concern the total cost of a specific project; a forecasting model may be an equation which links total cost to man-hours and man-hours to source lines of codes for the system; an estimate may be an assessment of the number of source lines that such a case might produce.

The utility of a forecasting model springs from the fact that it is often much more difficult to assess directly the variables of managerial interest (total effort, duration, staff necessary, quality, etc.) than to evaluate other variables (lines of code produced, number of programs...) used by the model itself. Forecasting models serve therefore to reduce the difficulty and the complexity of making estimates. In order to better the entire forecasting process, it is possible to take action with both the identification of the right model and the development of the estimating abilities of single employees.

Forecasting models are called "top-down" when the variables of interest are of a global nature, that is to say that they are macro-variables such as total cost, staff necessary for the over-all phases of the project, etc. Another more analytical type of forecast ("bottom-up") uses micro-variables and is based on the breaking down of a global project into increasingly elementary tasks (Work Breakdown Structure WBS or Project Breakdown Structure PBS) that can be directly evaluated with a certain reliablity. The former method of forecasting is useful in the early phases of a project and is not used very often; the latter is applied subsequently and more frequently, with the increasing availability information on the specific acitivities to develop. This second type of forecasting is often linked to the use of formal planning tools such as PERT, GANTT, Resource Load Diagram, etc. It is important to emphasize how a forecasting model is useful above all as a methodological guide to pay attention to those elements which might offer a relevant contribution to an estimate. A forecasting model cannot however eliminate human responsibility.

The elements of interest in the forecasting process are generally:
- cost of development, operation and maintenance of the system
- effort in terms of man-hours necessary for various phases
- number of personnel and their working periods
- duration of the development and life of the system
- size of the system
- quality of the system
- technical environment
- risks
- average productivity
- expected benefits
- methods of development (internal/external contracts)

The accurate forecast of the resources necessary for the completion of a project can be of great importance and requires a certain experience. Different Project Managers have different styles of estimating, and there is a growing need to standardize company forecasting procedures. The possibility of achieving homogeneity is tied either to the standardization of organizational structures (for example the creation of a group which occupies itself exclusively with estimates) or to the regularization of forecasting methods. An Expert System provides the possibility for the implementation of the latter solution, allowing for a greater decentralization.

The forecasting models chosen for the SEP prototype are those which result, after analysis of current documented experience, the most widespread, simple and trustworthy: Delfi method, the Function Point model, Tom De Marco's model, Putnam's model, CO.CO.MO. model, Mc Farlan's model (for their desription, please see bibliography). Each technique has a well-defined time spectrum of application.

A good forecasting process allows a correct evaluation of the alternatives for the investment of company resources in line with the development strategy of the company itself. Nevertheless, many firms demonstrate scarse interest in the betterment of their forecasting process, leaving estimates to the initiative and experience of individual employees. This situation can perhaps be explained by two different reasons. Firstly, the economic considerations of a project quite often are not passed from high organizational levels to Project Managers, with the result that the administration often makes estimates without knowing the technical aspects of the problem. At the same time, the Project Manager acts without the knowledge of the development and investment strategies of the company, not to mention the relationship between his own project and others in the company's project portfolio. Often small-scale optimizing causes a general loss to the systems development sector. Secondly, formal forecasting models adapt themselves with difficulty from one environment to another due to their dependence on variables, many of which tend to be constants within a company, yet assume a different though still constant value for another. Diagram 3 illustrates this concept.

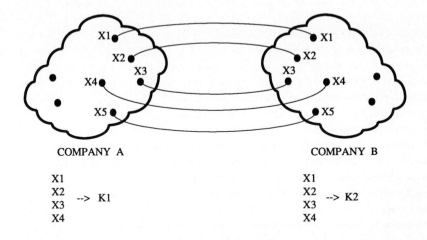

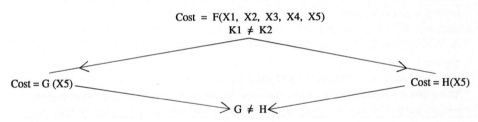

diagram 3

An example: within Company A there is a technological development environment equipped with fourth generation languages (4GL). This variable will surely influence the effort in terms of man-hours need to develop projects, yet will remain stable for a sufficiently long period to render constant its effect on the forecasting model. This and analogous factors will be incorporated in a constant of the model's equation. Within Company B, on the other hand, there is a technological development environment equipped with an Assembler language (2GL). Here too the environment and the influence remain stable but the value that the constant assumes will be different in equation A than that of equation B.

To sum up, we retain that a company cannot put to use a model developed by others without personalizing it for their particular environment. This personalization requires a certain commitment of time and money that, though limited, is often considered risky due to the impossibility to demonstrate an exact economic return. The majority of the specialists who have studied the problem share the opinion that such costs repay themselves many times over within the lifetime of the model.

Two other important aspects of forecasting are the frequency with which estimates are made and the relative methods of organization. A rigid process in which original estimates are not re-evaluated and modified during the course of a project, and which become administrative binds can represent a financial loss (due to inefficiency and waste). And so it becomes the task of the information systems Manager to sponsor a regularization of the forecasting process in order to pass from haphazardly individual estimates to the statiscal certainty of a standardized method at a corporate level. The construction and maintenance of forecasting models can be carried out by a group of staff members at an operative level. Such a group could also form the focal point for the development of an Expert System for forecasting.

3. EXPERT SYSTEMS AND THE FORECASTING FIELD
The characteristics of Expert Systems such as:
- the capacity to deal with euristics
- the ability to explain reasoning
- dialogue in a language similar to a natural one
- the management of knowledge of varying degree of validity
- the use of satisfying though not necessarily ideal solutions

can be considered adequate enough to confront automatically a forecasting problem.

Here follows a list of the problem's characteristics and those of the knowledge domain under examination that convinced us to choose the Expert Systems technology.

As far as the knowledge of the forecasting domain and the neccessary experience are concerned, one can observe:
- the knowledge necessary to form efficient estimates is made up of a strong euristic component combined with an equally strong algorithmic one. For example there are euristic procedures which select the most appropriate algorithm for a given situation, and can even help to understand if a certain algorithm will cause a deviation from the goal.
- the knowledge of the forecasting field has uncertain components,is expandable, evolveable, improvable.
- finally, the experience necessary for estimation is rare resource within a company. Once gathered in a knowledge base, it offers many possibilities: to consult the E.S., accede to the knowledge base written in a easily legible form (for example: if/then rules), receive explanations of reasoning given by the system itself. These activities allow a transfer of knowledge within a company useful for the training of new Project Managers and the achievment of consistent results.

Regarding the characteristics of the problem and those of the search for solutions:
- the problem is complex but self-contained and sufficiently autonomous from other types of knowlege. Moreover, it is divisable into smaller self-contained problems of minor complexity.
- it is impossible to determine "a priori" if a solution is ideal or not.

Regarding the use of an E.S. in the field of forecasting:
- its occasionally long response time (if compared to those of traditional systems) does not hinder the efficiency of its consultation.
- the man/machine interface in a language similar to a natural one renders the analysis easier. For example, the user's answers, supplied in qualitative terms, are transformed by the system into the quantitative responses required by the forecasting model.

From our point of view it is quite important, for the efficient introduction of an E.S., to accomplish an adequate preparation within the company, keeping in mind the following considerations:
- the access to the system should be extended gradually from a select group to the remaining personnel.
- the E.S. users should be aware that they are using a Decision Support System and not an infallible

forecaster (a wizard!), just as if they were to consult a "real" expert.

- an E.S. does not eliminate the human responsiblity for estimates.
- the existence of a managerial "sponsor" for the development and use of the E.S. is most important.
- the E.S. will be much more efficient if well-received by its users and not seen as an affront to their professionality.

3.1. Description of SEP (Sistema Esperto per la Pianificazione)

The objective of SEP is to furnish an automatic basis for the estimator to forsee project variables. Its general structure (see diagram 4) relies on a collection of knowledge bases and tables. The former contain various cost models, a consultation guide and a link with a software package for the implementation of PERT, GANTT etc. The tables contain synthetic information extracted from the elaboration of historical data of past projects, which serve as tuning for the equations associated with models and updated by means of a DBMS, a spreadsheet or an external program.

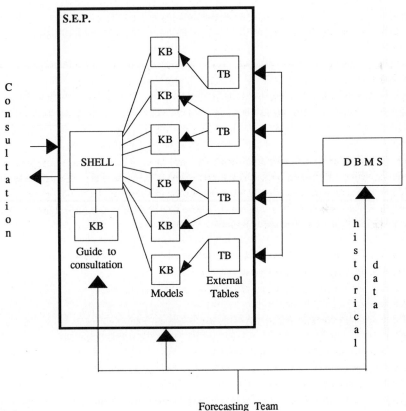

diagram 4

The separation of knowledge bases of cost models on the one hand, and of tables of parameters on the other, can be useful due to the difference in frequency with which the two parts of the system evolve. The former in fact are more stable than the latter.

3.2. The Consultation of SEP

The questions that one can ask SEP in the consulting phase concern the variables of interest for the project, like costs, manhours, personnel required, risks involved etc. It is also possible to make use of a corrective factor in forcasting which accounts for the different conditions surrounding various projects. SEP guides the user who does not know the models in the choice of that which is the most appropriate in a particular circumstance. SEP also has an interface which allows it to adapt itself during the consultation to the level of experience of its user. For example, the numerical parameter of a certain model can be given directly by the user (if expert), or inferred by the system by means of a series of increasingly detailed questions asked to the user (if beginner). Due to this possibility, SEP is able to train a junior estimator to use various models, as well as furnish a rapid means of support to a senior Project Manager. At any moment it is possible to put on "hold" the consultation in order to run a software package for network planning and then return to the consultation. It is possible to use an induction tool to compare the rules automatically generated by the system based on examples supplied by the user to those already included in SEP's knowledge bases. This comparison can facilitate the initiation of a neophyte and provide a departure point for the evolution of SEP itself.

3.3. The Technology Used

For the creation of SEP we used a MS-Dos compatible personal computer in order to widen the range of usage of the Expert System. As far as the software is concerned, we used a rule-based shell for the following reasons:

- forecasting knowledge lends itself to the use of rules and does not require hybrid formalisms for the representation.
- the reasoning is stable and of a deductive nature and needs only one paradigm of consultation.
- the possibility of interface with other software (such as packages for planning, graphics, spreadsheet, etc.)
- the facility of usage which provides a simple maintenance of the knowledge bases.
- short development times for this experimental phase.

Parting from these considerations, the design of the general architecture of the system (shown in diagram 4) followed.

Subsequently, the typical phases of construction of a prototypical approach were many times repeated: acquisition of knowledge, implementation of the base and test.

The shell used was the Xi Plus by Expertech Ltd. The induction tool was the Xi-Rule by Expertech Ltd. The fourth generation programming language used for the creation of the planning program was the Artemis 2000 by Metier Management Systems Ltd.

4. CONCLUSION

In this study we illustrated the fundamental concepts for the creation of an Expert System prototype for making estimates and forecasting. We saw how the field of business systems project forecasting lends itself to an experiment of advanced technology of this kind due to the simultaneous presence of both euristic and algorithmic components. We examined the concept of forecasting models and demonstrated the necessity of a personalization of the existing documented models for a correct use within any particular developement environment. A rule-based shell permits the implementation of such a personalization in a simplified manner (with respect to traditional technologies) and allows for the indispensable evolution of the forecasting model to adapt itself to a new environment. Among other advantages we evidenced the possible use of the tool SEP for the training of large numbers of junior personnel and the standardization of corporate methods and results of the forecasting process.

Roberto Meli is a trainer and consultant of the methodology of Project Management and is involved in the development of automatic supporting tools for management.

Elisabetta Tesi is responsible for the education and consultancy of themes related to Expert Systems.

REFERENCES

Regarding Project Management:

[1] R.D. Archibald , "Managing High Technology Programs and Projects", John Wiley & Sons, Inc., New York, N.Y. USA, '76.
[2] D.I. Cleveland, W.R. King, "Project Management Handbook", Van Nostrand Reinhold Company, '83.
[3] A.O. Awani, "Project Management Tecniques", Petrocelli Books, '83.
[4] Tom De Marco, "Controlling Software Projects", Yourdon Inc., '82.
[5] Boehm, "Software Engineering Economics", Prentice Hall, '81.
[6] Conte - Dunsmore - Shen, "Software Engineering Metrics and Models", The Benjamin Cummings Publishing Company Inc., '86.
[7] Albrecht & Gaffney, "Software function, source lines of code and development effort prediction : a software science validation", IEEE Transaction on Software Engineering SE-9 6 Nov 83.
[8] Hamid - Madnick, "The dynamics of Software Project Scheduling", Communication of the ACM, May '83
[9] Griffin E., "Real time estimating", Datamation, June '80

Regarding Expert Systems:

[10] Barr Feigenbaum, "The handbook of Artificial Intelligence", Pitman, 1981, Vol. 1
[11] Buchanan - Shortliffe, "Rule - Based Expert Systems", Addison Wesley, 1984
[12] Hammon King, "Expert Systems", Wiley Press, 1985
[13] Hayes Roth, "I Sistemi Esperti basati sulle conoscenze", Sistemi e Automazione, n. 275 Novembre 1986
[14] Rich E., "Intelligenza Artificiale", McGraw Hill Libri Italia, 1986
[15] Forsyth R., "Software Review Expertech Xi Plus" da Expert Systems, Feb 1987

Expert Systems in Economics, Banking and Management
L.F. Pau et al. (Editors)
© Elsevier Science Publishers B.V. (North-Holland), 1989

A MULTI-LEVEL MANIPULATION TECHNIQUE FOR STRUCTURING
ILL-STRUCTURED DECISION PROBLEMS: AN IMPLEMENTATION

Mohammed Ihsan Bu-Hulaiga

College of Industrial Management, King Fahd University of
of Petroleum & Minerals, Dhahran 31261, Saudi Arabia

Current implementations of DSS provide inadequate support for ill-
structured problems. This paper presents a rule-based implementation
of a multi-level technique for model manipulation. The technique provides a comprehensive framework that enables DSS of processing non-
routine queries. The queries range from pure retrieval (data oriented)
queries to analytical queries. The implemented technique is hierarchical with two main components: query management and model manipulation.
The former, dispatches queries to the appropriate processing facility
depending on the type of the query. The model manipulation component
generates efficient strategies for processing ill-structured queries.

1. INTRODUCTION

This paper presents an implementation of the plan-based model manipulation
technique [2]. The multi-level technique is instigated by the observation that
current implementations of DSS provide inadequate support for ill-structured
(i.e., ad hoc or non-routine) problems for which no solution path is established. In this context, strategies for solving ill-structured problems are, by
and large, decreed by the uncertainty, complexity and conflicting conditions of
the decision-making environment [9]. In order for a DSS to cope with such decisions, it comprises a database system, a model-base system and a dialogue
system. A model-base system contains a model-base and a model management system
(MMS). A number of model-units are stored in the model-base. The primarily
responsibility of an MMS is to manipulate model-units. Model-units are specific
formulations of decision situations amenable to contain generic normative
problem-solving techniques, such as mathematical programming. More precisely, a
model-unit may be characterized by its input-parameters, output-parameters,
preconditions, and solution procedure as follows:

[Model-unit identifier
    input-parameters
    output-parameters
    preconditions
    solution-procedure]

A fundamental requirement of a DSS is the ability to process ad hoc queries.
Queries range from pure retrieval queries to analytical queries. Processing
analytical queries is achieved (in the DSS environment) by the MMS. The two
interrelated components through which functionality of MMS is attained are model

representation and model manipulation [7].   Model representation includes the creation and storage of model-units.   Model manipulation is concerned with presenting viable model-units to solve the problem at hand.   Model manipulation includes building adequate integrated models (out of the stored model-units). The model manipulation component is, thus, concerned with the selection, activation, deactivation, sequencing, and synthesizing of models.

Section 2 presents a survey of related literature.   Section 3 is the crux of this paper.   It discusses a rule-based computer realization of the multi-level model manipulation technique.   Section 4 presents an example showing the mechanics of the implementation.   The paper concludes with section 5 which offers an assessment of the subject computer implementation and how it may be enhanced.

2. SURVEY OF RELATED WORK

It is well-recognized that providing DSS with a model manipulation capability increases its effectiveness [4].   Literature in model management proposes a number of approaches to model manipulation, the majority of which are based on the resolution principle.   Bonczek, Holsapple and Whinston [1] have suggested the use of this principle to deliver domain independent manipulation.   Dolk [3] shows how the resolution principle can be used in conjunction with model abstractions. Dutta and Basu [5] devise a two-phase (resolution and execution) proof procedure for manipulating the model-units in the model-base.   Liang [8] defined an algorithm for model manipulation that is based on input and output matching.   Bu-Hulaiga [2] proposes a plan-based model manipulation procedure.

The implementation discussed here is based on the planning paradigm of AI. The major function of any planning system is to produce a tentative plan based on a given description of the environment.   Planning is concerned with articulating a sequence of actions that transforms a current state into a goal state.   Thus, the function of a planning system is to search for the path linking a decision problem to a solution. Planning is necessary for complex problems for which no pre-established solution procedure is readily available. Planning for ill-structured decisions is difficult, as it is unclear at the outset what actions should be followed to bring about the desired state and in what sequence the operators should be applied to the current state of affairs. Actually, these are the two central conceptual issues of model manipulation: model selection and sequencing.

The literature on planning is centered around reducing the search of a state space by decomposing a problem into smaller ones.   A number of implementations contributed to the planning theory, such as STRIPS [6], ABSTRIPS [10], NOAH [11], MOLGEN [14], SAM [12], and PAM [16].   One of the characteristics of ill-structured problems is interactions among sub-problems.   A number of efforts that deal with resolving goal-interactions have been reported in the literature, such as meta-planning theory [17], constrains-based meta-planning [14], and critics [10].

Generally, the focus of research in goal-interaction is two-fold: to prevent goal conflict and to detect goal overlap. Wilensky [17] defines goal conflict as an unfavorable inter-action between goal relationships. On the other hand, goal overlap is a favorable interaction among goals. The goals are similar enough that a plan for realizing more than one goal may be derived.

3. COMPUTER REALIZATION OF THE MODEL MANIPULATION PROCEDURE

A computer research prototype, called ali, developed to provide a realization of the multi-level model manipulation technique. A problem is structured by ali when a plan for binding all of the problem's variables is generated. An active goal is satisfied when an adequate scheme for binding it is located.

3.1 Model Planning

ali attempts to locate an adequate model-unit for binding a given parameter if and only if it cannot be bound based on session knowledge or database. At such a time, a list of candidate model-units is constructed. As soon as elements of the candidate-list are instantiated, the goal decomposition process begins. The decomposition is achieved by selecting a single model-unit from the candidate-list. The unbound input-parameters of the selected model-unit represent an additional level to the search graph. The nominated model-unit must be a valid (i.e., with none of its preconditions known to be violated) member of the active goal's candidate list. Also, the evaluation function value of the model-unit needs to be less than that of any other member of the same candidate-list. When such a model-unit is found, it is called the most-promising model-unit. Such a model-unit represents, at the time of evaluation, the best alternative for binding an active goal.

For a most-promising model-unit to be selected to bind a parameter, the following conditions must be met:

1. all input-parameters are satisfied, and

2. all preconditions are satisfied.

By and large, neither of the two conditions is readily satisfied at the outset. Thus, in an attempt to satisfy the first condition above, the problem at hand is decomposed into sub-problems. Each of the sub-problems is concerned with satisfying one of the most-promising model-unit's input-parameters. The status of a precondition is checked against session knowledge. If no pertinent knowledge is available, the user is consulted about the situation. (This is done based on the premise that the user is an expert in the domain of the problem.) If the user gives a passive answer (e.g., I don't know), a default status is assumed for the precondition. If any of a model-unit's preconditions is violated, the model-unit ceased from being a most-promising, its status changes from "valid" to "violated", and the state of the concerned goal is changed from active to problematic.

The issue of model sequencing becomes relevant when a solution plan prescribes the use of a sequence of two or more consecutive model-units. Consecutive model-units are parameterically related such that an input-parameter of one is an output-parameter of the other. For example, in constant demand inventory models, an exponential smoothing and an economic order quantity model-units might be consecutive model-units, since demand-rate (an output parameter of exponential smoothing) is an input-parameter of the economic order quantity model-unit.

In the current implementation the sequencing of model-units is done recursively. The sub-goals (input-parameters of a model-unit) are parameterically related to their parent (output-parameter of the same model-unit). Using the simple running example above and assuming that the top-level goal were the optimal order-quantity, the manipulation procedure would search for model-units with order-quantity as an output parameter. Now, assume that the economic order quantity was the most-promising model-unit, with no binding for demand-rate. The manipulation procedure would create an instance of the goal's frame in an attempt to specify a means for binding the variable "demand-rate". If no adequate session knowledge or database entry found, the manipulation procedure would search the model-base for prospective model-units. Exponential smoothing might be used to fulfill this need (depending partly on the validity of preconditions). Note that model sequencing is latent in the sense that it is instigated by complex parameters that require decomposition into input-parameters which in turn require further decomposition. As alluded to earlier, this is achieved by recursive computing rather than by an explicitly called procedure. ali pursues the decomposition of model oriented active goals until all existing goals are either satisfied or no further improvement is possible. The former situation causes the articulated plan to be printed out by the system.

The latter situation—no further progress is achievable—forces the system to declare defeat.

3.2 Meta Model Planning

The meta-planning level handles exceptional situations. Primarily, it locates alternative plans for problematic goals. A goal is problematic if it cannot be satisfied via the regular planning cycle of the manipulation procedure. In addition, rules at the meta planning level look for overlapping goals and prevent conflicting goals. Rules of this level also inhibits circular goals. In the following paragraphs, various rules of meta planning are discussed.

3.2.1 Replanning Rules

Basically, replanning is backtracking on a previously generated solution path. The system resorts to backtracking if the following two conditions are satisfied:

- there is a problematic top-level goal, and
- an alternative model-unit is available in the goal's candidate-list for satisfying the goal.

Upon the satisfaction of the above two conditions, and the concerned goal's state is changed to active. A new value for the evaluation function needs to be computed for the "new" most-promising model-unit as the current most-promising model-unit was dropped from the candidate-list.

Now, if the candidate-list of a problematic goal is empty, the previous replanning rule is irrelevant. Such a situation is handled by a rule whose LHS contains a single condition element which is satisfied if there exists a goal with the state problematic and an empty candidate-list. The consequences of this rule are:

- to update the state of the subject goal from problematic to impossible, and
- to indicate that the model-manipulation process has failed to produce a binding for the top-level goal at hand.

Impossible goals are handed over to the user for his/her consideration.

3.2.2 Goal Interaction

As discussed earlier, goal interaction comes in two flavors: Positive and negative. The former is referred to as goal-overlapping; the latter is called goal-conflict. Two goals are overlapping if both can be satisfied by the same instance of a model-unit. That is, goals are output-parameters of the same model-unit. Two goals are conflicting when they have mutually exclusive preconditions and they are sub-goals of the same parent goal or one of them is a parent for the other.

The rule-based manipulation process takes advantage of goal overlapping by explicitly testing goals for such an inter-action. This is done by detecting any sibling relationships among active goals in the working memory. If a number of sibling goals can be satisfied by a single model-unit, then these goals are overlapping goals that can be satisfied by means of a single model-unit. The reason for considering interaction only among sibling goals is that goals at different depths of the search will not generally overlap, as they are not semantically related (i.e., don't belong to the set of output-parameters of the same instance of a model-unit). Additionally, if goal interaction is detected at a certain level, goals at subsequent levels are necessarily affected by this detection, as the overlapping goals share the same set of sub-goals if one needs to be created.

ali skirts goal conflicts by precluding model-units which have preconditions incompatible with the decision environment from being considered by the selection process.   Furthermore, preconditions that are violated by the current decision environment are kept in the working memory so that this knowledge can be used for checking preconditions belonging to subsequently created instances of model-units.   Instances of model-units with one or more violated preconditions are avoided by the manipulation process as follows:
- the model-unit instance with violated precondition is deleted from the candidate-list,
- the concerned model-unit is flagged so that it cannot be used during the current session, and
- the state of the current goal is changed from active to problematic, if the model-unit is a most-promising one.

Circular goals are also detected by the system's meta-planning rules.   The detection procedure is as follows:
1. the system searches the working memory for repeated goals (i.e., goals with equal definitions)
2. If the state of one of the repeated goal is "satisfied", the state of the rest is changed from active to satisfied.
3. If the state of one of the repeated goals is impossible, the state of the rest is changed from active to impossible.

The existence of a goal with a state of impossible motivates the firing of productions that perform chronological backtracking; they backtrack to the immediate parent of a goal and change the state of the parent to problematic.

It is necessary to distinguish between chronological backtracking and the one performed by the replanning rules, since the latter backtracks on model-units (and specifically most-promising model-units) rather than goals.

4.   EXAMPLE

The query to be analyzed in this section is a model oriented one that requires both selection and sequencing.   The single goal is decomposed into sub-queries and each is satisfied separately subject to being compatible with conditions specified by the decision-maker.   Results obtained by processing the sub-queries are combined so that a comprehensive plan for satisfying the top-level query is generated.

The essence of the query is to select a sequence of model-units so that an integrated model for computing safety stock for V-6 ENGINES is produced.   The AND/OR search graph for this problem is depicted in Figure 1.   The model-base contains three model-units with safety-stock as an output-parameter.   These model-units are

"safety-stock-number-of-stockouts,"

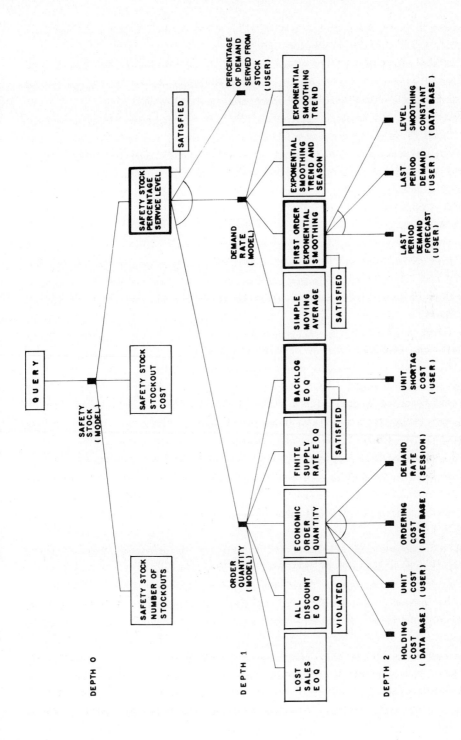

FIGURE 1:   SEARCH GRAPH FOR THE SAFETY STOCK PROBLEM

"safety-stock-stockout-cost," and

"safety-stock-percentage-service-level."

Based on the comparison of the respective values of the evaluation function of the three model-units, "safety-stock-percentage-service-level" is designated as the most-promising model-unit for binding the top-level goal.

order-quantity is an input-parameter for the current most-promising model-unit. Since no value is readily available (in database) for order-quantity, the model-base is searched. As a result, all valid model-units for which order-quantity is an output-parameter are included in the following candidate list.

economic-order-quantity

finite-supply-rate-EOQ

lost-sales-EOQ

all-discount-EOQ

At this point ali suffices with the progress made pertaining to order-quantity and focuses on the parameter demand-rate. This breadth-first search behavior is maintained to enhance ali's backtracking and detection of inter-acting goals.

The attempts to satisfy demand-rate without resorting to the model-base fail. The model-base contains a number of model-units that can be considered for bind-ing the parameter in question. These model-units are:

simple-moving-average

first-order-exponential-smoothing

exponential-smoothing-for-linear-trends

exponential-smoothing-for-trend-and-season

As explained earlier, at this point, ali temporarily shelves the processing of the demand-rate parameter to focus on the third parameter needed in order for a binding for safety stock to be computed. The parameter is "percentage-of-demand-served-from-stock," whose binding value is assumed to be known by the user.

Now, ali resumes its effort toward satisfying the parameter "demand-rate." As a result, the model-unit "first-order-exponential-smoothing" is designated as a most-promising model-unit. After interrogating the user about the decision-making environment, that model-unit is found compatible with the current environment, and hence, is selected as a means for binding the parameter demand-rate.

Order-quantity is the only remaining input-parameter of the most-promising model-unit "safety-stock-percentage-service-level" that is not yet satisfied. The economic-order-quantity (EOQ) model-unit is suggested by the system for satisfying this goal. However, the user indicates that shortages are allowed, a condition that cannot be sustained by the EOQ model-unit. Thus, EOQ is dropped from order-quantity's candidate-list, as well as all members of the candidate-list that do not allow shortages. This is depicted in Figure 1 by the word "VIOLATED." As a result, all model-units have been dropped from the candidate-list except for the model-units that allow shortages in stock, namely backlog-EOQ and lost-sales-EOQ. Based on the evaluation function backlog-EOQ is designated as most-promising. The model-unit is then selected (after binding all input-parameters and satisfying all preconditions) for binding "order-quantity."

Now that all its input-parameters are bound, the model-unit "safety-stock-percentage-service-level" is a primitive model-unit. This motivates the explicit interrogation of the user to find out the status of the model-unit's preconditions as perceived by the user. User interrogation leads the system to select the above primitive model-unit for binding the top-level goal "safety-stock." ali summarizes the plan and the actions to be taken in order for safety-stock to be correctly bound and prints out a concise plan for the consi-deration of the user. The selected model-units are represented as rectablges with bold boundaries in Figure 1.

5. CONCLUSION

The paper presents a computer implementation of a multi-level approach to model manipulation. The implementation uses frame-hierarchies representing model-units as a means for capturing a comprehensive definition of model-units. The manipulation is based on variables to be bound and preconditions to be observed. The technique attempts multiple sources (i.e., session knowledge, database, and model-base) for binding variables that appear in a user-posed query. Simple queries are satisfied from data-base. Structured analytical queries are satisfied from the session knowledge. Ill-structured analytical queries are satisfied from model-base, given that the adequate model-units are represented in the model-base.

The outcome of the model manipulation process is greatly affected by the com-patibility between the decision-problem at hand (i.e., the query) and the assumptions of the model-units available in the model-base. The system attempts to articular a plan that contains model-units consistent with the decision-making environment and among themselves. The implementation encompasses many of the issues of model-management especially model selection and sequencing. The current implementation has other capabilities, such as database access and knowledge management but these are not emphasized here. The multi-level mani-pulation system presented here is merely a plan-generation one. Further research is necessary so that the generated plan may be linked to a "plan executor".

REFERENCES

[1] Bonczek, R., Holsapple, R., and Whinston, A., "A Generalized Decision
     Support System Using Predicate Calculus and Network Data Base," Operations
     Research, Vol.29, No.2, March-April 1981, 263-281.

[2] Bu-Hulaiga, M., Model-Manipulation in Decision Support Systems: A Plan-
     based Approach, Ph.D. Dissertation, University of Wisconsin-Milwaukee,
     August 1987.

[3] Dolk, D., The Use of Abstractions in Model Management, Ph.D. Dissertation,
     University of Arizona, 1982.

[4] Dos Santos, B., and Bariff, M., "A Study of User Interface Aids for Model
     Oriented Decision Support Systems, "Management Science, Vol.34, No.4, April
     1988, 461-468.

[5] Dutta, A., and Basu, A., "An Artificial Intelligence Approach to Model
     Management in Decision Support Systems," IEEE Computer, Vol. 17, No.9,
     September 1984, 89-97.

[6] Fikes, R., and Nilsson, N., "STRIPS: A New Approach to the Application of
     Theorem Proving to Problem Solving," Artificial Intelligence, Vol.3, 1971,
     184-208.

[7] Hwang, S., "Automatic Model Building Systems: A Survey," in DSS-85
     Transactions, Elan, J. (Ed.), IADSS, 1985, 22-32.

[8] Liang, T., "A Graph-based Approach to Model Management," Proceedings of the
     Seventh International Conference on Information Systems, 1986, 136-151.

[9] MacCrimmon, K., "Elements of Decision Making," in Behavioral Approaches to
     Modern Management, W. Goldberg (ed.), Vol.1, Gothenburg, Sweden, 1970, 15-
     44.

[10] Sacerdoti, E., "Planning in a Hierarchy of Abstraction Spaces," Artificial
     Intelligence, Vol.5, 1974, 115-135.

[11] Sacerdoti, E., A Structure for Plans and Behavior, Elsevier, New York,
     1977.

[12] Schank, R. and Abelson, R., Script, Plans, Goals, and Understanding,
     Lawrence Erlbaum Press, Hillsdale, NJ, 1977.

[13] Sprague, R. Jr., and Carlson, E., Building Effective Decision Support
     Systems, Prentice-Hall, Englewood Cliffs, N.J., 1982.

[14] Stefik, M., Planning with Constraints, Stanford Heuristic Programming Pro-
     ject, Working Paper HPP-80-12, 1980.

[15] Stefik, M., Planning with Constraints (MOLGEN: Part 1)," Artificial
     Intelligence, Vol. 16, 1981, 111-139.

[16] Wilensky, R., "Understanding Goal-based Stories," Report #140, Yale Univer-
     sity, 1978.

[17] Wilensky, R., Planning and Understanding, Addison-Wesley, Reading, MA,
     1983.

Expert Systems in Economics, Banking and Management
L.F. Pau et al. (Editors)
 Elsevier Science Publishers B.V. (North-Holland), 1989

The Rubber Research Institute of Malaysia Environmax Planting Recommendation Expert System

LEONG YIT SAN*

The Environmax expert system recommends the most suitable rubber clones ranked in order of preference according to the specifications of the environment. The environment is classified in terms of disease susceptibility, terrain properties and the technological properties of rubber. The rule-based system, which has been distributed country-wide is implemented using EXSYS, an expert system shell and runs on any IBM compatible personal computer with two floppy disk drives and CGA colour monitor.

Computer knowledge or training is not required to run the system. Another important feature is its ability to alter specifications of the environment and observe the effects on the ranking of the recommended clones. A user can then obtain a printed copy of the picture of the clone together with its mean yield and characteristics as well as colourful yield graphs, soil map and maps of occurrence of rubber diseases throughout Peninsular Malaysia. He can also obtain detailed information on various diseases, their treatment and the performance of the clones in these environments. The clones recommended to estates by the expert system can be compared with the actual clones chosen by the rubber industry. Animation of the damage to rubber trees caused by strong winds serves as a caution. Response time is reasonably good as all files are usually disk-read once.

A strategy for a coherent total approach to what, how, where and why rubber is planted is outlined. By planting the proper clones, productivity in the Malaysian rubber industry will be enhanced.

1. INTRODUCTION

Developing countries like Malaysia have just begun to utilise artificial intelligence (AI) for applications requiring human or symbolic reasoning to solve problems pertinent to developing countries. Examples like MYCIN[1,2] for diagnosis of bacteriological blood infections, DENDRAL[3] for molecular structure elucidation from spectrometers, PROSPECTOR[4] for intelligent assistance in the search for mineral deposits, XCON (R1)[5] for configuring computers and CENTAUR[6], a combination of frames and rules for consultation in pulmonary diseases serve as a beacon for researchers in Malaysia to emulate.

One of the most effective ways to reduce rubber production cost is to replant all old and low-yielding fields with high yielding cultivars. The Rubber Research Institute of Malaysia (RRIM) recognises that it has the vital role of recommending the best cultivars.

In 1974, the RRIM introduced the Environmax Planting Recommendations[7] where areas under rubber in Peninsular Malaysia are divided into environments which display factors that act as constraints in the selection of rubber clones. Clones are recommended based on the underlying principle of maximising the yield potential of a particular locality, subject to the inhibitory influence of environmental factors such as known wind damage incidence, major leaf diseases, problematic soils and terracing and moisture stress (**Figure 1**). Clones are classified into three classes based on the amount of available information, the confidence of achieving high yields in actual planting by the commercial sector and the yield levels.

In addition to these refinements of the environment to maximise yields, due recognition has been given to rubber grades of higher commercial values.

---

* Address : Rubber Research Institute of Malaysia
    260, Jalan Ampang , 50450 Kuala Lumpur, Malaysia.

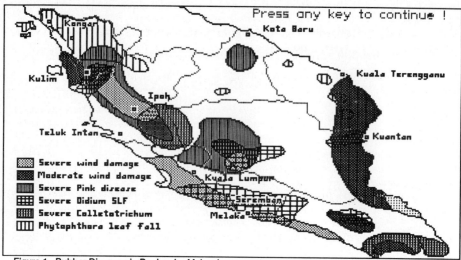

Figure 1. Rubber Diseases in Peninsular Malaysia.

This paper describes the Environmax rule-based expert system running on IBM compatible personal computer (PC) with two floppy drives and a colour monitor. The Environmax System was created using the EXSYS expert system shell.

2.   ENVIRONMAX EXPERT SYSTEM

The Environmax System which combines an expert system with graphics, conventional database, pictures of rubber trees and animation is described by the following seven modules:

o **The Environmax Expert System** contains the expert system shell and runtime module for running the knowledge base using the backward chaining inference engine with the two modules below serving as external programs.
o **The Presentation Graphics** module represents pictorially on maps the occurrence of various rubber diseases and wind conditions throughout Peninsular Malaysia.
o **The Yield Performance Graphs** are graphs of mean yield and cumulative yields for particular rubber clones.
o **The Clone Characteristics** module displays photographs of the various clones available together with information on annual yield, resistance to diseases and suitability to certain environmental conditions.
o **The Description of Characters and Other Information** module describes each clone character in detail as well as provides information on important characters not yet included in the Environmax recommendations.
o **The Wind Damage Animation** module provides an illustration of the damage to rubber trees caused by strong winds.
o **The Printer Setup** allows the user to specify the type of printer to print maps, graphs and pictures of rubber trees.

A presentation graphics external program is called at the start of the expert system run. A map of Peninsular Malaysia showing the delineation of areas under rubber according to the occurrence of wind damage and incidence of each disease is presented. The user can also select the state and obtain a more detailed map. From the Presentation Graphics module, a user can determine the diseases and wind conditions in a particular location.

The user then answers a set of multiple choice questions regarding other environmental factors such as soil, terrain conditions, tapping, trunk and bark characteristics, the preference for technological properties of rubber produced and the scale of planting.

The system employs an IF premise THEN action ELSE action production rule using the backward chaining inference engine to arrive at the goal of selecting the most suitable clones. An example of a rule is given as follows:

IF: THE CHARACTERISTIC OF YOUR AREA IS
    Severe Pink Disease Area
THEN:

	RRIM 600 (Class I Clone) - Probability = 2/10	
and	RRIM 712 (Class I Clone) - Probability = 6/10	
and	PB 255 (Class II Clone) - Probability = 4/10	
and	PB 260 (Class II Clone) - Probability = 8/10	

NOTE:
For this Severe Pink Disease Area, clones RRIM 600, RRIM 701 and RRIM 729 have poor resistance to pink disease. PB 217, RRIM 901, RRIM 905, PB 255 and PB 28/59 have below average resistance to pink disease.

REFERENCE:
You can refer to the map at the beginning of this Environmax Recommendation System or to Planters Bulletin No. 186, March 1986, page 10 published by the Rubber Research Institute of Malaysia.

The explanation facility consists of a note and a reference which can be viewed by typing **WHY**. Help is provided to assist a user on how to run the program. The 0-10 system of probabilities has been used and a probability of 0 excludes the clone from the final output. The program will continue asking questions until it has considered all of the possible solutions and will then display its results. The choice of clones will then be displayed arranged in order of preference by a final value which is computed by averaging the probabilities over the rules used. Sometimes a note such as "Individual holdings of 1 hectare or less may be planted with one clone" is included in the final output which can be printed together with the answers to the questions posted by the computer. These notes serve as additional advice to the user since they cannot be viewed as rules. The user has the option to select any clone recommended to view **HOW** the rules are used in its determination of the final probability.

The user may elect to change the answers to the questions such as changing from a Pink disease infested area to a wind damaged area and observe how this change affects the results. The new recommendation is then displayed alongside the previous recommendation for comparison. If he thinks several sets of answers are possible, he can produce a recommendation for each set of answers. A final recommendation can be obtained based on the weighted final probability of each set of recommendation.

By firing a rule, the yield performance graph module can be activated from the expert system. Annual yields averaged over fifteen years in the form of a histogram and cumulative yields for ten to fifteen years and five to ten years of yield recordings are presented.

The user may use the clone characteristic module to view photographs of the various clones recommended to examine the branching habit of the trees. Information on annual yield of the clone together with a description of its resistance to diseases and suitability to certain environmental conditions are provided.

The description of characters and other information module describes each character in detail and provides definitions of the characters and explanation of the effects on yield. Information on various diseases and their treatment is also included. Information on the number of rainy days, rubberwood and controlled upward tapping is useful even though these characters are not yet part of the Environmax system. The clones recommended to estates by the expert system can be compared with the actual clones chosen by the estate sector in 1985.

The character database is a simple database resident in memory to be used for quick browsing and printing of description of characters.

The wind damage animation module provides an animated illustration of the damage to rubber trees caused by strong winds as well as provides some computer assisted learning (CAL) and caution to smallholders. Branch snap, trunk snap and uprooting of trees due to strong wind and lightning are demonstrated. In areas where wind damage is prevalent, susceptible clones are not recommended. A 0 value of the probability will then be assigned to the susceptible clone in the rule on wind damage.

All text in the system can be printed. What remains to be printed is the graphics screen. By activating the printer setup module from the main menu and selecting the appropriate printer, a user can dump the screen to the printer by utilising the Shift Prt Sc keys. Colourful maps including a soil map, graphs and pictures of trees can be generated.

The main menu acts as a task or program selector to allow a user to select any of the seven modules and return to the main menu after completion of the task. The presentation graphics and yield performance graph modules are linked to the expert system to serve as external programs. The wind damage animation and clone characteristics modules can also be similarly linked but this was not implemented due to the limitation of the storage capacity of floppy diskettes and the requirement of non-excessive swapping of diskettes. A link to the clone characteristic database can automate the presentation of the top three clones recommended. The wind damage module can be included into the expert system on diskettes by utilising image compression techniques along the lines of factal image compression but the response time will be longer.

Floppy diskettes have been chosen as the medium of storage of the programs to enable the expert system to be widely utilised in the country with maximum effect but at minimum cost of hardware, program support and maintenance. The additional advantage of a floppy system is the ability to be physically moved to any place easily. This is important to a developing country as there are smallholdings in remote places without electricity. The Environmax Expert System can reach these smallholders by means of a portable PC brought by the Advisory Officers from the RRIM State office. Further, an extension man can have the system running in his home as well as his office. With the possible use of 3 mb floppy diskettes in the future, the entire system can be implemented on a single 3 1/2 inch floppy diskette small enough to be carried in the pocket of a shirt.

The probability attached to the choice of a clone in a rule has been obtained from the mean values of the results of field experiments which have been transformed to an ordinal scale. The precision of the mean values has been ignored and an additive model is assumed. The performance of a clone in a given environment will then be the sum of the effects of each sub-type of that environment. The performance is hence computed by averaging the "probabilities" or plot values over the rules used giving the clone mean over the individual sub-type of the environment. In an undefined area, the probability is based on the class of the clone and the average yields obtained. Clones of Class I carry a score of 5 and Class II a score of 4. The yields of the clone carry scores from 0 to 4. The scores for class and yield are added together to form the probability. In cases where the answer to the question is not from the above characteristics, the probability is derived from a scoring system based on weight on yield, class, secondary characters, terrain characters, tapping characters, soil characters and latex properties but excludes the characters mentioned in the question.

It is without doubt that yield is the more important primary character while other characters such as resistance to wind damage, diseases and tapping are secondary. It is therefore necessary for the system to incorporate this aspect. This can be achieved by adding the choice of clones, with the probability based on yield and class of the clone to nominal questions such as "Are you a smallholder or estate owner?" in an incremental fashion. As such choices of clones are added to each nominal question, the recommendations produced are examined until the system is tuned to reflect the emphasis on yield. Since the final probability is obtained by averaging over the rules used, it is additive in nature and hence allows incremental addition of emphasis on yield. In future when rubberwood becomes more important, additional weight on this character can easily be introduced to the knowledge base which is also incremental in nature.

Interaction of characters has not been incorporated even though the expert system can cater for it. The information on this aspect is limited as it is impossible to carry out experiments that take into account all possible interactions among all the characters.

When the Environmax Expert System was distributed country-wide, it was well received by the Malaysian rubber industry due to its coherent total solution approach to the problem of selection of clones for planting and its user friendliness.

There is no need to read any operation manual as all instructions are provided on the screen. An acid test though not following the Turing Test was performed for five users of English educated and non-English educated groups to determine the amount of knowledge required to operate the system and the extent of user friendliness of the system. These users had no previous experience in using a computer. All users had to be taught to make one of the choices in a menu by typing a numeric key and then the enter key to activate the selection. All five English educated users were able to obtain the recommendations and execute all the modules and most of them could print the graphics. All of them did not know that multiple answers could be given despite two pages of instruction. The non-English educated group did not understand how to key in E or 0 to end a selection and Y or N for Yes/No questions. On providing such instructions, they could obtain the recommendations. The findings of the test were used to construct a 16-point note or pest list to help users who could not operate the system. The two-page list contains instructions like differentiation between zero and letter O, type R for Retry when the message "Abort, Retry, Ignore?" appears and how to print graphics screens when the printer is not supported. The other notes contain information on how to start the system from DOS by using AUTOEXEC command, perform back-up procedures and print using the serial port. In an ideal situation, the pest list should be blank. Should it be blank, then a truly expert system exists without a user possessing any computer knowledge to operate the system. As it stands at the moment, the pest list contains a very small amount of computer knowledge which can be easily acquired by the user.

A rubber planter can have the recommendations and the specification of the environment of his land printed together with a picture of the selected clone and a description of its characteristics. If he is uncertain of what each character means, he can print the definition of the character together with a description of the effects on yield, treatment of diseases and other relevant information. This is a simplified form of computer assisted learning. To spread his risk, the planter can plant several clones based on the final probability. In cases where the top three clones obtain a final probability of eight out of ten, these three clones should be planted in equal proportion.

The greatest effect an expert system can have is to raise the quality of evaluation of clones especially among the smaller estates and progressive smallholders. Since they cannot afford to employ trained agriculturists competent enough to perform the complex evaluation, the expert system serves as a substitute. As the cost of the hardware is not prohibitive, they can afford to have the expert system running in their organisations. With about two million hectares of land planted with rubber yielding 1.5 million tonnes annually and earning more than US$1.5 billion in export revenue, replanting with proper clones will certainly increase export earnings and provide a competitive edge to the Malaysian rubber industry. Environmax can then be seen to have a positive impact on the efficiency, productivity and effectiveness of the Malaysian rubber industry.

A survey on the usefulness of the Environmax system to eighteen commercial estates was conducted. As expected, there were estates with users who had never used a computer before and Environmax was their first experience with a computer. All users rated the software easy to use without any problems except the inability to print graphics screen using unsupported printers. The two databases on description of clones and characters were rated most useful besides the recommendation while the maps, the bar charts and pictures were rated above average useful. Enhanced colour pictures were not required for the next version of Environmax. More description of clones, characters, CGA pictures and a hard disk version were identified as the area for improvement. A natural language interface was desirable but some users did not really want a voice recognition system.

3. DISCUSSION

What makes the system so successful is the mixture of expert system with conventional processing techniques at minimum hardware cost but with good response time. All files are usually disk-read only once and are usually placed in memory. The recipe for the Environmax expert system contains the following ingredients and characteristics:

Expert system shell with built in command processor,and interprogram communication
Presentation graphics, maps, bar charts, line graphs
Picture
Animation for CAL and entertainment
Memory-resident (RAM) Database
Printing of text and graphics in Colour
Modular structure with some modules written in C, Basic and Pascal
Computer assisted learning and help facility
Lowest possible cost of hardware
Floppy drive system
No thick manual to read only a Pest List
No phone-in consultancy service
Designed for first-time computer user
A strategy for a coherent total approach.

The only attempt at programming that failed was to incorporate the music of thunder, lightning and wind on the PC without music instrument digital interface even though it worked very well on a piano.

Additional desirable breadth-wise features not in the Environmax system but useful to expert system builders are:

o Inference Engine with forward and backward chaining mechanism and with different types of uncertainty factor taking into account Bayesian inference and theory of evidence
o A Blackboard
o Link to model-based system/structured objects containing frames and object-oriented programming methods, link to languages, Prolog and Lisp
o Interface to process control, video disk, music and voice synthesis.

By using all these features, a series of expert systems on rubber can be generated to function as an encyclopedia of knowledge. No distinction is made between the various types of knowledge representation as the outcome or output from the system is a user's only concern. It is preferred that these features or AI tools be interlinked with one another and with normal processing utilities to be more effective.

The Environmax expert system was built using the results of field experiments. It would be ideal if the expert system was built from raw data. In order for this kind of depth-wise system to be built, other types of inference engines have to be used. One of these would certainly be similar to REX[8] which utilises expert system techniques based on the Centaur structure as an interface to the S statistical system. REX provides a regression strategy whereby it guides the analysis by testing assumptions of regression, suggesting possible transformation when assumptions are violated, checking for missing data, outliers, heavy tails and autocorrelation. Frames are used to guide the invocation of rules as suggested by Aikins[6]. REX uses backward chaining to establish hypothesis and forward chaining to select additional hypothesis or specific actions. Definitions of statistical terms are kept in a lexicon module and reports are produced automatically.

Data analysis is a domain of knowledge which can be applied to data from another ground or core domain such as Environmax in this case. Data analysis can be termed as mantle domain. The formation of aims and questions the researcher wants to explore in the core domain, the translation into formal terms from ground domain into statistical terms together with the assumptions made, the numerical processing of data cleaning, transformation, estimation and test of hypotheses and the interpretation back to ground domain to update the rules in Environmax summarise the activities needed. Fuzzy reasoning using uncertainty factors, belief functions, Shafer-Dempster theory of evidence and subjectivist Bayesian inference[9] will be demanded by such expert systems. Particular attention should be paid to assumptions made and to the accumulated knowledge obtained so far as it is common to have different rules being articulated on different occasions for identical problems and scenarios but using different assumptions.

On top of the above core and mantle domains will be the surface domain consisting of natural language processing[10]. For practical purposes, it is not necessary to build a system such as D. Lenat's CYC or EURISKO [11] for a front end intelligent interface to enable the correct expert system to be fired during the dialogue session. All that is necessary is a more sophisticated Eliza[12] that can activate the various expert systems, access databases and parrot segments of the dialogue without truly understanding the conversation and generate new knowledge. It would be ideal if a voice recognition and synthesis system can be built on top of the natural language interface to allow a user to speak to the computer as though he is speaking to an expert.

What is presented is the rubber planting strategy as illustrated by Chambers[13.14] for a coherent total approach that can be defined as what, when, where, how, and why rubber is planted. With a planned strategy, a formal description of the choices, actions and decisions to be made can then be presented.

The tools in AI can be viewed as musical notes as described below:

Note	Description
Do	Domain -- core, mantle, surface
Re	Rule-based Element
Me	Model-based Element
Fa	Frames Action
So	Structured Objects, Scripts
LLa	Logic programming, Natural Language and Automated Reasoning
Ti	Tools (graphics, database, pictures, music,video) Integration.

These notes are available to a knowledge engineer. All he has to do is to string together the notes and attach words to the notes to form a song. The song will then sing the story of a strategy for a coherent total approach to his problems.

4. CONCLUSIONS

The strategy for a coherent total solution to what, how, where and why rubber is planted is the ultimate goal of Environmax expert system. Applications using a hybrid system of frames, rules, natural language processing with the usual data processing facilities like graphics, database, pictures, music, etc make artificial intelligence the centre-fold technology of today.

Implementation of the above strategy will enable important things requiring decision making to be simple. The Environmax experience indicates that simple things such as pictures, graphs, animation, databases, ease of use without manual to read etc are important to ensure the success and use of the system by ordinary people.

Widespread use of Environmax even in places without electricity can ensure that RRIM planting technology will be properly transferred and utilised by all sectors of the rubber industry. Productivity in the Malaysian rubber industry will therefore be enhanced.

REFERENCES

1   Buchanan, B.G. and Shortliffe, E.H., eds. (1984). Rule-Based Expert Systems.
    Reading, MA : Addison-Wesley.
2   Shortliffe, E.H. (1976). Computer-Based Medical Consultations : MYCIN.
    New York : Elsevier.
3   Buchanan, B.G. and Feigenbaum, E.A. (1978). DENDRAL and Meta-DENDRAL :
    Their applications dimension. Artificial Intelligence, 11, 5-24.
4   Duda, R.O., J.Gashing, and P.E.Hart. (1979). "Model Design in the Prospector
    Consultant System for Mineral Exploration" in Expert Systems
    in the Micro Electronic Age (D. Michie, ed.),
    Edinburgh University Press.
5   McDermott, D. (1980). R1: An expert in the computer system domain.
    Proceedings of AAAI-80, 269-271.
6   Aikins, J.S. (1983). Prototypical knowledge for expert systems.
    Artificial Intelligence, 20, 163-210.
7   RRIM Planting Recommendations 1986-8. RRIM Planters' Bulletin Published by
    Rubber Research Institute of Malaysia, No. 186, 1986, 4-22.
8   Gale, W.A. (1986). REX Review in Artificial Intelligence & Statistics in
    Artificial Intelligence and Statistics (Gale, W.A., ed.) Addison-Wesley.
9   Spiegelhalter, D.J. (1986). "A Statistical View of Uncertainty in Expert Systems" in
    Artificial Intelligence and Statistics (Gale, W.A., ed.). Addison-Wesley.
10 Obermeir,K.K. (1987). Natural-language Processing. Byte, 12, No. 4, 225-232.
11 Lenat,D. (1983). EURISKO : A Program that Learns New Heuristics and Domain
    Concepts. AI Journal (March, 1983), 21.
12 Weizenbaum,J. (1983). ELIZA - A Computer Program for the Study of Natural
    Language Communication Between Man and Machine.
    Comm. ACM 26, No. 1, 23-28.
13 Chambers, J.M. (1981). Some thoughts on expert software.
    Proceedings of the 13th Symposium on the Interface, 36-40.
14 Gale, W.A. (1986). "Overview of Artificial Intelligence and Statistics" in Artificial
    Intelligence and Statistics (Gale, W.A., ed.). Addison-Wesley.

Expert Systems in Economics, Banking and Management
L.F. Pau et al. (Editors)
© *Elsevier Science Publishers B.V. (North-Holland), 1989*

Managing AI Technology Transfer
for
Manufacturing Applications

Phaih-Lan Law, Digital Equipment Corp., Marlboro, Massachusetts, U.S.A.
Mitchell M.Tseng, Digital Equipment Corp., Marlboro, Massachusetts, U.S.A.
Peter Ow, Singapore Mfg.Plant, Digital Equipment Int.Ltd., Rep.of Singapore.

There are many AI applications that have been designed and developed in the laboratory environment but the transition to real world day to day operations has been difficult. At Digital, we have developed an AI technology transfer program which aimed at implementing AI applications by transferring ownership to the user organization. The program is also aimed at achieving business goals through developing local AI capability and competency, increase management understanding and confidence in the technology, and maintain Digital competitiveness and technical leadership. In this paper, we will describe the AI technology transfer program based on a case study at the Digital Manufacturing plant in Singapore.

Introduction

Artificial Intelligence, as a technology, has been around for several decades. However, productive uses of AI technology are still few and far between. While there are many AI applications that have been designed and developed in the laboratory environment, the transition to real world day to day operations has been difficult, particularly where critical business requirements depend on it. Obviously, there are technical issues, such as lack of stable software development environment and insufficient knowledge representation facilities. On the other hand, there are non-technical issues which are crucial to the successful implementation of knowledgebased systems. The issues include scarcity of knowledge engineers, system acceptance by the user organization, technology transfer, re-design of work assignment and change management. This paper attempts to address these issues and offer some alternatives for resolution.

Figure 1: Process for Building Expert Systems

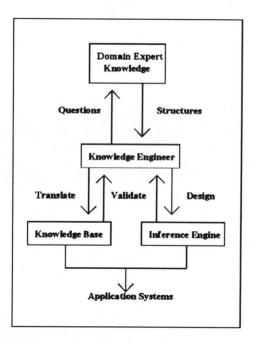

Fig.1 depicts the methodology used in most of the current AI applications development process [1]. Knowledge engineers play a key role in capturing the domain knowledge, and translating the knowledge acquired into knowledgebase. Historically, production rules have been an integral part of the knowledgebase production rules in most expert systems. Since knowledge engineers are scarce resources and often reside in developing organizations, the dependency of knowledge engineers to support and update the knowledgebase has resulted in unnecessary delays and inefficiency. These delays can make the system not responsive enough for serving the business needs. The solution is two folds, one is to train knowledge engineers to be more knowledgeable about domain knowledge, the other is to transfer AI expertise to the user organization. Because it is now technically feasible to segregate knowledgebase and inference engine, and make knowledgebase maintenance an easier task for the user organization, we need to increase the AI competency in the user organization so that the users can be more participative in application systems and business process design. Eventually, ownership of expert system applications can then be transferred to the user group so that the knowledgebased system is embedded in the business operations.

The segregation of the knowledgebase and the inference engine has to be incorporated into the design during the conceptual phase. The challenging issues for the user group are to augment understanding of AI technology and for the development group to gain insight of relevant business issues during this early stage, and carry on this learning process all the way through final implementation.

With that in mind, we at Digital have developed a technology transfer program for deploying the AI technology throughout the corporation. The program is aimed at achieving business goals through the following objectives:

- Develop local AI capability and competency
- Transfer ownership of AI application to the user organization
- Increase management understanding of the AI technology
- Increase management confidence in the AI technology
- Maintain Digital competitiveness and technical leadership

In this paper, we will use the case study of the Digital Manufacturing Plant in Singapore as an example to explain the above technology transfer program. The Singapore manufacturing plant is a high volume plant for Electronics Storage Devices (ESD), producing millions of dollars worth of Memory and Mass Storage products, including floppy disk drives and hard cartridge disks. The Singapore plant has been recognized for the timely delivery and high quality products, and is strategically important for the corporation.

Technology Transfer

In developing the technology transfer program, human resource issues have been identified as crucial factors in the successful, effective implementation of advanced technology [2]. The program has two major emphasis - communication and participation.

Communication is to keep the information flow between the development site and the user organization. It also means to set the right expectations for management and the users. By doing so, issues are addressed during the early stage of the development; it will then minimize the resistance to change [2].
Participation is based on the belief of "learning by doing". In order to master the AI technology, one way to learn it is through using the technology in development with the guidance of an experienced knowledge engineer. In addition, being a member of the development team will foster local ownership and develop confidence in the participant and the user organization.

The technology transfer program is broken down into seven phases.

1. Technology Awareness
2. Opportunity Identification
3. Candidate Selection

4. Formulation of Training Plan
5. AI Training
6. Advanced Fellowship Development Program.
7. Project Implementation

Each phase leads to the next phase. However, occasionally several phases overlap each other and run in parallel. The first five phases deal with educating management about the technology, setting the right expectations, and train the candidate on AI theory and implementation. The emphasis of the first five phases is to obtain management support and commitments to build local AI capability, and to provide the foundation for implementing AI applications. During the last two phases, intensive exchange of technology, i.e. infusion of AI technology to the user organization and importing domain knowledge to the development group occurs. The candidate will be part of the project team responsible for the development and implementation of the project in the user organization.

1. Technology Awareness

In the past, one of the major hindrance in transferring the AI technology is lack of management support and commitments. The hype about AI technology often set the wrong expectations which may result in mistrust of the technology. In order to overcome this problem, top management need to be educated to increase their understanding of the technology.

Technology awareness presentation is a solution we developed to communicate the information with top management. The goal of the presentation is to set the right expectations by increasing management understanding. The presentation include an overview of the technology - its impact and limitations, and results of some internal AI applications in manufacturing.
The presentation is given to management and individuals who may potentially use the AI technology in their jobs, of the sponsoring organization. For example, in the Singapore manufacturing plant, it is presented to the plant staff and the engineers. The outcome of these presentations foster information sharing on business requirements and AI technology. It was found that the presentation generated discussions around applicable technology and business impact. We were able to set the right expectations, and help increase the level of understanding of the technology.

2. Opportunity Identification

The process of opportunity identification is carried out by matching key business goals of the sponsoring organization and potential AI applications. The decision on choosing which area of AI application is based on the following criteria:

- Impact to the business goal - application need to have significant business impact to the sponsoring organization in order to be selected.

- Appropriateness of the AI application in achieving the business goal based on the reviews by local domain experts.

- Maturity of the AI application - application at the conceptual stage is inappropriate as it required experienced personnel to carry out the task. On the other hand, application that is near completion will not be able to offer the candidate opportunities to gain development experience.

- Accessibility to the domain experts.
- Availability of the information system in the sponsoring organization.

After going through the identification process, priorities on potential AI applications are agreed by the users, developers and management.

In the case of the Digital manufacturing plant at Singapore, implementing advanced process technology and quality excellence are the two areas chosen as primary business goals for the AI program. In particular, the evolving technological complexity around quality of the surface mount technology has been chosen as the initial project. The quality system today has difficulties in managing the information complexity and providing timely resolution to process problems. Moreover, the traditional system doesn't have the flexibility to change when new products and technology are introduced. Knowledge of the new process is often incomplete and evolves over time, this then resulted in fragmentary understanding of quality issues in term of quality levels, process capability and root-causes of the process problems. AI technology offers potential to provide a solution.

The D1 system (fig.2) [3], developed using AI techniques by the Applied Intelligent Systems Group at Digital in the US, is a system that addresses today's need of quality issues for process control and provides an architecture for future processes. It captures the process knowledge and matures over time as more knowledge is gathered. The Singapore plant has specified that the first phase of D1 system implementation is at the surface mount process since this technology has the greatest impact on present and future products.

Figure 2: Implementing of D1 System for Multiple Plant Applications

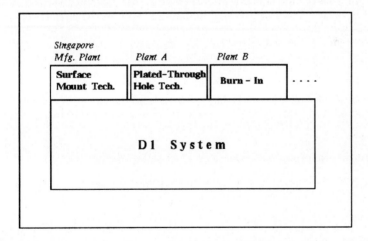

Fig.2 shows that the D1 system supports the knowledgebases developed at the user organizations. The user has the flexibility to customize the system according to the site requirements.

3. Candidate Selection

Once the project is selected, the next step is to select the candidate. The selection of the candidate is vital to the success of the technology transfer program. The individual will not only provide the expertise needed to apply AI technologies to business problems but also assume the leadership responsibility for the success of the AI project. Thus, candidates qualified for this program are motivated, capable, produce high quality work, able to deal with and effect change, and has personal commitment to learning the technology [4]. To aid the candidate selection process, a set of criteria is developed.

Candidate Selection Criteria [4]:

a. Behavioral/Organization
    - the ability to elicit and assimilate information quickly and effectively
    - high quality job performance
    - perceived by his/her peers as having been successful
    - good communication skills
    - self-motivated
    - the ability to use and develop formal and informal individual and organizational support networks
    - willingness to give and receive feedback non-defensively
    - awareness of his or her impact on others
    - the ability to work effectively as part of a project team
    - interested in and committed to learning and applying expert system technology.
    - understanding of the organization culture, preferably has been working with the group for 2-3 yrs.

b. Business/Strategic
    - a logical and creative approach to solving problems
    - the ability to deal with complexity and set priorities
    - the ability to manage time.

c. Technical
    - some programming background (e.g. PASCAL, BASIC, C)
    - a solid math background, particularly in logic
    - knowledgeable in the business/domain problem
    - software engineering, familiar with software development process
    - computer science - understanding of algorithms, abstract data types, language constructs, program design and organization

Based on the criteria, the Singapore plant has chosen a process engineer, who is knowledgeable about the surface mount process, to be the first candidate. The candidate will be able to contribute the domain knowledge and site requirements and participate as part of the development team for the D1 system. The candidate is accountable for the implementation of the system at the Singapore plant after he has finished the training.

4. Formulation of training plan

The formulation of a training plan is a management tool to finalize the logistics of the training program. During the development of the training plan, the following check-list is used:

- Is the candidate well qualified (i.e. meet the selection criteria)?
- Is there organization support?
- Is there management commitment?
- Does the AI project selected fit the business goals and have significant business impact?

This process is necessary to make sure that the right decisions are made before further investment in the technology transfer program. Another important factor that the training plan brought about is that it establishes the right expectations for the sponsoring and mentoring organizations, and most important of all, for the candidate.

The training plan contains information about the candidate, sponsoring and mentoring organization, the goal of the training program, duration of the training, and specific task during training. Its format varies from organization to organization, depending on the business needs. Fig.3 shows a sample of the training plan used.

Figure 3: Sample of Training Plan

Advanced Fellowship Program
Candidate's name

Sponsoring Organization : Singapore Manufacturing Plant

Mentoring Organization : Applied Intelligent Systems Group (AISG)

Fellowship Project : D1 System

Mentors - from mentoring organization :

Purpose : To gain significant practical experience working in an applied expert systems development project

Goals :
- Use D1 to acquire skills needed for expert systems implements
- Gain a broad perspective on various expert systems development approaches / methodologies
 ⋮

Candidate's Responsibilities :
- Drive continuous improvement of fellowship process :
  - submit monthly reports
  - feedback to management on any concerns or issues during the program; propose appropriate solutions to concerns / issues
 ⋮

Fellowship Review : AISG will be responsible to write the review of the canadidate at the end of the program

Fellowship Report : The candidate will submit a brief and concise report within a month of the end date

Fellowship Schedule : May 1, 1988 ....Start date, report to AISG
 ⋮

5. AI Training

The AI training program, developed by Digital's AI Technology Center, was designed to develop "knowledge engineers", individuals who can apply expert or knowledge-based systems technology to current business problems in Digital's environment. This program is established to reduce the company's dependency on university-based technical resources, and provide the state-of-the-art education necessary to maintain Digital's technological leadership in AI applications [5].

The program consists of two basic curriculum - business and technical. The business curriculum is a one-week seminar on "Introduction to AI in Business". It is targeted to give management an in-depth overview of AI technology. The technical curriculum is a 8-weeks program, providing the individual with base-level information and skills required of a knowledge engineer [5]:

- A broad understanding of the issues, principles, and tools of AI technology and their current and potential application in Digital's environment

- Familiarity with the syntax and application of several AI tools, including LISP and OPS-5

- An understanding of the behavioral and organizational issues and skills related to introducing technological change successfully.

Candidates selected for the technology transfer program are required to attend the technical curriculum, to acquire the fundamental skills in order to proceed to the next phase. Normally, the candidates are enrolled into the AI training program during the development of the training plan.

In the case of the Singapore plant, after the technical awareness presentation, the engineering manager from Singapore attended the one-week AI seminar before the commitment of developing AI capability in Singapore is made. Upon his return, he received the support from the plant manager to sign up for the technology transfer program. The technology transfer program team helped the engineering manager during phase 2 and 3 to come up with a training plan (fig.3). 3 months after the engineering manager attended the AI seminar, the candidate started in the 8-week technical program.

6. Advanced Fellowship Development Program

The advanced fellowship development program provides the candidates opportunity to continue their development by working on an existing AI application with the guidance of the experienced knowledge engineer. The AI application and the mentoring organization are identified during phase 2, and the training plan is developed at phase 3 of the technology transfer program. The program normally lasts 6-12 months, depending on the complexity of the business problems addressed. Besides "learning a new technology by doing", the advanced fellowship development program also brought about significant impacts to the technology transfer program:

- Remove the candidate from the old role for 6-12 months help the successful transition to the new responsibilities.

- Ensure management commitment and support at the senior level as well as at the local level in the sponsoring organization due to the significant financial and resource investment

- Help the candidate to develop confidence in applying the technology.

- Provide a laboratory environment for developing the AI application to meet the requirements/needs of the sponsoring organization. This then minimizes the interruption to the business operations (e.g. manufacturing production line).

- Provide an environment for the software engineers in the mentoring organization to share the AI technology, and learn the domain knowledge from the candidate, and vice versa.

- Help the candidate to establish the network and infrastructure in Digital's AI community.

Good planning and management of the fellowship program is essential in order to deliver a good knowledge engineer and the AI application. The plan takes into account of the technology learning, knowledge of managing an AI application implementation, and the transition to the sponsoring organization. The candidate, with the guidance of the mentor, is required to develop a project/implementation plan during the fellowship program. The benefit of developing a project plan is to identify the key issues that need to be resolved before implementation. This also helps to get management attention, especially for issues that need management commitment for resolutions.

Throughout the 6-12 month period, regular reviews were scheduled to measure the candidate progress. The review session is also needed as communication channel to discuss the candidate's expectation and needs from the fellowship program, and the expectations of the mentoring organization. To help the candidate broaden his/her perspective on AI applications, he/she is also introduce to other AI applications. At the end of the fellowship program, candidates are required to write a report to give feedbacks about the program so that the program can continue to improve.

In the case of the candidate from Singapore, he spent the first 2 months understanding the D1 system in term of how and why AI technology is applied and its application in other Digital manufacturing sites. From this learning, he developed a project plan for D1 implementation in Singapore.

As part of the fellowship program, the candidate returned to the plant to present to the Singapore plant management and the users information about the 8 week AI training program, the D1 system - its impact and limitations, and the implementation plan for the D1 system in Singapore. The outcome of the presentation is that management is well informed of his progress, and remains committed to transfer the AI technology. He also resolved some key issues that were identified, gained the users' perspective and feedbacks (i.e.user requirements), for the D1 system, and established a project team for implementing D1 in Singapore.

Based on the user requirements, the candidate developed the D1 system for the Singapore plant environment. This is when the engineer learned to apply the technical skill that he learned from the classroom to the system, with guidance from the mentoring organization. The candidate communicates constantly with the project team in the Singapore plant with the changes and obtain data from the plant to test the system. By involving the participation of the engineers in the plant during the fellowship program, the D1 system is no longer a new system; thus, reducing resistance to change and fostering local ownership.

7. Project Implementation

The last phase of the AI technology transfer program is to implement the AI application. After completing the advanced fellowship program (phase 6), the candidate returns to the sponsoring organization to implement the AI application. The implementation plan is based on the project plan developed. During this phase, the candidate communicates closely with the mentoring organization on the status of the project. Similarly, the mentoring organization reports to the candidate on any new system changes. This process is to ensure communication and to provide a supporting infrastructure for the successful implementation. The candidate's responsibilities include customization of the AI application to the site requirements, measuring system impacts, feedback to the mentoring organization, and initiating the next phase of development.

Program Result

The AI technology transfer program was developed in April 1987. In less than 2 years, the technology transfer program has been implemented in the manufacturing sites in the Far East, Latin America and the United States. A total of 13 managers have attended the 1 week AI seminar through this program and 8 engineers have completed the full technology transfer program. 100% of the engineers going through this program are currently the leaders in driving the technology in the manufacturing sites.

The candidate from Singapore has completed the program and is now implementing the D1 system in Singapore. The performance of the candidate and result of delivering an AI application has increased the confidence of the Singapore management in the AI technology. The management has already committed the second resources to go through the AI technology transfer program. The first candidate is playing a technical leader role to help the Singapore plant to identify the right project for the second fellowship program. We viewed the progress as success to the technology transfer program. Singapore manufacturing plant's continuation of sending engineers to this program is a positive sign to establish a critical mass for developing local AI capability.

Another success story of the technology transfer program is at the Digital manufacturing plant in Taiwan. The site has sent 3 engineers through this program, and they have successfully implemented 3 AI projects in less than 2 years. The 3 AI applications are now in production use. In addition, an AI group is formed by these 3 engineers to provide the technical focus to the site. The Taiwan site has just started designing and developing and AI system to solve computer system information problem.

Lessons Learned

We find that the critical component for the success of the technology transfer program is the management commitment. By requiring an organization to free up a resource for 8-14 months and the financial investment in training and relocation, ensures management commitment. In addition, taking the engineer away from his old role for 8-14 months helps the trained engineer to transition to his/her new responsibilities, and avoid their falling back to the old roles and old practices.
Secondly, the ability to deliver an application by the end of the program helps to increase the confidence of the candidate as well as the management confidence in the AI technology.

The technology transfer program also promotes knowledge sharing. We found that the software engineers in the mentoring organization has the opportunity to better understand the domain from the candidate, and the candidate also gains a better understanding of the AI technology from the software engineer.

Through the technology transfer program, we also learned that ownership by user organization is critical to the successful implementation of AI applications.

Acknowledgments

The authors wish to thank John Spencer, and the General International Area Manufacturing and Engineering Group at Digital for their support in this program.

References

1. Waterman, D.A., "A Guide to Expert Systems", Addison-Wesley Publishing Company, Reading, Massachusetts, 1986.

2. Majchrzak, A., "The Human Side of Factory Automation", Jossey-Bass Publishers, San Francisco, California, 1988.

3. Tseng, M.M., Cavanaugh, D., and Khorram, M., "Knowledge-based Systems Approach to Process Control Implementation", Winter Annual Meeting of ASME, 1987.

4. Clanon, J., "Guide to Knowledge Engineer Selection", Artificial Intelligence Guide Series, Digital Equipment Corporation, 1985.

5. Clanon, J., "Growing Your Own Artificial Intelligence Resources", Proceedings of the 1986 World Conference on Continuing Engineering Education, pp688-692 vol.2, 1986.

Expert Systems in Economics, Banking and Management
L.F. Pau et al. (Editors)
© *Elsevier Science Publishers B. V. (North-Holland), 1989*

KNOWLEDGE-BASED COORDINATION IN
DISTRIBUTED PRODUCTION MANAGEMENT

Juha E. HYNYNEN

Laboratory of Information Processing Science
Helsinki University of Technology
Otakaari 1, 02150 Espoo, Finland

In this paper, a framework for coordination of information processing in a distributed production management environment is discussed. For this purpose, a model coined as DREAM (Distributed Reactive Management) is specified. DREAM is based on a hierarchically decentralized set of opportunistically behaving decision-making subsystems, communicating with each other via message passing. The subsystems themselves are threefold entities, each comprising a Problem-Solving Subsystem, a Domain-Modeling Subsystem, and a Message Management Subsystem. An individual decision-making subsystem in DREAM is relatively self-contained, communicating with its environment on a reactive basis. The actual internode coordination is collectively in the hands of the individual Message Management Subsystems. They apply a set of temporal, topological, and application dependent rule-based heuristics to regulate the message traffic.

1. INTRODUCTION

A modern industrial enterprise engaged in manufacturing activities is a multilevel organization. A noticeable operational and structural aspect of a complex, hierarchical manufacturing system is the need for coordination of the activities [12]. Activity coordination takes place both in intrasubsystem and intersubsystem management contexts. The need to coordinate inevitably follows from specialization within the organization. Coordination is required to enforce coherence in the system by integrating the operation of the relatively self-contained subsystems in order to optimize some global criteria.

In addition to the requirement of coordination, as another result of the need for specialization, a hierarchical manufacturing system always exhibits some degree of decentralization of control. Moreover, several external factors dominating the markets clearly suggest that the degree of decentralization of control in a manufacturing system is - and should be - increasing. Recent development of the influencing factors has caused a shift in orientation of the competitive edge for industrial companies. This shift has taken place from efficient marketing and high quality products to integrated, cost-effective manufacturing and timely delivery of goods and services [11].

The basis of the research documented in this paper is that, taken the recent development towards production management systems with distributed control, a coordination framework at the information processing level of control is needed. The framework should take into account the special requirements, and use the potential opportunities the application environment lays down. It should also adapt the capabilities of the computerized control system to the distributed reality.

In any complete coordination framework for decentralized processing and problem solving, two different conceptual layers may be identified: the syntactic layer and the semantic layer. The syntactic layer is a domain-independent basis for the semantic layer. It gives a solution on the computational dimension of decentralized control, i.e., how to connect together the functionally and structurally distributed parts composing the system. Thus, it addresses the issues of distributed - possibly concurrent - processing of activity descriptions in the system. A coordination framework is insufficient, however, without a conceptually higher semantic level, tackling issues on the behavioral dimension of decentralized control. It gives an abstracted, metaphorical view of the coordination process: what, when, and according to what strategies to communicate between the subsystems, provided that the intersubsystem connections exist. The semantic layer, therefore, extends the computational framework to facilitate actual domain specific problem solving as opposed to mere distributed and synchronized execution of individual tasks.

It is the thrust in this paper that the semantic layer of a decentralized coordination framework in a manufacturing environment should draw heavily on heuristic, temporal, spatial, and experience-based domain knowledge present on the factory floor, rather than averaged algorithms. These algorithms (e.g., MRP, MRPII, etc.) are claimed, namely, to provide results with only a vague resemblance to what is actually happening in routine operations.

The vast majority of existing coordination frameworks in manufacturing contexts rely on a strictly hierarchical control architecture. For example, the use of intelligent electronic mail in passing control information in the AMRF model [10] which allows lateral communication for service request purposes only, the exploitation of fixed time windows with an assumption of total rescheduling in case of disruptions in the Esprit project #418 [7], and the advocation of decision frames with an emphasis on functional integration in the Esprit project #932 [13]. In addition and as opposed to those, it is claimed here that it is the lateral communication and horizontal structural integration - along the lines of the actual production processes - that exploits the real possibilities to coordinate behavior effectively in a manufacturing system. Coordination in a real-time and dynamic environment, namely, requires unnecessary authority-based communication to be reduced to its minimum. When inevitable disruptions in the operating environment arise, lateral cooperation between neighboring nodes at the same organizational level is needed to assure an intelligent adaptation to the changed circumstances with minimal disturbance regarding the overall system. By exploiting lateral communication the neighboring decision-making subsystems can temporarily join together in resolving a particular problem - without necessarily any intervention of the higher levels in the hierarchy.

2. OVERVIEW OF THE DREAM COORDINATION FRAMEWORK

DREAM (Distributed Reactive Management) is a modeling framework for decentralized problem solving in manufacturing contexts. As such, most essentially, DREAM may be characterized as permitting coordination of activities, opportunistic network behavior, and subtask integration:

- coordination of activities is achieved by exchanging application-oriented constraint knowledge between the relatively autonomous decision-making subsystems within the hierarchy;

- opportunism in the network behavior results from the local message-processing heuristics applied in regulating the internode information flow;

- integration is a consequence of the subtask allocation scheme based on a hierarchical decomposition of the high level goals, and enforcement of the constraints thus imposed both in generative and reactive problem-solving contexts.

The major task for DREAM is activity coordination. In general terms, activity coordination requires two types of control decisions [3]. One type is network control: tasks and responsibilities must be assigned to, and decisions must be communicated amongst each of the decision-making subsystems. The other type is local control: each decision-making subsystem must choose a task to execute next from among its assigned tasks. The choices concerning local task dispatching may be based on combinations of various preference, importance, and relevance measures, assigned to the individual tasks. These measures are usually adapted dynamically as changing problem-solving circumstances warrant.

The DREAM system architecture is based on an interconnected set of knowledge-based, "artificially intelligent", decision-making subsystems. The subsystems are connected to each other explicitly according to the underlying multilevel, hierarchical manufacturing system, and implicitly according to the various temporal, spatial, and authority <--> responsibility relationships amongst the subsystems. Local control in DREAM is facilitated by providing each local decision-making subsystem with a blackboard framework for problem solving [5], and a set of dedicated knowledge sources to provide local reasoning power. Network control in DREAM is achieved by having the nodes exchange constraint information to guide local decision making. Control over the exchange of information is assigned and distributed amongst the set of message management front-ends residing in individual subsystems.

Metaphorically, the coordination paradigm in DREAM combines a vertical, two-way communication protocol, usually associated with conventional organizational feedback control, and a lateral, market-oriented negotiating communication paradigm, normally seen in game theoretic and team-theoretic contexts. Moreover, DREAM relaxes the requirement for the coordination variables to be mathematical in nature. It applies, instead, knowledge-based techniques in general, and rule-based heuristics in particular, in facilitating opportunistic and integrating control.

DREAM = <S,M>, where

S = $(s_1, \dots, s_n)$, is a set of decision-making subsystems,

s_l = (D,K,I), is a triple object described subsequently,

M = $(m_1, \dots, m_m)$, is a set of messages, and

$m_k: s_j \to (s_r, \dots, s_t)$, is an implicit relation within S.

FIGURE 1
Formal definition of the DREAM coordination framework

Formally, the DREAM modeling framework is defined as illustrated in Figure 1. The basic building block in the framework, i.e., an individual decision-making subsystem is a threefold conceptualization. The dynamic set of messages in the framework provides an implicit mapping amongst the decision-making subsystems. An individual internode message is a one-to-many relation between neighboring system nodes. Coordination between the relatively self-interested agents in the framework is largely due to the hierarchical arrangement of the problem itself. Individual subsystems have no inherent need to coordinate their activities with other subsystems. Cooperation is thus achieved by decomposing and delegating the global system goals and by so doing enforcing individual agents to work towards those goals.

In an information system for distributed production management, control over the individual activities at different levels in the manufacturing hierarchy should be distributed throughout the management structure. Although some implicit global coordination stems from the authority <->responsibility relations inherent in the hierarchical organization, the major source of coherence is the set of individual subsystems and the behavioral characteristics of its components. In DREAM, a decision-making subsystem s_i is a triple object (D,K,I) comprising the following elements:

- **Domain model** (D), capturing all the manufacturing entities relevant to the particular subsystem. The entities may be either physical objects (products, resources, operations, etc.), or conceptual objects (customer orders, process plans, communication paths, temporal relations, etc.).

- **Knowledge** (K), capturing the local production management expertise required to run the particular subsystem. The Knowledge element is responsible for planning and monitoring production programs for the underlying portion of the manufacturing system in question. A local execution cycle is triggered either by the internal transactions generated during local problem-solving effort, or by the externally originated events forwarded to the Knowledge element from the local Interface element.

- **Interface** (I), capturing the local intersubsystem communication expertise required to adapt the plans of the subsystem to the surrounding system environment. A message-processing cycle is triggered either by internal plan deviations, i.e., the existence of outbound communications, or by external signals, i.e., the existence of inbound communications. The message-processing heuristics implicitly define the formal and informal organizational structures in question.

Figure 2 illustrates how the basic decision-making subsystem architecture discussed above is realized in DREAM: A Domain-Modeling Subsystem is associated with the Domain model element, a Problem-Solving Subsystem is associated with the Knowledge element, and a Message Management Subsystem is associated with the Interface element. The Domain-Modeling Subsystem is frequently consulted by the other two subsystems. Since the topic of this paper is coordination amongst a distributed set of decision-making nodes, the rest of it concentrates on the message management aspect of the DREAM framework. Readers interested in domain modeling or local problem solving within DREAM are referred to [8] for further details.

3. MESSAGE MANAGEMENT ARCHITECTURE IN DREAM

Each Message Management Subsystem in DREAM possesses a queue of inbound messages and a queue of pending outbound messages. Each prototypical message has associated with it a set of rule-based message-processing heuristics. These heuristics determine the appropriate courses of action triggered as a consequence of a receipt of a message. One possible proper action is to leave the corresponding message pending. In those situations, the content of the message indicates that the message is not "active" in the current problem-solving context.

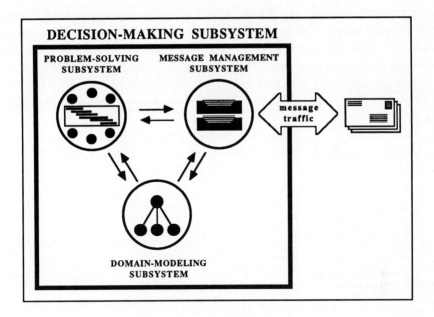

FIGURE 2
The node architecture in DREAM

In DREAM, a local reaction to "active" inbound messages is usually a set of relevant events forwarded to the local blackboard. These events describe particular transactions in the environment, requiring processing in the decision-making subsystem in question. A local reaction to all outbound messages is to deliver them to the appropriate recipients. The recipients are determined by consulting the local Domain-Modeling Subsystem. Rationale for this message delivery strategy is that it is the receiving decision-making subsystems which possesses the most detailed and accurate knowledge to judge the relevance of a particular communication.

Internode interaction within DREAM is governed by an underlying set of topological assumptions. These assumptions form a part of the communication strategy in the DREAM message flow. They drive, namely, a communication protocol determining the interpretation placed on communicated decisions by the recipients of the messages. The topological assumptions in DREAM are based on a distinction between three types of organizational internode relationships in a hierarchical system. Depending on the type of the relationship, the nature of the passed information belongs to one of three different categories (see Figure 3):

1. **Goal impositions**   from **managers upon subordinates**,
2. **Status updates**   from **subordinates to managers**, and
3. **Change announcements** from **peers to peers**.

An individual decision-making subsystem in DREAM is assumed to have a managerial relationship with those decision-making subsystems residing immediately below it in the manufacturing hierarchy. As such, downward communication of planning and control decisions is considered a goal imposition activity, and a subordinate decision-making subsystem always attempts to make its own decisions in accordance with the constraints and preferences imposed by its manager. This gives rise to the integrating top down behavior typically advocated in hierarchical production management system design [2, 6].

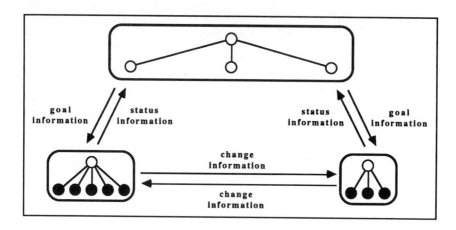

FIGURE 3
Nature of information in internode interactions in DREAM

In further respecting a management policy already advocated in downward control, upward communication of decisions in DREAM is viewed as a status updating activity. Given the local decision-making subsystem's more detailed knowledge of the current factory state and its more detailed view of the constraints on factory operation within its scope of interest, upward communication provides the more global decision-making subsystem with more accurate estimates of expected factory behavior. It may not be possible, for example, for a decision-making subsystem to satisfy all constraints imposed from above in generating or expanding its local plan of action. Similarly, reaction to unanticipated factory status changes may necessitate violation of globally imposed constraints. On the more fortunate side, upward communication of plan expansion or plan revision results relative to the local plan may point out opportunities for improvement of the global plan. In all such cases, upward communication provides the basis for reaction at higher levels.

Lateral communication of decisions and, therefore, announcement of possible changes in the decentralized hierarchy is seen as a crucial means in DREAM for reaction to unanticipated events in the manufacturing environment. If, indeed, something in the operating environment (e.g., machine breakdown, quality control rejection, etc.) implies that the downstream process plan has become infeasible as a consequence of disruptions beyond the immediate control of any decision-making subsystem, neighboring nodes in the manufacturing hierarchy may be able to resolve the conflict or at least reduce the severity of the conflict by clustering together in tackling the problem.

Lateral communication of changes in DREAM is an activity which has characteristics of both goal imposition and status updating. On the one hand, the decisions communicated laterally may be viewed as refinements of the constraints that have been posted from above (e.g., a refinement of the anticipated arrival time of an order to a given area of the factory). On the other hand, local considerations may suggest that the refinement is not acceptable and lead to an attempt to communicate a compromise, in this case treating the communication more as a status update.

4. MESSAGE-PROCESSING STRATEGY IN DREAM

The crux of the internode coordination strategy applied in DREAM is the behavior and contents of the individual Message Management Subsystems in the decentralized entirety. To fulfill their purpose of enforcing coherence, the Message Management Subsystems have to be able to handle the following questions:

1. **When to trigger communication,** i.e., at what point in time should local messages be communicated to the appropriate recipients ?

2. **What to say in a communication,** i.e., what does the decision-making subsystem inform about new plans or about deviations in existing plans to other nodes ?

3. **How to facilitate communication,** i.e., provided that a decision-making subsystem has something to inform other subsystems about, how does it go about in accomplishing the information transfer ?

4. **How to react to a communication,** i.e., if a decision-making subsystem receives information from another subsystem, how does it decide what to do, if anything ?

The first and second questions in the above list have already been answered previously. To combine it with the answer to the third question, in DREAM, outbound constraint information is delivered immediately and unconditionally to the appropriate recipients once it has emerged. To be more precise, the Message Management Subsystem of the originating decision-making subsystem sends a message containing the constraint information to the Message Management Subsystem of the receiving decision-making subsystem. The communication is asynchronous, and no acknowledgements are assumed.

The rationale behind the described delivery strategy is to enforce a timely reaction to changes in the environment. Should an individual decision-making subsystem temporarily break down, the rest of the distributed entirety could still continue and produce reasonably accurate control knowledge despite the disturbance. In case of such a local breakdown, it is only the subsystems next to the failed node which would potentially have slightly outdated plans. The thrust in reaction in DREAM, however, would enforce correction of those deviations immediately they become known to the system's sensory facilities.

The message-processing heuristics elaborated on subsequently assure that the resulting internode communication within the unconditional message delivery strategy will not be exhaustive. After all, the average number of recipients for a given message is rather small, and the filtering heuristics at the receiving ends prevent the communications from unnecessarily spreading all over the hierarchy.

The fourth issue in the message-processing strategy, i.e., the question about how to react to a received message, is answered in DREAM by a set of message-processing heuristics. The heuristics are directly attached to the messages which they manipulate. Heuristics are informal, judgmental rules-of-thumb that arise through specialization, generalization, and analogy and that are learned from past analogy [9]. Similarly to the mechanism according to which the event processing heuristics are used to assign subtasks to individual production management experts in the local Problem-Solving Subsystem, message-processing heuristics are used to filter and interpret the management information in inbound messages. In DREAM, four distinct classes of message-processing heuristics are identified. They represent general structural and time-related knowledge, as well as highly case-dependent processing information. As they all obtain, however, their specific contents with respect to a particular implementation, they can be discussed here in a classificatory manner only.

1. **Topological heuristics**: The position of a decision-making subsystem in the manufacturing hierarchy determines the portion of the manufacturing process over which it has authority and visibility. In this regard, a node in DREAM may be characterized as externally biased, locally biased, or unbiased: An external bias is exercised towards information received from above in the hierarchy. The principle of external bias assures that goal impositions originated in global contexts receive immediate attention, as opposed to problem-solving tasks based on purely local considerations. A local bias is exercised towards information received from below in the hierarchy. The principle of local bias is also meant to enforce global coherence. An unbiased view is taken towards information received from neighboring nodes in the hierarchy. The principle of unbias at the same hierarchical level enforces the forming of temporary clusters in resolving deviations from the original plans.

2. **Temporal heuristics**: Each decision-making subsystem in the DREAM framework is assumed to maintain its production programs over a designated time horizon. The objective is to tie the precision of decisions to the degree of uncertainty surrounding them, in this case using as a measure of uncertainty a node-dependent threshold value for urgent and nonurgent messages. For instance, at the shop level work orders falling within the next two weeks could be deemed urgent, whereas at the cell level a similar threshold could be, say, one day. Temporal heuristics in DREAM are related to the various decompositions of the problem along the timeline. Thus, they may either be associated with the time granularity in the involved decisions, or their time horizon. Heuristics on time granularity may suggest, e.g., that one should only consider changes with a magnitude significant enough to warrant reaction at the current organizational level. Heuristics about time horizon deal with the unpredictability of the future.

3. **Model-based heuristics**: The sensitivity of a particular decision-making subsystem to lower level deviations from its imposed constraints is regulated in DREAM by the model abstractions upon which its decisions are based. Assuming, for example, that the decision-making subsystem is operating with respect to a coarser granularity of time than its subordinates, then changes to posted operation time bounds resulting from local scheduling of the more detailed subprocesses that the operations abstract will not be perceived unless they in fact are significant enough to be detected at this coarser level of granularity. Such abstractions introduce flexibility in the constraints posted with subordinate decision-making subsystems, and tune the heuristics to reflect the particular implementation in question. Model-based heuristics in DREAM are related to the particular manufacturing system in question. They characterize the unique nature of a particular application. Besides the topological and temporal heuristics, there are many model-based idiosyncrasies in a manufacturing system which reflect the way the system interacts with its environment, and how the domain characteristics are distributed in the model. Model-based heuristics thus provide a domain-oriented, implicit "network index", connecting the coupled problem space areas together.

4. **Empirical heuristics**: One major problem in modeling a production management system in a discrete parts manufacturing environment is the lack of a solid framework or sound theory of the underlying concepts. The discipline of production management is, in fact, merely a loose and extremely dynamic collection of management principles, largely gained during several years of practice. In many reactive contexts, therefore, an "educated guess" is the best that can be made in solving a particular production management problem. The empirical heuristics in DREAM represent and encode the application-dependent "expert heuristics" or

production management practice. These rules-of-thumb are of utmost value to the success of the information system. It is often the case that different areas in the factory require alternating controlling principles depending on the type of production (e.g., make-to-order, make-to-inventory, emergency orders, etc.). This is very straight-forward to implement in DREAM.

5. CHARACTERISTICS OF THE DREAM FRAMEWORK

The presented DREAM model for coordination in distributed production management contexts is a framework to guide actual implementation efforts. As such, it advocates a particular computational system architecture, and a coordination protocol based on several approaches for the decomposition of the problem space. As a summary, there are a couple of important behavioral characteristics exhibited by the framework, and addressed below:

- **Immediate local reaction**: A subsystem always responds to a received message first locally before initiating any communication to other nodes. While such immediate local commitments are usually subject to subsequent revisions, an "eager" local reaction policy is viewed as crucial regarding overall system responsiveness in DREAM.

- **Nonselective internode communication**: All changes made to the local plans during local problem-solving activity are unconditionally delivered to the appropriate recipients. The rationale behind this nonselective communication policy is that the recipient of the information is the best expert in judging if the information is of any significance to it.

- **Selective intranode reaction**: Decisions as to when and in what order incoming messages are responded to are addressed by the message-processing heuristics. Knowledge related to the authoritative structure implied by the hierarchical model provides a partial basis for this message prioritization. However, the current relevance of the message to the local node, and the message's perceived urgency provide additional criteria.

- **Opportunistic adaptive intranode reaction**: Determination of the significance of an incoming message, and whether reactive action is warranted, is accomplished by updating the plans to reflect the communicated constraints and recognizing the problems that are introduced. It is important to emphasize, however, that this recognition process is "tuned" to the level of abstraction at which the node is operating. This has the effect of making minor deviations from imposed constraints transparent to the nodes operating at higher levels.

An implementation of the DREAM framework exists for factory scheduling. The system is coined as BOSS (<u>B</u>unch of <u>O</u>PIS-like <u>S</u>cheduling <u>S</u>ystems) as it is based on the OPIS (<u>O</u>pportunistic <u>I</u>ntelligent <u>S</u>cheduler) system [14, 15, 16] developed at the Intelligent Systems Laboratory of the Robotics Institute at Carnegie Mellon University (Pittsburgh, PA, USA). The BOSS system is implemented using Common Lisp and a frame-based knowledge representation facility called CRL™ (Carnegie Representation Language), running on a Texas Instruments, Inc. Explorer™ Lisp machine (courtesy of Sperry, Inc., nowadays Unisys, Inc.). CRL™ is part of a hybrid knowledge engineering environment called Knowledge Craft™ [1]. Due to physical resource limitations, structural decentralization in BOSS is simulated in an object-oriented style on a single Lisp machine. The BOSS software currently consists of about 1.0 Mb, or 32,000 lines of source code. The reader is referred to [8] for further details of the implementation.

6. CONCLUSIONS

A major behavioral characteristic of a coordination framework is how it finds a balance in being predictive enough in a generative, i.e., planning mode, and in being responsive enough in an interpretative, i.e., reaction mode. Being predictive in DREAM amounts to propagating goal imposition messages downward in the hierarchy, and operating locally within the constraints imposed by the messages. Roughly, it resembles the multi-agent planning approach [3]. In multi-agent planning, the nodes typically choose a node from among themselves to solve their planning problem and send this node all related information. The planning node then exploits a global view of the problem and forms a multi-agent plan that specifies the actions each node should take. It also distributes the plan among the nodes. In DREAM, in a distributed manufacturing environment, the chosen planning node at any given moment is implicitly defined by the resource abstraction hierarchy. No negotiation is needed, therefore, to choose the planning node. Since the main issue in manufacturing contexts, however, is not task delegation but coordination among highly dependent subproblems, the multi-agent paradigm has had to be extended towards an appropriate reactive capability.

Being responsive in DREAM amounts to propagating scheduling update and scheduling change messages upward and forward in the hierarchy, and adapting local plans opportunistically to changes severe enough to warrant consideration. As opposed to the functionally-accurate, cooperative (FA/C) approach for distributed problem solving [4], the nodes do not iteratively exchange tentative, partial solutions to converge to a final solution. In DREAM, in the reactive mode, a node commits to a new local plan without consulting the environment. An efficient overall adaptation is achieved by using a communication strategy which assures that conflicts and opportunities are absorbed in an opportunistic manner. This kind of behavior is found suitable in production management contexts because of the inherent structure of the problem domain.

In DREAM, there is a clear tradeoff between local operating flexibility and the globally posted slack in operation time intervals. The more freedom is given to an individual decision-making subsystem to organize its local activity plans, the more suboptimal the overall behavior of the system ends up, provided that things go along fairly smoothly. On the other hand, the tighter the constraints on an individual decision-making subsystem are, the more vulnerable the overall system is, even when facing minor deviations from the predicted future. Sometimes, it is even desirable to do nothing locally in a reactive context with respect to a real-time response and the computational cost. Resolving this tradeoff is largely domain-dependent and involves the unavoidable customization effort when putting DREAM into use.

ACKNOWLEDGEMENTS

The seeds of this work were sown when I held a Fulbright Scholarship in the Intelligent Systems Laboratory of the Robotics Institute at Carnegie Mellon University (Pittsburgh, PA, USA). I am indebted to Prof. Mark S. Fox and Dr Stephen F. Smith for providing me with guidance and an extremely inspiring working atmosphere. In Finland, I owe a lot to Prof. Markku Syrjänen, and to Mr Ora Lassila for his immense implementation efforts. This research has been sponsored in part by the Technology Development Centre in Finland (TEKES), and the Laboratory of Information Processing Science of the Computer Science Department at the Helsinki University of Technology.

REFERENCES

1. Carnegie Group, *Knowledge Craft User's Manual*. Pittsburgh (Pennsylvania, U.S.A.), 1986, Carnegie Group, Inc.
2. Dempster M.A.H., M.L. Fisher, L. Jansen, B.J. Lageweg, J.K. Lenstra, and A.H.G. Rinnooy Kan, *Analytical Evaluation of Hierarchical Planning Systems*. Vienna (Austria), 1984, The International Institute for Applied Systems Analysis, Research Report RR-84-4.
3. Durfee Edmund H., Victor R. Lesser, and Daniel D. Corkill, *Cooperation Through Communication in a Distributed Problem Solving Network*. In: Michael N. Huhns (ed.), Distributed Artificial Intelligence. London (Great Britain), 1987, Pitman Publishing.
4. Durfee Edmund H. and Victor R. Lesser, *Incremental Planning to Control a Blackboard-Based Problem Solver*. In: Proceedings of the Fifth National Conference on Artificial Intelligence. Philadelphia (Pennsylvania, U.S.A.), August, 1986, The American Association for Artificial Intelligence (AAAI), pp. 58-64.
5. Erman Lee D., Frederick Hayes-Roth, Victor R. Lesser, and Raj D. Reddy, *The Hearsay-II Speech-Understanding System: Integrating Knowledge to Resolve Uncertainty*. Computing Surveys 12(1980)2, pp. 213-253.
6. Hax A.C. and H.C. Meal, *Hierarchical Integration of Production Planning and Scheduling*. In: M.A. Geisler (ed.), Studies in Management Sciences, Vol. 1: Logistics. Amsterdam (The Netherlands), 1975, North-Holland.
7. Holmdahl Poul Erik, *Open CAM Systems*. Presentation at the CAM-I Intelligent Manufacturing Management Program (IMMP) International Meeting, Munic (West Germany), May, 1988, Computer Aided Manufacturing - International, Inc.
8. Hynynen Juha, *A framework for Coordination in Distributed Production Management*. Espoo (Finland), August, 1988, Laboratory of Information Processing Science, Helsinki University of Technology, Doctoral thesis (in preparation).
9. Lenat Douglas B., *The Nature of Heuristics*. Artificial Intelligence 19(1982)2, pp. 189-249.
10. McLean Charles R., Mary Mitchell, and Edward Barkmeyer, *A computer architecture for small-batch manufacturing*. IEEE Spectrum 20(1983)5, pp. 59-64.
11. Melnyk Steven A., *Production Control: Issues and Challenges*. In: Michael Oliff (ed.), Proceedings of the International Conference on Expert Systems and the Leading Edge in Production Planning and Control. Charleston (South Carolina, U.S.A.), May, 1987, pp. 243-276.
12. Mesarovic M.D., D. Macko, and Y. Takahara, *Theory of Hierarchical, Multilevel, Systems*. New York (New York, U.S.A.), 1970, Academic Press, Inc.
13. Meyer Wolfgang, Randolf Isenberg, and Martin Hübner, *Knowledge-based factory supervision - The CIM shell*. International Journal of Computer Integrated Manufacturing 1(1988)1, pp. 31-43.
14. Smith Stephen F., *A Constraint-Based Framework for Reactive Management of Factory Schedules*. In: Michael Oliff (ed.), Proceedings of the International Conference on Expert Systems and the Leading Edge in Production Planning and Control. Charleston (South Carolina, U.S.A.), May, 1987, pp. 349-366.
15. Smith Stephen F., Mark S. Fox, and Peng Si Ow, *Constructing and Maintaining Detailed Production Plans: Investigations into the Development of Knowledge-Based Factory Scheduling*. The AI Magazine 7(1986)4, pp. 45-61.
16. Smith Stephen F. and Peng Si Ow, *The Use of Multiple Problem Decompositions in Time-Constrained Planning Tasks*. In: Proceedings of the Ninth International Joint Conference on Artificial Intelligence. Los Angeles (California, U.S.A.), August, 1985, International Joint Conferences on Artificial Intelligence, Inc. (IJCAII).

Expert Systems in Economics, Banking and Management
L.F. Pau et al. (Editors)
© *Elsevier Science Publishers B.V. (North-Holland), 1989*

Intelligent Integrated Decision Support Systems
for
Manufacturing Enterprise

Mitchell M.Tseng, Digital Equipment Corp., Marlboro, Massachusetts, U.S.A.
Dennis O'Connor, Digital Equipment Corp., Marlboro, Massachusetts, U.S.A.

Abstract. In the last decade, three independent developments have started to make impacts on how we manage the manufacturing enterprise:

1. In business schools, we have developed a deeper understanding of the economic aspects of the business enterprise. For example, competitive analysis framework and value chain analysis have offered new insight into the complexity of the inner workings of modern business. It enabled us to articulate business strategies with more depth.

2. The computer-based information systems are prevalent in major aspects of our business. Tools such as Financial Systems, Materials Systems and Quality Systems have become widely accepted.

3. The technology for developing Knowledge-Based Systems has become more mature to better handle representations of complex relationships, heuristics and objects.

An Intelligent Integrated Executive Decision Support System has been developed at Digital Equipment Corporation by applying Knowledge-Based Systems Technology for capturing a deeper understanding of the economic aspects of business and integrating with conventional information systems. It assists managers making key decisions on demand, supply, and resource allocation. The results show significant reduction in the cycle time of decision making and improved consistency and quality of analysis.

Introduction:

In the last decade, the computer industry has witnessed the tremendous growth in our ability to design and manufacture new products. For example, VLSI designers have gained three orders of magnitude in design capability in less than ten years. At the macro level, Millions of Instructions Per Second (MIPS) per dollar for computing power and megabytes per dollar for storage have been doubled every two years. Product life has been shortened, the variety of products has been increased, and, more importantly, the complexity of our product functionality has experienced quantum jumps. This has been translated to the increasing number of new products introduced every year.

While the design engineers are using a new generation of CAD tools, and manufacturing professionals are using new equipment with high flexibility and precision to produce consistent quality at reduced cost, the management decision making process was left to utilize conventional spread sheets. Key strategic decisions are still based on information gathered through the manipulation of rows and columns in a two dimensional formation in a static mode. With the tremendous amount of information in-flow, these tools are not only inadequate to address the complexity of product lines, but also make it difficult, if not impossible, to respond to the dynamic nature of competitive market pressure in areas such as pricing changes, new product positioning and resource balancing.

The purpose of this paper is to address this new set of requirements. It will also discuss an Intelligent Integrated Executive Decision Support System developed at Digital to meet these needs. While the computer industry has lead the 1980's in rapid deployment of technology, the issues and challenges discussed here should by no means be limited to the computer industry. Its implications and potential applications, although different in degree, could reach well beyond the manufacturing industry.

Requirements for a New Executive Decision Support Systems:

In the 1970's, American industries experienced a period of declining growth in productivity, inadequate product quality, sluggish response to market requirements, and deceleration in innovation. This lead to a broad based search for a deeper understanding of the economic relationships of competition, supply, demand, and the customer's requirements [1]. For example, the success of Michael Porter's competitive analysis framework and value chain analysis has enabled us to articulate economic understandings of our business in a more substantial manner [2]. In addition, the wide spread adoption of separate information systems in key business functions such as finance, materials, services, and quality has made relevant information in these functional areas readily available. However, most of these information systems were developed and implemented with clearly defined justifications. Attempts to integrate them solely at data interface and data translation levels have failed because they were either too costly to maintain or therein appeared confusion in data definition. On the other hand, our new conceptual understanding remains pretty much in the business school arena or strategic planning departments. The difficulty to relate them to reality has not been trivial. The advent of technology for developing Knowledge-Based Systems has made representation of complex model a much easier task. It is our belief that a new generation of executive decision support systems is now becoming feasible. By applying knowledge-based systems technology, abundant information residing in separate information systems can be integrated with our new understanding of economic relationships and the analysis framework developed in the recent years. This new avenue bridges the conceptual understanding of business and the reality residing in the data. Indeed, the whole arena of business analysis can move away from simplicity with the following new objectives:

- Assist executives to manipulate "what-if" scenarios with pertinent data and his own framework of understanding simultaneously. This could lead to substantiate business strategy formulation with backup information and analysis.

- By verifying their own understanding of business framework with real data, executives can acquire new knowledge and modify old framework. This will accelerate executives' gaining insight of new business environment and learning the causal relationships between decisions and effects.

To achieve these objectives, we believe the basic requirements include the following:

1. The ability to effectively represent complicated relationships. A sound executive decision should take into consideration the many structural and infrastructural dimensions. These dimensions include capacity, facility, technology, sourcing, work force, quality, product line, production planning, control and organization. Analysis which does not represent these dimensions and the forces that drive them is incomplete. Thus, in designing a useful executive decision support system for the manufacturing enterprise, one has to be able to effectively take the above dimensions into consideration.

   Representation for different dimensions should be able to capture the complexity of each dimension and the intricate relationship among these dimensions. For example, when the decisionmakers are contemplating the price change, its implications are not only in financial areas (such as gross margin, profit and loss), but it also impacts capacity by increasing or decreasing demand which may in turn change the sourcing strategy, process technology, and workforce plan, and affect the country content dictated by the marketing requirements. Although these relationships have been understood as heuristics, they are seldomly used for serious analyzing purposes. The current numerical based methodology, though with a high degree of precision, fails to capture the important aspect of representing the intricacy of multiple dimensions of these decision criteria.

2. The ability to integrate with existing database and information systems. Effective Decision Support has to be able to relate to the information stored in existing management information systems. Through existing information systems, the quality and credibility of decision support systems can be validated with real life data. Furthermore, it is only by looking at planned scenario versus actual performance simultaneously that one can sharpen the decision making skill by applying the capability of Executive Decision Support Systems. The systems need to have access to multiple information resources in a timely manner with data integrity.

3. The facility to support, verify, and maintain the intricate relationship captured in the systems, since relationships among different decision criteria will not be well understood at the beginning, and may never be fully clarified in the long run. This is particularly true when we try to deal with different perspectives in a given dimension. Therefore it is critical to provide the facility to identify conflicts

in defining criteria to criteria relationships and to input or modify these relation-ships. The ability to handle ambiguity distinguishes executive decision making from clerical level problem solving. Competent executive decision making pro-cess requires taking uncertainty into account by trading off degrees of details and exactness of data. The uncertainty can then be reduced by applying the in-flow of new information as time elapses. For example, the communication product division prepares a 5 to 10 year plan with probable market sizing in different technology area such as fiber optics, radio frequency transmission, satellite com-munication and others. At this stage, it will not be productive to prepare product plans with detailed breakdown of the proposed product with model number and quantities. However, for a mid-range plan (3-5 year), it will be feasible and useful to plan with product families, for example, a 10 Mega Baud family, 100 Mega Baud family, and others. As the time frame pulls in closer to the current state, new pieces of information, such as the wide acceptance of micro computer- based workstations demand higher baudwidth for Local Area Networks (LAN), should be taken into consideration to reduce uncertainty for market sizing, allocation of resources, etc.

4. Ease of use: Because the target user base is executives whose priority is to make de-cisions in a very short timeframe, the system has to provide ample capability with relatively short response time. In general, it is difficult to expect executives to go through extended training sessions. The system must provide facility to navigate users through system functionality and be alerted with potential discrepancies in interpretation. Furthermore, a robust system design has to offer proactive capa-bility to alert users of potential imbalance in the use of resources, the discrepancy between plan and actual, and to guide users through "zoom in" analysis sessions. Because of the differences in emphasis and requirements, different sets of function-ality with different perspectives of business can be designed with the same core systems. This core system provides scale of economy, and integration/sharing of data, information and knowledge. The specific executive requirements are also met with customized front end to suit users capability and needs.

An Intelligent Integrated Executive Decision Support System:

Balancing demand, supply, and resource utilization is a classical example of execu-tive decision process in the manufacturing enterprise. Manufacturing executives in a competitive environment have to constantly review inventory, shortage, revenue, market share, profit margin, and over- or under-utilization of resources. It normally involves several information systems such as MRP, Finance, Human Resources, and others to address some key questions such as "Do we have the capacity to meet next year's volume plan and also achieve financial metrics?" The overall system design follow the general architecture developed by Tseng and O'Connor [5].

Figure 1:　An Intelligent Integrated Executive Decision Support System

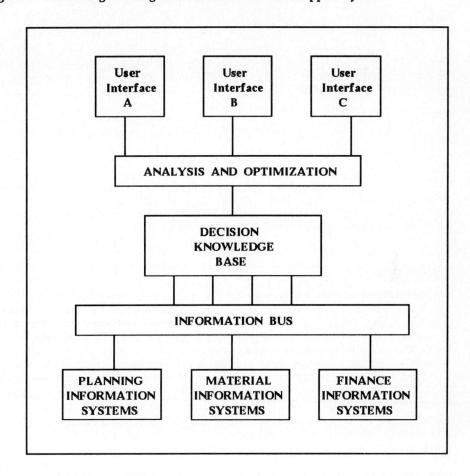

Figure 1 depicts the overall architecture which includes several key components: Decision Knowledge Base, Information Bus, Analysis and Optimization Module, and User Interface.

1. Decision Knowledge Base

Because the relationship among business entities often are more complicated than object-attribute-value triplets can capture, a frame-based representation system is selected for representing facts and relationships. A frame is a description of an object that contains slots for all of the information associated with the object. Slots, like attributes, may store values, pointers to other frames, sets of rules or procedures by which values may be obtained [3].

For example, a product can be represented with a frame consisting of data (such as price, quantity of orders, etc.), pointers to descendent frames (such as a network of configurable peripherals or product options), sets of rules for manipulating product to product relationships and pointers to other frames for calculating cost and price. Once the relationship is defined, a change in the price data in a frame will propagate a corresponding update in the price data of a related frame, for example, the automatic updating of the system price when a peripheral price is changed. Likewise, the user can manipulate the network of relationships and frames. For examples, we can modify the number of peripherals connected to certain system orders.

2. Information Bus

An information bus is set up to routinely pull in data and information from several information systems for pertinent data (such as product cost data from financial information systems). The information bus is designed with a VMS/RDB data base to serve as a buffer to populate the knowledge and maintain its current state. Precaution has been taken to check data integrity and security.

3. Analysis and Optimization Module

The analysis module includes a repertoire of analysis and optimization routines. The user query is first translated to mathematical formulation appropriately so that analysis and optimization can be performed. Most of these routines are implemented in conventional software. A report generation routine coupled with graphic presentation then converts the results from mathematical routines to the user interface.

4. User Interface

To meet the ease of user requirements, the system is designed with the following approach:

a. The emergence of windows (such as DEC windows) and interactive graphics front end enable user to interact with the system with a minimal amount of front end.

b. On the human factor aspect, the use of analogy and metaphor has proven to be very important for ad-hoc queries and infrequent users.

c. Customized interfaces to serve specific groups of user needs so that their specific analysis pattern and requirements can be addressed.

Figure 2: Screen layout for an Intelligent Integrated Executive Decisi on Support System

DIVISION OF DATA [HELP]	SALES PROGNOSIS [HELP]	MANUFACTURING OPERATIONS CONSULTANT	DIGITAL Has it Now!
VERSION QUARTER — Q1 89 | from Aug 88 | Next	APPLICATIONS — Change Product Mix	PLAN ANALYSIS [HELP]	TOOLS — HELP | SAVE
INDUSTRY — Food & Bev | Pharm — Gas & Oil | Auto — Aerospace | Electronic	SUPPLY PLAN [HELP] — Change Mfg / Fabricated Ingredient Availability	What is the financial impact? — Are Demand and Supply well balanced? — What is the critical resources path?	RESET — EXIT

HARDWARE SUBDIVISION FINANCIAL SUMMARY FOR IN Q189 :

PRODUCT	UNIT	SALES ($K)	TRANSFER COST ($K)	MARGIN ($K)	TC-%	UV ($)
COMPUTER A	4000	14.99	7.93	4.06	66.14	2.79
COMPUTER B	6000	6.47	4.08	2.39	63.11	1.69
COMPUTER C	12000	7.47	4.80	2.68	64.18	0.49
HARD DISK A	500	13.66	9.04	4.63	66.14	2.79
HARD DISK B	1000	8.39	5.29	3.09	63.11	1.69
HARD DISK C	1500	6.52	4.18	2.33	64.18	0.49
TERMINAL A	200	11.01	7.28	3.73	66.14	3.89
TERMINAL B	400	8.23	5.20	3.04	63.18	1.09
TERMINAL C	600	6.54	8.80	2.34	62.14	1.69

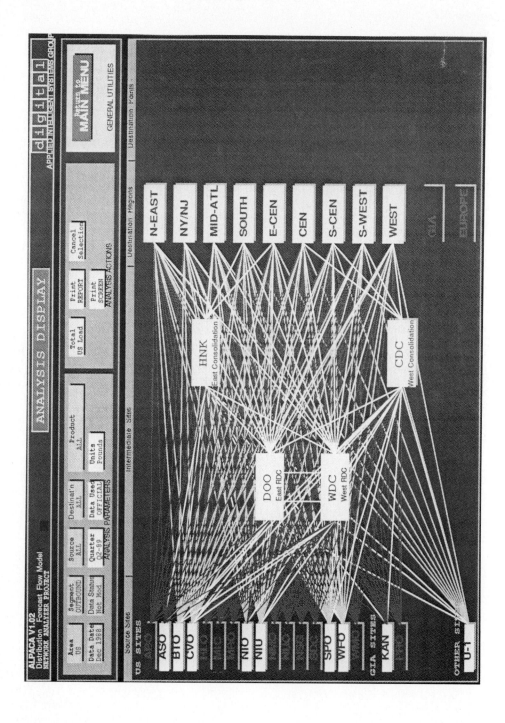

Results:

The system was originally designed to serve a well- defined group of Digital executives who handle specific responsibilities in balancing supply, demand and resource allocations. It was written on Knowledge Craft and run on MicroVAX GPX Workstations. Figure 2 shows a sample screen layout.

- The result of using such an executive decision support system reduces the amount of time needed to analyze available resources and current inventory for the business volume plan from months to a matter a minutes, if not seconds.

- Because of the drastically reduced planning cycle time, several functions and business units previously had different sets of planning data because of differences in scenarios can now use one unified set of data. As a result, customer satisfaction has increased while inventory is decreased and resource utilization has improved.

- Other applications such as distribution network planning to answer questions such as "How many trucks are required to move the new increased demands?" have propagated to different organizations by using the core set of data and representation. Figure 3 shows an example of the distribution planning system.

Acknowledgment

The authors wish to thank Erik Sand, Phillip Soo, and Mary Lewis who have carried out the design from vision to full implementation. In addition, numerous Digital executives have made their many years of management expertise available for developing this system. We especially want to thank William C. Hanson, Vice President of Manufacturing, and Donato A. Infante, Vice President of Information and Technology. Their forsight and commitment to excellence have nurtured this and other Knowledge-Based Systems projects.

References

1. Frederick, P. and Venkatrawan, N., "The Rise Of Strategy Support Systems", Sloan Management Review - M.I.T., Spring 1988.

2. Porter, M.E., "Competitive Advantage", Free Press, 1985.

3. Hayes, R. and Wheelwright, S. and Clark, J., "Dynamic Manufacturing", Free Press, 1988, pp. 148-152.

4. Harman, P. and King, D., "Expert Systems", John Wiley & Sons, Inc., 1985.

5. Tseng, M. and O'Connor, D., "Augmenting CIM With Intelligent Systems", Knowledge-Based Expert Systems for Manufacturing, American Society Of Mechanical Engineers, edited by S. C. Lu, New York, December 7-12, 1986.

Expert Systems in Economics, Banking and Management
L.F. Pau et al. (Editors)
© *Elsevier Science Publishers B.V. (North-Holland), 1989*

Utilizing knowledge intensive techniques in an automated consultant for financial marketing

Chidanand Apté, James Griesmer, Se June Hong, Maurice Karnaugh
John Kastner, Meir Laker, Eric Mays

IBM Research Division
Thomas J. Watson Research Center
P.O. Box 218
Yorktown Heights, NY 10598
USA

Financial marketing represents a new and challenging domain for expert systems. For our purposes, the term financial marketing denotes the specialized problem solving skills and practices that are required in the marketing of mainframe computing products. When making large equipment acquisitions, financial considerations often become as important as technical considerations to a buyer. The FAME system is an interactive problem solving assistant that takes these considerations into account for preparing marketing proposals. To build this system we have been developing a spectrum of techniques, ranging from object centered knowledge representation mechanisms to specialized goal directed heuristic problem solvers. These have been successfully employed in the system, which is currently being tested on active marketing situations. The paper will cover our experiences with this system, and describe our methodologies for dealing with large knowledge based systems.

1. Introduction

This paper discusses our experiences with using knowledge based techniques for an automated problem solving consultant in financial marketing. Financial marketing presents a class of problem solving activities that are fairly common in the marketing environments of companies that produce capital equipment. Successful solving of these problems requires combining a wide latitude of skills with a vast repository of market data (past, current, and projected). Typically, such problems are tackled today by experienced human experts in conjunction with popular computational tools such as spreadsheet packages and database systems. The advent of knowledge based technologies makes it possible today to build systems that automate a larger portion of the problem solving activities. We have been experimenting successfully in the past few years with such an approach to build a prototype system, FAME [1, 2], that provides integrated interactive problem solving expertise for financial marketing. In this paper, we will present an overview of our application and a summary of advances that we have made to knowledge based techniques for realizing our prototype. We will take the position that for building comprehensive intelligent problem solving assistants for business and finance one needs to integrate and use a wide cross-section of knowledge based methodologies and techniques, and that the contribution of our research is an evolving framework for implementing such systems.

2. The domain of financial marketing

Financial marketing as an activity is mainly pursued by manufacturing companies that are in the business of producing capital intensive goods, i.e., goods that have extremely high monetary values. These range from items such as jet aircraft and oil tankers to very large mainframe computer systems. The buyers of such goods have not only to be convinced that they address and solve some requirements of the buyers in a technical sense, but that the acquisition of these goods does not adversely impact some financial constraints of the buyers. The manufacturing companies that produce these goods therefore have an additional burden of coming up with attractive financial mechanisms that may be employed by a customer to acquire these goods. *Financial marketing therefore is an activity that determines an offering which is most beneficial to a customer within an agreed to set of financial parameters*. Needless to say, the item must also satisfactorily address the customer's technical requirements and be competitive with other similar offerings in the marketplace. This process is usually extensively supported and carried out by the manufacturer's marketing teams. *Financial marketing is knowledge intensive in nature*. That is, not only does successful financial marketing require good marketing and financial skills, it also requires skill in mapping the technology being marketed onto the customer's requirements, and the ability to combine all these into meaningful, efficient actions, utilizing a vast amount of market data on products and services, historical trends, competition, and the customer's corporate financial profile. Given the high volume of information, problem solving has to deal very frequently with incomplete or uncertain scenarios. This naturally gives rise to multiple solutions based on varying assumptions.

This characteristic of financial marketing makes it necessary for any marketing proposal to be supported with extensive arguments for it to be of sellable value. There are usually no well defined criteria for determining the best solution for a customer's problem. This domain is highly characterized by this lack of single answers, even from a single seller's viewpoint. It therefore becomes very important to be able to strengthen one's proposal by providing appropriate justifications and alternatives.

Here is an example of a simple problem that will require the skills of financial marketing to come up with reasonable solutions: *A customer currently has an IBM 3081 KX3 processor that was installed two years ago. The customer is close to exceeding the capacity of that machine and is expecting his computing requirements to grow at 35% on an annual basis. The machine is on a 3 year lease from a third party leasing firm. The customer is soliciting proposals for solving his expected shortfall in available computing. The proposals will be examined and evaluated by an executive whose concerns include the customer's MIS budget as well as its short term debt holdings*. There may be a number of solutions to this problem. Since the existing machine still has a year to go on its lease, there will be a penalty incurred if the machine is prematurely removed. However, if the customer goes with the third party's proposal, that penalty may be waived. On the other hand, a manufacturer may be able to provide much newer technology that offers much better cost/performance. Manufacturers' credit subsidiaries may be able to offer proposals that satisfactorily address the customer executive's concerns about budget and debt. The skill of financial marketing lies in the ability to anticipate what the competition is, and then structure proposals that can be shown to be better. It is this skill that FAME has attempted to capture, and offer to users in a highly interactive mode.

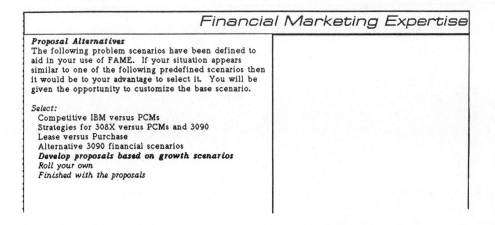

Figure 1. Presenting customer financial data for verification

Financial Marketing Expertise
Proposal Alternatives
The following problem scenarios have been defined to aid in your use of FAME. If your situation appears similar to one of the following predefined scenarios then it would be to your advantage to select it. You will be given the opportunity to customize the base scenario.
Select:
Competitive IBM versus PCMs
Strategies for 308X versus PCMs and 3090
Lease versus Purchase
Alternative 3090 financial scenarios
Develop proposals based on growth scenarios
Roll your own
Finished with the proposals

Figure 2. Choices for automated marketing proposal generation

3. The FAME system

The FAME system that we have been evolving since early 1986 is a knowledge based advisory system that helps in the preparation of comprehensive financial marketing recommendations for the mainframe computer business. It runs on Lisp workstations, and extensively utilizes the advanced I/O features that are commonly available on these workstations. The system operates in the mode of an interactive assistant, i.e., the user remains in complete control during a problem solving session. Typically, a user begins by identifying a customer to the system. If the customer's profile (installed computer base as well as corporate financial information) is already available in the system's knowledge base, it is extracted and presented to the user for verification. Alternately, if the profile is not already available, the system will generate reasonable defaults and present them for verification. Figure 1 illustrates an instance from the series of windows the user will sequence through while setting up the customer profile. The next step requires the user to select one of several *automated* marketing proposal generators that are available. This selection is dependent upon the nature of the marketing situation that the user is in. For example, if the situation is that of anticipating competitors' responses to a particular proposal that the user has in mind, the user can select the appropriate problem solver to generate the required proposals. Alternately, if the user is in a situation where the customer's install base is known and a proposal is sought for upgrading the install base for satisfying the customer's growth in computing requirements, then a selection will let the system generate a capacity satisfaction proposal that makes acquisition recommendations for only a particular vendor's technology. Figure 2 illustrates the window that shows the user the choice of automated proposal generators that are available for use in any given context. Once marketing proposals are generated, a variety of reporting mechanisms can be invoked to compare and contrast the proposals. In addition, an automated impact analyzer can be invoked that will analyze a competitive situation and recommend minimal changes to a marketing proposal to make it better than the competition's. Figure 3 and Figure 4 illustrate some of these capabilities.

4. Architecture and technical underpinnings

FAME may be viewed as a large heterogeneous knowledge base system. The term heterogeneous refers to the nature of the knowledge used by FAME to solve typical problems in the domain. A variety of techniques are used to capture this knowledge, ranging from rule based classification models and heuristic search algorithms to conventional and hybrid analytical techniques. To service this cross-section of problem solvers, so that they may communicate, share, and be controllable in an autonomous fashion, it is important that a model of the problem domain and the evolving problem solving situation be uniformly accessible to all the components.

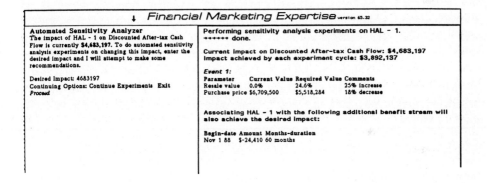

Financial Marketing Expertise vₑ

Summary of analysis for XYZ International Inc.:

Proposals and their key numbers (ranked by Discounted After-tax Cash Flo

Proposal	Before-tax Cash Flow	After-tax Cash Flow	Discounted After-tax Cash Flow	P&L Impact
ZLC - 3	6,243,567	3,791,094	3,892,137	3,791,094
HAL - 1	7,484,039	4,544,309	4,683,197	4,544,309
M2R - 2	8,267,392	5,019,960	5,149,762	5,019,960

Annual budgetary impact:

Proposal	Year 1	Year 2	Year 3	Year 4	Year 5	Year 6
ZLC - 3	462,463	632,530	679,916	663,522	647,127	705,536
HAL - 1	568,450	772,676	806,832	786,680	766,529	843,141
M2R - 2	609,198	834,309	902,144	880,548	858,952	934,810

Figure 3. Comparing a particular financial aspect of competing proposals

↓ *Financial Marketing Expertise* version 65.32

Automated Sensitivity Analyzer
The impact of HAL - 1 on Discounted After-tax Cash Flow is currently **$4,683,197**. To do automated sensitivity analysis experiments on changing this impact, enter the desired impact and I will attempt to make some recommendations.

Desired Impact: 4683197
Continuing Options: Continue Experiments Exit
Proceed

Performing sensitivity analysis experiments on HAL - 1.
→→→→→ done.

Current Impact on Discounted After-tax Cash Flow: **$4,683,197**
Impact achieved by each experiment cycle: **$3,892,137**

Event 1:
Parameter	Current Value	Required Value	Comments
Resale value	0.0%	24.6%	25% increase
Purchase price	$6,709,500	$5,518,284	18% decrease

Associating HAL - 1 with the following additional benefit stream will also achieve the desired impact:

Begin-date Amount Months-duration
Nov 1 88 $-24,410 60 months

Figure 4. Recommendations of an automated impact analysis

Our paradigm for this requirement is the pervasive use of structured inheritance networks for modeling the problem domain. Thus, we have captured in the FAME knowledge bases the essence of objects and their inter-relations as encountered in the domain, and relevant to intelligent problem-solving in it. For financial marketing in the mainframe computer business, one needs to model entities such as the products in the market today, their historical trends in terms of price and performance, the vendors who manufacture these products, the third parties who finance their use and acquisition, and customers. This broad base of knowledge about the domain is then usable by a variety of expert problem solvers. These *expert sub-systems* help a user in the interactive construction of a customer's financial profile, and subsequently, in designing marketing proposals. Among them, they offer a variety of automated services that can be utilized for generating competitive proposals and explanations, information walk-throughs, and related tasks. Figure 5 illustrates the multi-layered architecture of FAME, which our experience has indicated to be a very suitable one for large and heterogeneous knowledge based systems.

We have also used the domain of financial marketing to develop and advance methodologies for building knowledge based systems. In the area of *knowledge representation*, we have been experimenting with an object centered knowledge representation mechanism, K-Rep [3], which views knowledge as a collection of objects in a structured inheritance network, very much influenced by, and in the style of KL-One [4]. K-Rep provides a mechanism for representing the very common and most natural styles of objects and their inter-connections using the fundamental algebraic relations of subsumption and attribution.

The primary object in K-Rep is called a concept. Concepts may be specializations of other concepts, in which case the more specific concept inherits attributes from the more general. Attributive information about concepts is given via a binary relation (called a role relation) to some other concept. Thus one can form fairly complex descriptions, since the roles of concepts may in turn be other (complex) concepts, as well as numbers, strings, and arbitrary Lisp objects. K-Rep also provides a facility for performing definitional classification on new concepts. Based on the role relations of a new concept the classifier places it in the most specific and most general place with respect to specialization of existing concepts. Using the classifier one can perform a restricted pattern match by creating a new concept corresponding to the pattern, classifying the new concept, and retrieving those concepts which are its specializations.

K-Rep is a robust knowledge representation service, enabling the building of extremely large knowledge bases that can be efficiently manipulated. Other useful features of K-Rep that help in the building of large yet practical knowledge bases include multiple knowledge base management, role-value caching, facet definability, reverse inheritance, integrated rule based programming, and database integration. This knowledge representation service is described in greater detail in [3].

We have essentially developed a *knowledge modeling discipline*, which forces us to examine the domain world and model it using K-Rep's enforced semantics. Our experience indicates that such models can be very powerful. We have successfully modeled the vast domain of the computer mainframe market using this approach.

Utilizing an object centered knowledge representation service like K-Rep for modeling financial marketing enabled us to capture fairly complex domain structures and their inherent abstractions and aggregations in an elegant fashion. This object centered modeling allowed efficient access to tremendous amounts of inter-related knowledge that is typically required for producing detailed arguments and justifications for problem solving steps.

Various types of objects that play a major role in financial marketing were identified, and their interconnections were studied. Relations between various objects were

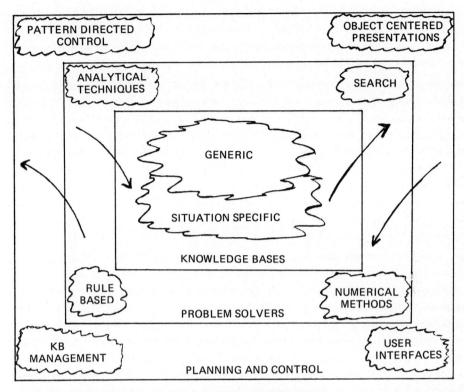

Figure 5. Multi-layered organization of the FAME system

developed using only the two fundamental algebraic relations of subsumption and attribution. Classifying the domain in terms of objects allowed us to quickly build hierarchies and taxonomies of objects by their different classes. These classes included, but were not limited to, financing mechanisms, manufacturers, products (past, present, and future), customers, financiers, etc. as relevant to the market of mainframe computers. Subsumption allowed us to build abstractions of these classes. This categorization not only makes it easy to build such knowledge using structured inheritance networks, it also allows acquisition of such knowledge from experts either via a knowledge engineer and/or computer based acquisition tools.

Tightly coupled with knowledge engineering is the requirement for some form of computer based support for knowledge acquisition. The success of fully automated knowledge acquisition (e.g. *self-learning*) tools has been quite limited to date. Our experience with the FAME system indicates that semi-automatic support in the form of advanced graphical interfaces for browsing and editing knowledge bases can be a powerful medium for both the managing and use of very large knowledge bases. Other experiences [5] [6] also indicate this to be the case. In this spirit, we have been evolving an approach to develop object-centered interfaces on advanced workstations that allow a structured retrieval of all knowledge stored in the knowledge bases that support FAME. This technique eases tasks such as maintaining very large knowledge bases and their use as an educational medium. In this activity we are developing and extending capabilities similar to those reported in Hypertext systems [7] and systems such as XCON-in-RIME [8].

Knowledge acquisition and maintenance are important issues for knowledge based systems, even more so when we deal with very large knowledge bases. Hypertext systems have traditionally taken the approach that by fully exploiting the more advanced features that are available on today's high resolution bit-mapped monitors and fast desk top computers, one can build fairly powerful interfaces to large amounts of stored data. These interfaces have had the goal of providing access to large databases with much the same ease and flexibility one has when using dictionaries and encyclopedias. Our experience with FAME suggests that by providing such interfaces to large knowledge bases, we not only have we made them easy to use, but also made more amenable the maintenance and modeling of the knowledge in them.

We have been successfully using an object-centered interface to FAME's knowledge bases for both knowledge engineer and end user. This interface is highly domain independent, though it does have the capability to present objects from a knowledge base on a screen, using certain presentation mechanisms that allow these objects, even when appearing on a screen in many different ways, to be selectable by a user as a unit object. By selecting objects on a screen, the user (whether a knowledge engineer or a end user) may be allowed to carry out a variety of activities, all controlled by essentially where the object is located in the underlying knowledge base. Thus the user may traverse or browse through the knowledge base by searching through the object's subsumption and attribution links. This link-driven traversing is extremely powerful for browsing large pieces of non-linear organizations, which is exactly what large knowledge bases are in their structure. This philosophy also provides a single coherent interface to knowledge bases that relies upon the semantics of the underlying object-role network, rather than some forced artificial interaction.

The object centered browser was used to good effect when knowledge was being acquired and engineered into the FAME knowledge bases. It was extremely easy to identify sub-areas in the knowledge bases in which objects needed to be added, modified, copied, or deleted. Specialized methods associated with these objects were provided for these operations that could be dynamically invoked by selecting objects on a screen. This methodology turned out to be an extremely powerful semi-automatic knowledge acquisition and maintenance support tool.

5. Concluding Discussion

The model of the mainframe computer market that currently drives FAME consists of well over 2000 complex objects connected in a K-Rep network. By complex objects, we mean that typical objects usually have multiple inheritance links, and in addition their roles themselves are restricted by other complex objects. By keeping the types of links allowable in this network to just two different algebraic relations, it has been very easy to build tools and support programs that aid in the acquisition and maintenance of objects in this knowledge base.

Our modeling methodology allowed us to develop an adequate model of the mainframe computer market. This comprehensive model has permitted us to build intelligent planning, control, and problem solving in FAME. An important issue in building large heterogeneous knowledge based systems is that of *planning and control*. It becomes crucial to dynamically plan problem-solving sequences in the presence of incomplete information to achieve some goals. For this it is important that we can build pattern-directed models that will drive this activity. We have been experimenting with a framework called KROPS [9] that allows a RETE net based [10] pattern matching of K-Rep based models. In the area of *automated problem solving*, we have had some interesting results using search based techniques and qualitative reasoning mechanisms. For a large and complex domain such as financial marketing, using the purest forms of search algorithms like the A^* is just too inefficient. We have been experimenting with alternative heuristic search control techniques to achieve rapid search termination [11]. This has resulted in very positive performance in our domain. Intelligent problem solving in financial marketing requires one to reason symbolically and heuristically about quantitative relations and the mathematics that governs these. We have been evolving techniques for qualitative reasoning about financial arithmetic and employing these in automated sensitivity analyses [12] [13].

We have reached a stage where the experimental prototype of FAME has received sufficient positive feedback from experts of the potential user community. An effort has begun to plan the transfer and solidification of the prototype into a field usable system. Systems like FAME represent an emerging class of very large heterogeneous knowledge based systems. Such systems, with multiple developers and users, pose their own peculiar types of problems. We hope to address some of these issues in the the coming years.

Acknowledgements

We would like to thank IBM US Marketing & Services for providing us with assistance and support during various phases of this project.

References

[1]   J. Kastner, C. Apté, J. Griesmer, S.J. Hong, M. Karnaugh, E. Mays, and Y. Tozawa.
A Knowledge-Based Consultant for Financial Marketing.
AI magazine, VII(5):71-79, Winter 1986.

[2]   E. Mays, C. Apté, J. Griesmer, and J. Kastner.
Organizing Knowledge in a Complex Financial Domain.
IEEE EXPERT, 2(3):61-70, Fall 1987.

[3] E. Mays, C. Apté, J. Griesmer, and J. Kastner.
Experience with K-Rep: An Object Centered Knowledge Representation Language.
Proceedings of the IEEE CAIA-88, pages 62-67, March 1988.

[4] R. Brachman and J. Schmolze.
An Overview of the KI-One Knowledge Representation System.
Cognitive Science, 9:171-216, 1985.

[5] G. Abrett and M. Burstein.
The KREME knowledge editing environment.
Int. J. Man-Machine Studies, 27:103-126, 1987.

[6] J. Boose.
ETS: A system for the transfer of human expertise.
in J. Kowalik, editor, *Knowledge Based Problem Solving*, pages 68-111, 1986.

[7] J. Conklin.
Hypertext: An Introduction and Survey.
IEEE Computer, pages 17-41, September 1987.

[8] E. Soloway, J. Bachant, and K. Jensen.
Assessing the Maintainability of XCON-in-RIME: Coping with the Problems of a VERY Large Rule-Base.
Proceedings of the AAAI-87, pages 824-829, 1987.

[9] T. Daly, J. Kastner, and E. Mays.
Integrating Rules and Inheritance Networks in a Knowledge-Based Financial Marketing Consultation System.
Proceedings of the HICSS-88, January 1988.

[10] M. Schor, T. Daly, H.S. Lee, and B. Tibbitts.
Advances in Rete Pattern Matching.
Proceedings of the AAAI-86, pages 226-232, August 1986.

[11] M. Karnaugh and R. Min.
Mainframe Equipment Planner: A Case of Industrial Strength Search.
IBM Research Division RC 13558, 1988.

[12] C. Apté and S.J. Hong.
Using Qualitative Reasoning to Understand Financial Arithmetic.
Proceedings of the AAAI-86, pages 942-948, August 1986.

[13] C. Apté and R. Dionne.
Building Numerical Sensitivity Analysis Systems Using a Knowledge Based Approach.
Proceedings of the IEEE CAIA-88, pages 371-378, 1988.

Expert Systems in Economics, Banking and Management
L.F. Pau et al. (Editors)
© *Elsevier Science Publishers B.V. (North-Holland), 1989*

APPLICATION OF EXPERT SYSTEM TECHNIQUES
FOR ANALYSING FIRM'S FALL IN MARKET SHARE

R.S. Dhananjayan * V.S. Janaki Raman # K. Sarukesi #

The object of this study is to develop an Expert System (ES) involving multiple-loop causal factor interaction model, in an interactive mode, for analysing a firm's fall in market share. The use of computers in economics and management, tapping the application potentials of Artificial Intelligence (AI) towards judgemental subject matter knowledge has been considerably slower as compared with the use of computers for solving problems in computational arithmatic logic. One reason why judgemental knowledge is unavailable, rests with the fact that the use of expert system, requires the expert's knowledge base, in symbolic rather than numerical or analytical form. Thus to make available, the expert knowledge, the knowledge and the relevant data base need a new orientation. Only then, it could render the scope for convenient manipulation by a computer towards analysing problems in any well defined area of economics and management. An attempt in this study is made to develop an inference system which uses the knowledge base and data base to make a 'brute search' and /or 'heuristic search' of the causal factors so as to identify the factor /factors responsible, in the event a firm is faced with a situation characterising a fall in market share.

INTRODUCTION

Research in the field of industrial economics and business management has made great progress during the past two decades with the statistical testing of hypotheses about the effects of the structures of the market on the performance of firms in a competitive system. New paradigms are provided to comprehend the behavioural pattern of firms in an industry [1]. The technological progress made possible on account of the rapid advancement in science and technology, has helped the firms to cut across the size and scale barriers. Firms are forced to adopt high-technological base so as to successfully face the changing competitive environment in the market. Economic theorists emphasized more on the principle of allocative efficiency for the optimal performance of firms. Of late, the evidence that market share of firms play a more central role in determining the economic performance, in the ways predicted by the managerial and behavioural theorists of the firm has brought into focus new dimensions in the management objective of firms [2,3,4,5,6].

Competition policies of the firms in most industrialised countries now attempt to combat fall in market share. Hence the code of conduct, in the determination of

---

* Department of Economics, Bharathiar University, Coimbatore - 641 046, India

\# Department of Computer Science, Bharathiar University, Coimbatore - 641 046, India

market structure has become more crucial to firms today than what has been in the past [7]. The competition policies include both price and non-price competitive domains. The behavioural strategy chosen by firms, heavily depend in the short-run on market structures that surrounds them. But it has important random components. Conduct patterns can however, feedback and influence the market share in the long-run.

The traditional profit maximization objective, consistent with the principle of resource allocative efficiency , to guide the conduct patterns of firms fail to explain fall in market share of firms in the event of economic crises and uncertainties originating due to market intervention by the government. Hence, the firms besides the profit maximization objective also now take into account such crucial factors as that of dynamic shifts in the production technology, government / public policies, rival / competitive firm's strategies relating to both price and non-price domains, the changing structure of the market with specific reference to market concentration and market share [8].

WHY EXPERT SYSTEM TECHNIQUE

In this context, the use of Artificial Intelligence faculty of the computer science has the great scope to play a vital role in applied research in economics and management. Intelligent computer systems are developed incorporating cognitive nature of human knowledge such as understanding language, ability to learn and reason and the capacity to solve problems and arrive at meaningful decisions [9,10,11]. These features of knowledge helps them to arrive at solutions in well defined problem domains. The explosion of knowledge (information) in every field of human reasoning as resulted in expanding the knowledge base. The need for expert knowledge in well defined problem areas became indispensable because of this explosion in knowledge base. However, the complexity of the real world situation has made it difficult, even for the expert, to analyse comprehensively involving all the casual factors and arrive at a meaningful solution, purely depending upon his natural mental faculties of memory and intelligence. The development of AI in computer systems aid the human in such domains of human knowledge which required complex reasoning at several hierarchial levels. Expert Systems, of late, in great measures have been developed in disciplines like the Engineering, Chemistry [12], Medicine [13], Computer Configurations [14], Economics and Management [15], etc., Expert Systems are basically knowledge intensive programs with capabilities to solve problems in domains requiring considerable amount of human expertise. Architectural details and the working methodology of expert systems are well brought out by Waterman [16], Hayes-Roth [17] and Jackson [18].

The voluminous knowledge that the expert system possess are stored in the knowledge base. The relevant support for the ES is drawn from the required data base. The data base assists the knowledge base in the process of analysing, solving and arriving at a decision. The knowledge is typically represented by i) Production Rules [19, 20], ii) Semantic Nets [21] and iii) Frames [22]. Of these, production rules are easy to implement.

PROLOG has the inherent advantage of being problem oriented rather than solution oriented [23]. The built-in inference engine performs a depthfirst searching coupled with backtracking. Further it is ideally suited in the codification of expert's knowledge using production rules. PROLOG is used in the expert system developed for analysing the fall in market share of firms in the present study.

STATEMENT OF THE PROBLEM

Typical of a situation where an event is caused by multiple-loop causation system, required for the application of expert system technique, the fall in market share, targeted by firms does depend upon a system of causal factors rendering the scoipe to analyse the problem using the ES Technique. The study is based on a hypothetical situation, in which a firm faces the problem of a fall in market share. It is a difficult proposition, to decide on an 'a priori' basis an 'optimal market share' for a firm operating in competitive market structures. It requries the firms not only to have an effective and complete control, in a planned manner on its internal factors but also requires the firms to have an ingenious comprehension and intelligent assessment of the external environment that have a bearing upon firms's share of output in the market. The present study does not outline the strategies involved in setting an optimal level of market share for a firm. It aims only in developing an expert system in order to analyse the factor/factors responsible in the event that a firm faces a fall in market share less than the level targeted for. The expert system developed here, relies on the data which are typically available with the enterprise's data base such as financial accounts, labour turnover, market statistics, production statistics, machine hour utilization data etc. The variables involved in the knowledge base of the program can be computed from the data base through properly structured report generating and reporting procedure. The list of variables that are required to interact with the expert system is given in figure 1.

FACTORS AFFECTING MARKET SHARE

The system of causal factors that affect the market share of firms are identified at different hierarchial levels. They are grouped under internal factors, based upon the criteria whether the factors are at the immediate and direct control of firms or not. [Details in Figure 1].

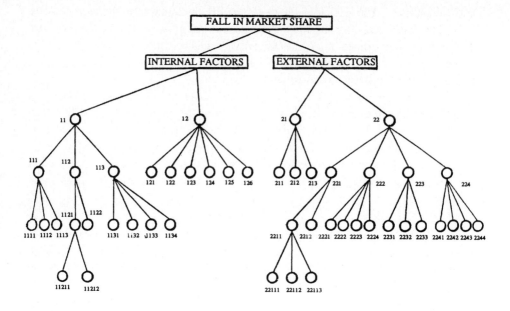

FIGURE 1 : KNOWLEDGE TREE OF THE SYSTEM SHOWING CAUSAL FACTORS

11	Fall in output	21	Rival/Competitive firms
111	Factor constraints	211	Entry of rival firms
1111	Machine breakdown	212	Price cut/war by rival firms
1112	Loss of mandays of labour	213	Output expansion by rival/
1113	Inadequate energy & fuel		competitive firms
112	Finance constraints	22	Government/public decisions
1121	Diversion of funds	221	Fiscal policy
11211	Borrowings diverted to capitalisation	2211	Specific restriction on firm's share
11212	Financial assets are capitalised	22111	Output restriction
1122	Portfolio Mismanagement	22112	Price restriction
113	Material constraints	22113	Resource use restriction
1131	Shortage of raw material	2212	Discriminated tax structure
1132	Stock depletion of semi finished goods	222	Monetary policy
1133	Inadequate stock of spares, components and stores	2221	Lending rate variations
1134	Depletion of finished goods	2222	Restrictions on soft loans
12	Uncompetitive price	2223	Specific borrowing restrictions on the firm
121	High input cost	2224	General price disturbs relative price of firm's output
122	Inefficient Technology		
123	Bad market survey	223	Industrial policy
124	Bad sales network	2231	Liberal licensing of new firms
125	Bad advertisement	2232	Withdrawl of market support
126	Cut in selling and customer service expenses	2233	Import of project
		224	Import policy
		2241	Product import
		2242	Raw material and technical knowhow restrictions
		2243	Change in foreign trade relations
		2244	Protectionist and tariff regulations

* On factors involved in the set consisting of the internal variables, the firms have a direct control. A failure in any one or more of the causal factors in this set such as Fall in output and/or uncompetitive price would account for the non achievment of the targeted level of market share. Once if any one of the above factor stand a possibility to cause the fall in market share, then each of these factors are traced down below to locate the factors which are responsible at further decomposed levels.

* The factors which lie external to a firm are beyond the control of individual firms. The working mechanism of external factors on the market share of individual firms is complex in nature. In typical real world environment, two major external factors could account for the fall in market share of firms viz. the rival/ competitive firm's behaviour and the government/public policy decisions. In economies where market intervention by the government is limited, then external uncertainities causing fall in market share are likely to orginate from the conduct patterns of rival/competitive firms. In other economies, public/government policy decisions would greatly influence the market share of firms. Since, the expert system developed here deals with a hypothetical situation of a firm, the answers from the user towards analysing the problem is deliberately kept exhaustive. However it is possible to use the E.S., to be exactly precise in dealing with the problem involving the system of causal factors, in particular case studies also. [Details in Figure 1].

METHODOLOGY

An AND / OR graph [Knowledge Tree] is a devise to explicitly represent the relationship between all situations and options that may be encountered in the solutions of decomposable problems. The nodes in an AND / OR graph represent sub-problems to be solved or sub-goals to be achieved, with the top node representing the specification of the overall problem. The nodes are connected by two type of directed links : the OR links are the ones that represent alternative options and the AND links are the ones that connect a parent problem node to the individual sub-problems of which it is composed. AND / OR graphs lend themselves to systematic search methods such as the backtracking, depth-first, breadth-first and various forms of heuristic best-first algorithms [24]. In our ES the tree is an OR tree which allows the search for the multiple loop causation system. Each loop and its hierarchially decomposed sub-loops are assumed to be capable of independently causing the market share of a firm to fall. In all, 68 rules imply the different causal factors accounting for the fall in market share of a firm.

The following section describes how the rules are used to analyse the factor responsible for the fall in market share, assuming fall in output is true on account of Material Constraints affecting the firm.

Rule : * #

IF	Fall in market share
AND	Ratio of Total Inventory Planned to total inventory being held at the end of the current planning period is more than unity i.e. $TINV_{Pt}/TINV_{Rt} > 1$
AND	Expost output is less than exante output i.e. $Q_{Rt} < Q_{At}$
THEN	Material Constraints.

Rule

IF	Fall in market share
AND	the ratio of raw material inventory planned for acquistion during the current period to the planned measure of raw material to be provided is less than unity
AND	the ratio of raw material inventory planned for acquistion during the current period to the raw material stock as held at the end of the previous period is less than unity
AND	exante output more than expost output during the current planning period
THEN	Raw Material Constraints

---

* EXPLANATORY NOTE

Inventory Management occupies a central role in ensuring smooth and steady supply of adequate material inputs at the appropriate time in the production process of an enterprise. Since in manufacturing enterprises, production underlines a value adding process, 'Stock-run out' situation in any one category of the inventory would hamper the enterprise and prevent the realization of exante output levels consequently the firms would face either a fall in output below the target levels of output not only in regard to the current planning (t) but also the realised output levels of the previous period (t-1). Stability in the structural composition of various categories of inventories occupy great importance both in respect of the planned total levels inventories ($TINV_{Pt}$) and also in terms of what the firms have ended up in thier total inventory levels being provided at the end of the current planning period ($TINV_{Rt}$). It can be deduced from the above, that planned or exante output (Q_{At}) will be in harmony with $TINV_{Pt}$ and expostor realised output (Q_{Rt}) will be in harmony with $TINV_{Rt}$. Inorder that a firm is able to check whether or not material constraints have led to the fall in output that has caused the nonrealization of targeted market share, the expert system will require te user to give such data that could be computed from the informations available with the firm relating to Inventory Accounts, production Accounts etc. The rule is based on the logic that

$Q_{At} = Q_{Rt}$ only when $TINV_{Pt} / TINV_{Rt} = 1$. Hence

RULE :

IF	Fall in market share
AND	$TINV_{Pt} / TINV_{Rt} > 1$
AND	$Q_{At} > Q_{Rt}$
THEN	Material Constraints.

Detailed explanatory notes for all the 68 rules used in the Expert System are available with the authors.

Rule
    IF   Fall in market share
    AND   the ratio of the stocks of spares, components, and stores at the end of the current planning period to that of the total inventory at the end of the current period is less than the ratio of the stocks of shares, components and stores to be provided during the current period to that of the total inventory provided
    AND   the ratio of the stocks of spares, components and stores at the end of the current planning period to the total inventory at the end of the current planning period is stable
    AND   exante output is greater that expost output of the current planning period
    THEN   Inadequate spaces, components and stores inventory

Rule:
    IF   Fall in market share
    AND   ratio of the stock of the semifinished goods at the end of the current planning period to that of the stocks at the end of the previous period is less that unity
    AND   the ratio of the stock of semifinished goods at the end of the current planning period of the total inventory at the end of the current planning period is less than the stock of the semifinished goods planned to be held during the current planning period to that of the total inventory provided
    AND   exante output is greater that expost output of the current planning period
    THEN   stock depletion of semifinished goods.

Rule:
    IF   Fall in market share
    AND   ratio of the stock of the semifinished goods at the end of the current planning period to that of the stocks at the end of the previous period is less than unity
    AND   the ratio of the stock of semifinished goods at the end of the current planning period to the total inventory at the end of the current planning period is less than the stock of the semifinished goods planned to be held during the current planning period to that of the total inventory provided
    AND   exante output is greater than expost output of the current planning period
    THEN   stock depletion of simifinished goods.

Like the above rules which lie within the boundry conditions of the internal factors under the sub-head material constraints, the system is incorporated with rules to trace the factors that would account for the fall in market share on account of external factors.

INFERENCE PROCEDURE

The knowledge for analysing the fall in market share, consisting of internal and external factors at different levels of decomposition, is represented in the form of production rules, in the knowledge base. The system is built with depth first search procedure pinpoint the causal factor responsible for the reported fall in market share. The following section proceeds to illustrate how the inference procedure works if material constraints faced by the firm has caused the fall in the market share. Material constraints could develop in a firm, typically due to shortage of raw materials, inadequate stocks of spares, components and stores, depletion of semifinished goods stock and the depletion in the stock of finished goods. The tree diagram in Figure 2 represents the situation.

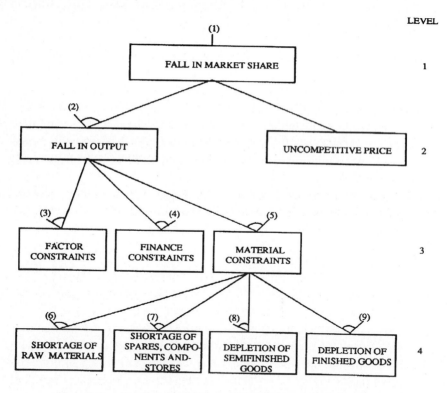

Figure 2: A section of the knowledge tree describing the inference algorithm

The system at level 4, indicates the definitive causes for the fall in market share. The numbers given in the parantheses indicate the observable facts. Event at level 1 (Fall in market share) is assumed to be occuring. The left most cause at level 4 is examined first. This is true if and only if (6) is true and material constraints (level 3) is true. Material constraints is true only when (5) is true and fall in output (level 2) is true. Fall in output is true only when (2) is true and fall in market share is true.

Since it is presumed that fall in market share is true, the system tries to confirm fall in output by asking the user to confirm (2)

If (2) is confirmed, the system proceeds to confirm factor constraints by asking (3)

If (3) is false, the system proceeds to ask (4). It is because the tree is OR in nature.

If (4)is false, it is confirmed that the finance constriants are not the cause.the system now proceeds to confirm material constraints by asking (5)

If (5) is true, questions with regard to shortage of raw material, shortage of spares, components and stores, depletion of semifinished goods and depletion of finished goods are asked.

Assuming that the user confirms (9) and not (6),(7) and (8), depletion of finished goods is the cause for the fall in market share experienced by the firm. The system now backtracks to uncompetitive price (level 2) and checks for the various causal factors associated with it. The system uses the same procedural principles for analysing the causal factors considered under the external factors.

UTILITY OF THE EXPERT SYSTEM

The business corporations operating in a market with the following characteristics will find the expert system more useful:
* The market is oligopolistic.
* Product loyalties change due to selling and advertisement costs.
* Sweeping technological modernisation charaterises shifts in production function of firms.
* Products have extended durability and have high income elasticity of demand.
* Product differentiation is subtle but crusial for firms to survive in the market.
* Sudden entry of firms on account of technology development breaks the plant scale and size of operation.

This expert system, is useful to firms associated with the manufacture of :
* Consumer electronics
* Automobile industry
* Cement, Paper, Chemicals, Machine tools etc., (Mostly in controlled/regulated economies)
* Wine and distilleries
* Cigarette and Tobacco
* Airlines
* Hotel industry
* Camera and Opticals
* Tea, Coffee etc.

SUMMARIZING REMARKS

The entire system works on the assumption that the user will have the details and the required data base to answer the questions raised by the expert system. As such the system does not provide for facilities to accomadate answers to questions as "Don't know ". The user has to have with him the detailed information from the data base which is exclusively designed with a reporting system to support the expert system.

REFERENCES

[1] Mach1up F., Theories of the Firm: Marginalist, Managerialist, Behavioural, American Economic Review 1967.

[2] Bain J S., Economies of scale, Concentration and the condition of Entry in Twenty Manufacturing Industries, American Economic Review 1954.

[3] Bhagwati J N., Oligopoly theory, Entry prevention and growth, Oxford Economic Papers, 1970. [4] Baumol W J., Models in Economic competition in Townsend (ed) Reading in price theory, Penguin, Middlesex, England, 1971.

[5] Marris R and Woods A (ed)., The Corporate Economy (Macmillan, New York, 1971)

[6] Cyert R M and March J G., A Behavioural Theory of the Firm (Prentice Hall, New York, 1963)

[7] Caves, Richard E., The Determinants of Market Structure: Design for Research in Jacquemin A P and de Jong H W (ed) Markets, Corporate Behaviour and State, Neigenrode studies in Economics Vol. I, Martinus Nizriff, The Hague 1976.

[8] Koutsoyiannis A., Non-price Decisions, The firm in a Modern Context (Macmillan, New York, 1982).

[9] Charnaik E and Mc Dermott J., Introduction to Artificial Intelligence (Addision Wesely Reading, MA, 1985).

[10] Rich, Elaine., Artificial Intelliegence (McGraw Hill Publishing Company, Tokyo, 1985)

[11] Nilsson N J., Principles of Artificial Intelliegence (Tioga Publishing Company, Palo Alto, California, 1980)

[12] Buchanan B G and Feigenbaum E A ., DENDRAL and META DENDRAL; Their Application Dimension, Journal of Artificial Intelligence 11

[13] Shortliffe., Computer Based Medical Consultation: MYCIN (American Elsevier / North Holland, New York, 1976)

[14] Mc Dermott J., R1: A Rule Based Configurer of Computer Systems, AI (19) 1982.

[15] Holsapple C W and Whinston A B ., Business Expert Systems (Galgotia Publications, New Delhi, India, 1988)

[16] Waterman D A., A Guide to Expert Systems (Ad 'ltion Wesely, MA, 1986)

[17] Hayes-Roth F, Waterman D A and Lenat D B (ed) Building Expert System (Addition Wesely, Reading, MA, 1983)

[18] Jackson P., Introduction to Expert Systems, (Addition Wesely, England, 1986)

[19] Davis et.al ., Production Rules as a Representation for a Knowledge Based Consultation Program. AI(8) 1977

[20] Janaki Raman V S ., Expert Systems in Chande BK (ed) Lecture notes on Artificial Intelligence and Fault tolerance in Computers, ISTE Notes 1987.

[21] Minsky (ed) Information Processing, (MIT Press, Cambridge, 1968)

[22] Minsky., A Frame work for Representing Knowledge in Psychology of Computer Vision, (McGraw Hill, New York, 1975)

[23] Frenzel Jr, Louis E., Crash course in Artificial Intelligence and Expert System (Howard Sam Publishing Company, New York, 1987)

[24] Shapiro (ed) Encyclopedia of Artificial Intelligence Vol 1, (Wiley Inter Science Publication, 1987)

Expert Systems in Economics, Banking and Management
L.F. Pau et al. (Editors)
© *Elsevier Science Publishers B.V. (North-Holland), 1989*

A PROLOG-BASED EXPERT SYSTEM FOR PRICE DECISION MAKING
UNDER INCOMPLETE KNOWLEDGE

Alan Tse

Department of Marketing, Massey University, Palmerston
North, New Zealand.

The expert system reported in this research is a rule-
based system that simulates expert wool exporters'
price decision making under incomplete knowledge. The
uncertainty caused by the incompleted knowledge base is
handled by fuzzy logic. The system is capable of
accepting fuzzy inputs from the user in the form of
linguistic variables. Following these inputs, the
system performs a set of fuzzy operations to produce a
nonfuzzy recommended price. The research shows that
fuzzy set theory is a powerful tool in modelling
entrepreneurial judgement, subject to the reservation
that a more pragmatic procedure be devised to get the
fuzzy membership functions from experts without causing
severe channel deterioration.

1. INTRODUCTION

The objective of the study is to build an expert system that
simulates wool marketer's price decision making under incomplete
knowledge. There are three specific objectives:

1.   To model entrepreneurial price decision making in the
     export wool industry;

2.   To determine whether fuzzy set theory is effective
     in modelling such kind of decision making; and

3.   To establish whether the delphi technique can be used to
     improve the results of knowledge engineering.

As a result of the de-regulated economy and the currency-
float, New Zealand wool marketers are now operating in an
increasingly turbulent, uncertain and risky environment. To
survive, these companies need expert decision makers.

So far, the application of Artificial Intelligence in
Marketing has been very limited. The primary objective of this

research is to determine whether a computer can be used to model entrepreneurial judgements. The system would be capable of accepting fuzzy inputs and subsequently producing a nonfuzzy recommended price using fuzzy mathematics. The research also investigates whether fuzzy set theories are effective in modelling the decision making process of marketing managers.

The system is made up of a main program driving four different modules. The first module is the user interface, which accepts inputs from the user and provides capacities for answering 'why' and 'how' type questions. The second module is the accounting subsystem that provides the user with a graphical display of the company's overdraft situation in the previous twelve months. The third module is the price forecasting subsystem. The forecasting model is the result of a competition using three different approaches: the Box–Jenkins model, the Fama model and the author's own model (Tse [1]). This module allows the user to examine the probable future market conditions by viewing a graphic display of the model's extrapolation. The last module performs the fuzzy transformation. The entire system is a rule-based system written in turbo Prolog (Kemp, Tse, Greenwood, Eagle [2]) and implemented on an IBM PCXT microcomputer. To enable Prolog to be used, all the clauses in the system were expressed as horn clauses, designed according to the top–down backward inference mode of logical thinking.

All the rules and facts in the knowledge base were obtained through depth interviews with marketers in the wool industry. The delphi technique was then used to refine these decision rules and facts. Given that the most serious obstacle in the construction of an expert system is the extraction of sound knowledge from experts, the delphi technique appears to have great potential in this problem area of knowledge engineering.

2. KNOWLEDGE ENGINEERING

Human expertise, in particular entrepreneurial expertise, is a scarce resource. However, experts typically do not structure their decision making in any formal way, and they may have great difficulty in isolating and describing their steps of reasoning. Different means of improving the process of knowledge engineering have been suggested. Hayes-Roth, Waterman and Lenat [3] have published guidelines about knowledge engineering. Buchanan [4] offered a five step approach to knowledge acquisition. Wrelinger and Breuker [5] also identified three stages of knowledge engineering.

The above paradigms, however, still have not solved the problem of extracting reliable and sound knowledge from the experts. The method of knowledge acquisition using personal depth interviews is subject to different forms of biases, and, more importantly, its ability to enable experts to isolate and describe their decision making dynamics is highly questionable. To date, there is still no scientific framework for knowledge engineering.

An alternative that the author believes may address the problem is the delphi technique.

Linstone and Turoff [6] describe delphi as a method used to structure group communication processes so that the process is effective in allowing a group of individuals, as a whole, to deal with a complex problem. To accomplish a structural communication, the process provides a channel of feedback to the participants, some methods of assessing their judgements, an opportunity for an individual to revise his/her opinions and some degree of anonymity for the participants. The procedure for conducting a delphi exercise can be found in Riggs [7].

After its inception, delphi has been applied to a wide range of areas, such as forecasting and future studies, with very satisfactory results.

Of course, there are still some unresolved issues in using delphi. Some methodological problems in using delphi have been addressed by Dalkey [8] and Martino [9]. Dalkey's study found that respondents were sensitive to the scores of the whole group and that they tended to move to the direction of the perceived consensus. Also, less confident members exhibited a larger degree of movement. Dalkey, Brown and Cochran [10] studied the feedbacks of delphi and suggested that with more sessions, a

consensus might be achieved more easily. Hence, to avoid
artificial consensus, stability of the distribution of the
responses over successive rounds was used as a stopping criterion
rather than degree of convergence in the author's study.

Ten companies were invited to participate in the study.
These ten companies comprise all the medium size wool exporters
in the North Island that are moderate in terms of their attitude
towards risk taking. Medium size companies are defined as
companies employing 10 to 14 full-time employees, or with a sales
turnover of 40 to 80 million in the financial year from April
1986 to March 1987. Their risk taking attitude is determined
subjectively by using a five-point scale ranging from very risk-
aversive to very risk-taking. The standard for including
companies in the study could not be more stringent because,
according to Turoff's study [11], reliable results can only be
obtained using 10–15 experts.

All the companies are making a profit in the financial year
under study; the participating marketing managers are thereby
regarded as experts.

The delphi procedure for this study consisted of three
iterations and took place over a three-month period from March to
May 1988. Stability in response was achieved after three rounds.
During each iteration, summaries of decision rules and membership
functions were sent to each manager together with his/her own
decision rules as well as membership functions. The managers
were in turn invited to revise their rules and membership
functions. The initial set of decision rules and membership
functions for the first iteration were obtained by depth
interviews with the ten participating managers. The
questionnaire consisted of a number of broadly designed open
questions. The funnelling technique was used so that additional
probing questions could be asked until the author was satisfied
that he had obtained all the information. Meanwhile, the
original levels in the membership functions were obtained by the
method of just noticeable difference involving two marketing
managers in the Palmerston North region.

The table below shows participation in the delphi study.   A

subsample of 2 of the 3 nonresponding companies in the first
iteration were interviewed by telephone for reasons of
nonresponse. Both these managers were on overseas trips and were
therefore unable to participate. The main reason for surveying
nonrespondents was to ascertain that the reason for nonresponse
was not because they had specific formula for making price
decisions and did not want to disclose these to the other
participants.

Iteration	Number of Experts asked to Participate	Number of Complete Returns	Percentage of Complete Returns
1	10	7	70.0
2	7	5	71.4
3	5	5	100.0

The mode of decision making in the industry is basically cost-
plus pricing. That is, if an offer is received for a certain
amount of wool to be delivered several months later, the price of
buying the wool is first ascertained, and different costs are
then added to this. A five percent profit margin is then added
to the total cost of the product to get a preliminary price
quote. The final price is determined after taking into account a
number of important factors in the decision making environment.
For simplicity, only these four fuzzy variables ranked as being
most important were incorporated in the system: exchange rate,
market situation, competition and cashflow.

3   THE INFERENCE ENGINE

The inference is based on fuzzy logic. The reasons for using
fuzzy logic are as follows.

First of all, the ordinary bayesian approach requires a lot of
measurements, and the reliability of the methods used to obtain
the priors and the likelihoods is sometimes problematic. This
approach would be complicated with the addition of a new decision
criterion as the system is usually not modular. The use of

confidence factors, on the other hand, do not have a strong
theorectical base. Fuzzy logic, however, is built upon a sound
foundation of the theory of fuzzy subsets. More importantly,
there is no requirement that a.â = 0 and a + â = 1 (a is a
boolean variable and â is its complement), which forms the basis
of probability theories. One can then easily see that the theory
of probability is related to the theory of boolean lattices (a
boolean lattice is distributive and complemented) and that the
theory of fuzzy subsets is related to the theory of distributive
lattices, which is connected to a still more general concept of a
preorder structure. That is, if E is a reference set, L is a
lattice and L^E is the power set, then for a fuzzy subset $\underset{\sim}{A}$ of E,
we can associate with each x ∈ E an element ∝ ∈ L, such element∝
will be the grade of membership of x in $\underset{\sim}{A}$. It is clear up to this
point that if the lattice is distributive and complemented, then
working with the membership function of E is identical to working
with probabilities. If the lattice is not complemeted, we are
working with fuzzy subsets (the notion of complementation used by
Zadeh in his papers is actually pseudo-complementation).

In addition to the above benefits, the use of fuzzy
propositions involving linguistic variables enable the author to
model in a more precise manner the decision making process of
managers.   It is commonly accepted that the process of
entrepreneurial decision making is too complex and ill-defined to
be amenable to quantitative characterization. Experts think in
terms of linguistic variables rather than descrete numbers. The
use of linguistic variables provides the inference engine with a
unit of measurement, giving the logic the power virtually
identical with the ordinary mechanistic systems.

The following example illustrates how the inference works:

Consider a typical membership function of a fuzzy linguistic
variable as shown follow.

Percentage price decrease   Grade of membership
                                     in fuzzy set
                                     slight price
                                     decrease

1%	0.41
2%	0.71
3%	0.85
5%	0.59
7%	0.50
10%	0.15
15%	0.09

The grades of membership are mean grades of membership at different levels of price decrease. Convex fuzzy sets were assumed. The percentages of price decrease in the above table represent the possible range of price decreases. The levels were established by the method of just noticeable difference.

A typical decision rule would be as follow:

If the cashflow is unfavourable, then the price should be lowered slightly.

The linguistic variables 'unfavourable cashflow' and 'slight price decrease' will be used as the base variable [Zadeh 12] for generating elements in the term set.

The above decision rule could be represented in the form of a fuzzy relation involving the base variables. Given that the membership function for unfavourable cashflow is:

unfavourable cashflow = 0.50/5% + 0.70/10% + 0.75/15%
$$+ 0.80/20\% + 1.00/30\% + 0.90/40\%$$
$$+ 0.83/50\%^{1}$$

Given also that slight price decrease is:

slight price decrease = 0.41/1% + 0.71/2% + 0.85/3%
$$+ 0.59/5\% + 0.50/7\% + 0.15/10\%$$
$$+ 0.09/15\%$$

Then the decision rule "If cashflow is unfavourable, then decrease price slightly" can be represented by the following

relational matrix using the operator min[1, 1 - u1(x) + u2(x)]
[Zadeh 13], where u1(x) is the membership function representing
unfavourable cashflow and u2(x) is the membership function
representing slight price decrease.   The   operator is consistent
with the definition of implication in Lakasiewicz's logic.

	1%	2%	3%	5%	7%	10%	15%
5%	0.91	1.00	1.00	1.00	1.00	0.65	0.59
10%	0.71	1.00	1.00	0.89	0.80	0.45	0.39
15%	0.66	0.96	1.00	0.84	0.75	0.40	0.34
20%	0.61	0.91	1.00	0.79	0.70	0.35	0.29
30%	0.41	0.71	0.85	0.59	0.50	0.15	0.09
40%	0.51	0.81	0.95	0.69	0.60	0.25	0.19
50%	0.58	0.88	1.00	0.76	0.67	0.32	0.26

Suppose the user input of the cashflow situation is very
unfavourable.   Based on the membership function of unfavourable
cashflow, the membership function of very unfavourable cashflow
could be defined as:

very unfavourable cashflow
$$= (\text{unfavourable cashflow})**2$$
$$= 0.25/5\% + 0.49/10\% + 0.56/15\% + 0.64/20\%$$
$$+ 1.00/30\% + 0.81/40\% + 0.69/50\%$$

The method that can be used to generate the membership
functions of linguistic variables modified by hedges is well
documented in Zadeh's paper [12].

Using the generalized modus ponens [Zadeh 13], the induced
decision space is:

$$0.61/1\% + 0.81/2\% + 0.85/3\% + 0.69/5\% + 0.67/7\% + 0.45/10\%$$
$$+ 0.39/15\%$$

The decision is to recommend a 3% drop in price because the 3%
drop correponds to the degree of membership of 0.85, which is the
highest grade of membership in the induced decision space.

If the decision space is unimodal the crisp maximizing decision rule mentioned above is used for the action. If the function is not unimodal, then the recommendation will be based on random choice subject to a number of constraints.

Upon the completion of the system, the program was sent to the five participating companies at the end of the third iteration for evaluation. The marketing managers were asked to test the system and rate the effectiveness of the recommendations produced by the system on a five point scale ranging from very poor to very good. The average rating was 3.2, indicating that the perception of the usefulness of the system is only slightly above fair.

4 Discussion

Fuzzy logic is undoubtedly very attractive in modeling imprecision in the marketing decision making environment. However, one important finding in the author's study is that the estimation of grades of membership is as tedious and subjective as the estimation of probabilities and certainty factors. It was a painful experience for both the interviewer and the interviewees to get the decision rules and the grades of membership for the different linguistic variables used. In fact, the value of the membership function cannot be determined rationally.

Also, the different definitional algorithms and operators are selected arbitrarily without sufficient empirical support, more analysis needs to be undertaken in this area to get more scientific definitional algorithms for the operators. Finally, counter examples can be given to show that cognitive processes do not follow the distributive axiom required for fuzzy algebra.

As far as the delphi technique is concerned, it appears that the technique is very useful in solving the problem of knowledge engineering in expert system construction. However, some issues remain to be solved.

First of all, attrition in later iterations is common in using the delphi technique. A sufficiently large sample must therefore

be selected at the outset. In the author's opinion, the problem
of improving the quality and quantity of the response is similar
to problems incurred in mail surveys.

Another problem is the question of how to choose a good expert
group. In this research, the marketing managers or directors in
the respective sampled companies were considered as experts so
long as the company made a profit in the previous year; this
definition might not be appropriate.

FOOTNOTE
1   The percentages in the denominators are the percentages of
     overdraft above the credit line permitted by the bank. The
     numerators are grades of membership.

REFERENCES
[1] Tse, A., A   Price Forecasting   Model on New Zealand Wool,
     Paper presented to the 1988 NZ Conference on Statistics.
[2] Kemp, R., Tse, A., Greenwood, J. and Eagle, C., Maintaining
     Flexibility in Expert Systems Design,   Proceedings of the
     Third New Zealand Annual Conference on Expert Systems,
     (1988) pp. 143-54.
[3] Hayes-Roth, F., Waterman, D.A. and   Lenat, D.B., ed.,
     Building Expert Systems, (Addison-Wesley, Reading, 1983).
[4] Buchanan, B.G. and   Shortliffe, E.H., Rule-based   Expert
     Systems, The MYCIN Experiments of the Stanford Heuristic
     Programming Project (Addison-Wesley, Reading, MA, 1984).
[5] Jackson, P., Introduction to Expert Systems (Addison Wesley,
     1986).
[6] Linston, H.A. and Turoff, M., The Delphi Method, Techniques
     and Application (Addison-Wesley, 1975).
[7] Riggs, W.E.,   The   Delphi Technique, An Experimental
     Evaluation, Technological Forecasting and Social Change Vol.
     23 (1983) p.90.
[8] Dalkey, N.C., An Experimental Study of Group Opinion, Santa
     Monica (1969).
[9] Martino, J.P., The Optimism/Pessimism Consistency of Delphi
     Panelists, Technological Forecasting 2, No.2 (1970) pp.221-
     24.
[10] Dalkey, N.C.,   Brown, B. and Cochran, S., The Delphi Method
     IV: Effect of Percentile Feedback and Feed-in of Relevant
     Facts, Rank Corporation (1970).
[11] Turoff, M., The Design of a Policy   Delphi, Technological
     Forecasting and Social Change 2, No.2 (1970).
[12] Zadeh, L.A.,   Outline of a New Approach to the Analysis of
     Complex Systems and Decision Processes,   IEEE Trans. System,
     Man & Cybernetics, SMC-3, (1973) pp. 28-44.
[13] Zadeh, L.A., Fuzzy Logic, Computer (1988) pp. 83-93.

Expert Systems in Economics, Banking and Management
L.F. Pau et al. (Editors)
© *Elsevier Science Publishers B.V. (North-Holland), 1989*

Configuring Knowledge-based Systems to Organizational Structures: Issues and Examples in Multiple Agent Support

Peng Si Ow
IBM Research Division
IBM Thomas J. Watson Research Center
Yorktown Heights, NY 10598

Michael J. Prietula
Graduate School of Industrial Administration
Carnegie Mellon University
Pittsburgh, PA 15213

Wen-Ling Hsu
School of Urban and Public Affairs
Carnegie Mellon University
Pittsburgh, PA 15213

In the presence of stable environments as operations-level decision-making, organizations evolve particular *sympathetic structures* to handle distributed decision-making tasks. Efforts to provide automated support to the agents of these structures must attend to the structure's distinguishing characteristics. In this paper we describe our experiences in designing two distributed, cooperative knowledge-base systems which solve operations-level decisions in a manner consistent with the relevant sympathetic structure of the organizations for which they were designed.

1. Introduction

For an organization to function, countless decisions must be made at all levels of the firm. Over time, organizations adapt to the internal and external environmental demands and constraints in a manner which yield structures that reduce the complexity of such decisionmaking tasks [e.g., Cyert & March, 1963, March & Simon, 1958; Simon, 1976]. What the "appropriate" structures might be and how they might get that way have been, and are continually being, researched and debated [e.g., Galbraith, 1977; Hax & Majluf, 1981; Malone & Smith, 1985]. In any event, these structures are comprised of a variety of formal and informal components which are sometimes quite difficult to articulate or explicate; therefore, modifications to such structures can lead to unanticipated and possibly undesirable results [Schein, 1985].

The lessons learned from organizational theory are quite relevant to information systems. As our capability and effort turn to assisting decisionmakers with information technology, it is essential that we understand and appreciate the interaction between the systems we build and the organizational structures in which we embed them. The systems we build must be compatible with those structures [Markus, 1984]. Additionally, relevant interesting and innovative results are emerging from distributed artificial intelligence (AI) research [Bond & Gasser, 1988]. As organizations begin to develop and rely upon AI-related technologies (e.g., knowledge-based systems), the notion of configuring collections of problem solving agents comprised of both humans and machines offers a powerful form of solution for important classes of problems occuring in organizations.

Whereas earlier researchers have proposed a link between organization structures and information systems, we further propose that because problem solving procedures are embedded in information systems, the design of these procedures affect, and are affected by, both the information systems and the organizational structure. In this paper we discuss observations drawn from two case studies on distributed knowledge-based systems design and their organizational fit. One case involves the task of scheduling tests for hospital patients while the other is a system that integrates the quotation of work-order completion dates with work-order scheduling in a jobshop of a large aircrafts manufacturer.

2. Operations Level Decision-Making

Our research focuses on systems which (1) are concerned with assisting in operations-level decisions and (2) involve distributed, multiple-agent decision-making at that level. At the operations-level of an organization, many decisions are made on a routine basis by groups of individuals. The decisions at that level typically span a relatively short horizon in the immediate future and are fairly well-structured [Simon, 1977] where the constraints and goals are clearly stated. Examples of operations-level decision-making include customer order processing, inventory control, and shop floor scheduling. Multiple-agent decision-making suggests that there are more than one decision-making agent involved. Additionally, any decision-making agent could be a person or a computing entity (e.g., a knowledge-based system). As noted, both of our case studies involve multiple operations-level decision-makers. We present a brief overview of the problems underlying each case.

Case 1: General Hospital Patient Scheduling. Patients in General Hospital reside in *units* that are organized by branches of medicine, such as orthopedics or neurosurgery. Each day, physicians request certain tests and/or therapy to be performed as part of the diagnosis and treatment of a patient. We will use the term *test* to refer to both types of requests. Tests are performed by separate, independent, and distally located *ancillary departments* in the hospital. The radiology department, for example, provides X-ray services and may receive requests from a number of different units in the hospital. After receiving a request from a physician, the unit secretary conveys the test request to the secretary of the relevant ancillary department. In turn, the ancillary secretary then determines the appropriate time for the test to be run. The unit secretary is notified immediately prior to that scheduled time slot and not sooner. The actual time the patient is scheduled is known only to the ancillary secretary (i.e., it is not relayed back to the requesting unit). Since each ancillary department schedules independently (and without knowledge) of all other ancillaries, conflicts arise when a patient is scheduled in overlapping (or near overlapping) time slots in different ancillaries. Such conflicts must be resolved by the unit secretaries. However, as the unit secretaries are made aware of the the scheduled ancillary times only when the request to "deliver" the patient comes from the ancillary, little slack time remains to resolve scheduling conflicts and delays. This can disrupt the care of the patient.[1]

Case 2: Max Aircraft Completion Date Quotations. This is a metal working jobshop comprised of approximately 1000 machines grouped into 170 work-centers. As part of the process of negotiating on a customer order, the Materials Control Department supervisor is responsible for making a

---

[1] Additional problems may also ensue. For example, in some cases the *sequence* of multiple tests are important -- a wrong sequence can result in patient stay delays as the residual effects of one test may influence the earliest start time of another test.

bid that includes an estimate of the *completion date.* This estimation is performed by consulting data supplied by the work-center load report -- an output of a computer system. Should the customer accept the bid, the awarded job is then given to the machine schedulers. The job completion date promised to the customer is again reviewed by the schedulers at a daily meeting with the process planners and industrial engineers. Schedulers have responsibility for the scheduling of a job and/or a work-center; therefore, detailed information on work loads and job priorities is readily available so that a more realistic projection of the completion date of the new job may be made. More often than not, the original promised due date is revised. From there, a work-order is created for eventual release to the shop floor.

Max Aircrafts was dissatisfied with the reliability of the completion date quoted. However, it was too time consuming to have the schedulers meet face-to-face to estimate completion dates on all requests for quotes. Max Aircrafts was interested in a system that would not change the existing assignment of responsibilities, but would closer integrate the quotation process with the scheduling process for greater accuracy. In particular, the department supervisor would continue to be responsible for the completion date quotation and the schedulers would keep the responsibility for the work-center schedules. After a work-order has been awarded, a scheduler would be assigned responsibility for tracking the order. The company realized that significant changes to the current methods of quoting and scheduling may be needed.

3. The Emergence of Sympathetic Structures

In both of the cases studied, the decision-making process had evolved a clearly defined set of procedures where the responsibility of each participant was specified and known. We propose that in a relatively stable environment,[2] the routine nature of operations level decision-making will lead the group responsible to adopt a structure (possibly informal) that will enable the decision process to be *collectively admissible* -- acceptable for each participating agent and for the group as a whole. Note that this does not imply each agent will seek to maximize the efficiency of its part in the process, nor that the adopted structure is optimal for the entire group. What forms is a *sympathetic structure* evolved by the group in the presence of task characteristics, human characteristics, and organizational realities (e.g., organizational memory, authority structures, distribution of expertise [Simon, 1976]). Such sympathetic structures have several specific characteristics.

Each group agent has a well-defined role in the decision-making process embodied in the structure. Roles include control and coordination of the process (such as that played by the nurses in the hospital), the execution of tasks (the scheduling of tests in the hospital, the estimation of work-order completion times), and information dissemination (the roles played by the unit secretaries, Max Aircraft's computer system). Typically, a group may assume several roles with each role defining a set of responsibilities for the group agent in the decision-making process. Furthermore, each agent's role is known to the rest of the group. In this model, the group agents are cooperative (i.e., they will not intentionally act, misinform, or withhold information to the detriment of other agents).

---

[2] For example, one in which there is a stable manufacturing process, a low employee turnover rate and employees remain in their job positions for long periods, and where employee evaluation methods and organizational goals do not frequently change.

Each group agent has individual goals in carrying out responsibilities; these individual goals are not necessarily shared by all group members. Individual goals typically include the criteria against which the agent is evaluated. In Max Aircraft, schedulers are evaluated by the throughput of their work-centers and the timeliness of those jobs for which they are responsible. The ancillary secretaries in General Hospital try to provide a fast response time to the test requests while the unit secretaries watch out for schedule conflicts and ensure that a patient's stay is not affected by bad test schedules [Kumar, 1988].

There is a well-defined communication protocol. The fact that all group members know each other's responsibilities reduces uncertainty in communication -- each member knows what should be communicated, to whom, when, and how. In Max Aircrafts, a well-defined protocol assures that meetings accomplish their goals in a relatively short period of time. In the case of General Hospital, the unit secretary knows which ancillaries should be sent the test requests and that the requests should include times during which the patient is unavailable for the test.

4. Issues in Supporting Multi-Agent Decision-Making

Distributed problem solving occurs when distributed, loosely coupled, multiple agents cooperate to solve problems [Smith & Davis, 1981]. When (some or all of) these agents are artificial intelligent programs, it is referred to as a distributed artificial intelligence (DAI) system. DAI systems involve unique design tradeoffs and difficulties. The literature on DAI is replete with interesting and creative ways of configuring systems that allow problem-solving to proceed. For example, HEARSAY III [Erman, London & Fickas, 1981], used the blackboard model as the problem-solving paradigm. Lesser and Corkill [1981, 1983] investigated the issues of distributed, cooperative problem-solving system design through a vehicle monitoring problem. Durfee, Lesser and Corkill [1985] later extended the original work to explore the issue of sharing partial solutions among the multiple problem-solvers so as to increase the level of cooperation of the system. Smith and Hynenen [1987] explored a hierarchical approach to production scheduling based on a corresponding hierarchical representation of the factory. Theirs also focused on a centralized, globally accessible knowledge base, the blackboard model, for communicating developments to the schedule. Others such as Smith and Davis [1981] concentrated on models of negotiation of the communication protocol used by the distributed problem-solvers. All in all, the primary focus of these DAI researchers has been on exploring problem-solving paradigms for systems that were intended to operate independent of human interaction.

Many of the models for DAI were drawn from beliefs and observations of group problem-solving and principles of organizational design [Fox, 1981; Lesser & Corkill, 1981; Malone, 1987; Wesson et al., 1981]. As such, the methods and techniques subsumed within these approaches permit configurations appropriate for the particular group of problem solving agents. Operations-level decision-making presents an ideal environment to begin examining the issues of designing knowledge-based systems based on the sympathetic structure of the organization. Insights into which features of DAI systems are useful for a particular context are gained by examining the evolved sympathetic structure itself. Our study of two cases revealed several characteristics of the sympathetic structures to which design attention had to be paid.

Multiple perspectives: The multiple agents play different roles in obtaining a solution for the problem.

All or a subset of these roles represent a particular decomposition of the problem that has been adopted by the group. Those agent roles that do not reflect effort toward solving a specific subproblem tend to serve control and coordination roles in the process. Thus a distributed system to support operations-level decision-making needs to be able to present multiple perspectives of the problem that is consistent with each role. A particular perspective may be limited to a subproblem in the decomposition or an alternative view of the same problem.Smith and Ow [1985] discuss this need for multiple perspectives reflecting alternative decompositions of a problem. Smith and Hynenen [1987] describe the use of multiple perspectives in the design of a distributed scheduling system.

> **Model Consistency:** Each perspective may require its own unique problem-solving model that not only assists the decision-maker in fulfilling its responsibility but also addresses the set of personal goals local to the agent.

No computer system can assure that each agent's goals are compatible with the other agents. Such issues must be resolved through negotiation and areconsidered to be outside the scope of this paper. However, it is recognized that the implementation of a distributed system may make goals more explicit so that goal inconsistencies are more apparent. Because these multiple agents interact, they must make certain assumptions about the behavior of other agents. One way to accomplish this is to embed in each agent a model of the other agents [e.g., Corkhill, 1979; Georgeff, 1984]. As a consequence, one then needs to consider the validity of problem-solving model assumptions across subproblems and agents [Kumar, 1988].

If the assumptions are incorrect or insufficient, performance and quality of the outcome will be affected. Consider two agents, α and β. α releases jobs to the floor and β schedules the jobs on the machines. α assumes that β can make reservations for jobs anytime in the future and hence releases the high priority jobs first even though they may not be ready to start until some time in the future. α wants to be sure that β will have these jobs scheduled as early as possible, and so does β. However, β only makes reservations forward in time. When scheduling a new job, β only considers available capacity after the last reservation made, so that lower priority jobs that can start immediately are not scheduled before higher priority jobs -- even if there is available capacity. Alhough α and β may have compatible goals, incorrect or insufficient model assumptions severely jeopardize the quality of the solution.

> **Location of Data/Knowledge:** The group structure may make it necessary to logically, if not physically, partition the knowledge or data or both, thus giving individual agents control over accessibility to the various partitions.

Each perspective should also be configured so that most of its data and knowledge requirements come from the agent's locale or a locale to which the agent has access rights. The work of Durfee and Lesser [1986], for example, provide insight into the sharing of knowledge and results. Unfortunately, the research to date is sparse on issues of distribution, consistency and integrity of knowledge representations and sources.

> **Communication protocol:** The problem-solving efforts of multiple agents needs to be controlled and coordinated with a well-specified, known, and consistent protocol.

The concern here is not with hardware, but with the logical design of how data and control is transferred between participating (and sometimes non-participating) agents. The contract net models of Davis and Smith [1983], the interrupt mechanism proposed by Durfee and Lesser [1986], the blackboard scheduler of HEARSAY III [Balzar et al., 1980], and the task and event list of OPIS [Smith & Hynynen, 1987] provide alternative approaches to designing communication protocols.[3] In the next sections we describe the knowledge-based systems that were designed

---

[3]Jarke [1986] also describes a variety of approaches for multiple agent communication.

for the two cases studied, and indicate how the group organization structure shaped those designs.

5. The General Hospital Patient Scheduling System

The *units* of General Hospital have responsibility for the welfare of their patients and the complete records of each patient is kept at the unit in which the patient resides. The *ancillary departments,* on the other hand, are "service" departments concerned with the prompt delivery of the specific services ordered for a patient; however, because of the high cost of medical equipment, they are also concerned with maximizing equipment use. The units and ancillaries incorporate two different perspectives of the patient scheduling problem. Furthermore, no information on patients is shared between units and no schedule information is shared between ancillaries.

We designed two types of subsystems -- an ancillary subsystem and a unit subsystem -- to provide for the different perspectives. Each *unit subsystem* is capable of being tailored to the needs of the unit where it is housed. It is intended to monitor the test schedule of each patient as well as collecting and disseminating test requests to the ancillary systems. Each *ancillary system* collects the test requests sent to it by the unit subsystems and schedules them. The test schedules are returned to the appropriate units as soon as they are determined. The ancillary system incorporates heuristics for scheduling tests and these heuristics may be tailored to the particular scheduling objectives of the ancillary (e.g., minimize setups, maximize throughput, etc.). A *global objective* was formulated which stated that the length of time taken to complete all tests are met should be minimized. To ensure this, the ancillary systems all have local goals striving (a) to minimize the response times to individual test requests and (b) not to exceed a particular date, called the *flow due date,* which is supplied along with the test request by the unit secretaries. The flow due date is the date before which all tests for a particular patient should be scheduled. The units' patient-oriented perspective of the problem makes it ideal for estimating this date for their patients.

In this system we provide a *primary* communication protocol which maintains the directions of information flows -- unit-ancillary communication with virtually no lateral communication between units or between ancillaries. We also have a *secondary* communication protocol which is unapparent to the user and serves as a substrate upon which the functioning of the primary protocol relies. The secondary protocol includes a broadcast-type communication between ancillaries concerning times that have been "blocked out" for each patient because of a scheduling decision made by an ancillary system. These blocked times are time intervals within which a patient cannot be scheduled and serve to prevent ancillaries from making conflicting scheduling decisions. It is not necessary for ancillaries to reveal their identities in broadcasting blocked times in the secondary protocol; therefore, the information content exchanged between agents-types (ancillaries and units) has not changed. Only the timeliness of information is affected. By incorporating this layered approach to defining protocols, the dominant (and visible) characteristics of the sympathetic structure are retained by the primary protocol while the secondary (and invisible) protocol overcomes a serious drawback inherent in the sympathetic structure.

A high level view of the system is shown in Figure 1. Each unit subsystem collects test requests for the patients in its unit. A flow due date is estimated by the unit secretary for each patient based on the tests requested. This date is communicated to the appropriate ancillaries together with the test information and blocked times. As the ancillaries schedule the tests, the schedules are communicated back to the appropriate units and the blocked times are broadcast to the other ancillaries. To provide the ancillary subsystems the most accurate estimates possible, the unit subsystems continuously update the flow due date estimates as tests are scheduled. A detailed description of this system may be found in Kumar and Ow [1988].

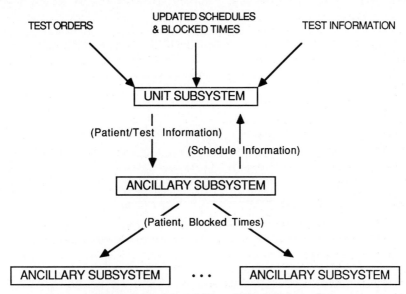

Figure 1. Overview of General Hospital System

6. Max Aircraft Completion Date Quotation and Scheduling System

The many decision-makers involved in the quotation and scheduling process for Max Aircraft suggested that a distributed system might be appropriate. The departmental supervisor's perspective of the problem was oriented around a single work-order at a time and getting an acceptable completion date quotation. For the vast majority of cases, this meant getting the work-order fulfilled as early as possible. In contrast, the workcenter schedulers were only concerned with those operations of the work-order that had to be performed at the workcenter and maximizing the utilization of the equipment. To address the conflicting goals of utility maximization and minimization of production lead time, Max Aircrafts agreed to modify the criteria for evaluating the schedulers' performance to include the response time of their workcenters. This forced the schedulers to evaluate trade-offs between fast turnaround time for a work-order and lower productivity on the machines due to machine setups. Our system had to be designed in such a way that the department supervisor had access to the schedulers' schedule without seemingly making the scheduling decisions.

Figure 2 shows an overview of the Max Aircraft system. Again, two types of subsystems were designed toprovide the two very different perspectives held by the problem-solving agents. The role of each scheduler is supported by a *resource broker*. The resource broker includes an up-to-date schedule of the work-center and can identify time intervals during which an operation may

316 P.S. Ow, M. Prietula and W.L. Hsu

be scheduled, including shifting existing reservations on the schedule to make room. A broker can also create a reservation in one of these time intervals if desired. The department supervisor's role is supported by a *work-order manager*, or WORM. The WORM is capable of collecting candidate time intervals for operations from the brokers and searching among them for a schedule that minimizes work-in-process and completion dates.The communication protocol between the brokers and the WORM is based on Davis and Smith's notion of contract nets [1983].

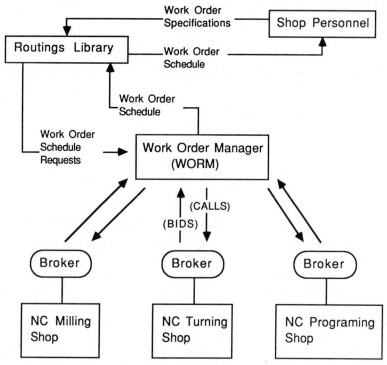

Figure 2. Overview of Max Aircraft System

After receiving a request for a quote, the departmental supervisor instructs the WORM to search for a good completion date. The WORM is also given a process plan with information about operations and machines needed to perform them. The WORM proceeds from the first set of operations on the process plan and puts out a *call for bids* on when these operations can be completed to those brokers that are associated with the work-centers capable of performing the operations. This call includes information on *constraints* such as the earliest start time and specific machining requirements. Each broker examines its current schedule and returns one (or more) candidate time intervals for performing the requested operation. The brokers select only those time intervals that are "good" with respect to the schedulers' local goals. The WORM reviews each bid submitted and selects the best bid with respect to the department supervisor's goals and proceeds to schedule the next set of operations that can be performed (using the bids selected to determine the start time constraints on these operations). The WORM, in effect, sprouts a search tree whose nodes are the bids returned by the brokers. When the last bids have been selected, the WORM has a feasible completion date to return to the department supervisor. Should the customer accept the quote from Max Aircraft, the selected bids are returned to the brokers as *awards* which the brokers will then schedule. Note that the WORM has several bids to select from for each operation. This can be assured either by requiring a broker to return a time interval *greater* than that required for an operation or by requiring that more than one bid be returned. The brokers have flexibility as the call for bids from the WORM do not tightly constrain the end-time of an operation as well as the start-time so that more than one candidate interval may be found. A detailed description of this system may be found in Ow, Smith, and Howie [1988].

This system demonstrates a cooperative problem-solving approach where the goals of each agent may be different, but when goal conflicts occur, the conflicting goals belong to the same agent therefore that agent may consider the trade-offs between goals. Furthermore, this system demonstrates that each agent can maintain control and privacy of its own knowledge-base without restricting the flexibility of other agents, where flexibility is measured by the number of alternatives an agent has when making a decision.

7. Conclusion

We have described two case studies to illustrate systems that were designed to fit the existing sympathetic structure of a problem-solving group in an organization. Our research focuses on distributed knowledge-base systems and is a subset of a growing body of effort toward understanding and designing "group" decision support systems [e.g., DeSanctis & Gallupe, 1987; Jelassi & Beauclair, 1987; Beauclair, forthcoming]. We have proposed that the design of problem-solving procedures to support multi-agent decision-making must be compatible with the organizational structure of the group of agents. Toward that end, we find that operations-level decision-making often presents a structured, distributed, multi-agent decision-making environment. Based on our experiences on two research projects involving operations-level decision-making, we have attempted to characterize those aspects of the group that affect our system design choices. We also identified how some of the system features developed by DAI researchers provide the knowledge-based systems designer the ability to support these group characteristics by exploiting features of the sympathetic structure. Clearly, two case studies are insufficient for a theory of how to design problem-solving procedures and systems for organizational fit. We hope that this paper has provided some insight on the issues of design and encourages further work that will lead to the crystallization of such a theory.

8. References

Beauclair, R. [forthcoming]. "Group Decision Support Systems and their effect on small group work." In Phillips, G. (Ed.) *How Groups Work*. Norwood, NJ:Ablex.

Bond, A. & Gasser, L.(Eds.). *Readings in Distributed Artificial Intelligence*. San Mateo, CA: Morgan Kaufmann.

Cammarata, S., McArthur, D. & Steeb, R. [1983]. "Strategies of cooperation in distributed problem solving," *Proceedings of the 8th International Joint Conference on Artificial Intelligence*, 767-770.

Corkill, D. [1979]. "Hierarchical planning in a distributed environment," *Proceedings of the 6th International Joint Conference on Artificial Intelligence*, 168-175.

Cyert, R. & March, J. [1963]. *A behavioral theory of the firm*. Englewood Cliffs, NJ: Prentice-Hall.

Davis, R. and Smith, G. [1983]. Negotiation as a metaphor for distributed problem solving. *Artificial Intelligence, 20,* 63-109.

DeSanctis, G. & Gallupe, B.[1987]. "A foundation for the study of group decision support systems," *Management Science,* 33(5), 589-609.

Durfee, E. & Lesser, V. [1986]. "Incremental planning to control a blackboard-based problem solver." *Proceedings of the Fifth National Conference on Artificial Intelligence,* 58-64.

Durfee, E., Lesser, V. & Corkill, D. [1985]. *Coherent Cooperation Among Communicating Problem Solvers.* Depart of Computer and Information Science Technical Report, University of Massachusetts, Amherst, MA.

Erman, L., London, P. & Fickas, S. [1981]. "The design and an example of Hearsay-III,"*Proceedings of the Seventh International Joint Conference on Artificial Intelligence,* 409-415.

Fox, M. [1981]. "An organizational view of distributed systems," *IEEE Transactions on Systems, Man and Cybernetics,* SMC-11(1), 70-80.

Galbraith, J. [1977]. *Organizational design.* Reading, MA: Addison-Wesley.

Georgeff, M. [1984]. "A theory of action for multiagent planning," *Proceedings of the 4th National Conference on Artificial Intelligence,* 121-125.

Hax, A. & Majluf, N. [1981]. "Organizational design: A survey and an approach," *Operations Research,* 29(3), 100-120.

Jelassi, M. & Beauclair, R. [1987]. "An integrated framework for GDSS design," *Information & Management.*

Kumar, A. [1988]. *A scheduling system from an organizational structure perspective.* Graduate School of Industrial Administration Summer Paper, Carnegie Mellon University.

Kumar, A. & Ow, P.S. [1988]. "A study of distributed problem-solving for patient scheduling." ORSA/TIMS Meeting, Washington DC.

Lesser, V. & Corkill, D. [1981]. "Functionally-accurate, cooperative distributed systems," *IEEE Transactions on Systems, Man, and Cybernetics,* 11(1), 81-96.

Lesser, V. & Corkill, D. [1983]. "Functionally-accurate, cooperative distributed systems," *IEEE Transactions on Systems, Man and Cybernetics,* SMC-11(1), 81-96.

Malone, T. [1987]. "Modelling coordination in organizations and markets," *Management Science,* 33(10), 1317-1332.

Malone, T. & Smith, S. [1985]. *Modeling Organizational Structures: Analogies between Human Organizations and Computer Systems,* MIT Sloan School of Management, Cambridge, MA.

March, J. & Simon, H. [1958]. *Organizations.* New York: Wiley.

Markus, ML [1984]. *Systems in Organizations: Bugs + Features.* Cambridge, MA: Ballinger.

Ow, P.S., Smith, S. & Howie, R. [1988]. "A cooperative scheduling system," *Proceedings of the Second International Conference on Expert Systems and the Leading Edge of Production Planning and Control.*

Schein, E. [1985]. *Organizational Culture and Leadership.* San Francisco, CA: Jossey-Bass.

Simon, H. [1976]. *Administrative Behavior -- Third Edition.* New York: Free Press.

Simon, H. [1977]. *The New Science of Management Decision - Revised Edition,* Prentice-Hall.

Smith, R. [1980]. "The contract-net protocol: High-level communications and control in a distributed problem solver," *IEEE Transactions on Computers,* 29(12), 1104-1113.

Smith, R. & Davis, R. [1981]. "Frameworks for Cooperation in Distributed Problem Solving," *IEEE Transactions on Systems, Man and Cybernetics,* 11(1), 61-70.

Smith, S. & Hynynen, J. [1987]. "Integrated decentralization of production management: An approach for factory scheduling," *Proceedings of the ASME Annual Winter Conference.*

Smith, S. & Ow, P.S. [1985]. "The use of multiple problem decompositions in time-constrained planning tasks," *Proceedings of the Ninth International Joint Conference on Artificial Intelligence.*

Expert Systems in Economics, Banking and Management
L.F. Pau et al. (Editors)
© Elsevier Science Publishers B.V. (North-Holland), 1989

EVALUATING ORGANIZATIONS USING AN EXPERT SYSTEM

Richard M. Burton and Børge Obel *

Organization theory exists as a large body of loosely related languages, definitions, hypotheses, analyses and conclusions. Yet, there is an underlying core of knowledge which can be used in a rule-based expert system. This requires that the knowledge be distilled and augmented to produce a set of clear, consistent, and operational generalizations. The result would be a knowledge base for an expert system that is *useful*. The resulting expert system can be used to analyze firms, help us teach our students, and aid us in the scrutiny of the knowledge in the organization theory literature.

This paper presents our best attempt to capture some of the literature in organization theory as a rule-based expert system and use it to prescribe an organizational structure in terms of centralization, formalization, and complexity. The paper discusses the structure of the knowledge base and how various features in expert system methodology can be used in this particular application. Particularly, the use of both positive and negative certainty factors are discussed. European as well as American firms have been used to validate the system.

I Introduction

Organization theory is a large body of knowledge of loosely related languages, definitions, hypotheses, analyses and conclusions. Organization theory is multidisciplinary where the separate disciplines have created the questions, hypotheses, methodologies and conclusions - each built on related yet distinct views of the world.

Organization design is an equally important complement to organization theory. Organization theory is a positive science which focuses on an understanding of organizations. Organizational design is a normative science which focuses on the creation of organization to obtain given goals. Of course, organizational design must incorporate the knowledge from organization theory; otherwise, it is an exercise in abstraction without empirical content.

In this paper we report on an attempt to create an expert system as a decision support system in the design process of organization. The system incorporates knowledge from the literature on organization theory as well as expertise derived from experts.

An expert system is composed of three parts (Harmon and King, 1985): a knowledge base, an inference engine, and a user interface. The knowledge base contains what we know about the issue - herein, our understanding from the positive science of organization theory. It consists of concepts like organizational structure, divisional structure, decentralization, formalization etc. The expert system requires that the knowledge base be stated using consistent and clear definitions of terms and concepts. Relationships between concepts are also a part of the knowledge base. Statements such as "mass production is a technology definition" and "analyzer is a strategy" are examples.

The knowledge base concept in expert system is mostly recognized due to its use of facts and if-then production rules to represent knowledge. Facts like "The organization is large" and rules like "if the organization is large then the formalization is high" are examples. In the next section we argue that the knowledge in organization theory does not have consistent definitions and conclusions. However, the construction of a knowledge base for the expert system requires a clarity and consistency which forces us to ask new questions about the knowledge of organization theory.

---

* University of Odense, 5000 Odense, Denmark

The inference engine is the part of the expert system which controls the way the rules are inspected and how conclusions are made based on these rules. The inference process accumulates conclusions inspecting a number of relatively simple "if-then" rules. As we shall show many hypotheses in organization theory are stated in relatively simple "if-then" rules. We therefore use the machinery of the inference processes in expert systems to combine the many separate hypotheses in organization theory into a comprehensive model.

A distinct feature of most expert systems is the ability to explain why the system reached a particular conclusion. This feature has been used both in the validation process as well as in the actual use of the system. The system contains the particular definitions of the concepts used. This enables the user to get a better understanding of the basic organization model used in the system. The user interface is the way the system communicates with the user - using window's, pull down menus, icons etc. The system presented in this paper does not use a sophisticated user interface. It communicates with the user asking relatively simple questions. The user answers by choosing from a prespecified menu of legal answers. One general answer is "unknown". Thus the system can operate using incomplete information from the user. As will be discussed later the way these questions are phrased is very important.

The expert system is a tool to help us as students, teachers and researchers, who want to use existing organization theory, create new understanding, and design organizations which serve us.

II The Knowledge Base in Organization Theory

What is known about the theory of organization and its implications for design? There is a very large knowledge base in the literature and common knowledge where both academics and practitioners are experts. However, this vast knowledge is fragmented in many different theoretical constructs and practical knowledge. There is not a single coherent structure for our knowledge on organizational design. The beginnings of such an effort is the consideration of normative recommendations as well as efficiency and effectiveness hypotheses from the literature.

Frequently, research treatises, review articles, and textbooks attempt to develop integrated views of knowledge-information systems. Robbins (1987) has attempted to state such an integrated view. The task is formidable. There is a very large literature to consider each normally emphasizing a particular paradigm. There are many descriptions of the environment and technology as well as different relational statements (Duncan 1972, 1975; Perrow 1967). Perrow (1967) is one description of technology along the dimension of task variability and problem analyzability. Woodward (1965) uses batch, continuous, and process on a nominal scale. Thompson (1967) uses pooled, sequential, and reciprocal. Burton and Obel (1984) apply Simon's (1981) decomposibility measure of technology, and suggest that Thompson may have confused technology for structure. In addition, the contingencies for organizational design potential include strategy, size and power control (Robbins 1987, p. 22) as well as environment and technology.

The relational (IF-Then) statements are involved, complicated, and numerous as well as stated in different, if not disjoint, spaces. Given the state and form of our knowledge, it is to be expected that any integrated view, such as Robbins' (1987), will be less than totally complete, comprehensive, and operational. Our knowledge is fragmented, diverse, and largely disjoint. An expert system approach demands a discipline which forces us to consider these issues. Our knowledge base shows that it is possible to combine different views. However, new concepts and precision of concepts my be required. There are basic concepts for organizational design which can guide the further development of expert systems.

III Expert System for the Organization Theory Literature

Despite the diversity and vastness of the literature, contingency theory is the dominant theme in organization theory (Robbins, 1987; Daft 1986). Size, strategy, uncertainty, environment, power have all been offered and argued as imperatives to determine the organization's structure. The controversy over which organizational imperative is the correct one has largely disappeared. The more general contingency concept would suggest that each factor is important in structuring the organization. The organization must fit with one or several of these determining factors in order to be efficient, effective, or at least viable. In Figure 1, these contingency concepts are summarized. For the fit criteria, the contingency factors lead to an appropriate organization structure and properties.

THE CONTINGENCY MODEL OF
ORGANIZATIONAL THEORY

The Contingency Factors for
Organizational Structure:

Properties and Structure
of the Organization:

Strategy
Size
Technology
Environment
Power Desires

Structure:
Simple, functional,
divisional, machine
bureaucracy, matrix, etc.
Properties:
Complexity and differentiation
Centralization
Span of Control
Rules
Procedures
Professionalization

Fit Criteria:
Effectiveness
Efficiency
Viability

Activities
Meetings
Reports
Communications

Figure 1

Our knowledge about these relations can be stated in a series of conditional imperatives, or rules in a rule-based knowledge base in an expert system. One rule (Duncan, 1979) is:

if the environmental uncertainty is stable then the centralization is high.

Our knowledge base for a contingency theory of organization contains more than 150 such rules. These rules are gleaned from the literature. Another rule which is readily recognized is:

if size is large then decentralization is high.

This rule is a statement that the size and a decentralized organization will provide a good fit. Similarly another rule, is:

if the strategy is prospector then the decentralization is high

This business strategy indicates that the organization should be decentralized. This is consistent with a strategy - structure hypothesis. These rules illustrate the large number of such statements which summarize our knowledge of organization theory.
    A less obvious rule is:

if the strategy is prospector and the product innovation is low then a situational misfit exists.

This rule states that a situation which includes a prospector strategy and a low product innovation is not a good fit, and would require a change in the situation, before the fit between the organizational structure and the situation can be established.
    The construction of a knowledge base for an expert system is a statement of our knowledge about organization theory. Definition of terms must be clear and operational. For the expert system, the knowledge statements must be precise and consistent. Many textbooks are written with these criteria in mind. In a text, one can say that environment is important to determine a good structure; and that strategy is too. Further refinement may be desirable, but is not mandatory. For the knowledge base in an expert system, the weighing and balancing of the contingency factors must be addressed explicitly. The composition of the rules is central to the development of the knowledge base. For the expert system, the two rules on environment and strategy are not independent, but are part of the total statement of our knowledge and understanding of organizations.
    Either statement would be an over-statement. To make the statements more correct and to reflect our knowledge of organization theory, we must add to each statement to indicate the strengthening of the statement. The contingency imperatives are then balanced. A certainty factor (cf) can be used to modify each statement to more adequately summarize our understanding and knowledge. Rewritten, the two statements are:

if the size is large then the decentralization is high (cf 30)
if the strategy is prospector then the decentralization is high (cf 20)

Now let us assume that both antecedents are true; i.e. both "if" conditions are met, then the rules for combining the strengthening of our conclusion on the structure is given by:

decentralization is high cf 44

where the calculation follows the rules from the MYCIN concept. In this case $30 + (100-30) 20/100 = 44$.
    The resulting conclusion is stronger than either statement would be above. Each contingent factor adds to the conclusion, but neither condition is sufficient to make a certain conclusion or recommendation. These two rules both have a positive relation with decentralization. We may

also have knowledge that tells when a relationship is not positive. For example: if structural complexity is low then decentralization should not be high. In an expert system framework we can handle this by using negative certainty factors:

if structural complexity is low then
decentralization is high cf - 30.

By taking all three statements together we get that decentralization is high cf 20. Thus we get a balancing of positive and negative impacts.

In terms of contingency theory, we are combining the various imperatives into a unified and consistent statement of our knowledge. The literature is rather silent on the appropriate combination (although there is evidence for using each factor). Thus, the validation of the knowledge base requires a continuing revision through application in real situations and cases. We shall discuss this issue in a later section.

So far, we have only discussed the creation of the rule-based knowledge base which represents our knowledge of organization theory. We now turn to the organization design problem. Here we want to apply our knowledge about organizations to help specify appropriate structures and properties for given contingencies. It is the reverse problem. Referring again to Figure 1, the goal is to determine the structure and properties for the organization. So, the expert system begins to seek a value for structure. The expert system inference engine begins a query process seeking the needed information to specify the structure and properties. Beginning with the goal to find a structure and properties and running backwards through the rule-based knowledge, it will eventually find that it needs to know the conditions of the environment, strategy, technology, etc., and it can only determine the environmental condition by asking the user. Thus it asks for responses for the contingency factors. This process is called backward chaining. That is, the inference engine begins with a goal, and works backwards through the knowledge base, and requests fundamental information. The expert system then recommends a structure - simple, functional, divisional, matrix, etc.

These are the three elements to the expert system: 1) the knowledge base of organization theory, 2) the inference engine which guides the search to determine the organization design, and 3) the contingency factor values, e.g., the environment is changing. General knowledge and a means to use it in a particular situation make up the necessary ingredients to recommend a structure and properties for an organization.

IV Organizational Consultant

The *Organizational Consultant* expert system analyzes the current organizational structure by queering the user about 27 facts related to the functioning of the organization. The structure is then described in the terms that are later used to describe the recommended structure.

Next the expert system asks for input related to 14 major situational variables. The input is given again answering a number of specific questions about the organization's situation - in the current version a maximum of 25 questions depending on the particular situation. These answers are then translated into values for the internal concepts used in the system.

Based on this input the system recommends the most likely structure that gives the best fit with the specified situation. The situation itself is analyzed and possible situational misfits are given. Finally, the current and prescribed organizational structure is compared and possible changes recommended. The system includes a feature that enables the user to change input values and rerun the consultation thereby providing a way to perform sensitivity analysis. A sample output is shown in Figure 2:

* * * * * * * RESULTS FROM ORGANIZATIONAL CONSULTANTS * * * * * * * *

EXISTING ORGANIZATIONAL STRUCTURE

Test organization has a functional structure.
The organization has a high complexity.
The horizontal differentiation is medium.
The vertical differentiation is medium and the spatial differentiation is high.
The formalization is high and the centralization is high.

EXISTING BUSINESS SITUATION

You provided the following information about Test-organization's situation:
size(Test-organization) = medium (100%) because kb-59.
age(Test-organization) = mature (100%) because you said so.
diversity = few (100%) because kb-71.
technology-routineness = yes (100%) because you said so.
technology-type = 0 (100%) because rule-u.
technology-divisibility = little (100%) because you said so.
strategy = defender (100%) because you said so.
ownership = private (100%) because you said so.
wish-of-power-concentration = yes, indeed (100%) because you said so.
environmental-complexity = some (100%) because rule-auncer.
environmental-uncertainty = changing (100%) because rule-uncer.
environmental-hostility = medium (100%) because you said so.
capital-requirement = high (100%) because you said so.
product-innovation = high (100%) because you said so.

THE SUGGESTED NEW ORGANIZATIONAL STRUCTURE

Based on the input you provided it is most likely that the best structural
form for Test-organization is a functional structure (cf 70).
The formalization should be high (cf 56) and the centralization should be
medium (cf 53).
The complexity should be low (cf 52) with a low vertical differentiation.
The span of control should be wide and coordination and control should be obtained
through the following means: planning-and-rules.
The structure of Test-organization should not be a divisional structure (cf -100).

POTENTIAL PROBLEMS

Test organization has both a defender strategy and a non stable environment. The organization is in a high risk situation as a market change may lead to serious losses. This may cause problems!!!

Test organization has a high capital requirement, but is not a large organization. This may cause problems!!!

Current and prescribed complexity do not match.
Current and prescribed centralization do not match.

The current version of the expert system is developed using the expert system shell M1 version 2-1 (Tecknowledge, 1987) and has 367 knowledge base entries (156 rules, 64 facts and 147 meta-facts). M1 was chosen because it is relatively easy to use and it runs on a PC. We found it was important to be able to bring the expert system to the organization. A portable PC and printer are used. The analysis is performed where the executive chooses it.

The design problem covered is relatively large. With 14 variables describing the situation and assuming three possible values for each variable then $3^{14} \approx 4.8$ million different situations are covered by the system. The basic result is described by structural form, centralization, complexity and formalization where the expert system has $7x3x3x3 = 189$ fundamentally different designs to choose from.

V The Structure of the Knowledge Base

The knowledge base in *Organizational Consultant* is divided into 4 major sections, which have been developed and tested somewhat independently.

The first section is a data section which queries about some fundamental facts about the organization that is analyzed. The second section relates to the current organization as described above. The third section deals with the organization's situation and is partitioned into a number of subsections. One subsection asks the user about relevant information. The second subsection is a database which maps the situation onto overall organizational designs, and finally the third subsection which analyzes the situation in more detail both with respect to situational misfits and more detailed recommendation about the prescribed structure. The knowledge base is concluded by a section which prints the output, compares the prescribed and current organization and finally controls the looping necessary for the sensitivity analysis where the user can change any input item and get a new analysis.

The knowledge base has been structured in this way for a variety of reasons.

When one uses a relatively small expert system shell like M1 the knowledge bases often become very complicated to write, debug and maintain. (Rauch-Hindin 1988, p. 134). Therefore, a specific structure of the knowledge base was developed. Actually the first version of the part related to the current structure and the part related to the prescribed structure were developed as independent expert systems. Later in the design process they were merged. However, they can still be run independently if only the conclusions made in the first part are transferred to the second part. This shows another reason for the structuring of the knowledge base. In many PC based expert system shells the number of rules become the bottleneck. We have not reached that yet with M1, but should it happen we can separate the knowledge base into two without ruining the system. In principle M1 uses a backward chaining inferencing process. However, M1 allows more than one goal. The separability of the various parts of the knowledge base has also been enhanced by using relatively many goals related to the various subsections of the system. Another advantage has been that the sequence of the questions, which the system asks, has been strictly controlled, so that they appear in a logical sequence. For example, when the system prompts questions about the environment it basically asks all relevant questions about the environment given the situation. The system may in rare cases ask a question, where the answer does not have any impact on the conclusion.

The use of certainty factors to combine the partial organizational theories was an integral part of our development process. The use of positive and negative certainty factors turned out to have some important effect on the use of our system. The first version of our system used only positive certainty factors. M1 allows multivalued variables which we used to encounter for one important issue in organization theory: How to average! If one says that the organizational environment is medium uncertain, does this mean that for all parts of the environment the uncertainty is medium, or does it mean some parts are very uncertain and some are relatively certain. Using only positive certainty factors enabled us to run each of the multivalued answers on a parallel basis using the same rules. However, when we started adding knowledge about what should not be in terms of rules with negative certainty factors this parallelism collapsed and we had to control the above two situations directly in a more complicated rule structure.

VI Validation

Validation is an ever ongoing process for an expert system. We have validated the expert system using two different methods. The first one, especially useful in the early stages of the development of the system, used tests based on textbook cases. We have assembled a number of text book cases which are rich enough in their description to provide input for our system. We - as experts - have then solved these cases, and/or we have consulted the recommended solution provided from other sources e.g. instructor's manual. The system is then constantly confronted with this set of tests. When a revision is made this first part of the validation is used to tune the combination of the partial theories described earlier. The second part of the validation was a test using American and European executives from companies of various sizes and in various industries. This includes a large US pharmaceutical company, a large telecommunication organization, a small Danish retail store, a division of a large Danish company in the machinery industry, a retail and wholesale chain in the building industry in Denmark, and a new TV channel.

These validation tests follow a general format. The executive chooses the organization, usually his own firm or division. The expert system then asks questions, and gives a summary of the current situation and the recommended organizational design. The executive then discusses whether the questions are clear and can be answered. Do the questions seem reasonable as input to determine an organizational design? Is the summary correct and does it represent what you wanted to say? Then, are the recommendations reasonable? Why? Have new issues been surfaced? Will you implement the recommendations? Why or why not? It is an interactive verbal protocol which brings out the executive's own expertise and juxtaposes it with the expert system. Of course, an executive's agreement with the expert system results is more satisfying to the developer, but less constructive than disagreement. Something must be wrong. The error may be with the executive, or with the expert system. The developer must apply his judgement after listening to the executive's rationale.

The technique to modify and fine tune the expert system begins with the executive's observation and rationale that "it doesn't make sense". The expert system then searches the system to see why this result obtains. There is a sequence of rules which yielded the result. e.g., the recommendation that centralization is high was by a sequence of rules being applied. The developer then investigates this sequence of rules in detail. Have we captured the knowledge adequately? Usually the situation is that the general statements are appropriate, but that the relations among the rules need to be modified, i.e., the cf's must be changed or there are specific circumstances with this particular organization which have to be taken into account. This often means that more precision is built into more general rules. On occasion, one finds rules in error and format errors, but it is the composition of the rules which usually creates the problem.

In the test with the executives we encountered the specific problem that some executives found that some questions were difficult to understand and/or answer. Generally the executives preferred very detailed and specific questions to more general and less specific questions. We are currently reviewing the expert system to enhance the level of details both with respect to inputs and outputs.

VII Conclusion

One may ask what are the major benefits from an exercise of building this kind of expert system.

First, it forces one to look very critically at the definition of concepts and hypotheses. It creates a need to look into the explicitly used definition of terms in the many studies on organizational theory. Additionally one has to synthesize the many partial theories and hypotheses into a comprehensive whole. This often highlights gabs and inconsistencies which could form a platform for new research.

Second, one of the major benefits of using the expert system techniques in the process of combining the disparate field of organization theory is that rules can be added and deleted incrementally. The inclusion of different versions of a hypothesis can easily be tested and the best one for the purpose be chosen. It also provides a means for combining scientific and heuristic knowledge.

The expert system can be used at least in three different situations. As discussed above it can be a tool in the basic research in organization theory both in theory testing and in the generation of new research questions.

We have also used the system successfully as an educational tool in an organization theory course. The students solved cases along with the system and the results were compared. The system provided an explanation of why it made the recommendation, and thus taught the student some fundamental principles. Finally and probably most importantly it showed the students that the proper organizational design depends on many factors, some of which may require different solutions. It thus provided a basis for the discussion of trade-off's in the design of organizations.

The most obvious use of an expert system to design organizations is to use it for designing organizations. As described above the system has been used in a number of companies and it has been an excellent tool for starting a discussion about how appropriate the situation and the organization was. It has also, by asking surprising questions, forced the executives to think of issues which they had not incorporated before in their own analysis. The work on this project is continuing. In this paper one expert system based on theories and concepts from the literature has been presented. This system is a part of a larger project which includes a description of organizational design using new precisely defined concepts and relations (Baligh and Damon, 1980; Baligh and Burton, 1981; Baligh, 1986 and Baligh, Burton and Obel, 1987) and the development of an expert system based on these concepts and relations.

References

Baligh, Helmy H. "Decision Rules and Transactions, Organization and Markets." *Management Science*, Vol. 32, No. 11, Nov. 1986, pp. 1480-1491.

Baligh, Helmy H. and William W. Damon. "Foundations for a Systematic Process of Organizational Structure Design." *Journal of Information and Optimization Sciences*, Vol. 1, 1980, pp. 133-165.

Baligh, Helmy H. and Richard M. Burton. "Describing and Designing Organization Structures and Processes." *International Journal of Policy Analysis and Information systems*, vol. 5, December 1981, pp. 251-266.

_____. "The Process of Designing Organization Structures and Their Information Substructures." S.K. Chang (editor). *Management and Office Information systems*, New York, Plenum Press, 1984, pp. 3-25.

_____ and Børge Obel. "Designing Organizational Structures: An Expert System Method" presented at Economics and Artificial Intelligence Conference, Aix-En-Provence, September 1987.

Burton, Richard M. and Børge Obel. *Designing Efficient Organizations: Modelling and Experimentation*. Amsterdam, North-Holland, 1984.

Daft, Richard L. *Organization Theory and Design*, West Publishing Company, 1986.

Duncan, Robert. "What is the Right Organization Structure?" *Organizational Dynamics*, Winter, 1979, pp. 59-79.

Duncan, Robert B. "Characteristics of Organizational Environments and Perceived Environmental Uncertainty." *Administrative Science Quarterly*, Vol. 17, September 1972, pp. 313-327.

Harmon, O. and King D. *Expert Systems. Artificial Intelligence in Business*. Wiley 1985.

M1. Reference Manual for Software version 2.1, Tecknowledge, 1987.

Perrow, Charles. "A Framework for the Comparative Analysis of Organizations". *American Sociological Review* vol. 32, April 1967 pp. 194-208.

Rauch-Hindin, W.B. *A Guide to Commercial Artificial Intelligence: Fundamentals and Real-World Applications*, Prentice Hall, 1988.

Robbins, Stephen A. *Organizational Theory: The Structure and Design of Organization*, 1987, Englewood Cliffs, NJ, Prentice-Hall, Inc.

Simon, Herbert A. *The Science of the Artificial*, 1981, Cambridge, MA, The MIT Press, 1981.

Thompson, James D. *Organizations in Action*, 1967, New York, McGraw-Hill, Inc.

Woodward, Joan. *Industrial Organization: Theory and Practice*, 1965, London, Oxford University Press.

Expert Systems in Economics, Banking and Management
L.F. Pau et al. (Editors)
© *Elsevier Science Publishers B.V. (North-Holland), 1989*

A Computerized Prototype Natural Language Tour Guide

Hwee Tou Ng

Department of Computer Sciences
University of Texas at Austin
Austin, Texas 78712

This paper describes a computerized prototype natural language tour guide. The computer system serves as a tour guide and provides the user with travel information through an interactive question answering session. Based on the travel information stored in its database, the system processes the user's query, accesses the database and returns an answer. The system is capable of providing cooperative response when appropriate, and it can also handle simple sentence fragments(ellipsis).

1   Introduction

Getting computers to understand natural language is a very difficult task that still requires extensive research efforts. Vast amount of both linguistic and world knowledge are necessary to any computational process that attempts to understand unrestricted natural language. As such, practical natural language systems have so far focused on understanding a habitable, restricted set of natural language in carefully circumscribed domains so as to achieve a level of performance acceptable to the specific applications while still keeping the complexity of the systems under control. [Waltz 82]

One such class of applied systems is natural language interfaces to databases that provide users with information in the database by accepting users' queries in natural language [Hendrix et al 78]. In this paper, we describe one such prototype system that serves as a tour guide by providing the user with travel information stored in a database through an interactive question answering session.

More specifically, the implemented system has the following capabilities :

- process user's natural language requests (Wh-questions), access the database and return an answer,

- provide cooperative response when appropriate,

- handle simple sentence fragments(ellipsis).

As such, the system demonstrates capabilities typically found in systems like LADDER [Hendrix et al 78], CO-OP [Kaplan 82] and SOPHIE [Burton, Brown 79]. The prototype system has been completely implemented and tested. It is written in Common Lisp and runs on the HP 9000 Lisp machines.

The remainder of this paper is organized as follows : Section 2 presents a short sample annotated dialogue of the system. This will give the reader a good feel of what the prototype system can do. Section 3 describes the overall system architecture, showing the functions of the various system components and how they fit together. Section 4 gives the details of how the system parses the user's sentence into an internal database query. We show an example of the parse tree and the database query for a typical user input sentence. Section 5 elaborates on the cooperative response generation component, arguing why cooperative response is essential and showing how the system actually accomplishes it. Section 6 describes the handling of sentence fragments by the system. We discuss the issues of limitations and possible extensions of the system in section 7, followed by a concluding section.

2   Sample Dialogue

This section presents a short, representative, annotated interactive question answering session with the prototype system. Note that the added comments are preceded by ;

```
HI! WELCOME TO THE CITY OF LOS ANGELES.
I AM YOUR FRIENDLY TOUR GUIDE, HERE TO PROVIDE YOU
WITH MORE TRAVEL INFORMATION. WHAT CAN I DO FOR YOU ?

>Tell me the outdoor tourist sights in LA
DISNEYLAND
UNIVERSAL-STUDIO

>Where is Holiday Inn located ?
(2200 WILSHIRE)

>List the single rates of Holiday Inn
60

; the system processes the next sentence fragment as
; "List the double rates of Holiday Inn"

>double rates
TRYING ELLIPSIS...
90

>Which are the deluxe hotels in east LA with single rates
 below 100 dollars
HOLIDAY-INN

; the system processes the next sentence fragment as
; "Which are the deluxe hotels near the airport with single rates
; below 100 dollars"

>near the airport
TRYING ELLIPSIS...
RAMADA-INN

; the next query demonstrates the system's capability to
; generate cooperative response. Since Disneyworld is not in
```

```
; LA (hence not in the system's database), the system reports so
; and in addition gives the admission fees of the other tourist
; sights in the database.

>What is the admission fee of Disneyworld ?
I DONT KNOW OF ANY DISNEYWORLD
BUT YOU MAY WANT TO KNOW THE FOLLOWING
ADMISSION-FEE        NAME
10                   DISNEYLAND
5                    UNIVERSAL-STUDIO
2                    WAX-MUSEUM
3                    MUSIC-CENTER


; another instance of cooperative response.

>Give me the deluxe hotels in downtown LA with double rates
 below 150 dollars

I DONT KNOW OF ANY DELUXE HOTELS IN DOWNTOWN LA
BUT YOU MAY WANT TO KNOW THE FOLLOWING
NAME            TYPE            LOC             DOUBLE-RATES
HOLIDAY-INN     DELUXE          EAST            90
RAMADA-INN      DELUXE          AIRPORT         95

>Thanks for your help
GOODBYE
```

Other typical queries that the system can handle are :

```
When does Disneyland close daily ?
What is the opening time of Universal Studio ?
What are the Italian restaurants in east LA ?
What is the specialty of restaurant Bistro ?
Show me the economy class hotels
List the restaurants serving Spanish food in downtown LA
What are the hotels with double rates below 20 dollars ?
```

3   System Architecture

1. The main loop repeatedly gets the next input sentence query from the user and calls the parser to parse the sentence into a parse tree and an internal database query. If the parse is successful, the internal database query is used to access the database and provide an answer to the user's query. Details of how the system parses an input sentence into a parse tree and an internal database query are in section 4 of this paper.

2. If the parse fails, the system attempts to parse the current input sentence as a sentence fragment(ellipsis). If this succeeds, then the system proceeds as in 1. above. If this attempt fails, the system responds with "SORRY I DONT UNDERSTAND.

PLEASE REPHRASE AND TRY AGAIN". Details of how the system handles ellipsis are in section 6 of this paper.

3. In 1. above, when the answer resulting from the database query is null, the system will generate some cooperative response instead of simply giving the null response. More specifically, the system will inform the user that some subset(which can be all) of the conditions in the query sentence cannot be satisfied. In addition, the system will generate an alternative, suggestive answer such that it satisfies as many of the user's query conditions as possible. Details of the cooperative response generation are given in section 5 of this paper.

4   Parsing Sentences into Database Queries

The parser used in this system is a topdown, left-to-right, depth-first, backtracking ATN (augmented transition network) parser, analogous to that used in [Hendrix et al 78]. The system uses a semantic grammar, in which semantic as well as syntactic knowledge are embodied in the grammar. This semantic grammar technique has proven to be a successful approach in building restricted natural language interfaces, as demonstrated in both LADDER [Hendrix et al 78] and SOPHIE [Burton, Brown 79]

The following shows a fragment of the semantic grammar used in this system.

```
<s> --> <present> [the] [<hotel-type>] hotels [<loc-pp>] [<rate-pp>] [?]
<present> --> what | which | what is | what are | which is | which are |
              list | show | tell me | show me | give me
<hotel-type> --> first class | deluxe | economy class | four starred |
                 three starred | two starrred
<loc-pp> --> <loc-prep> <loc>
<loc-prep> --> in | near
<loc> --> downtown LA | east LA | west LA | north LA | south LA |
          the airport | town
<rate-pp> --> <poss-mod> <rate-type> rates <rate-prep> <num> dollars
<poss-mod> --> has | have | having | with | that has | which has |
               that have | which have
<rate-type> --> single | double | single room | double room
<rate-prep> --> below | at
```

Given this grammar fragment, the system can parse the input sentence "What are the first class hotels in east LA with single rates below 60 dollars ?" The parse tree of this sentence produced by the system is shown in figure 1. The figure also indicates how the internal database query is produced at the end of the parsing.

Note that in this system, the semantic representation of the user's input sentence is the internal database query that is produced as a result of the parsing. (That is, there is not an extra semantic processing phase) We assume in the current system that all the information that is needed to answer a single user query is contained within a single relation in the database (the system uses a relational database), and that the input sentence can be translated into an internal database query of the following form :

Example : "What are the first class hotels in east LA
with single rates below 60 dollars ?"

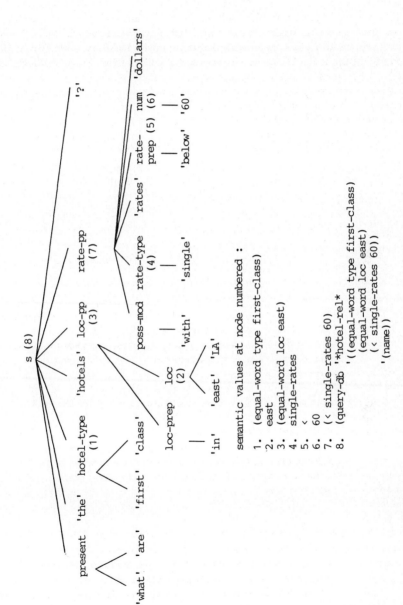

semantic values at node numbered :

1. (equal-word type first-class)
2. east
3. (equal-word loc east)
4. single-rates
5. <
6. 60
7. (< single-rates 60)
8. (query-db '*hotel-rel*
        '((equal-word type first-class)
          (equal-word loc east)
          (< single-rates 60))
        '(name))

FIGURE 1   A sample parse tree

```
(query-db relation-name
          (condition-1 condition-2 ... condition-n)
          (field-1 field-2 ... field-m))
```

where each condition is of the form : (compare-p field value)

This database query will retrieve all the tuples in the relation named `relation-name` that satisfy *all* the n conditions and print out the values of the m fields of each selected tuple. [1]

In order to accomplish the construction of a database query at the end of parsing a sentence, there is a *semantic action* associated with each grammar rule. This semantic action returns a *semantic value* for the left-hand-side category of the current grammar rule. This semantic value is built up by composing the semantic values of the constituent categories of the current rule. The semantic action of a grammar rule is executed upon successful parsing using the rule. The semantic value of the top-level sentence category will be the internal database query corresponding to the input sentence. In other words, we have assumed in this system that semantics is *compositional* – the meaning of the entire sentence is composed of the meanings of individual components of the sentence.

In figure 1, we show the semantic value returned at each node in the parse tree. For example, the semantic value of <hotel-type> is (equal-word type first-class), the semantic value of <rate-pp> is (< single-rates 60), which is composed of the semantic values of <rate-type> (single-rates), <rate-prep> (<) and <num> (60).

Before moving on to discuss cooperative response generation, we note here that the use of semantic grammar has the following advantages :

- reduce syntactic ambiguity

  Since semantic knowledge is embedded directly into the grammar, this tends to reduce syntactic ambiguity during parsing and prunes away many interpretations which the system has to otherwise contend with. For example, in the sentence "What are the hotels near the airport with single rates below 100 dollars ?", the use of semantic grammar in this system prevents it from considering the interpretation in which the prepositional phrase "with rates below 100 dollars" modify "the airport".

- no additional semantic processing

  When parsing is completed, no additional semantic processing is required, since the system has already built up the internal database query upon parsing. Note that the internal database query is the semantic representation of the user's input sentence in this system. As such, this approach results in an efficient and practical system.

- ignore syntactic details unimportant to the sentence semantics

  The use of semantic grammar allows the system to accept ungrammatical but semantically meaningful sentences like "What restaurants in downtown LA ?". A syntactic parser following strictly the grammar rules of English would have rejected this sentence as one without a verb.

---

[1] As far as this prototype system is concerned, we do not want to be bothered with the complex but uninteresting details (from the computational linguistics point of view) of more complex database queries that may involved the join of several relations and with arbitrary combinations of boolean conditions. As such we only consider conjunction of conditions over single relations here.

In all fairness, semantic grammar does have some drawbacks. It fails to capture syntactic generality, and can result in uneven coverage. Also, as the system expands, the number of grammar rules required can become very large, and this will have an adverse impact on the efficiency of the parser. On the whole, however, semantic grammar is very useful and appropriate for natural language interfaces in well circumscribed, restricted domain of application.

5   Generating Cooperative Response

As mentioned earlier in this paper, when the answer to a user's query sentence is null (ie. no tuples in the database satisfy all the conditions specified in the user's sentence), the system will generate a cooperative response, as illustrated in the sample dialogue presented in section 2.

5.1   Why Cooperative Response ?

Before discussing the details of how the system goes about generating cooperative responses, let us first give some motivation of why cooperative response is desirable in the first place. Consider the following 2 dialogue fragments :

```
Dialogue (1) :
> What are the first class hotels in north LA ?
  None
> What are the economy class hotels in north LA ?
  None
> What are the hotels in north LA ?
  None


Dialogue (2) :
> What is the admission fee of Disneyworld in LA ?
  Zero
> What is the opening time of Disneyworld in LA ?
  None
> Is Disneyworld in LA ?
  No
```

In the first dialogue, the user starts by asking about the first class hotels in north LA. In actual fact, there are no hotels in north LA that the system is aware of. Instead of reporting this fact, the system simply replies 'None', resulting in the user asking the otherwise unnecessary and unproductive second and third question. A more cooperative response by the system to the user's first question would be "I dont know of any hotels in north LA. But the first class hotels in downtown LA are ..."

Similarly, in the second dialogue, the system should have pointed out in the first answer to the confused traveller that Disneyworld is not in LA, such as "I dont know of Disneyworld in LA. But the admission fee of Disneyland in LA is 10 dollars"

The two dialogue fragments illustrate that a sentence conveys the *intentions* and *beliefs* of the speaker in addition to its *literal* content. For example, in the sentence "What is the admission fee of Disneyworld in LA ?", besides asking about the amount of money one needs to pay to get into Disneyworld, there is an implicit *presupposition* of the speaker implied by the sentence, namely, that the speaker believes that Disneyworld is in LA. Similarly, in the sentence "What are the first class hotels in north LA ?", the speaker presupposes that there are hotels in north LA.

In addition, there is strong evidence that participants in a conversation follow certain general rules, among them is the Grice's conversational maxim of quantity [Grice 75], which states "Make your contribution as informative as is required (for the purposes of the current exchange)" Given this rule of conversation, and the observation above that a sentence conveys speaker's intentions and beliefs, we can justify why cooperative response is necessary. When the user inputs the sentence "What is the admission fee of Disneyworld in LA ?", we can infer that the speaker believes (falsely) that Disneyworld is in LA. Following Grice's maxim, the system should then give the suggested cooperative response so as to be *informative*. If the system simply responds 'zero', then it has misled the user into confirming his false beliefs, and thus would violate Grice's maxim to be an informative participant in the conversation.

5.2   Algorithm to Compute Cooperative Response

Now that we have justified the need for cooperative response, let us turn to the question of how the system actually accomplishes it.

To generate cooperative response, the system must determine *when* an indirect, cooperative response is required and also *what* that response should be.

In the context of a database query system, a cooperative response is called for when the answer to the user's query is null, zero, none or some trivial responses. The actual response itself has two components :

1. correct user's false presupposition

2. provide some helpful, suggestive alternative response

To understand how the system computes cooperative response, first note that a database query in this system can be viewed as the selection of tuples in a relation satisfying all the select conditions $C_1, C_2, \dots , C_n$. There is one set S_i of tuples satisfying each C_i condition. The response is null if

$$S_1 \cap S_2 \cap \dots \cap S_n = \emptyset$$

It then follows that :

1. to correct user's false presupposition amounts to finding the *smallest* k such that

$$S_{i_1} \cap S_{i_2} \cap \dots \cap S_{i_k} = \emptyset \qquad 0 < k \leq n$$

Then report to the user that the corresponding k conditions cannot be satisfied, in the form "I DONT KNOW OF ANY ..." Note that we find the *smallest* k since if there are no tuples satisfying these k conditions, then it definitely follows that there are no tuples satisfying any more condition in addition to these k conditions. Hence, reporting this would give the user maximal information and correct his false presupposition that there are tuples satisfying the k conditions.

2. to provide helpful, suggestive alternative response amounts to finding the *largest l* such that

$$S_{i_1} \cap S_{i_2} \cap \ldots \cap S_{i_l} \neq \emptyset \qquad 0 \leq l < n$$

Then report to the user all the tuples that satisfy these l conditions, along with values for fields corresponding to the remaining $(n - l)$ unsatisfied conditions, in the form "BUT YOU MAY WANT TO KNOW THE FOLLOWING ..." Note that we find the *largest l* since we will give the user the most information by trying to satisfy as many of the user's query conditions as possible. This would be considered the most helpful suggestive response in the absence of other apriori knowledge. Also we give the values for the fields of unsatisfied conditions so that the user could consider the available alternatives.

Notice that although it is *always* the case that there are *unique* numbers k and l satisfying the above criteria, the corresponding k or l S-sets may *not* be unique. In the absence of any apriori information, the current system will select one of them arbitrarily. (We will discuss at the end of this section the issue of which of the sets to pick if we have other relevant sources of information)

As an illustration of how the algorithm works, consider the last user query "Give me the deluxe hotels in downtown LA with double rates below 150 dollars" appearing in the sample dialogue shown in section 2. In this case, there are 3 conditions giving rise to 3 S sets :

1. S_1 = the set of all deluxe hotels

2. S_2 = the set of all hotels in downtown LA

3. S_3 = the set of all hotels with double rates below 150 dollars

In this example, there are no hotels in the database satisfying all 3 conditions. That is, the intersection of S_1, S_2 and S_3 is the empty set. So the system attempts to generate cooperative response. It first determines the smallest k such that the intersection of the k sets is empty. It turns out that in this database, there are hotels in each of the sets S_1, S_2 and S_3. However, there are no hotels in the intersection of S_1 and S_2. (ie. the system happens to not know of any deluxe hotels in downtown LA). The system announces this fact by responding "I DONT KNOW OF ANY DELUXE HOTELS IN DOWNTOWN LA". This surface sentence can be generated easily since it follows very closely the user's own input sentence. Basically, the response generation routine simply collects all the terminal words in the parse tree corresponding to the nodes that contributed these k conditions.

To generate a helpful, suggestive response, the system finds the largest l such that the l S-sets have nonempty intersection. In this case, it so happens that the database includes hotels that are deluxe and have double rates below 150 dollars. (ie. the intersection of S_1 and S_3 is nonempty) Hence the system reports this as its suggestive response, along with the LOC field indicating the alternate locations of the hotels listed.

Lastly, we note that we have so far selected arbitrarily among the possible candidates for the S-sets when there are more than one such set of k or l S-sets, under the assumption that we have no other apriori knowledge. However, if from other relevant sources, such as the context of the discourse, we can determine that the user prefers some set of conditions to hold in favor of some other sets, then we should take that into consideration in generating the cooperative response. For example, if we know that the user is looking for hotels with cheap rates from previous part of the dialogue, then we might try as far as possible to satisfy the low cost requirement of visiting a restaurant in a subsequent restaurant query.

6   Handling Sentence Fragments

Ellipsis, or sentence fragments are utterances that do not express complete thoughts, (ie. they are not a completely specified question or command), but only give the differences between the intended thought and an earlier one. Ellipsis occurs commonly among dialogues. As such, it is important for any natural language dialogue system to be able to handle ellipsis.

The current prototype system is capable of handling simple sentence fragments. When the parser fails to parse the current user input as a complete sentence, it will try to parse it as a sentence fragment of the previous complete sentence. It treats the current utterance as the terminal words of some syntactic category of the previous complete sentence, and attempts to parse it as such.

For example, in the sample dialogue in section 2, consider the sentence fragment "near the airport" after the previous complete sentence "Which are the deluxe hotels in east LA with single rates below 100 dollars". The syntactic categories of the complete sentence include s, present, hotel-type, loc-pp, loc-prep, loc, rate-pp, poss-mod, rate-type, rate-prep, and num. For each syntactic category (except s) in the given list, the system will try to parse the sentence fragment by replacing the terminal words of that syntactic category with "near the airport", and then takes the substituted sentence to be the intended complete sentence of the user and attempts to parse it. The system performs this substitution for each syntactic category until it either succeeds parsing or fails. If it succeeds on any one of the syntactic category, it proceeds as per normal. If it fails on all syntactic categories, then the current input sentence cannot be parsed.

7   Limitations and Extensions

As implemented, the current prototype system has its limitations. We will discuss them in this section. Among the limitations and possible future extensions of the system are :

- anaphoric reference

  Anaphoric references occur very frequently in dialogues. Even in restricted natural language interfaces, the user often expects the system to understand the referent of pronouns like 'it', 'them' and definite noun phrases like 'the hotel', 'the restaurant' when they are used to refer to preceding entities mentioned in the dialogue. To be able to handle anaphoric references, the system must no longer treat each user utterance as an isolated sentence by itself.

- mixed initiative

  In a natural dialogue between human participants, control of the conversation passes between the participants. A natural language interface would be much more helpful if it has mixed initiative, taking the control of the conversation at appropriate times. For example, when faced with the user query "Tell me all the interesting places I can visit in LA", a mixed initiative system may take control of the conversation at this time by asking the user what his interests are, and then selectively gives the appropriate places of interests depending on the user's response.

• model of user's beliefs and intentions

It is well known that people do not say exactly what they mean. Rather, the speaker expects the hearer to infer his goals, beliefs and intentions from his utterances. In the context of natural language interface, this implies that the system must infer the user's beliefs and intentions beyond the sentence's literal interpretation, since users fully expect the system to be responsive to their unstated desires. To achieve this, the system needs to maintain an explicit model of user's beliefs and intentions.

In fact, in [Cohen 82], the authors argued that question answering systems, like the natural language database query system described in this paper, should be viewed as a special case of natural language dialogue system, and that techniques for engaging in question answering conversation should be special cases of general conversational abilities. In other words, "the ultimate tour guide" is a dialogue system.

8   Conclusion

In this paper, we have described a computerized prototype natural language tour guide that provides the user with travel information stored in its database through an interactive question answering session. The system is capable of providing cooperative response when appropriate, and it can also handle simple sentence fragments(ellipsis). As we have seen, the present system has its limitations which should be addressed if one desires to build a more powerful system. Nonetheless, the prototype system demonstrates that in a particular well circumscribed application domain, one can build a useful natural language system of manageable complexity that still achieves an acceptable level of performance.

9   References

1. Bobrow, D., R. Kaplan, M. Kay, D. Norman, H. Thompson, T. Winograd. GUS, a Frame-Driven Dialog System. Artificial Intelligence 8, 1977 155-173

2. Burton, R.R., J.S. Brown. Toward a Natural Language Capability for Computer Assisted Instruction. 1979. in Readings in Natural Language Processing, edited by B. Grosz, K. Sparck-Jones, B.L. Webber 1986

3. Cohen, P.R., C.R. Perrault, J. Allen. Beyond Question Answering. in Strategies for Natural Language Processing, edited by W. Lehnert, M. Ringle 1982

4. Grice, H.P. Logic and Conversation. in Studies in Syntax Vol 3, edited by Cole, Morgan 1975

5. Hendrix, G., E. Sacerdoti, D. Sagalowicz, J. Slocum Developing a Natural Language Interface to Complex Data. ACM Trans. on Database System 3(2) 1978 105-147

6. Kaplan, S.J. Cooperative Responses from a Portable Natural Language Query System. Artificial Intelligence 19(2) 165-188 1982

7. Waltz, D.L. The State of the Art in Natural Language Understanding. in Strategies for Natural Language Processing, edited by W. Lehnert, M. Ringle 1982

Expert Systems in Economics, Banking and Management
L.F. Pau et al. (Editors)
© Elsevier Science Publishers B.V. (North-Holland), 1989

DERIVATION OF VERBAL EXPERTISES FROM ACCOUNTING DATA

Prof. Dr. Peter Mertens
Universität Erlangen-Nuremberg
Betriebswirtschaftliches Institut
Lange Gasse 20
8500 Nuremberg 1
Federal Republic of Germany

With the expert system tools NEXPERT and HEXE, a tool developed at the Institute of Business Administration of the University of Erlangen-Nuremberg, systems were built for a knowledge-based derivation of verbal reports from company data. This paper describes examples of applications, aspects of technical realization with emphasis on text generation and the application of graphics, experience in practice and opportunities for further developments by the implementation of user models and learning capabilities.

1. Introduction

It is said that the methodology of expert systems (XPS) respectively knowledge-based systems (KBS) is well suited for diagnostic tasks. This hypothesis was confirmed many times theoretically and practically, e.g. by technical and medical diagnoses [1]. It seems reasonable to transfer these findings onto diagnoses in business. I am specially thinking of advisers and managers in business who write reports based on a huge amount of data for themselves and for others.

Such results are presented by numeric tables, graphics and verbal reports. The stylistic and optical design of these reports is often very complicated (therefore diagnostic systems for economic tasks usually differ from those for technical or medical tasks). One of the classical functions of data processing is the development of structure and output of *tables* and *graphics*. With the increasing use of PCs presentation graphics have gained importance.

The development of *reports* is more challenging than the development of tables and graphics. Thus the question arises whether expert systems could be of any help for this particular task. The creation of verbal text is somehow similar to the recognition of speech by means of Artificial Intelligence. The text generation is of course much easier.

I will call KBS *expertise systems* if they generate verbal reports from data material and in some cases integrate graphics and tables. With this contribution I like to give an impression of the state of the art by using expertise systems developed at our institute as examples.

2. Background of experience

There are several expertise systems developed at our institute:

1. Expert systems designed to diagnose the relative position of companies based on annual reports (in cooperation with DATEV e.G., a large computer service company for tax advisers). These systems are in detail:

a) *GUVEX* (XPS to analyse the profit and loss statement)

This system analyses the profit situation of companies on the basis of two consecutive annual profit and loss statements. Figure 2./1 shows an extract of an expertise.

Figure 2./1   Extract of a GUVEX expertise

Compared to 1985 the profit before interest shows a significant increase (13.5%). In 1985 the profit added up to 44,459.0 TDM[*], this year to 50,447.7 TDM. This is due to an increased annual surplus (9,684.4 TDM) and a reduction of interest costs by 3,695.7 TDM. The reduced interests are not due to a decrease of the interest rate.

Stock situation

It is remarkable that the inventory has increased progressively compared to sales. Stock increased by 17.39% from 138,279.0 TDM in the previous year to 162,327.2 TDM this year. As stated there are several indicators for large orders or improved sales opportunities. Therefore this negative tendency does not really count.

Material expenses

The personnel expenses dropped significantly. Simultaneously there was a remarkable shift from personnel to material expenses. It is remarkable that the material expenses developed favourable in relation to the operational earnings.

---

b) *BILEX* (XPS to analyse the balance sheet)

This system is related to GUVEX and supports the analysis of companies on the basis of the data of two consecutive balance sheets.

c) *FINEX* (XPS to evaluate a company's financial situation)

FINEX complements GUVEX and BILEX and focuses on an interpretation of financial ratios, especially the cash flow. See Figure 2./2.

Figure 2./2   Extract of a FINEX expertise

Inspection of the current ratio:

The short-term current gross working capital (in terms of liability less than one year) amounts to 72% of the short-term liabilities (last year 65%). It is still remarkable lower than the standard of 100%. During the period analysed there was a slight increase in short-term receivables (including other assets and liquid funds). The short-term liabilities remained almost the same as last year.

In the observed period the capital requirements amounted to 400 TDM on the application of funds in the flow statement. For a long-term 250 TDM were needed (62.5% of the total capital requirements). The short-term capital required 37.5%.

---

[*] TDM = Thousands of German Marks

d)   *MEVEX* (XPS to compare the data of several years)

   MEVEX has much in common with GUVEX, BILEX and FINEX however the analysis is based on *five* consecutive annual reports.

e)   *BVEX* (XPS to compare companies)

   BVEX presents expertises based on a comparison of annual reports of similar sized companies operating in the same industry.

f)   *TYPEX* (XPS to classify companies)

   TYPEX tries to position a firm within a company classification. The analysis is based on annual reports. (Figure 2./3). The system selects companies that require particular attention and need a more detailed analysis by a human analyst.

Figure 2./3   Extract of a TYPEX expertise

Interpretation of the type of enterprise

For the last two years this company can be classified as "cumulation of problems". This type of company is characterized by a heavily charged material sector and personnel sector on the one hand and a shrinking sales sector on the other hand.

1. Profitability situation

The analysed company did not succeed in improving its profitability which was lower than that of competitors during the reported year. This is due to sales profitability and capital profitability. With 1.2% respectively 2.1% it could not reach its previous values of 1.5% and 2.4%.

For further information it is recommended to analyse the profit and loss statement (GUVEX) and the balance sheet (BILEX).

---

2.   *CONTREX* (controlling expert system) processes data produced by different SAP accounting programs (SAP ist one of the largest German software firms; it is specialized in cost accounting software packages). Its output are different reports about the cost and return situation of the company, especially of its divisions (lines of business, profit centres and cost centres etc.). CONTREX also supports the user in "navigating" through the variety of reports generated by accounting programs. CONTREX helps to discover hidden causes of favourable as well as unfavourable developments. These conclusions are drawn from symptoms that appear on different levels of cost accounting reports. Figure 2./4 shows the abstract of an expertise.

   The expertise consists of several texts and tables. It is also planned to add graphics to the results. It is remarkable that the KBS will recommend to call off lists generated by the traditional SAP accounting software if verbal reports need to be clarified. In some cases the user has the opportunity to ask for additional reports as a special form of an explanation facility, e.g. in order to check a verbal conclusion.

3.   *LOGEX* (logistics expert system) processes extensive numerical information about the readiness to deliver, to meet shipping deadlines, the stock situation, the rearrangement of deadlines etc. The analysis is provided for a plant of a large electrical company in order to give a brief presentation of the logistic situation ("logistics barometer"). Figure 2./5 shows an example.

Figure 2./4   Extract of a CONTREX expertise

	actual past deviation cumulated	**target actual deviation**	target actual deviation cumulated	target predicted deviation	target predicted deviation cumulated
Gross sales	-2,00	**6,90**	23,70	8,70	4,90
Revenue decrease	-6,50	**16,70**	28,90	23,30	12,30
Net yields	-1,40	**5,60**	23,00	6,90	4,00
Variable costs	-1,30	**-15,40**	-51,80	-16,30	-12,70
Contribution margin I	-7,20	**-12,00**	-28,90	25,90	28,60
Fixed costs	1,10	**-4,40**	-11,10	-5,60	-8,30
Contribution margin II	-15,90	**-30,40**	-73,50	-27,60	-34,10

For further information you can ask for SAP reports:

Please indicate with (x)

It turns out that the negative deviation can be traced back to an extension of volume only if the result of the contribution margin flow analysis is combined with the relative cost variance of -15.40%. This means that the unit costs remained the same. The relative increase of income by 6.90% is caused by higher *sales* due to reduced prices. The price reduction proved to be favourable.

The *break-even point* had been exceeded in the past, i.e. all fixed costs planned until the end of the year are covered by the contribution margin I, however the real profit was much smaller than planned.

In comparison to the previous year the *power of the contribution margin* dropped remarkably. In the previous year 25% of the income was obtained as contribution to fixed costs and profit whereas it was only 19.79% in the past months of the year.

For further information you can ask for *SAP reports*:

Please indicate with (x)

4.   DIPSEX (expert system to diagnose production drawbacks), a pure laboratory system, is part of a larger project to support production planning and control by KBS. It detects and comments drawbacks in production planning and material management of the previous period and makes suggestions for possible "therapies". It is based on the DuPont pyramid of ratios. We extended this pyramid by ratios that are particularly suited to measure the quality of production control. Figure 2./6 shows an extract of a report.

Figure 2./5   Extract of a LOGEX expertise

An analysis of factory XY shows the ability for on-time deliveries (target 80 ; actual value 78). This is an improvement of 6 points compared to last year's value. The result, however, is not as satisfactory as it shows because it was achieved by compensatory effects in subordinate sectors. The extraordinarily bad ability of delivering in time in business line 4711 (63) was compensated by a high value of 94 in business line 4712.

It is favourable that the reduction of delivery time was accompanied by a decrease in inventory. In the reported month the inventory was down by 17% compared to the average month of the previous year. Variations of the sales volume are considered.

Figure 2./6   Extract of a DIPSEX expertise

In the past production periods the average processing time for an order amounted to 6.73 days with a standard deviation of 2.78 days. This very high standard deviation is caused by a high portion of orders with many and orders with only few operations.

The throughput termination resulted in an average processing time of 5.80 days. The huge difference of 0.93 days was based on a very large variation between the real average idle time and the predicted values.

Orders that were manufactured during the last production period had an average throughput time of 7.73 days. This is a deterioration by the factor 1.14 compared to the value of the preceding periods.

The prototypes were developed by using the shells HEXE and NEXPERT. The possible range of applications is not restricted to the listed examples. Expertise systems could become very useful in reports of the sales department where prediction values, target values and actual values of sales volumes, turnovers and different types of contribution margins need to be compared. Based on these data patterns detailed judgements can be provided as well as instructions for the determination of appropriate forecast parameters.

3. Technical realization
3.1. Knowledge base
According to Rauh [4], the knowledge base of an expertise system consists of four components:

1.   The *structural knowledge* describes the way the underlying data material is organized for the diagnosis. BILEX e.g., assigns single items of the annual statement to superior values (e.g., balance sheet items like real estate and buildings or certain parts of the securities are added up to give the fixed assets). Furthermore rules indicating the degree of detail of the balance sheet are used. They depend on the size of the company.

2. The *goal-oriented knowledge* enables the transition from the data material of the
    analysed object to the diagnosis, e.g. by providing information how a certain ratio is
    defined.

3. The *meta knowledge* describes possible attributes of the considered ratios. It represents
    all possible causes for potential symptoms. The increase of the ratio 'fixed assets/total
    assets' e.g. is a primary indicator for an increase of fixed costs. This presumption will be
    revised if the potential increase of the fixed assets is due to an increase of financial
    assets.

4. The *analogy knowledge* enables the system to adapt to different environmental
    conditions. If the system knows, for instance, that the average equity capitalization of
    enterprises within a certain industry has been falling for a longer time a particular
    statement in the expertise will be made only if the equity ratio of the analysed firm is
    decreasing considerably more than the average ratio of the industry.

In the previously mentioned expertise systems the knowledge is represented by production
rules or objects.

3.2. Data acquisition

Due to their nature expertise systems get the largest amount of facts required from databases
within an integrated data processing environment. These databases are provided by
administrative programs. For many business applications we will gain benefits only if the
input of data is reduced to a short man-machine dialogue or entirely abolished.

For a verification of the advice we have to distinguish between conditioned and
unconditioned questions.

In the financial statement analysis e.g., *unconditioned questions* ask whether certain areas
have to be inspected more closely or should be excluded. *Conditioned questions* appear only if
the ratios reach certain parameter values. For instance, if the enterprise shows clearly extended periods of payment compared to the previous year GUVEX will ask whether the introduction of a new product is accompanied by granting longer periods of payment to the customers. If BILEX concludes that the company should take advantage of the leverage effect
(substituting owners' capital by borrowed capital) it will ask whether the firm plans risky investments because in this case the company should retain enough owners' capital before giving such an advice.

3.3. Inference mechanism

In the solution space HEXE works with a goal-driven strategy. It proved to be useful,
however, to include elements of a data driven strategy, too.

A part of the knowledge base serves to gather all quantitative data. With this solution the
data is available for the rule interpreter at the beginning of the actual analysis though the
system uses a "backward chaining" strategy.

During the development of the prototype, performance problems appeared. The system
GUVEX with its 1200 rules required one minute of cpu-time in certain data constellations,

even on a mainframe. Therefore, control rules had to be implemented. Parts of the knowledge base will be excluded from the analysis if the data variation is of a smaller percentage than a default threshold value or a threshold value determined by the user.

With an increasing size of the rule base so-called meta rules had to be introduced that check the variations between different annual values. In GUVEX a double-layered filter was formed. After passing this filter only certain areas of the knowledge base are remaining. So the run time could be improved considerably without any negative influence on the analysis. For example, in GUVEX this led to a run time reduction by the factor ten.

3.4. Parameter setting

A difficult job within the "calibration" of expertise systems is to separate the 'area of ignorance' where a further investigation of index figures is unnecessary from the area where a deeper analysis is important [5]. In this case a compromise will be made between the danger of first class errors (insignificant deviations are declared as significant) and second class errors (significant deviations are not identified at all). E.g. in GUVEX there is a positive tolerance for extraordinary profits of 2% and a negative tolerance of 4% because of the possibilities to hide failures in the area of extraordinary expenses and profits. Thus data of areas that are crucial for the prosperity of the enterprise are gathered more precisely than data of less important areas.

3.5. Concept of text generation

The text concept is the nucleus of each expertise system. This is also indicated by the fact that in CONTREX, an implementation with the shell NEXPERT, only 250 of 650 rules represent business knowledge. The rest of the rules is used to generate text. Therefore, a special text facility has been integrated into HEXE that makes the system different from many other shells.

Each rule type (boolean, bayesian etc.) in HEXE can be linked to text frames during the knowledge engineering process by indicating a text key. These frames are filled with variables that have to be replaced by appropriate chunks of text or numbers.

There are conditioned and unconditioned text frames. *Unconditioned text frames* are not linked to certain facts and appear in each expertise. E.g. in GUVEX there is a statement to what extent the total annual profit is based on ordinary and extraordinary components. *Conditioned text frames* are used for special diagnostic areas. They will only be selected if special constellations occur. E.g. the personnel expenses rose progressively. Part of the examination is to compare the relative variation of the personnel expenses with the relative variation of the output. If the difference extends a threshold value the system will issue the information that the personnel expenses have risen progressively compared to the output. In addition, so-called '*immediate texts*' were implemented to explain the inference process to the human analyst during the dialogue.

Considering the immediate preceding phrases in the expertise several text elements are necessary to connect sentences like

- "Simultaneously the ... decreased"
- "In contrary to ..." or
- "A similar critical trend is shown ...".

A particular linguistic problem arose with the presentation of significant variations. A number of practitioners for instance preferred a statement like "has more than doubled" instead of "rose by 112%". Another suggestion in the same direction is to substitute "the capital turnover takes place in 0.42 years" by "... approximately five months" (but on the other hand the expression "... capital turnover takes place in 3,5 years" sounds better than "... in 42 months"!).

No practicable solution for the text summary which is very important in daily business has been found so far. Theoretically the whole rule base would have to be processed for a consideration of important interconnections. Another analysis would be necessary to look for criteria that ought to be summarized. For the technical realization a huge number of combinations would have to be considered. At this point we abandoned further efforts.

3.6. Graphics component
When mixing texts and graphics in expertises two questions arise:

1. What kind of facts should be presented graphically instead of verbally?
2. How should the graphics be presented?

The answer to the first question depends on the user's preference. Therefore in general it should be sufficient to determine his preferences as part of the dialogue, e.g. in a user model (see chapter 5), and edit graphics in the eligible positions.

It is advisable to delegate the decisions concerning the second question to a large extent to the expertise system. This assumption is based on the following considerations:

1. Modern computer-based presentation graphics provide a large number of alternatives difficult to select.
2. Partly, well-based recommendations can be made for the graphical design according to the data constellations resulting from analysis and diagnosis. The recommendation can be stored in a small part of the rule base.
3. From experience we know that some users commit 'malpractices' when transforming data into graphics. Many of these can cause misunderstandings.

Therefore a graphics component was integrated into the tool HEXE [6].

4. Gained experience
None of the prototypes has yet been subject to any well defined analysis of acceptance by its potential users. Most of the systems however were presented to a larger audience on several congresses and well-known fairs like the CeBIT in Hannover. These potential users had different experience concerning the subject. At that time the prototypes had different states

of development and their errors were not known completely even to the demonstrators. The feedback of these fairs was also influenced by various perceptions of the test persons (regularly/sometimes, by inexperienced users/specialists etc.). Because of all these "disturbing influences" we have to be cautious when generalizing our observations.

Most of the time it was emphasized that a lot of effort and time required by routine business (calculating, condensing and preformulating of reports) will be cut down by applying expertise systems. There was a general consensus to consider expertises as mere guidelines that need to be revised with a text processing system, not necessarily because of stylistic aspects (compare chapter 3.5.) but for introducing background information. Tax advisers and accountants repeatedly pointed out that, during a final personnel editing, targets or sensitiveness of the recipient of the expertise should be regarded.

Frequent statements were: "When the expertises are generated automatically, you can be sure that nothing is forgotten during the analysis" or "The adviser just has to tick off mentally the statements made by the system. Thus the expertises serve as checklists within the analysis of the enterprise".

Some of the people specialized in the analysis of enterprises saw a problem that often occurs when the decision support is refined by technical data processing methodologies: The new techniques could tempt users who are not familiar with this job to trust the statements of these systems too much. The following statement is characteristic: "The hasty euphoria of temporary users should not blind someone to disregard the fact that undiscovered mistakes in the automatically designed expertises may have aggravating consequences."

5. Further developments

According to the mentioned experience the design of expertise systems should concentrate on two aspects: adaptability and machine learning capability. *Adaptability* is defined as a static adjustment of the expertise system to the user. The results of the adaptation will be stored as a set of parameters and remain constant for a longer time. With its *learning capabilities* the system will adapt dynamically to new situations or new behaviours of the addressee.

Adaptability is implemented with user models. In a prototype that was developed as an extension to GUVEX the following issues were considered:

1. User model parameters are implemented for directing the dialogue, i.e., they consider user expectations concerning the length of the dialogue. This is determined by the time the user plans to spend for a session and by the analyst's detailed knowledge about the company. If (s)he has no internal information corresponding questions will not be asked.

2. The design of the expertise can be directed by the user model. This means that the optional output of tables complementing the text of the expertise, the selection and design of graphics (see chapter 3.6.), and the different "sharpness" in the verbal evaluation of data can be based on threshold values of different levels. E.g. an "angry young manager" who needs the expertise to convince his colleagues that a cost cutting program is inevitable is interested in very critical statements. On the other hand a

businessman who intends to send the expertise to his bank to apply for a credit doesn't like phrases which sound too severe (at this point we see that expertise systems are not only instruments to interpret data but also to manipulate them).

Learning capabilities are important to design expertises efficiently, e.g. in order to minimize the number of questions the user has to answer during a dialogue. Additionally it is often useful to avoid stereotype repetitions in consecutive expertises. This requires that the new expertise is based on the previous one and assumes that the user remembers the latter.

Two examples for learning by refinement that are implemented in our prototypes are:

1. Over several years an adviser acquires knowledge about characteristics of his client. Similarly an expertise system should use information about the company or a division from *several* periods to improve the comparison of *two* periods by long-term aspects. The learning component in GUVEX for instance stores evaluations of the equity ratio. If it is considered too high for several periods the system will draw the conclusion that this higher portion has strategic reasons. Then the corresponding negative remark will not appear in the expertise.

2. If the expertise system made recommendations in the previous year, the system could refer to these recommendations in the next year as a kind of feedback and check whether they have caused any reaction.

References

[1]   Puppe, F., Diagnostisches Problemlösen mit Expertensystemen, Berlin et al. 1987.

[2]   Mertens, P., Borkowski, V., Geis, W., Betriebliche Expertensystem-Anwendungen - Eine Materialsammlung, Berlin et al. 1988, p. 7.

[3]   Borkowski, V., Allgeyer, K., Rose, H., Wedel, Th., Benutzerhandbuch zum Expertensystemtool HEXE, Teil 1: Einführung und Überblick, Arbeitspapiere der Informatik-Forschungsgruppe VIII der Universität Erlangen-Nürnberg, Erlangen 1987 and Benutzerhandbuch zum Expertensystemtool HEXE, Teil 2: Detaillierte Beschreibung, Arbeitspapiere der Informatik-Forschungsgruppe VIII der Universität Erlangen-Nürnberg, Erlangen 1987. Allgeyer, K., Das Expertensystemtool HEXE und seine Anwendung zur Schwachstellendiagnose in der Produktion, Ph.D.Thesis, Nürnberg 1987, p. 12.

[4]   Rauh, N., Wissensbasierte Systeme zur Unternehmensdiagnose auf der Grundlage von Jahresabschlußdaten und Branchenvergleichswerten in der Steuerkanzlei, Ph.D. Thesis, Nürnberg 1988.

[5]   Altmann, E., Financial Ratios - Discriminant Analysis and the Prediction of Corporate Bankruptcy, Journal of Finance 23 (1968) 4, p. 606. Bowen, T., Payling, L., Monitoring Organizational Performance Using Expert Systems, in: Duffin, P. (ed.), KBS in Government - Proceedings of the Conference Nov. 1987, London 1987, p. 182. Mertens, P., Developments and Applications of Expert Systems in Germany, in: Roos, J. L. (ed.), Economics and Artificial Intelligence, Aix-en-Provence 1986, pp. 251 - 256.

[6]   Schorr, G., Krug, P., Entwicklung einer Grafikkomponente für das Expertensystemtool PC-HEXE, Arbeitspapiere der Informatik-Forschungsgruppe VIII der Universität Erlangen-Nürnberg, Erlangen 1988.

Expert Systems in Economics, Banking and Management
L.F. Pau et al. (Editors)
© *Elsevier Science Publishers B.V. (North-Holland), 1989*

A PRODUCTION MODEL CONSTRUCTION PROGRAM: MATH PROGRAMMING TO STRUCTURED MODELING

David A. Kendrick

Department of Economics
The University of Texas
Austin, Texas 78712, USA

This paper provides a description and critique for mathematical programmers and economists of a portion of the knowledge-based production and transportation modeling construction program developed by Krishnan (1987).

This paper describes a portion of Krishnan's (1987) knowledge based model development system for constructing linear programming production and distribution models. The original discussion by Krishnan was written for persons with a background in logic programming. In contrast, the discussion here is prepared for mathematical programmers and economists who are familiar with linear programming production and distribution problems but who are new to the field of logic programming. Also, the discussion here employs a model fragment which helps to elucidate the working of the system.

Krishnan's systems has three parts. The front end has been discussed in Kendrick, Krishnan, and Lee (1988), the main part of the model construction program was the subject of Kendrick (1988) and the present paper focuses on the last part of the model construction program and the back end. In order to keep this paper short only a little of the material in Kendrick (1988) is repeated. Therefore the reader is encouraged to begin with that paper and then progress to this one. Also, this paper assumes some knowledge of Structured Modeling from Geoffrion (1987). Alternatively the reader who is familiar with GAMs can get a brief introduction to Structured Modeling from Kendrick and Krishnan (1986).

The previous paper ended with the development of the mathematical programming form of the model with is called canonical objects. From that form the model could be translated into any of a number of modeling systems such as AMPL by Fourer, Gay, and Kernighan (1987), GAMS by Meeraus (1983) or Structured Modeling by Geoffrion (1987). Krishnan's implementation of the system translates the model into the Structured Modeling form in two steps. The first step remains within the realm of logic programming by using the predicates in the canonical objects form of the model to create the predicates for the equational form. The equational form uses the concepts of Structured Modeling such as primitive entities and constant and variable attributes while maintaining the model in a predicate logic style. The second step reformats the equational form into the style required by Structured Modeling. In this step the predicates are removed and the model looks like any other structured model which was created without the use of a knowledge based system.

1. CANONICAL OBJECTS TO EQUATIONAL FORM

The previous paper ended with the example model in a mathematical programming form which is called canonical objects. These canonical objects are shown in Table 1.

Table 1
Canonical Objects

activity_level_obj (*iron_production_level, iron, iron_production, mills, years*, [r,p,i,t]).
process_obj (*iron_production*, [p]).
resource_obj (*input, iron_production, mills, years*, [c]).
resource_util_obj (*iron, iron_production, mills, years*, [r]).
util_rate_obj (*io_coef_matl_iron, input, iron,iron_production, mills, years*,[c,p,i,t,r]).

Recall that the model fragment used is one in which an input-output coefficient is multiplied by an activity level to determine the total use of the input commodities. The input-output coefficient is called the util_rate_obj and the activity level is called the activity_level_obj. Also there are canonical objects for the input commodities, i.e. resource_obj, and for the production processes, i.e. process_obj.

At first it would seem that each form of the model depends only on the previous version, i.e. that

PM representation --> domain independent predicates
domain independent predicates --> canonical objects
canonical objects --> equational form
equational form --> structured modeling

However, the picture is more complicated. A part of the equational form is created not just from the canonical objects but also by reaching back all the way to the PM representation of the model. Figure 1 provides a graphic description of the dependence between the various forms of the model.

There would be some gain in ease of understanding if each form of the model depended only on the previous version. This could be done in a modified version of the PM system but only at some cost in computational efficiency.

Since the construction of the equational form is based not only on the canonical objects but also on aspects of the PM representation of the model that statement is repeated here in Table 2.

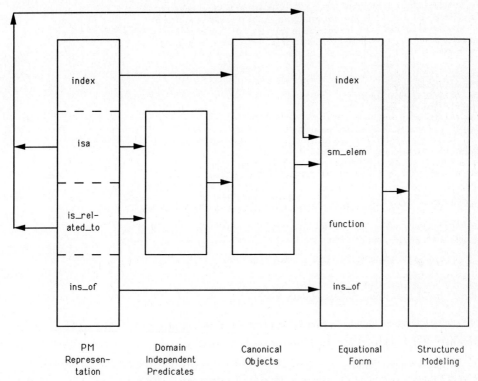

Figure 1 Dependence Among Model Forms

Table 2
PM Representation

context (prod).
model_name (io_for_iron).

index (*years*, [t]).
index (*mills*, [i]).
index (*input*, [c]).
index (*iron*, [r]).
index (*iron_production*,[p]).

isa (*years*, **planning_period**).
isa (*mills*, **plant**).
isa (*input*, **raw_material**).
isa (*iron*, **product**).
isa (*iron_production*, **production_process**).

is_related_to (*material_input*, **raw_iprocess** , [*input*, *iron_production*, *mills*, *years*])

is_related_to (*iron_output*, **prod_oprocess,** [*iron, iron_production, mills, years*])
is_related_to (*material_in_iron_out*, **prod_raw,** [*material_input, iron_output*])
is_related_to (*io_coef_matl_iron*,**raw_material_util_rate,** [*material_in_iron_out*, **re**])
is_related_to (*iron_production_level*,**production_level,** [*iron_output*, **re**])
is_related_to (*input_usage_plan*, **raw_production_plan,** [*input, mills, years*])

ins_of ([1989], *years*).
ins_of ([hylsa], *mills*).
ins_of ([coking_coal], *input*).
ins_of ([iron_ore], *input*).
ins_of ([pig_iron], *iron*).
ins_of ([pig_iron_production], *iron_production*).

ins_of ([coking_coal, pig_iron_production, hylsa, 1989], *material_input*)
ins_of ([iron_ore, pig_iron_production, hylsa, 1989], *material_input*)
ins_of ([pig_iron, pig_iron_production, hylsa, 1989], *iron_output*)

ins_of ([coking_coal, pig_iron_production, pig_iron, hylsa, 1989], *material_in_iron_out*)
ins_of ([iron_ore, pig_iron_production, pig_iron, hylsa, 1989], *material_in_iron_out*)

ins_of ([coking_coal, pig_iron_production, pig_iron, hylsa, 1989, 0.8], *io_coef_matl_iron*)
ins_of ([iron_ore, pig_iron_production, pig_iron, hylsa, 1989, 1.2], *io_coef_matl_iron*)

ins_of ([pig_iron, pig_iron_production, hylsa, 1989, n/a], *iron_production_level*)

ins_of ([iron_ore, hylsa, 1989], *input_usage_plan*)
ins_of ([coking_coal, hylsa, 1989], *input_usage_plan*)

The canonical objects form is discussed here using elements from Structured Modeling, i.e. primitive entities, compound entities, attributes and constraints.

1.1. Primitive Entities

Primitive entities which are like sets in other modeling languages are specified with isa predicates in the PM representation of the model as is shown below.

    isa (*years*, **planning_period**).
    isa (*mills*, **plant**).
    isa (*input*, **raw_material**).
    isa (*iron*, **product**).
    isa (*iron_production*, **production_process**).

In the equational form of the model the sets are specified with the sm_elem (structured modeling element) predicates and marked as primitive entities with the symbol pe as is shown below. This translation process is as straightforward as it appears.

    sm_elem (*years*, **pe**, [ ]).
    sm_elem (*mills*, **pe**, [ ]).
    sm_elem (*input*, **pe**, [ ]).
    sm_elem (*iron*, **pe**, [ ]).
    sm_elem (*iron_production*, **pe**, [ ]).

1.2. Compound Entities

The compound entities of Structured Modeling are also relatively simple to create. An example is given below where the is_related_to predicate for material_input from the PM representation is used to create the equivalent statement in the equational form.

is_related_to (*material_input*, **raw_iprocess**, [*input, iron_production, mills, years*])

As is apparent, index information from the PM representation is also used in the process of creating the sm_elem predicate for a compound entity which is marked with symbol ce as is shown below.

sm_elem (*material_input*, **ce** , [[*input*, [c]], [*iron_production*, [p]], [*mills*, [i]], [*years*,[t]]]).

1.3. Attributes

Structured modeling has two kinds of attributes: constant attributes which are parameters and variable attributes which are variables. When the equational form is created no distinction is made between the two kinds of attributes. Rather that distinction is made at the next step when the equational form is reformatted into the Structured Modeling form.

The is_related_to predicates for the input-output coefficient io_coef_matl_iron and for the variable iron_production_level as shown below are used to create the corresponding

is_related_to (*io_coef_matl_iron*,**raw_material_util_rate**, [*material_in_iron_out*, **re**])
is_related_to (*iron_production_level*,**production_level**, [*iron_output*, **re**])

sm_elem(...,atrib,...) predicates. Also index information which is developed in the index portion of the model construction program is used to create these sm_elem predicates.

sm_elem (*io_coef_matl_iron*, **atrib**, [[*material_in_iron_out*, [c,p,i,t,r]]])
sm_elem (*iron_production_level*, **atrib**, [[*iron_output*, [r,p,i,t]]]).

1.4. Constraints

The example model used in this paper involves only a portion of a constraint but that portion is sufficient to illustrate the workings of this part of the PM system. The model contains the information required to compute the use of coking coal and iron ore inputs by multiplying the input-output coefficient by the activity level for pig-iron production. This function would of course be a part of a materials balance constraint in a complete model. The four canonical objects which are required to specify the function are shown below

resource_util_obj (*iron, iron_production, mills, years*, [r]).
process_obj (*iron_production*, [p]).
util_rate_obj (*io_coef_matl_iron, input, iron,iron_production, mills, years*, [c,p,i,t,r]).
activity_level_obj (*iron_production_level, iron, iron_production, mills, years*, [r,p,i,t]).

if all of these canonical objects exist than the PM system will create a resource utilization function by asserting the following four predicates.

index (**utilization**1, [c,i,t]).
index_set(**utilization**1, *input_usage_plan*).
sm_elem (**utilization**1, **function**,
   [[*io_coef_matl_iron*, [c,.,i,t,.]],[*iron_production_level*,[.,.,i,t]]]).
function(**utilization**1, [[sum,[p]],[sum,[r]],
   [*io_coef_matl_iron*,[c,p,i,t,r]],*, [*iron_production_level*, [r,p,i,t]]]]).

The index predicate provides the index for the function and the index_set provides the variable for the left hand side of the function. The sm_elem predicate declares the function and the function predicate defines the function. The last of these is the most interesting since it contains the specification of the right hand side of the function. In that function the use of inputs is determined by summing over processes and types of iron output of the product of the input-output coefficient and the activity level for iron production. This illustrates one of the important capabilities of the PM system - the ability to create the mathematical structures for a model from a verbal description elicited from the user.

    In summary, the equational form of the model is created in three steps. In the first step the sm_elem predicates for the primitive and compound entities and the attributes are translated directly from the PM representation to the equational form. The second step is much more protracted. In this step the functions of the equational form are created by using the PM representation to create the domain independent predicates, then the canonical objects, and finally the equational form. In the third step the ins_of predicates are copied from the PM representation to the equational form directly with no translation. The complete equational form for the model at hand is shown in Table 3.

Table 3
Equational Form

model_name (io_for_iron).

index (*years*, [t]).
index (*mills*, [i]).
index (*input*, [c]).
index (*iron*, [r]).
index (*iron_production*, [p]).

index (*material_input*, [c,p,i,t]).
index (*iron_output*, [r,p,i,t]).
index (*iron_production_plan*, [r,i,t]).
index (*input_usage_plan*, [c,i,t]).
index (*material_in_iron_out*, [c,p,i,t,r]).

index (*io_coef_matl_iron*, [c,p,i,t,r]).
index (*iron_production_level*, [r,p,i,t]).

index (**utilization**1, [c,i,t]).
index_set(**utilization**1, *input_usage_plan*).

sm_elem (*years*, **pe**, [ ]).
sm_elem (*mills*, **pe**, [ ]).
sm_elem (*input*, **pe**, [ ]).
sm_elem (*iron*, **pe**, [ ]).
sm_elem (*iron_production*, **pe**, [ ]).

sm_elem (*material_input*, **ce** , [[*input*, [c]], [*iron_production*, [p]], [*mills*, [i]], [*years*,[t]]]).
sm_elem (*iron_output*, **ce**, [[*iron*, [r]], [*iron_production*, [p]], [*mills*, [i]], [*years*,[t]]]).
sm_elem (*iron_production_plan*, **ce**, [[*iron*, [r]], [*mills*, [i]], [*years*,[t]]]).
sm_elem (*input_usage_plan*, **ce**, [[*input*, [c]], [*mills*, [i]], [*years*,[t]]]).
sm_elem (*material_in_iron_out*, **ce**, [[*material_input*, [c,p,i,t]], [*iron_output*, [r,p,i,t]]]).

sm_elem (*io_coef_matl_iron*, **atrib**, [[*material_in_iron_out*, [c,p,i,t,r]]]).
sm_elem (*iron_production_level*, **atrib**, [[*iron_output*, [r,p,i,t]]]).

sm_elem (**utilization1, function,**[[*io_coef_matl_iron*, [c,.,i,t,.]],[*iron_production_level*,[.,.,i,t]]]).
function(**utilization1**, [[**sum**,[p]],[**sum**,[r]],
      [*io_coef_matl_iron*,[c,p,i,t,r]],*, [*iron_production_level*, [r,p,i,t]]]]).

ins_of ([1989], *years*).
ins_of ([hylsa], *mills*).
ins_of ([coking_coal], *input*).
ins_of ([iron_ore], *input*).
ins_of ([pig_iron], *iron*).
ins_of ([pig_iron_production], *iron_production*).

ins_of ([coking_coal, pig_iron_production, hylsa, 1989], *material_input*)
ins_of ([iron_ore, pig_iron_production, hylsa, 1989], *material_input*)
ins_of ([pig_iron, pig_iron_production, hylsa, 1989], *iron_output*)

ins_of ([coking_coal, pig_iron_production, pig_iron, hylsa, 1989], *material_in_iron_out*)
ins_of ([iron_ore, pig_iron_production, pig_iron, hylsa, 1989], *material_in_iron_out*)

ins_of ([coal, pig_iron_production, pig_iron, hylsa, 1989, 0.8], *io_coef_matl_iron*)
ins_of ([iron_ore, pig_iron_production, pig_iron, hylsa, 1989, 1.2], *io_coef_matl_iron*)

ins_of ([pig_iron, hylsa, 1989], *iron_production_plan*)
ins_of ([iron_ore, hylsa, 1989], *input_usage_plan*)
ins_of ([coking_coal, hylsa, 1989], *input_usage_plan*)

ins_of ([pig_iron, pig_iron_production, hylsa, 1989, n/a], *iron_production_level*)

2. EQUATIONAL FORM TO STRUCTURED MODELING

This is the most straightforward part of the PM system since all of the information for the Structured Modeling form of the model is in the equational form and most of the work at this stage is simply a matter of reformatting. For example the index predicates and some of the sm_elem predicates shown below are used to create the primitive entities part of the Structured Modeling

      index (*years*, [t]).
      index (*mills*, [i]).
      index (*input*, [c]).

index (*iron*, [r]).
index (*iron_production*, [p]).

sm_elem (*years*, **pe**, [ ]).
sm_elem (*mills*, **pe**, [ ]).
sm_elem (*input*, **pe**, [ ]).
sm_elem (*iron*, **pe**, [ ]).
sm_elem (*iron_production*, **pe**, [ ]).

input. This is primarily a matter of changing lower case to upper case letters and rearranging the information.

YEARSt   /pe/
MILLSi   /pe/
INPUTc   /pe/
IRONr   /pe/
IRON_PRODUCTIONp   /pe/

Another example of the reformatting is the function. In the equational form the function is written as

function(utilization1, [[**sum**,[p]],[**sum**,[r]],
        [*io_coef_matl_iron*,[c,p,i,t,r]],*, [*iron_production_level*, [r,p,i,t]]]).

and in the SM form it is written

UTILIZATION1
    (IO_COEF_MATL_IRONc.it., IRON_PRODUCTION_LEVEL..it) /f/
        Select {INPUT_USAGE_PLAN} ;
        SUMp SUMr (IO_COEF_MATL_IRONcpitr *
            IRON_PRODUCTION_LEVELrpit)

This too is simply a matter of changing the case of terms and rearranging the information.

There is one exception to the rule that only reformatting takes place at this stage. The exception is in the attributes of the equational form. These must be separated into constant and variable attributes and that is not done at the equational form level but rather only at the last step when the SM form of the model is created.   Except for this minor exception the SM form can be created entirely from the equational form without going back to earlier forms of the model. However, for this step it is necessary to reach back to the PM representation of the model. Cleaner interfaces could be maintained if the PM system were modified so that all information for the model is contained in the equational form.

The complete SM form of the model is given in Table 4.

Table 4
Structured Modeling Form

&IO_FOR_IRON

    YEARSt   /pe/
    MILLSi   /pe/
    INPUTc   /pe/
    IRONr   /pe/
    IRON_PRODUCTIONp   /pe/

    MATERIAL_INPUT
            (INPUTc, IRON_PRODUCTIONp, MILLSi, YEARSt) /ce/
            Select {INPUT} x {IRON_PRODUCTION} x {MILLS} x {YEARS}
    IRON_OUTPUT
            (IRONr, IRON_PRODUCTIONp, MILLSi, YEARSt) /ce/
            Select {IRON} x {IRON_PRODUCTION} x {MILLS} x {YEARS}
    IRON_PRODUCTION_PLAN
            (IRONr, MILLSi, YEARSt) /ce/
            Select {IRON} x {MILLS} x {YEARS}
    INPUT_USAGE_PLAN
            (INPUTc, MILLSi, YEARSt) /ce/
            Select {INPUT} x {MILLS} x {YEARS}
    MATERIAL_IN_IRON_OUT
            (MATERIAL_INPUTcpit,IRON_OUTPUTrpit) /ce/
            Select {MATERIAL_INPUT} x {IRON_OUTPUT}

    IO_COEF_MATL_IRON
            (MATERIAL_IN_IRON_OUTcpitr) /a/
            Select {MATERIAL_IN-IRON_OUT} :R+

    IRON_PRODUCTION_LEVEL
            (IRON_OUTPUTrpit) /va/
            Select {IRON_OUTPUT} :R+

    UTILIZATIONN1
      (IO_COEF_MATL_IRONc.it., IRON_PRODUCTION_LEVEL..it) /f/
            Select {INPUT_USAGE_PLAN} ;
            SUMp SUMr (IO_COEF_MATL_IRONcpitr *
                            IRON_PRODUCTION_LEVELrpit)
    YEARS
    1989

    MILLS
    HYLSA

    INPUT
    COKING_COAL
    IRON_ORE

    IRON
    PIG_IRON

IRON PRODUCTION
PIG_IRON_PRODUCTION

IO COEF MATL IRON
COKING_COAL ‖ PIG_IRON ‖ PIG_IRON_PRODUCTION
              ‖ HYLSA ‖ 1989 ‖ 0.8
IRON_ORE   ‖ PIG_IRON ‖ PIG_IRON_PRODUCTION
              ‖ HYLSA ‖ 1989 ‖ 1.2

3. CONCLUSIONS

The PM system which was created by Krishnan as a knowledge-based tool to develop linear programming production and transportation problem offers a new approach to economic modeling. It provides an important test bed for gaining information about the potential usefulness of knowledge-based system in microeconomic modeling. Hopefully, this paper will facilitate that process by helping to decrease the cost of entry for mathematical programmers and economists into the field of knowledge-based system.

REFERENCES

[1] Fourer, R., D. M. Gay, and B. W. Kernighan (1987), "AMPL: A Mathematical Programming Language", Computing Science Technical Report No. 133, AT&T Bell Laboratories, Murray Hill, NJ 07974, January.
[2] Geoffrion, A. M. (1987), "An Introduction to Structured Modeling", *Management Science*, Vol. 33, No. 5, May, pp. 547-588.
[3] Kendrick, David A. and Ramayya Krishnan (1986), "A Comparison of Structured Modeling and GAMS", Paper 86-24, Center for Economic Research, The University of Texas, Austin, Texas.
[4] Kendrick, David A. (1988), "A Production Model Construction Program: User Conception to Math Programming," Paper No. 88-5, Center for Economic Research, The University of Texas, Austin, Texas 78712.
[5] Krishnan, Ramayya (1987), *Knowledge Based Aids for Model Construction*, Unpublished Ph.D. Dissertation, The University of Texas, Austin, Texas, 78712.
[6] Krishnan, Ramayya, David A. Kendrick and Ronald M. Lee (1988), "A Knowledge-Based System for Production and Distribution Economics", *Computer Science in Economics and Management*, Vol. 1, No. 1, pp. 53-72.
[7] Meeraus, Alexander (1983), "An Algebraic Approach to Modeling", *Journal of Economic Dynamics and Control*, Vol. 5, No. 1, February, pp. 81-108.
[8] Murphy, F. H. and E. A. Stohr (1986), "An Intelligent System for Formulating Linear Programs," *Decision Support Systems*, Vol. 2, pp. 39-47.
[9] Pau, L. F. (1986), *Artificial Intelligence in Economics and Management*, North Holland Publishing Company, Amsterdam.

Expert Systems in Economics, Banking and Management
L.F. Pau et al. (Editors)
© Elsevier Science Publishers B.V. (North-Holland), 1989

KNOWLEDGE-BASED COMPONENTS OF SOFTWARE DEVELOPMENT EFFORT ESTIMATION:
AN EXPLORATORY STUDY

Tridas Mukhopadhyay
Michael Prietula
Steve Vicinanza

Graduate School of Industrial Administration
Carnegie Mellon University
Pittsburgh, PA   15213
USA

An exploratory study was conducted to determine the nature
of human expertise in software effort estimation and how it
compared to a commonly used analytic model.   Using data
from ten software projects that ranged from 39,000 to
450,000 lines of code and varied from 23 to 1,107
man-months to complete, a detailed analysis was made of a
project manager's estimation technique.   Over the ten
projects, the human expert was remarkably accurate with a
coefficient of determination of 0.96, while the analytic
model performed at a level of 0.71. The human expert had an
average margin of relative error of 32% compared to 758% of
the analytic model. The results of the study are discussed
with respect to an explanation of estimation based on
qualitative and analogical reasoning.

1.   INTRODUCTION

Software is a major bottleneck in management efforts to successfully
compete in the marketplace with information technology. As the hardware
performance-cost ratio has been improving, the use of computer based systems
in both commercial and governmental organizations has been increasing
sharply. Consequently, in recent years the real investment in software has
been growing rapidly and is expected to follow this trend for the remainder
of this century [4]. Despite the increasing investments in software, a
substantial backlog of software development exists in most organizations
[11]. In addition, there is an even greater "invisible" backlog of user needs
which are not formally placed in the queue of pending applications in view of
the large existing backlog [8]. In short, software development has become a
dominant factor in the computerization of business.

A fundamental issue of the software problem concerns the estimation of effort and time required for the software development process. This process is often characterized by overruns in both budgets and schedules [5]. Instances of actual costs and schedules running two or three times the estimated amounts are quite common in the data processing environment [8]. Furthermore, information system managers are frequently unable to understand why some projects finish on target while others miss their targets completely.

We contend that the key to the timely completion of software projects within budget lies in integrating the skill of the project manager to accurately estimate the efforts required for development with the algorithmic methods currently (but often ineffectually) in use. Little research, however, has addressed the task of explicating the knowledge-based components of software estimation. Our goal is to elicit the reasoning components used by experienced software project managers. For this project we (a) examine the components of reasoning that several highly-skilled managers bring to bear on project estimation, (b) develop a knowledge base for effort estimation from those studies, and (c) validate our approach using actual (rather than artifactual) software project data. In this paper, we discuss our rationale, describe our approach, and report the preliminary results.

2. ALGORITHMIC METHODS

Many algorithmic models have been developed for software development effort estimation. A common criterion often used to classify these models is whether or not they use lines of code (LOC) as the primary independent variable. Two well known models using LOC as the primary variable are COCOMO and SLIM. Based on the size of the software measured in LOC, COCOMO [2] produces a nominal estimate of effort which is later modified using ratings on fifteen cost drivers that include attributes of products, computers, and personnel. SLIM, [10] on the other hand, uses the Rayleigh curve to produce an effort estimate based on the software size expressed in terms of LOC. The models involving LOC are often criticized because they require estimating LOC before development begins and fail to account for differences in coding languages [5]. These problems are overcome by some recent models such as the function point method which involves counting the user functions requested and adjusting for processing complexity to estimate the programming effort [1].

The algorithmic approach to software estimation does not often produce an accurate estimate of development effort. A recent study reports that the average error rate expected from using existing models typically falls in the 500-600 percent range unless the models are explicitly calibrated using past data of the specific development environment [6]. Despite the large number of models developed in recent years [e.g. 2, 7], the software estimation task remains an unsolved and difficult problem.

3.   THE ROLE OF KNOWLEDGE

Given the large magnitudes of error exhibited in estimates by the well known algorithmic models, we are looking for opportunities to reduce this error rate by incorporating the knowledge-based methods of experienced project managers.   Such research is beginning to address several significant issues concerning software estimation.   First, how accurate are the experts' estimates compared to the algorithmic methods?   If they differ from the models' estimates, where, how and why do these differences occur?   Second, do the experts differ from each other?   Expertise is based on specific task adaptation mechanisms, therefore, it is imperative to determine how experts vary in the methods they incorporate [e.g., 10]. Third, what general forms of reasoning are being used?   Augmenting human decision making with either AI-based or algorithmic-based systems should not make excessive demands on or be incompatible with the experts' methods.

4.   THE STUDY

A preliminary study was conducted which compared a software development professional with ten years of software development scheduling experience against an analytic model, COCOMO. Data from ten completed software projects were obtained which consisted of a large set of project attributes, including the actual LOC and total time taken to completion. These data were collected by project managers at a large management consulting firm specializing in data processing, and were originally used by Kemerer [6] in a comparative study of software cost estimation models.   The ten projects ranged in size from 39,000 to 450,000 LOC, and took from 23 to 1,107 man-months of effort to complete.   The COCOMO inputs for these projects were also obtained.   Each project attribute and its value were placed on an individual 3 by 5 inch index card.

The subject was first asked to sort a set of index cards which listed the project attributes (without any values). The purpose of this task was to both familiarize the subject with the nature of available project data as well as to gain insight into the relative importance the subject attached to the project data.   The subject was then asked to estimate the number of

man-months taken by each of the ten projects, one at a time. The subject was
given a list of the available project attributes and, for each project, had
to request attribute values from the experimenter, who then supplied the
value on a 3 by 5 inch card. The subject was asked to verbalize his thoughts
as he proceeded, and the session was audio-tape recorded for subsequent
analysis [see 3].

5.   RESULTS

5.1 Sorting Task

The subject expressed reservations about sorting and ordering the
productivity factors, and found this part of the experiment more difficult
than formulating the project estimates.   The subject described two major
problems with the sorting task.   First, when estimating, a factor becomes
important only when its value is out of the ordinary.   For example, if a
project requires "normal" reliability then reliability is not an important
factor.   However, if "high" reliability is required then reliabiity can have
a major impact on the effort estimate. It is difficult to relate reliability
to another factor, such as reusability, in the absence of values for each
factor. Second, the subject noted that there are instances of joint effects
of two or more factors on development effort.   One factor that was frequently
mentioned as interacting with other factors was programmer capability.   If
programmers are highly capable, then other factors such as reliabilty and
reusability do not exert as strong an influence on development effort as they
might otherwise.   Consequently, such joint effects preclude the assignment of
a strict linear ordering of the factors.

5.2 Accuracy of Estimates

The accuracy of the subject's estimates was evaluated by two criteria:
the average margin of relative error (MRE) and the coefficient of
determination.   MRE refers to the absolute value of the percentage error of
the estimate with respect to the actual development effort.   The coefficient
of determination measures the degree of correlation between estimates and
actuals.

The subject's estimates had a mean MRE of 32%. When used as predictors
of actual development effort the resultant linear model had a coefficient of
determination of 0.96.   In comparison, the estimates of the COCOMO model had
a mean MRE of 758% and coefficient of determination of only 0.71.   Thus the
subject's estimates are much more accurate and sensitive to the effects of
project attributes on software development effort. Figure 1 illustrates the
performance across the ten projects for the COCOMO model and the expert.

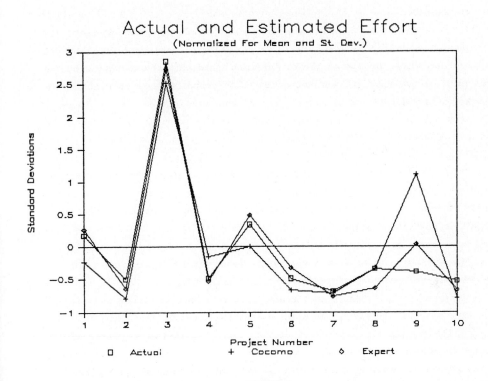

FIGURE 1

A comparison of the expert performance against the COCOMO model

5.3 Estimation Strategy

The strategy employed by the subject in this estimation task is quite different from that used by COCOMO (and other algorithmic models). Rather than relying on lines of code and a base productivity function to generate an initial estimate, the subject carefully analyzes the project data in an attempt to decipher the type of application that was developed. Lines of code is used primarily to verify that the guess about application type is sensible. Once the application type is decided upon, the subject forms an analogy between the application to be estimated and a similar application that he had managed in the past. Where the analogy is not in correspondence, the estimate is adjusted to compensate for the difference. By adjusting the estimate for each productivity factor that differs from one project to the other, the subject is able to produce accurate estimates.

6.   DISCUSSION

The expert did not attempt to "build a model" of the application described by the project data; rather, the subject used the data to help determine the most relevant "model of the application" with which he was familiar. Once that was determined, the propriety and "worth" of the project data was reviewed in the context of that application. This, in part, explains why the expert had such a difficult time sorting and ranking the project parameters -- they are essentially meaningless until they are given values and considered with respect to an invoked application context.

This implies that a review of project data is a quite active process and tightly integrated with the estimation process. A review of the expert's protocol when examining the data indicated that several different types of cognitive activities occur:

  *strategies to reduce the number of parameters considered are invoked
  *inferences being drawn concerning the "importance" of the data
  *causal attributions are made to explain data values
  *between-data (in)consistencies are checked
  *the value of data adjusted with respect to values of other data

The first activity reflects the nature of the limited capacity of the cognitive mechanism. One strategy to accomplish this is to rely on the history of the effects of parameters on delays. Our expert noted this strategy in this protocol segment for one of the projects:

"I'm going to have to start eliminating all the useless options but I'll have to ask for all the cards...(expert starts to review cards)...I'm eliminating those options that rarely have an effect and I want to make sure that this is not one of those occasions..."

In implementing this strategy, it was apparent that each parameter was reviewed to see if it was "important" or not. For example, one parameter identified the type of hardware involved ("IBM mainframe. Doesn't have an effect..."). The critical issue was more what the hardware was not; that is, not

"one of these rare machines that only one or two people in the world know how to use... not an obsolete machine that goes down 95% of the time."

Data values were rarely examined without an attempt to understand (or confirm) them, both independently and in the context of other values obtained. In reviewing a piece of data that noted the influence of the loading of the target system on the application design, the expert observed that "this is really an issue... knowing this I want to confirm it with some

other factors." Additionally, the values of one parameter can affect the
importance or relevance of another (i.e., significant interaction effects).
For example, when given a relatively inexperienced staff and a need for
reusable code, the expert noted that "they might not know when they have
really reusable code."

The overall strategy used by the expert depended heavily on invoking a
referent context (application), reviewing the data, determining where the
important differences in the parameter values occur (e.g., experience of the
staff), and then envisioning how the situation *described by the referent
model* would have been altered with those parameter values. It appears that a
mental model of the current project is generated by successive refinement
derivations of the referent model. Furthermore, the key to an effective
estimate is not based on how similar the original referent model is, but
rather on how accurately one applies the derivation operators to that model.
This is born out strikingly by the protocol for Problem 1. In this protocol,
the initial referent application had a duration of 90 man-months. Upon
reviewing and refining the data, the expert concluded that the current
project would take around 250 man-months -- a difference of 270%. The actual
value was 287. Figure 2 presents an overall algorithm depicting this
process.

7. CONCLUSION

This paper has noted the preliminary results of a study that seeks to
examine how highly-skilled software professionals estimate an important
aspect of project costs: development effort. The initial findings from a
detailed analysis of a single subject indicate that under certain conditions,
an expert can accurately estimate software project costs. This knowledge of
the software development process should be useful to researchers who intend
to refine current models of the devleopment process or develop new models.
One approach to software effort estimation that appears to be promising is
the incorporation of analogic problem solving techniques in effort estimation
tools.

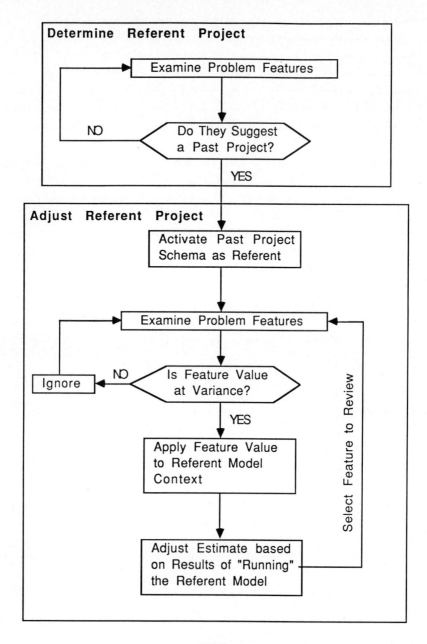

FIGURE 2

A high level algorithm of expert behavior

REFERENCES

1.   Albrecht AJ & J. Gaffney (1983) "Software Function, Source Lines of Code, and Development Effort Prediction," IEEE Transactions on Software Engineering, SE9, 639-648.

2.   Boehm, B. W. (1984) "Software Engineering Economics," IEEE Transactions on Software Engineering SE10, 4-21.

3.   Ericsson, K. A. & Simon, H. A. (1984) Protocol Analysis: Verbal Reports as Data, MIT Press: Cambridge, MA.

4.   Gurubaxani V. & H. Mendelson (1987) "Software and Hardware in Data Processing Budgets," IEEE Transactions on Software Engineering SE13, 1010-1017.

5.   Jones, C. (1985) Programming Productivity, McGraw-Hill: New York.

6.   Kemerer, C. F. (1987) "An Empirical Validation of Software Cost Estimation Models," Communications of the ACM, 30 (5), 416-429.

7.   Li, H. F. & W. K. Cheung (1987) "An Empirical Study of Software Metrics," IEEE Transaction on Software Engineering, SE13, 697-708.

8.   Martin, J. & C. McClure (1983) Software Maintenance: The Problem and its Solutions, Prentice-Hall: New Jersey.

9.   Prietula, M. & Dickson, G. (1987) "Flexible Interfaces and the Support of Physical Database Design Reasoning." In L. Kerschberg (Ed.) Expert Database Systems, Prentice-Hall: New Jersey.

10. Putnam, L. H. (1978) "A General Empirical Solution to the Macro Software Sizing and Estimating Problem," IEEE Transactions on Software Engineering, SE4 (4), 345-361.

11. Sprague, R. H. & B. C. McNurlin (1986) Information Systems Management in Practice, Prentice-Hall: New Jersey.

Expert Systems in Economics, Banking and Management
L.F. Pau et al. (Editors)
© *Elsevier Science Publishers B.V. (North-Holland), 1989*

EXPERT SUPPORT FOR INFORMATION RETRIEVAL USING GRAPHICAL AND OBJECT-ORIENTED TECHNIQUES

Hiirsalmi, Mikko and Hämäläinen, Matti

Laboratory for Information Processing, Technical Research Centre of Finland, Lehtisaarentie 2 A, 00340 Helsinki, Finland*

Information retrieval has been gaining importance as publicly accessible, online information databases have entered the market. Vast amounts of unstructured, rapidly changing information is being stored into these databases. The end-users having the information need should be able to search by themselves without the help of information retrieval specialists. However, as the area is rather unstandardized there are both technical and administrative difficulties hindering the efficient utilization of this multitude of information. For some time these problems have been attacked by building special front-end systems that are aimed at providing a common user interface to multiple retrieval systems hiding the system specific details from the users. This paper describes our approach to constructing a user friendly intermediary system for assisting end-users in accessing textual databases via heterogeneous information retrieval systems. Our prototype consists of personal computers using data communications lines to access some of the information retrieval systems available in Finland. External support programs may also be accessed via data communications lines. The system provides facilities for specifying queries using a graphical search profile editor, automatic retrieval session management, automatic translation of the tree representation of the search profile into the corresponding command language as well as facilities for browsing expert advice included into the system. The current prototype system has been implemented on IBM/PC computers running MS/DOS operating system using Smalltalk/V programming environment.

1. INTRODUCTION

1.1. Motivation for Building Intermediary Systems

Currently thousands of publicly accessible, online databases are commercially available and their number is increasing. These databases serve different purposes and contain information from various fields. It is often useful to search multiple databases to gain good coverage of the problem area and separate retrieval systems are sometimes required. Usually casual users find it difficult to access online databases especially if multiple retrieval systems are involved. Therefore few people actually perform searches by themselves - professional intermediaries, such as librarians, are used instead. They are better informed about potential information sources, even about those that are not available online, such as manual reference indexes. They are also familiar with the technical details of using the various information retrieval systems. However, librarians are not always available and they are not familiar with every subject domain - only the person

* This research was carried out as a part of the FINPRIT research programme, funded mainly by the Technology Development Centre of Finland (TEKES). Financial support to this project was provided also by DEC, Finnish PTT, Nokia, VTKK and Wärtrsilä Marine.

needing the information may judge the value of the retrieved information. More advanced interfaces to the retrieval systems might help especially the end-users.

1.2. Background for Information Retrieval

Information retrieval systems provide the interfaces to textual databases. A typical retrieval command language consists of commands for opening and closing databases, viewing documents in various formats and matching the database against a logical combination of constraining search terms. A few logical connectives, such as AND, OR, NOT and ADJ (adjacency) are available for specifying the desired query. In some systems every command changes the global state of the retrieval system; in others separate retrieval sets are formed concerning every retrieval command (later commands may reference these retrieval sets). Below we have an example of a typical retrieval command and the appropriate system response indicating that retrieval set 1 was formed and 15 applicable records were found in the selected database(s):

Find user$ AND (interf$ OR model$)

- Search 1: 15 records.

In the 1980's some efforts have been made to build computerized intermediary systems for assisting the use of heterogeneous textual databases. These systems attempt to hide data communications as well as database and retrieval system related peculiarities from the user. Typically these intermediary systems assist by supervising the retrieval session, providing a common user interface language for the specification of the query and performing a transformation from this representation to the corresponding retrieval command language.

The basic command set is conceptually relatively uniform among various systems but the system responses tend to vary a lot and may be caused by different parts of the overall computer system (data communications may fail, a retrieval command may fail matching no database objects and may require backing up to the previous context, the system may request the user to change the password etc.). A perfect intermediary system should be able to recognize the system's state at all times which is a very difficult task.

2. TÄLLI - AN INTERMEDIARY SYSTEM FOR INFORMATION RETRIEVAL

2.1 Project Background

There are 77 information retrieval systems and about 200 public databases in the Nordic countries; in Finland we have 51 databases and 8 retrieval systems. It was considered important to improve the usability of these retrieval systems by developing an intelligent intermediary system. Our project was started in late 1986 for exploring the technical feasibility of such a system.

Our most concrete objective has been to develop methods for assisting users in accessing heterogeneous information retrieval systems, especially in the Finnish environment. Main goals have been to [1]:

- help in dealing with variations among heterogeneous retrieval systems
- provide automated management of the retrieval session
- provide easier ways for describing information wanted
- help with problems related to the Finnish morphology
- support the users in the analysis of the retrieval results.

2.2. Architecture of the Overall System

All available publicly accessible retrieval systems are accessed via existing computer or telephone networks using already existing interactive command languages. We have wanted to share generally applicable support programs among the potential users. As personal computers are gaining popularity we chose to distribute our application into the network with the user interface software in a commonly available personal computer and external support programs located in a network computer (maintained by the National Telecommunications Administration). These programs may be accessed using terminal emulation via available computer networks or telephone lines. The overall architecture has been sketched in figure 1. A prototype of a knowledge-based intermediary system for information retrieval has been implemented on IBM/PC compatible personal computers.

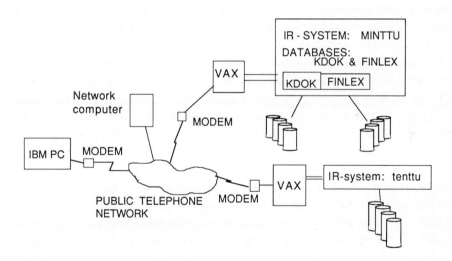

FIGURE 1 The system environment

In order to develop a user friendly interface a multi-windowed display with graphics capabilities was considered potential. As Smalltalk/V provided these facilities as well as a terminal emulation package we decided to develop our prototype system using object-oriented techniques on an IBM/PC. Currently only one support program is being used - a natural language related program producing all possible stems of the given Finnish words. This facility is being used to improve gain as the Finnish words have been stored in the inverted indexes in their conjugated forms. A Finnish noun may have about 2000 conjugated forms but only up to 12 stem forms which cover all the conjugated forms if truncated.

The data communications peculiarities have been hidden from the user as well as possible by accessing them through a graphical, multi-windowed user interface and by maintaining the data communications lines automatically. The personal computer based software has been written using Smalltalk/V and Prolog/V [2]. We have provided the user all essential information concerning the retrieval process using a multi-windowed workspace with graph editors, pull-down as well as pop-up menus and information as well as rule browsers. We have attempted to make the user interaction as easy as possible using interactive techniques whenever possible. In order to control the various workspace objects a global context had to be defined. Using this the users may define their preferences and the context is also used for passing data between objects. [3]

3. IMPLEMENTATION PRINCIPLES BEHIND TÄLLI

3.1. Structure of the User Interface

The user interface is based on the direct manipulation principle: The user is shown all information retrieval related information graphically and operations are performed directly with graph editors, by menus and by cutting/pasting with the mouse. The system does not have any command interface. Multiple windows are open at the same time providing the user the possibility to view different information concurrently in separate workspaces. The most important ones are search profile editor, results browser and advice browser. Figure 2 shows us a snapshot of the user interface with pull-down menus at the top, rule browser at the upper left corner, search profile editor below the rule browser and results browser at the bottom right. Above the results browser one may see the retrieval commands equivalent to the search profile.

No expressive power will be lost using the search profile editor as the user is allowed to define as complex logical queries as are possible with the traditional command languages. Search keys are entered into the workspace either by typing them or by gathering them from previously retrieved documents using the results browser. Logical connectives may be used while entering the search keys. On the other hand, the search keys may be interactively grouped with graph manipulation operations. The stem forms of Finnish words are automatically queried from an external support program. One may check what the corresponding command sequence would look like in the chosen retrieval system. When desired the search profile may be used for retrieval and the quantitative hit information is shown on the graph editor together with the corresponding search concepts. The user does not have to worry about the command syntax and about establishing a data communications session - these are done automatically.

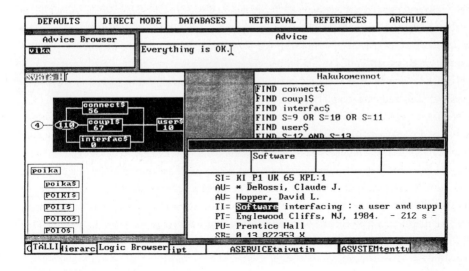

| DEFAULTS | DIRECT MODE | DATABASES | RETRIEVAL | REFERENCES | ARCHIVE |

FIGURE 2 A snapshot from the display of the prototype system

The quantitative feedback information may be analyzed using expert's rules which have been integrated into the search profile editor. Information retrieval researchers have identified useful online search strategies which are used in our intermediary systems as a basis for expert advice [4], [5]. The pieces of advice are visualized as a tree on an advice browser letting the user focus into the appropriate ones. Expert rules identify potential sources of trouble in the search profile and provide also advice for improving the search profile. These advices may be browsed through by using the advice browser and the concepts affected by the advice are highlighted in the search profile editor.

The search profile may be altered at all times. When the number of references is in suitable limits some sample references may be retrieved and their relevance may be determined by the user. This process of enhancing the search profile and evaluating the number of results and their relevance is continued until one is satisfied with the results. The major benefit of this type of visual user interaction is that one sees the state of the query thereby avoiding the interpretation problems inherent to the traditional textual command language interfaces. Retrieved documents may be browsed through using a results browser. New search terms may be picked up from these documents and added into the profile.

3.2 Knowledge Representation in the Prototype

Smalltalk provides an object-oriented paradigm where application-specific concepts may be directly modeled via classes and their instances. Object-specific data may be naturally represented in the instance variables of the objects but there is no natural way to represent rule type of knowledge in the pure object-oriented paradigm. On the other hand, logic programming provides a good vehicle for representing this kind of declarative knowledge.

Various types of knowledge have been included in the prototype: We have knowledge about the command languages of the information retrieval systems as well as about their most common responses. Some 'rules of thumb' have been provided by the information retrieval experts. These rules deal with the selection of the appropriate search terms, with the interpretation of the retrieval results and with the possible improvements of the query in order to get the desired number of references   Transformation rules guide the transformation of the internal (logical) representation of the query into the appropriate target command language.

Search profiles, specifying the desired logical relations between the search terms, are represented as a tree structure using a set of classes, representing different types of relations and search terms. Instances of these classes contain all the required information. They contain routines for drawing themselves on the profile editor, graph manipulation methods, menus and retrieval specific information such as number of retrieved hits for the appropriate search term in a database query.

Prolog databases are used for representing the expert rules, retrieval system specific commands and their restrictions as well as some tree transformation guide-lines. In Prolog/V predicates may be grouped into hierarchies that may be consulted separately. Prolog databases may be consulted from Smalltalk objects and these objects may also be accessed by Prolog predicates. This provides a sufficiently flexible interface between the two programming paradigms.

Command transformations have been described using a common command language (CCL) proposal as a reference model [6]. For each retrieval system it has to be described how the most important CCL-commands can be implemented with the command set of this specific system. Also the restrictions of the retrieval systems have to be represented. For example, if each command is not associated with a result set of its own the scope of possible logical queries may be reduced.

The representation of the systems responses is a bigger problem since they have originally been intended for interactive usage and therefore vary a lot. Some procedural code had to be used to overcome these problems.

3.3.   Connections to External Services

As we can not require any changes to be made to the external online services and to their software, we use terminal emulation to communicate with them. For each of the services one or more communication paths may be specified by the user by defining the required communication conventions (i.e. login, line configuration, timeout values etc.) both to establish and to close a retrieval session. The definition is done interactively with a communications browser and the given information is used by the intermediary system when establishing the connection.

4. COMPARISON TO OTHER SYSTEMS

In the 1980's a few efforts have been made to build computerized intermediary systems for assisting in the use of heterogeneous textual databases. Pioneering work has been done at MIT since the late 1970's, where an intermediary system, called CONIT, has been developed. The system takes care of the data communications tasks and the translation of the commands and the responses into a standard format [7], [8]. An expert system containing some online retrieval related knowledge was also developed at MIT using a consulting rule-based approach [9]. Our intermediary system contains many features from both of these early systems. The main contribution of our system is that we have put much more emphasis on the development of the user interface integrating the expert advices into the intermediary system. The development and implementation of the system has been carried out by using personal computers commonly available in the user organizations.

In addition to the CONIT/EXPERT type of approach several other approaches to support for information retrieval have been proposed. Many of them have prerequirements concerning the information retrieval systems accessed and are thus not feasible in our environment. There are also a few commercial systems providing interfaces to some of the major information retrieval systems. EasyNet (a gateway system) and Pro-Search (a front-end system) provide good examples of such systems.

5. CONCLUSIONS

All of the goals mentioned earlier (in chapter 2.1) have been achieved to some degree by the demonstration prototype which has been developed in the course of the project. Currently it supports two of the Finnish information retrieval systems. One of them is a library database, called TENTTU, and maintained by the Helsinki University of Technology Library. The other one is MINTTU, maintained by the Finnish State Computing Center. It contains databases ranging from library data and research documents to Finnish judicial documents. As their command languages and usage conventions differ from each other they provide a good environment for evaluating the potential benefits of the interpretive approach described in this paper.

So far the evaluation of the system has been based primarily on the demonstrations and - to some extent - on the experiments carried out by the information retrieval experts of the project team. The combination of graphical and object-oriented techniques have provided more flexible means to integrate expertise into the system. Smalltalk/V has provided us with a unique environment for prototyping with personal computers. However the version of the language we have been using has also its drawbacks as the response times tend to get longer with large applications (currently the application contains 40 classes, 800 methods and about 60 Prolog-predicates in addition to the standard Smalltalk/V definitions).

After the prototype environment for this project was selected some new highly interactive programming environments have entered the market in the personal computer field. For instance hypertext-based tools (we include also HyperCard to this group) have become very popular. It seems that for the development of advanced intermediary systems integration of a flexible user-interface tool with efficient programming languages is needed.

ACKNOWLEDGEMENTS

We would like to thank the members of the TÄLLI-project team, especially the information retrieval specialists Eero Sormunen and Riitta Alkula at the Information Services of the Technical Research Centre of Finland.

[1]   Sormunen, E., Nurminen, R., Hämäläinen, M., Hiirsalmi, M., Knowledge-based intermediary system for information retrieval Requirements specification, VTT Research Notes 794, Espoo, 1987.

[2]   Smalltalk V, PC World November 1986, p. 168-171.

[3]   Hiirsalmi, M., Design of a knowledge-based intermediary system for information retrieval, M.Sc. Thesis, Helsinki University of Technology, 1987.

[4]   Schroder, J. J., Study of strategies used in online searching: 3.   Query refining, Online Review, 1983, Vol.7, No.3, pp. 229- 236.

[5]   Shaw, D., Nine sources of problems for novice online searches, Online Review, 1986, Vol.10, No.5.

[6]   de Brisis, K. & Manders, I., Language requirements for the intelligent interface facility, Statens bibliotekhogskole, Brodd report 871151, Oslo, 1987, p. 155.

[7]   Marcus, R. S. & Reintjes, J., A Translating Computer Interface for End-User Operation of heterogeneous Retrieval Systems. Journal of the American Society for Information Science, July 1981. pp. 287-317.

[8]   Marcus, R. S., Development and Testing of Expert Systems for Retrieval Assistance, MIT, ASIS Proceedings 1985.

[9]   Yip, M., An Expert System for Document Retrieval. Master of Science Thesis in Electronical Engineering and Computer Science, Massachusetts Institute of Technology. MA. 1981.

Expert Systems in Economics, Banking and Management
L.F. Pau et al. (Editors)
© *Elsevier Science Publishers B.V. (North-Holland), 1989*

TRANSFORMATION OF A SEMANTIC NETWORK INTO OBJECT-ORIENTED AND RELATIONAL DATABASE DESIGN

Chan Huang Seng

Por Hau Joo

Information Engineering Services
16 Arumugam Road #07-00
Teck Chiang Industrial Building
Singapore 1440

Institute of Systems Science
National University of Singapore
Heng Mui Keng Terrace
Kent Ridge, Singapore 0511

This paper presents an approach in modelling an application using semantic network techniques and then followed by transformation of the semantic networks into an object-oriented design. As an added benefit, a relational database is designed to support the object-oriented environment, to enhance its reliability and recoverability, and to support an expert system shell for knowledge based system application. The analysis of internal controls within an order processing system is used as a case study to illustrate the concepts and techniques presented in this paper.

1. KNOWLEDGE REPRESENTATION USING SEMANTIC NETWORKS

1.1 Audit Flowcharts

Reviewing and evaluating internal controls are key concerns of organizations, and main functions of internal as well as external auditors. Commonly practised among auditors is the use of flowcharts to record accounting procedures and flow of documents. These audit flowcharts represent the control and flow of documents of transaction activities that are carried out during business operations. They also served as main sources of information for auditors to check and validate accounting procedures within an organization, and to enable them evaluate the extent of internal controls within the transaction [1].

1.2 The Sales Cycle

Generally, there are many types of transactions handled by an organization. For a given business cycle, there are a number of related transactions. For example, the audit flowcharts as shown in Figure 1a and Figure 1b described diagramatically transaction activities related to order processing within a sales cycle.

1.3 From An Audit Flowchart To Semantic Networks

The audit flowchart as described earlier clearly represents the activities within a sales cycle. An auditor uses it to check, validate and evaluate internal controls within that cycle. But if intelligent computer programs are to be developed to perform some of these tasks, then a more suitable representation scheme is required.

Semantic networks have been used in representing knowledge for solving problems [2]. For this auditing problem, they can be used to represent the knowledge contained in an audit flowchart. An in-depth analysis of the sales cycle produces several high-level semantic networks that represent the knowledge for solving the auditing problem.

An *agent* is defined as an actor who performs an action. It can be an employee of the organization, a department or even an external body such as the customer. Figure 2 shows only the classes of the *AGENT* semantic network, the actual instances are left out to avoid "congestion" in the diagram.

An *item* is defined as an object that is acted upon by an actor during an action. For example, a document is an item. An item could have some attributes like stock quantity, order amount, which are important to the auditors for purpose of evaluating internal controls. The *ITEM & ATTRIBUTE* semantic network is shown in Figure 3.

A *repository* is a storage facility for items of similar type. Cabinet, paper file and incoming basket are some examples of repository. This is shown in Figure 4.

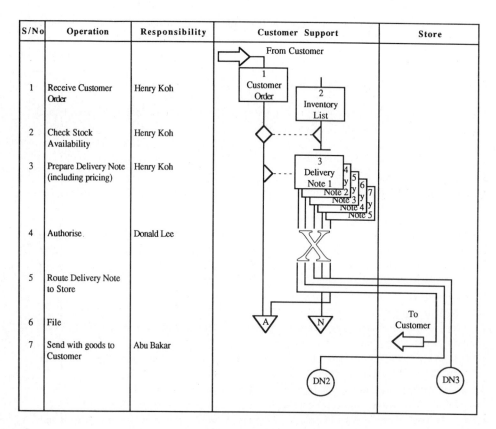

S/No	Operation	Responsibility	Customer Support	Store
1	Receive Customer Order	Henry Koh		
2	Check Stock Availability	Henry Koh		
3	Prepare Delivery Note (including pricing)	Henry Koh		
4	Authorise	Donald Lee		
5	Route Delivery Note to Store			
6	File			
7	Send with goods to Customer	Abu Bakar		

Figure 1a : Audit Flowchart Of A Sales Cycle

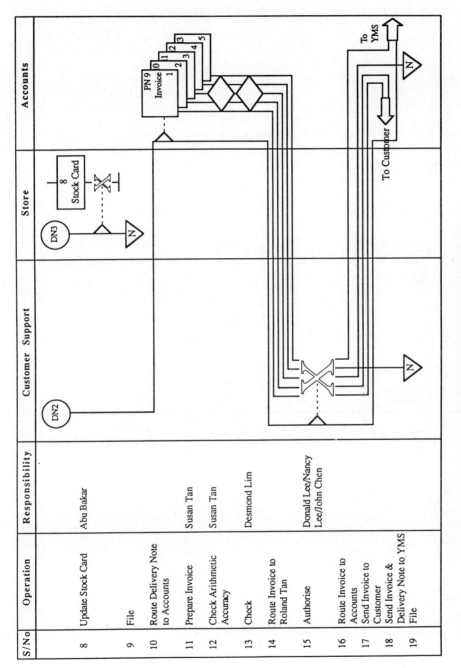

Figure 1b : **Audit Flowchart Of A Sales Cycle**

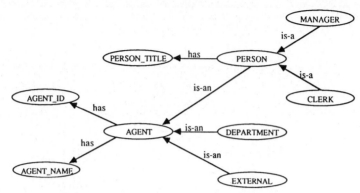

Figure 2 : The *AGENT* Semantic Network.

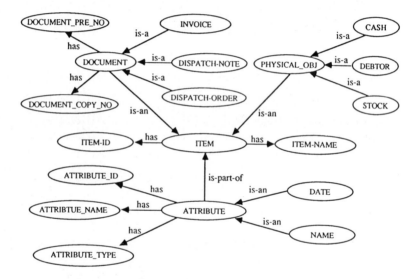

Figure 3 : The *ITEM & ATTRIBUTE* Semantic Network.

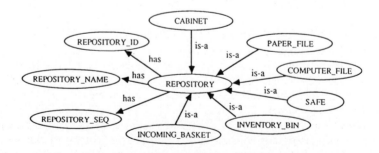

Figure 4 : The *REPOSITORY* Semantic Network.

An *action* indicates an activity that involves an actor acting on an item. A *command* is a collection of one or more related actions. The objective of introducing command is to simplify the declaration of detailed actions. This is shown as follows :

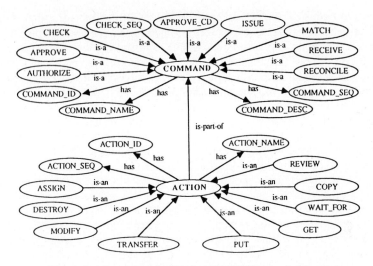

Figure 5 : The *COMMAND & ACTION* Semantic Network.

Finally, the individual semantic networks as described earlier are bound together using a token node. This is to show that they are all related to the same event in any transaction activity. The following figure illustrates this concept.

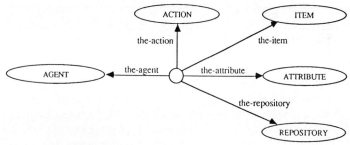

Figure 6 : The *ACTIVIY* Semantic Network

2.   DESIGN USING OBJECT-ORIENTED APPROACH

2.1 Object-Oriented Languages & Environment

Object-oriented programming languages and environments have recently become very popular tools for designing and developing application and/or knowledge based systems.   These tools introduce new approaches in solving business problems, by representing entities, concepts, events, etc in the form of object classes. Each object class may have slots attached to it, and procedures for manipulating values of these slots may be defined. An object class is not only a collection of slots (commonly called *variables*) but also includes a set of procedures (commonly called *methods*). An object class is just a definition, an instance of that class is called an *object* [3].

Objects communicate with each other by sending messages, which invoke the procedures of the "message-receiving" object. Some of these procedures are called *demons*, they are invoked automatically within the object whenever the value of a slot changes.

An object class can be related to other classes in one or more ways, such as : (i) generalization, (ii) aggregation and (iii) association [4]. A *generalization* relationship assimilates the concept of a *is-a* relationship commonly found in semantic networks. Object classes that are related in this manner are arranged in a multi-level structure, with object classes at the lower level being subclasses of the higher level. Furthermore, object classes at lower levels inherit the properties of all the slots and procedures of the object classes above them. An *aggregation* relationship assimilates the concept of *a-part-of* relationship that is well known in any "Bill-of-Materials" system. Object classes that are *a-part-of* or components of another object class are also arranged in a multi-level structure, with lower level object classes combined to form a composite object class at the higher level. An aggregation relationship indicates dependency among object classes but does not necessarily implies inheritance property as exhibited in a generalization relationship. An *association* relationship assimilates the concept of *one-to-one*, *one-to-many* or *many-to-many* association between two or more objects. These relationships are used widely in entity and/or data modelling techniques. Inheritance property is not implied by an association relationship, and it differs from an aggregation relationships in that the related objects are not necessarily a component class of one or the other.

2.2 Object-Oriented Design

In designing an object-oriented application system, one of the most important tasks is to identify the object classes required by the application. Slots relevant to each object class are then identified, and relationships among different object classes are established. The audit of an order processing transaction can be assisted by a computer-aided application using a variety of tools, including an object-oriented tool. If this is the case, then we must transform the semantic networks into an object-oriented design.

From Figure 2, *AGENT, DEPARTMENT, EXTERNAL, PERSON, MANAGER* and *CLERK* are relevant object classes. *AGENT* and *PERSON* have specific slots attached to them, *EXTERNAL, DEPARTMENT, MANAGER* and *CLERK* do not, but they are expected to inherit the slots from either the *AGENT, PERSON* or both object classes. This is a generalization relationship. For object classes without slots, depending on how their objects are manipulated, it may not be necessary to establish them for the design. For example, a new slot called PERSON_TYPE can be introduced in *PERSON* to distinguish a manager from a clerk so that their object classes need not be created.

Apart from above considerations, a person works for a department and a department has many workers. This is an association relationship between *DEPARTMENT* and *PERSON*, which can be represented in several ways :

(a) By having a PERSON_ID slot within the *DEPARTMENT* object class and making it a list data type, i.e. one that can take several values. It can be used to store the identifications of the *PERSON* objects who work for a *DEPARTMENT* object.

(b) By having a DEPARTMENT_ID slot within the *PERSON* object class so that each person works for a *DEPARTMENT* object.

(c) By having both (a) and (b) in the design to achieve maximum flexibility.

Depending on how the *DEPARTMENT–PERSON* association relationship is to be manipulated, one of the above ways can be selected. The second one is chosen here because it reflects the relational approach as advocated by E. F. Codd [5]. This approach is most logical and flexible in design and therefore easier to maintain and manage. Figure 7 shows the result of this transformation.

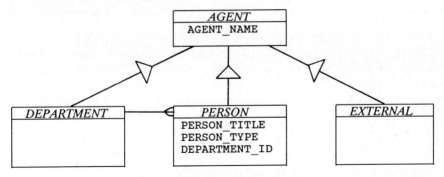

Figure 7 : The *AGENT* Object Classes.

Using the same techniques as described earlier, Figure 3 is transformed into an object-oriented design with *ITEM*, *DOCUMENT*, *PHYSICAL* and *ATTRIBUTE* object classes. The result is shown as follows :

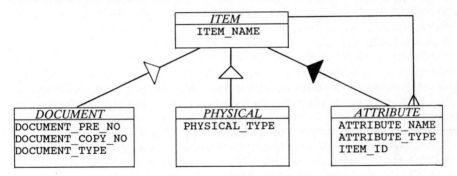

Figure 8 : The *ITEM & ATTRIBUTE* Object Classes.

Similarly, Figure 4 can be transformed into an object-oriented design as follows :

```
REPOSITORY
REPOSITORY_NAME
REPOSITORY_SEQ
REPOSITORY_TYPE
```

Figure 9 : The *REPOSITORY* Object Class.

The *COMMAND & ACTION* Semantic Network indicates an aggregation relationship (an action is a part of a command) as well as an association relationship (a command has one or more actions). An activity is an actor acting upon some items, such as *DOCUMENT*, *PHYSICAL*, *ATTRIBUTE* and/or *REPOSITORY* objects. Since it is the action that drives an activity, the *ACTION* object class can be expanded to support this concept by having AGENT_ID, ITEM_ID, ATTRIBUTE_ID and REPOSITORY_ID slots attached to it, so that the identifications of these objects can be kept together with an *ACTION* object. This concept is illustrated using the following figure.

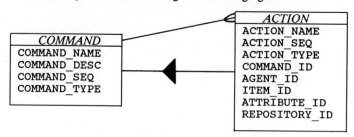

Figure 10 : The *COMMAND & ACTION* Object Classes.

3.   DESIGN USING RELATIONAL DATABASE APPROACH

3.1 Relational Database Management System

Relational database management system (RDBMS) is well known for its simplicity and flexibility in data management. The relational model, based on mathematical theory and foundation, is now accepted by industry and widely used for managing operational and strategic data in production environments. In the development of any application and/or knowledge based system using an object-oriented approach, it is definitely an added advantage to have a direct, or even indirect, interface to RDBMS.

In a RDBMS, data are organized into relations (commonly called *tables*), usually normalized to third or higher normal forms. Each relation represents an entity type, described by a collection of attributes (commonly called *fields* or *columns*). Occurrences of an entity type are stored in a relation as tuples (commonly called *rows* or *records*) [6].

A relation is related to another if both have an attribute in common. However, the relationship is limited to association only, generalization relationship with inheritance property is not supported by the relational model, and aggregation relationship is not clearly defined. Therefore only *one-to-one*, *one-to-many* or *many-to-many* relationship links can be established between relations in a relational database.

RDBMS can be used to manage objects, i.e. instances of object classes that are created by an object-oriented application. These objects can be stored as tuples and they can be manipulated using a high-level language called Structured Query Language (SQL). Using SQL, query programs could be developed for the auditors to access the database and to interrogate the objects for purposes of checking, validating and evaluating internal controls of the order processing transaction.

3.2 Relational Database Design

A key step in relational database design is identifying the relations and attributes required by the application. To support an object-oriented environment, relations are needed only for those object classes for which their objects are required to be stored as tuples in some relations in the database. These relations form the base relations of the database, to support the SQL queries initiated by the auditors.

From Figure 7, object classes *DEPARTMENT*, *PERSON* and *EXTERNAL* require a relation each. No relation is needed for object class *AGENT* as it is there merely for the purpose of inheritance. Similarly, from Figure 8, relations and attributes are required for object classes *DOCUMENT*, *PHYSICAL* and *ATTRIBUTE*. From Figure 9, a relation for *REPOSITORY* object class is required. From Figure 10, relations and attributes for the *COMMAND* and *ACTION* object classes are identified. These are shown in Figure 11.

RELATION	ATTRIBUTES
DEPARTMENT	DEPARTMENT_ID, DEPARTMENT_NAME
PERSON	PERSON_ID, PERSON_NAME, PERSON_TITLE, PERSON_TYPE, DEPARTMENT_ID
EXTERNAL	EXTERNAL_ID, EXTERNAL_NAME
DOCUMENT	DOCUMENT_ID, DOCUMENT_NAME, DOCUMENT_TYPE, DOCUMENT_PRE_NO, DOCUMENT_COPY_NO
PHYSICAL	PHYSICAL_ID, PHYSICAL_NAME, PHYSICAL_TYPE
ATTRIBUTE	ATTRIBUTE_ID, ATTRIBUTE_NAME, ATTRIBUTE_TYPE, ITEM_ID
REPOSITORY	REPOSITORY_ID, REPOSITORY_NAME, REPOSITORY_SEQ, REPOSITORY_TYPE
COMMAND	COMMAND_ID, COMMAND_TYPE, COMMAND_DESC, COMMAND_SEQ
ACTION	ACTION_ID, ACTION_TYPE, ACTION_SEQ, COMMAND_ID, AGENT_ID, ITEM_ID, ATTRIBUTE_ID, REPOSITORY_ID

Figure 11 : Relational Database Design.

3.3 Defining Userview & Query Processing Using SQL

An advantage of RDBMS over non-relational ones is that userview can be defined easily and dynamically, and SQL commands can be embedded in the userview. This mechanism allows complex JOINs involving multiple relations be made totally transparent to the auditors. An example is provided as follows :

```
CREATE VIEW AUDIT_ACTIVITY AS
SELECT ACTION_ID, ACTION_TYPE, PERSON_ID, PERSON_NAME,
       PERSON_TITLE, DEPARTMENT.DEPARTMENT_ID,
       DEPARTMENT_NAME, DOCUMENT.ID, DOCUMENT_NAME,
       DOCUMENT_TYPE
FROM   ACTION, PERSON, DEPARTMENT, DOCUMENT
WHERE  AGENT_ID = PERSON_ID AND ITEM_ID = DOCUMENT_ID
AND    PERSON.DEPARTMENT_ID=DEPARTMENT.DEPARTMENT_ID
```

From the above userview, the following queries can be executed :

(a) To determine what actions, and on what documents Susan Tan has executed :

```
SELECT ACTION_TYPE, DOCUMENT_NAME, DOCUMENT_TYPE
FROM   AUDIT_ACTIVITY
WHERE  PERSON_NAME = "Susan Tan"
```

(b) To determine the persons who have authorized any documents of type "Invoice", and showing their names, job titles and departments :

```
SELECT. ACTION_TYPE, PERSON_NAME, PERSON_TITLE,
        DEPARTMENT_NAME
FROM    COMMAND, ACTION, AUDIT_ACTIVITY
WHERE   COMMAND.COMMAND_ID = ACTION.COMMAND_ID
AND     ACTION.ACTION_ID = AUDIT_ACTIVITY.ACTION_ID
AND     COMMAND_TYPE = "Authorize"
AND     DOCUMENT_TYPE = "Invoice"
```

For complex queries that are frequently asked by the auditors, a set of userviews can be created to simplify access to the database. For adhoc queries, SQL commands can be issued directly to the RDBMS.

4. CONCLUSIONS

The transformation of a set of related semantic networks into an object-oriented design requires the identification of object classes, slots and relationships among object classes. Object classes without specific slots may be omitted without losing information by introducing an *object-type* slot in their respective higher level object classes. As an added advantage, a relational database should be designed to support the object-oriented environment by allowing objects to be stored as tuples and manipulated using SQL. This results in increased usability, reliability and recoverability of the system. Finally, the relational database may act as a source knowledge on auditing and internal controls for a knowledge-based system which has an interface to the RDBMS [7].

ACKNOWLEDGEMENT

Since October 1987, a joint project by Information Engineering Services (IES) and PG Management Consultants (PGMC) was formed to develop an intelligent computer application to assist auditors in checking, validating and evaluating internal controls within an organization. A prototype was built at the Knowledge Engineering Resource Center (KERC). KERC is established by the Information Technology Institute (ITI) of the National Computer Board (NCB) to help organization develop expert systems. The prototype was completed, showing the feasibility of performing evaluation of internal controls and deriving at the appropriate conclusions. The project is now in its second cycle, with collaboration between the three parties (IES, PGMC and ITI), and major developments are now underway to expand it into a full system.

The initial project team consists of the following members :

Domain Expert :   Wee Phui Gam, Consultant, PGMC

Application   :   Chan Huang Seng, Senior Software Specialist, IES
Developers   Teow Poh Choo, Senior Systems Engineer, IES
                           Tham Kai Yuen, Systems Engineer,IES

Project   :   Patrick Ong Swee Hock, Systems Engineer, HP Singapore
Advisors   Por Hau Joo, Member, Technology Application Staff, ISS
                           Tan Sian Lip, Knowledge Engineer, ITI

The approach presented in this paper is not the design that is implemented in the above mentioned project. However, the learning, experiences and ideas gained from the project have provided a starting point for this paper. The authors would like to acknowledge and sincerely thank all team members for these experiences.

REFERENCES

[1] Alvin A.Arens, James K.Loebbecke, "Auditing: An Integrated Approach", Prentice Hall (1984)

[2] Ronald J.Brachman, "On the Epistemological Status of Semantic Networks", from "Readings in Knowledge Representation" edited by Ronald J.Brachman and Hector J.Levesque (1984)

[3] Gerald E.Peterson, "Tutorial: Object-Oriented Computing", Volume 1: Concepts, Volume 2: Implementations, from the Computer Society of IEEE (1987)

[4] Michael R.Blaha, William J.Premerlani and James E.Rumbaugh, "Relational Database Design Using An Object-Oriented Methodology", CACM 31, No. 4 (April 1988)

[5] E.F.Codd, "A Relational Model of Data for Large Shared Data Banks", CACM 13 No. 6 (June 1970)

[6] C.J.Date, "Relational Database: Selected Writings", Addison-Wesley (1986)

[7] A. Alzobaidie and J.B. Grimson, 'Expert Systems and Database Systems : How can they serve each other ?', 2nd International Expert Systems Conference, London (1986)

Expert Systems in Economics, Banking and Management
L.F. Pau et al. (Editors)
© *Elsevier Science Publishers B.V. (North-Holland), 1989*

A MODEL FOR THE EMPIRICAL INVESTIGATION
OF KNOWLEDGE ACQUISITION TECHNIQUES

Jasbir Singh Dhaliwal and Izak Benbasat

Faculty of Commerce and Business Administration
University of British Columbia
Vancouver, B.C.
Canada V6T 1Y8*

This paper calls for the empirical investigation of various knowledge acquisition tools and techniques, and presents a research model for guiding such investigation and integrating their findings. The model identifies the salient factors influencing both the choice of knowledge acquisition techniques, and the process and product of knowledge acquisition. Empirical measures for the independent and dependent variables identified by the model are discussed.

I. THE NEED FOR RESEARCH IN KNOWLEDGE ACQUISITION TECHNIQUES

Knowledge-based systems (KBS) are intelligent computer programs that use knowledge and inference procedures to solve problems that are difficult enough to require human expertise for their resolution (Feigenbaum, 1982). Knowledge engineering (KE) is the development process of eliciting/acquiring, representing and manipulating knowledge consisting of descriptions, relationships, and procedures in a specialised domain of interest. Although various KE methodologies and tools now exist for the acquisition and representation of expertise (Buchanan et al., 1983; Welbank, 1987), there is a need for more research in determining which techniques are more effective for acquiring and transferring knowledge from expert sources to computers. This is the new version of the old knowledge acquisition (KA) problem that has been regarded as a major bottleneck in the efficient development of KBS (Hayes-Roth, 1983).

Early work on KA dealt largely with the computerised refinement and maintenance of *already existing* knowledge bases (KB) such as TEIRESIAS (Davis and Lenat, 1986). Recent work, however, has focused on approaches, tools, and techniques for the computerised elicitation of knowledge from human experts for the *initial development* of KB. The focus of KE on the refinement of existing KB and on developing new KA tools has led to the critical task of evaluating the various KA techniques, especially the nonautomated ones, which are being largely overshadowed and ignored. This has prompted calls for research (Fellers, 1987) on the following: 1) Is there one best elicitation technique for KA? 2) If not, what is the best combination of techniques? 3) Which techniques are most suitable under which circumstances? and 4) What skills are

* This work has been supported by operating grant OGP2421 from the Natural Sciences and Engineering Research Council of Canada.

required in order to utilise each of these techniques? Current techniques of KA suffer from both the lack of an empirical and a theoretical basis to guide the elicitation process. As a result, the knowledge engineer involved in a KBS development is forced to make many *ad hoc* and arbitrary decisions regarding how to proceed with the task.

In calling for the empirical investigation of the various KA techniques, this paper proposes a research model that identifies the salient factors influencing both the choice of KA technique used, and the *process* and *product* of KA. The next section describes the various dependent and independent variables that constitute the research model (see Figure 1).

II. ELEMENTS OF THE RESEARCH MODEL

The objective of the KA process is to *efficiently* develop a KBS of *high quality*. It is also important to ensure that the system developed is accepted and utilised by its intended users (i.e., it is usable and of value). The two major dependent variable categories shown in Figure 1, quality of the product (KB/KBS) and quality of the KA process, are influenced by a number of factors that bear upon any KA effort. Warbelow (1986) identified three categories of such factors, including: 1) the attributes of the domain expert whose expertise is being sought, 2) the attributes of the domain itself, and 3) the KA techniques used. To these we add: 4) the attributes of the knowledge engineer involved in the development, 5) application characteristics, 6) the system development approach used, and 7) the organizational environment in which the KBS is being developed.

These independent variables influence the quality of the resulting KB or KBS (if implemented) and the quality of the KA process. Note that *the choice of KA technique used is influenced by these variables, and it in turn mediates the influence of the other independent variables on the dependent variables*. For example, while an upper limit on the quality of the KBS developed is directly imposed by the level of expertise an expert possesses, it is also mediated by the ability of the KA technique utilised to capture the knowledge that the expert has to offer. An appropriate KA technique that matches the expert's characteristics could elicit the most from the expert, but the KA technique cannot acquire more than what the expert could initially offer. In such cases, KA techniques that elicit knowledge from multiple sources might be appropriate. Therefore, the model in Figure 1 posits both direct and indirect influences (through their influence on the KA technique to be selected) of the independent variables.

INDEPENDENT VARIABLES
A. Knowledge Acquisition Techniques

The process of building an expert KB can be viewed as being composed of three distinct task phases: capturing, structuring and representation. The first two together constitute KA, while representation involves transcribing the expertise acquired into an appropriate machine-readable representation. The capturing and structuring phases can

INDEPENDENT VARIABLES   DEPENDENT VARIABLES

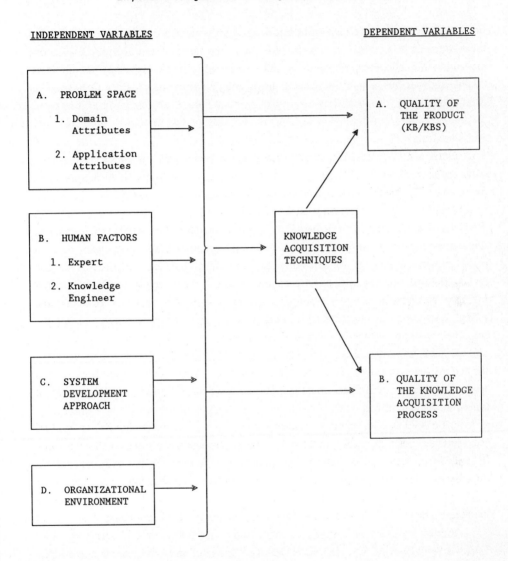

FIGURE 1
A Research Model for Investigating Knowledge Acquisition Techniques

be thought of as iterative cycles which are closely intertwined. *Capturing* relates to the techniques used to elicit the knowledge from the expert, and *structuring* involves organising the elicited knowledge to make sense of what is captured. Thus, while structuring specifies a form for what is being sought, capturing provides the means of acquiring it.

A.1 Capturing

Johnson (1984) describes three categories of techniques for capturing expertise from human experts: 1) descriptive techniques, 2) observational techniques and 3) intuitive techniques. *Descriptive* techniques capture expertise as described by a source expert. This is commonly done by interviewing and by creating for the expert's direct use formalised computer based description languages that are closely related to the representation software being used. The latter approach has been widely used to build automated systems for updating and modifying KB, e.g., TEIRESIAS. KA techniques that are applications of personal construct theory (such as KSS0) also fall into the descriptive category. Expert descriptions of the entities, attributes and ratings constituting the expert's conceptual structure serve as the basis for further KB refinement and expansion (Gaines and Shaw, 1981).

As the expertise being sought is by nature cognitive rather than physical, techniques of cognitive *observation* are required rather than visual observation techniques. Such techniques include protocol analysis (Ericsson and Simon, 1984), multidimensional scaling, and cluster analysis of expert performance data, e.g., on a set of real case studies or hypothetical scenarios.

Intuitive techniques take two forms. An expert could, by training and the study of knowledge engineering, attempt to capture his own expertise. Alternatively, a knowledge engineer could, by training and study of the domain, attempt to become an expert and then through introspection capture the expertise. Johnson (1984) provides a detailed evaluation of the advantages and disadvantages of these techniques.

Another category of techniques that could be added to the above three is *inductive techniques* of KA. Examples include the use of inductive learning algorithms such as the Aq algorithm (Michalski, 1983) and the ID3 algorithms (Quinlan, 1983). Since the subject matter for using such techniques has to be obtained from either expert descriptions of examples or from observing expert performance on a set of examples, it may not warrant being categorised separately. However, in cases where a KBS is being developed based on observed phenomena, then such inductive learning techniques of KA warrant separate consideration.

A.2 Structuring

KA techniques can also be classified according to the structuring formalism used. While some of these, e.g., production rules and semantic networks, have a machine knowledge representation tradition, others have been adopted from other fields such as decision analysis (decision trees), information requirements analysis (user views or screens) and psychotherapy (repertory grids). Such structuring formalisms, besides facilitating the organization and management of the knowledge captured, also serve a useful purpose in assisting knowledge engineers to form a quick and precise conceptualization of the KBS domain.

Rules have been the most commonly used structuring formalism. Since the bulk of current KBS technology utilises rule-based representations, knowledge engineers attempt to obtain synergy by using rules in KA as well. Although it may be advantageous to utilise rules at the KBS implementation level, the benefits of their use as KA structuring formalisms has yet to be empirically demonstrated. Another commonly used formalism in nonautomated KA, especially in conjunction with rules, is the decision tree or the decision table version of it.

Although we know of at least one study that has directly compared KA capturing techniques (Burton et al., 1987), there are none that directly compared KA structuring formalisms, or KA techniques that are based on different formalisms.

B. Human Factors
B.1 Attributes of the Source Expert

Sources of expertise can be classified into two general categories -- authentic sources and reconstructed sources (Johnson, 1983). Human experts exemplify the former category. Reconstructed knowledge (or expertise) flows from textbooks, nonexpert introspection, databases, normative mathematical/computer models, etc. Feigenbaum (1978) advances a somewhat identical taxonomy comprising expertise private to a human expert and that which is in the public domain. The KA problem is restricted to knowledge transfer from authentic or private sources despite the fact that the bulk of existing KBS utilise reconstructed expertise.

Attributes of the expert that impact KA are: 1) the stage of expertise development attained, 2) personality variables, and 3) the degree of motivation or commitment the expert has in the project. Of these, the first is considered to have the most impact on the selection and use of KA techniques and will be discussed here.

Expertise is considered to be a function of domain-specific knowledge evolving with practice into well developed mental schemas. The stage of expertise development directly impacts an expert's ability to articulate the expertise, and thereby the KA method selected. No explanation of expertise, no matter how persuasive, can be deemed adequate without an underlying theory to explain how such expert skill is acquired in the first place. Thus, the stage of expertise development variable can be related to the three stages of expertise development of Anderson's (1982) theory of skill acquisition. It views the skill learning (or expertise acquisition) process as a sequence of phases or stages termed the declarative (cognitive) phase, the knowledge-compilation (association) phase and the procedural (autonomous) stage.

During the *cognitive* stage the novice learns from instruction (advice) or from the observation of the consequences of actions undertaken.   His initial performance involves the operation of general strategies utilising declarative knowledge to guide performance.   The *association* stage involves the conversion of the slow and conscious declarative knowledge interpretations into faster compiled procedures.   At this stage, the individual is beginning to develop an initial mental model.   In the final *autonomous* stage, the newly acquired schemas are refined and tuned through the process of over-practicing and reinforcement to the point of automation and unconsciousness, termed the the paradox of expertise (Johnson, 1984).

It is the expertise of experts at stage three of the theory that is usually sought to build KBS.   However, the paradox of expertise suggests that *stage three* experts are not conscious of or able to describe their thought processes.   This implies that *stage two* experts may provide better descriptions of their expertise than *stage three* experts although they will be of a lower quality.   A more important implication is that since *stage three* experts are not able to describe their expertise directly, descriptive techniques of KA such as interviewing experts may have limited potential as compared to observational techniques.   Observational techniques such as protocol analysis that probe into the "black box" of *stage three* experts' minds avoid the limitations inherent in the expert's ability to articulate his knowledge.

B.2 Attributes of the Knowledge Engineer

A knowledge engineer handles the various aspects of KA. Among the particular attributes that impact the KA process include the knowledge engineer's familiarity with the domain, technical expertise, experience with the KA methodologies, and background in developing KBS.   Attributes such as interaction within and between teams of knowledge engineers are not considered here as it is assumed that one knowledge engineer handles all the KA and knowledge representation tasks.

C. Problem Space Aspects
C.1 Attributes of the Domain

Many different criteria can be used to distinguish between domains.   These include levels of complexity, levels of risk or uncertainty, number of alternatives and attributes, size of the search space, and levels of structure.   Of these the existence of structure in domains can be singled out as being of paramount importance in KA. Johnson (1984) notes that:

> "In well-structured problems, reconstructed methods of reasoning and authentic methods of reasoning may be quite similar since the number of ways for a task to be done is small.   In more ill-structured domains, however, the two types of methods are often quite different, and authentic methods of reasoning become an important source of expert level algorithms...."

Based on Keen and Scott-Morton's (1978) assertions that structure often reflects knowledge, and structure exists only to the extent that it is perceived, Warbelow

(1986) posits that both the extent of underlying "deep structure" (Chomsky, 1971) in a domain and the extent to which it is specified, and thereby perceived, will impact KA. The underlying deep structure of a domain specifies the relationships in its problem space. Thus, while chess has high deep structure, weather forecasting possesses low deep structure. Perceived structure, on the other hand, is the extent to which experts in the domain have a well-defined and specified body of knowledge with which to work. KA would be most difficult when both the specificity of the knowledge and the actual existence of deep structure are low, as in natural language interpretation. However, in domains such as accounting, both deep structure and specificity of the domain knowledge are high; thus knowledge acquisition would be relatively simpler.

C.2 Nature of the Application

Hayes-Roth et al. (1983) classify knowledge engineering applications into the following classes: interpretation, prediction, diagnosis, design, planning, monitoring, debugging, repair, instruction, and control. Chandrasekaran (1983) proposes that a domain (e.g., medical problem solving) is naturally decomposed into knowledge substructures each of which specialises in one type of problem solving (e.g., diagnosis). Each of these substructures in turn is further decomposed into small knowledge sources of the same problem-solving type, but specialising in different concepts in the domain (e.g., clinician, pathologist, radiologist). Thus, identification of the knowledge substructures for different task types can organise a body of knowledge in that task domain. This body of knowledge, even if developed in rudimentary form, can assist both in the development of automated KA tools and in guiding the knowledge engineer about what approach to take, or method to use.

D. System Development Approach

The KA technique used and the two dependent variables are also influenced by the system development approach taken for the KBS development. The two alternatives here are the rapid prototyping approach and the traditional life cycle approach. The former is most commonly used, although some of the nonautomated versions of KA techniques such as cluster analysis, factor analysis, and sorting are more suited to the latter approach which does not require a prototype system to be constructed until after acquiring the bulk of the knowledge.

E. Organizational Environment

The resources that an organization puts into the development of a KBS (in terms of the time and cost of source experts and knowledge engineers) and consequently the commitment that the organization has in the project will depend on: the strategic importance of the KBS to the organization, its past experience with KBS use and development, and its technological culture. In an organization that is experimenting with KBS technology by undertaking a trial development, it can be expected that the

KA method used will be one that produces a working prototype utilising the smallest amount of resources. On the other hand, in organizations where the importance of, and commitment to, KBS development is greater, the KA technique selected will be one that is more specifically appropriate for the particular application, and multiple techniques might also be used. This may be done at the expense of a longer KA period to achieve a KBS quality level commensurate with the importance of the project. Similarly, organizations with more KBS development experience and strong technological cultures can be expected to use more complex KA techniques.

DEPENDENT VARIABLES

Measuring the two dependent variables of the model, 1) the quality of the KBS or KB developed (product), and 2) the quality of the KA process, are the most difficult aspects of undertaking KA research because of various problems related to the operationalization of the constructs.

A. Quality of the KBS/KB

As a construct, the quality of a KBS/KB is difficult to operationalize as a reliable, valid measure. Four different aspects of quality could be considered:

1) the representational *validity* of the KB/KBS to its source;

2) the *value* of or the perceived benefits obtained from utilizing the KBS;

3) the *acceptance* and use of the KBS/KB by its intended users; and

4) the *design* aspects of the KB especially in terms of its ease of maintenance and change.

A.1 Validity

Benbasat and Dhaliwal (1988) propose that the validity of a KBS is the degree of its *representational homomorphism* with the source system it is intended to replicate (e.g., a human expert), and that such validity has two components: structural and behavioural. Behavioural validity involves comparing the KBS output to the source expert's recommendations. Structural validity is determined by obtaining the following measures of homomorphism between the KBS and its source: domain and range correspondence, operational (event) correspondence, grain size (level of detail) correspondence, abstraction level correspondence, construct correspondence, meta-knowledge correspondence, and correspondence in terms of the set of primitives used.

Johnson's (1983) view of validity is similar, with the quality of KBS/KB construct having outcome (behavioural validity) and reasoning (similar to operational correspondence of structural validity) components. He further suggests that KBS which reason using the same process as the expert and arrive at the same conclusion can be considered to be superior to those that arrive at the same conclusion, but with a different line of reasoning. Thus both reasoning and outcome evaluations should be obtained.

A.2 Value

This measures utility as identified by users based on actual or perceived benefits as applied to their problems. Specific measures would be user's opinion as to how well the KBS solves the problems for which it was built and actual cost savings that the KBS generates after being put into use (e.g., in the case of R1/XCON at DEC).

A.3 Acceptance

Hayes-Roth et al., (1983) argue that the ultimate test of the quality of a KBS is the level of acceptance of the system by the end users, and the extent to which the users depend on it for expert consultation. Thus, such a measure of quality would be the degree to which the KBS is being used by its user community as compared to the source expert. Other measures would include evaluations of *usability* such as different aspects of the interface: ease-of-use, naturalness, and flexibility.

A.4 Design

The quality of the KB design can provide useful measures of the dependent variable. These include measures of completeness, modularity, cohesiveness of subunits (e.g., rules), coupling between subunits, consistency between rules, ease of maintenance and ease of expansion. Such measures can be obtained by objective benchmark testing or through judgement by a panel of KBS experts.

B. Quality of the KA Process

The quality of the KA process is associated with the resources put into the development of the KBS/KB. The effort, cost, and time of the source expert(s) and the knowledge engineer are the major determinants of the quality of process. Since both knowledge engineers and source experts are scarce and costly resources, minimizing their individual efforts and their interaction time is clearly desirable. This has been the major motivation for building automated KA tools that reduce the need for interaction and communication between the two parties. However, since the central objective of KBS development is to build high quality KBS, it makes little sense to build KA tools that optimize the KA process at the expense of system quality. This may be especially relevant to the use of automated KA tools that efficiently capture only a fixed subset of the total set of different types of knowledge required for a particular KBS application.

III. CONCLUDING COMMENTS

Given the paucity of empirical work in investigating the efficacy of various KA techniques and the factors that lead to selection of the appropriate KA technique, we believe that the model proposed in this paper is a logical starting point to guide studies in this increasingly important area relating to the development and use of KBS technology in organizations.

BIBLIOGRAPHY

Anderson, J.R., "Acquisition of Cognitive Skill," *Psychological Review*, Vol. 89, 1982, pp. 369-406.

Benbasat, I., and Dhaliwal, J.S., "A Framework for the Validation of Knowledge Acquisition," *Proceedings of the Third Knowledge Acquisition for Knowledge-Based Systems Workshop*, AAAI, Banff, November, 1988.

Buchanan, B.G., et al., "Constructing an Expert System," in Hayes-Roth, R., Waterman, D.A., and Lenat, D.B., (eds.), *Building Expert Systems*, London: Addison-Wesley, 1983.

Burton, A.M., Shadbolt, N.R., Hedgecock, A.P., and Rugg, G., "A Formal Evaluation of Knowledge Elicitation Techniques for Expert Systems," *Proceedings of the First European Workshop on Knowledge Acquisition for Knowledge-Based Systems*, Reading University, September, 1987.

Chandrasekaran, B., "Towards a Taxonomy of Problem Solving Types," *The AI Magazine*, Winter/Spring, 1983, pp. 9-17.

Chomsky, N., *Aspects of the Theory of Syntax*, Cambridge, Mass.: MIT Press, 1971.

Davis, R. and Lenat, R.B., "Knowledge Acquisition," *Knowledge-Based Systems in Artificial Intelligence*, 1986, pp. 276-408.

Ericsson, K.A. and Simon, H.A., *Protocol Analysis*, Hillsdale, NJ: Erlbaum, 1984.

Fellers, J.W., "Key Factors in Knowledge Acquisition," *Computer Personnel*, Vol. 11, No. 1, May, 1987.

Feigenbaum, E.A., "The Art of Artificial Intelligence: Themes and Case Studies of Knowledge Engineering," *Proceedings from the AFIPS Conference of the 1978 National Computer Conference*, 1978, pp. 227-240.

Feigenbaum, E.A., "Knowledge Engineering for the 1980's," Computer Science Dept., Stanford University, 1982.

Gaines, B.R., and Shaw, M.L.G., "New Directions in the Analysis and Interactive Elicitation of Personal Construct Systems," in *Recent Advances in Personal Construct Technology*, Shaw, M.L.G., (ed.), London: Academic Press, 1981, pp. 147-182.

Hayes-Roth, R., "The Industrialization of Knowledge Engineering," *Proceedings from the Symposium on Artificial Intelligence Applications in Business*, New York, May 1983.

Hayes-Roth, R., Waterman, D.A., and Lenat, D.B., *Building Expert Systems*, Reading, MA: Addison-Wesley, 1983.

Johnson, P.E., "What Kind of Expert Should a System Be?," *The Journal of Medicine and Philosophy*, Vol. 8, 1983, pp. 77-97.

Johnson, P.E., "The Expert Mind: A New Challenge for the Information Scientist," in Bemelmans, M. A. (ed.), *Beyond Productivity: Information System Development for Organizational Effectiveness*, Amsterdam: Elsevier Sciences Publishing, 1984.

Keen, P., and Scott-Morton, M., *Decision Support Systems: An Organizational Perspective*, Reading, MA: 1978.

Michalski, R.S., "A Theory and Methodology of Inductive Learning," in Michalski, R.S., Carbonell, J., and Mitchell, T.M., (eds.), *Machine Learning*, Palo Alto: Tioga Press, 1983.

Quinlan, J.R., "Learning Efficient Classification Procedures and their Application to Chess Endgames," in Michalski, R.S., Carbonell, J., and Mitchell, T.M., (eds.), *Machine Learning*, Palo Alto: Tioga Press, 1983.

Warbelow, A., Knowledge Acquisition for Expert System Development. Unpublished Research Proposal, Harvard Business School, 1986.

Welbank, M., "Knowledge Acquisition: A Survey and British Telecom Experience," *Proceedings of the First European Workshop on Knowledge Acquisition for Knowledge-Based Systems*, Reading University, September, 1987.

Expert Systems in Economics, Banking and Management
L.F. Pau et al. (Editors)
© *Elsevier Science Publishers B.V. (North-Holland), 1989*

DATA-DRIVEN ASSESSMENT AND DECISION MAKING

Stuart L. Crawford, Robert M. Fung, & Edison Tse

Advanced Decision Systems, 1500 Plymouth Street, Mt. View, California 94043, U.S.A.

In domains such as market research, insurance, and forecasting, accurate and timely assessments in the face of uncertainty, and rational decisions based upon those assessments, are crucial to success. This paper describes a multidisciplinary approach to decision support systems with which decision makers can use a database of observations to automatically generate probabilistic judgments. Using these judgments, specific evidence from the situation at hand, and the possible decision alternatives, the decision support system generates a prototype decision model. Using this model an optimal decision is calculated, as is the value of gathering additional information.

1 INTRODUCTION

In domains such as market research, insurance, and forecasting, accurate and timely assessments in the face of uncertainty, and rational decisions based upon those assessments, are crucial to success. Although rule-based expert systems for assessment and decision making are emerging as tools in these domains, inadequate mechanisms for combining uncertain information are often used and, in addition, such systems depend on experts for all judgments (*e.g.*, rules) in the presence of uncertainty. However, it has been established [7] that it is difficult to make unbiased, consistent judgments in the presence of uncertainty. Making important business assessments and decisions based upon the use of inadequate mechanisms for combining suspect judgments is clearly undesirable.

Consider, however, a software system where a decision maker interactively uses a database of observations to generate probabilistic judgments. Using these judgments, specific evidence from the situation at hand, and the possible decision alternatives, the decision support system generates a prototype decision model. Using this model an optimal decision is calculated, as is the value of gathering additional information. The end result of such activity is a report citing previous cases, the pros and cons of various decisions and, finally, a recommendation for action.

We feel that the realization of this scenario will benefit assessment and decision making. From this scenario, we abstract four guiding principles:

1. the ability to induce domain knowledge from observed data,

2. the use of a theoretically sound evidential reasoning mechanism,

3. a normative, decision theoretic approach to forming recommendations, and

4. an understanding that the system's goal is to *support*, not replace, the human decision maker.

Although AI has much to offer, a multidisciplinary approach to these problems seems most promising, and the fields of decision analysis and statistical data analysis appear particularly suitable for integration with AI. Our efforts have concentrated on the integration of specific tools from these fields into a testbed for experiments in interactive, data-driven decision making. In particular, we have built upon work in *influence diagrams* [6, 9] and *CART* [1]. In this paper, we describe:

- how these tools are augmented and fused to provide the ability to induce probabilistic models from data (principle 1),
- how the induced models can be used in combination with evidence from the specific situation in order to derive decision theoretic recommendations (principles 2 and 3), and
- how this process fits into a decision support environment (principle 4)

In the sections to follow, both the CART and influence diagrams approaches are described, as is the technique by which these tools are integrated. A simple market survey dataset is used to illustrate the data-driven technique.

2   GENERATING DECISION TREES WITH CART

This section provides a brief description of the CART algorithm. For a more detailed treatment refer to [10], for a complete analysis of alternative procedures for tree error rate estimation, refer to [3, 2] and for the definitive description of CART, refer to [1].

Overview: CART takes as input a learning set, $\mathcal{L}$, consisting of N cases, each of which consists of a *known* class θ and a vector of attribute values that may be boolean, integer, real or nominal. In addition, the data may be both noisy and sparse. The system user has the option of specifying both a *loss function* and *prior probabilities* of class membership, parameters which can be of crucial significance, particularly in diagnostic situations. A classification tree, T, initially consists only of the root node τ_1, containing all of the cases in $\mathcal{L}$. A search is made through the set of possible binary splits of τ_1 until an optimal split s_{opt} is found. For real-valued attributes A, splits take on the form $A \leq r$, where r is a midpoint of any adjacent pair found in the set of unique values attained by A. For categorical attributes which can attain possible values $D_1, \ldots, D_M$, splits take on the form $A \in \{D\}$ where $\{D\}$ is one of the subsets of $\{D_1, \ldots, D_M\}$. Once s_{opt} is located, the root node acquires two descendants, τ_L and τ_R, each of which now contains a subset of $\mathcal{L}$. Geometrically, s_{opt} describes a partition orthogonal to one of the coordinates of the measurement space. The partitioning process is applied recursively to each leaf, continuing until all leaves are too small, contain cases from a single class only, or contain identical measurement vectors. When partitioning ends, the initial tree has grown to become a terminal tree T_{max}. Figure 1 shows how a two dimensional measurement space can be partitioned.

Since, with a noisy domain, T_{max} almost certainly overfits $\mathcal{L}$, it is pruned backwards, yielding a unique, nested sequence of subtrees $\{T_{max} \preceq, \ldots, \preceq \tau_2 \preceq \tau_1\}$, and an error estimation procedure is then applied to the sequence in order to select an optimally sized subtree. Subsequent observations are dropped down the selected tree, and classified according to the class membership of the plurality of cases populating the leaf into which they fall.

Splitting Criteria: Since the tree building mechanism attempts to generate a tree with increasingly homogeneous (pure) nodes, a natural splitting criterion is one which tends to maximize some index of purity. For C classes, using an impurity function ϕ, and defining $p(j|\tau)$ as the pro-

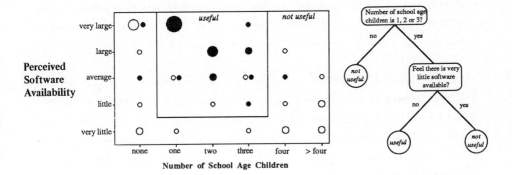

Figure 1: *A simple partitioning of a space spanned by two nominal-valued attributes. Since the space is discrete, points can overlap, and so the area of the circles are proportional to the number of points they represent.*

portion of class j cases at node τ, the impurity of node τ is defined as: $\iota(\tau) = \phi(p(1|\tau), \dots, p(C|\tau))$. Any split s on τ sends a proportion p_L of cases to τ_L and a proportion p_R to τ_R, and the decrease in impurity obtained from splitting τ by s is defined by $\Delta\iota(s,\tau) = \iota(\tau) - p_R\iota(\tau_R) - p_L\iota(\tau_L)$. The optimal split of node τ is selected as the split that yields the maximum decrease in impurity as determined by $\Delta\iota(s,\tau)$.

It turns out that the performance of the classification tree algorithm is relatively insensitive to the choice of ϕ, as long as certain concavity requirements are met. Most commonly used, however, is the *Gini* criterion, which measures class *diversity* at a node.

Pruning the Tree: As described previously, CART avoids the pitfalls of stopping rules by first growing a tree of maximal size, and then pruning backwards in an appropriate manner. The pruning approach is based upon the notion of assigning a *penalty* to the growth of large trees. Defining the cost complexity of tree T as $R_\alpha(T) = \hat{R}(T) + \alpha T$, where α is a real-valued penalty parameter, T is the number of leaves in T and $\hat{R}(T)$ is the *resubstitution estimate* (obtained by classifying the cases in $\mathcal{L}$ by the *same* tree generated from $\mathcal{L}$) of the *true* error rate of T, it is possible, without exhaustive search, to locate that *unique* smallest subtree $T(\alpha)$ of T_{max} which minimizes $R_\alpha(T)$ for fixed α. Although it is not implemented in this manner, minimal cost-complexity pruning can be thought of as a procedure in which α is steadily increased, with pruning occurring at threshold values α', thus yielding a nested sequence of minimizing subtrees.

Error Estimation: Once the sequence of minimizing subtrees has been obtained, a minimum risk subtree, T_{opt} is sought. If $\hat{R}(T)$ is the criterion used to select T_{opt} then T_{max} will always be selected, since $\hat{R}(T)$ decreases with increasing T. However, since $\hat{R}(T)$ is obtained as a result of resubstituting $\mathcal{L}$ into a tree generated from $\mathcal{L}$, $\hat{R}(T)$ is a *downwardly biased* estimate of $R^*(T)$ and therefore inappropriate.

If an independent test sample (*i.e.* a set of training cases *not* used in the initial tree growing procedure) is available, then those cases can be used to select T_{opt} by simply calculating the misclassification rate associated with each subtree in the nested sequence, and choosing the subtree with the best performance. Unfortunately, however, such test samples are rarely available and so the availability of independent training cases is *simulated* via the statistical error estimation technique of *cross-validation* (refer to [1] for details).

3 INFLUENCE DIAGRAMS

Influence diagrams [6] is a technology for probabilistically representing and reasoning with uncertain beliefs, decisions, and preferences. The technology is based on Bayesian probability and utility theory. Although influence diagrams have been most often applied to decision analysis in which the decisions and preferences of a decision maker are central, their utility for situation assessment is increasingly recognized [9, 5].

A successor to decision tree technology, influence diagrams have been shown to be to be more understandable and computationally more tractable than the older technology. These advantages are achieved primarily through the representation of conditional independence assumptions.

The binary independence relation states that two random variables are independent *iff* knowing the value of one does not affect one's beliefs in the value of the other. Conditional independence is a generalization of binary independence and adds a third argument, the conditioning set of variables, to the independence relation. A random variable A is conditionally independent of another variable B *given the value* of variable C *iff* knowing the value of B does not affect one's beliefs about the values of A under those circumstances when the value of C is known.

The representation of conditional independence relations allows for a very compact graph representation, requiring less detail than tree representations. This is because variables represented in the graph need only be connected to their conditioning set. Conditional independence has also been shown to correspond well to concepts of causality [8] Because of these features, influence diagrams tend to be more understandable and computationally tractable to users than decision trees are.

Representation: An influence diagram models a situation with respect to some problem-solver and may involve states of the world, decisions, or preferences. An influence diagram is a collection of nodes and arcs organized into a *directed acyclic graph.* There are four different types of nodes: state nodes, decision nodes, value nodes, and evidence nodes, each of which have meaning only with respect to their *predecessors.* The predecessors of a node X are defined as those other nodes that have arcs pointing to X, and a node, along with its predecessors, can be thought of as a model of a process. The conditional independence assumptions state that a node's "value" is determined by the "values" of its predecessors and that given a set of values no other knowledge will affect the result. Throughout this discussion, Figure 2 is used as to illustrate each kind of node.

A *state node* represents a set of mutually exclusive and exhaustive states in the world about which the problem-solver is uncertain. A state node, along with its predecessors, represents a model for determining one's belief in the values of the node. In Figure 2, for example, the "product usefulness" state node represents a set of states ({*useful, not-useful*}) about which the decision maker is uncertain. A *decision node* represents a state of the world over which the problem-solver has control, and predecessors of a decision-node represent information known at the time of the

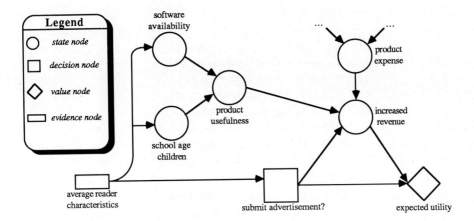

Figure 2: *An influence diagram for the market survey dataset.*

decision. In Figure 2, for example, the "submit advertisement?" decision node has evidence nodes as predecessors, and this evidence is information known at the time of the decision. A *value node* is a deterministic node which represents the problem-solver's preferences based on selected world states. Predecessors to a value node represent the world states in which the problem-solver has direct interest. Finally, *evidence nodes* represent acquired information bearing upon a particular situation. In Figure 2, for example, the evidence nodes contain information about the typical readers of the publications under consideration.

Inference: Several techniques are available for making inferences (*i.e.*, reaching conclusions) from an influence diagram. If decisions are represented in a diagram, the typical result of inference is an optimal decision strategy based on the preferences of the problem-solver and uncertainties about the world's state. If only states and evidence are involved, the typical result is posterior beliefs of a set of states based on all of the evidence. Two primary inference techniques have been proposed by Shachter [9] and Pearl [8].

Structure Composing: In rule-based systems, it is often the case that one wishes to use the *same* knowledge under different circumstances. This is also the case for influence diagrams, and this need is met via the technique of *structure composing*, which allows large, complex, situation-specific models to be built (composed) from smaller, more generic models. Structure composing involves the construction of models that typically rely on general models of behavior as building blocks. These general models are activated by a pattern matching process and at some later time may be added to the base model being built. The set of activated models change as new evidence is received about the situation and as models from the set are added to change the base model.

The model fitting and addition tools are the core structure composing tools. They provide the machinery for building up new models using existing models as building blocks. The model fitting tool finds how building models can be "fitted" to a base model, and displays the information to the user. The user or application program chooses a building model and uses the model addition

Category	Description	Collection Method
Personal	Descriptions of the potential customer	Questionnaire
Perception1	Potential customer's perceptions of the computer's attributes	Questionnaire
Perception2	Manufacturer's perceptions of the computer's attributes	Internal Interview
Actual	Actual computer attributes	Technical specifications
External	External economic indicators	Newspaper

Table 1: *Attribute categories for the market survey data.*

tool to modify a base model with the chosen building model. In model addition, models are fused by "docking" nodes of the base model with nodes in the building model. The docking process involves matching pairs of nodes, such that each pair consists of a base model node and a building model node. To be docked together, two nodes must meet certain compatibility requirements. Modifications are often necessary to make a pair of nodes compatible and such modifications can change other nodes in the models. This is the primary difficulty in matching models since attempts at docking multiple pairs of nodes can cause inconsistencies between the models and therefore make a docking infeasible. Docking of a building model to a base model can often take place in multiple consistent configurations. The function of the model fitting tool is to determine all the consistent configurations that a building model can be docked (*e.g.*, connect) to the base model. A docking configuration is specified by a model-substitution.

Given a model-substitution, the model addition tool rechecks the consistency of the model-substitution and then modifies the base model with the particular docking configuration of the building model called out by the model-substitution. Checking consistency is necessary for two reasons. Since model fitting does not fully go through the process of model addition some of its suggestions are infeasible. The second reason for inconsistencies is that model addition can be performed after other changes to the base model — changes which could make the base model inconsistent with the model-substitution. Comparing the docking process with blackboard systems, model fitting is analogous to the triggering of a knowledge source onto the agenda of a blackboard and model addition is analogous to the execution of a knowledge source.

4 DATA-DRIVEN ASSESSMENT & DECISION MAKING

4.1 Introduction

Consider a scenario in which a microcomputer manufacturer must decide whether to place advertisements in a variety of different publications. Using the data-driven assessment and decision process, the manufacturer collects data from a sample of the target population. This data consists of attributes whose categories are shown as the first two rows of Table 1. The manufacturer then collects data on the set of attribute categories shown as the last three rows of Table 1. The entire set of collected attributes is shown in Table 2.

Once data has been collected, a model for decision making is constructed, as described in more detail in Section 4.2 below. For each publication that is being considered, the manufacturer then

Personal	Perception1	Perception2	Actual	External
SES	sw availability	sw availability	CPU	U.S. inflation
income	sw quality	sw quality	clock rate	local inflation
residence	sw power	sw power	architecture	U.S. unemployment
age	user friendliness	user friendliness	RAM	local unemployment
sex	state of the art	state of the art	disk type	trade imbalance
job type	portability	portability	access time	
education	price	price	operating system	
schoolage children	usefulness	usefulness	printer type	
marital status	market penetration	market penetration	print speed	

Table 2: *Attributes for the market survey data.*

obtains, from mailing lists, information characterizing the "average reader". The mailing list data for each publication is transformed into *evidence* nodes, which are then attached to the model. Finally, for each publication, the model is updated with the newly acquired evidence, and the manufacturer is provided with *a posteriori* distributions for state nodes in the model, as well as optimal decisions with respect to whether or not to invest in advertising. Figure 3 schematically illustrates this process, and each step is described in more detail below.

4.2 Data-driven Assessment and Decision Processes

Data Acquisition: The process of data-driven assessment and decision-making relies upon the assumption that data are readily available. Typically, datasets will consist of sets of *records*, each of which contains a *value* for each of a series of *attributes*. Often, one will wish to acquire data consisting of attributes that are thought to be important yet costly or difficult to obtain (the *model set*). Once acquired, a decision model is built from the model set, and later updated upon the acquisition of more readily obtainable *evidential* attributes (the *evidence set*) that are correlates of attributes in the model set. For example, the directly observable attribute "area of residence" is *evidence* for the routinely unobservable attribute "income".

Note that data acquisition may be an *incremental* process and when the dataset is small, the incremental updating of models as new data is acquired is particularly important. To this end, we have *extended* the CART algorithm [2] so as to allow induced trees to be incrementally updated as new training data is acquired.

CART Application: A single application of CART to the collected dataset will return an explanatory model for the *single* attribute chosen as the class descriptor. Since the goal is to derive a model of the relationship amongst *all* attributes in the dataset, CART is repeatedly applied to the data, using a different attribute as the class descriptor during each iteration. In this way, a *set* of induced models is generated. For datasets with many attributes, some of which may offer little explanatory power, this process is extremely useful in that those attributes that do not contribute to the CART trees will not appear in the final explanatory model, thus simplifying eventual interpretation. CART application is shown *as step 1* of Figure 3. Note that the CART

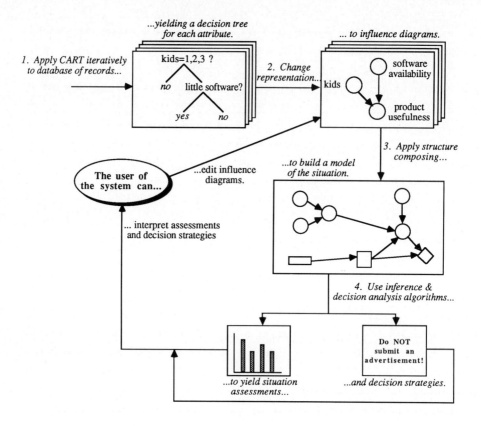

Figure 3: *An overview of the entire data-driven assessment and decision making process*

tree shown in this figure is the same one as is illustrated in Figure 1.

Once an explanatory model for an attribute has been induced by CART, that attribute is *removed* from the dataset for all subsequent iterations. The removal of attributes eliminates the tendency for "explanatory cycles" to be generated. An explanatory cycle occurs when attribute $A1$ is explained in terms of attribute $A2$ during iteration n and then, during iteration $n + p$, attribute $A2$ is explained in terms of attribute $A1$.

When a *causal* ordering of attributes is suspected *a priori*, then choosing those attributes as class descriptors according to the causal ordering will tend to result in simpler decision models being generated. For example, in time-series data, it may be clear that the value of attribute $A1_t$, measured at time t, is dependent upon attribute $A1_{t-1}$ which, in turn, depends upon attribute $A1_{t-2}$. If this is so, supplying CART with class descriptors in the order $\{A1_t, A1_{t-1}, A1_{t-1}\}$ will ensure simplicity in the eventual decision model.

Model Building: Each of the *tree models* generated by CART is transformed into an *influence diagram*. The class descriptor attribute becomes a state node with no successors, and each attribute represented as a CART decision node becomes a predecessor of the class descriptor node. The conditional probability matrix associated with the class descriptor node is filled in based upon probability estimates obtained via attribute proportions in the original dataset. Since the predecessors of the class descriptor node may eventually acquire their own predecessors, prior probability estimates for these nodes are not computed. Once again, attributes with no explanatory power do not appear in the CART trees and therefore never contribute to the structure of the influence diagrams, thus ensuring a parsimonious representation. If a domain expert disagrees with the structure of any of the generated influence diagrams, intervention to alter the form of the diagrams can occur during this step. Model building is shown as *step 2* of Figure 3. Note that the influence diagram shown in this figure is obtained via transformation of the CART tree shown in Figure 1.

Evidence Acquisition & Model Updating: For each situation, *evidence* is acquired and represented separately from the *situation independent* CART induced influence diagrams. Although this perspective is new to decision analysis practice, the incorporation of evidence is strictly Bayesian and thus theoretically sound. On the basis of the evidence that is acquired, the influence diagram fragments obtained during the previous step are assembled into a larger, contiguous model. Assembly occurs by simply connecting diagram fragments that contain the same nodes. When assembly is complete, prior and conditional probability matrices are provided where necessary, as described above. In addition, decision points and values are included as nodes in the larger network. This process is shown as *step 3* of Figure 3. The updated graph shown in Figure 3 represents the final decision model for the market research problem, also shown as Figure 2.

Inference & Decision Analysis: Using techniques of Bayesian inference, *a posteriori* distributions can be obtained for any state node, and quickly updated as new evidence is acquired. In addition, the techniques of decision analysis can be applied to the induced model, resulting in assessments of optimal decisions, the value of added information, the *sensitivity* of the decision to uncertain quantities, and the decision maker's impact on the situation. This process is shown as *step 4* in Figure 3. The top half of step 4 illustrates the display of an *a posteriori* distribution for a state node, and the bottom half shows a recommended decision for a given publication.

5   SUMMARY

Bayesian methods have been criticized due to difficulties in eliciting consistent, stable probabilistic judgments from domain experts. Furthermore, the elicitation process is expensive and time consuming. This phenomenon is commonly referred to as the knowledge engineering "bottleneck" [4]. However, when sufficient data is available, a data-driven approach to model *induction* provides a feasible means to overcome this bottleneck.

Until recently, most decision-rule induction algorithms were inadequate in domains where available data is real-valued, errorful and sparse. The CART algorithm, however, provides a theoretically justified mechanism for dealing with data of this kind. CART takes as input a training set consisting of a set of observations, each of which is composed of a *known* class assignment and a vector of observations. The output from CART is a disjunctive set of decision rules, represented in the form of a binary decision tree. The tree is a parsimonious, easily interpretable representation of induced domain expertise with which new observations can be quickly classified. Iterative application of CART using each attribute as a class descriptor generates a set of trees which, *en masse*, explain the entire dataset. Transforming the CART trees into separate influence diagrams yields a set of parsimonious, consistent, readily interpretable models that represent the relationships among *all* the attributes in the situation. Finally, the process of *structure composing* allows the influence diagram representation to be augmented, thus providing the ability to build large, situation-specific models from smaller, more generic models.

To summarize, we have developed a new mechanism which allows for the induction of models from observed data. The induced models can subsequently be used in a decision analytic framework. This mechanism is part of a larger effort to provide an environment based upon the principles enumerated in Section 1. We believe adherence to these principles can substantially improve upon current approaches to the computer support of decision making.

REFERENCES

[1] L. Breiman, J. H. Friedman, R. A. Olshen, and C. J. Stone. *Classification and Regression Trees.* Wadsworth, Belmont, 1984.

[2] Stuart L. Crawford. Extensions to the CART algorithm. *International Journal of Man-Machine Studies*, 1988. In print.

[3] Stuart L. Crawford. *Resampling Strategies for Recursive Partitioning Classification with the CART Algorithm.* PhD thesis, Stanford University, Stanford, California, 1987.

[4] Edward A. Feigenbaum. Expert systems in the 1980's. In A. Bond, editor, *State of the Art Report on Machine Intelligence*, Maidenhead: Pergamon-Infotech, 1981.

[5] Robert M. Fung. *Structure Composing for Situation Assessment.* PhD thesis, Stanford University, Stanford, California, 1988.

[6] R.A. Howard and J.E. Matheson. Influence diagrams. In R.A. Howard and J.E. Matheson, editors, *The Principles and Applications of Decision Analysis, vol. II*, Menlo Park: Strategic Decisions Group, 1981.

[7] D. Kahneman and A. Tversky. Judgement under uncertainty: heuristics and biases. In P. Slovic D.Kahneman and A. Tversky, editors, *Judgement Under Uncertainty: Heuristics and Biases*, Cambridge: Cambridge University Press, 1982.

[8] Judea Pearl. Fusion, propagation, and structuring in belief networks. *Artificial Intelligence*, 29, 1986.

[9] Ross D. Shachter. Intelligent probabilistic inference. In L.N. Kanal and J.F. Lemmer, editors, *Uncertainty in Artificial Intelligence*, Amsterdam: North-Holland, 1986.

[10] Terry. M. Therneau. *A Short Introduction to Recursive Partitioning.* Technical Report ORION 021, Stanford University Statistics Department, Stanford, California, 1983.

Expert Systems in Economics, Banking and Management
L.F. Pau et al. (Editors)
© *Elsevier Science Publishers B.V. (North-Holland), 1989*

A METHODOLOGY FOR CAPTURING TECHNOLOGY VIA NEURAL NETWORKS

Arie Ben-David* and Yoh-Han Pao**

*School of Business Administration, The Hebrew University of Jerusalem, Mount Scopus, Jerusalem 91905, Israel. Phone: 02-8832235, 883449

**Center for Automation and Intelligent Systems Research, Case Western Reserve University, Cleveland, Ohio 44106, USA. Phone: 216-368-4040

ABSTRACT

The tasks being addressed here are automated process design and multiple fault troubleshooters for complex industrial applications. The processes of interest are nonlinear and they are of high dimensions. Typically, they are not supported by a well established theory. Traditionally expert systems techniques are likely to be inadequate for such tasks. A tremendous knowledge engineering effort may be involved, and potentially a huge set of rules can result by using pure rule based approaches. Traditional statistical methods, on the other hand, such as nonlinear regression analysis, may be found inadequate as well. They require prior knowledge regarding the phenomenon under investigation.

A methodology is presented which effectively deals with such applications. It is based upon a hybrid of neural networks and the rule based approaches. By using the methodology, one can construct self improving expert systems which combine actual examples and domain knowledge. The architecture has been successfully implemented in a major Cleveland based chemicals manufacturer facilities. We describe the application and also discuss some interesting implementations issues.

Keywords: Neural networks, learning from examples, rule based systems, nonlinear regression, process simulation.

1. INTRODUCTION

Neural networks are gradually being accepted as a suitable tool for various applications, as demonstrated by the long list of applications presented by Caudill [1]. Pattern recognition application of neural networks is described by Hinton and Kevin [2]. Utilization of the model for signal analysis can be found in Sejnowski and Rosenberg [3]. Hopfield and Tank [4] used neural nets for optimization. Pao and Sobajic [5] proposed means for incorporating them in adaptive control applications.

To date, less has been said about the usefulness of neural networks for capturing knowledge about complex manufacturing processes. We report here some very encouraging findings regarding this issue, hoping this will assist in paving the way for a wide spread harnessing of the model for such applications.

We show that by utilizing the models in an appropriate architecture, one may not have to use super or special purpose computers for solving practical industrial problems. Rather, there are very good chances that by using existing hardware one can accomplish very useful results. This observation is based upon several neural networks related projects we were and are involved in. One of these applications, currently running at a major Cleveland based chemicals manufacturer, will be shortly described.

2. THE DOMAIN

The domain being studied is chemistry. After fifteen components, in particular application discussed here, are mixed and processed in order to meet certain product properties, such as heating temperature, color, acid resistivity, etc.

The designer's problem is to find a composition which will eventually meet the product's specifications. Up to date, no theoretical model of the process of interest is known. Consequently, domain experts are relying upon the history of previous compositions, stored in a database, and upon their experience. They fetch the 'closest neighbor' formula from the database and gradually modify this 'basic formula' to meet the specifications.

Components have conflicting effects on the various properties. Furthermore, some of the effects are state (or composition) dependent, and may vary both in magnitude and in sign. As a result, experts prefer to attack one property at a time. At each iteration, up to three ingredients are changed in order to bring one property closer to its constraint without causing a deterioration with respect to the rest. An attempt to deal with more than one property at a time may easily get out of hand.

Each iteration involves substantial cost, since the new properties are to be measured at a lab (a procedure which takes a couple of hours). Getting to the proper formula can last a couple of days to several weeks.

The system recommends a base formula and iteratively guides a lab technical what changes to make to the current composition in order to faster meet the product's specifications. Program users need less expertize relative to what has been necessary before using this tool.

2.1 The Role of Neural Networks

A designer of a computerized process design or troubleshooting system of the above nature must resort to a simulation of the process. One may attack the problem in one or more the following ways in order to construct an appropriate model:

- Express the model as a rule based system
- Use regression analysis of some sort
- Utilize neural networks

The first approach has been used, for instance, by Herrod and Richel [6] for glass annealing simulation, and by Kumar and Ernst [7] in the WAX system. Process simulation using production rules can be very complicated in terms of knowledge acquisition when no theory exists for a complex phenomena. Rule-base maintenance and response time may also be severe obstacles. In particular, the task is difficult when nonlinear and high dimension processes are involved. Learning, too, is a problem, and the resulting systems are typically resorting to complicated meta-rules.

Regression analysis is a very attractive alternative when compared to the first, since no knowledge engineering effort is required, just examples. However, the major problems with the utilization of regression models is the need to assume the function and layer to evaluate its fitness. The complexity of a regression analysis explodes exponentially. Assuming a composition of N statistically significant components, one needs T^N trials for evaluating just T functions of each independent variable. For example, checking just linear, quadratic, logarithmic and geometric forms of each of the 12 components involves $1.677 \times (10^7)$ combinations.

A neural nets model is another alternative by which one can reconstruct an approximation of the mapping functions from inputs to outputs. The procedure of defining neural networks also involve trial and error. However, the search space is significantly smaller when compared to the one using regression.

Before discussing this point let's have a brief look at the computational model itself. We consider here a feedforward neural net described by Rumelhart [8]. Figure 1 shows a typical semi-linear neural network configuration.

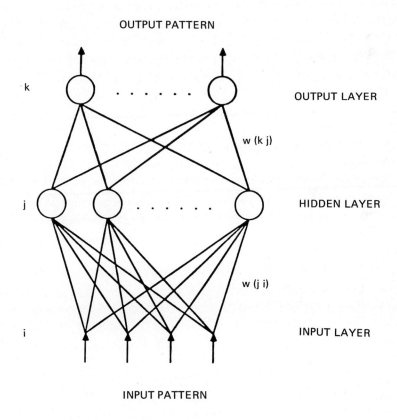

FIGURE 1
Schematic Illustration of Semi-linear Feedforward Net

The output of the j-th node, o_j, is a sigmodial function of its inputs:

$$o_j = 1/\{1+\exp[-(net_j + \theta_j)]\} \tag{1}$$

where θ_j is a threshold and net_j is the sum $w_{ji} * o_i$ over all incoming connections.

A network configuration is determined by its topology, thresholds and weight. The target is to find a configuration which will minimize the energy, or the total error. Minimization of a net's energy can be achieved by using a gradient descent algorithm, where the thresholds and weights are modified during backward propagation of the errors, possibly by using the formula:

$$\Delta w_{kj}(n+1) = \eta * \delta_k * o_j + \alpha * \Delta w_{kj}(n) \tag{2}$$

$\Delta w_{kj}(n)$ indicates a change in the kj-th weight during the presentation of the n-th example. 'η' is a learning rate parameter and 'α' is a smoothing factor which assists in preventing oscillations.

There is no guarantee that an arbitrary neural net will actually converge to a global minimum energy state. In this respect, determining the net's configuration is equivalent to the establishment of a nonlinear regression function, where one cannot guarantee that the chosen function is the best possible indeed.

Determining a neural net configuration involves the following decisions:
• number of layers
• number of processing unit in each layer
• learning rate
• momentum factor

Our original problem has, therefore, been reduced. Instead of guessing a regression function with twelve independent variables, one has to deal now with only four parameters. Please note that unlike regression analysis, the number of parameters of the net's configuration is fixed (regardless of the problem size).

In practice, for many applications, one can try three to four learning rates and about the same number of momentum factors. Furthermore, an incremental increase in the number of layers and the number of processing units in each of them generally makes no substantial difference with respect to the convergence behavior of the net. Increasing the number of layers and the processing units does not necessarily improve the net's behavior. On the contrary, a deterioration may result while increasing the net's size too much.

For many practical applications, a configuration of four to six layers, each composed of three to fifteen processing units, is sufficient. A comprehensive 'bag of tricks' is beyond the scope of this paper. For now it is sufficient to mention that we have found more than twenty trials for finding a proper network topology to be very rare. Furthermore, a 'bad' configuration can usually be detected very early.

3. THE ARCHITECTURE

Neural nets have many advantages, as has been mentioned above. The more examples presented to the system, the better. However, one cannot entirely rely upon predictions, regardless of the method being used. For that reason, the nets are augmented with rule based components.

Figure 2. shows the general architecture of the system. Two types of pretrained nets are used for process simulation. The first net provides the composition out of desired properties. The second deals with the inverse problem and predicts the properties given a composition.

The neural net at the top of Figure 2 provides the base formula. This component constitutes an associative memory and it is much more efficient compared to the simple 'nearest neighbor' retrieval from previous examples stored in some sort of a data base. Forward propagation of a layerwise fully connected net of size N (layers) on M (units in each) involves $(N-1) * M^2$ addition operation and $M * N$ logistic function evaluations. Typical values of N and M in the domain we deal with are five and twelve, respectively. Consequently, very decent computation effort is involved, even for a common microprocessor. Unlike nearest neighbor algorithms, the complexity of a prediction computation is determined by the net's parameter - it is not a function of the training set size.

Any prediction is naturally susceptible to errors. Field tests must be carried out in order to verify the products' properties before any mass production can take place. When the predictions are accurate, within pre-defined margins - the algorithm successfully terminates, and no new information can be gained for future use.

Cases of inaccurate enough predictions are handled differently. The results of the lab test , that is, the actual properties, are stored for further network training. We will discuss this point in the Implementation Section. Meanwhile, though the network has failed to predict accurately enough, due to lake of sufficient relevant examples, an actual product design problem is to be solved.

At this point, a rule based component is invoked. This component iteratively suggests possible modifications to the base formula by applying actual versus desired properties on a set of production rules.

The rule based module also drives the second neural network shown in Figure 2. All the potential actions are filtered through the network in order to evaluate the effects of possible changes in the composition on the various properties before recommendations are issued. The selected plans are those which are anticipated to bring the composition to an acceptable state faster and cheaper than the others.

The main advantage of this architecture is that it enables to avoid defining many complicated rules which must explicitly take into account the effects of each possible change on every property. Rules in the system are rather few and simple. They assume monotonicity of the effects on the properties and deal with one property at a time. What enables these simplified assumptions not to disturb the correctness of the recommendations is the neural net which filters out inaccurate rules, rather cheaply. One can rightfully treat the rule based component as a driver, or the generator, component of the process simulation, and the neural nets as the testing module.

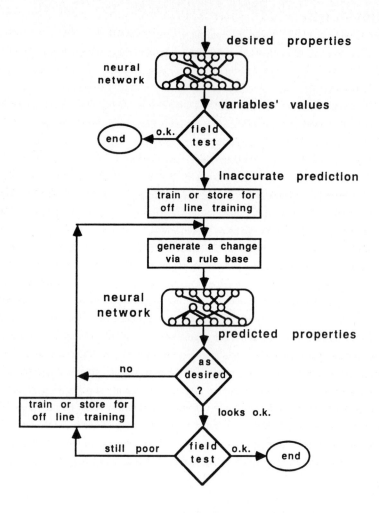

FIGURE 2
A Hybrid of Neural Nets and Rule Base

A lot of knowledge engineering effort has been saved by using this strategy. Conflicts occasionally occur between the rules and the net's predictions. This is not surprising, taking into account the simplistic nature of the rules and the fact that examples for training the nets, as well as computer resources, see the Implementation Section, were quite limited. Since two different sources of information are inherent in the system - expert rules and actual observation, only those actions in which both the net and the rules agree, are selected.

About 75 percent agreement rate and the existence of multiple possible solutions leaves three to five agreeable candidate actions in most cases. The above approach is by far better and more cost effective when compared to an attempt to bring the production rules module closer to perfection, as done in most expert systems. Recommendations which are agreeable both the experts' rules and the neural nets are displayed, closer-to-target first. Once selected, a plan is carried out and a field test is performed. Again, bad predictions are stored with their respective actual properties for further training, such that future predictions will improve. The rule based component, however, is static. We have found the use of meta-rules in this case to be too expensive and unjustified.

4. IMPLEMENTATION

Neural networks become synonymous to inefficient computation on general purpose machines. This reputation is not entirely justified should one carefully engineer and tailor the application to existing hardware and software capabilities.

Five neural nets are responsible in the system for composition to properties simulation. Each net has 24 inputs and one output. Two hidden payers of sizes seven to ten and six to four, respectively, are used. Each net provides the predictions with variable degrees of accuracy, as required by the specific application.

Although the target machine was an IBM AT of 10 MHz., we have found it too slow for training. Training has been done on DEC's VAX 780 using its efficient Fortran compiler. Training of one of the above nets requires about three cpu hours on the average with 200 examples. The resulting trained nets were imported to the AT, where the system is currently running. Training, is, therefore, done off-line, a fact which does not adversely affect the implementation. Some measures, which are beyond the scope of this paper, were successfully taken later in order to further decrease the training cpu time.

The implementation on the AT was done using TI's Personal Consultant, a general purpose expert system shell written in LISP. This programming tool is responsible for the man-machine interface and for the rule based component of the system. The neural networks were implemented on the AT via AI-WARE's AI-NET, which is a C based neural networks development toolkit. A meaningful demo version was available on the AT at the sponsor's facility for beta tests in about three months after the project's starting date. A full version for one line of products was ready in six months. This timetable was definitely impossible had a pure rule based approach been adopted.

5. LIMITATIONS AND CONCLUSIONS

While neural nets are useful tools for AI applications, it is also important to understand their limitations for the type of applications being described. First, neural nets behave as black boxes. It is tough to explain their predictions in terms which are natural to the user. Secondly, although examples are generally easier to derive than rules, they are not always handy.

The architecture described provides partial solution to these difficulties. In term of explanations, one can use the rule base component as a source for explanations. Also, were examples are scares, a rule base component can partially compensate for inaccurate predictions. Consequently, the system may be operational without having to wait for the neural nets to completely 'mature'. As more examples are introduced, the predictions will eventually improve and the reliance upon the rules will decrease.

Neural nets, in general, are taking off from labs to commercial markets. We do hope this paper will contribute to this trend by the introduction of a methodology by which an important class of industrial applications can be implemented on available hardware with relative ease.

REFERENCES

[1] Caudill, M., Neural Networks Primer, IEEE Expert, Vol. 2 No. 12, Vol. 3 No. 2 and 6 1987-1988.

[2] Hinton, G. E. and J. L. Kevin, Shape Recognition and Illusory Conjunctions, Proceedings of IJCAI, pp. 252-259, 1985.

[3] Sejnowski, T. J. and C. R. Rosenberg, NETtalk: A parallel network that learns to read aloud, TR-JJHU/EECS-86/01, Electrical Engineering and Computer Science Dept., John Hopkins University, 1986.

[4] Hopfield, J. J. and D. W. Tank, Neural Computation of Decisions in Optimization Problems, Biological Cybernectics 52, pp. 141-152, 1985.

[5] Pao, Yoh-Han and D. J. Sobajic, Connectionist-net Technology for Intelligent Robotic Control, Technical Report 87-117, Center for Automation and Intelligent Systems Research, Case Western Reserve University, Cleveland, Ohio, 1987.

[6] Herrod, R. A. and Kevin, J. L., Knowledge Based Simulation of a Glass Annealing Process, An AI Application in the Glass Industry, Proceedings of AAAI-86, pp. 800-804, 1986.

[7] Kumar, G. S. and Ernst, G. W., An Expert System Architecture for Predictive Monitoring, Proceedings of the Winter Annual Meeting of the ASME, 1987.

[8] Rumelhart, D. E., Learning Internal Representations by Error Propagation, in: Rumelhart, D. E. and McClelland, J. L., (eds.)Parallel Distributed Processing, Vol. 1, (The MIT Press, 1986).

Expert Systems in Economics, Banking and Management
L.F. Pau et al. (Editors)
© *Elsevier Science Publishers B.V. (North-Holland), 1989*

Representing Commonsense Business Knowledge:
An Initial Implementation

Phillip Ein-Dor & Yaakov Ginzberg
Faculty of Management, Tel-Aviv University
Tel-Aviv 69978, ISRAEL

ABSTRACT

Work on the development of a knowldege base of commonsense business
concepts is described. Two central concepts, *value* and *negotiation*, are
discussed in greater detail.

1. INTRODUCTION

The objective of this report is to describe ongoing work on the
development of a commonsense knowledge base of everyday business
activities; by commonsense knowledge we mean that naive knowledge
generally possessed by every person. This work lies at the nexus of two
important issues - representing common sense in general and representing
business knowledge. On the one hand, the artificial intelligence community
has long recognized representing commonsense knowledge as a most
important and difficult problem and the relative lack of progress with respect
to it has been amply documented, e.g. [1, 2, 3, 4]. On the other hand, business
is one of the most pervasive of human activities, economic transactions being a
feature of all but the most primitive social systems [5]; thus, there is a large
corpus of common sense knowledge which applies to it. Consequently, there
have been calls for representing commonsense business knowledge [6] and
many researchers in commonsense knowledge representation provide
examples with business connotations, e.g. [7, 8, 9].

The preceding considerations motivated the modular implementation of a
knowledge base of business common sense. The modularization follows Hayes'
[10] suggestion to identify and formalize concept clusters relating to specific
areas of knowledge. The first module, described here, deals with the
exchange concept cluster which incorporates concepts such as *buy, sell,
trade, give, take*, etc. Future modules will be devoted to additional concept
clusters including *media of exchange, contractual obligations,* and
employment.

The main focus of this paper is the evolution, in several phases, of the
knowledge base of commonsense concepts related to *exchange*.

2. PHASE 1. CONCEPTUAL DEPENDENCY

The first phase of development was based on Schank's theory of conceptual dependency [11, 12]. In particular, the semantic primitives PTRANS (physical transfer) and ATRANS (transfer of ownership) were exploited in this phase.

Each concept in this phase was represented by a definition frame and expectations. The frames contain a number of fixed slots; additional slots are added as expectations are realized. To demonstrate, the following is a partial definition (in LISP) of the concept *buy*:

```
(setf (get 'buy 'def)
   '(buy (type verb) (meaning atrans)))
(setf (get 'buy 'demons)
   '(((op expect) (slot actor_1)
      (fill        ((check_element_before  (type human))
            (no_gap st_id actor_1)
            (not_same st_id actor_1 actor_2)
      (destroy  ((gap_filled st_id actor_1)
            (end_of_sentence))))).
```

The fixed slots in the *buy* definition are its syntactic role, verb, and its semantic significance, ATRANS. The actor_1 slot, representing the seller, is filled if the expectation to identify a seller is realized. The expectations are represented by functions known here as demons (see also [7] and [11]). In the example, the expectation for actor_1 is evaluated by three demons in the function *fill*. The *check_element_before* demon verifies that the entity before the verb "buy" is represented by a *type human* frame. The *no_gap* demon verifies that this slot is still vacant. The third demon, *not_same*, ensures that the content of the actor_1 slot is not identical to that of the actor_2 slot, i.e. that the seller and the buyer are not the same person. If the three conditions are met, the expectation is realized and the frame under consideration is linked to the actor_1 slot of *buy*.

The actor_1 slot is not necessarily filled, and if any of the demons listed under *destroy* is successful, the expectation concerning actor_1 is cancelled.

The full definition of *buy* contains, in addition to the actor_1 slot, expectations concerning actor_2 (the buyer), obj_1 (the object sold), and obj_2 (the remuneration). Following is the memory structure which results from processing the sentence "DANNY BOUGHT A BOOK FROM SARAH."

```
(1 (danny  (type human) (gender male) (name danny)))
(2 (bought (type verb) (meaning atrans)
        (actor_1 (id_1))
        (obj_1 (id_3))
        (actor_2 (id_5))
(3 (book   (type object) (meaning reading_obj) (quantity one)))
(4 (from   (type preposition)))
(5 (sarah  (type human) (gender female) (name sarah))).
```

The frame for the concept *bought* contains the core meaning of the sentence. The expectations for a seller, a buyer, and an object exchanged are realized by "Danny", "Sarah", and "book", respectively. Thus, the *bought* frame for the sentence under consideration contains pointers to the concepts for these instantiations. The expectation for a remuneration (obj_2) is not realized and so has, as yet, no slot in the frame. The determiner "a" is ignored, as are all determiners, since it does not contribute to the semantics of the sentence.

Following are some examples of the interrogation of this structure. In all examples, Sn ::= assertion n; Q ::= question; A ::= answer; An ::= answer of type n; ====> ::= goal reference.

Q: DID DANNY BUY A BOOK FROM SARAH?
A: YES.
The question completely replicates the original statement so the answer is obvious.

Q: DID DANNY BUY A BOOK?
A: YES.
Q: DID DANNY BUY SOMETHING?
A: YES.
Details from the original statement are omitted in the two preceding questions, but the structure of the original is retained.

Q: DID DANNY BUY FROM SARAH A BOOK?
A: YES.
There is no significance to word order in processed concepts, so the answer is still positive.

Q: WHAT DID DANNY BUY?
A: (book (type object) (meaning reading_obj) (quantity one))
This time the question required reference to a particular slot rather than a simple yes or no.

Q: DID SARAH SELL A BOOK?
A: YES.
Q: WHAT DID DANNY GET FROM SARAH?
A: (book (type object) (meaning reading_obj) (quantity one))

The concept structures for *buy* and *sell* are identical so there is no problem in interpreting the episode as a sale rather than a purchase

Q: DID SARAH SELL TWO BOOKS?

A: NO.

The system knows of only one book sold by Sarah.

Q: HOW MUCH DID DANNY PAY FOR THE BOOK?

A: UNKNOWN.

Q: WHERE DID DANNY BUY?

A: UNKNOWN.

Unrealized and non-existent expectations cause the answer *unknown*.

Although conceptual dependency permits quite impressive surface understanding of concepts, it does not permit deeper implications to be understood because only explicit input statements are represented. From the sentence "Danny bought a book," it should be possible to infer, for example, that the book was transferred to Danny's possession (physically), that Danny now owns the book (contractually), and that Danny can now read the book; these additional consequences are all part of the semantic primitive *buy* but are rarely stated explicitly.

Even more seriously, a purchase episode is much deeper than a mere list of who bought what from whom, when, where, and for how much. For example, the question "Why did Danny buy a book?" brings to mind many potential motivations such as he liked it, he thought it might be interesting, the seller influenced him, or to fulfill some other need, e.g. to give as a gift. Implicit inferences such as these are the essence of common sense.

3. PHASE 2. THE DEEP STRUCTURE OF "EXCHANGE"

This phase was motivated by Hayes' work on commonsense knowledge representation [10, 13]. The principal ideas adopted here are the need to define dense clusters of concepts with multiple interconnections in order to capture the full meaning of the concepts defined and the development of complex knowledge bases by iteration.

The main task in Phase 2 was the definition of many additional, mainly abstract, concepts relevant to a deeper understanding of *exchange*. These include the concept of a transaction (*deal*), awareness (*know_of*), interpersonal communication (*tell*), motivations (*need, like, influence*), preference (*more_than*), value (*val*), and influences on value (*affect_val*).

The additional concepts were defined in frames similar to those of Phase 1. The major difference was that it became necessary to define a new type of expectation concerning relationships between concepts, i.e. inferences. Each concept now contained expectations concerning other relevant concepts in addition to the previously defined expectations concerning slots.

In order to demonstrate this phase, consider the statements:

S1: DANNY DIDN'T LIKE RED PENS.
S2: HE NEEDED A BALL-POINT PEN.
S3: HE SAW A RED BALL-POINT PEN.

We will now assume that all concepts explicit in the input have been mapped into frames, as demonstrated earlier. The following diagram schematically illustrates the resulting process:

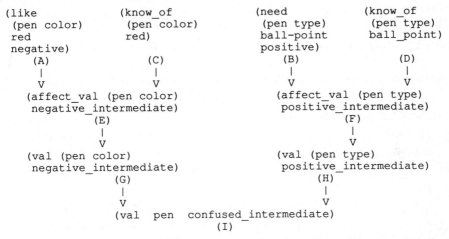

```
(like              (know_of           (need              (know_of
 (pen color)        (pen color)        (pen type)         (pen type)
 red                red)               ball-point         ball_point)
 negative)                             positive)
    (A)                (C)                (B)                (D)
     |                  |                  |                  |
     V                  V                  V                  V
 (affect_val (pen color)             (affect_val (pen type)
   negative_intermediate)              positive_intermediate)
        (E)                                  (F)
         |                                    |
         V                                    V
 (val (pen color)                    (val (pen type)
   negative_intermediate)              positive_intermediate)
        (G)                                  (H)
         |                                    |
         V                                    V
 (val   pen   confused_intermediate)
              (I)
```

S1 results in frame (A), S2 is mapped into frame (B), and S3 into (C) and (D). Inference then proceeds as follows:

1. The concepts (A) and (C) create the concept (E), the meaning of which is that the pen's color negatively affects its value for Danny. This is the result of Danny's aversion to red pens and his awareness of the pen's redness. The *intermediate* qualifier refers to the strength of the effect, alternatives being *strong* and *weak*.

2. The negative effect of the pen's redness (E) gives rise to a negative evaluation of the pen's color(G).

3. The negative effect of the pen's color (G) negatively influences Danny's concept of the pen itself (I). The *confused* evaluation is a result of further processing explained in 6 below.

4. Danny's need for a ball-point pen (B) and his awareness of the pen's ball-pointedness (D) lead to a positive effect of the pen's type (F).

5. The positive effect of the pen's type leads to the inference of a positive evaluation of the pen's type by Danny (H).

6. Concept (H) positively influences Danny's evaluation of the pen itself (I). However, there is already a negative influence on the value of the same pen from concept (G). In the absence of any additional information, and given the inconsistency between (G) and (H), the system infers Danny's confusion concerning the value of the pen.

A feature of the system is its ability to explain its conclusions at any stage of their development. For example:

Q: WHY DID DANNY FEEL CONFUSED ABOUT THE PEN?
A: PROBABLY, BECAUSE THE TRADE-OFF BETWEEN
      POSITIVE: DANNY LIKED THE PEN'S TYPE
      NEGATIVE: DANNY DIDN'T LIKE THE PEN'S COLOR
    WAS CONFUSING TO DANNY

The qualifier *probably* indicates that the conclusion was drawn by the system, and is not explicit in the text.

One way to resolve confusion is by introducing a preference. For example:

S4: BUT DANNY REALIZED HE NEEDED A BALL-POINT PEN MORE THAN HE DISLIKED
    RED PENS.

The effect of the additional information cascades through the inference process, weighting the outcome in favor of a positive evaluation of the pen, as in the following diagram:

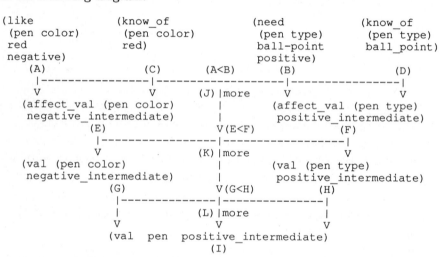

```
(like              (know_of                (need               (know_of
 (pen color)        (pen color)             (pen type)          (pen type)
 red                red)                    ball-point          ball_point)
 negative)                                  positive)
   (A)                  (C)       (A<B)       (B)                  (D)
   |-----------------|--------------------|-----------------|
   V                  V         (J)|more    V                    V
 (affect_val (pen color)          |      (affect_val (pen type)
  negative_intermediate)          |       positive_intermediate)
        (E)                    V(E<F)              (F)
   |-----------------|------------------|
   V                  (K)|more          V
 (val (pen color)        |           (val (pen type)
  negative_intermediate) |            positive_intermediate)
        (G)           V(G<H)             (H)
   |--------------|---------------|
   |              (L)|more         |
   V                 V             V
 (val   pen  positive_intermediate)
               (I)
```

Contrary to the previous case, the conclusion now is that Danny's perception of the pen is positive. This arises from the preference of the concept (H) over (G) as expressed by (L); this in turn was caused by the preference for (F) over (E), expressed by (K), which originated in the explicit statement in the text concerning the preference for (B) over (A) as represented by (J).

This is explained by the system as follows:

Q: WHY DID DANNY LIKE THE PEN?
A: PROBABLY, BECAUSE THE TRADE-OFF BETWEEN
      POSITIVE: DANNY LIKED THE PEN'S TYPE
      NEGATIVE (BYPASS): DANNY DIDN'T LIKE THE PEN'S COLOR
    WAS POSITIVE TO DANNY.

The negative effect of the color is *bypassed* because of the explicit preference expressed in the text.

Continuing the example:

S5: DANNY WAS OFFERED THE PEN FOR TEN DOLLARS, BUT HE DIDN'T LIKE THE DEAL.

This complicates the situation with a further inconsistency between Danny's positive perception of the pen versus his negative view of the transaction offered. The system explains this as follows:

Q: WHY DIDN'T DANNY LIKE THE DEAL?
A: PROBABLY, BECAUSE THE TRADE_OFF BETWEEN
      POSITIVE (BYPASS): DANNY LIKED THE PEN
      NEGATIVE: DANNY DIDN'T LIKE THE PEN'S PRICE (TEN DOLLARS)
  WAS NEGATIVE TO DANNY.

The system infers that Danny's negative evaluation of the deal arose because he values the pen less than its price.

4. CONVERGENCE

It is obviously impossible to demonstrate here the many possible developments of the previous example, not to mention additional examples. Nevertheless, it is clear that the system is far from complete and the process of adding concepts and relations to the knowledge base is virtually endless. An encouraging aspect of the process, however, is that as work progressed, the knowledge base clearly began to converge on a central concept, that of *value*.

In the initial phases, it was invariably necessary to introduce many changes in existing concept definitions and to add or modify relations between concepts every time a new example was introduced. Eventually, however, the knowledge base became able to cope fully, or almost fully, with more and more examples while fewer additions and changes were required. This is not a new phenomenon and it has been reported in at least two earlier attempts to formalize commonsense knowledge [10, 14]. Convergence thus becomes an indicator that one is on the right track.

5. PHASE 3. NEGOTIATION

The example in the previous section refers mainly to the choice of objects in trade. The concept of *value* plays a central role in achieving a deep understanding of this process. Once an object has been chosen, the natural sequel is to initialize negotiations with the owner of the object in order to acquire it. This process is much more dynamic than the previous one; different offers may be made in the course of a negotiation with different prices and conditions. Elements of goals and interests enter the picture and are expressed as bargaining, attempts at persuasion, etc. The concept of *value* still remains crucial, as people do not decide to buy objects, even after long negotiations, unless the value of the deal is positive for them. However, the concept of *value* alone is not sufficient for a full understanding of negotiations.

Schank's [9] memory organization packets (MOPS) were adopted in representing negotiation concepts. These knowledge structures are suitable for representing the dynamics of negotiations, participant's goals, and plans for achieving them, in addition to the value concepts. Space does not permit full description of these concepts, which will be demonstrated by means of an annotated example.

S1: DANNY SAW JOHN'S PEN.
S2: HE OFFERED JOHN FIVE DOLLARS FOR THE PEN.
S3: JOHN SAID HE LIKED THE PEN VERY MUCH.
Q: DID DANNY LIKE THE DEAL?
A: PROBABLY, YES.
Q: WHY?
A: BECAUSE DANNY OFFERED THE DEAL.

From the fact that Danny offered the deal, the system infers that he likes it.

Q: DID JOHN LIKE THE DEAL?
A: PROBABLY, NO.
Q: WHY DIDN'T JOHN LIKE THE DEAL?
A: PROBABLY, AS A RESULT OF
        NEGATIVE (STRESS): JOHN LIKED THE PEN.

The stress originates in the words "very much" expressing the strength of John's affection for the pen.

Q: DID THE NEGOTIATION SUCCEED?
A: PROBABLY, NO.

This conclusion follows from John's (inferred) negative attitude to the transaction.

Continuing the example:

S4: DANNY SAID THAT THE PEN WAS NOT VERY GOOD.
Q: WHY DID DANNY SAY THAT THE PEN WAS NOT VERY GOOD.

There are three answers:

A1: DANNY LIKED THE DEAL; PROBABLY, JOHN DIDN'T LIKE THE DEAL;
        DANNY WANTED JOHN TO LIKE THE DEAL TOO.

This is the most general answer.

A2: PROBABLY, DANNY TRIED TO PERSUADE JOHN TO LIKE THE DEAL TOO.

This answer is slightly more detailed than A1 and contains the inference of Danny's attempt to persuade John to agree to the deal. The third answer details the way in which Danny tries to persuade John:

A3: DANNY SAID THAT HE DIDN'T LIKE THE PEN
        ===> JOHN WOULDN'T LIKE THE PEN
        ===> JOHN WOULD LIKE THE DEAL.

Additional developments in the negotiation which the system can follow include:

a. Danny offers a higher price in order to persuade John,
b. John himself asks for a higher price,
c. both sides agree,
d. one of the sides withdraws,
e. negotiation shifts to a different object.

6. DISCUSSION

The uniqueness of this system is in the area of commensense knowledge with which it deals, namely business common sense. To the best of our knowledge this is the first reported attempt to build a knowledge base in this field. A number of important business concepts have been formalized for the first time, including the concepts of *value* and *negotiation*; these enable the system to make inferences on the basis of knowledge implicit in the domain even though not stated explicitly in the text provided.

Many previous ideas and developments were found to be applicable to this domain. In particular, the implementation was influenced by Hayes' theory of concept clusters [10], employs Schank's theory of conceptual dependency [15], represented in frames [8] embedded in goals, plans, and MOPS [9]. The main problem was not so much in identifying the appropriate heuristic representations as in identifying the central concepts and processes around which the knowledge base should be assembled.

A major conclusion of the search for representation formalisms is that there is as yet no comprehensive theory of knowledge representation sufficient to permit adequate formalization of a complex domain such as business. It appears that developing systems of the kind demonstrated here may provide heuristic solutions until a general theory is available. Furthermore, much can be learned from system development efforts concerning the requirement of a general theory of knowledge representation.

Given the pervasiveness of business activity, it is not difficult to visualize potential applications for a knowledge base in this domain; they span the gamut from expert systems to advise consumers on business problems to translating business texts from one language to another.

Three promising directions for further development of the system are 1) inferring the degree of satisfaction of the parties after conclusion of a transaction, 2) deepening the concepts on obligations and legal consequences of transaction, possession, etc., and 3) the addition of knowledge relating to the consequences of deviations from the norms embodied in the knowledge base. Work in this area has already been done by Dyre [7] and the knowledge structures he has defined seem appropriate in the business domain as well.

REFERENCES

[1] Doyle, Jon. "Expert Systems Without Computers, or Theory and Trust in Artificial Intelligence." *AI Magazine* 5, 2 (1984) pp. 59-63.

[2] Israel, David J. "The Role of Logic in Knowledge Representation." *Computer* 16, 10 (1983) pp.37-41.

[3] McCarthy, John. "Programs With Common Sense" in: *Proceedings of the Teddington Conference on The Mechanization of Thought Processes.* (Her Majesty's Stationery Office, London,1960).

[4] McCarthy, John. "Applications of Circumscription to Formalizing Common Sense Knowledge." Stanford University: Working Paper (1985).

[5] Levi-Strauss, Claude. *The Naked Man: Introduction to A Science of Mythology: 4.* (Harper & Row, New York, 1981).

[6] McCarthy, John. "The Common Business Communication Language" in: Albert Endres and Jurgen Reetz (eds.) *Textverarbeitung und Burosysteme.*(R. Oldenbourg Verlag, Munich, 1982).

[7] Dyre, M. G. *In Depth Understanding: A Computer Model of Integrated Processing for Narrative Comprehension* (MIT Press, Cambridge, Mass. 1984).

[8] Minsky, Marvin. "A Framework for Representing Knowledge" in: Patrick Henry Winston (ed) *The Psychology of Computer Vision* (McGraw-Hill, New York, 1975) pp. 211-277.

[9] Schank, Roger C. "Language and Memory" in: Donald A. Norman (ed) *Perspectives on Cognitive Science* (Ablex, Norwood, NJ 1981) pp. 105-146

[10] Hayes, Patrick J. "The Naive Physics Manifesto" in: Donald Michie (ed.) *Expert Systems in The Micro Electronic Age* (Edinburgh University Press, Edinburgh, 1979) pp. 242-270.

[11] Schank, Roger C. and Christopher K. Riesbeck. *Inside Computer Understanding: Five Programs Plus Miniatures* (Lawrence Erlbaum Associates, Hillsdale, NJ, 1981).

[12] Schank, Roger C. and Charles J. Rieger III. "Inference and the Computer Understanding of Natural Language." *Artificial Intelligence* 3, 4 (1974) pp. 373-412.

[13] Hayes, Patrick J. "Naive Physics 1: Ontology for Liquids." University of Essex. Working Paper (1978).

[14] Lenat, D., M. Prakash, and M. Shepherd. "CYC: Using Commonsense Knowledge to Overcome Brittleness and Knowledge Acquisition Bottlenecks." *AI MAgazine* 6, 4 (1986) pp. 65-85.

[15] Schank, Roger C. "Conceptual Dependency: A Theory of Natural Language Understanding." *Cognitive Psychology* 3 (1972) pp. 552-631.

Expert Systems in Economics, Banking and Management
L.F. Pau et al. (Editors)
© *Elsevier Science Publishers B.V. (North-Holland), 1989*

FUNCTIONAL PROTOTYPING:
USING AI TECHNIQUES TO UNTIE KNOTS OF SYSTEMS COMPLEXITY

CHUNKA MUI, LARRY DOWNES, AND LISA C. CURTIS

Andersen Consulting, Arthur Andersen & Co.
33 West Monroe Ave.
Chicago, IL 60603

ABSTRACT

As user sophistication and hardware capability have simultaneously increased, software engineers are asked to build increasingly complex management information systems. Consequently, conventional software engineering practices now collide regularly with application *knots of complexity* which defy traditional analysis and system specification techniques. The result is an incomplete specification that poses a significant risk to the successful development of the target system. In this article, we describe our experiences in the use of functional prototyping to manage these knots of complexity. Functional prototyping is a rapid prototyping approach which incorporates Artificial Intelligence techniques and tools to develop an executable specification of detailed functional requirements.

1.   THE IMPORTANCE OF FUNCTIONAL SPECIFICATIONS

Requirements analysis and specification are the first phases of the conventional software life cycle model. They are concerned with defining the problem that is being addressed and establishing objectives and constraints on the system that is to be built. Specifically, requirements analysis is the process of understanding and recording in a clear form the needs to be met by the target system. Specification, on the other hand, is the process of describing the proposed system to meet the established requirements.[1]

A *functional specification* is the main deliverable of the specification phase. It documents the understanding of the analysis team and communicates this understanding to several important audiences: 1) management, who sponsored the system, 2) users, whose problems the system will address, and 3) the development team, who will build the system. In many ways, the functional specification is the key to the success of the development project. It is used by all parties involved as the definitive statement of the functioning and behavior of the system.

The contents of the functional specification are: 1. External Interfaces, 2. Overall Data Flow, 3. Functional Decomposition, 4. Process Specifications, 5. Expected Changes, and 6. Testing Criteria. While all of these items are important, the focus of our attention is on the detailed functional specification, which is comprised of the functional decomposition and the process specifications. The functional decomposition is a hierarchical breakdown of the processes to be performed by the target system. Then, for each process, a process specification describes the inputs, outputs, and detailed processing logic:

- Inputs describe the information required by the process. This includes incoming data and their sources.
- Outputs describe the information generated by the process. This includes returned data, screens, and reports.
- Detailed processing logic describes the operations that make up the process. This includes logical algorithms, exception conditions, and flow of control.

ption is crucial because it describes the core of the proposed system.
It is a key input to a number of other phases of the development process, such as:

User Acceptance - The detailed functional specification communicates the analyst's understanding
of the requirements back to the user. It serves as the primary vehicle of communication both during
and after the analysis and specification processes. It is the agreement between the users and the developers as to what the system will do.

Design - The detailed functional specification feeds both the architectural and detailed design activities. In architectural design, the functional decomposition and input/output flow of the processes
is used to design the structure of the system to be built. This involves the definition of subsystems
and modules and the interfaces between them. In detailed design, the architectural design and the
detailed processing logic descriptions are considered together for the definition and selection of algorithms and data structures for each process.

Testing - The detailed functional specification represents part of the shared understanding of the
analysis team concerning what the system should do and, as such, it is one of the documents against
which the finished system is tested. It is used to develop test conditions and expected results for both
unit and system testing.

Project Management - The detailed functional specification also represents the understanding of
the size and complexity of each module. It is used to plan resources needed to develop software components. Resources include required skill levels of the project team, time allocated to develop the
components, and tools to support the development process. The detailed functional specification is
also used to identify the potential problem areas that may be encountered during development.

2. KNOTS OF COMPLEXITY

Unfortunately, the complexity of large applications often makes it difficult to develop adequate detailed functional specifications. Our experience is that today's large management information
systems tend to have areas of functionality which cannot be correctly specified using conventional
software engineering methods and tools. We refer to these difficult functions as knots of complexity
within the overall system both because of their complexity vis-a-vis the other parts and because of the
effect they have on the stomachs of project managers.

The majority of functions in an MIS system are concerned with simple transformations of data,
which can generally be specified cleanly with traditional structured analysis and algorithm design.
The knots of complexity usually arise when complex rules or regulations need to be encoded, or when
extensive decision-making processes are being automated.

Examples of knots of complexity are well known: tax calculations in payroll systems, pricing in
order entry systems, and inventory allocation in distribution control systems. These are the functions
often associated with software development horror stories--stories in the "we've built this module five
times and it still doesn't work right" vein. One can probably imagine at least one such function in any
major system. In earlier generations of the application, these functions may have been considered un-
doable and left to manual procedures, or worse, the failure to ever get that portion of the system
working may have meant indefinitely delayed implementation and eventual cancellation of the
development project. Theses are cases where analysts, in order to understand the processing of low
level subtasks, often must dig through manuals describing remarkably complex procedures that cross
departments and personnel, many of which are ad hoc and often contradictory.

Later in this article, we present a case study from an oil and gas accounting system. That system
contained a knot of complexity in the form of a materials transfer accounting function which codified
complicated accounting procedures for the recording of material transfers between oil lease sites.

3. CONVENTIONAL APPROACHES

Conventional approaches such as Structured Analysis[2] and SADT are typically used for developing detailed functional specifications. These approaches rely on a process in which the analyst elicits the requirements from the user and translates those requirements into specifications. Typically this is done in a top down manner where the processes are decomposed using tools such as data flow diagrams, structure charts, and data dictionaries. The detailed processing logic for each process is then specified using tools such as structured English, decision tables, or decision trees. The resulting documents are discussed and confirmed with users. This analysis process relies upon the user having sufficient understanding of the functional requirements in order to support the analyst. It also relies upon the analyst being able to adequately communicate the proposed specification to the user in order to obtain feedback and confirmation.

Several problems emerge from the application of conventional structured analysis techniques to knots of complexity. Since these are functions that users themselves have trouble "getting their hands around," it becomes correspondingly difficult for them to be communicated as systems requirements. In these situations, the analyst, who is generally not an expert in the application domain, is unable to obtain an acceptable level of understanding of the function. The result is almost certainly an incomplete and incorrect specification.

The methods and tools of structured analysis exacerbate these problems in understanding and communication because they are informal and are not designed for complex processes. They also do not support any verification of consistency, completeness, or correctness of the specification. The more complex the process, the less users are able to follow and review documentation that is generated, leaving neither analyst nor user confident of the validity of the specification. Moreover, the long feedback loop inherent in the standard software development process leads to errors in the specification that are often not even identified until after the system is implemented.

Thus knots of complexity often translate into an incomplete and faulty specification which poses a significant risk to the successful development of the system. Initial misconceptions can have an enormous impact upon the rest of the development effort.[3] Errors in specification can propagate dramatically into the target system, leading to widespread software bugs that are very costly to correct. As is now well understood, the interdependencies of code heighten the impact of changes in the later phases of the system life cycle. A requirements analysis error which might have been easily fixed during analysis could take 100 times as long to fix if detected during the operational phase of the system.

In addition to the added cost of correcting software errors that stem from errors in analysis and specification, a number of other critical problems are propagated to related development phases[4]:

1. *User acceptance* is impossible. The user is effectively locked out of the development process, because there is no clear statement of what is going to be built.
2. *Design* is impossible. There is no accurate specification of the system from which designers can form the basis for a good architectural or detailed design.
3. *Testing* is impossible. There is nothing to test against.
4. Effective *project management* is impossible. There is no basis for accurate planning, resource allocation, or monitoring.

4. PROTOTYPING

Prototyping has been demonstrated to be one approach for overcoming some of the inadequacies of the conventional structured approach to specification and design.[5] It is the process of building an early working version of the system that can be exercised. This allows the understanding of the requirements and the validity of the system specification to be tested and verified during the specification process--instead of waiting until after design and implementation.

Prototyping has become a generally accepted technique for enhancing software quality by resolving ambiguous system requirements in the early phases of the software development process.

It has typically focused on modeling the inputs and outputs identified in the functional specification, such as screens, reports, validation messages, and conversation flows, since these are the components of the application that most directly affect the end-user's job.

In fact, a range of commercial products including screen painters, report generators, and conversation simulators, are widely available to support the development of prototypes. As a result, the development team can give users concrete examples of the external behavior (look and feel) of the ultimate system. This enables the users to evaluate the interface and helps them to articulate their preferences and needs. Prototyping used in this manner has proven to be effective in the development of proper user interaction requirements.[6,7]

Since they focus on *system externals*,[8] however, current prototyping approaches are not suitable for unraveling knots of complexity. By definition, knots of complexity embody complexity in *system internals*. Thus what is needed is a new type of prototyping, *functional prototyping*, which allows us to build working models of the internals of an application's ambiguous components, and do so in a way that will be as accessible to user review as are conventional prototypes.

5.   FUNCTIONAL PROTOTYPING

Functional prototyping is used to model the detailed processing logic of the functional specification, and has become a standard feature of our application development methodology. As with conventional prototyping approaches, working models of the system are built during the analysis phase to clarify requirements and are then used to help in the specification of the target system. But the focus of functional prototyping is on clarifying ambiguous detailed processing logic. It is geared towards specifying complicated decision-making functions, which may involve convoluted reasoning paths, large numbers of intermediate variables, and/or many possible exception conditions.

The functional prototyping methodology relies heavily on concepts and methods pioneered in the AI community for the building of knowledge-based systems. Specifically, a rapid prototyping environment based on the rule-based paradigm is used. In this paradigm, the specification is stated in the form of rules which describe the detailed processing logic of the target system. The rules become an executable specification of the system and allow both the analyst and the user to observe the system's functional behavior. Iterative development and refinement of the specification is supported.

The rule-based paradigm is appropriate for analysis and specification of knots of complexity for a number of reasons:[9]

- Rules provide a natural medium for specifying complex processing logic, since the steps that people employ when solving problems and the laws and regulations which dictate many functions are naturally expressed in rule-like format.

- The modular nature of rules allow for quick and easy modification of the specification as the understanding of the requirements changes and grows. This allows for incremental requirements analysis, which is essential for difficult problems. It also allows the analyst to concentrate on one part of the problem at a time and to explore various reasoning paths in parallel.

- Rules can be expressed in near-natural language and can be used as a communication medium between the analyst and the user. The fact that these easy-to-understand rules are also executable enables and encourages rapid and constant feedback from the user to the analyst.

- The structure of rule-based architectures shield the analyst from early control flow and data typing considerations and allows him to concentrate on the essential functional requirements of the system.

- The rule set is relatively free from design and implementation information and can therefore be used as part of the functional specification without major revision.

It is important to note that even though AI tools and techniques are being applied, functional prototyping is not restricted to the class of problems generally considered for "expert systems." Rather, any decision-making process in an application, even those normally performed algorithmically in procedural programming languages or manually by lower-level users, may be appropriate candidates for the rule-based specification prescribed by functional prototyping. AI simply provides a more appropriate way of representing the logic of complex processes and an automated, highly productive environment for the analyst.

6.   METHODOLOGY

In order to develop the functional prototype, the analyst follows a six phase methodology designed to extract the detailed functional requirements and to develop a rule set representing the specification to meet those requirements. This methodology is shown in Figure 1 and described below:

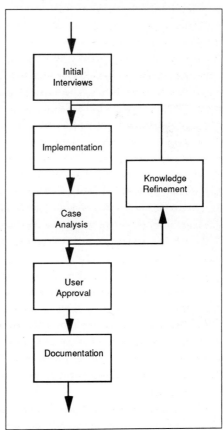

1. *Initial Interviews.* The analysis conducts initial interviews with the user and utilizes actual case data to develop a basic understanding of the function.
2. *Implementation.* In the initial iteration, a working prototype is built as early as possible. In later iterations, the specification is modified and enhanced to deal with refined requirements.
3. *Case Analysis.* The analyst uses both the prototype and additional case data to draw out user feedback.
4. *Knowledge Refinement.* User feedback, prototype test results, and additional case data is used to refine the specification and identify additional requirements. This feeds back into the Implementation phase to iteratively develop de next version of the functional prototype.
5. *User Approval.* The user is satisfied with the prototype and accepts the correctness of the specification.
6. *Documentation.* The specification is translated into the appropriate format for use during the rest of the development effort.

FIGURE 1:
Functional Prototyping Methodology

This methodology relies heavily on the expressive and executable nature of the rules, the rapid feedback allowed by the environment, and the use of actual case data. The analyst strives to build the initial prototype as quickly as possible. This initial implementation is not intended to be complete, but instead acts as a means of quickly gaining user confidence and driving the analysis process. The analyst takes advantage of the executable nature of the specification to elicit user feedback and to continually test the prototype against actual case data.

The methodology also calls for the users to be constantly involved in the evaluation and refinement of the specification. In conventional analysis and specification approaches, this would require users to review actual specification documents, such as structured English, program description languages, and decision tables. But the functional prototyping approach allows them to review actual test cases and results. This allows for more effective user input and makes it easier to develop user confidence in the correctness of the specification. It also makes it easier to obtain user approval once the prototype is finished.

Once all parties involved are satisfied with the correctness of the prototype, the rule set can be translated into the appropriate form for input to other development phases. In current functional prototyping efforts, this has usually been in the form of a manually developed paper specification. We will describe other options, such as automatically produced documentation and code generation, in a later section.

7.   FUNCTIONAL PROTOTYPING TOOLS

The appropriateness of the rule-based paradigm allows us to make use of existing expert systems building tools for the development of functional prototypes. In selecting an appropriate functional prototyping environment, we have developed the following criteria:

1. *The product must support the basic rule-based paradigm.* This includes a high-level rule representation that is easily understood. In addition, a basic inference engine supporting either forward or backward-chaining reasoning is required, as this frees the analyst from having to develop detailed control strategies.

2. *It must be easy to learn.* This is a primary requirement and is quite crucial since the tool will be used by analysts more accustomed to conventional approaches. The tool must allow for widespread use and not be labelled as a tool usable only by specialists.

3. *It must support rule base partitioning.* This allows the analyst to functionally decompose the target function and to separately deal with each subtask. This supports iterative development and also helps in the mapping of the rule base to the specification for the target system.

4. *It must have easy-to-use user interface development facilities, such as screen design and report building features.* This is important for two reasons. It frees the analyst from having to spend a large amount of time developing the user interface, allowing him to focus instead on the system internals. It also encourages user interaction with the prototype, which is important for obtaining feedback.

We have found that the more sophisticated, workstation-based expert systems shells are not appropriate for functional prototyping, since they utilize formalisms which do not map easily back into conventional applications. Most of these products were designed to handle complex problems and include sophisticated representations, such as frames or semantic networks, which do not have corresponding constructs in conventional languages. On the other hand, PC-based shells such as Aion Development System (ADS) and Personal Consultant are rule-based and meet the above criteria.

8. CASE STUDY

In this section, we present a case study based on our experiences during the development of a mainframe-based oil and gas accounting system for a major oil company. The case describes the functional prototyping effort for the materials management function within the inventory control module of the system. Functional prototyping was undertaken because conventional analysis and specification methods were not successfully dealing with the function's complexity. Project management felt that the ambiguity surrounding the function represented a significant risk to the project. A description of this case has also been presented by Weisman.[10]

The materials management function accounted for the transfer of equipment from one oil lease or warehouse to another. The accounting guidelines governing these movements were very complex, especially in cases where the properties were co-owned by more than one oil company. They were also relatively new, so that even the users were not fully comfortable with them. These guidelines dealt with about 35 different types of transfers and contained a large number of permutations of exception conditions.

For example, consider the transfer of a motor from the Independent Oil Company's wholly owned warehouse to a co-owned well site, where Independent owns 70%. Independent may post the book value of the motor as a credit to the warehouse, but they must post the current market value as a debit to the well site. This is because the transfer is considered a change of ownership, so the well-site must be charged the current market value as the purchase price. The difference in prices (book value is usually lower than market value), creates an anomaly on Independent's books. The difference between Independent's portion (70%) and the non-Independent portion (30%) must be clearly accounted for. In addition to the percentage of ownership, other factors such as the condition of the motor, its tax depreciation status, and the location of both the warehouse and the well-site (for tax purposes) must also be considered.

The analysis team consisted of two full-time analysts, one half-time senior analyst, and one part-time user representative. The entire functional prototyping effort lasted approximately five weeks and followed the previously described six phase methodology:

1. *Interviews.* The user spent one day explaining the materials movement function to the analysis team. She described the general process and discussed specific examples. She also gave the team case data for ten different types of material transfers along with the resulting accounting journal entries.

2. *Initial Implementation.* Within a week, the team developed an initial functional prototype that successfully processed the 10 cases. This quick result gave credibility to the process and the user became eager to continue with the development.

3. *Case Analysis.* Additional discussions were held with the user to identify other types of material movements. Additional historical data was retrieved to aid in the analysis and supplemental data was created for situations where historical data could not be found.

4. *Knowledge Refinement.* The functional prototype was refined as errors were uncovered and new situations were identified. After five weeks of development, the prototype was able to process correctly all 35 general types of materials transfers. With the user's further assistance, a total of 95 cases were eventually developed to test the functional prototype.

5. *User Approval.* The output of the functional prototype for each test case was a one page report that identified the case parameters and showed the resulting accounting journal entries. These were used by the user to review the prototype's logic for each type of materials movement. Once all cases

were dealt with adequately, the user endorsed the prototype and approved it as a correct specification.

6. *Documentation.* Once user approval was achieved, the rule-based specification was translated into the standard detailed functional specification format for the project. This included functional decomposition information for 12 processes and process specifications for each of those processes. The process specifications included input/output data element information and detailed processing logic descriptions. The prototype's 25 states and their associated rules, for example, were translated to 98 pages of Warnier-Orr structure charts. In addition to this information, the analysis team also produced a set of test cases which included conditions, cases, and expected results. These were approved by the user for subsequent testing of the final implementation. The documentation process required approximately 3 days.

The functional prototyping effort was considered highly successful. A high quality detailed functional specification was developed and a critical understanding of a very important function was gained. This lead not only to a better design, but also to better user relations and more informed project planning and management. The entire task required 60 workdays, an average of five days per process. The user's time represented only 5% of the total effort.

The functional prototype modeled a new set of accounting rules that the new system needed to support, but the user was so impressed by its capabilities that another prototype was built that modeled the existing rules. The user employed the second prototype as a decision support system until the new application was built.

9.   KEY SUCCESS FACTORS

Our experiences in this and subsequent functional prototyping efforts have identified a number of factors that are crucial for organizations wishing to use functional prototyping tools and techniques. These are:

Incorporate functional prototyping into the overall development effort. Since functional prototyping is a new technique, there is a natural tendency to make it an isolated task performed by a team of specialists. In order to maximize its benefits, functional prototyping should be treated as simply an alternative means of developing the detailed functional specifications. The analysts who develop a functional prototype should be regular members of the project team who will remain with the team throughout the development effort. This will ensure that the knowledge gained during functional prototyping will remain with the project team and be incorporated into the overall system design, implementation, and testing.

Manage and control the functional prototyping effort. As with its structured analysis and conventional prototyping counterparts[11], functional prototyping needs to be planned, budgeted, managed, and controlled. The effort must be planned in advance, with time and resource commitments set. Explicit procedures for control and coordination must be established and the parts of the system to be prototyped need to be identified. The iterative nature of functional prototyping, the ambiguity of the functional requirements, and the "newness" of the approach all serve to make management and control more difficult. But these factors also increase the importance of proper project management.

Manage user expectations and system enhancements. Once users begin seeing the power and development productivity of the rule-based paradigm, they tend to request greater system functionality. Analysts, working closely with project management, must work to manage user expectations of what functionality can go into the production system and understand when that functionality goes beyond the scope of the target system. As with conventional prototyping, there is also a tendency to assume the prototype is a full-function version of whatever it models. Users need to understand the limitations of the model and the need to build the "real" system.

ACKNOWLEDGEMENTS

The authors wish to acknowledge Randy Weisman. Her contributions were of critical value both to the topic discussed and this paper itself.

REFERENCES

[1]   P. Freeman, "Requirements Analysis and Specification," *Advances in Computer Technology—1980,* American Society of Mechanical Engineers, August, 1980.

[2]   DeMarco, T. *Structured Analysis and System Specification,* Yourdon, Inc., New York, NY, 1978.

[3]   Boehm, B.W., "Verifying and Validating Software Requirements and Design Specifications," *IEEE Software Magazine.* January 1984.

[4]   Royce, W.W., "Software Requirements Analysis, Sizing, and Costing," in *Practical Strategies for the Development of Large Scale Software,* E. Horowitz, Ed., Addison-Wesley, Reading, Mass., 1975.

[5]   Agresti, W. W., "What Are the New Paradigms?" in *New Paradigms for Software Development,* E. Agresti, Ed., IEEE Computer Society, New York, NY, 1986.

[6]   Gomaa, H. and Scott, D., "Prototyping as a Tool in the Specification of User Requirements," *The Proceedings of the 5th International Conference on Software Engineering,* 1981, Pages 333-342.

[7]   Boehm, B.W., Gray, T.E., and Seewaldt, T., "Prototyping Versus Specifying: A Multiproject Experiment," *IEEE Transactions on Software Engineering,* Volume SE-10, Number 3, May, 1984.

[8]   Taylor, T. and Standish, T.A., "Initial Thoughts on Rapid Prototyping", *ACM SIGSOFT Software Engineering Notes,* Volume 7, Number 5, December 1982.

[9]   Brownston, L., et. al., *Programming Expert Systems in OPS5, An Introduction to Rule-Based Programming,* Addison-Wesley, Reading, Mass., 1985.

[10] Weisman, R., "Six Steps to AI-Based Functional Prototyping", in *DATAMATION,* August 1, 1987, pp. 71-72.

[11] Alavi, M., "An Assessment of the Prototyping Approach to Information Systems Development," *Communications of the ACM,* Volume 27, Number 6, June 1984, pages 556-563.

Expert Systems in Economics, Banking and Management
L.F. Pau et al. (Editors)
© Elsevier Science Publishers B.V. (North-Holland), 1989

Comparison of Rule Based Expert Systems with Traditional Technology
Selected Examples

W. Geis & M. Schumann
University Erlangen-Nuremberg
School of Management
Information Systems Department
Lange Gasse 20
8500 Nuremberg 1
Federal Republic of Germany

Some people argue that knowledge based systems are nothing else than a realization of decision support systems with a new kind of technology. At least some of the simpler expert systems could have been realized with one of the traditional technologies like third generation languages, decision tables, spreadsheet based software etc. Therefore, the question comes up, whether the use of expert system methods and expert system shells really results in major advantages.

The following paper presents an attempt of a comparison based on three selected business examples. The three applications were developed at our institute.

We implemented all systems with our own rule based expert system shell. Alternative implementation technologies were simple COBOL programming, a COBOL/decision table generator combination and an integrated dBASE/LOTUS approach.

1. INTRODUCTION

These days expert systems gain significant interest from the academic audience as well as practitioners. In such a situation it is important to compare the expert system approach with traditional technologies. This is of help for the identification of advantages and disadvantages of the new decision support technique from a user's point of view and a system developer's position, too.

Some people, for instance, argue that knowledge based systems are nothing else than a realization of decision support systems with a new kind of software technology. Therefore, the question comes up whether the use of expert system methodology and expert system shells really results in development advantages and offers new opportunities for application areas.

The following paper presents an attempt of a comparison based on three selected business examples. The three applications were developed at our institute.

We implemented all systems with our own rule based expert system shell. Alternative implementation technologies were simple COBOL programming, a COBOL/decision table generator combination and an integrated dBASE/LOTUS approach.

2. DESCRIPTION OF THE APPLICATIONS

2.1. STAKNETEX - an Expert System for Subsidy-Selection

In recent years the amount and variety of subsidies within the Federal Republic of Germany, for example for the promotion of new enterprises, have increased significantly. On the one hand it can hurt a young entrepreneur in a small or medium-sized company badly if he does not apply for subsidies that his competitors claim for their business. On the other hand it means a lot of effort to keep up with the most recent developments in subsidy-law. In this situation the new profession of a subsidy-consultant is coming up.

Therefore, the question arises whether those consultants, who advise in subsidy affairs only occasionally such as tax advisers or clerks in banks can be supported effectively by an expert system. For an evaluation of this idea a prototype called STAKNETEX was developed at our institute (1). More than 400 different subsidies are implemented within the knowledge base.

STAKNETEX identifies characteristic strategies and conditions of an enterprise by means of an intelligent dialogue. Then the system matches recognized characteristics with subsidy requirements. Finally, the possible subsidies are displayed. Figure 2.1./1 shows questions and answers of a particular dialogue (extract).

Figure 2.1./1	Sample of Questions of a Dialogue	
Questions in short form:		Answer
Is it a start-up of an enterprise?		N
Is an increase of owner's capital planned?		N
Is the applicant a fugitive, expellee, etc.?		N
Are investments on environmental protection intended?		Y
Is an increase of the work-force planned?		N
Is R&D carried out by other companies?		N
Does the company export products?		N
Will environmental pollution be reduced substantially?		N

STAKNETEX actually consists of about 3000 rules. The system was demonstrated to various experts in subsidy consulting. Their common impression was that the consulting quality of an experienced counsellor is not reached by the system. But they think that the system is of valuable help to an inexperienced consultant. After further improvements the system has been in practical use since the end of 1987.

2.2. Analysis of incoming mail

Task of this application, that can be seen as part of an office system, is the automatic distribution of incoming mail to identified recipients or affected business units of companies. It is assumed that the mail arrives via an electronic network or letters are scanned into the system. The following tasks should be supported by the system (2):

1.   automatic distribution of the mail to identified clerks, managers etc. (if they are not specified in the letter),
2.   combination of the mail with affiliated processes,
3.   identification of redundant mail,
4.   determination of the importance of the mail,

5. deletion of unimportant information, e.g. advertising letters,
6. answering of routine letters,
7. storage of letters in an office database that allows easy retrieval (e.g. all complaint letters for product x),
8. presentation of the mail on a certain date and/or within a certain context.

The developed prototype consists of two parts, a formal analysis and a content analysis of the mail. Rules for the formal analysis are those especially used to identify the sender, recipient or subject line of the mail. A rule base that contains the knowledge about the formal structure of letters is utilized for scanning the mail for these items. For an identification of the sender, for instance, it is used that in German letters the sender address is positioned on the upper third of a page and usually covers the left side of the page. Examples of these rules are shown in figure 2.2./1. The underlying document data base contains links between already processed documents, its senders and recipients. This enables a selection of all documents that belong to one sender. If the rough classification is not sufficient to identify a recipient clearly, then this selection will help to make a connection to the responsible employee and affiliated process.

Figure 2.2./1   Sample Rules for a Rough Mail Classification

Rule to identify an information unit:
      if information unit $\geq$ 3 rows and $\leq$ 8 rows
      and information unit located on the upper 1/3 page
      and end of the unit column $\leq$ 1/2 of the width of the pagerow
      and sender unit already identified
      then recipient unit identified

Rule to identify document indentification data:
      if sender unit found
      and textrow (1) = specifies a company name
      then sender firm identified

2.3. GUVEX - an Expert System to analyze Profit and Loss Statements

Objective of our so far largest project is to improve the evaluation of the situation of medium-sized firms at DATEV e.G., a large computer service company that was founded by German tax advisers. This analysis will help to diagnose the relative position of a company in the market and among competitors. It is based on accounting information and annual financial statement data which DATEV gathers by preparing those for thousands of tax advisers and their clients (German enterprises) every year.

GUVEX analyzes the situation of companies on the basis of two consecutive annual profit and loss statements. It generates verbal expertises, that describe the company's situation (3). Figure 2.3./1 shows a small example. The application examines income and expense items and takes also the valuation area into account.

Figure 2.3./1	Extract of an Expertise by GUVEX

The profit on sales will be used to start with the analysis of the profit and loss statement. In the investigated period it added up to 9.9 % (profit 79,000 DM; sales = 800,000 DM) while in the previous year it had only reached 5.6 % (profit = 56,000 DM; sales = 1,000,000 DM).

In comparison to the preceding period the earnings show a significant increase (41.1 %). Nevertheless it is critical that this rise was not caused by the ordinary profits but only by the noncurrent profits. The first ones dropped drastically from 21,000 DM to -20,000 DM while the latter ones increased considerably from 30,000 DM up to 84,000 DM.

The enterprise tried to diminish its operation expenses according to the reduced operating revenues. This was only partially successful (operating revenues = -110,000 DM; operating expenses = -80,000 DM).

It is remarkable that the goods in stock have increased progressively in comparison to sales. Since there is no large contract or a better market situation, this trend should be watched carefully. It should be checked whether the production program is outdated or whether the capacity is to large.

DM = German Marks

3. TOOLS USED FOR THE COMPARISON

3.1. The expert system shell HEXE

HEXE (German: Hilfsmittel zur Expertensystemerstellung) is an expert system shell specially tailored to business applications (4). It is used for the development, consultation, test and maintenance of rule based expert systems. Figure 3.1./1 shows the architecture of HEXE. The shell is based on the classical separation of program, knowledge base and data. HEXE uses production rules for the representation of expert knowledge in the knowledge base. Theoretically, rules can contain as many premises as necessary and one conclusion. The action part of a conclusion, for instance, can fire another rule, display a consultation result or initiate a question to the user.

Figure 3.1./1	Architecture of HEXE

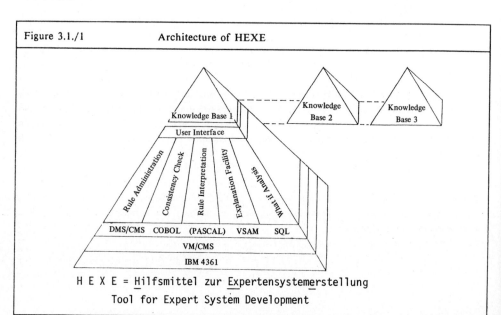

H E X E = Hilfsmittel zur Expertensystemerstellung
Tool for Expert System Development

HEXE offers a feature which generates fluent text based on text frames and text keys for the generation of expertises. Single text frames are linked to rules. Depending on rule conclusions a text is selected or rejected.

In addition HEXE contains a component that checks the formal correctness of the rule base. The program considers missing rule premises, isolated knowledge areas or potential loops within the knowledge base etc.

The inference component of HEXE is using a goal driven backward chaining strategy. In addition certain rules can be excluded from firing. For example, the use of a rule can be dependent on the conclusions of certain other rules. The results of these other rules have to be within a certain probability range. If these requirements are not met, then the other rule will not be used for the inference process. This mechanism allows to exclude complete knowledge areas from consultation dynamically, depending on intermediate results. A combination of these "block rules" can influence the order of the rule processing and even support a simulation of a data driven strategy.

Besides, HEXE offers an explanation facility. It supports the user with three different modes. The first mode offers additional information for questions that are asked by the system. The second shows the context of the question that is asked and the third describes the sub-goal that is pursued by a question. In addition the user can perform a sensitivity analysis of system results. This feature of the shell enables the user to change input parameters.

For the administration of the knowledge base as well as the consultation mode of HEXE a menu driven user interface is used. All expert system solutions that are compared later on were developed using HEXE.

3.2. The decision table generator DECTAT
The decision table generator DECTAT (Decision Table Translator) is a simple to use tool that transforms a decision table based upon conditions and actions into a sequence of COBOL program statements. Finally, these COBOL code is compiled into machine code. DECTAT does not require knowledge of a special programming language, since the instructions represented in the decision table - with few exceptions only - are similar to the usual COBOL syntax. The system checks for completeness and consistency of the decision table, e.g. whether it is free of redundances, during the generation of the COBOL code.

DECTAT only processes single strike decision tables. That means, that the action part of a rule is fired as soon as all rule premises are satisfied. Subsequently, control is given back to the calling program. The system does not analyze whether other rules are met too. Therefore, the order of the rules is of general importance for the time necessary to process the decision table.

DECTAT was used for the development of STAKNETEX and the analysis of incoming mail.

3.3. Other tools used for system development
Additionally, GUVEX was developed with a combined dBASE III+/LOTUS 1-2-3 solution. The main tasks of the system are covered by dBASE. It is used for the storage of the data, calculation of ratios and output of selected text paragraphs. LOTUS is used to select and display graphics only. The third GUVEX alternative was developed with the programming language COBOL on a Mainframe.

4. GENERAL EXPERIENCE

For the following results of our comparisons we have to consider that the expert system solutions had already been available when the development of the alternative system started. Therefore, it was possible to base the follow-up solutions upon the concepts that had been developed for the expert systems. This implies that on the one hand the concept phase for the following implementations was decreased significantly. On the other hand disadvantages of the expert system applications were known at the beginning and the development could concentrate on avoiding these problems.

Another aspect that must be considered for the description of the results is the experience of the system developer or knowledge engineer in using the development tools and development environment. All developers had at least basic COBOL knowledge. A special training was required for the expert system shell HEXE and the decision table generator. However, it seems reasonable to present a rough estimation of the times necessary for instruction.

- Training times of approximately ten days are required to work with the expert system shell HEXE.
- In general for the development of a COBOL solution advanced COBOL knowledge was necessary. This was obtained by extensive programming experience. A similar statement is valid for the fourth generation programming languages dBASE III+ and LOTUS 1-2-3. Especially, this will become true, if we consider that the developed applications contain a high degree of complexity for this kind of programming languages.
- COBOL knowledge is required for the use of the decision table generator DECTAT. For DECTAT only a training time of three days should be sufficient.

We identified the development technique of an application as a main criterion that influences the quality of the solution. Especially, it is important to separate the procedural parts from the basic application knowledge. We distinguish between subject knowledge and control knowledge. We define subject knowledge as knowledge that makes a contribution to the solution of the problem. Control knowledge determines the use of subject knowledge.

While HEXE supports the distinction of knowledge, with our conventional approaches this separation was only partly (DECTAT), in most cases not at all feasible (COBOL, dBASE). In contrast, it is a disadvantage of HEXE that the construction of control structures is supported conditionally only and sometimes it needs high efforts. The main reason for this problem can be seen in the limited knowledge processing capabilities of the inference mechanism in HEXE.

We could recognize a difference between the classical approaches and the use of an expert system shell for the process of application development too. The classical procedure was only successful when a very detailed concept was available that was implemented in a second step. A main characteristic of the development process by HEXE is an incremental proceeding. This is very similar to a prototyping methodology. Starting point is a small running system. It represents a small portion of the knowledge base only. This is changed and enhanced by a gradual procedure.

5. EXPERIENCE IN PARTICULAR APPLICATION AREAS

5.1. Subsidy counseling

The development of the decision table system took 3.5 months. During this time only the program modules were developed that are used for the administration and processing of the subsidies. That is similar to an environment already available with the expert system shell. During the same time approximately 100 subsidies could be implemented in the HEXE knowledge base (5).

Since the COBOL/DECTAT solution was tailored to the special task of subsidy counseling, the implementation of subsidies was much more efficient than it could be with HEXE. The average implementation time for one subsidy by the conventional solution took only two-third of the time needed for the expert system application.

On one hand this time advantages of the conventional system are due to a strong application oriented user interface. On the other hand the implementation of the control knowledge has a major influence. With the conventional approach the control structure was completely included in the basic system, whereas the knowledge engineer had to implement the control structures for the subsidies in addition to the subject knowledge within the knowledge base of the expert system. This became increasingly complex and time consuming with a growing size of the knowledge base

We have to make a distinction between a new subsidy that is added to an existing subsidy area and a completely new subsidy area that is implemented for the extension of the knowledge base. The addition of new subsidies is simple for both solutions. Small advantages can be seen for the conventional solution, since the earlier described problem of the control knowledge is not experienced (6).

The enhancement of the expert system with new subsidy areas does not vary from the introduction of a single new subsidy. This is a major difference of the COBOL/DECTAT solution. Here, extensive programming is required.

Modules were built for the conventional application that support the easy selection of subsidies performing certain requirements. This has proven to be a major advantage for changes of the knowledge base. For example, it allows a fast selection of an area that is changed and assures the completeness of the changes. These changes are more complicated for the expert system solution since a good knowledge of the rule base is required.

The expert system supports a check of the semantical consistency of the knowledge base. The consistency of the contents of the knowledge base has to be secured by the knowledge engineer. An additional facility aiming at the evaluation of subsidies was programmed for the conventional solution. This is another advantage. The knowledge based system offers the general documentation facilities only, e.g. a sequential printout of the knowledge base.

The following are more user oriented comparisons. The expert system as well as the COBOL/DECTAT solution are equipped with a menu driven user interface and additional help modes. The user without any experience is guided through the expert system application as well as through the conventional program.

Both, the expert system and the conventional program, offer a what-if facility. It supports the search for alternative solutions after a first utilization of the system. There is no difference between the quality of the results of the knowledge based and the conventional system.

A comparison of the run time of the expert system application and the conventional application shows a ratio of 1 to 10 in favour to the COBOL/DECTAT solution. Primarily, the reason for the big difference is the interpretive inference process of the knowledge base.

5.2. Classification of incoming mail

At the beginning of the description for this application it must be mentioned that it is a batch system. Explanation facilities, a major characteristic of dialogue oriented expert systems are of no importance.

The development took 3.5 months for the COBOL/DECTAT solution and 5 months for the HEXE application (7). This difference is explained by the fact that the problem of structuring the knowledge for the application and the development of a concept for the procedural flow was done for the expert system solution only. The conventional programming was based on this concept. If we assume that such a concept takes at least 50 percent of the development time, then we can certify clear development advantages of the expert system approach. The development of the conventional program started from the data represented by the incoming mail. In difference, an incremental development procedure, as it was utilized for the expert system solution, was nearly not applicable. The program that supervises the analysis was developed as a single algorithm. For the implementation of the knowledge based solution the goal (e.g. identification of the mail recipient) was used as a starting point. This was separated into sub-goals of the problem solution by a stepwise approach.

For the extension of the developed application we experienced similar results compared to the subsidy counseling. However, for the analysis of incoming mail the case that we have to add whole knowledge areas happens more often. Therefore, the advantage of the expert system application that offers a much easier addition of knowledge areas is of more importance. In addition there is only a program listing for the documentation of the conventional program. As a result we experienced also advantages for changes of the expert system solution as compared to the COBOL/DECTAT system.

There is no real difference between the power of the two solutions. This is not surprising, since both developments are based on the same global concept. A major difference is the order of the analysis, where the expert system starts to analyze secure information and comes to uncertain information later on. This helps to reduce errors based on uncertain data. The COBOL/DECTAT solution uses a much more sequentialized analysis for the incoming mail. Therefore, qualitative improvements can be expected much more from the enhancement of the expert system than an improvement of the conventional program.

Once again, the run time was a disadvantage of the expert system. But for the application of analyzing incoming mail this is of minor importance, since it is a batch oriented application. The COBOL/DECTAT system analyzes a letter approximately twelve times faster than the knowledge based version.

5.3. Profit and Loss Statement analysis

For the generation of expertises based on profit and loss statement data we have to compare three implementation methods, a HEXE based solution, an application programmed in COBOL and a dBASE/LOTUS development.

The concept and realization of the HEXE system took six months. One of these months was used for the development of a fundamental concept for the proceeding of a profit and loss statement analysis, without any substantial results for the later implementation. The other five months were characterized by a recursive process of conception and implementation.

The other two implementations were based on the concept that was a result of the expert system development. If we separate the conception time, then this will take approximately two to three months. The further development of the concept for the dBASE application as well as the COBOL program took about one month. For the dBASE programming 2.5 months were used and the COBOL programming required four months.

For the representation of the knowledge nearly 1,200 rules were necessary using the expert system. The similar knowledge implemented in COBOL took approximately 5,000 lines of code.

A huge advantage of the expert system is the implementation of text frames and text keys. They are always linked to corresponding rules. The COBOL program does not offer such a direct connection. Therefore, the problem emerges that text frames may be linked to the wrong program statements.

The knowledge based solution allows an easy extension of the rule base. It offers this opportunity since the entire number of possible premises of rules was not used during the development process.

Extensions for the dBASE solution and the COBOL program can be made only with major efforts. In any case interventions into the program code are necessary. This problem even increases with an improved performance of the application, because this is combined with more complexity for the program code. Therefore, the explicit knowledge representation of the expert system has major advantages in this area. A change of the dBASE or COBOL application requires difficult operations, similar to those for an extension. But in this case the expert system results are weaker too. Especially, the problem of the control knowledge comes up again.

Based on the before mentioned and the complexity of the systems changes of the dBASE and COBOL applications are very time consuming. They should be performed by the system developer only.

The statements already made for the consistency check of the previous two expert systems also fit for this application. But for the dBASE and COBOL application not even a similar kind of support tool is available. As a result the documentation is of upmost importance for the maintenance or check of correctness of the dBASE and COBOL system. But the documentation is insufficient too, since there exists a program listing only, hopefully complemented by commentaries added by the programmer.

The three alternatives show no difference in user friendliness. All systems offer a menu driven user interface and have an explanation facility available. In addition the expert system has the advantage to offer a reasoning for its proceeding. Neither for the dBASE nor the COBOL application a what-if facility is available.

There is no difference between the power of the implemented solutions. But we have to consider that "deeper" knowledge can be implemented much easier within the expert system than within the other solutions.

Since the system was implemented on different computer systems run time comparisons have no real evidence.

W. Geis and M. Schumann

6. CONCLUSION

Based on our described experience global statements about general advantages or disadvantages of expert systems or conventional techniques are not possible. But at least some tendencies or conclusions can be derived from those examples where we could notice the same results.

All conventional systems had evident run time advantages compared to the expert system solutions. However, this should be of minor importance only, since an increasing number of powerful shells is able to generate an efficient run time version from a knowledge base. We have recognized that well structured knowledge or knowledge which contains a recurrent structure can be represented sufficiently using decision tables. Nevertheless, expert systems offer better opportunities for the representation of complex knowledge and knowledge that is combined with probabilities. This is an advantage of the rule based expert system technology. An important factor is that extensions and changes of the knowledge base can be done easily. Another advantage of our expert system based solutions was the high degree of user friendliness which was provided for dialogue applications. For instance, it can be very cumbersome to add functions of an explanation facility to a conventional program. In addition great efforts are required to provide a user interface similar to the standard interface offered by the expert system shell.

The ability to represent also procedural knowledge easily would be a major advantage for expert system shells in business areas. As our experience shows this kind of control knowledge, especially used for an integration into other application areas, is an important part of an expert system application in business.

We have learned that the recursive procedure of expert system development based on a stepwise representation of the knowledge area and subsequent implementation and modification fits nicely for the development of complicated application problems.

Our results show that a combination of both development technologies might be useful in approaching similar tasks. For example, we can think of a prototype development supported with an expert system approach. Based on the experience gained during this process an efficient solution can be produced using conventional technologies.

This approach would allow to combine the advantages of both techniques:
-   Expert systems are well-suited for the fast development and stepwise refinement of a prototype ("rapid prototyping").
-   Conventional solutions are characterized by major advantages in run time efficiency and by offering a more problem oriented user guidance.

REFERENCES:
(1)   Effenhauser, R. and Krug, P., Stand des Expertensystems zur Subventionsanalyse, Arbeitspapiere der Informatik Forschungsgruppe VIII, 2. Aufl., Erlangen 1987.
(2)   Schumann, M., Eingangspostbearbeitung in Bürokommunikationssystemen - Expertensystemansatz und Standardisierung, Berlin et al. 1987, pp. 57.
(3)   Mertens, P., Derivation of Verbal Expertises from Accounting Data, paper presented at this conference.
(4)   Allgeyer, K., Das Expertensystemtool HEXE und seine Anwendung zur Schwachstellendiagnose in der Produktion, Thesis, Erlangen 1987.
(5)   Geis, W., Ludwig, H. and Straßer, N., Vergleich von regelbasierten Expertensystemen mit Entscheidungstabellen anhand ausgewählter Beispiele, Arbeitsberichte des IMMD, Bd. 21, Nr. 5, Erlangen 1988.
(6)   Straßer, N., Entwicklung eines Entscheidungstabellenansatzes zur Subventionsberatung und Vergleich mit einer Expertensystemlösung, Student-Thesis, Nuremberg 1988.
(7)   Ludwig, H., Konzeption und Realisierung eines Entscheidungstabellenansatzes zur Grobklassifikation der Eingangspost und Vergleich mit einem Expertensystem, Student-Thesis, Nuremberg 1988.

Expert Systems in Economics, Banking and Management
L.F. Pau et al. (Editors)
© Elsevier Science Publishers B.V. (North-Holland), 1989

A Knowledge–based Formulation of Linear Programming Models using UNIK–OPT

Jae Kyu Lee, Seok Chin Chu, Min Yong Kim

Department of Management Science
Korea Advanced Institute of Science and Technology
P.O. Box 150, Cheongryang, Seoul, Korea

Sung Hoon Shim

S/W Quality Division, Quality Assurance Center
Korea Telecommunication Authority
100 Sejongno Chongno–gu, Seoul, Korea

To assist in the formulation of linear programming models, a knowledge–assisted formulation support framework is proposed. In developing this framework, modeling is viewed from three levels : semantic, notational, and tabular, and twelve normative evaluation criteria for modeling systems are discussed. A frame–based knowledge representation is adopted, and the prototype UNIK–OPT is developed. UNIK–OPT is applied to the case of petroleum industry. It supports both the formulation process and the management of multiple linear programming models.

1.   INTRODUCTION

Though there have been numerous studies on the algorithmic efficiency of linear programming (LP) models, not enough attention have been paid to research on formulation support for LP models. Previous research on this topic can be classified into the following four categories.

(1) Matrix Generators

(2) Modeling Languages

(3) Structured Modeling

(4) Knowledge–based Approach

1)   *Matrix Generators*

Matrix generators accept input data in a predefined format so that an initial table of algorithms can be generated. In this approach, there is no practical support for the formulation process itself. Well known matrix generators include APEX–II MRG, DATAFORM, DATAMAT, GAMMA, MaGen, OMNI/PDS, IBM MGRW, MPSX, MODELER[FOU 83].

2)   *Modeling Languages*

In general, modeling languages are designed so that LP models can be easily formulated by using the modeling language. Since it is not easy, however, to become familiar with these languages, they can not be widely propagated among managers. Some modeling languages are ALPS, GAMS LMA[MIL 77], LPMODEL[KAT 80], MAGIC, MGG, UIMP, EZLP, LINDO, MPOS, UHELP, PAM[WEL 87], LAMP, RPMS.

3) Structured Modeling

The notion of structured modeling is a conceptual framework for the modeling process GEO 87]. Recently, Park [PAR 88] has developed a language that uses the structured modeling approach.

4) Knowledge–based Approach

Ma, Murphy and Stohr [MUR 86, 87, MA 86a, 86b] have designed a graphical interface so that the problems associated with the development of large, complex LP models can be overcome. This rule–based system is mainly for OR experts. Stohr [STO 87] has tried to translate problem specifications to graphical notation rather than mathematical notation generating the algebraic terms and their subsequent combinations into constraint equations. Although the above studies are very important, they are all focused on supporting OR experts. Binbasioglu and Jarke [BIN 86], however, have suggested a domain–specific approach to supporting OR–naive users using both syntactic knowledge about LP and domain knowledge.

In this paper, we assume that LP formulation is an extraction of relevant linear knowledge from a corporate knowledge base. For this approach, knowledge engineers and LP modeling experts should, of course, prepare the knowledge base beforehand. Although the preparation of a knowledge base is not cheap, once formed it can be shared by many OR–naive users as well as OR experts whose models can be built as subsets of the knowledge base. The proposed process of knowledge–assisted LP formulation is graphically depicted in Figure 1. This approach also supports Post–Model Analysis which supports the tradeoffs between the objective function in the LP model and the objectives in the associated knowledge base [LEE 88, 87a]. So far, there has been no known knowledge–assisted LP formulator. We propose UNIK–OPT, which we apply here to the formulation of LP models in the petroleum industry.

2.   MODELING VIEWS

To systematize the model formulation process, we propose three modeling views: *Semantic View, Notational View,* and *Tabular View* whose relationships are graphically shown in Figure 2.

2.1.   Semantic View

The *semantic view* describes the problem in aggregate, descriptive and understandable terms for decision makers. Thus, it is desirable to be able to revise as well as formulate models at this level. The semantic view, however, often includes ambiguities which require resolution. For example, a constraint may be described as "the production, inventory and sales amount should be balanced". On a semantic level, this constraint does not say anything about associated products, time units, etc. At this level, the model is described independently of algorithms or data.

2.2.   Notational View

The notational view can be further classified into two views : *aggregate notational view* and *individual equation view.*

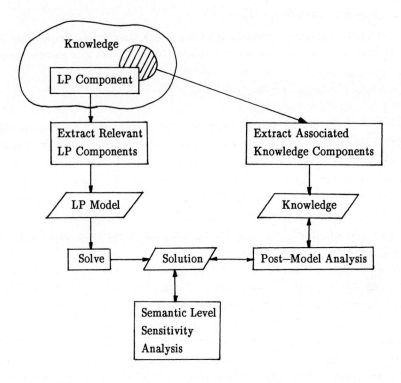

Figure 1. Knowledge–assisted LP Model Formulation Process

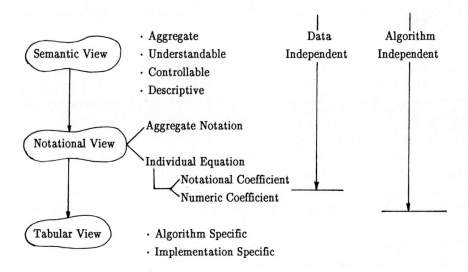

Figure 2. Three Modeling Views

(1) Aggregate Notational View

The term "aggregate" refers to aggregation with respect to constraints and terms. Aggregation with respect to terms implies summations as illustrated in equation (1).

$$\sum_{i=1}^{m} P_{it} + \sum_{i=1}^{m} I^{+}_{it} + \sum_{i=1}^{m} I^{-}_{it} = \sum_{i=1}^{m} S_{it} \tag{1}$$

On the other hand, aggregation with respect to constraints implies aggregate representation of constraints in "for all $t=1,....,12$" form. For example, the equations in (2) are effective for m items and n time units.

$$P_{it} + I^{+}_{it} - I^{-}_{it} = S_{it} \qquad\qquad \begin{matrix} i=1,...,m \\ t=1,...,n \end{matrix} \tag{2}$$

(2) Individual Equation View

Aggregate notation can be further broken down into individual equations and terms as illustrated in (3) and (4).

$$P_{11} + P_{21} + ... + P_{m1} + I^{+}_{11} + I^{+}_{21} ... + I^{+}_{m1}$$
$$+ I^{-}_{11} + I^{-}_{21} + ... + I^{-}_{m1} = S_{11} + S_{21} + ... + S_{m1} \tag{3}$$

$$\left.\begin{matrix} P_{11} + I^{+}_{11} - I^{-}_{11} = S_{11} \\ P_{12} + I^{+}_{12} - I^{-}_{12} = S_{12} \\ ... \\ P_{m,n-1} + I^{+}_{m,n-1} - I^{-}_{m,n-1} = S_{m,n-1} \\ P_{m,n} + I^{+}_{m,n} - I^{-}_{m,n} = S_{m,n} \end{matrix}\right\} \tag{4}$$

In the above examples, all coefficients are fixed as constants. However, the coefficients a_{ij}'s in example (5) are notational.

$$\left.\begin{matrix} a_{11}P_1 + a_{12}P_2 + ... + a_{1m}P_m \leq b_1 \\ a_{21}P_1 + a_{22}P_2 + ... + a_{2m}P_m \leq b_2 \\ ... \end{matrix}\right\} \tag{5}$$

Upto this point, the model is data independent. To feed data into the model, data from the database must be transformed into a format compatible with the coefficients in the LP model. Thus, after having fed in the data, model (5) becomes model (6).

$$\left.\begin{matrix} 0.1\,P_1 + 0.2\,P_2 + ... + 0.1\,P_m \leq 1,000 \\ 0.2\,P_1 + 0.3\,P_2 + ... + 0.4\,P_m \leq 1,500 \\ ... \end{matrix}\right\} \tag{6}$$

2.3.   Tabular View

The *tabular view* is the initial tabular form of an algorithm. It can be the initial table of the Simplex Method, Revised Simplex Method, or the input format of MPSX. The tabular view is thus algorithm–specific and implementation–specific. Roughly speaking, the modeling process can be considered a conversion process from the semantic view to the tabular view of a model.

3. REPRESENTATION OF MODELING KNOWLEDGE

To realize knowledge–assisted modeling support, a prototype UNIK–OPT (<u>UNI</u>fied <u>K</u>nowledge – <u>OPT</u>imization) is proposed. UNIK–OPT adopts a frame–based knowledge representation method. There are four categories of knowledge:

(1) Modeling Structure of Linear Programming

(2) Domain Context

(3) Constraints

(4) Reusable Models

We will illustrate these knowledge categories by examining the domain of the petroleum industry.

3.1. Modeling Structure of Linear Programming

Desirable features of frames in representing the LP modeling structure include the distinction between class and instances, graphical relationships between frames, and a hierarchy among the instances of a frame to reflect the level of abstraction. Class frames for LP model structure are shown in the syntax of UNIK–OPT.

```
{{ LP–MODEL                              {{ OBJECTIVE
      is–a : CLASS                             is–a : CLASS
      has–objectives :                         has–term : }}
      has–semantic–constraints : }}

{{ SEMANTIC–CONSTRAINTS                  {{ CONSTRAINT–EQUATION
      is–a : CLASS                             is–a : CLASS
      has–constraints : }}                     has–LHS :
                                               has–RHS : }}

{{ TERM                                  {{ COEFFICIENT
      is–a : CLASS                             is–a : CLASS
      has–coefficent :                         has–attribute :
      has–variable :                           has–index : }}
      has–index : }}

{{ VARIABLE                              {{ INDEX
      is–a : CLASS                             is–a : CLASS }}
      has–attribute :
      has–index : }}
```

An instance model CRUDE–SELECTION–MODEL can be represented as follows:

```
{{ CRUDE–SELECTION–MODEL
      instance–of : LP–MODEL
      has–objectives : COST–MINIMIZATION
                       PROFIT–MAXIMIZATION
      has–semantic–constraints : MATERIAL–BALANCES
                                 CAPACITY–LIMITS
                                 BLEND–QUALITY–CONSTRAINTS }}
```

```
{{ MATERIAL–BALANCES
      instance–of : SEMANTIC–CONSTRAINTS
      lower–instances : MATERIAL–BALANCE–FOR–CRUDE
                        MATERIAL–BALANCE–FOR–CDU–STREAM
                        MATERIAL–BALANCE–FOR–FINAL–PRODUCT }}

{{ MATERIAL–BALANCES–FOR–CRUDE
      instance–of : SEMANTIC–CONSTRAINTS
      higher–instances : MATERIAL–BALANCES }}
```

The frames MATERIAL–BALANCES and MATERIAL–BALANCES–FOR–CRUDE show the hierarchy of instances within the SEMANTIC–CONSTRAINTS frame.

3.2.   Domain Context

3.2.1.   Knowledge about Indices

Illustrative types of domain knowledge for the petroleum industry include products, crude oils, facilities, and time units. This knowledge will be used as indices of decision variables.

(1) *Knowledge about Products*

There are two types of products : refining products and distillation products. Each type of product can have many instances as in the following examples.

```
{{ PRODUCT
      is–a :
      description :
      index–symbol : i
      related–attributes : PRODUCTION–AMOUNT  INVENTORY }}

{{ REFINING – PRODUCT
      is–a : PRODUCT }}

{{ RC3
      description : "propane gas"
      instance–of : REFINING–PRODUCT }}
```

In this example, REFINING–PRODUCT is treated as a class, while RC3 is an instance of REFINING–PRODUCT. The inheritance of slot names and inheritance of default slot values are necessary. The *related–attributes* slots provide the links to possibly connective attributes in building the decision variables. Knowledge about crude oils can be represented in a similar way.

(2)   *Knowledge about Facilities*

Knowledge about facilities has special slots like *a–process–of, succeed, precede* and *may–be–used–for.*

```
{{ FACILITY
      is–a :
      description :
      index–symbol : f
      related–attribute : PRODUCTION–AMOUNT
      a–process–of :
      precede :
      succeed : }}
```

```
{{ PLANT
     is—a : FACILITY
     has—process : DISTILLATION—UNIT  REFINING—UNIT }}

{{ PLANT1
     is—a : PLANT
     description : "Plant in Ulsan"

{{ DISTILLATION—UNIT                    {{ REFINING—UNIT
     a—process—of : PLANT                    a—process—of : PLANT
     index—symbol : f1                       index—symbol : f2
     precede : REFINING—UNIT }}              succeed : DISTILLATION—UNIT }}

{{ C3—C4—MEROX—UNIT
     a—process—of : REFINING—UNIT
     precede : GAS—CONCENTRATION—UNIT }}

{{ GAS—CONCENTRATION—UNIT
     a—process—of : REFINING—UNIT
     succeed : C3—C4—MEROX—UNIT
     precede : NAPHTHA—BLENDING—UNIT  GASOLINE—BLENDING—UNIT
     may—be—used—for : RC3  RC4 }}
```

Knowledge of storage facilities can be represented in a similar way.

(3)   *Knowledge about Time Units*

Time units are important indices. To reconcile mismatches in the units in the model and data base, data units should be automatically transformed. Illustrative frames for time units are the following:

```
{{ 1988
     instance—of : YEAR
     has—quarter : 1ST—QUARTER  2ND—QUARTER  3RD—QUARTER
                   4TH—QUARTER
     has—month : JAN FEB MAR APR MAY JUN JULY AUG SEP OCT NOV DEC
     has—weeks : WEEK1  WEEK2  WEEK3  ...  WEEK52
     before : 1989
     after : 1987 }}

{{ 1ST—QUARTER                    {{ FEB
     instance—of : QUARTER             instance—of : MONTH
     year—of : 1988                    description : Febraury
     has—month : JAN FEB MAR           year—of : 1988
     before : 2ND—QUARTER              has—weeks : WEEK5 WEEK6 ... WEEK9
     after : }}                        has—days : 1 2 ... 29 }}

{{ WEEK5                           {{ WEEK6
     instance—of : WEEK                instance—of : WEEK
     beginning—month : JAN             beginning—month : FEB
     ending—month : FEB                ending—month : FEB
     days—in—beginning—month : 31      days—in—beginning—month :
     days—in—ending—month : 1 2 3 4 5 6    days—in—ending—month :
     has—days : }}                     has—days : 7 8 9 10 11 12 13 }}

{{ NO—WORKING—DAY                 {{ HOLIDAYS
     days : SUNDAY                      days : NEW—YEAR  THANKSGIVING  X—MAS }}
            HOLIDAYS }}
```

```
{{ NEW–YEAR                          {{ CURRENT
     instance–of : HOLIDAYS               current–year : 1988
     date : (Jan (1 2 3)) }}              current–month : OCT
                                          current–day : 20 }}
```

3.2.2.   Knowledge about Attributes

Attributes like production amount, purchase amount, and inventory are important characteristics of decision variables. Notationally, an attribute is represented as the body "X" of a decision variable X_{ij} . To link attributes with indices, the *related–indices* slots can be utilized.

```
{{ ATTRIBUTE
     symbol :
     related–indices : }}

{{ PRODUCTION–AMOUNT
     symbol : X
     related–indices : PRODUCT  FACILITY  TIME–UNIT }}

{{ PURCHASE–AMOUNT
     symbol : P
     related–indices : TIME–UNIT  CRUDE–OIL }}

{{ INVENTORY
     symbol : I
     related–indices : PRODUCT  TANK  CRUDE–OIL  TIME–UNIT }
```

3.3.   Constraints

3.3.1.   Types and Levels of Constraints

Constraints are the must relationships between terms. They can be broken down in two types : *hierarchical terms* and *procedural terms*.

Hierarchical terms are the components which constitute the upper level term. For example, the terms "sales amount of gasoline" and "sales amount of kerosene" constitute the "sales amount" of both products.

On the other hand, procedural terms describe the processes that comprise the overall operation. By using the concept of level of abstraction [SMI 77], modeling for different levels of decision making can be supported.

3.3.2.   Relationships among Constraints and Terms

Top level constraints are composed of terms described by attributes without making distinctions by indices. As the constraint level goes down to specify in greater detail the context and intention of models, indices are defined accordingly. Terms are eventually composed of decision variables and coefficients, while decision variables and coefficients are composed of attributes and indices. Possible variables and coefficients which can constitute terms can be pre–defined so that model builders can select the one appropriate for definition of a specific model.

3.4.   Reusable Models

To reuse models, the formulated specific instance model needs to maintain its *Title,*

Description, Built–Date, Built–By, User–Department, and *User–Level* slots so that subsequent users can find the model according to these criteria. The titles of instance models may include relationships each other.

4. FORMULATION OF LP MODELS USING UNIK–OPT

The LP model formulation can be assisted by the following procedure.

1) *Context Identification and Selection of Decision Variables*

Using the frames on domain context, the context and aggregation level of decision models can be defined which will be used as indices. By tracing related–attributes, decision variables can be identified.

2) *Identification of Objective Functions*

Using the constraint net, potential objective functions can be traced and selected. Once an objective function is selected as a primal objective, related objective function values will be computed based on the primal objective function for reporting purposes.

3) *Elicitation of Constraints*

The UNIK–OPT automatically elicits constraints associated with the decision variables and objective functions. The model builder can decide whether certain terms will be treated as decision terms or as given constants. They can also decide which parts of terms will be located in the RHS. If ambiguities remain about summation of terms or about units of constraints, these ambiguities should be eliminated through dialogues with the decision maker.

4) *Generation of LP Models*

Based on the definitions made during the previous stages, descriptive and notational LP models can be synthesized.

5) *Provision of Coefficient Data*

Relevant data from the data base should be transformed into the values in the unit used by the models. Then input data should be generated that is suitable for the format of the appropriate algorithm.

6) *Saving and Reuse of the Model*

The model can be saved for later use. The saved model may be linked to the data base at the time of use to accomodate future data changes that may occur. The model may be changed in terms of context, level of decision, objective function, etc. Sensitivity analysis at the semantic level can be supported through context and data modification.

5. CONCLUDING REMARKS

This paper has proposed a framework for knowledge–assisted LP model formulation. The framework is applied to the petroleum industry, and a prototype UNIK–OPT is developed. By applying this approach, the assistance in the formulation and management of models can be effectively provided.

Acknowledgement

This research is funded by Korea Ministry of Science and Technology and Yukong Limited. We thank researchers of Yukong Limited for their cooperation in this research, particularly Mr. Youn–sung Lee who is almost a co–author of this paper.

REFERENCES

[BIN 86] Binbasioglu, M. and M. Jarke, "Domain Specific DSS Tools for Knowledge–Based Model Building," *Decision Support Systems*, Vol. 2, No. 3, 1986, pp. 213–223.

[FOU 83] Fourer, R., "Modeling Languages Versus Matrix Generators for Linear Programming," *ACM Transactions on Mathematical Software*, Vol. 9, No. 2, June, 1983, pp. 143–183.

[GEO 87] Geoffrion, A., "Introduction to Structured Modeling," *Management Science*, Vol. 33, No. 5, May, 1987, pp. 547–588.

[KAT 80] Katz, S., L. J. Risman and M. Rodeh, "A System for Constructing Linear Programming Models," *IBM Systems Journal*, Vol. 19, No. 4, 1980, pp. 505–520.

[LEE 87a] Lee, Jae K. and E. Gerald Hurst, Jr., "Multiple Criteria Decision Making Including Qualitative Factors : The Post–Model Analysis Approach," *Decision Sciences*, Vol. 19, No. 2, Spring, 1988, pp. 334–352.

[LEE 88] Lee, Jae K., M. S. Shin and W. K. Lee, "The Integration of Linear Programming with Rule–based System by the Post–Model Analysis Approach," submitted to *Management Science*, 1988.

[MA 86a] Ma, P., F. H. Murphy and E. A. Stohr, "Design of a Graphics Interface for Linear Programming," Graduate School of Business Administration, New York University, Working Paper Series, GBA #86–101, September, 1986.

[MA 86b] Ma, P., F. H. Murphy and E. A. Stohr, "LPSPEC : A Language for Representing Linear Programs," Graduate School of Business Administration, New York University, Working Paper Series, GBA #86–104, October, 1986.

[MIL 77] Mills, R., R. Fetter and R. Averill, "A Computer Language for Mathematical Programming Formulation," *Decision Sciences*, Vol. 8, No. 2, 1977, pp. 427–444.

[MUR 86] Murphy, F. H. and E. A. Stohr, "An Intelligent System for Formulating Linear Programs," *Decision Support Systems*, Vol. 2, No. 1, March, 1986, pp. 39–47.

[MUR 87] Murphy, F. H., E. A. Stohr and Ma, P., "Composition Rules for Building Linear Programming Models from Component Models," Graduate School of Business Administration, New York University, Working Paper Series, GBA #87–30, March, 1987.

[ORL 86] Orlikowski, W. and V. Dahr, "Imposing Structure on LP Problem : An Empirical Analysis of Expert and Novice Models," *AAAI–86*, 1986, pp. 308–312.

[PAR 88] Park, Sung J. and Jin Y. Park, "Structured Modeling Support System (SMSS) : A Computer–aided Tool for DSS Development," *APORS '88*, 1988, p. 181.

[SMI 77] Smith, J. M. and D. C. P. Smith, "Database Abstraction : Aggregation," *Communications of the ACM*, Vol. 20, No. 6, 1977, pp. 405–413.

[STO 87] Stohr, Edward A., "Automated Support For Formulating Linear Programs," Working Paper, Information Systems Area, Graduate School of Business Administration, New York University, October, 1987.

[WEL 87] Welch, J. S. Jr., "PAM : A Practitioner's Approach to Modeling," *Management Science*, Vol. 33, No. 5, May, 1987, pp. 610–625.

Expert Systems in Economics, Banking and Management
L.F. Pau et al. (Editors)
© *Elsevier Science Publishers B.V. (North-Holland), 1989*

DEGREE ANALYSIS AND ITS APPLICATION IN DECISION MAKING

Peizhuang Wang† Dazhi Zhang# Kwok-Chi Yau* Hongmin Zhang†

†: Department of Mathematics, Beijing Normal University, Beijing, China
#: School of Business, University of Kansas, Lawrence, Kansas 66045-2003, U.S.A.
*: American Center of Chinese Medicine, 3121 Park Avenue, Soquel, CA 95073, U.S.A.

ABSTRACT

In this paper, we offer a clarification process, called degree analysis model, for measuring and aggregating various degrees by employing expert judgement, variable weights, and the theory of set-valued statistics, especially the concept of fall-shadow proposed therein. The model is applicable to various kinds of synthetic decision problems.

1. INTRODUCTION

We are encountered quite frequently with the problems of estimating or evaluating the degree to which some aims or requirements are met. We often use such words as "satisfying", "feasible", "compatible", "stable", "reliable", ... etc. to express our feelings and perceptions to a certain project. However, up to now, effective mathematical method is lacking in giving a measurement scale or in conducting a quantitative analysis, basically because of the nature of fuzziness of these degrees as well as the difficulty to measure by using a single-point value. On the other hand, it is relatively easy to measure various degrees by using set-values (intervals, for instance).

In what follows, we first introduce a few basic concepts of set-valued statistics and fall-shadow in Section 2, then we discuss various methods of expert judgement (partially based on set-valued statistics) in Section 3, and variable weights in Section 4. Based on these techniques and methods, a model for synthetic decision making is presented in Section 5.

2. SET-VALUED STATISTICS AND FALL-SHADOW OF RANDOM SETS

In classical statistics, one gets a definite point in the sample space from each experiment. But in many decision problems in the real world, one gets a subset (a ordinary subset or more generally, a fuzzy subset) from every experiment. We call such a statistical experiment a *set-valued statistical experiment* [9, 10, 12, 14,].

The classical statistical experiment, which are familiar to us, are mostly used to measure some physical quantities, and are rarely based on the psychological reflections of human beings. The set-valued statistics, however, is closely related to psychological processes.

As is well known in psychophysics that there is a precise power function law between the changes in the quantities of psychological reflection obtained by various sense organs (such as those of vision, hearing, smelling, etc) and the changes in the quantities of physical stimulations (such as degrees of brightness, loudness, sweetness, and fragrance), a scientific method of psycological measurement can objectively reflect the real world. For those objects which can not be measured by physical or chemical or any other ways, the psychological measurement is really a very important quantifying method. We may say that bringing psychological measurement into set-valued statistics is an advantage rather than a disadvantage.

An important concept which is closely related to set-valued statistics is that of *fall-shadow*. To avoid distraction and to save space, we will not go into the mathematics of set-valued statistics and fall-shadows here. For more discussions, refer to [8, 9, 10, 11, 13, 16, 17] for details. Here we only sketch the basic concepts which are related to the discussions in the following sections.

DEFINITION 2.1 Given the universe (or domain) U. Let

$$\theta_1, \theta_2, ..., \theta_n \qquad (\theta_i \in \mathbb{P}(U), i = 1, 2, ..., n)$$

be a random sample for some *random set* ξ (for a mathematical definition of random sets refer to for example [6, 10]), Then

$$\bar{\theta}(u) = \frac{1}{n} \sum_{i=1}^{n} \chi_{\theta_i}(u) \tag{2.1}$$

is called the *covering frequency* of ξ to u, where χ is the characteristic function.

The covering frequency defined above is the estimation function of the fall-shadow function of ξ. We usually call (2.1) the *fall-shadow formula*. In addition, this estimation satisfies the law of great numbers [11].

3.EXPERT JUDGEMENT

If a degree to be evaluated relies upon psychological measurement, then we invite some experts to give their opinion and judgement on the degree. The following are some of the ways.

3.1 INTERVAL METHOD

We use the degree of satisfaction (with respect to a certain project) as an example. First we draw a line segment with left endpoint "0" and right endpoint "1". Here number "0" means very unsatisfying while "1" stands for very satisfying. Then we ask each expert to give his/her judgement: (i) He/she may evaluate (independently or dependently) several times and mark his/her evaluations on the corresponding points on the line segment. We use the interval [x, y] to represent the opinion of this expert, where x is the first point from left and y from right; (ii) He/she may directly give a interval measurement if he/she prefers to do so.

Let $\theta_i = [x_i, y_i]$ be the evaluation of the ith expert (i = 1, 2, ..., n). Then we calculate $\bar{\theta}(u)$ according to (2.1). $\bar{\theta}(u)$ is a fuzzy degree of satisfaction, which stores more information than single point estimation. We may further calculate

$$\alpha = \frac{1}{n} \sum_{i=1}^{n} \frac{x_i + y_i}{2}$$

(3.1)

and

$$\bar{\lambda} = \frac{1}{n} \sum_{i=1}^{n} (y_i - x_i)$$

(3.2)

α is a *point estimation* of the degree of satisfaction, while $\bar{\lambda}$ is called the *blindness* of the point estimation. The smaller the value of $\bar{\lambda}$, the more trustworthy the estimation is. $\bar{\lambda} = 0$ means quite sure.

3.2 CONFIDENCE METHOD

We ask each expert to give only one point evaluation x_i (i.e., put only one point x_i on the line segment) but have a positive integer $k \cdot (0 \leq k \leq 10)$ associated with it. This integer k indicates his/her degree of confidence α_i to the point put. Therefore, we obtain the following sample from confidence method:

$$(x_i, \alpha_i) \qquad (i = 1, 2, ..., n)$$

(3.3)

Using weighted average, we get the point estimation as follows:

$$\alpha = \Sigma \, \alpha_i x_i / \Sigma \, \alpha_i$$

(3.4)

The interval method and the confidence method can be transformed from one to another. The more concentrated the points are (in the interval method), the more confident the participant is (in the confidence method).

Let ϕ be the degree of confidence when given the evaluation by using the confidence method, and δ be the radius of the estimation interval in the interval evaluation. Then we can find a functional relationship $\delta = f(\phi)$ between ϕ and δ by applying some statistical methods. Given (x_i, ϕ_i), a result from the confidence method, we can transform it into $[x_i - f(\phi_i), x_i + f(\phi_i)] \cap [0,1]$, which may be regarded as a result from interval method; and vice versa, as long as we change $[x_i, y_i]$ into $((x_i + y_i)/2, f^{-1}((y_i - x_i)/2))$.

The *transformation relationship* between the interval method and the confidence method is of great significance. It shows that the set-valued statistics is likely to be transformed into another statistics, in which the data are of different membership degrees to the problem in hand instead of having equal importance. They were called "*colored data*" in [3]. The idea of adding weights to data has been applied to the regression of weight functions in mathematical statistics [7] and to the Krige method in geological statistics [11].

3.3 TABLE METHOD

We use a discrete form of the interval [0,1]. Each expert is asked to put marks "X" on the table as is shown in Table 3.1:

very unsatisfying	unsatisfying	middling	satisfying	very satisfying
		X	X	

Table 3.1

By calculating the covering frequencies we obtain Table 3.2, which is a fuzzy degree of satisfaction.

very unsatisfying	unsatisfying	middling	satisfying	very satisfying
0	.3	1	.9	.2

Table 3.2

3.4 MULTI-STAGE TABLE METHOD

Each expert is given the same table as in table method. However, he/she is asked to fill in a number (an integer between 0 and 10) in every box on the table. This number represents his/her degree of confidence in using the corresponding word (e.g, satisfying) as the evaluation [4, 5]. Therefore, the sample from each expert is of the following form:

very unsatisfying	unsatisfying	middling	satisfying	very satisfying
0	5	10	8	2

Table 3.3

By calculating the average for each box, we get a fuzzy degree of satisfaction (All numbers are divided by 10 in the final results.). The multistage table method is a kind of fuzzy set-valued statistics.

4. VARIABLE WEIGHTS

In this section, we introduce the concept of *variable weights*. It is a very important concept in synthetic decision making as we will discuss below. Furthermore, variable weights can also be studied by employing the theory of *factor space* [11, 14, 15, 16], which offers a more mathematical reasoning.

4.1 VARIABLE WEIGHTS FOR TWO FACTORS

Suppose we want to evaluate two projects A and B in terms of two equally regarded standards: feasibility and necessity. Suppose that A is very necessary (necessity ≈ 1) and extremely infeasible (feasibility ≈ 0); and that B is middling in both necessity and feasibility (≈ .5) Are we going to undertake project A? Surely not! However, if we use constant weights distribution (.5, .5) in the weighted average, the synthetic degrees for both A and B will be the same (.5) !

The above paradox led us to the study of variable weights. That is, the weight distribution (w_1, w_2) is a function of the levels of the corresponding factors:

$$\begin{cases} w_1 = w_1(u_1, u_2) \\ w_2 = w_2(u_1, u_2) \end{cases}$$ (4.1)

where u_1 and u_2 are respectively the levels of the two factors or degrees to which the two standards are met.

Generally, given the constant weight ratio $k = w_2 / w_1$, we can revise it to obtain a variable weights distribution:

$$\begin{cases} w_1(u_1, u_2) = \dfrac{u_2}{k u_1 + u_2} \\[2ex] w_2(u_1, u_2) = \dfrac{k u_1}{k u_1 + u_2} \end{cases}$$ (4.2)

This formula expresses such an experiential law: when a factor is at a relative low level, its weight must increase.

Now let us reconsider the situation described at the beginning of this section. Applying the variable weights proposed in (4.2), we get the synthetic degrees for both A and B, which are respectively approximately 0 and .5. Therefore, the application of variable weights provides with us reasonable results.

4.2 VARIABLE WEIGHTS FOR MULTIPLE FACTORS

Now we generalize the above discussion to the case of multiple factors. Suppose we have in total r factors under consideration. We want to determine the variable weights $w_i(u_1, u_2, ..., u_r)$ $(i=1, 2, ..., r)$ which satisfy

$$w_i(u_1, u_2, ..., u_r) \geq 0 \quad i = 1, 2, ..., r$$ (4.3)

$$\Sigma w_i(u_1, u_2, ..., u_r) \equiv 1.$$ (4.4)

We have the following procedures:
(i) First we choose arbitrarily a pair of factors, say the ith and the jth. We determine their variable weights $w_i(u_i, u_j)$ and $w_j(u_i, u_j)$ as if we are only concerned with these two factors. Let

$$R_{ij}(u_i, u_j) = w_i(u_i, u_j) / w_j(u_i, u_j)$$ (4.5)

be the ratio of the variable weights.
(ii) Then we impose the following conditions on $w_i(u_1, u_2, ..., u_r)$ $(i=1, 2, ..., r)$:

$$w_i(u_1, u_2, ..., u_r) / w_j(u_1, u_2, ..., u_r) \equiv R_{ij}(u_i, u_j).$$ (4.6)

Combined with

$$\Sigma \, w_i(u_1, u_2, ..., u_r) \equiv 1, \qquad\qquad (4.7)$$

we get the following simultaneous linear equations (for simplicity, we denote $w_i(u_1, u_2, ..., u_r)$ by w_i for $i = 1, 2, ..., r$):

$$\begin{cases} w_1 - R_{11} w_1 = 0 \\ w_1 - R_{12} w_2 = 0 \\ ...\quad...\quad...\quad... \\ w_r - R_{rr} w_r = 0 \\ w_1 + \cdots + w_r = 1 \end{cases}$$

$$(4.8)$$

(iii) Under the following natural (consistence) assumptions:

$$\begin{cases} (1)\quad R_{ij} > 0 \ , \ R_{ii} = 1 \\[6pt] (2)\quad R_{ij} = 1 \,/\, R_{ji} \qquad (i, j, k = 1, 2, ..., r) \\[6pt] (3)\quad R_{ij} = R_{ik}\, R_{kj} \end{cases}$$

$$(4.9)$$

it is easy to show that (4.8) has a unique solution [16], which is of the following form:

$$\begin{cases} w_1 = \dfrac{R_{1r}}{1 + \sum\limits_{i=1}^{r-1} R_{ir}} \\[10pt] ...\quad...\quad...\quad... \\[6pt] w_{r-1} = \dfrac{R_{(r-1)r}}{1 + \sum\limits_{i=1}^{r-1} R_{ir}} \\[10pt] w_r = \dfrac{R_{rr}}{1 + \sum\limits_{i=1}^{r-1} R_{ir}} \end{cases}$$

$$(4.10)$$

This distribution depends on $(u_1, u_2, ..., u_r)$, it is the variable weights distribution when all the factors have been taken into account.

The following are worth noting.

(1) The ratios $R_{ij}(u_i, u_j)$ $(i,j = 1, 2, ..., r)$ can be determined as follows:

Suppose that for each pair of factors, the constant weights are known. Then so is k_{ij}, the ratio of the weight of the ith factor to that of the jth factor($i, j = 1, 2, ..., r$). Thus we obtain the variable weights by applying (4.2). Finally, we get $R_{ij}(u_i, u_j)$, which is

$$R_{ij}(u_i, u_j) = k_{ij}(u_j/u_i) \qquad\qquad (4.11)$$

Furthermore, it is easy to prove that if k_{ij} $(i, j = 1, 2, ..., r)$ satisfy (4.9), then so do $R_{ij}(u_i, u_j)$ $(i, j = 1, 2, ..., r)$. Therefore, we obtain the variable weight distribution by applying (4.10).

(2) $R_{ij}(u_i, u_j)$ (i, j = 1, 2, ..., r) may also be found by the evaluation of experts. At first, the experts are asked to determine (from the state space) the subspaces in which the (variable) weights are relatively stable, then determine the weight ratios in the subspaces, and finally obtain the ratios of variable weights in the whole space. For details, refer to [11, 16].

(3) In an actual problem, the ratios k_{ij} (i, j = 1, 2, ..., r), when directly given, may not satisfy some or all the conditions in (4.9). Therefore, (4.8) is generally unsolvable. However, we can use least square method to get a variable weight distribution $w_i(u_1, u_2, ..., u_r)$ (i = 1, 2, ..., r).

(4) If we have already got a constant weight distribution, then the associated ratios satisfy (4.9) automatically.

In closing this section, we offer a method to determine the constant weight distribution for multiple factors. It is essentially rooted in the set-valued statistics.

Given factors F_1, F_2, ..., and F_r. We ask each expert to evaluate the importance of these factors. Obviously, it is much easier for an expert to choose a set of factors he/she thinks to be important than to choose only one. Thus we let each expert to answer the question "which factors are important?". (Therefore, it is a kind of set-valued statistics.) The data from each expert is a subset of $\{F_1, F_2, ..., F_r\}$. Thus we get the following sample:

$$\Pi_j = \{F_{j_1}, F_{j_2}, ..., F_{j_{s_j}}\} \qquad (j = 1, 2, ..., n). \qquad (4.12)$$

Applying (2.1), we get the covering frequency for each factor:

$$\theta(F_i) = \frac{1}{n} \sum_{j=1}^{n} \chi_{\Pi_j}(F_i) \ (i = 1, 2, ..., r) \qquad (4.13)$$

After normalizing, we get the constant weight distribution w_i (i=1,2,...,r), where

$$w_i = w(F_i) = \frac{\theta(F_i)}{\sum_{i=1}^{r} \theta(F_i)} \qquad (i = 1, 2, ..., r) \qquad (4.14)$$

5. A DEGREE ANALYSIS MODEL OF SYNTHETIC DECISION MAKING

The goal of degree analysis is to make synthetic judgements and decisions. Given a set of projects (alternatives) and a set of factors (standards, criteria) to be considered, how can we find the "optimal" one? To give a illustration of the degree analysis method, we assume (without losing generality) that the only factors to be considered are necessity and feasibility.

(1) For every given alternative, each expert is asked to evaluate in terms of both necessity and feasibility, according to the method provided in Section 3.1. The data from each expert are two intervals $[x_1, y_1]$ and $[x_2, y_2]$, where $[x_1, y_1]$ is his/her evaluation about necessity and $[x_2, y_2]$ about feasibility. Or a sub-rectangle $[x_1, y_1; x_2, y_2]$ inside the unit rectangle in the two-dimensional space. Therefore, for each alternative, we have the following sample:

$$[x_1^{(j)}, y_1^{(j)}; x_2^{(j)}, y_2^{(j)}] \qquad (j = 1, 2, ..., n) \qquad (5.1)$$

(2) Using fall-shadow formula (2.1), we get

$$\theta\,(\,u_1,\,u_2\,)=\frac{1}{n}\sum_{j=1}^{n}\chi_{[x_1^\varphi,y_1^\varphi;\,x_2^\varphi,y_2^\varphi]}(u_1,\,u_2)$$

(5.2)

where $[u_1,\,u_2]$ is an arbitrary point in the unit rectangle.
(3) For each alternative, we calculate

$$d=\frac{\displaystyle\int_0^1\!\!\int_0^1\,(u_1 w_1(u_1,\,u_2)+u_2 w_2(u_1,\,u_2))\,\theta\,(u_1,\,u_2)\,du_1\,du_2}{\displaystyle\int_0^1\!\!\int_0^1\,\theta\,(u_1,\,u_2)\,du_1\,du_2}$$

(5.3)

where $w_1(u_1,\,u_2)$ and $w_2(u_1,\,u_2)$ are variable weights. d is called the _synthetic degree_ of necessity and feasibility.
(4) Our decision is to choose the alternative which has the highest synthetic degree.

This model can obviously be generalized to the case of multiple factors. We propose the following model:

$$d=\frac{\displaystyle\int_0^1\!\!\int_0^1\cdots\int_0^1\left(\sum_{i=1}^{r}u_i\,w_i\,(u_1,\,u_2,\,...,\,u_r)\right)\theta\,(u_1,\,u_2,\,...,\,u_r)\,du_1 du_2...du_r}{\displaystyle\int_0^1\!\!\int_0^1\cdots\int_0^1\,\theta\,(u_1,\,u_2,\,...,\,u_r)\,du_1 du_2...du_r}$$

(5.4)

where $w_i(u_1,\,u_2,\,...,\,u_r)$ ($i=1,\,2,\,...,\,r$) are variable weights, $\theta(u_1,\,u_2,\,...,\,u_r)$ is the fall-shadow function. The computer program has been given in [16].

The degree analysis model has been applied to various synthetic decision making problems, including that of multi-objective decision making, group decision making (which yields a preference ordering over the alternatives), as well as the rule building for fuzzy inference machines [1, 2, 16].

6. CONCLUSION

In this paper, we introduced the degree analysis model, a brand-new way to deal with synthetic decision problems, by employing the theory of set-valued statistics and fall-shadows, and the concept of variable weights. Applying this model, it is possible and easy for us to measure and aggregate various degrees. The using of variable weights in the model makes it more reliable than those models using constant weights. In addition, the model provides us with a ranking over the alternatives rather than giving only the "optimal" solution.

REFERENCES

[1] Chuan, K., Wang, P. Z., Liu, X. H., & Zhang, D, (1985) Degree Analysis and Its Application in the Plan Choosing Problem in the Construction of Hydropower Stations. Presented to the International Conference of Fuzzy Sets and Systems, Spain

[2] Chuan, K., Zhang, D, & Wang, P. Z., (1984) Multiobjective Decision Making in Fuzzy Environments (in Chinese), The Second National Conference on Multiobjective Decision Making, Beijing, China.

[3] Kandel, A., (1979) On Fuzzy Statistics, Advances on Fuzzy Sets Theory and Applications, Gupta, M. M., Ragade, R. K., & Yager, R. R. (eds.). North-Holland.

[4] Ma, M. C., & Cao, Z. Q., (1982) The Multistage Evaluation Method in Psychological Measurement: An Application of Fuzzy Sets Theory to Psychology, Approximate Reasoning in Decision Analysis. Gupta, M. M. & Sanchez, E. (eds.) North-Holland

[5] Ma, M. C., & Cao, Z. Q., (1983) A Fuzzy Set Model for Classification and the Method of Multistage Evaluation, Journal of Psychology, No.2

[6] Matheron, G., (1974) Random Sets and Integral Geometry, John Wiley & Sons, New York.

[7] Stone, C. (1977) Consistent Nonparametric Regression, Ann. Statist.

[8] Wang, P. Z., (1983), From the Fuzzy Statistics to the Falling Random Subsets, Advances on Fuzzy Sets Theory and Applications, Wang, P. P. (ed.) Pergamon Press.

[9] Wang, P. Z., (1983) Fuzzy Sets Theory and Applications (in Chinese), Shanghai Publishing House of Science and Technology, Shanghai, China

[10] Wang, P. Z., (1983) σ- Hyperfield and the Measurability of Set-Valued Mappings. KEXUE TONGBAO, Vol.28, No.12

[11] Wang, P. Z., (1984) Fuzzy Sets and the Fall-Shadow of Random Sets (in Chinese). Beijing Normal University Press, Beijing, China

[12] Wang, P. Z., Chuan, K., & Zhang, D., (1984) Set-Valued Statistics and Fuzzy Decision Making, Working Paper, Department of Mathematics, Beijing Normal University, China.

[13] Wang, P. Z., & Sanchez, E., (1982) Treating a Fuzzy Subset as a Fallable Subset, Fuzzy Information and Decision Processes, Gupta, M. M., & Sanchez, E., (eds.) North-Holland.

[14] Wang, P. Z., et al (1984) Set-Valued Statistics, Journal of Engineering Mathematics (in Chinese) Vol.1, No.1.

[15] Wang, P. Z., & Zhang, D., (1986) An Exploratory Study on Mathematical Form of Ideology (in Chinese) , Applied Mathematics. A Journal of Chinese Universities, Vol.1, No.1 Hangzhou, China

[16] Wang, P. Z., & Zhang, D., (1985) Fuzzy Decision Making - Theory and Applications (in Chinese), Beijing Normal University, Beijing, China

[17] Wang, P. Z., & Zhang, L., (1983) The Fall-Shadow Spaces - A Probabilistic Description of Fuzzy Sets (in Chinese). Journal of Mathematical Research and Exposition, Vol.3, No.1.

POSTER PRESENTATIONS

1. A stock market investment strategy shell (SMISS)
   Chong Chin Nyak, Loo Lee Saulan, University of Malaya

2. Expert system building in reinsurance
   Torben Tambo, Technical University of Denmark

3. Economic information through simulated programming
   Choong Yeow Wei, Loo Lee Saula, University of Malaya

4. Distributed AI and the intelligent enterprise
   Rolf Müller, Daimler-Benz AG

5. A knowledge based filter and visualizer for an office knowledge base
   Frank Martial, GMD; Hiroshi Ishii, NTT Human Interface Labs

6. SAFIR - An intelligent information retrieval front-end
   Volkmar Haase, Technical University Graz

7. INVEST - An expert system for inventory control in an Indian Oil Company
   Mark Huffman, Nixford Computers

AUTHOR INDEX

SUBJECT INDEX